A B

CW01020194

3|6°   3|8°   4|2°

-4°

Lake Stefan

TURKANA

Lake Rudolf

-2°

Mt. Kulal

Lorian Swamp

Lake Baringo

-0°

Mt. Kenya

R. Tana

Lake Naivasha

Machakos

-2°

R. Athi

Lamu

Mt. Kilimanjaro

Mt. Meru

Taveta

Malindi

-4°

MOMBASA

INDIAN

Pemba

-6°

Pangani

OCEAN

ZANZIBAR

0   100   200

Miles

Bagamoyo

Over Land and Sea

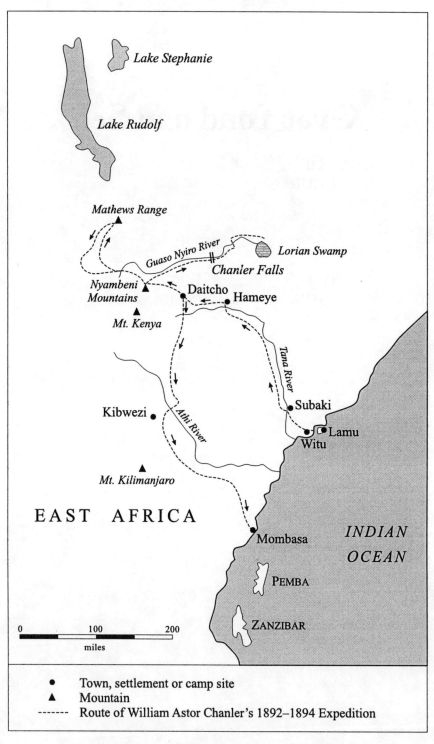

Lake Stephanie

Lake Rudolf

Mathews Range

Guaso Nyiro River

Lorian Swamp

Chanler Falls

Nyambeni
Mountains

Daitcho

Hameye

Mt. Kenya

Tana River

Kibwezi

Athi River

Subaki

Lamu
Witu

Mt. Kilimanjaro

EAST AFRICA

INDIAN
OCEAN

Mombasa

PEMBA

ZANZIBAR

0   100   200
miles

●   Town, settlement or camp site
▲   Mountain
------   Route of William Astor Chanler's 1892–1894 Expedition

William Astor Chanler's 1892–1894 route in East Africa. (Pascal James Imperato).

Over Land and Sea

MEMOIRS OF AN AUSTRIAN REAR ADMIRAL'S LIFE IN EUROPE AND AFRICA, 1857–1909

Ludwig Ritter von Höhnel

Edited by
Ronald E. Coons and Pascal James Imperato

Consulting Editor
J. Winthrop Aldrich

Foreword by
Sir Vivian Fuchs

HM
HOLMES & MEIER
New York / London

End paper map: Count Samuel Teleki's route in East Africa. (From Charles Richards, *Some Historic Journeys in East Africa*, 1961, by permission of Oxford University Press).

Published in the United States of America 2000 by
Holmes & Meier Publishers, Inc.
160 Broadway • New York, NY 10038

BOOK DESIGN BY BRIGID McCARTHY

TYPESETTING BY ALPHA GRAPHICS

This book has been printed on acid-free paper.

Library of Congress Cataloging-in-Publication Data

Höhnel, Ludwig Ritter von, 1857–1942
    Over land and sea : memoir of an Austrain rear admiral's life in Europe and Africa, 1857–1909 / by Ludwig Ritter von Höhnel; edited by Ronald E. Coons and Pascal James Imperato ; with an introduction by J. Winthrop Aldrich, Ronald E. Coons, and Pascal James Imperato.
      p. cm.
    Includes bibliographical references and index.
    ISBN 0-8419-1390-0 (alk. paper)
    1. Höhnel, Ludwig, Ritter von, 1857–1942. 2. Admirals—Austria—Biography.
3. Austria—History, Naval. 4. Austria—Foreign relations—Africa. 5. Africa—Foreign relations—Austria. I. Title. II. Coons, Ronald E. III. Imperato, Pascal James. IV. Aldrich, J. Winthrop (John Winthrop)
    V64.A92 H66 2000
    359'.0092—dc21
    [B]   94-045080

Manufactured in the United States of America

CONTENTS

FOREWORD

When I met Rear Admiral Ludwig Ritter von Höhnel in Vienna in 1935, he was one of the few remaining links with the Africa of David Livingstone and Henry Morton Stanley. For he had traveled through Africa during that bygone era when vast stretches of land were uncharted and when most indigenous peoples were unfamiliar with Europeans. Although nearly a half century had elapsed since he had trekked through what is now Kenya and Tanzania, he still had a command of Kiswahili and vividly remembered the day in March 1888 when he and Count Samuel Teleki von Szék first laid eyes on a great inland sea, which they named Lake Rudolf in honor of Austria-Hungary's crown prince. They also charted a second lake, which they named Stephanie for the archduke's wife.

Not only were Lakes Rudolf and Stephanie "discovered," but Höhnel also brought back excellent topographical maps of vast stretches of previously uncharted country. In addition, his industry resulted in the collection of large numbers of geological, zoological, and botanical specimens, together with a mass of detailed information. He produced several scientific papers, as well as a general account of the expedition, which was published in English in 1894 under the title *Discovery of Lakes Rudolf and Stephanie*. The excellence of his scientific studies, as well as his writings, quickly established him as a leading explorer who had made major geographical discoveries in Africa.

Because of his fame as an Africa explorer, Höhnel came to the attention of William Astor Chanler, who was organizing an expedition into the East African interior. Chanler, a descendant of John Jacob Astor, had previously traveled in East Africa in 1889. He now planned to explore the Tana and Guaso Nyiro rivers and strike for Lake Rudolf and Ethiopia. Höhnel accepted Chanler's invitation to join the expedition, and in 1892 they set out for the interior with sixty men. During the year that he was with Chanler, Höhnel mapped the region to the east of Mount Kenya and the lower reaches of the Guaso Nyiro River. Unfortunately, in August 1893 he was seriously injured by a charging rhinoceros and had to be carried back to the coast. Although he led a diplomatic mission to Ethiopia in 1905 on behalf of Austria-Hungary, he never returned to those parts of East Africa he had so carefully mapped years before.

Höhnel went on to have a distinguished naval career, interrupted for a few years when he served as an aide-de-camp to Emperor Francis Joseph. He later commanded the torpedo cruiser *Panther* and the armored cruiser *St. Georg*.

I became interested in Höhnel and his scientific work in Africa at a fairly early age, when I participated in the Cambridge Expedition to the East African Lakes in 1930–32. A few years later, in 1933–34, I served as leader of the Lake Rudolf Rift Valley Expedition. My own work at Lake Rudolf gave me a greater appreciation of the importance of Höhnel's scientific accomplishments some forty-five years before. I also came to admire the tremendous courage and physical stamina he and Count Teleki had demonstrated in trekking for a thousand miles on foot through unknown terrain often inhabited by hostile peoples.

When I visited Höhnel in 1935, he still cut an impressive figure. He was tall, erect, and white-haired, and he possessed an innate dignity that did not overshadow his warm and engaging personality. Although he was a renowned Africa explorer with a rich and varied naval career, he was consistently modest when speaking about his own significant accomplishments. He was also extremely well informed about the other European expeditions that had visited Lake Rudolf following its "discovery." Given his encyclopedic knowledge of this subject, I encouraged him to write up this history, which was later published as a two-part series in the *Journal of the Royal African Society*.

Höhnel maintained a keen interest in naval matters. In fact, one of his hobbies was to follow the movements and exercises of the Royal Navy, for which he had an unbounded admiration. He had a wide circle of friends among former Austro-Hungarian naval officers, and he greatly enjoyed reminiscing with them about his years at sea.

I was truly delighted when I learned of the existence of an unpublished English version of Höhnel's memoirs. He wrote them over seventy-five years ago at the urging of William Astor Chanler, who hoped that their publication would provide his impecunious friend with some badly needed income. While Chanler was unsuccessful in finding a publisher, his relatives carefully cared for the manuscript over the decades, thus ensuring its survival and ultimate publication.

J. Winthrop Aldrich, the consulting editor of this volume and the Chanler family historian, sought the help of the two very able co-editors in order to make the publication of this volume possible. They bring to this memoir complementary areas of expertise. Professor Ronald E. Coons is an experienced student of the maritime and political history of the Habsburg Monarchy, while Professor Pascal James Imperato possesses an extensive knowledge of Lake Rudolf and its early European visitors. The result is a highly readable book in which Höhnel's remarkable life and career are presented in his own words, but also in a broader historical context through the use of appropriate annotations.

Ludwig Ritter von Höhnel's long-lost memoir is an historical treasure not only because it vividly chronicles his own life story, but also because it provides a first-hand and unique look into the bygone worlds of explorers, emperors, and Austro-Hungarian naval officers. It was written by a man who was widely respected for being a sensitive, objective, and meticulous observer, and has been carefully edited so as to preserve its originality. As such, it will appeal to a broad audience interested in topics as diverse as the Habsburg Monarchy, naval history, and the exciting story of late nineteenth-century African travel.

I am sure that Ludwig von Höhnel would have delighted in the publication of his *Over Land and Sea*. Through it, he can now speak to younger generations and bring to them the excitement and drama of worlds that have long since disappeared.

Sir Vivian Fuchs, F.R.S.
Former President
The Royal Geographical Society

ACKNOWLEDGMENTS

In expressing their appreciation to the many individuals who have made this edition possible, J. Winthrop Aldrich, Ronald E. Coons, and Pascal James Imperato would first like to thank one another for the remarkable spirit of cooperation that has guided their collective undertaking. They further wish to thank their editors, Katharine Turok, Brady Kahn, and Maggie Kennedy, for their continuous and enthusiastic support of the project and to acknowledge the interest, help, and encouragement of William Astor Chanler's sons—William Astor Chanler, Jr. and the late Ashley Chanler—and his niece, Margaret DeMott.

For his part, Pascal James Imperato wishes to recognize a number of persons who provided aid, especially in the early stages of the project. George E. Galvin, Jr., made available archival materials concerning his father; Robert Baker, former Director of the United States Information Agency Regional Program Office in Vienna, kindly put him in contact with a number of institutions in Austria that hold archival materials related to Höhnel's career; Lajos Erdélyi, Count Samuel Teleki's biographer, provided important insights into Höhnel's first trip to Africa and kindly provided some rare photographs that are reproduced in this volume; the Rev. Paul Tablino of Marsabit, Kenya, an internationally respected authority on the peoples and history of northern Kenya, provided research assistance concerning Höhnel's first and second trips to Africa; and Géza Teleki generously allowed access to Count Samuel Teleki's personal diary of his expedition with Höhnel to Africa in 1886–89. In addition, Irma A. Erickson of the Medical Society of the State of New York and Professor Frederick Hueppe of the Department of Modern Foreign Languages, St. John's University, Jamaica, New York, translated a number of documents and letters from German into English; Richard Pankhurst, a leading authority on the history of Ethiopia, greatly assisted in finding modern equivalents for Höhnel's Ethiopian geographic place names; officials at the Austrian National Library and at the library of the University of Vienna located and photocopied materials related to Höhnel's career; Dr. Christina Unterrainer of the library at the University of Salzburg provided bibliographical help; and Herr Erwin F. Sieche, an authority on Austrian naval history, assisted in many ways over the years, most recently by providing some of the photographs that accompany Höhnel's memoirs.

Ronald Coons is also deeply indebted to Herr Sieche, who was always quick to give advice and information, often on short notice via e-mail. During three brief research trips to Vienna, two long-time Viennese friends, General Director Dr. Lorenz Mikoletzky of the Austrian State Archives and Dr. Leopold Auer of the Haus-, Hof- und Staatsarchiv, rendered valuable assistance by facilitating access to archival materials. In the United States, Gerald Lombardi, a freelance editor in New York City, offered sage advice on technical matters; Professors Paul Halpern of Florida State University and Lawrence Sondhaus of the University of Indianapolis, two distinguished American experts on Austrian naval history, provided valuable comments on the manuscript; and the Interlibrary Loan Department of the Homer Babbidge Library at the University of Connecticut cheerfully complied with numerous requests for printed materials.

In addition, a number of individuals and institutions provided assistance in various stages of the project, for which the editors are deeply thankful: Frau Ildikó Cazan-Simanyi; Dr. Rainer Egger, Director of the Kriegsarchiv in Vienna; Dr. Lidia Ferenczy of the National Széchenyi Library in Budapest; Dr. Erich Gabriel of the Heeresgeschichtliches Museum in Vienna; Lieutenant Commander John D. Harbron, Senior Research Fellow at the Canadian Institute of Strategic Studies; the Library of the State University of New York, Health Science Center at Brooklyn; the Manhasset Public Library; the New York Historical Society; the New York Public Library; Monty Brown of Naro Moru, Kenya; and Errol and Sbish Trzebinski of Mombasa, Kenya. Special thanks are extended to Cornelia Wright for her expert copy editing of the manuscript and to Chris Brest for drawing the map of William Astor Chanler's 1892–94 travels in East Africa. The editors also wish to extend special thanks to Lois Hahn, who over the years prepared much of the research correspondence for the project, and to Cynthia Skeete and Roberta Lusa for their clerical assistance.

Though many persons have aided in the preparation of this English edition of Ludwig Ritter von Höhnel's memoirs, only the editors are responsible for any errors, oversights, or inconsistencies that readers may find in the pages that follow.

INTRODUCTION

I

While preparing his informative and engaging book on the Lake Rudolf region in East Africa's Rift Valley, the Austrian geologist and ethnographer Herbert Tichy conducted an experiment. In 1980 he first asked ten well-educated Austrian acquaintances if they could identify Ludwig Ritter von Höhnel,[1] who with Count Samuel Teleki was the first European to explore the area in the course of an expedition that Teleki financed and led almost a century earlier. During a visit to London, Tichy then posed the same question to ten English acquaintances with similar educational backgrounds. To his surprise, only one of the ten Austrians he approached knew that Höhnel and Teleki had "discovered" Lake Rudolf in March 1888 and had named it after the heir to the throne of the Austro-Hungarian Monarchy. In contrast, three of Tichy's English respondents knew at least something of Höhnel and his accomplishments.[2]

Tichy attributes the English advantage in what he confesses was an unscientific survey to Britain's still living colonial past. For the educated Englishman, the history of the exploration of Africa was by no means an arcane subject to be learned only at school from dry textbooks. For most Austrians it was. Even Tichy admits that as a student at the University of Vienna in the 1930s, when he had already developed a fascination with distant lands, he was more than merely unaware that he could have interviewed the last living major European explorer of Africa at Reisnerstrasse 61 in the city's Third District.[3] He had never even heard of Ludwig Ritter von Höhnel.

Tichy had every reason to be embarrassed by his own youthful ignorance and to be dismayed by the poor showing of his countrymen on the quiz he administered them. Had he and they been better acquainted with the history of Africa exploration and of the Habsburg Monarchy, they would have known that Höhnel was a notable figure in the three distinct worlds in which he had been active. In the first place, he was a distinguished explorer of Africa in the era of Livingstone and Stanley who, along with Count Teleki and the wealthy American William Astor Chanler, explored and mapped vast areas of what is now Kenya and Tanzania.[4] In 1888 he and Teleki not only "discovered" Lake Rudolf (today Lake Turkana) but soon thereafter found a neighboring smaller body of water which they named Lake Stephanie (today Lake Chew Bahir) in honor of

Crown Prince Rudolf's Belgian-born consort. Subsequently, between 1892 and 1894, Höhnel and Chanler mapped new areas of East Africa beyond the two lakes; Chanler has left a vivid account of this ill-fated expedition.[5] In turn, these experiences inspired the Austro-Hungarian Foreign Office to appoint Höhnel to lead the diplomatic mission it sent to Addis Ababa in 1905 to conclude the Habsburg Monarchy's first commercial agreement with Ethiopia, this at a time when travel to the capital still constituted an adventure.

A second area in which Höhnel achieved distinction was as an officer in the Austro-Hungarian Imperial and Royal Navy. Entering the service following his graduation from the Monarchy's naval academy in 1876, Höhnel rose steadily in rank, was assigned ever greater responsibilities, and in all probability would have ended his career with a high command had he not chosen to seek early retirement in 1909. And thirdly, Höhnel was one of the relatively few naval officers ever appointed to the prestigious post of aide-de-camp to Emperor Francis Joseph, whom he loyally served—and closely observed—between 1899 and 1903. As one of Höhnel's fellow officers, Admiral Alfred von Koudelka, notes in his autobiography, "Höhnel was one of the most impressive persons I ever met: sea-dog, Africa explorer, and polished court official in one person, and a man of the utmost integrity."[6]

Höhnel describes his participation in these vanished worlds of Africa exploration, the Austro-Hungarian navy, and the Habsburg court in the memoirs that follow. During the 1920s, when Höhnel was living in impecunious retirement in Vienna, William Astor Chanler urged him to write a memoir of his career in English, emphasizing that his associations with the Habsburgs and with Africa would be especially marketable in the English-speaking world. Höhnel's correspondence with Chanler reveals that he had already begun to write his autobiography in German shortly after the conclusion of World War I. Urged on by Chanler's occasional badgering and sustained by his financial subsidies,[7] he completed an English-language manuscript in August 1924 and quickly set about seeking a publisher. After failing to find interest in Great Britain, he sent the manuscript to Edward Motley Pickman of Boston, a gentleman-scholar specializing in medieval history who was married to Chanler's niece Hester and who had offered his help in finding a publisher.[8] A German version of Höhnel's autobiography appeared in Berlin in 1926.[9] Pickman's efforts on behalf of the English manuscript, on the other hand, proved futile, in part because he devoted little sustained energy to a task for which he appears to have volunteered primarily out of respect for his wife's uncle. A disappointed Höhnel then turned to Chanler, who soon discovered that there was no market for the memoirs of an admiral in the navy of a monarchy that no longer existed.[10] The onset of the worldwide economic crisis in 1929, Chanler's death in 1934, and the outbreak of war in Europe in 1939 caused the project to languish, seemingly forever.

In 1965, while clearing out Pickman's large library at Bedford, Massachusetts, his widow came across the labeled package containing Höhnel's manuscript, set aside and forgotten for over three decades. She passed it on to J. Winthrop

Aldrich for inclusion in the Chanler family archives at Rokeby, the family's ancestral seat in Barrytown-on-Hudson, New York, where numerous documents and artifacts of the Chanler-Höhnel expedition to East Africa had already been assembled. A grandnephew of Chanler, Aldrich was at the time an undergraduate at Harvard College majoring in European history. In no position to undertake the task of editing the manuscript himself, he nevertheless recognized its significance and the need to have it appraised by scholars for possible publication. In this he was encouraged by Chanler's niece, Margaret Aldrich DeMott, who spent many years in Kenya and who would publish, in 1967, an article about her uncle's African travels.[11]

Education, marriage, and career long prevented Aldrich, who is currently New York State's Deputy Commissioner for Historic Preservation, from actively working to seek publication of Höhnel's memoirs. Still, in his capacity as Chanler family historian he did not abandon his interest in the manuscript, thanks in part to his association with Dr. Pascal James Imperato, a specialist in tropical medicine and public health who is Distinguished Service Professor and chairman of the Department of Preventive Medicine and Community Health at the State University of New York Health Science Center at Brooklyn. While preparing a monograph on the exploration of the Lake Rudolf area, Imperato had occasion to consult Aldrich for materials on the Chanler-Höhnel expedition.[12] Through this connection he learned of the existence of Höhnel's manuscript and came to share Aldrich's interest in having it published.

Imperato's long experience in East Africa and his extensive knowledge of the exploration of the region fully qualified him to evaluate the chapters dealing with Höhnel's African adventures. What was needed was a scholar fluent in German who was familiar with the maritime and political history of the Habsburg Monarchy and could devote the time required to edit the manuscript. In the early 1990s, Aldrich remembered that the tutor at Harvard who had directed his senior honors thesis had been working on a doctoral dissertation with an Austrian maritime theme. Imperato tracked down Professor Ronald E. Coons at the University of Connecticut in Storrs, where he was then serving as Director of Graduate Studies in the Department of History. Coons offered to bring to the project the experience he had gained while conducting research in the Austrian State Archives,[13] Aldrich and Imperato accepted the offer, and a Höhnel-based triumvirate was formed.

Upon receiving a copy of Höhnel's partly typed and partly handwritten manuscript, Coons set about comparing the English and German texts to determine whether the Rokeby manuscript was simply a translation of the memoirs that had appeared in Germany in 1926. A close examination of the two texts indicated that it was not. Whereas the English manuscript contains virtually all of the material published in the book, it includes many lengthy passages that either had not been a part of the text submitted to Höhnel's German publisher or had been deleted in the interest of economy. Recognizing that in either case the English manuscript was more than a translation of an already published book,

Aldrich, Coons, and Imperato decided to proceed with the project. Coons began to transcribe the text in the summer of 1995, correcting obvious errors and infelicities of style in the process. During the following summer and a sabbatical leave in the fall semester of 1996, he then undertook the more challenging task of thoroughly revising the text. Though Höhnel had had help in translating portions of his German text, much of the English manuscript is in his own handwriting and can be assumed to have been his own work. In general, the English was surprisingly good, with few errors in grammar or diction. The prose was not, however, idiomatic. All too often, sentences were heavily Germanic in structure, occasionally awkward to the point of obscuring the author's meaning. The challenge was to render the text more readable while maintaining the integrity of prose translated into English in the 1920s by an author and his helper who had learned their English in the nineteenth century.

Once Coons had edited Höhnel's text to his and his colleagues' satisfaction it was necessary to reduce the manuscript to manageable length. Höhnel wrote extensively about such matters as his travels, his social obligations during his visits to foreign ports, and his love of animals, and on a number of occasions this material impeded the flow of his narrative. In consultation with the staff at Holmes & Meier, the manuscript was therefore cut wherever possible. Of the passages omitted, only one, a lengthy discussion of Höhnel's role in stocking New Zealand with Austrian chamois, was sacrificed with regret.[14] Otherwise the excised materials are at best of only passing interest. In no case have the editors suppressed passages that might damage Höhnel's reputation; to the contrary, they have retained offensive racial epithets that they would have preferred to omit in the interest of good taste. In further consultation with their publisher, the editors decided against imposing a ponderous scholarly apparatus upon the reader and chose to keep explanatory footnotes to a minimum. Pascal James Imperato wrote most of the notes in chapters 4, 6, 7, and 11 dealing with Höhnel's experiences in Africa; Ronald Coons assumed responsibility for writing those in the remaining chapters.

II

As William Astor Chanler recognized over seventy years ago, Höhnel's discussion of his experiences in Africa will probably evoke the greatest interest in the English-reading world. From a scientific point of view, his first expedition, which led to the "discoveries" of Lakes Rudolf and Stephanie, was the most significant as far as contemporaries were concerned. For if Höhnel's detailed maps of large areas of present-day Kenya and Tanzania evoked little interest in Vienna, they were of paramount importance to Great Britain, which was a major colonial competitor in this part of Africa. Indeed, it was primarily because of these colonial territorial ambitions that the Royal Geographical Society in London failed to invite Teleki and Höhnel to address its members. As the society saw it, an invitation to speak would have represented recognition of their claim to be the first Europeans to have visited Lake Rudolf.[15] And in the scramble for Africa that was then underway, such claims normally gave sponsoring colonial powers the right of territorial annexation.

Teleki, who had confided all of the scientific aspects of the expedition to Höhnel, subsequently asked his partner to write up an account of their adventure, which was published initially in German and later in English.[16] This two-volume work and the scientific papers that Höhnel authored about the trip established him as a leading explorer and as an authority on East Africa, just as the Eurocolonial scramble for Africa was at its height. The book quickly became a travel classic in the English-speaking world and made his name familiar to several generations of readers of the genre.

One of those who admired Höhnel's accomplishments was William Astor Chanler, who had already traveled in 1889 to Mount Kilimanjaro.[17] Chanler knew East Africa well, and in 1892 he set his sights on exploring the extensive uncharted territory that lay to the north of the Tana River (in present-day Kenya) between Lake Rudolf and the Juba River (in present-day Somalia). Chanler was determined that his expedition should be a serious scientific endeavor. Thus he wrote to Höhnel out of the blue in March 1892, asking that he join him. Höhnel's fame as a seasoned traveler in Africa had already brought him a number of lucrative government and corporate offers to return to East Africa, but during a visit to Vienna in April, it was Chanler who was able to recruit him. Höhnel may have been attracted to Chanler's offer because, like Teleki's, it came from a private patron under whom he could engage in independent scientific inquiry.

Chanler and Höhnel left the coast for the interior on September 18, 1892. As he had done on Teleki's expedition, Höhnel marched at the rear of the column with his surveying instruments so that he could carefully chart the line of march and the prominent geographic features he observed. Over the next eleven months the two men explored the distant reaches of the Guaso Nyiro River, as well as a huge tract of land north of the Tana River in what is today Kenya, an area never before visited by white men. The expedition's fortunes were dealt a serious blow in August 1893, however, when Höhnel was seriously gored in the groin and lower abdomen by a charging rhinoceros. Chanler cared for him as best he could and eventually had him carried in a hammock for several hundred miles to Kibwezi, where a missionary physician, amazed by his survival, debrided his wounds. From there Höhnel returned to Vienna to recuperate, while Chanler planned to strike for Lake Rudolf.

Increasingly anxious that Chanler might make an American claim on the territories he and Höhnel had charted, British officials in Zanzibar successfully sabotaged the expedition by inducing the men who served as guides and porters to desert.[18] As a result, Chanler was forced to return to the coast in February 1894. Despite this disappointment the expedition was a success,[19] thanks to Chanler's tenacity and Höhnel's excellent scientific and cartographic efforts.

The ensuing lifelong friendship between Höhnel and Chanler was forged, moreover, during their year together in Africa under life-and-death circumstances. Its foundations ran deep, and it was able to sustain the stresses that these two strong-willed personalities brought to it. When Höhnel fell on hard financial times during his retirement, it was his friend Chanler who came to his aid with a monthly remittance.

Höhnel's final expedition to Africa came in 1905, when he led a diplomatic mission to the Emperor Menelik II of Ethiopia. Höhnel had briefly visited Ethiopia with Teleki in 1889 and was familiar with the country. The commercial treaty he signed with Addis Ababa on behalf of the Monarchy never led to meaningful commercial ties, however, primarily because neither party had much to export that was in demand by the other. Both countries, in fact, took several years to ratify the treaty, and it was not until 1912 that an Austro-Hungarian consulate was established in the Ethiopian capital.[20] In retrospect, therefore, Höhnel's final visit to Africa was but a footnote to his earlier two trips, during which he had established himself as a leading scientific explorer.

As stirring as Höhnel's accounts of his exploits in Africa frequently are, it is to his career as a naval officer that he devotes the major part of his memoirs. Indeed, for the study of Austrian naval history the significance of his autobiography may well lie in its very existence. For whereas there is abundant literature on the history of the Habsburg Monarchy's land forces, much less has been published on the history of the Austro-Hungarian navy, even in German. In recent years a number of important books have indeed appeared on the topic in the United States, some of which—particularly those by Lawrence Sondhaus of the University of Indianapolis and Paul G. Halpern of Florida State University—are of a very high quality.[21] Their authors primarily concern themselves, however, with the formulation and execution of naval policy at the highest level and say relatively little about such matters as the education of cadets or the experiences of officers and sailors in port and at sea. As improbable as it may seem, one of the few available sources of knowledge about everyday life in the Austro-Hungarian navy is not a work of scholarship at all but rather the recent fiction of the British author John Biggins, who brings a profound knowledge of naval lore to the novel he has written about the Habsburg submarine service during World War I.[22]

Höhnel's account of his career in the Austro-Hungarian navy confirms the impression Biggins gives of an institution that was inappropriately faithful to the central-European stereotype of inefficiency. Surely not all Austrian naval officers were as idiosyncratic as some of the characters Höhnel encountered during his career, and it is entirely possible that he uses his memoirs now and again to settle old scores. Nevertheless, precisely because he makes no attempt to hide his own deficiencies, there is no reason to believe that he fabricated any of the stories he has to tell. From his memoirs it is clear, for example, that he was an indifferent student, that he paid less than full attention to the technical details of the service, that he chafed at the important representational obligations he was required to fulfill as commander of a warship calling at foreign ports, and that he demonstrated a lack of some of the more important skills required of a diplomat during his 1905 expedition to Ethiopia and his subsequent visit to New Zealand.

Höhnel's honesty in these matters in no way diminishes, however, his notable professional accomplishments. A modern geographer writes that even today his sketches and his publications associated with the Teleki expedition to East Africa continue to inspire "astonishment and respect," suggesting that he possessed considerable intelligence and was able to give sustained and systematic attention to exacting tasks.[23] Equally important, on more than one occasion he safely brought a warship through treacherous waters; while in foreign ports he ably and diligently performed his burdensome duties and charmed his hosts in doing so; and his missions to Addis Ababa and New Zealand achieved their purpose despite his lack of diplomatic savoir faire. It is noteworthy, moreover, that Höhnel's colleagues and superiors recognized his talents and consistently praised his exemplary sense of duty. The earlier quoted judgment of Admiral Koudelka, who served under his command on board the cruiser *Szigetvár*, corresponds closely to that of the naval historian Heinrich Bayer von Bayersburg, who before and after World War I had ample opportunity to come into contact with Höhnel's former subordinates. "Höhnel was," he writes, "a 'personality'— a distinguished mariner, a hunter of wild animals, a scientific explorer, and a strict and exacting superior, under whose hard outer core there nevertheless beat a warm, golden heart that revealed itself, however, to only a few."[24] Höhnel's superiors were equally positive in their evaluations. In 1899 Count Eduard von Paar, the adjutant general to Emperor Francis Joseph, wrote concerning Höhnel's service as aide-de-camp: "Of strong, honorable character; sincere, upright, very energetic. Is mentally very gifted and is quick and accurate in grasping matters; has a comprehensive knowledge. . . . A very able, distinguished officer." Ten years later Rear Admiral Lazar Schukić wrote an equally favorable evaluation on the eve of Höhnel's retirement: "Entirely military and correct toward his superiors; strict toward his subordinates. Sets an example as a zealous and conscientious naval staff officer."[25]

As forthright as Höhnel is in describing his naval career, he nevertheless suppresses the truth in one important matter. Most likely in order to spare his wife embarrassment, in chapter 13 he gives a misleading account of his decision to retire from the navy in 1909. Earlier in his memoirs Höhnel mentions in passing that at some point during the 1890s he made the acquaintance of the family of the woman he would eventually marry. Regrettably, little is known about the life of Valeska van Oestéren (1870–1947) either before or after she met Höhnel—with one important exception. As a young woman of considerable charm and modest literary talent she enjoyed a brief "flirtation" in 1896 with the poet Rainer Maria Rilke.[26] Precisely when she subsequently began her relationship with Höhnel is uncertain, but the couple did not embark upon marriage impetuously. In submitting a formal request in February 1907 for the permission to marry that naval regulations required of officers, Höhnel explained that his forthcoming promotion to *Linienschiffskapitän* (captain) would at last provide him with a salary sufficient to enable him to realize a long-desired goal.

Though Höhnel planned to marry as soon as he received the requisite permission, he abruptly withdrew his petition less than a month after submitting it, referring only to "unanticipated events." What he had failed to anticipate was the formidable opposition of the heir to the throne, Archduke Francis Ferdinand, who occupied a powerful position within the Habsburg Monarchy's military-naval hierarchy.[27] A year earlier, Höhnel's future brother-in-law, Friedrich Werner van Oestéren, had published a fiercely anti-Jesuit novel that had incurred the archduke's wrath.[28] According to the testimony of the well-informed Alfred von Koudelka, who at the time was serving at the Admiralty, the archduke intervened and forced the petitioner to choose between marriage and his career.

For the time being Höhnel opted to remain with the navy. On March 12, 1907, he withdrew his request, and his promotion was allowed to take effect on May 1.[29] Then, two years later, Höhnel unexpectedly requested permission to retire, explaining that his hearing had deteriorated in the line of duty and that his general health had suffered during his adventures in Africa. The reasons he advanced for retirement may well have been pretexts, however, for on July 17, 1909, only a few days before he left active service, Höhnel married Valeska van Oestéren in Vienna, with William Astor Chanler and, provocatively, the bride's brother serving as two of the four witnesses. The marriage having quickly come to the attention of Francis Ferdinand, the archduke's military chancellery wrote the Admiralty on July 20 demanding to know how Höhnel could have taken such a step without having first gained permission from higher authority. In response, the Admiralty coolly informed the heir to the throne that in light of Höhnel's impending retirement, no official permission was necessary. Mere notification was sufficient, and Höhnel had complied with that obligation in a timely manner.[30]

If, as is probable, the circumstances surrounding Höhnel's retirement left him with bitter feelings, it is significant that he did not direct them against the House of Habsburg. Aware as he must have been of Archduke Francis Ferdinand's role in thwarting his desire to continue serving in the navy as a married man, he is remarkably restrained in his comments in chapter 9 on the heir to the throne, whom he encountered during his appointment as aide-de-camp to Emperor Francis Joseph. About the emperor himself, moreover, he writes with immense respect and affection. If Höhnel ever entertained doubts about the monarchical system of government, he did not express them in his memoirs, where he in fact says little about whatever political views he may have held. Here and there he drops hints that he opposed democracy, and in chapter 9 he indicates that he disapproved of the extreme Magyar nationalism he observed during his sojourns with Francis Joseph in the Kingdom of Hungary. Otherwise he ignores politics altogether, with the curious result that his memoirs give not the slightest evidence that he lived through what were in fact turbulent times in the internal history of the Habsburg Monarchy. When he wrote his memoirs in the 1920s, Höhnel either consciously chose to avoid commenting upon political matters, or he demonstrated that as a naval officer he had failed to devote much attention to them.[31] In all probability Höhnel, the son of a high-ranking provincial bureaucrat and the graduate and servant of imperial institutions, retained throughout his career the allegiance to the House of Habsburg that had permeated the atmosphere in which he had been raised and educated.

It is precisely Höhnel's acceptance of the monarchical order, combined with his critical powers of observation, that lifts his account in chapter 9 of his contact with Francis Joseph above the level of the memoirs of a mere courtier. A contemporary observer indicates that Höhnel declined to surrender his intellectual integrity even in the all-highest presence. In his autobiography, the emperor's long-time valet notes:

> Ludwig v. Höhnel was Corvette-Captain when he came as *aide-de-camp* to the Emperor; he knew many languages and had a high degree of general knowledge. With all his devotion to his imperial master—devotion which in some quarters was thought to border on servility—he never wavered one hair's-breadth from his opinions, and permitted himself, even if in a perfectly humble manner, to contradict His Majesty. Thus it came to pass that the Emperor did not care for him especially, but he impressed His Majesty, who always valued his opinions.[32]

In a recent political biography, Steven Beller views Francis Joseph as an anachronistic ruler and severely criticizes him for his "disdain for constitutionalism, his paternalistic vision of 'his peoples' and his stress on dynastic and personal loyalty."[33] In the present context it is irrelevant whether such a critique is accurate in every respect. What is striking is the degree to which Höhnel's observations support at least some of Beller's judgments. To be sure, Francis Joseph was no cipher, for he possessed considerable political acumen and was the very incarnation of imperial dignity. He also did not lack endearing qualities, one of which was the politeness that sometimes comes from good breeding. For example, he showed consideration for the deteriorating hearing in Höhnel's left ear by failing to insist that his aide-de-camp sit or walk to the right, as protocol prescribed.[34] Yet as flattered as Höhnel must have been by such courtesy, he was too intelligent and was too experienced in the ways of the world not to be aware of the vacuous private lives the monarch, the imperial family, and their courtiers led. From Höhnel's memoirs, Francis Joseph emerges as a remote ruler who was inexorably bound to the past, this at a time when the Habsburg Monarchy confronted a host of political and social problems that cried out for imaginative solutions.

III

Although extensive archival research may someday expose major lapses in Höhnel's memoirs—regrettably his private papers disappeared after his death and must at present be considered lost—where the documentary record has been consulted it largely substantiates the account he gives of his career.[35] On the basis of the present state of research there are, indeed, only four instances in which Höhnel clearly suppresses the truth. The first concerns his treatment of his decision to retire from the navy in 1909 and has already been discussed. In a second instance, Höhnel errs in asserting in chapter 7 that Count Teleki killed game during the expedition that led to the "discovery" of Lake Rudolf only when it was absolutely necessary to gain food to sustain human life. Having included an extract from Teleki's game-book as an appendix to his published account of their adventures, Höhnel had already provided striking proof to the contrary.[36] In a University of Vienna master's thesis in which she surveys and evaluates Höhnel's career, Ildikó Simanyi—now Cazan-Simanyi—explains that in all probability, by the time he wrote his memoirs he had abandoned the nineteenth century's acceptance of the wanton slaughter of animals in the wild and had begun to move toward a more modern attitude of conservation, causing him to forget—or repress—Teleki's aristocratic passion for the hunt.[37] His uncharacteristic lack of candor on this matter may, therefore, have been unconscious rather than deliberate.

On two further occasions there is evidence that Höhnel allowed William Astor Chanler to influence the contents of his final manuscript. In 1923 Höhnel asked Chanler to comment on the drafts of three chapters he had recently completed. In a lengthy response, Chanler indicated on November 4 that he was generally pleased with the material he had read, but he raised objections to two passages in which his former companion had been truthful to the point of embarrassment. Chanler was distressed, for example, that Höhnel had referred to George Galvin, who had accompanied their expedition and had demonstrated invaluable organizational skills, as Chanler's "servant." Chanler insisted that Höhnel change the reference:

> Our friend George Galvin, it is true, was my servant. He is now [however] in a high situation in the hotel business and it would do him no good to have you allude to him in this book as *my servant*. He has . . . six children and has built up a dignified position for himself. When I wrote my book I stupidly mentioned the fact that he was my servant; but happily this book is out of print and is long since forgotten. I hope you will understand this and find it not too difficult to allude to him *as being employed by me*. The world is stupid enough to attach great importance to words.[38]

In fact, Galvin was the son of a gardener on the estate of the Delano family adjacent to Rokeby.[39] Nonetheless, in the final text Höhnel describes Galvin in so vague a manner—"George Galvin came of a less illustrious family [than William Astor Chanler], but he also hailed from Rokeby on the Hudson, where the Chanlers had their family seat" (p. 100)—that uninformed readers would have no reason to believe that he came from anything other than solid bourgeois origins.

Chanler also objected to a passage in the draft of what appears below as chapter 7, "About Africa." In comparing the leaders of the two expeditions in which he had participated, Höhnel had written that Chanler, unlike Teleki, had gone "for things rashly and irresponsibly." In calling for revision, a displeased Chanler explained that the passage in question "would be construed in America where I happily have many political enemies . . . as an attack upon my own personal character." He therefore suggested that Höhnel simply write "that I appeared at times willing to run risks which were not commensurate with the value of the object to be achieved. This in itself is a criticism; but nevertheless it is not offensive, at least to me."[40] Confronted with a critical William Astor Chanler, Ludwig Ritter von Höhnel, who more than once in Africa had bravely faced a charging rhinoceros, lost his courage. In his final manuscript he abandoned his earlier formulation and meekly followed Chanler's lead, simply noting that "it was indeed a sight to watch my young traveling companion running risks that were not always commensurate with the object to be achieved. He often needed to be cautioned." As in the case of his reference to Galvin, Höhnel revealed that on occasion he could be loyal to a friend to a fault.

IV

That it was not his only failing is apparent from the memoirs that follow. In chapter 10, for example, Höhnel seems almost proud of his sometimes cavalier attitude toward his obligations as commander of a warship. Throughout the memoirs, moreover, he makes no attempt to hide that he could be arrogant, petulant, and aloof—qualities that cannot have made serving under his stern command an unmitigated pleasure. The memoirs also show that Höhnel shared some of the late nineteenth century's least edifying characteristics. Thus even if the Habsburg Monarchy itself harbored few realistic or sustained colonial ambitions in Africa,[41] he fully shared in the culture of the new imperialism that had such a profound impact upon the African continent during the last decades of the nineteenth century. Höhnel's memoirs leave little doubt that he supported German and British colonial activities in the pre-war period, while following World War I, he expressed the hope and the conviction that Germany would soon succeed in regaining its lost African colonies.[42] And finally, he was guilty of the racism that afflicted so many Europeans of his generation. Not only do his memoirs frequently betray a prejudice against native peoples, but his post-war correspondence with William Astor Chanler includes a number of undeniably anti-Semitic remarks.

Yet as disturbing as these statements surely are, in all probability they were written not out of conviction but out of self-interest. Höhnel had been associated with William Astor Chanler long enough to know that his American friend was indiscriminately bigoted. Obsessed in his later life with a belief that the Vatican was intent on world domination, Chanler was also anti-Semitic. A large portion of his extensive correspondence with Höhnel after 1918 survives, and it reveals both that he repeatedly drew his friend's attention to an alleged "Jewish world conspiracy," and that he expected Höhnel to share his views. Writing on March 22, 1923, for example, Chanler complained: "You don't seem disturbed by the fact that your town is overrun by Jews. You accept it in a sort of fatal way."[43]

Höhnel may have risen to the challenge for a highly personal reason. Although there is no certainty in the matter, it is possible that Höhnel wrote his anti-Semitic comments as a smokescreen to hide a potentially damaging piece of information. According to Nazi records from 1943, Valeska von Höhnel, née van Ostéren, was of Jewish origin.[44] There is unfortunately no proof that Höhnel was himself aware of this fact, and it is not even certain that his wife, who had been born into a family that had fully assimilated into German culture, was well informed on her family's background. One thing is nevertheless certain. If Chanler had known of Valeska van Ostéren's background, he never would have served as a witness at Höhnel's wedding in 1909, and he would not have maintained the friendship that closely bound him with the couple until his death in 1934.

There was, however, a more important reason than mere friendship for Höhnel to express anti-Semitic sentiments in his correspondence with Chanler following the collapse of the Habsburg Monarchy. During the post-war period he came increasingly to rely upon the wealthy American for financial support. As inflation seriously reduced the buying power of his pension, Höhnel continually drew Chanler's attention to his deteriorating financial situation. At first Chanler responded with occasional handouts. Then, in October 1925 he ordered his bank in Paris to send Höhnel a monthly remittance of 1,000 French francs.[45] Ever more dependent upon a patron who badgered him on the issue of anti-Semitism, Höhnel seems to have responded on cue. It would not, of course, have been unusual for a retired Austrian naval officer to have harbored anti-Semitic thoughts in the 1920s. In Höhnel's case, however, it is far more likely that his occasional anti-Semitic remarks were written primarily to assure Chanler that he was worthy of continuing aid. It may not have been the action of a moral hero. Nevertheless, it enabled a retired Habsburg naval officer to supplement his meager post-war pension so that he could continue to lead the bourgeois lifestyle to which he and his wife had become accustomed before 1914.

As far as Höhnel's views on native African peoples are concerned, moreover, even here there are mitigating factors. That he was guilty of racist attitudes is not open to question. To his credit, however, on more than one occasion he was able to transcend the intellectual limitations of his class, his profession, and his time. His experiences in Abyssinia demonstrate, for example, that knowledge eventually tempered prejudice. At first undeniably biased against Ethiopians, by the time he completed his mission to Addis Ababa in 1905 he had developed a measure of admiration and respect for them. He also showed genuine compassion for the lot of local peoples who were employed as porters on Count Teleki's expedition to Lake Rudolf, while he recognized the major contributions Africans had made to the success of European expeditions. Moreover, in explaining to his readers how Teleki, his expedition facing the very real possibility of starvation, had ordered food to be taken by force from natives who had nothing to spare, Höhnel indicates a measure of shame that was hardly characteristic of the majority of the explorers of his generation. "Acts of violence of course do not go off without bloodshed, and this grieved us more than I can say, for the natives had been friendly, and we were the first Europeans they had ever met." With cool if macabre objectivity, Höhnel elsewhere regretfully recognizes the grim realities of survival in the wild: "One may well believe that we would have preferred to act as apostles of peace in the heart of Africa. In truth, it is no pleasure to fire with repeaters and other modern rifles into a crowd of defenseless natives."

The most striking example of Höhnel's refusal to submit fully to the cultural bias of his time comes, however, in a passage that appears in only the German version of his memoirs:

> We met, albeit rarely, individuals who had been entirely untouched by any sort of civilizing influence and yet who were on so high a moral level and who possessed such intelligence that we could not help but ask ourselves if so great a cultural difference in fact exists between Europeans and primitive native peoples, as is generally assumed, and if the tiny bit of civilization that we have to our advantage justifies the superiority that we claim for ourselves.[46]

In his book on the Lake Rudolf region, Herbert Tichy finds this passage so astonishing that he declares Höhnel to have been a "humane explorer" who was "far in advance of his time."[47] Yet as extraordinary as the passage undoubtedly is, its impact is diminished by Höhnel's failure to translate it into English. Why he omitted it from the manuscript he hoped to publish in the United States must unfortunately remain a mystery, but it is possible that once again William Astor Chanler exerted his influence, albeit only indirectly. In his long letter of November 4, 1923, in which he responded to Höhnel's request for comments on chapters he had sent for evaluation, Chanler strongly advised him to delete a statement in which he admitted that he had found at least some of the African women he had encountered physically attractive—a statement prompted, Höhnel later confided, "by the memory of a delightful maiden, whom I met in Turkana, who at the time made my heart beat quite strong."[48] Though Chanler's ostensible reason for striking the statement was practical, his own racism may well have played a role. "Remember," he advised Höhnel, "[that] the big sale of this book, if it has one, will be in America; and there we have a hatred of negroes—perhaps entirely unjustified;—but nevertheless it dominates our whole life. And I fear that perhaps the allusions you make might arouse hostile criticism and hurt the book."[49] Eager to reap royalties from the sale of an eventual American edition of his book, Höhnel dutifully followed Chanler's advice and struck the statement from the final version of his memoirs. Having done so, he may also have taken Chanler's warning to heart and decided against including a passage in which he admitted admiring the morals and the intelligence of some of the African peoples with whom he had come into contact. Given his loyalty to Chanler and his dependence upon his friend for financial support, it would have been entirely in character for him to have done so.

V

Almost seventy-five years after Ludwig Ritter von Höhnel sent his completed manuscript to Edward Motley Pickman in the hope of finding an American publisher, his memoirs at long last appear in English. Virtually without exception, the words that follow are Höhnel's own. As indicated earlier, however, the order in which those words appear within sentences has frequently undergone revision in the interest of clarity and felicity of style. Other editorial interventions have been kept to a minimum. Because the first two chapters of Höhnel's manuscript, which deal with his childhood and choice of profession, are unusually short, these have been combined, with the result that while the German edition of the memoirs has fourteen chapters, the English edition has but thirteen. On those few occasions when it has been necessary to provide additions to the text, these appear either as footnotes or, in cases where the editors have been able to supply first names to persons Höhnel identifies by last name only, in brackets. As far as geographical locations are concerned, Höhnel consistently refers to these as they were known to him at the time he served as an officer of the Austro-Hungarian navy—that is, as they appeared on maps published before the major territorial changes that followed the conclusion of World War I. The editors have allowed these now archaic names to stand, but they have provided modern nomenclature in parentheses on first mention. In the case of Ethiopia, on the other hand, they have replaced Höhnel's cumbersome Germanic renderings of Amharic place names with modern English transliterations. Finally, because the memoirs end abruptly with his retirement from the navy, Ronald Coons has prepared an epilogue that covers the little that is known of Höhnel's life between 1909 and his death in Vienna on March 23, 1942, at the age of 84.

J. Winthrop Aldrich
Ronald E. Coons
Pascal James Imperato

1

Family, Youth, and Choice of Profession (1857–1876)

Of my ancestors on my father's side I only know that during the reign of the great Empress Maria Theresa three brothers had emigrated from Bromberg (Bydgoszcz) in Posen (Poznań) to Austria, where they separated and settled in different German-speaking provinces. The branch from which my father descended settled in Vienna as silk manufacturers. As far back as can be remembered, my ancestors on my mother's side had lived in Bruck an der Leitha, a little German town on the Hungarian border, where they had been well-to-do landowners. None of the lines had known how to amass riches, however. To the contrary, in the course of time their fortunes declined, so that instead of going into the business of his forefathers my father was obliged to seek out another profession. He studied at the University of Vienna, and his transcript shows that he was an excellent student. He then went into the civil service, rising in later life to a prominent position. In turn he was entrusted with the organization of the customs administration of the former "military frontier," then of Venetia, and finally of Trieste and Istria; in 1864 he was appointed provincial director of customs at Trieste.[1]

My father must have married around the age of thirty, and he had several sons and daughters. Without being in the least of a coarse nature, my father was nevertheless a hard and inflexible man whose chief trait was an exaggerated sense of justice and duty. All through his life he refused even the smallest and most obvious privilege for his own person, and the fear that his perfect integrity might in any way be questioned was quite morbid. If, for example, my mother wished to have a hot salt bath at home, such as the doctor had ordered, then she, the wife of the customs director, had to submit a written petition like every other mortal, because sea water, containing salt, was a state monopoly and could not be drawn without permission, even though it flowed directly below our windows. On another occasion he acted in a most stern manner toward one of my brothers, who had failed his final exams at the classical *Gymnasium*. He would not allow him to repeat the year but instead gave him a post in his office as an unsalaried clerk. Normally one remained on this

1

lowest plane for one or, at the most, two years. But so that no one could say that he was showing favoritism toward his son, he made him remain in the same lowly position for three whole years. Toward my eldest brother he also proceeded in a most strict and rigorous fashion. This does not mean that he was an unkind man or that he was a tyrant. Rather he was extremely conscientious and was faithful to a severe ethical code.

I was born the youngest of four brothers in the Hungarian coronation city of Pressburg (Bratislava) on August 6, 1857. I was therefore relatively young when we moved to Trieste. In an official's family, even though the father may occupy a comparatively high position, means are often limited when there are many children. In those days salaries were extremely low, and my father had no private fortune. Certain luxuries, such as visiting a spa or going away for the summer, were luckily unknown at that time. But many of the economy measures that were part of our daily routine were similar to those that were characteristic of so many families after the Great War. Memory tells of worn-out suits being passed on to me from my brothers, and torn shoe soles were a familiar sight. But I am afraid that I was neither tidy nor careful in that respect—my nether garments would have shown tears and grass stains whether they had been new or old.

We brothers all harbored a special predilection for natural science, a fact that caused us to neglect the usual pastimes of youth. I remember that in my earliest childhood some of our chief pleasures were catching beetles and butterflies, collecting plants, and arranging herbaria. At home we always had a galaxy of crickets, lizards, snakes, and capricorn and stag beetles; these we fed in order to keep them alive so that we could observe them for as long as possible. To this end we often made long excursions, from which we generally returned laden with rich booty. Later we went in for botany, wherein my brothers and to a lesser extent I excelled. The teachers in the higher schools that I later attended did not hesitate to say that I was better informed on this subject than they were.

In general my parents failed to exercise a positive pedagogical influence. I rarely saw my father. He lived unto himself and did not take his meals in the family circle but alone in his room, which was taboo for the rest of us, probably because his strictly kept office hours did not tally with the usual dinner hour. As he was a very serious and reserved man, we had very little contact with one another. For her part my good mother, who was an excellent housewife, had her hands full trying to cope with her numerous household duties, whereby she—and this is merely a supposition—found little support from my father. In our house there was no lack of harmony—I cannot remember anything in the nature of a scene—but at the same time we did not have a really happy family circle. When addressing our parents, we children did so in the most formal manner, which with Germans meant a lack of affectionate relations.

At Trieste I first attended an elementary school where instruction was in Italian; at the age of nine I passed into the German Gymnasium, where I failed in the very first year. Though I was not a keen student, perhaps one would have shown me some indulgence, but in that year, 1868, my father died, and the school no longer had to make allowances for the son of the director of customs. The death of the head of the family was more of a catastrophe in officers' and officials' families than it was for others. In comparison with my father's modest income, my mother's widow's pension was a mere pittance, which made life a hardship for her. The estate my father left behind him amounted to a total of about 700 florins. She could, however, count on a modest subsidy from her mother, and no doubt that was the reason we moved to Vienna. After my unfortunate experience in the Gymnasium I was made to try the *Realschule* or scientific secondary school, but even in the lowest class I had no luck. The schools of the capital stood on a far higher level than those in the provinces. Thereafter I was again sent to school in a classical Gymnasium as an external pupil in the Theresianum, where I had to start at the bottom of the ladder for a third time. Study was hardly my special gift, but I was finally able to steer clear of the biggest shoals and to avoid any further shipwreck. As I had a talent for languages and a predilection for their study, I did not find Latin and Greek very hard. Incredibly, I had been dismissed from the Realschule because I had failed religion. I therefore became aware of just how highly the school authorities regarded this subject, and I later acted accordingly. The other subjects we learned at the Theresianum were so few that it was quite possible to pass, though my inclination drew me in another direction.

I very much missed the attractive life of the port town, and the long distances in the capital were an obstacle to wandering about in the country. From my days at the Realschule I had a good friend who had the same tastes as I, and we remained close. He was the only son of an amiable and kind widow whose bourgeois home did not disclose the fact that her husband had once belonged to the French Foreign Legion. Their son was my permanent and only companion, all the more as he willingly followed my inclinations. Already at an early age powder and lead fascinated me. At first I manufactured gunpowder myself, and though it is true that I only managed to produce a gray dusty mixture, it nevertheless made the desired noise. I also fashioned my own gun using the mortar of my sister's dolls' kitchen, inside of which I pasted a well-annealed chalk cylinder, filling the form with lead. The chalk was removed, a vent bored, and the gun was ready. As it consisted of soft lead it was not durable, but it was absolutely safe, and it could be loaded with gunpowder until it burst. With a firmly fixed clay stopper, the little contrivance went off with a tremendous bang. My friend and I often went outside the city, preferably to the Vienna Woods, where on Sundays thousands of nature-loving citizens animated its glades and not a few policemen could also be found. When the coast was clear and we thought the moment had come, we fired off our miniature cannon in the silence of the woods and then promptly pocketed it. With the most innocent mien in the world we then took to our heels, vastly enjoying the ensuing excitement.

At the Theresianum I had some fellow students with whom I was friends, but only among the boarders. Being good at Latin, I often was able to assist weaker colleagues with their lessons. A few students collected stamps, something that did not interest me. But since I could obtain a profusion of these from my brother-in-law, a rich merchant in Trieste, this earned me many a friend. Another boy who became my friend spoke Spanish fluently and had been with his father in Mexico at the court of the unhappy Emperor Maximilian. This was my first incentive toward enthusiasm for this language, and later I learned it perfectly and raved about everything that had any connection with the land of the hidalgos. It sufficed for somebody to have been in Spain for only a short time for me to feel attracted to him in envious admiration, even though he might not be a pleasant person in any other respect.

Besides descriptions of travel, Spanish and later on classical writers formed my exclusive reading. In my choice of books I was solely dependent on my instinct, which drew me to serious and, strange to say, foreign-tongued writings. I only read novels in later years, and never liked works of poetry. I must confess that to the present day I have but a poor acquaintance with classical German literature. Grown older, I regret never having had any training in this respect, just as I also lament that even today the schools exercise so little influence on the younger generation regarding what they read, so that they are not familiar with the titles of those hundred standard works that every man who claims to be a cultured individual ought to know.

I used to spend my holidays every year at Bruck an der Leitha in the house of my aged but still very active grandmother. I had no playmates of my own age there, but I could freely wander about all over the countryside, learn to handle carts and horses, and make myself generally useful. I was not in anybody's way, and I shirked no kind of work. I was not a strong but rather a lanky boy, but I was tough and persevering, hardened against heat and cold, never ill, and free of every other passion excepting that of cigarette smoking. In general I look back on a very joyless childhood, perhaps because Providence had encumbered me with too serious a nature.

I think I was about eight years old when my father, on the occasion of one of our rare interviews, asked me for the first time what I should like to be in life. My answer was that I was quite sure that I would become a sailor. My father nodded his head and responded, "That's right." I had always longed for the sea, and I can truly say that I would decide in the same manner if I should come into the world a second time. This idea occupied me even in Vienna, where we were far from the sea, ships, and the bustle of the harbor. Whenever I could, I wandered to the Danube River, where extensive works for the regulation of its course were going on at the time. There I watched for hours the work of the rattling dredgers, the moving to and fro of the fast tenders, and the towing of the large lighters laden with rubble, and I envied the men who had a share in this activity. Here there was an end in view, whereas my days passed away on the school bench without meaning. As I have mentioned, it was books on travel and especially on voyages of discovery that gave me the greatest reading pleasure, even those that were much too serious and scientific for my years, much to the astonishment of my teachers. These travel books, which I borrowed from the school's library, referred to all parts of the globe, and I wished to become acquainted with every one of them. One day to my great joy I chanced to hit upon K. R. Brommy's well-known book *The Navy*,[2] and that enabled me to enter more deeply into the mysteries of seamanship. I at once took to carving a large model ship out of wood, working on it for months, and I rigged it with masts and yards to the best of my knowledge. Later I happened to find in one of the newspapers the advertisement of a school for seamanship in Hamburg, and that made me think and dream of nothing else; I sent off for a catalogue and studied it day and night. My mother did not take any interest in my visionary life, however, and whenever I expressed my enthusiasm for the sea she always cut me short, saying, "You'd better take to learning more diligently." That caused me to think of simply running away from home and enlisting in some port as a cabin boy, in case I should not be permitted to follow my heart's desire—though being without any means, I was at a loss to know how I could get there.

The years glided by without bringing any change in the situation until the close of my third year at the Theresianum. The instruction we received there was quite inadequate, and even in that I had not partaken with any zeal, since the material we were taught did not appear to me to be of any use for my aims. What good would Latin and Greek do me at sea? Accordingly, my report card at the close of the third class was mediocre except for geography and the classical languages. This I flung on the table, telling my mother that it was the last one I would ever bring home. These words and the serious way in which I uttered them finally made an impression. My mother deliberated what should be done with me and finally launched a petition to the Admiralty requesting my admittance to the naval college at Fiume (Rijeka). This was not entirely to my taste, for I would far more have preferred to be thrown at once into stirring adventures on distant seas, even if only as a cabin boy. I therefore did not like the idea of having to spend four more years under strict discipline in a military academy. In time the ministerial reply came, which at first caused not a little embarrassment. I had frivolously idled away—and therewith lost—two years and therefore had become too old for entrance into the first class of the naval college. For entry into the second class, however, I was granted a free scholarship "in case the petitioner will comply with the terms of admission." And there was the rub. The entrance examinations were given in Fiume. In my grammar school I had learned wretchedly little in all branches excepting the classical languages. I was certainly at home in geography and matters of natural science, but in other subjects I had in fact not passed beyond the first elements. To be admitted into the second class of the naval academy a knowledge of various subjects, in particular mathematics, physics, and chemistry, was demanded. Yet I had never even heard, for example, of trigonometry. To gain all this knowledge I had no more than fourteen weeks at my disposal. There being very little hope as to my admission to the naval college, a second possibility was to enter the nautical school at Trieste so that I might join the merchant marine. But even to go there I would have to pass the required examinations in Fiume.

Thereafter such cramming went on as I had never known before, under the surveillance and guidance of an older brother, who not only possessed extraordinary qualifications but who was also prepared to be severe and even brutal, to the point that soon sight and hearing began to fail me. My brother, who was six years my senior, was very talented and exceedingly diligent, and he had always been an excellent student. The scholastic wisdom that I lacked, he relentlessly drummed into my head from morning until late at night, with terms of endearment or, if necessary, with scolding and knocks. These were awful, hard times for me, added to which I had to attend my regular school classes except for Greek, which I very sensibly dropped.

The hot summer months passed in such a manner, during which I was never allowed to stroll about in the surroundings of the town, not even to see the great Vienna World's Fair of 1873. Only on Sunday afternoons was I permitted to have a swim in the Danube, where there were very primitive bathing accommodations. Yet despite my uninterrupted and diligent studies I did not seem to be making much progress. To the contrary, I had the feeling that the chaos in my head was increasing day by day. My tyrant of a brother was utterly dissatisfied with me, and when the last hour had gone by he dismissed me with words that were as little adapted to fortifying my assurance as they were suitable to be transmitted to my contemporaries. With little comfort and still less confidence, at the end of August I set out on my journey to Fiume, where my fate was to be decided.

There I was again near the beloved sea, where I saw real ships with towering masts or with funnels puffing away clouds of smoke. But my heart was weighed down by anxious feelings as heavy as lead, which nipped all cheerfulness in the bud. The sight of the naval college building, although it was only partially to be seen behind iron railings, amid high poplar trees and green bushes, made an uneasy impression upon me. In Fiume I did not know a soul, but I was furnished with a letter of recommendation to the retired Captain Heinrich von Littrow, a brother of the well-known astronomer.[3] I called on him in the course of the first day and found myself in the presence of a friendly, gray-haired gentleman with merry blue eyes in a reddish face, who at first remained mute. Then suddenly, as if struck by a very interesting discovery, he looked at me sharply and told me I most certainly was well qualified for the navy, having eyes that could see particularly well at night. This was not much, but it filled me with a certain satisfaction.

The slight comfort with which Littrow had filled me vanished the following morning when I faced the stern commander of the academy, Captain von Lindner. He was a strikingly handsome man with fine lines, a head of carefully parted grayish hair, and a short-cropped beard. Bundles of paper were lying on his desk, giving evidence of the burdensome office he had to administer. After a piercing glance of his clear gray eyes had superficially glided over me, he asked with a metallic, clear, and severe voice, though not in a gruff manner, "What's your name?" Then, after a short silence, he continued, "You wish to enter the second class, having been only in a grammar school for four years? That's out of the question, quite impossible. What have you learned?" Accustomed from school to a certain order of the various subjects of instruction, I slowly and shyly began by saying, "Religion." And when he thereupon burst forth with an angry "Confound it!" I went on to say, "Latin and Greek." I did not get any further, because a flood of angry ejaculations cut me short. The storm was followed by some seconds of quiet. Then, with a softened voice he said, "After all, you may try it. The examinations begin tomorrow; we shall see."

It is obvious that thereafter I lost all hope of being admitted to the academy. When the examinations began the next day, however, a certain change had taken place within me thanks to my seven-day rest from studying. The chaos in my fully crammed brain had settled down somewhat, and there did not prevail the same mathematical, physical, and chemical confusion as before. This feeling improved with every examination that I took, and my mind was better able than ever before to concentrate upon the subject at hand. In short, I succeeded in passing the examination with preference, to the great astonishment of the commander. Twelve candidates had applied, but only two places were vacant, and I had passed with by far the best marks. That made so strong and lasting an impression upon the commander that he not only favored me during my years in college but continued to be my great admirer even later on, when I was in active service.

The academy was housed in a building three stories high, situated in a park, hard by the high road leading from Fiume to Volosca (Volosko). From the upper stories one could enjoy a wonderful view encompassing the entire Gulf of Fiume. In the distance, far to the south, were to be seen in azure tints the steep shores of the rocky islands of Cherso (Cres) and Veglia (Krk). To the right the view spread over the surroundings of Abbazia (Opatija), at the time still lost in dreams, its beauties being as yet unknown, with the graceful outlines of Monte Maggiore in the background, in winter covered with snow. To the east one could survey the denuded shores of Croatia, which are frequently haunted by furious bora gales.

In former years the academy had been a military school for the training of infantry cadets and therefore did not answer its present purpose. I think it was in consequence of a request from the Hungarian government that the naval college had been transferred to Fiume, on Hungarian territory, after having first been in Venice, later on in Trieste, and then on board the training ship *Venus*. From the academy's windows one surveyed the sea, which was bordered by huge cubic concrete blocks, but one could not get there because of the railroad tracks of the nearby station, which were shut off by a high stone wall. There was, of course, no landing place, and the naval college did not dispose of even a launch or a bathing place or any practical educational tools referring to the sea, which was obviously a great drawback for a naval college. The classrooms, which were on the second floor of the building, and the dormitories situated over them, were tolerable. But there were no instructional models or plans on the walls, nor were there any manuals, except a few copies of a book referring to the art of ship's maneuvering and rigging and a handbook on oceanography. The pupils were compelled to jot down the lectures of the teachers and to make fair copies of them, which burdened them with work beyond measure. In one corner of the park there was a ship's mast for sailing exercises, and nearby there was an imitation of a battery deck, showing several old muzzle-loading guns on truck carriages and two cast-iron Wahrendorf breech-loading guns—and this in the days of Armstrong and Krupp guns! The interior of the building and the walls of the corridors and rooms were plain and showed no object whatsoever that referred to the sea. There were not even pictures of battles and ships calculated to arouse enthusiasm and love for their vocation in the souls of the young inmates, whose home it was for four long years. Only the entrance hall showed the row of Werndl carbines needed for infantry drill. The academy did possess, however, a fine large chapel, in which Mass was celebrated on Sundays.

Various teachers were appointed as instructors. A frigate captain instructed us in the art of ship's rigging and maneuver, and a boatswain taught us how to make the many knots, bends, loops, and hitches. A naval architect lectured on his special subject and also on steamship engineering, using sketches that he made on a blackboard in default of plans and designs. Our instruction in maritime law, tactics, military history, and oceanography was committed to retired Corvette Captain Attlmayr, who in 1866 had been Vice Admiral Tegetthoff's chief of staff during the Battle of Lissa (Viz).[4] The other subjects were entrusted to various teachers, some of whom were civilians. The paymaster taught us to speak Croatian; the chaplain, who had experienced the famous circumnavigation that the frigate *Novara* had accomplished in the years 1855–57, taught us Italian; and assistant teachers were appointed for French and English. Several officers of the now disbanded Marine Infantry Corps acted as superintendents; they had no prestige and no educational influence. In summing up, I am sorry to state that everything concerning our education and instruction was far from adequate. Indeed, it was deficient even in the most indispensable areas, and it was entirely due to the incredible zeal and application of the pupils that astonishing results were obtained. At the time of which I am speaking the navy was not yet well known in the interior of our Monarchy and was by no means as popular as it was to become a decade or two later. The boys who joined the navy in my day were all well suited to this vocation or were at least filled with an adventurous spirit.

The four classes were normally twenty-four to thirty in size, and between them there was no intercourse whatsoever. During the leisure hours a separate part of the park was allotted to each of them for recreational purposes. The several classes confronted each other reservedly, sometimes even with hostility. Among the pupils of one and the same class, on the other hand, harmony prevailed, and coarse or oppressive acts never occurred. Some boys attached themselves to others with more or less warm feelings of friendship, but nobody was slighted or bullied. One could often see a better man help a less-qualified mate in his studies; we were all too much engrossed in our studies to think of mischief or nonsense. The boys came from all parts of the Monarchy. Very few were natives of our seashores, and as a rule they were lacking in the knowledge of the German language, in which all lectures were given. The pupils were mostly the sons of officers or civil servants; only one out of a hundred came from wealthier circles, but a large number could boast a noble title. Of this, however, not much fuss was made. The navy, without thinking or premeditation, was to a certain extent rather democratic. This circumstance and an apparent indifference regarding religious matters were characteristic of our navy, at least for the staff.

Hard times began for all of us as soon as the lectures started, not the least for me. We had to get up at 5:00 A.M. in summer and at 6:00 in winter, and we were kept busy until bedtime at 9:00 in the evening. We were free from noon to 2:00 P.M. and for a half hour in the afternoon. Every minute of the rest of the day was profitably employed, and the days passed in hard studies and other work, the zeal of all pupils knowing no bounds. The subjects that had to be mastered were so wide-ranging that the teachers could barely cover the material, and only the last two weeks at the end of the half-year term were left for examinations. These were the hardest weeks of all, during which we used to plunge into our notebooks even at dinner time and at night in our beds. It was of course impossible to be prepared for passing an examination on all subjects on every one of these last days. The more considerate teachers therefore allowed us to report to them when we were ready to be examined. But not all of them were so humane, and that frequently led to catastrophe.[5]

The fiery zeal with which every one of the pupils was filled during the examination period can be explained by the fact that a student's final transcript determined the rank of enrollment in the navy. It was a particularly difficult period for me, since my preparatory training had been insufficient, and the branches connected with mathematics gave me particular difficulties. Unfortunately, these were precisely the most important subjects, and they counted fourfold, while the others were counted treble, double, or simple according to their importance. The total number of points decided the rank in the class and the rank at which one entered the navy. Thanks to the good entrance examination I had passed, I was at once valued as one of the "select" pupils, and at Christmas time I was even gratified with two gold braids on the collar, the corresponding distinction. These I kept during all my years at the college, though only by virtue of the commander's authority. The certificate of a pupil belonging to the select order could not show anything less than a "satisfactory" mark in any subject. I knew very well how to produce technical designs and drawings, and my handwriting at the time was excellent, but with regard to freehand drawing I truly deserved the lowest mark. It would have been absurd to rank me in the last category, but my teacher was furious when the commander ordered him to judge my skill in freehand drawing more leniently.

Very little was done in the way of recreation, for there was no spare time left for that. On very rare occasions we were taken to a play at the theater in Fiume. Once a week we had a dancing lesson, and once every year the academy held a ball. I had no liking whatever for dancing, thinking it to be a very unmanly kind of amusement, and I therefore kept aloof from any such activity, which I much regretted in later life. Of course we engaged in such practical exercises as gymnastics and fencing—in both of which I showed some skill—as well as infantry and sailing drill on the mast in the park, but not in exaggerated measure; there was no opportunity for us to have a swim. On Sunday afternoons the three lower classes—the pupils of the uppermost class were allowed to promenade where they liked—frequently undertook excursions in common to the surroundings. If there happened to be an opportunity, one put up at an inn or coffeehouse to eat a little something, for which, however, the pupils themselves had to pay. On such occasions some of the boys made off without paying for what they had taken. During my stay in the academy these bamboozlements were twice committed to such an extent that the wronged innkeepers lodged complaints with the commander. The offenders did not deny their guilt but rather laughingly confessed that they had been hungry and had had no money, which one could readily believe. This trait in the pupils' demeanor was all the more astonishing as in every other respect they revealed a very highly developed sense of honor. It may be that at the bottom of this nuisance lay only the recollection of some piratical novel they had read.

As is more or less the case everywhere, the academy was not exempt from protection, prejudice, and injustice. For example, if one had the good fortune to begin as a select pupil, then he remained such, for the law of inertia made itself felt. If, on the other hand, one had a bad beginning, then it was very hard and almost impossible to work one's way up to a higher order, as I learned all too well. I do not know why, but the physics teacher took a dislike to me from the first, and I would not have obtained a mark better than "satisfactory" even if all the wisdom of modern science had been at my disposal. I had another sad experience with the navigation teacher, instruction in which started in the third year. This was a very important subject, counting as it did fourfold. This teacher had barely mastered his subject, although he had been teaching it for many years. After having lectured until near the end of the half-year term, he announced that on the following day he would begin examining us. This was not the case, however, for he began by repeating for some time what he had just discussed the previous day. Only later in the class did he ask who was prepared to pass an examination. As it turned out, nobody was. Everyone sat tight on the bench with his face deeply plunged into his notebook. In spite of the teacher's repeated inquiry, several painful minutes passed, with no one willing to be the victim. I was in no way better prepared than the others and was certainly not the best student in the class, but being unable to stand the unpleasant situation any longer and incited by a certain sense of shame, I stepped up, thoroughly convinced it was merely a question of killing time until the remaining half hour had elapsed.

This was a mistake for which I was to pay dearly. The teacher busied himself with confronting me with some of the more difficult problems and continued after the hour had struck. Thereupon one of my lynx-eyed mates, who was seated next to the lecturing desk, revealed to me that he had plainly seen how the teacher had marked an "insufficient" in his notebook. That was certainly not calculated to set me at ease. I therefore ran after the navigator and questioned him whether this was true. He did not answer with a "yes" or a "no" but continued on his way, saying only: "Don't worry; a single swallow does not make a summer." In the future, however, no properly solved problem got me any mark better than "satisfactory."

There were both oral and written parts to the final examinations in navigation. The latter portion consisted of solving three nautical problems within one hour in the presence of the teacher, who sat at his desk and watched us with Argus eyes. The calculations that had to be worked did not vary with every one of the pupils, for there were only three varieties for the whole class, and these were graduated in difficulty according to the qualification of the three categories into which the class was divided. At the end of the hour the teacher collected the sheets and took them to his office, locked the door, and went his way. If he only once would have thought of comparing the calculations that we had initially delivered to him with those which a few hours later were lying on the table in his office! From time immemorial there had been a picklock in use. Nobody knew where it came from, but there it was, passed down from one student to another, year after year. Soon after the noon meal the whole class stole one by one into the classroom, where strange things came to pass. Someone unlocked the teacher's office, fetched the sheets he had collected, and distributed them among the several pupils. The best navigators in the class were busy solving the problems on the blackboard. The others copied them, whereby the lesser qualified were wise enough to intersperse one or more indifferent errors into their work. As soon as all were ready, the sheets wandered back again into the office. This occurred year after year. These proceedings were of course not useful to the instruction of the lesser qualified pupils. But if one considers how small the percentage of officers was who, in the course of their careers, were ever employed as navigating lieutenants on long voyages, which is the only occasion when a greater knowledge of the nautical art is essential, then one will not tax so very high the inconvenience of this abuse.

The end of the scholastic year wound up with a six-week cruise on board a frigate or corvette, which took the pupils to one and the other of the nearer ports in the Mediterranean. This was the high point of the year, to which all the pupils enthusiastically looked forward. One could see them for days in advance spying about to see whether the vessel destined for their accommodation had arrived. At the same time they envied the lucky chaps who, after having lived in seclusion and strict discipline for four long years, had overcome the time of suffering and were now going to face life, freedom, and their vocation. Now that these had completed their schooling, they walked about as proud as kings in long frock coats, gilt sword dangling at their side, and they could go and come just as they liked, until the train carried them off to their respective homes.

On board ship we were of course instructed only in practical matters. We were at last taught to row and sail in boats and had in general to work the mizzenmast, the pupils of the oldest class doing the duty of midshipmen. The officers treated us more or less kindly, according to their temper, though some were brutal, making us sweat and not allowing us much sleep during the night watches. But that taught us to sleep as sound as rats anywhere—in hammocks, on wooden planks, or even in a coil of rope. We did not get coffee and milk for breakfast but plain boiled potatoes, salt herring or cheese, and, of course, hard biscuits. The worst was the drinking water, which in those days was not distilled, because of the myriad of animalcules that swarmed in it in all shapes and sizes. Even this water was made spare, and for washing purposes we had to use salt water. The program of the cruise, which allowed the ship to stay half of the time in port, had to be strictly observed. The weather conditions in our waters during the summer are generally fine, but now and then there were some stronger breezes, and not a few of the young naval heroes had to make a sacrifice to Neptune. Some of the boys became terribly seasick, and they used to take a solemn oath not to join the navy but rather to serve their term on horseback in one of the cavalry regiments. On the occasion of a rough passage on our way from Malta to Zante (Zakynthos) almost all pupils were down with seasickness. I have never suffered from it in the least, and to my mind there is nothing more impressive than a hard gale with a correspondingly agitated sea. I always, at least in my younger days, enjoyed a great uproar, when the sea foamed and the wind whizzed through the rig. Many a time of my own accord I relieved seasick mates who were stationed as lookout men on the forecastle.

A fourteen-day furlough closed the scholastic year. In order to relate a few more characteristics of life at the academy, I must record that on two occasions students came to blows—once a fight broke out between the boys of my class and the next inferior, and some months later between the third class and the uppermost one. At the bottom of these encounters lay as a rule a pert answer or a jostle or some such offense committed by a junior pupil against a senior one. The fights wound up with some swollen noses and black eyes, whereupon peace was restored. The smoking of cigarettes was prohibited, but violation of this interdiction was not severely censured; smoking was officially allowed for the two upper classes when I rose to the third class.

Sometime during the last half year in the surveying course the class was sent somewhere in the surrounding territory for about ten days to carry out a survey of a port and its seashore. We were sent to a small village and port lying on the island of Veglia. There we led a happy outdoors life, cheerfully busy with our work all day long, and we did not mind that we were rather uncomfortably quartered in very simple peasant houses. The mayor of the village had been in California and had returned to his native place with some wealth. He was married to a young wife of dazzling beauty, of whom, of course, we all became madly enamored, to the exasperation of the very jealous husband. A scorching heat rose from the bare and stony ground, and we soon looked like mulattos. That suited us well, because a bronze face and rough, hardened hands were considered smart and were much appreciated by the boys. The rocky land, dried up by a torrid sun, swarmed with innumerable poisonous vipers, which, judging by their liveliness, seemed to enjoy the heat. None of us was bitten, however.

This practical course in surveying was followed by another, so to speak, traditional abuse. The cartographic elements gathered in this survey were afterward used for the construction of a beautiful map. The drawing was performed in the teacher's office by the pupils who were best qualified for this kind of work. It was an old, sacred tradition that on this occasion the teacher was robbed of a good part of his annual store of pencils, colors, inks, brushes, India rubbers, drawing paper, and rulers. These proceedings were quite absurd, because nobody knew what to do with the plunder. Provided this "clearance" was not committed in too outrageous a manner, the teacher contented himself with reproaches and some bitter remarks. But when he was grossly harmed, he insisted on getting at least a part of the goods returned. This nuisance had no other evil consequences.

The academy was of course provided with lockups. Although I was a very serious and well-behaved pupil and although the commander was favorably disposed toward me, I nevertheless made their acquaintance on two occasions. The first time was because I persistently refused to be confirmed. An archbishop had arrived, and the pupils who had not yet been confirmed were ordered to enter into this sacred bliss. I did not think this to be so very necessary and preferred to go to prison for twenty-four hours as a martyr to my conviction. The second time was because I stubbornly declined to go to a ball given by the city.

Even four—or, in my case, three—years must have an end, and so for my class the dreaded last two weeks arrived—an atrocious span of time on account of the uninterrupted studying that went on, day and night. At the end of these examinations the faces of all the newly nominated midshipmen looked pale and tired, plainly showing the exhausting nature of these last weeks. The first examination day was already at hand when a surprising circumstance suddenly put an end to our cares and fears. An epidemic of a contagious kind of eye complaint had broken out, and the telegraphic order came to desist from all examinations and to dismiss the pupils at once on furlough. Overjoyed by this unexpected piece of good luck, we slipped into our frock coats and hurried to the chapel, there to take the service oath. With grave emotion we swore faithfully to serve the emperor-king and the realm by day and by night, on land and at sea, at any time. Thereafter we had to sign a certificate pledging never to join any secret society, by which Freemasonry was meant. Then at last we were free.

2

Three Years as a Midshipman
(1876–1879)

Although my youth was not very bright, far more awkward feelings surface when I think back on the decade following my days at the academy. Perhaps these first disillusionments subsequently got me out of the ordinary groove and influenced my life in such a remarkable way. The well-earned furlough I spent at home in Vienna came to an end at the beginning of August 1876; the old longing for the sea and activity had been reawakened, and my parting from relatives did not fill me with a heavy heart. In Pola (Pula), the main port of our navy, I met with my fellow students from the academy, who like myself had now joined the ranks. We had to report to quite a number of offices, running about for several days in full dress from one department to the other. But I can remember only one visit vividly, the one we made to the old port admiral, Baron Bourguignon.[1] A number of funny stories were told about him that were strikingly similar to Baron Munchhausen's tales. Bourguignon was an odd type. He always spun his yarns in such a pompous manner that nobody dared even to smirk when he told the same story for the hundredth time.

On the day we had to call on the admiral as a group, it so happened that his son, an older midshipman, also had to report, and this afforded us an occasion to witness a sample of his ways. He behaved toward his son just as a mighty lord might treat an utter stranger. After receiving his son's prescribed report, he asked him who he was. No matter what he said, no answer would satisfy his father, who stubbornly went on saying, "And, and?" Finally the young man explained that he was the son of a great admiral of worldwide fame. This, of course, was precisely what the admiral wanted to hear and was meant to impress us midshipmen. Surely he gained his end, but I am afraid not in the sense he had in mind.

After making our many calls we were no wiser concerning the authorities to which we were to report, because we were an embarrassment for every one of them. No one wished to be encumbered with such a lot of greenhorns. It was finally decreed that we were to work in the various departments of the navy yard. That sounded fine, although we had no idea precisely what services we

14

were to perform. For the moment, however, we were at least out of the way. Of course, we were of no use to the people at the navy yard, and we, too, were unhappy with the situation. We therefore went on infesting the different pubs and coffeehouses of the town, just as before. After a while, as a result of some offense we had committed, we were transferred on board the watch vessel, the old, worm-eaten frigate *Bellona*, from which we were only allowed to see the town by means of our telescopes. The captain was naturally furious about the disturbance caused by such a number of unbidden guests who were of no use to him whatsoever and for whose accommodation his ship was in no way prepared. It is obvious that we were treated like a herd of sheep and that everyone considered us a nuisance. This delivered the first blow to our childish belief in our importance. On board the *Bellona*, however, we were at least protected from the dark side of Pola and its expensive life. Already several of the sextants and telescopes with which we had been provided upon leaving the academy had found their way to the shop of a well-known money changer, who used to buy them cheaply and then sell them to members of the merchant marine.

The reason that Pola did not know what to do with us was that the vessel destined for our one-year cruise was not ready. The brand-new corvette *Donau* had been designated for this purpose, but her completion had unexpectedly been delayed. The authorities could not, however, let us idle away our time on board the watch vessel forever, and we were ultimately ordered on board the gunnery ship *Adria*, there to complete our training. The prospect of sitting on school benches again after so many years of studying was certainly not a cheery one and was not at all to our taste, but since the *Adria* was connected with the shore by a bridge, we could go and enjoy the charms of Pola whenever we liked. That comforted us somewhat.

Superficially viewed, Pola was picturesque. Not many years ago this place had been little more than a fishing village, and it never rose to a very high level. But the place could boast quite a number of ancient Roman buildings, including even a monumental amphitheater, all of which contributed to its interest. On the shorefront some larger modern houses, built in the artless style favored by military architects, attracted some attention. The large harbor, with its evergreen hilly shores, crowned here and there by a fort, looked quite pretty. The expanse of water was made narrow by two islands, the Scoglio Franz and Olive Island, which, with the fact that the northern half was reserved as a commercial port, made the harbor inadequate for the fleet. The shores of the man-of-war harbor were wholly taken up by the navy yard. Whereas only brick-red walls and some abandoned fortifications rose out of the dark undergrowth of Scoglio Franz, the bare, flat Olive Island was covered with shipyards, factories, and repair shops. Two beautiful dry docks, blasted out of solid rock at great expense, gave additional value to the island, which in later years was linked to the town by an iron bridge.

In those days the harbor showed little life. Ordinarily there were no ships to be seen on the buoys except for the above-mentioned watch vessel and a small paddle steamer that was used for harbor purposes. Ships of the fleet that were out of commission were moored close together along the town's shore. On top of the hill that dominates the town one could see the overgrown remnants of ancient fortifications that once had been the citadel. On another hill near the town stood the observatory, while a large square house situated farther away to the south was the very clean and efficient naval hospital. The ugliest feature of Pola was the high stone wall that separated the whole area of the navy yard from the outer world. Situated at the periphery of the old town, but right in the center of what may be properly named Pola, was the navy club, half hidden by the luxurious growth of a pretty garden. Being the only decent retreat Pola offered to the many hundreds of officers who lived in this out-of-the-way place, it was a real oasis for the eye and offered culture, as well.

Still farther away from the town, where Pola already began to open out into the environs, were a number of plain, two-story houses that the government erected for the families of officers and civil servants. They surrounded a pretty park, which was ornamented by a fine bronze statue of the late Archduke Maximilian, who had been commander of the navy before going to Mexico to meet his fate.[2] This group of about fifteen barracks-like houses formed a suburb that was officially named St. Policarpo, but for reasons that one may easily guess it was generally known under the pseudonym *Klatschhausen*, or Gossip Town.

Halfway between the old town and St. Policarpo were the well-kept naval barracks, the parade grounds, and the nearby children's boarding school. As already suggested, the navy club was literally the only resource the officers had at their disposal in Pola. It afforded its members comparatively splendid accommodations: a good coffeehouse; a restaurant, which unfortunately was never well-managed; rooms for billiards, games, and writing; a large dance hall where the young people could enjoy themselves in wintertime; and even a library. But the principal amenity lay in one paragraph of the club's regulations that stated that all members were equal inside the house, be they high or low in rank. Everyone was free to greet or to introduce himself to others. This paragraph explained why the club's promoters had only succeeded in getting it established after a lengthy fight with the Admiralty,[3] why it never enjoyed any support, and why it was always deeply in debt. The membership fee was small, only two florins a month, so that even the lowest grades could easily afford to join. As the years passed, the club's indebtedness increased, a state of affairs that was deliberately allowed to continue. It served as a safety valve for its continued existence, since a subsequent Admiralty opposed to the democratic regulations could not as easily dissolve an organization heavily burdened with mortgages as it could one free of debt.

One would assume that this club was the regular rallying point for naval officers, but this was not necessarily the case. Above all, the civilian bureaucrats of the city did not like to frequent it, feeling uneasy there as only guests and not members. But quite a number of officers also preferred to stick to their accustomed taverns, be it for love of convenience or for the sake of some pretty bar-maid. The total ebb in their purses also explains why some planted their tent now here, now there, on credit. The town taverns were all low-grade, but as a rule they had female attendants, and that lured many. Other hosts knew how to retain their customers through the delicacy of certain dishes, the good quality of their drinks, or moderate prices. Besides, a young mariner feels happy wherever he is, so long as he is away from superiors. In those days the presence of a single one of them could spoil the humor of all the youngsters in a locality.

It would be logical to suppose that the main naval port was treated primarily as a military installation, but no minister of war or naval commander had succeeded in attaining this object. Though our Monarchy had a military tinge to it, only politicians had power. No small danger for the navy arose from Pola's dual nature as both a naval harbor and a commercial port. Although the port admiral, who was at the same time commanding officer of the fortress, was high in rank, in a certain way a much younger civilian functionary outranked him. The directions the former issued were in force only with the garrison, while the latter's decrees were law for all. It is therefore no wonder that under such circumstances Pola was always a hotbed of politics. The navy was also well aware that our neighbor on the other side of the Adriatic knew exactly what was going on in Pola at all times. Pola was a commercial harbor open to trade—and also to espionage. This knowledge did not inconvenience naval officers very much, for they were used to the feeling that they were living on hostile ground. Now and then the absurdity of the situation was discussed, but the subject was soon dropped.

During Vice Admiral Baron Pöck's era, the navy had virtually come to a standstill.[4] There was a squadron, consisting of three or four ships in commission, which permanently navigated in Greek waters, with Smyrna (Izmir) as headquarters. To stay there was more interesting than on the Dalmatian coast, for there were pretty Levantine women to be admired, life was pleasanter and cheaper, and one also received a higher salary, paid in gold—reasons enough to forget the home waters, with their many islands and channels. As a result, however, these waters were a *mare incognitum* for many officers. No one in authority seemed aware that the large sums of money that were spent by the squadron in Greece would have much benefited the poor population on our own coast. There, in the Adriatic, only two small gunboats bored themselves to death, year in and year out, nonsensically watching the two Turkish enclaves that ran through our territories to the coast.[5] There was no possibility whatever for spending any money on these forlorn anchorages, and since life cost almost nothing, these appointments were much sought after by officers who were deep in debt. The small paddle steamer *Taurus* was forever stationed in Constantinople, at the disposition of the ambassador, and another steamer as a rule remained in Zara (Zadar) for use by the governor of Dalmatia. Add to these ships the corvette that made the short cruise with the pupils of the academy for a few weeks during the summer and the vessel that made the one-year voyage with the young midshipmen, and you have the total of the ships in commission in our fleet. That number only permitted naval officers to spend twelve months on board ship after a three-year stay on shore, certainly not enough to make them experienced sailors. Ironically, the surgeons had a far greater chance of becoming old salts, since their numbers were insufficient. If only they had taken a greater interest in their trade; as it was, they only complained of getting too much of the sea.

The corvette *Donau*, whose completion meant the realization of so many of our dreams and hopes, was ready to receive us midshipmen by the end of October. We had often impatiently admired her from afar, with her black sides slashed by a bold streak of white and her bow adorned by a rather full-bosomed river nymph. Most of all we were impressed by her exceptionally high masts, which made her look like a real clipper. The lectures on gunnery were cut short, and lustily we joined our ship. Later, after the initial enthusiasm had abated and our eyes had grown more discerning, it became obvious that the proud *Donau* would not be a pleasant home as far as our accommodations were concerned. The midshipmen's mess room, where we had to live, take our meals, and make our nautical reckonings, was a dark hole on the lower deck, lit only by two small round bull's-eyes. A large table screwed down to the floor took up almost the whole space; it was surrounded on three sides by a bench with leather cushions. Along the wall and the fore and aft bulkheads were ten small flat cupboards, which with some good will could be used for storage. A brass oil lamp, two suspended bottle holders, a mirror on the wall, and half a dozen bentwood chairs completed the luxurious furniture of our abode. Outside, on the bulkhead, were attached six wash basins, which could be put down; there was no bathroom. Such were the accommodations with which we twenty-eight middies had to be satisfied.

The midshipmen in our navy kept their belongings in a wooden chest of considerable size, and since there was not enough room in the aft lower deck to store them, someone had hit upon the expedient of assigning the ten cupboards in the mess room to the first ten in rank. Here the favored few kept their property, and their chests were sent to the navy yard for storage. I was one of these unfortunate favorites. As only a few of the midshipmen were ordinarily on duty at one time, most of us lived in the mess room. We were packed so closely together, however, that there was no room for more than twelve and certainly for no more than fourteen of us at a time. We therefore had to take our meals in two shifts. But how on earth were the favored ten to get to our clothes, underwear, and books, which were crammed in the hold of the benches and the cupboards? That was always a dilemma, and the consequence was that after the year had passed the preferred ten did not have much more property than what they wore on their backs. Our cocked hats in their bulky leather coverings, our cloaks, oil cloths, and jack boots were hidden away in one of the boatswain's storerooms, where they lay higgledy-piggledy and got dusty and musty.

We had, of course, to sleep in hammocks. Three sailors were assigned as our attendants, who had to tear themselves to pieces to barely accomplish what was required of them. One may imagine how many clouts these poor devils got in the course of the year. The table requisites were left unwashed for hours, and as a rule the hammocks were badly slung or left unlashed. In short, conditions were such that they continuously led to quarrels, to no end of recriminations on the part of our superiors, and soon to general discontent.

Another circumstance helped diminish our already much-reduced enthusiasm. We had dreamt of making a fine voyage to the tropics, and we willingly would have gone through much discomfort to that end. But the brandnew ship, with her clipperlike features and her exceptionally high masts, had aroused doubts in the minds of some experts as to her seaworthiness. This situation made it inadvisable to send her into the Atlantic. Instead, the *Donau* was ordered first to join the squadron and then to proceed to Malta, Naples, Port Mahon, and Gibraltar, where her subsequent fate would be decided. Young as we were, we knew that life in squadron was not especially pleasant, but most of all we grieved that we had to bury our hopes for a tropical cruise. Fortunately, however, the formalities by which a ship is put in commission and the hustle and bustle of the first days left little time for sentimental thoughts. The continuous roll calls and exercises of the first days made us tired, and by the time the watch vessel's signal ordered the *Donau* to set out on her mission, we were resigned to our fate.

I do not remember how the outward voyage to Smyrna passed off, probably because my duties as midshipman of the hold made me spend most of my time on the lower deck. Our major task was to reconcile ourselves to conditions as best we could and to acquaint ourselves with the gods to whose discretion we had been delivered. In those days strange things happened in our navy, the more so as there were no printed regulations. Everything was based on tradition, customary rights, the personal conceptions of superiors, and on sheer arbitrariness. Our boss was an elderly frigate captain [Julius Dauflick], whose bearing and appearance were not very impressive; indeed, they were rather shabby. We did not think for a moment that we would have to fear him, and what he was worth as a man and sailor we could know only in time. He was nearsighted, always wore glasses, and had a funny habit of snorting twice through his nose before speaking as if to gain time for thinking. Next to him in rank came the executive officer, a lieutenant who on account of his gray hair appeared to be older than he probably was. His pleasant demeanor, good looks, dazzling white teeth, and friendly eyes in a face that was reddened, we thought, by sharp sea breezes won us over from the first. What we admired in him above all was his wonderfully clear and far-reaching voice, which attracted favorable attention whenever he commanded the sea drill. Of the other officers I would single out the one appointed as superintendent of the midshipmen. He was a rather common person who saw his task as annoying rather than as helpful to us. Instead of showing us consideration or giving us instruction, he preferred to blame and revile us on every occasion, and our fate would have been very miserable if he had been able to have his way. As it was, the captain and the executive officer often took our side and warded off the thunderstorms that the other had vowed to unload upon us.

Our days were taken up with duties or exercises of various kinds, but the evening hours were spent in the mess room in frightful closeness, with a glass or two of grog and a secretly smoked cigarette. We were not always cheery but were surely in a very animated mood until the night round passed by. As smoking is strictly forbidden in the lower deck, we had to be careful, especially because the aft magazine was situated close to the mess room and was watched by a sentry day and night. But we could not resist the temptation to smoke, although we often had to suffer for it.

Such were the conditions we experienced on our way to Smyrna, where we arrived to find our squadron at anchor. With its oriental features, the town was quite interesting. Though I am far from being musical, one French song—*La clef* was its name—still tingles in my ear. It was sung every night in one of the coffeehouses by a worn-out but gaudily made-up performer who in our young eyes was the most charming creature we had ever seen. Night after night she succeeded in drawing us into her magic circle. We were nevertheless quite pleased when, after a fortnight's stay, the flagship's signal gave the *Donau* permission to set out on her cruise for the second time.

Stormy weather persevered during our voyage to Candia (Crete), where we suddenly met with a furious western gale, against which it was impossible to work to windward. What we gained during the day was lost again at night, which of course the captain did not mind. At that time we did not yet know that he would have been pleased to be able to keep to the sea the whole year round, if such were possible; of this we midshipmen only became aware much later. Before taking command of the ship, the captain had legalized a love affair that had not remained without hostages of fortune. However, he only received the Admiralty's consent to this union, which did not correspond with his social position, on the condition that he retire from active service as soon as his present period of service at sea had come to an end. This condition weighed heavily upon him, since it affected his material future to no small degree. Being poor, he was filled with only one thought—to save as much money as possible for as long as there was a chance to do so. This aim governed all his actions. Rarely could a captain be found who was so pleased with contrary winds as he, and when the grim western gale slowed us on our way to Malta, he rubbed his hands in glee. It was therefore quite a blow for the captain that one of the midshipmen came down with typhoid fever and was so ill that he had to be consigned to a hospital at any cost. The proper thing to do would have been to proceed to Suda (Souda) Bay, which was the nearest port. But it annoyed the captain so much to call at any place, even an uncivilized Turkish one, that he decided merely to anchor the ship in the Gulf of Gonia (Khania) and send the sick man with the steam launch to get medical care on land. The midshipman was, however, doomed, and we suffered the first rent in our ranks.

Although a grim gale was raging, at this forsaken anchorage the ship lay as snugly as in Abraham's bosom, the gulf being thoroughly sheltered by a high mountainous peninsula from whatever puff of wind that came from the west. But malice quite often knows how to deceive by candid looks, and we were lulled into a false sense of security by the reigning stillness. The Sailing Directions speak ill of the Gulf of Gonia, saying that it is a dangerous anchorage, and they do not conceal that the anchors of many a ship lie there at the bottom of the sea, the loss of which has forced careless skippers to pay for their improvidence. After having enjoyed two days of wonderful rest, we again put to sea. We had hardly shown our head outside the sheltering Cape Spatha, however, when the same furious westerly gale drove us back, forcing us to return to the very anchorage we had just left. Two more days were spent in dreamy peace— festive Christmas days, though unfortunately we had nothing to celebrate with but an extra glass of grog.

A few nights later the ship had passed the southernmost promontory of Greece, with a cold sharp wind blowing from the north. When we came on deck on the following morning, our eyes were struck by a strange sight, for a countless number of all kinds of terrestrial birds, among them thousands of swallows, filled the air, circling in anxious flutter round the ship, which for them was like an island in the broad sea. As time progressed, more and more of the tired birds took a nest in the rig, and many of them fell exhausted into the sea or onto deck. They followed us for several days and nights; their number decreased rapidly until the hecatomb was accomplished.

The picturesque outlines of Malta and its capital, La Valetta, were not new to us midshipmen. I do not remember how long the ship remained there, certainly only a few days, or in what way we enjoyed ourselves. After a brief call we again took to the sea on our way to our next goal, Naples. For some length of time the gods were the allies of the captain, for it took us two weeks of tacking to get to the Strait of Messina. The majestic Etna and the bold forms of the Aspromonte became as familiar to us as if we had been brought up in their shade. Sugar and coffee ran short and then were finished, but we nevertheless went on, passing close to the sunlit town of Messina, and continued our cruise northward. Sailing on the port tack with a fair breeze, one fine afternoon the *Donau* finally found herself close to Naples. In approaching the harbor, the watch officer sent his report to the captain over and over again, but the latter's answer was always a disinterested, "All right." Finally we were so near to the place that we could easily distinguish individual houses, and the ship could not continue any farther under sail. When I, now being midshipman of the watch, reported this to the boss, at first I could not think he was in earnest, since he said that it would be a sin to spend such fine days idly in port; the watch officer had to put the ship about. After so many days passed at sea, this monstrous order enraged everyone on board, but that did not change matters. This time, however, the gods apparently did not wish to be trifled with, for the captain's punishment quickly followed. In the evening the wind and the sea rose, and during the night a fresh gale began to blow that defied all the captain's seamanship and ended with the loss of the main yard. We had to make steam up in all four boilers, and finally, after a great waste of coal, we arrived back at where we had been twenty hours before. There we made the ship fast on a buoy in the face of the lively, fire-spitting Vesuvius.

We midshipmen knew Naples from a former cruise, but we were neverthe-less delighted to be there again. Since Carnival was at its height, we would see it at a time of special merriment. I hope that even the severest reader will be lenient enough not to condemn us if I confess that after we had passed so many days under very unpleasant conditions, we took life only from the easy side. So while carpenters busied themselves on board completing the main yard, we cheerfully entered into the whirl of the many tempting amusements this easy-going place offered.

After a week of gaiety and high spirits our thirst for life was not yet quenched, but our purses were empty, and with feelings well described by the saying Vedi Napoli, e poi muori—"See Naples and then die"—we left the harbor to return to the odious island of Candia. The mere thought of this did not please anybody, not even the captain. Our passage was much delayed by contrary winds, and one night the weather was so rough and the ship so unsteady that while mounting the ladder to the bridge, the captain lost his balance and fell headlong on deck. He could rise by himself and even stayed for some time on the bridge, but he complained of all sorts of pains. Curiously, he insisted that his accident be entered in detail in the ship's journal and that it be duly documented by medi-cal certificates. Days later we were in the quiet Bay of Suda, which served as our headquarters for the next five weeks.

Our next destination was Port Mahon on Minorca. That was pretty far away, and the captain was at liberty to give vent to his desire for a long passage. This he did thoroughly; it took us thirty-seven days to get there. After passing south of Malta in very foul, boisterous weather, we had to work our way against a stiff but steady northwester to the sheltering east side of Sardinia. There we met a great number of merchant sailing vessels that had gathered there for the same reason. One day, when sailing north of Sicily, for twenty-four hours we passed through waters that were literally covered with giant turtles. This was certainly connected with their course of propagation and may be a periodic phenom-enon, but I have never heard of a similar occurrence in the Mediterranean.

In the shelter of Sardinia, with a steady stiff breeze and comparatively smooth sea, one afternoon we conducted inclination experiments with the ship, which was sailing with two reefs in the topsails, close hauled to the wind. Observing all necessary caution, we gradually passed over to all sails set, and it was excit-ing to watch how the increase of sail area influenced the inclination of the ship, which finally was considerable. A ship can carry such an amount of sails only for a short while, for the masts, stays, and backstays would not stand the strain for any length of time.

The long duration of the passage led to various discomforts, the more so as the staff's cook had seen fit to leave the ship at Suda Bay. Officers and midshipmen had to take the victualling into their own hands. One of the midshipmen had offered to do the marketing and to attend to the management, probably because this freed him from regular service. One may imagine how this inexperienced youngster performed what is in fact a difficult task. For some time we certainly lived in revelry, until nothing was left except flour and lard, unless we wished to partake of the loathsome salt horse of the men. We tried this once but immediately gave it up, and for ten days we had to fare on flint-hard biscuits and what we had. What could even the best cook in the world have done with only flour and fat? Not only we midshipmen had to accept the situation, but also the captain, who had left the officer's table and joined our mess after some difference there. The ward room was not much better off, as nobody had taken such a prolonged passage into consideration. Even the drinking water ran short. The ship was furnished with a distilling apparatus, but this was new and had not yet been used. It may also have been badly handled, since the water it produced, though pure, had such a strong tallowy taste that it could only be swallowed with a closed nose. The chief engineer did all he could but was unable to mend matters. The officers were in a fury about this water and objected emphatically to the captain, but that was of no avail, for their remonstrances glanced off him without effect. He declared the distilled water to be good, went to the forecastle with a bottle of it and a glass, and made the men taste it. When he asked them whether the water was all right, the poor devils of course answered "Si Sior," and there the question rested. As may be imagined, it was a relief for all on board when the outlines of Minorca finally came into sight and we could pass the narrow entrance to the harbor of Port Mahon.

The corvette was never kept in good condition. Of this we were not quite conscious until we arrived at this inviting little town, where everything glittered in remarkable neatness. I have heard of the extreme cleanliness of certain places in Holland, but I cannot imagine that it beats what we encountered here. Among the friendly population of Port Mahon we half-starved midshipmen felt as if we were in paradise. When we entered one of the posadas, the innkeeper put before us a row of pans with delicious roasts that came directly from the oven. We could help ourselves as many times as we liked, and for all that and a bottle of good Alicante wine we had to pay but a mere song. In one respect only did Port Mahon disappoint me. Years before I had read a description of the island that praised the beauty of the girls to the skies. This race of heavenly creatures was apparently extinct, for I looked in vain for an opportunity to lose my heart. Yet in spite of all the amenities and blessings of the place, our land-shy captain was not willing to remain for more than two days—and I wished so much to stay somewhat longer on Spanish soil, the land of my earliest dreams, where I had set foot for the first time.

Sixteen storm-free days brought us to Gibraltar. Most of the time we sailed in a crowd with scores of merchant vessels that, like us, had been detained by the continuously blowing westerly winds and were now striving for the Straits of Gibraltar with all sails set. The incomparable beauty of this maritime stronghold made a great impression on us. No other place on earth symbolizes so emphatically the might of the British lion. We confirmed materialists were less attracted by the defiant heights, however, than we were by the town lying snugly at their foot. To tell the truth, I must state that officers and midshipmen took little interest in the sights of the places we visited. On shore they rarely ventured far from the harbor. It could not have been otherwise; after days of privation, one is above all drawn to material gratifications. And in any event, in those days the staff was not allowed to leave the ship before the termination of the afternoon schools and exercises—and what on earth could a man tired out from service do with the few hours that remained until sunset? Only in later years did more liberal views in this regard gain ground, but in these earlier days our men were badly off. Their life on board ship was hard, and the time accorded to them for rest was insufficient, for they never had more than three and a half hours of uninterrupted sleep. Their fare was inadequate, moreover, and in general their treatment was not very friendly. The boatswains and petty officers often dealt with them with revolting brutality, but since they were for the most part a tractable and submissive lot, it very rarely came to outright insubordination.

On board almost every one of our ships there were some devil-may-care fellows who moved in the rig like rope dancers, often filling the onlookers with anxious suspense. It was quite uncertain whether they held themselves fast with their teeth or their toes. We midshipmen were used to feeling at home in the upper regions of the rig and often had to lend a hand to the royal yard men, but that was nothing compared with the feats of these rope dancers. They knew that everybody on deck watched and admired them, and they liked to show off. The greater part of our men consisted of Dalmatian coastal people. They were a patient, hardened, good-natured lot, of rather distrusting and parsimonious inclination, lacking any higher ideals. They willingly did what was asked of them, but not a bit more. Those in our navy who were in some way distinguished in knowledge, cleverness, efficiency, and spirit were without exception men from the interior of the Monarchy.

The *Donau* was allowed to make only one further stop in the Atlantic—at Lisbon, the capital of Portugal, so beautifully situated on the Tagus River, and like Rome built on seven hills. Here some members of the staff and I had the honor of being introduced to His Majesty the King of Portugal, Luis I [reigned 1861–1889], whose predilection for the navy was manifest by the pride with which he spoke of his miniature battleship *Vasco da Gama*, which he invited us to inspect. Then, following a short stay in Tangier and in Algiers, we anchored off La Goulette, the port of Tunis. Summertime had meanwhile set in, and as a rule the weather was fine. Conditions on board had somewhat bettered, for we no longer had to put up with all sorts of inconveniences—or perhaps it only seemed so because we had grown accustomed to them. The midshipmen's berth had not undergone much change, though it was certainly cleaner and in better order, and on every Sunday morning it was inspected by the officer of the hold. Nevertheless, the fearful closeness continued as before, and the first ten of the class still had to fight whenever they wished to get to their belongings. Indeed, it was often quite impossible for them to store away the underwear they had just changed. This was therefore left lying about somewhere until Sundays, when the responsible midshipman of the hold simply flung it overboard if its owner was not on the spot. Thus it came to pass that we unfortunate ten had very little to call our own when we finally left the ship.

For some reason I never understood, after leaving Lisbon I was appointed as the sole master of the steam launch. In the future no other midshipman was to act as her skipper. I had seen real neatness at Port Mahon, and after having picked out a fine crew for the boat, I set to work. The paint soon looked bright, and after the little launch had been adorned with a number of glistening brass fittings and mountings she became quite a jewel and did honor to the ship. But because the steam launch was always in use, I could never go on shore, as neither I nor any of her regular crew would think of allowing someone else to handle her. On account of my fine handwriting, the captain frequently made use of me for scribbling, and in Lisbon he even appointed me his secretary. In the meanwhile he had undergone a certain change, frequently complaining of pains caused, he said, by his fall on deck from the bridge. He was often confined to bed for a week or two and rarely came on deck; during the last month he hardly left his cabin and looked very pale. In port he pulled himself up a little but then complained that he felt all the more miserable. I had to spend most of my time in his cabin and kept him company for hours.

At La Goulette we were anchored four miles from shore. Because of a continually blowing wind there was much swell on the roadstead, and to run the small steam launch, with her low freeboard, was not without danger. I therefore was only allowed to use her with a boat in tow. The captain enjoyed the reigning quiet, and we remained there for ten days. Much of this time I spent in the steam launch, running her back and forth to shore, so that I was rarely off duty for more than two or three hours at a time. Besides the normal traffic I also had to supply the ship with fresh water. Many a time I brought the launch with the canvas tank full of fresh water, only to see the contents emptied out again into the sea as unfit for use, it being impossible to avoid shipping breakers. This restless activity tired me and my men so much that it sometimes happened that one of us fell asleep while under way.

The general discontent with our caterer had grown to such an extent that a change was unavoidable. Another midshipman offered his services in his stead, but that only moved us from the frying pan into the fire. This frivolous fellow was so irresponsible that he spent the whole last—and certainly most important—purchase day shooting flamingos far in the interior. He came on board very late at night, bringing five hundred live chickens, but he had no fodder for them, and as the ship was leaving the anchorage early on the following morning for Alexandria, matters could not be changed. We had reckoned with a fortnight's passage and had spent our money in purchasing victuals for that length of time. As it was, however, we had the bad luck to reach Alexandria already on the eighth day. Our many chickens had managed to stay alive for some time by devouring one another's feathers; we could consume some of them, but in the absence of proper food we had to feed the greater half to the fish in the sea. In harbor, therefore, amidst all the delicacies of Egypt, we were without the necessary funds to buy anything. Quite a number of the midshipmen suffered terribly from hunger, and we had to live on half rations until the next monthly pay day.

Our captain's career came to a close in Alexandria, where we learned that his successor was on his way. Before the latter's arrival the invalid captain was to return home on board a Lloyd steamer. During the last two months I had known him only groaning and moaning. On the morning of his departure I was therefore much surprised to find him running about in his cabin as lively as a weasel, picking up his belongings and packing them away in trunks. This done, the boat for his transfer to the Lloyd steamer could come alongside. When I entered the cabin to say that the boat was ready, for the second time I could hardly believe my eyes. For now the same man who had just been so lively had changed into a dejected and moaning creature, sunk down in an armchair with his head bent forward. Only with great difficulty could I and his servant drag him to the companionway leading on deck, where the officers and crew were ready to bid him farewell. A steward midshipman jumped to our aid, and with our united forces we succeeded in getting him on deck. But there his strength began to fade, and a chair had to be brought quickly so that he could sit down. Then, with a voice hardly audible, he thanked the officers and men for their services. Not a few of the hardened sailors had a heavy heart, and in some of their eyes one could even see a glittery tear. "*Povero commandante*," one heard them murmur. He had led the ship with manifest skill and composure through many a storm and peril, and now they saw him broken down, a wreck, a victim of his vocation. Slowly and with all possible care he was lowered down into the boat by means of an invalid's chair, and the hurrahs that followed him were honest and heartfelt. *La comedia é finita*. For that is exactly what it was. An officer invalided in active service gets 400 florins added to his annual pension; it therefore pays a poor devil to play a part for a short while.

A few days later drama followed comedy. The new captain had arrived, and for his reception the officers and crew again fell in on deck. This went off with less cordiality than the recent leave-taking, however. No tradition or days of storm and stress linked us midshipmen with the new captain, of whom we knew nothing. Had we only had some knowledge of mankind, the cold, searching look with which he glanced along the ship and over her crew would have told us that nothing good awaited us. The officers knew him and made serious faces. Captain v[on] L[und] was a Swede, one of the foreigners who had entered our navy at the time of its beginnings.[6] There were several of them still in service, and while the others were in no way remarkable, v. L.'s sternness, sense of duty, and orderliness could not be questioned. Otherwise he was a dry soul and a man of few words. I am pretty sure that he dismissed the officers, whom he had summoned to his cabin shortly after his arrival, with something like the following words: "Gentlemen, the ship is a pigsty, and that must change in the shortest possible time. I will see to it. As long as this is not done, nobody is allowed to go on shore." Of this nothing leaked out, but the morose faces of the officers clearly revealed that they were shamed by the reception they had received.

After engaging two excellent Italian cooks—who for many years to come were the most coveted in our navy—we left Alexandria and proceeded to Smyrna to join the squadron. The passage was not favorable, for it took several weeks to get there, during which time we became acquainted with a kind of service that was far different from that to which we had been accustomed. The captain ruled over the officers and midshipmen with an iron rod and treated both with equal brutality, which was possible in those days of arbitrary despotism. Although the men were also not spared, they were not maltreated or persecuted, the vials of his wrath being poured chiefly over the staff's heads. His methods were of course crowned with success, and when the *Donau* reached Smyrna, she almost needed not to be ashamed. The inspection by the admiral, who was a weak man, went off fairly well, but there was nevertheless no shore allowance for anyone on board, including the gray-haired executive officer. The latter had even been deprived of certain traditional rights. For instance, the midshipmen now had to ask not him but the captain himself for shore leave, which most of them simply would not do. And if one did have the pluck to ask, he then had to appear with diary and nautical calculations before the severe lord, who then looked through them carefully until he found a pretext to refuse the request for shore leave. I personally stood in the captain's good graces, whether on account of the fine steam launch or my good handwriting I do not know. But when after a few weeks I asked permission to go on shore, after having thoroughly searched my diary and calculation books he merely said, "Why do you wish to go on shore? It is far better for you if you stay on board." He himself, on the other hand, went every afternoon for one hour, but only to one of the coffeehouses near the landing, from which he watched the *Donau* and the proceedings on board with his telescope. On his return he did not restrain his pitiless critique. It was a hard time for us all, though luckily for me I was frequently in the steam launch, which even the commander of the squadron preferred to use.

Besides our squadron, which consisted of four ironclads, there were several French ships and the American navy's sloop *Trenton* at anchor in the harbor. I was often sent on duty on board these ships, which I liked very much. Only one ship, one of our own, I always approached with a palpitating heart. She was the oldest ironclad in our navy, and her official name was *Salamander*. Generally, however, she passed under the name of "*Warthog*" on account of the innumerable fist-sized rivet heads with which her sides were studded. This epithet could certainly not be applied to the inner conditions and the boats of this ship, for I was indeed dazzled by the neatness, brilliance, and order that reigned there. This was the work of her executive officer, who was an outrageous fellow and a real tyrant. Only such a man could succeed in maintaining a ship in an excessively clean state. His almost deaf captain did not take much interest in the ship. Life on board must have been hell for officers and crew alike. Whenever we midshipmen came near the ship, we could see her executive officer lying in wait at the gangway like a Cerberus. As we stepped on board he snarled at us, before we had said one word, "What are you here for! Go away!"

After some months the *Donau* was sent on station to Salonica, but we did not remain there long. Meanwhile wintertime had set in, and a terrible winter it was. An icy cold storm wind continually blew with such fury that communication with land was only possible by means of the launch under storm sails. After a fortnight, all on board were very glad when the ship was ordered to Pola. The homeward voyage was tedious and very uncomfortable. I vividly remember only one incident that occurred one afternoon. The ship was cruising off Cape Matapan, close-hauled to the wind with two reefed topsails, when she was suddenly struck by a violent squall that made her heel over so alarmingly that the topsail sheets had to be let fly. In a moment the main deck was flooded with water that came rushing in through the open portholes, and all hands hurried on deck. I also recollect the somewhat paler face of the captain, who nervously grasped the breastwork of the bridge and observed, "That was the most furious squall I have ever experienced."

I have only a faint recollection of how the first days passed after our arrival in Pola, where we were unshipped and the *Donau* was put out of commission. I and a half-dozen other midshipmen were quartered on board a rather cold, dark, unoccupied hulk for ten awful days, but there we were at least under cover without having to pay for it. We could not really think of going on shore because of the disreputable condition of our clothing, though in those days no great weight was attached to such trifles. As yet there existed no written rules concerning uniforms, so that individual taste had full scope as to color, fashion, size, and style. Our stock of clothing was exhausted, however, and badly needed to be renewed. Our first steps were therefore to find a tailor who would supply us with what we needed on credit.

Ten days later I found myself with some chums from the *Donau* and a few older midshipmen on board the small ironclad *Kaiser Max*, again on the way out to Smyrna to join the squadron. After having lived for sixteen months in a dark hole, the fine, spacious midshipmen's berth on board the *Kaiser Max* seemed like a room in a palace. The captain was another of the foreigners hailing from the north, but a weakling. The reins of government were held by the executive officer, a blustering, fat-bellied corvette captain who was always hungry and thought of nothing but eating. He took a dislike to me from the outset, and I had to suffer many an injustice on his part.[7] As far as I remember we only remained in Smyrna for two months, whereupon the whole squadron was ordered home to receive a new commander.

After our arrival in Pola the squadron was dissolved. The *Kaiser Max* was placed in a new squadron that was put in commission under the command of Rear Admiral A[lois von] P[okorny]. The new commander was far more able than his predecessor, but he was not in much favor at the Admiralty, being too dangerous a candidate for the command of the navy. The squadron was therefore not to return to pleasant Levantine waters but had to be content with the certainly picturesque but by no means delightful Dalmatian coast. Here we got to know our home waters better, which was certainly profitable, but as a rather unwelcome addition there was much more schooling and drill. According to regulations, our monthly pay was to be made at the lowest rate, which probably grieved the admiral as much as it did everyone else. To improve matters he hit upon an ingenious scheme. The pay schedule in our navy knew an imaginary so-called "silver line" that linked Cape Linguetta on the island of Saseno (Sazan) with the Italian Cape Sta. Maria di Leuca. Ships that happened to be south of this line on pay day not only drew higher wages, but also got them paid in gold. The admiral now made his squadron cruise on the first day of the month near that line. At noon it was ascertained by exact astronomical observations that the squadron happened to be one or two miles south of the line— and the rest was the paymaster's business. The Admiralty, alas, was only fooled twice and thereafter exercised an absolute veto of this practice. In later years such behavior on the part of a commanding officer would have been unthinkable, and I have related the story only to characterize the conditions as they existed in our navy at that time.

The days in squadron went off rather monotonously, and only once was there some passing excitement. The ships were at anchor at Megline (Meljine) in the Bocche di Cattaro (Kotor). It being a Sunday, half of the crews had been granted shore leave and were widely dispersed in the surrounding villages. The executive officers of the squadron and some midshipmen, I among them, were invited to dinner by the admiral and were just enjoying the feast when a dispatch was handed to the host. He read it calmly, scribbled some words on the backside, gave it to the orderly, and therewith the evidently unimportant matter seemed settled. Indeed, the incident was hardly noticed by any of the guests. A few moments later, however, to the astonishment of all, the holy peace of the day was suddenly interrupted by the thunder of a cannon shot, and only now did the admiral divulge that the order had come for the ships in the squadron immediately to make ready for sea, with steam up in all boilers. Thereupon the executive officers jumped up to hurry back on board their ships, but they were stopped by the admiral's calmly saying, "The others will know how to do what's necessary." It was indeed a proud sight to see how skillfully the ships' reduced crews managed to hoist in the heavy launches and get the ships ready for sea, how quickly the men at liberty on shore responded to the urgent signal to come on board, and how soon one ship after the other reported to be ready. Hardly one hour after the arrival of the telegraphic order, the squadron was sailing at full speed northward, filled with curiosity and making wild guesses as to its destination, which the admiral had kept secret to all.

The Austro-Hungarian Monarchy had occupied Bosnia and Hercegovina in accordance with the stipulations of the Treaty of Berlin. In the course of this operation a Turkish general, Ali Pasha, had surrendered and had rallied with his troops, amounting to some 6,000 men, at Neum, one of the two Turkish enclaves, to be shipped by the squadron and some Lloyd steamers to Preveza. That was what had caused the alarm.[8]

After having spent eight months on board the *Kaiser Max*, the prescribed two years of sea service for taking the officer's examination had expired for me and the other midshipmen of my class. We unshipped at the Bocche and went by Lloyd steamer to Pola. This examination was a serious matter. One first took the practical half at Pola and then moved to Fiume for the theoretical part. One was allowed to repeat one or even both parts once, but lost thereby in rank. It so happened that we had three months in which to prepare, which was an exceptionally long time. This was not quite to our taste, since even on board ship a low-salaried midshipman could make shift with his monthly pay only with difficulty. The thought of having to live so long on a reduced income in the expensive city frightened us not a little. A friend and I having agreed to live together for the duration, we now went in search of a cheap room, bought a teapot, and procured the necessary textbooks. When all was ready, we started to study from morning until night. We could not do otherwise, for our means barely sufficed for a frugal noon meal and for coffee with milk and half a dozen rolls in the afternoon; we could not think of having a supper. It certainly was a very hard time, but we were cheered up by our conviction that we would be able to face even the most rigid examination with calm. Our secret hope to pass "with distinction" was not, however, realized, this being primarily a matter of luck that occurred but once in our navy. In Fiume I learned that the professors of physics and of navigation were not inclined to appreciate my knowledge. I comforted myself with the thought that it was of no consequence whatever, and I showed my feelings by simply answering their questions with undisguised unconcern.

We were now first-class—"passed"—midshipmen, and as a mark of distinction we wore a narrow golden braid on the shoulder as support for our epaulets, of which we were very proud. The pecuniary side of the promotion consisted of ten more florins a month. With these, as before, we could not make do. With such beginnings it is no wonder that the lifestyle of all our officers, whether high or low in rank, was always very modest. We were all used to a hard life and did not know any better. The pay of the lower grades was so insufficient that if one transgressed the minimum limit in one's standard of living by just a little, one easily fell into debt. A "passed" midshipman who did not enjoy an extra allowance from home—such lucky chaps were very rare in our navy—could not afford to rent even the cheapest room for any length of time.

We therefore thought of all sorts of expedients. Some housed directly on board an unguarded hulk until they were discovered and turned out. At night others stole into the hospital, there to sleep in one of the empty beds, making off in the morning before the medical inspection of the rooms began. Others preferred for their night's rest the corner of a sofa or the billiard table in their accustomed coffeehouse. The authorities had some knowledge of what was going on in this respect and either overlooked things or put a stop to the nuisance, as they saw fit. These conditions ceased in 1879 with the end of the command of Admiral von Pöck, who had shown little interest in the woe and welfare of his inferiors. His successor, Admiral Baron Sterneck,[9] took care that the midshipmen embarked on seagoing ships as much as possible.

Soon after passing our examinations, three of my classmates and I had the rare chance to be shipped on board the imperial yacht *Miramar*, on which Crown Prince Rudolf was to undertake a hunting trip to Spain. In this assignment we could see a certain distinction, and since I would again be able to visit the land of my dreams, I was overjoyed. The *Miramar*, a fine 1,830–ton paddle steamer that could easily steam 20 knots an hour, was put in commission for a cruise of three to four months' duration. The voyage, which we made in the finest season of the year, would have been ideal in every respect had we not sailed under the command of a captain who much embittered the midshipmen's lives. Captain M. v. M. was an inconsiderate and insolent fellow who hailed from Friuli or some other Italian part of southern Austria, which he betrayed by the crooked way in which he spoke German.[10] His long, forward-bent, hump-backed figure was not a pleasant sight, and the petty officers and men spoke of him only as the *brutto gobbo*, or the "hideous humpback." On his breast, however, shone the Maria Theresa Order, the Monarchy's highest military decoration, which in higher and lower circles alike enjoyed an almost pathetic esteem. This distinction, which was bestowed for a spontaneous act of conspicuous bravery of great importance in warfare, he had chanced to get in 1866 by mere luck. Only three navy officers were decorated with the Maria Theresa Order: Vice Admiral Wilhelm von Tegetthoff for his victory of Lissa, in which he defeated a far superior Italian fleet; his flag captain, Baron von Sterneck, for boldly ramming the Italian admiral's former flagship *Re d'Italia*; and Captain M. v. M. In 1866 the latter was commanding a flotilla of small gunboats on Lake Garda. Before Field Marshal Archduke Albrecht, the commander in chief in the Italian theater of war,[11] undertook to strike the decisive blow against the Italians at Custoza on June 23, he summoned all his generals and the commander of the flotilla and questioned the latter about whether he could rely on his holding the lake front. M. v. M. thereupon answered on the spur of the moment, without considering the importance of his words, with bold pathos, "Your Imperial Highness, this I guarantee with my neck." This neck would not have been of any use to the field marshal, but the brisk answer flattered his ears and made a favorable impression upon him. When finally the decisive battle was won, the triumphant commander in chief remembered the pert speaker and graciously allowed the horn of plenty to shower its favor upon him. So it came about that M. v. M. could boast of the Monarchy's highest military distinction.

The *Miramar* at first coaled at Messina and then proceeded to Villefranche, where Crown Prince Rudolf, his brother-in-law Prince Leopold of Bavaria, and Dr. A. E. Brehm, the well-known zoologist,[12] were to come on board. We had to wait several days for them, but in view of the beautiful scenery we did not mind the delay. The midshipmen's funds were at a very low ebb, which roused our desire to seize the opportunity for making a coup at the gambling tables at nearby Monte Carlo. Of course, we were sure that we would be successful, perhaps even break the bank. The only one of us who owned a civilian garment was to pay a visit to the goddess Fortuna in the name of us all; to him we intended to commit the entire riches that were due to us on May 1, the day after our arrival. But the captain must have foreseen some such scheme; he thwarted our plan by ordering that we could not draw our pay, which legally was due on the first of every month. This was an unparalleled interference, but it would have been useless to rebel, for the old man was not to be trifled with. The presence of such high persons on board ship inclined us to be accommodating, and in any event a complaint would have only made things worse. In a military organization, an inferior never gets his rights, because only in this way can strict and unbounded discipline be enforced and maintained.

The ship first called at Barcelona and then entered the estuary of the Ebro, where the first shooting took place. There a large number of common black coots were bagged but no more interesting game birds. On this occasion a nasty-looking brown mongrel dog behaved remarkably well, swimming for hours in the reed-overgrown river and fetching and carrying the many birds that had been shot; this prodigious animal belonged to a Catalonian peasant. The crown prince wished to own the dog very badly and saw his wish fulfilled, but coming to terms with the owner cost him a fabulous sum. This dog subsequently proved to be absolutely worthless. He only got visibly fatter and lazier, and after some weeks of idle existence on board he could have roused special interest only by his astonishing plumpness.

The ship remained one whole week at its next port of call, Valencia, because the crown prince, his guests, and, to our satisfaction, the captain went to Madrid to pay their respects to King Alfonso XII [reigned 1875–1885]. Of these days I can only record that soon after our arrival I met with the first love of my twenty-year-old heart. It was on the occasion of a special bullfight, a so-called *corrida blanca*, at which all the most distinguished nobles of Valencia were present. The ladies wore white mantillas, and noble artillery officers acted as picadors. Although this awful spectacle was new to me, soon a pair of fawn-colored eyes in the face of a marvelous black-haired beauty fascinated me and held me in their spell, not only on that afternoon, but for many a week to come. It had not escaped the attention of my companion, a very amiable Spanish midshipman, that his fair countrywoman had made a tremendous impression upon me. He did not know who she was but comforted me somewhat after her departure by assuring me that I would see her again. This was indeed the case, but the few fleeting glances that I caught of my idol only increased the flame of my love. There was nothing else on earth for me thereafter; ship and service were entirely neglected, and every free hour found me on shore in search of the object of my desire. Unfortunately, daughters are well supervised in Spain, so that all my efforts were in vain. I saw the days pass away and the hour of our departure approach.

During the crown prince's absence from the ship many persons belonging to the best social circles had come on board to visit, but our daily guests were a number of young noble artillery officers who had become great friends of us midshipmen. They all knew how matters stood with me and took a sincere interest in my love affair. Hundreds of ladies had already come on board, but "she" had not been among them. When the last afternoon came and I was standing absent-mindedly on the poop deck in the midst of the jolly artillery officers, one of them suddenly caught my arm and said, "Mira, mira, la Joaquina que vien!" —"Look, look, Joaquina," which was her first name, "is coming!" I was not sure whether I should trust his words, but sure enough, there was a boat nearing the ship with an old lady and two girls, and a moment later there was no doubt that one of them was she whose sight I so eagerly desired. One may imagine that I was at once at the gangway to receive the visitors and show them round the ship, and for half an hour I was the happiest man alive. But finally the dreaded moment of farewell arrived. The ladies were again at the gangway and thanked me for the courtesy I had shown them, and soon my lovely star would vanish forever, leaving behind nothing but a deep longing in my heart. In that sad instant my eyes were struck by a bunch of scarlet carnations on her breast, which suddenly filled me with the ardent wish to be made happy with them. I do not remember with what words I asked for them, only that my beauty blushed and with charming confusion and hesitation asked her companions, "Que le he de decir? Que le he de decir?"—"What shall I say to him?"— whereupon the kind old lady answered: "Dele los claveles, dele," therewith making an end to the indecision. So the land of my youthful longing had become the source of my first infatuation.

The morning after the crown prince and his guests returned from Madrid, we left Valencia to proceed to Malaga. Until now the booty had been very disappointing. It was therefore planned to start on a more distant hunt in the Sierra Nevada. This did not live up to expectations. Because of a special kind of seagull that is only to be found on this island, we next touched lonely, rocky, and rarely visited Alborán, which lies forlornly in the midst of the Mediterranean. The crown prince chanced to bag several of these rare birds, and that somewhat appeased the anger caused by repeated disappointments. There followed a short call at Gibraltar, for a reason that was never made clear to us. At

Cadiz we only stopped to take on board a pilot to take the ship up the Guadalquivir River, where we lay for several days at anchor in the midst of a wilderness. Here, finally, the crown prince succeeded in shooting a lynx, certainly a rare and acceptable booty.

According to plan, the *Miramar* was to proceed upriver as far as Seville. The chief pilot who had been sent out by the Spanish government came on board and declared his readiness to take the ship there. But when, in the course of the preceding deliberations, which I interpreted, it turned out that in some places the ship would only have one or two inches of water under her keel, the knight of the Maria Theresa Order flatly declared that he would not think of going to Seville under such circumstances.

The hunting tour to Spain had been made at the instigation of Dr. Brehm. The crown prince, who was deeply interested not only in shooting but also in zoological studies, particularly ornithology, held this scientist in high esteem. The prince's repeated disappointments during this trip, upon which he had probably ventured with high expectations and at no slight expense, surely must have had an effect on the relations between the two men. To a sportsman like the crown prince, who was wont all his life to bag large numbers of game whenever he went out for a shoot, a country so entirely void of game as Spain was hardly a proper destination. This twenty-year-old prince showed just how indefatigable he was by how he lived on board. He never enjoyed more than four hours' sleep. Regularly at midnight he left his guests, and before dawn he was already up again, ready for whatever undertaking was scheduled. We were amazed that the prince's much older and more experienced retinue acquiesced in so ruinous a lifestyle.

Except for the captain, the crown prince had little intercourse with the ship's staff. Of us midshipmen, who were exactly his age, he took hardly any notice. Imperial princes, especially when they are heirs to the throne, are older in their ways of thinking than their years would suggest. Prince Leopold of Bavaria was a great sportsman, but being older and more considerate, he had quickly realized that though Spain was certainly the land of chestnuts and bullfights, it was not an El Dorado for hunters; he therefore soon showed little interest in the trip. In consequence of the unsatisfactory experiences that had been made as to shooting, the itinerary was shortened. From the Guadalquivir the ship made only one more step out into the Atlantic, to the little port of Ribadesella, situated in the Gulf of Biscay, the hinterland of which was said to be the haunt of bear. However, because of the torrential rain that poured down during the following days, the crown prince did not sight a single one of them. The party made a short, very unpleasant roundabout, and we reached the coast at Santander drenched to the bone. There the crown prince and his guests took leave of the *Miramar* and, disgusted with Spain, sped home by rail by the shortest possible route.[13]

On her homeward voyage the *Miramar* called at Cartagena and Palermo. Of this passage, the only remarkable thing was that its entire course was accomplished in a sea literally as smooth as a mirror. To our joy, after our arrival at Pola we midshipmen were freed from the care of house-hunting by being shipped on board of the old familiar watch vessel *Bellona*. This time we were not received by her executive officer as bothersome intruders. On the contrary, we were allowed to look forward in peace and comfort to our impending promotion to ensign.

3

Life as a Subaltern Naval Officer
(1879–1886)

On the first day of November 1879 I was promoted to the rank of ensign
and received the coveted golden sword knot. Once again I thought I
had become a monarch in miniature—an illusion that I soon had to
abandon. A consequence of the promotion was that I had to serve for at least
three years as a landlubber and content myself with the amenities of Pola. Unfortunately, newly promoted ensigns did not have much of a choice as far as opportunities; one was appointed to do duty either in the barracks or at the navy
yard. Only one or two lucky chaps chanced to be shipped as watch officers on
board the old, rotten hulk *Vulkan*, where at least they were delivered from worry
about lodging and were able to enjoy regular—and inexpensive—fare.

Promotion to the rank of ensign by no means eased our financial status. To
the contrary, prolonged expensive shore life and the greater requirements regarding clothing and demeanor made the situation more acute. A midshipman
may temporarily content himself with all sorts of privations, and he may even
suffer from hunger for some time and still be quite happy. But to exact from a
young officer a life full of abnegation is, I think, more than unfair, and I therefore look back on those years in horror and with reproaches against the supreme
powers of the state. In the barracks one was junior officer in one of the eleven
companies, which as a rule were only fifteen to twenty strong. The daily routine consisted of inspecting the quarters of the men, which in general were kept
very clean, and going through some infantry drill with them, whereby no satisfactory results could be achieved because of constant changes in personnel. The
main work of the barracks officers consisted of standing about in groups on the
parade ground for hours and in gossiping. Not a few young ensigns remained
attached to the barracks for three full years and even got to like this vapid and
idle existence; they forgot, however, the little seamanship they had learned and
became thorough infantry men, but bad sailors. The mere thought of possibly
being ordered to the barracks made me shudder. I was therefore overjoyed that
I escaped this ordeal, at least for a while, and was attached to the navy yard as
officer of inspection. That, too, was a sinful waste of skill and time, but if noth-

ing else I remained in indirect contact with ships and the water and did not come hopelessly to anchor, since there was always a chance of going to sea for a day or a week.

I used the many leisure hours that I enjoyed in the navy yard studying Arabic and Turkish. I cannot say what led me embark upon this venture, and perhaps it was only the circumstance that I happened to hit upon an Arabic grammar. As it was, I quickly got stuck on *alif*, the first letter in the alphabet. I therefore turned to one of our staff officers, who was well versed in Oriental languages. He kindly led me on the right path, and after having overcome the first difficulties I pursued these studies both day and night with untiring zeal and astonishing results—but for four months only. I finally knew how to write Arabic characters as easily as if they were German or English, and I attained such perfection that fourty-four years later I still can master them, even though I did not continue my studies.

This pastime came to a sudden stop when I was ordered on board the transport *Pola*, which had to undertake several voyages to and from Trieste. The amusing aspect of this appointment was the odd commander, who bore an English name. He cared very little about what was going on, and in turn the very able executive officer paid still less attention to him. One could often hear the commander shout an order from the bridge, whereupon the executive officer simply answered, "Yes, Sir," and then did whatever he thought was appropriate, which was often quite the reverse of what had just been ordered. The captain apparently did not mind this, for though he might look puzzled for a while, he kept silent. The captain's mania consisted in telling tall tales whenever there was an opportunity to do so. These for the most part dealt with tiger hunts, and to make his stories appear more authentic he liked to embellish them with English terms. One night, after having listened to a dozen of his cock-and-bull stories, the executive officer gravely insulted the captain by boldly asking him whether he had ever really seen a live tiger in the wild. Although very much astonished, the captain was honest enough to answer, after hesitating a while, with a simple "No." But thereafter he no longer honored the doubting Thomas with his amusing adventures, and we watch officers had to serve as the sole victims of his mania.

After this six-week *Pola* intermezzo, I came as watch officer on board the *Vulkan*, a hulked old paddle steamer serving as watch vessel to the ships of the fleet that were out of commission. She was moored at the quay, one could come and go as one pleased, and the watches were not strictly kept, particularly during the night. The fare on board was good and cheap, so that as a rule some outsiders also partook of the board. After dinner, gambling went on quietly, as was generally the case with idlers in garrisons. Here for the first time I got acquainted with games of chance, first keeping aloof from them, but later casting myself all the more recklessly into the arms of the demon of gambling. In general, life in Pola was altogether decadent in those days, for it offered nothing positive. Social intercourse hardly existed; the conditions were those of a medium-sized garrison town whose spiritless inhabitants were without higher aims and were content to wade through the lowland of everyday routine. The streets of the town showed the same sights day after day, and everywhere one met the same officers, men, and civilians. It is not pleasant always to see the same faces, and it was irritating continually to have to raise one's hand to salute a superior or to return a salute. Nowhere did one feel alone or undisturbed.

These conditions induced many to avoid the town as much as possible in favor of walking in the surrounding countryside, which, with the exception of the Kaiserwald, was little more than a stony desert. Pola could nevertheless pride itself on having a prosperous hunting club, which probably had more members than the country had hares, and many officers devoted their entire interest and time to this sport, keeping pointers and setters and looking upon them as their darlings. Whenever they could they raced with them through the country, rain or shine, and though as a rule they came home empty-handed, they were cheerful in spite of their repeated disappointments. It looked as if these Nimrods were driven by an irresistible impulse, perhaps the desire to expend their excess energy in whatever physical exercise they could find. Some took to hook and line, while others contented themselves with visiting their favorite pub in the company of some like-minded friends. Intellectual occupations were less favored. There was a well-stocked library connected with the observatory and a small book shop in town. The former was rarely used, and the latter shrunk visibly year by year, being kept alive with considerable difficulty. Whenever the shopkeeper wished to sell anything, he had to give it on credit, for he could hardly expect men who were often compelled to buy their daily bread on credit to make payment for dry books in cash. The navy club offered quite a number of daily papers and weekly and monthly publications, however, which sufficed for the spiritual edification of the majority, while occasional concerts given by the always brilliant navy band afforded recreation for those who reveled in the like.

Since Pola in those days was not yet popular in the inner circle of the Monarchy and did not enjoy a good reputation, it was not much frequented by visitors. The town was not yet sufficiently developed—and never was—to offer the gentle sex the comfort to which it is accustomed. Until later years, when it was made accessible and exploited by the venturesome Mr. Kupelwieser, Brioni (Brijuni) was still an ill-famed fever island to be avoided.[1] The navy's attitude toward the town's civilian population was always negative. Some of the wives of the older generation were not admitted to society because of their ancestry, and there were only a few genteel creatures who could make the hearts of men quiver. For some length of time only three stars dominated the social heavens. All three were celestial embodiments of the first magnitude, shining in equal luster, and as provident nature would have it, one was blond, the second was brunette, and the third was a black-haired beauty. This permitted the various worshipers to follow their preference and to find in the one or the other of these stars an idol worthy of their adoration.

Pola differed from other garrison towns insofar as the colonel's wife did not dare to think herself superior to the major's wife, and so forth and so on down the ranks. Only the port admiral's lady throned above them all, but no social obligations were imposed upon the officers. Discipline on base was willingly borne, but on shore one wished to be one's own master. In later years, when the number of married people had increased tenfold in consequence of more liberal regulations concerning the allowable percentage of married officers, social life in Pola assumed other forms; villas and tennis courts sprang from the soil like mushrooms, and the sport of sailing took on considerable dimensions. These improvements occurred after the Pöck era had come to a close. Vice Admiral Baron Sterneck, his successor as naval commander in chief, did everything in his power to infuse new life into the navy. This took considerable time, however, since the hinterland, above all the political centers of Vienna and Budapest, did not think much of the navy, their hearts being only with the army. That von Sterneck finally succeeded in directing public attention toward the needs of the navy is perhaps his greatest distinction, for it is always difficult to set an inert mass into motion. He was precisely the right man for this task. The cross of the Maria Theresa Order that adorned his breast granted him respect and weight, and to the end of his days he remained as daring and pert as he had been at the Battle of Lissa in 1866. He did not care which way he had to go and what means he had to use to attain his goal of improving the navy. Some of his measures did not meet with approval in Pola, but he knew the world well and was aware that it is easier to lead it by the nose in gentle waltz time than in brisk march tempo. He would order the fleet to perform all sorts of marine spectacles in the presence of crowds of influential visitors amid the roar of cannon; in this way he obtained more battleships than the witty navy club members ever imagined possible. Coming ages will be reminded of Baron von Sterneck by a delightful little church that was built at his instigation in precious marble and dedicated to the Madonna del Mare.[2]

I have devoted only a few lines to social life in Pola, lacking as I do much insight into the matter. My life passed on board the *Vulkan* or in the open air, rather aside from the social highways. I did not become a member of the hunting club, but I did join a shooting association, not merely out of love for this sport but also because I was a good marksman and could therefore count on winning prizes, which was indeed the case. Being a good hiker and fond of long walks, I hit upon the idea of spending my next furlough on an extended walking tour through some of the wilder parts of southern Austria, and to have a partner I procured a very big and powerful dog, which I inconsiderately trained against man when it was still young. This subsequently caused me not a little trouble. To begin with, I did not get the leave, and the projected walking tour fell through. But then I still had the ferocious beast, who was a real danger in town. He used to attack any shabbily dressed person who came too near to me, and things did not always end with just torn trousers. Every morning he also had the habit of fetching his meat ration for himself from one of the butcher shops without paying for it, always returning on board with a pound or more of meat in his jaws, until one fine day he returned limping and profusely bleeding from a deep wound in his hind leg. This brought his predatory days to a close. His repeated misdeeds finally caused the city fathers to declare my dog a public danger, and I was only allowed to go out with him if he were muzzled and on a leash. I consequently seized the opportunity to favor the Austrian Arctic Expedition with the dog. However, on the way out on board the transport *Pola* he bit so many of the men that the captain sentenced him to death. At the urgent entreaties of the superstitious crew, however, he was allowed to live until the ship reached Gibraltar, where a splenetic Englishman took a fancy to the dog and was delighted to get him.

In contrast, a fox cub that I reared from youth became everyone's pet. He developed into a delightful rogue whom we all enjoyed immensely. He felt quite at home on board the *Vulkan*, but he was much in dread when taken on shore. He was also afraid of the sailors and was only perfectly at ease among the officers. He was allowed to move about at liberty, and he never ventured far from the wardroom. Once we missed him for one whole week, finally discovering him half-starved in one of the empty deck cabins. During the repasts he used to sit near me, putting his paws on my knees and waiting to be stuffed with food. Sometimes he crept into hiding places unknown to us, and if we wished to have him come out we only had to rattle a plate and a fork to make him think it was mealtime. Then we saw our darling emerge from somewhere, yawning and stretching his limbs. It was extremely funny to watch him tease a monkey that was on board and to see how he made fools of the astonished hounds that now and then came with their masters to see him. Alas, he met a sad end. On hot days he liked to hide inside the boiler of a small paddle steamer that lay alongside the *Vulkan* and was connected with the latter by a wooden bridge. One day that vessel had to put to sea in haste. The manhole of her boilers was closed, steam was made up, and our pet was done for.

To my great disappointment, after having wasted two years in this way, I had to get acquainted with the barracks. At this time I had unfortunately already taken to gambling and had even come to like it. The number of gamblers had increased to the point that the *Vulkan*'s wardroom could not hold them all. The gambling hall therefore moved into a room in the coffeehouse on the marketplace. There we spent our nights, month after month, with the chief of police in our midst as one of the most enthusiastic violators of the law. When the evil grew, we gamblers abandoned the coffeehouse den and boldly established ourselves in the navy club, although games of chance were forbidden there—as indeed they were on board ship. At first the gambling went on secretly, but later on, after the public mind had become vitiated, we did not recoil from gambling quite openly. Instead of the original baccarat we now played a pokerlike game, and the sums that changed hands were larger. Many a gambler lost all his money and had to drop out, and others took his place. I was not much favored by luck but managed to keep *à fleur d'eau* [above water]. One got to know the character of the gamblers, which was quite interesting. But one also got acquainted with various loan societies and professional money lenders, moved about at daytime drowsily, and neglected one's duties. Many a time the commander of the barracks—my protector at the naval college—returned my salute with a friendly smile when he saw me hurrying toward the parade ground in the morning, thinking that I was already bent on doing my duty so early in the day, when in fact I was only hurrying home to have a good, long sleep after a night of gambling. The dissipating life that we led was very apt to undermine one's health and also one's good morals. As for me, it came to an end in consequence of my being employed for some special work.

This had to do with the introduction of a stronger cartridge and an altered moveable notch for the Werndl carbines that were used in our navy, requiring every one of these ten thousand carbines to be tested anew. A bonus amounting to thirty florins a month was promised to the two officers who did this work, and since I sorely needed the money and was a good marksman, I volunteered. Day after day a friend and I, along with half a dozen artificers, spent the hours from six in the morning until sunset on the practice ground in dull monotony, firing at a target only one hundred yards distant. Some three thousand rifles passed through my hands. The breech mechanism of many of them did not stand the increased gas pressure, and many a fire flash imperiled our eyesight. After our day's work we walked home in an enervated, apathetic frame of mind, half-deafened by the detonations. Some years before, when I was under water in a diving suit, the drum of my left ear had been crushed, and these months of continual shooting hardly improved my hearing. The payment of the promised bonus was put off from one month to the next, and when the Admiralty finally declared that our exhausting work had to be treated as any other regular service, I felt indignant, made an end of it, and returned to gambling.

As already mentioned, I lived with one of my classmates in the barracks in one of the cheap, badly furnished lodgings provided there. My friend was one of the few officers who got a respectable monthly allowance from home. Although he never gambled and was in no way a spendthrift, he was nevertheless in debt as often as I. It was always a puzzle to me just how he spent his money; having different interests, we went our separate ways without caring much about what the other did. We lived very simply, and after the various restaurant keepers refused to give us further credit we even procured our meals from the rather unappetizing canteen. The only visible extravagance in which my companion indulged was that he had our orderly rigged out in a really fine and showy livery. Whether it was a matter of taking a note or a bunch of flowers somewhere—perhaps to one of the three stars—I cannot say, for my friend was very discreet in this regard.

From what I have narrated, the reader probably will have learned that I was not a person belonging to the species of "carpet knights." I had no fondness for society and therefore did not have much social intercourse. I kept aloof from the three stars, whose charms I perhaps resisted because of my gambling, which

I think is indeed a nostrum against other passions. But I liked to frequent the families of two brothers, twins, both of whom accepted me with warm feelings and signs of true friendship. They were much older and higher in rank than I, were very capable and dutiful officers, and as such were admired by all. Being very strict and even severe in service, however, they were not loved but were rather feared. I knew only their private side, never having served under their command. At the time of which I am speaking these twin brothers looked so much alike that one at first never knew who was who. Although they were men of wide experience, they apparently valued my judgment, for they always used to confer with me whenever an important question arose, listening to my opinion. They were both married, and I spent many a pleasant hour in the company of their families; on Sundays there was a place regularly reserved for me at their table. They often pressed me to give up my dissipating life of gambling, but their exhortations were of no avail. From my vice I could only be freed by being appointed on board ship, after my three years of shore duty had expired.

On Christmas Day 1882 the paddle steamer *Andreas Hofer*, the vessel placed at the disposal of the governor of Dalmatia, arrived at Pola for repairs. The ship had run aground somewhere, and her navigating officer, who was not the only person responsible for the accident, was removed and severely punished. I was to replace the unfortunate man. At the beginning of his command, Vice Admiral Baron von Sterneck dealt pitilessly with whoever had the slightest accident. I did not quite like the idea of having to spend my one-year term of service at sea on the Dalmatian coast on board a small old paddle steamer, but there I was, at the least delivered from the constant pecuniary embarrassment that had worried me for so long. At the same time, I would have the opportunity to get to know our sea coast better, which I considered an important gain. The ship's captain, [Karl] S[eemann] von T[reuenwart], was a smart-looking officer who pleased me all the more for having manfully, though unsuccessfully, defended the navigating lieutenant, a proceeding that was not usual in our navy. I cared less for the executive officer, who was a dry soul. In the wardroom there were two ensigns, both older than I. The one was a count with a Russian name, with very aristocratic looks and demeanor; the other was an upright Styrian, a passionate huntsman and brilliant marksman, with whom I had started the shooting tests of the Werndl carbines. Finally there were two midshipmen, a surgeon, and a paymaster on board.

The governor's residence was in Zara, a small town surrounded by abandoned ramparts. A bridged-over moat severed the town from the mainland, and a weekly mail steamer was her only connection with the outer world. The governor was a well-known field marshal with pleasant, affable manners; his wife was a charming lady, and their only daughter was a fresh and pretty girl. But a single swallow does not make a summer. There was a large number of civil servants, who always looked awfully bored, and then there were the officers of the garrison, who preferred to live apart. The civilian inhabitants of the place were not worthy of consideration. After the first excitement of novelty had passed, the monotony in our lives made itself much felt, although our duty as watch officers kept us busy. Unfortunately our relations with our two bosses soon became troubled in consequence of a complaint that we lodged against the executive officer, with which the captain did not comply. Thereafter we conspired against them both and exhibited passive resistance on every occasion. As none of the parties felt inclined to give in, these unpleasant conditions continued for many months, in fact until our adversaries left the ship.

Now and then the *Andreas Hofer* made an inspection tour along the Dalmatian coast with the governor on board. In between we spent weary weeks on our moorings, which made us hail even the arrival of the weekly mail steamer as an event of great interest. The wardroom officers had no social contact with us, and with the captain and the executive officer we were on a war footing, which in time took on even rougher forms in consequence of further complaints. Since the surgeon and the paymaster did not count, we three ensigns had to depend on ourselves, and since one of us was always on duty, there was not even the possibility of playing cards. The Styrian owned a gun and frequently went out shooting, though he rarely found an occasion to fire off a shot. For my part I took up fishing with hook, groundline, fish spear, and net. Only the last proved enjoyable or rewarding, done on the sly at night on forbidden fishing grounds. This soon appeared to me to be not quite safe, however, and not wishing to be caught red-handed or to get mixed up in some awkward legal affair, I soon gave it up. Now and then I took the dinghy and rowed along the coast, amusing myself by shooting at diving birds, which were quite common.

I need not say that this way of living failed to satisfy me. Where were the extended voyages and stirring adventures I had anticipated upon joining the navy? In former years I had already harbored the thought of trying my luck in the Turkish or Argentine navy, the latter because I was fully conversant in Spanish. Subsequently I became animated to an even greater degree by a desire to explore Africa, having been bewitched by the many travel books I had read. I had already offered my services to one of the African explorers, but he did not deign to answer. In Zara my longing for the dark continent began to torment me again and made me write the chairman of the Comité d'Études du Haut Congo, asking him for employment. His answers were all couched in friendly but evasive terms. I did not abandon the hope of finding work in the Congo, however; on the contrary, in my mind's eye I was already in desert and wilderness, and I set to work with fiery zeal to train myself for coming hardships. The next thing I did was to procure a gun. Bearing it on my shoulder, I moved out into the country, making forced marches and other such nonsense. At a goodly distance from Zara there was a reed-overgrown, swampy lake, which I represented as either Lake Chad or Lake Bangweulu, and its surroundings became my favorite sporting field. To enjoy this fun I had to start out after my middle watch at 4:00 A.M., because only then was I free from duty for the next twelve hours. It being wintertime, the lake was covered with a paper-thin sheet of ice. These circumstances certainly did not tally with my African fantasies, but they did not detain me from wandering thither after a night watch, clad in jackboots and thin drill knickerbockers. In the darkness of the night I indulged in dreams of ambushes and attacks of savage hordes and thereby gave evidence of my cold-bloodedness.

In some rare instances the *Andreas Hofer* was used by distinguished persons for a trip. Once we had on board for ten days Field Marshal Archduke Albrecht, who was on an inspection tour to various places of strategic importance. The archduke was in no way an inconvenience, being always affable and discreet in his demeanor. He was a thorough soldier, and in spite of his advanced age was filled with an unquenchable interest in all military matters. Another time Prince Nicholas of Montenegro used the ship for his passage from Cattaro to Trieste. Since he was a bad sailor, we saw very little of him, for he hardly left the captain's stateroom. At the time he also suffered from a toothache, and the tooth had to be extracted. According to our surgeon, the prince did not behave on this occasion as heroically as would have befitted one of the proud sons of the black mountains.

In time, the day came for the captain and the executive officer to be relieved. Before he left the ship for good, the former kindly offered me an opportunity for reconciliation by asking me to take him along on one of my duck hunts. But we only wandered a short distance, leisurely talking all the while of this and that, and returned on board without having fired a shot; we remained friends for all times to come. His place was taken by the former executive officer of the so-called *Warthog*—that is, the *Salamander*—whom I mentioned in the previous chapter. Since I served with him, the "bugbear of Smyrna" had married and now seemed much tamer than before. As for the new executive officer, years ago he had been a member of the Austrian Arctic Expedition that had discovered the Franz Josef Land in 1873 under the command of Lieutenant Weyprecht.[3] His merry blue eyes revealed a cheerful mind, which he proved by amusing us with many a droll yarn and witty tale. A few days after this change in the ship's staff, the governor was pleased to undertake an inspection tour. As was usual, the ship had gone alongside the quay for his convenience, and in order to leave port she had merely to steer straight ahead and pass through the admittedly narrow entrance. The paddle boards had hardly begun to turn round when to my astonishment the new captain requested me to take command of the ship, since he was feeling too nervous to do so himself. Such, then, was the true nature of the Cerberus of Smyrna! Thereafter he no longer had any teeth as far as I was concerned.

After having spent fourteen months on board the *Andreas Hofer*, I was relieved and had to take charge of the 12th Company in the barracks, a special formation about 250 strong. The men, all qualified mechanics, were employed in the navy yard. It had always been a select company, for they were a serious lot. They kept busy at work all day long, were always neatly dressed, and kept their quarters in an exaggerated state of order. My duty consisted mainly of leading some infantry drills on Saturday afternoons. Every ten days I also had to fetch the funds for the payment of the men, merely committing the money to the sergeant major, who did the rest. I had to attend to very little myself, and I soon fell back into the clutches of the demon of gambling. As before, I passed the hours of the day in drowsiness in expectation of the evening. The number of gamblers had grown larger, as had the prevailing stakes, and the card tables were not left before daylight had set in. During the night the gamblers did not live as they had before, on strong coffee and countless cigarettes, but now reveled in the very best that kitchen and cellar could offer. That was quite sensible and allowed the gamblers to continue their exhausting way of living for any length of time. It is true that the heavy bills consumed their funds, but when one lost thousands, these hundreds could well go with them. About this time the emperor made one of his rare visits to Pola. One day he was to inspect the barracks. Accordingly, the officers and men were presented to the all-highest war lord on the parade ground, where my fine company excelled and was distinguished by the monarch with an approving nod of the head. Surely none of the worthy spectators was aware that I, the wanton leader of the company, had been seated at a gambling table until close to that very hour.

I was left in charge of the 12th Company for only eight weeks, after which I was ordered on board the gunnery ship *Novara*. There I did not have so much leisure, but my needs were less and my salary was higher, which served me well. The negative side of the appointment was that the gambling vice had also quartered itself on board this ship, which offered an additional opportunity for dissipation. The majority of her officers used to gamble in the afternoons, not caring about the exercise and instruction hours. They secured themselves against an unpleasant surprise by posting sentinels. I do not know whether or not the captain had any inkling of what was going on, but in any event he would have been too weak a person to proceed against the disorder in a determined manner.

One of the duties of the gunnery ship was to execute the practical part of trial shootings whenever such had to be made, under the control of the Permanent Artillery Committee. This board was composed of twelve to fifteen artillery engineers and two navy officers under the chairmanship of a rear admiral. The other officers on board the gunnery ship did not care for these trials or want anything to do with the artillery committee. I, on the other hand, was very fond of shooting and volunteered whenever a trial was to occur. At that time the question had arisen whether the newly invented brown prismatic powder should be introduced in our navy in place of ordinary black prismatic powder. This new powder not only developed 20 percent higher gas pressure but was also much cheaper in price—advantages that certainly were not to be despised. To decide the question, a long series of trial shootings with guns of all calibers had to be made. These were performed over two months on the shooting ground in the presence of the whole artillery board, and measurements of gas pressure and other investigations were made. My participation was minimal, and I understood that I was only the mechanical assistant to the committee. After the conclusion of these trials I did not hear of the matter for several weeks, which made me think that the question had been settled in favor of the brown pow-der. One forenoon, however, when I had been on duty as officer of the deck and was lying drowsily on the sofa in the deck cabin, an artillery engineer—our former teacher from the naval college—entered and placed a large bundle of documents on the table. He explained that these were the proceedings of the trial shootings and asked me to put my signature on the Permanent Artillery Committee's final vote. He would return at 2:00 P.M. I said "Aye, aye" and there-with left the papers where they were. But though I was very sleepy, after some time I became interested in knowing the tenor of the committee's final deci-sion. I began to leaf through the documents until I hit upon the verdict. There, to my astonishment, I read that the brown prismatic powder was not to be in-troduced in our navy because of certain reasons of secondary importance, which were specified; underneath were the signatures of the whole board. It was a unanimous vote, and no doubt the powerful and cheap brown powder had been condemned for some paltry reason. It was then time to go to the wardroom to have my noon meal, but my mind was so absorbed by the monstrosity I had just read that I could hardly eat.

When the meal was over, my mind was made up never to put my signature to a vote of that kind. I therefore retired to my cabin, took a sheet of paper, and began to write a separate vote. Then, after some deliberation, I stated the rea-sons—there were nine—why the brown powder unquestionably had to be in-troduced in our navy; underneath, in letters as big as if I were a mighty admi-ral, I put my humble ensign's name. Punctually at 2:00 P.M. the engineer returned, received the paper bundle without any remark, and went his way. I had not given the matter any further thought when on the following day the captain summoned me and covered me with reproaches, declaring it to be an imperti-nence that I had dared to submit a separate vote in the face of the unanimous verdict of the artillery board and, having participated in the trials as the repre-sentative of the gunnery ship, to give it as his judgment. I begged to observe that I had only expressed my private opinion and not his, which indeed was the case. Two days later I was surprised by the order to appear at a meeting of the artillery board. This circumstance bothered me to some degree, and I made up my mind in the future to be more circumspect when stating my opinions—not because I thought I had been wrong, but because in my present state of mind I did not care a bit whether our guns were booming with black, brown, or blue powder.

Before the beginning of the dreaded meeting I was struck by the fact that the chairman, a rear admiral of rough manners and few words, had returned my salute with a friendly smile. Still more was I astonished by what followed at the council table, where I sat at the end as the youngest member in rank, in the midst of a crowd of eminent artillery engineers. The chairman opened the ses-sion by declaring that a divergence of opinion had arisen as to the value of the brown powder and that further deliberations were therefore necessary. What was the meaning of this? Had it not been a unanimous vote? I am not going to relate the course of this session in detail, but beginning with the chief artillery engineer and going down to the lowest in rank, all, at first cautiously and then more boldly, followed the path I had defined in my separate vote. When I was finally asked again to offer my opinion, I simply replied that I had nothing to add to what the previous speakers had said. Consequently the brown powder was introduced, and thanks to a disorderly ensign who was entirely devoted to gambling, the artillery of the Austro-Hungarian navy had overnight been increased in power by fully 20 percent. The affair was of course hushed up, and for my part I kept quiet about the whole matter. In order to allow the first vote to disappear, just for show, a short series of trial shootings was hurriedly arranged, which I was not asked to attend. I had to participate in these matters only once more, when my former artillery instructor at the naval college had to pass judgment on an altered cannon's breech action. On my arrival at the shooting ground he held out his hand to me, anxiously beseeching me not to raise any difficulties. I hastened to reassure him and smilingly let him do and write what he pleased. I signed his report without even looking at it.

In the course of time I had been promoted to the higher ranks without having passed any one of the prescribed special instruction courses. One usually remained on board the gunnery ship for one and a half years. I was disappointed, however, when I was relieved after less than five months and ordered to return to the watch hulk *Adria*, which had meanwhile replaced the *Vulkan*. I do not like to remember the six and a half months I spent at my new assignment, for they were entirely devoted to gambling, whereby fortune did not smile upon me. The burden of debt increased and finally was crushing. Others had fared as badly as I, and the number of gamblers was very much reduced. Not knowing of any further source of money that I could possibly tap, I was bound to make an end of it. These were terrible days, for just as the opium eater longs to get the cherished drug when the time for it has arrived, so did I feel drawn to the card table when the evening hours set in. But I had exhausted all available resources and it could not be. Though it made me suffer agonies to resist the temptation, I manfully held my ground.

Several weeks had already passed in this way without my touching cards, and I certainly was on my way to recovery, when temptation approached. One night a much older and higher-ranking officer could not wait for the usual time for gambling, but I flatly refused to join him. After a while he returned and pressed me hard. In answer I merely showed him my empty purse. The officer accosted me a third time and beseeched me to join the party; others would come, he explained, and then I could withdraw. When he finally called me a spoilsport, I grew weak. As things turned out, after the first game a heap of bank notes lay before me, and when I returned home late that night my pockets were full. On the following two nights I was again no loser but was less fortunate. After that, gambling came to an end because of changes in personnel.

On March 1, 1886, I was appointed navigating officer on board the yacht *Greif*, a paddle steamer destined to convey Crown Prince Rudolf and his consort Archduchess Stephanie to Lacroma (Lokrum), a small, picturesque island lying in Dalmatia close to Ragusa (Dubrovnik). The high personages boarded the *Greif* at Trieste, where they had resided for some time in Miramare, a beautiful seashore castle built by the unfortunate Emperor Maximilian of Mexico. From there we proceeded south and reached our destination in cold, snowy weather. The princely couple took their abode in an old, unused monastery, the only building that exists on Lacroma; the yacht had to remain there for the duration of the all-highest visit. The crown princess was not feeling well and had selected this place for the sake of her health, taking with her only a small retinue; the conveniences in the monastery were too limited to allow for a greater display of royalty.[4] The snowy weather was soon followed by fine, sunny days, which enticed us to take quiet walks over graveled pathways in balmy air scented by the countless jasmine blossoms that abound on this lovely island. Very few foreign visitors came to disturb the idyllic quiet—only the brother- and sister-in-law, Prince Philip of Coburg and his consort, stayed for some time. I repeatedly had the honor of taking this royal couple around to one of the many interesting sites in that beautiful section of the Dalmatian coast. At the time I never would have thought that this gentle, fair lady would one day attract attention to herself on account of her conduct. Perhaps her thoughts were already brooding over things far away when she, sitting quietly in the boat with apparent indifference, was absorbed in contemplating her polished, rosy fingernails, as was mostly the case. To me at the time she seemed the personification of virtue itself.[5]

We officers rarely got a glimpse of Crown Prince Rudolf and Archduchess Stephanie—I should almost like to say luckily, for the archduchess was young, beaming with grace, very affable, and simple in her ways, and when we chanced to meet her on her lonely walks she always condescended to favor us with some kind and friendly words. It would not have been surprising if a young and heedless heart had lost its equanimity in the face of so much charm. Although the captain was a daily guest at the princely table, we were only rarely distinguished with an invitation to dinner, usually when it was a matter of avoiding the ominous number thirteen. For this very reason I was one day twice invited to dinner, only to have the invitation finally recalled. The ship had to be ready to obey the all-highest orders whenever they arrived, and we therefore could not think of absenting ourselves for more than an hour or two. The days glided by very quietly, as was proper for an Arcadia, until it pleased fate to rouse me quite unexpectedly to a new life.

As a rule the captain used to return to the ship from Lacroma late at night and tell the watch officer before retiring what had happened on shore. Once, when I luckily was on duty—for otherwise I would not have learned about it— he quite incidentally mentioned that a Hungarian count had arrived in order to take leave of the crown prince before starting out on an African expedition. The captain had no idea that his remark touched the most sensitive string of my inner life, and he was therefore much surprised when I emphatically said, "In this I must have a share!" My longing for Africa had temporarily calmed down somewhat, but it was still strong. The captain, who liked me, volunteered to see the count and communicate my wish to him, even going on shore earlier than usual the following morning, while I nervously waited on board for what would develop. At the time I was nearly twenty-nine years old and had made up my mind to dismiss any further thought of Africa after reaching the age of thirty. And now, all at once, the possibility, even the probability—nay, the certainty—of the realization of my most ardent desire had drawn near!

The captain returned with the news that Count Samuel Teleki would come on board at 3:00 P.M.[6] He also told me that the count had at first decidedly declined the thought of associating himself with anyone, especially with a person unknown to him and possibly unfit. That he finally consented to get in touch with me was thanks to the crown prince and the archduchess, who both spoke strongly in my favor. The count came on board with Professor Schweinfurth's famous travel book *Im Herzen von Afrika* under his arm.[7] In the deck saloon he silently spread out the map of the book, pointed to a penciled line on it, and said, "This is where I want to go." So far, the count had hardly taken any notice of me, and I was too excited to pay much attention to his exterior looks. Just for the sake of politeness, however, I furtively peeked at the penciled line, which as far as I remember ran from Zanzibar toward Lake Tanganyika and from there in a northeasterly direction toward Abyssinia. I was absolutely indifferent where the expedition was to go or how the count looked—if only he would allow me to have a share in it! I therefore assented to everything he said. As the count had to leave Lacroma that same evening, we agreed to settle all further questions by letter, and he gave as his address the name Sáromberke, a small village in Transylvania. It was a name that at the time meant nothing to me, but it was one with which I would soon become quite familiar. I could not then foresee what incisive consequences would result from this first short interview, for years of true friendship would knit us together for as long as the count lived.

It was a lucky circumstance, and one of decisive importance, that the narrated preliminaries had come to pass under the auspices of the crown prince, because it was virtually certain that I would be granted a furlough of several years' duration. One may imagine that my mind was now too preoccupied to allow me to enjoy a peaceful life, even on this delightful island. I therefore felt relieved when a few weeks later, at the beginning of May, the princely residence at Lacroma came to an end and we could begin the homeward voyage.

4

My First Expedition to Africa
(1886–1889)

I had agreed with Count Teleki that we would meet in Vienna about the middle of June to discuss some details concerning the expedition. Meanwhile I had no difficulty obtaining leave for an indefinite term and was even granted full pay for the duration of my absence. Years ago, the commander in chief of our navy, Vice Admiral Baron Sterneck, had himself made a short tour in Arctic regions, and he favored any enterprise that would help make the navy popular.

My discussions with the count did not concern the route that the expedition was to take but only the outfitting, which we agreed to share, I purchasing items in Vienna and he in London. I was well acquainted with African travel literature and at least in theory was no new hand as far as the dark continent was concerned. Also, my qualifications regarding scientific training probably answered the purpose. I was in any case a person serious enough for such an enterprise and was certainly burning with enthusiasm. As a mere ensign, however, I was of no consequence and knew hardly anybody in the large city. My brother Franz, who had meanwhile become a professor at the Technical University in Vienna,[1] was a very talented and highly trained person, knowledgeable in all branches of science, but he did not take very much interest in my plans and only gave me occasional hints. In Vienna nobody spoke of or took an interest in the expedition, and the few who had knowledge of it did not take it very seriously. I therefore received little help from others and had to depend largely on my own devices. It took me no end of research before I could begin to purchase, pack, and ship the thousand and one items that were needed. It was our firm intention to make the expedition a creditable enterprise with regard to all branches of science, insofar as this lay in our power, but special attention was devoted to geographical detail. I procured the newest editions of E. G. Ravenstein's and Lannoy de Bissy's maps of Africa—which, however, proved to be of no use to us whatsoever[2]—and requested the observatories at Vienna and Pola to provide us with chronometers; other special instruments had to be made to order. The accessories needed for scientific collections were assembled. I had to learn and practice photography and the preservation of skins, insects, and plants. I also needed to learn the art of skinning birds; I practiced it until I could do it properly, even with a goat sucker, a bird that sheds its feathers if these are so much as touched. As it was not our intention to take a surgeon with us, we also had to acquire some medical knowledge. To equip the people of our caravan, two hundred old military muzzle-loading rifles and eighty breech-loading Werndl carbines were bought inexpensively at an ironmonger's shop. As for foodstuffs, which we intended to take with us in large quantities, only Knorr's pea soup, ship's biscuits, salt, and some sugar were considered. These were soldered in special tins that could be opened without damaging them.

One day I was drawn from my quiet and assiduous activity by an invitation to a court dinner by Crown Prince Rudolf and his consort, Archduchess Stephanie, who at the time were sojourning at Laxenburg near Vienna. I knew that Count Teleki had not been thinking of taking a companion on his expedition and that it was only through the urgent instigation of both the crown prince and princess that he had finally consented to travel with me, an unknown outsider. I was therefore greatly pleased to be allowed to express my heartiest thanks to my illustrious patrons for their kind intervention. The crown prince advised me to call on the chief of the Imperial Military Chancellery, General Popp,[3] for the sake of a subsidy destined for my personal outfit, which, according to the crown prince, I was to be granted by His Majesty the Emperor. I did so at once on the following morning but regretted having been so rash, for instead of hearing some friendly words from the general, as I had expected, I was received in a most ungracious manner. Not knowing what to think and what it meant, I listened quietly to his flow of angry words, and when he had finished I only said that I had come by order of His Imperial Highness, Crown Prince Rudolf. I thereafter called on Count [Karl] Bombelles, the crown prince's lord high steward, and gave him a vivid account of the way in which I had been treated. I could see that the count was indignant, but he only said, "Do not mind it; this Popp is a boor."

We intended to climb Kilimanjaro, then the highest unconquered summit in Africa, whose higher parts are covered with eternal snow. Not being familiar with the Alpine world and its dangers, I felt it advisable to pass a short course in mountaineering. I did this under the guidance of my brother, who, having climbed most of the highest peaks in Europe, was experienced in this regard. He chose the Grossglockner region as a suitable training ground, and in the course of ten days we climbed not only the main peak (3798 m), but also other mountains of nearly the same height.

On my return to Vienna, I was greatly alarmed by a letter I received. The hundreds of cases that contained the objects I had procured had successively been forwarded to Trieste, there to await my arrival. Among other things, they contained rifles, cartridges, rockets, guncotton, and kindred items that ships do not like to take on board. Therefore the Steam Navigation Company of the Austrian Lloyd had at first refused to have anything to do with them. It had taken long and tedious negotiations before the Lloyd had finally consented to ship this ticklish consignment to Aden with a freighter that was to sail to that port at an earlier date. This took a great weight from my mind, as there would not have been any other way for shipping these items. Now, to my amazement, the Lloyd informed me it could not transport this load, the landing of arms or ammunition at Aden being strictly prohibited. Since the freighter in question was to leave within forty-eight hours, I had no time to waste; two hours after my return from the Alps, I was sitting in a train on my way to Trieste. There I hurried to the directors of the shipping company to beg and implore them, but I only succeeded in getting them to promise that they would take further counsel regarding the matter and would let me know their final decision at 2:00 P.M. When I put in an appearance at the desired hour, I was told that the Lloyd could not ship arms and ammunition without first gaining permission to land them at Aden. As it was, the Lloyd insisted on getting assurance from the British Colonial Office that the port authorities in Aden had been accordingly advised; of this the Lloyd of course had to be informed before the steamer's departure.

Barely thirty hours were at my disposal to pull this off. The only thing for me to do was to wire Count Teleki at once in London to request that he move heaven and earth in order to do away with the difficulty that had arisen so unexpectedly. Thereafter it was time to think of my return to Vienna. I had hardly arrived at home and had not yet shaken off the dust of the journey when I received an astonishing telegram from the count in London, which soon set me going again. It ran thus: "Arrange difficulty in Vienna with Foreign Office." Tired as I was and not in the best of humor, I slipped on a uniform and hastened to the Foreign Office at the Ballhausplatz. The minister had not yet put in an appearance, but I could see his representative, who was a type of official certainly not common in Austria. He patiently listened to my explanation, which he found not quite comprehensible because he had never heard anything of our expedition. He therefore finally asked me what I wished him to do. We then jointly drafted a long, urgent dispatch to our embassy in London covering the matter. More we could not do. Twelve hours were still left for the settlement of the transport question, which I passed in perfect quiet, having conscientiously done everything possible. It is true, however, that I jumped with joy when a wire arrived from the Lloyd the following morning announcing that the required consent had been received, putting an end to all uncertainty.

On October 5, after a short farewell visit to Gorizia, not far from Trieste, where my mother had moved because of my sister's ill health and the mild climate, I stepped on board the *Titania*, the vessel that was to bring me to Aden. No farewell pangs burdened my heart, and I abandoned myself to the spell of an uncertain future. This I did with the utmost unconcern, but not with exalted feelings, although my most ardent hopes were finally being realized. I cared very little for my life at the time, but I could not know in advance whether I was truly made of the proper stuff for such an enterprise. This thought did not allow me to indulge in immoderate illusions.

A naval officer may accomplish long voyages and call at many a port yet still have little experience with the ways of the world. His life is ordinarily too much restricted to his ship and the accustomed circle of his mates. This being my first longer voyage on board a passenger vessel, I joyfully looked forward to this new experience, if only for the opportunity to gain the rest I needed after the exciting months devoted entirely to travel arrangements. Nowhere can one better enjoy such rest than at sea, on the way to a distant destination. The ship was full of passengers who at first roused my curiosity, which could best be satisfied at dinner time. To my surprise, when I entered the crowded saloon and looked around for a table and a chair, I was taken to the captain's table and seated next to him. At that time I did not yet know what an honor this was in the eyes of my fellow passengers and how much attention I would attract. As Captain Mersich explained, he was glad to have at his side a colleague who would not bother him with silly questions. I am sorry to relate that this was his penultimate voyage. On his next trip, to the Far East, his ship was caught in an extraordinarily vehement typhoon, and Captain Mersich found an untimely watery grave.

The many passengers who were seated in the brilliantly lit saloon were of the usual type. For me, however, this animated crowd, which was talking in half a dozen different languages and was obviously enjoying the voyage, fascinated me for some time because of its novelty. When I sat down for my last luncheon on board, the brown forbidding rocks of Aden were already in sight. Knowing that I would have it less like Lucullus the farther away from the world's highways my steps would lead me, I enjoyed this meal all the more, as for the first time champagne was served. Thinking such was always the case whenever one of the main stations was reached in the course of the ship's voyage, I was curious when one of the passengers, an English judge in India, rose, lifted his glass, and began to make a speech. One may imagine my bewilderment when I heard him express the wish in the name of all the passengers that my journey might be successful and that I would be granted a safe and happy return. I had kept up very little intercourse with my fellow passengers and had spoken of my intentions with hardly any of them, and I was deeply moved by this demonstration of kind feelings.

A few days later I boarded a steamer of the Imperial British India Line, which had natives of Goa as stewards and which was infested with innumerable cockroaches. Her captain, Frohawk by name, was a sturdy, sailorly type who had already beaten this track for ten years. He knew the very intricate currents that run along the East African coast, which at that time had not yet been fully investigated. He jealously guarded the sea chart on which he had noted his observations like a treasure; only once did he allow me a furtive glimpse at it. Aside from me, the only other passenger was Mr. William O'Swald, our consul in Zanzibar. It was lucky for me that I met with Mr. O'Swald here, because he initiated me into the mysteries of the Kiswahili language, the lingua franca of vast tracts of central Africa. I picked up this idiom with so much facility that my teacher was lost in amazement and praised me as if I were one of the seven wonders of the world. It is true, however, that when I arrived in Zanzibar after eleven days, I already spoke Kiswahili as fluently as most of the Europeans who had already resided there for several years.

On her way to Zanzibar the ship called at the picturesque and historically interesting port of Mombasa. There a Mr. Gustav Denhardt came on board as a passenger. For several years he and his elder brother Clemens had served as ministers of all departments to the Sultan of Witu, a small Negro realm in the hinterland of Lamu.[4] Our ship reached Zanzibar on October 31. With her arrived 140 of our cases; our ammunition stores had been left in Aden because they could only be shipped to Zanzibar by way of an Arabian dhow, which our consul in Aden had promised to arrange. On board the British India liner I had only taken two smaller cases, which I had hidden underneath my couch. They contained 120 lbs. of guncotton, and it amused me when turning in at night to read a notice hanging in my cabin which threatened a heavy penalty in case I was caught. My luggage was at first taken to the customs house, where the native officials searched my many cases with great curiosity. They had probably seen everything before except compressed and stearinized guncotton. Even Mr. Denhardt asked what these yellowish, square things were. I enlightened him and was greatly amused when he promptly told the inquisitive blacks that they were *sabuni*, that is, soap. Mr. Denhardt and I then moved to the Hotel Criterion, a new, unfinished building with bare rooms that offered no comfort whatsoever.

The count's arrival was quite unexpectedly delayed for four weeks. I had to live in Zanzibar that long without being able to make any preparatory arrangements, being neither authorized to do so nor having the necessary funds at my disposal. In general I lived a secluded life. The number of Europeans residing in Zanzibar in those days was limited, and the arrival of anyone new caused not a little sensation. I let them talk, however, and did not trouble about either Sultan Sayid Barghash[5] or the Europeans of the place, did not visit the numerous British and German men-of-war that lay in the roads, and in no way put myself forward, so that the excitement caused by my arrival soon subsided. Having been away in Europe for some time, Mr. O'Swald was busy with his own affairs, so for the most part my social relations were restricted to Mr. Denhardt and a native of Goa who spoke English well and whom I engaged as my tutor in Kiswahili.

In the course of my conversations with Count Teleki we had spoken of a common sailor by the name of James Martin, a native of Malta, of whom Mr. Joseph Thomson speaks in commendable terms in his book *Through Masai Land*.[6] Since the count was of the opinion that it would be good to have this man as caravan leader, I looked for him but discovered that he had already been engaged by some English sportsmen who were to arrive later in the month. At the time I was sorry that he was unavailable, but when I got to know him better later on I was glad not to have him in our service. He was not the right man for a difficult and dangerous expedition through unknown countries, for he was lacking in spirit and would have had an unfavorable influence on the morale of the men. Besides, he did not know how to read and write, which would certainly have been a great drawback in an enterprise that required the keeping of many lists and registers.

Among the most influential figures at that time was General Lloyd William Mathews,[7] the commander in chief of the sultan's troops. Years before he had come to Zanzibar as a lieutenant on board a British man-of-war, had remained at the place after the ship had been hulked there, and had entered the services of Sultan Sayid Barghash. James Martin was in the general's good graces and used to live in the latter's country house, situated out of town. The general's conduct toward me was at first distant, until one day to my surprise he demanded my word of honor that our expedition would not pursue any political goals. Of this I could assure him without restraint, whereupon he became quite obliging.

Whenever I called on James Martin I found him surrounded by a number of caravan people, among whom were several who had participated in one or even more famous travels of discovery. I was greatly interested in these men, whose names were familiar to me from travel books by Livingstone, Cameron, Stanley, and others.[8] Another more important acquaintance was brought about by Mr. Denhardt. From Joseph Thomson's book I knew that he had made his successful trip through Masailand in the train of a prominent ivory trader named Jumbe Kimemeta.[9] He was a half-Arab living at Pangani and was reputed to know the Masai and their country better than any other man. The ivory districts in Africa form, so to speak, domains that are exploited by people who are acquainted with the natives, their languages, and their customs and who are well informed in the various current trading goods. I mention these facts because they forcibly influenced the count's somewhat vague plans, causing him to decide on the direction that the expedition would take.

Jumbe Kimemeta happened to be in Zanzibar. In the course of his many travels he had never penetrated farther inland than Lake Baringo and the Ngamatak, an uninhabited deserted border district lying between countries peopled by the Suk and the Turkana tribes—peoples at the time still unknown to science. By then Jumbe Kimemeta had heard of a lake which, he was told, lay somewhere farther north, but he could not say how far away and how large this lake was. E. G. Ravenstein's large atlas showed little more in this direction than blank spaces and a few lines based entirely on doubtful information. To fill in these blanks was certainly better than following the much-trodden route to Lake Tanganyika, as the count had initially intended. This new direction would take us past Mounts Kilimanjaro and Kenya, the two highest elevations in Africa (5895 meters and 5195 meters, respectively), the exploration of which would most certainly lead to valuable scientific results. In an interview with Jumbe Kimemeta a nonbinding agreement was reached: he would remain in Zanzibar against the payment of a fixed daily allowance until the count's arrival, and would eventually enter our service as the leader of our caravan in an expedition directed to those unknown regions north of Lake Baringo. In this way the expedition's itinerary was determined.

To my relief, the count arrived on November 29. My way of living now underwent a great change, since I was no longer allowed to bloom in the dark like a violet. We visited General Mathews, the sultan, the British ships, and the German men-of-war, which were in the charge of Rear Admiral [Eduard] von Knorr. A lively intercourse was kept up with General Mathews because we frequently needed his intervention. We enjoyed very friendly relations with Rear Admiral von Knorr, who revealed a sincere interest in our doings. Apart from appreciating his very sympathetic and sailorlike exterior, I also saw in him the hero of the only naval encounter that occurred in the course of the Franco-Prussian war, in 1870. His aide-de-camp was a Commander von Holtzendorff, and he, too, made a pleasant impression. The admiral and his aide-de-camp apparently worked very well together, both being men who made light of the serious side of life. Von Holtzendorff was some years older than I, took little notice of me, and was closer to Count Teleki.

Our honorary consul, Mr. William O'Swald, was a citizen of Hamburg and the eldest son of the commercial firm of this name. It originally had been engaged in the shipping trade, and like all such had faced hard times when steam shipping came into existence. The firm thereafter expanded into the East African trade and soon attained new prosperity. In our day it maintained several thriving factories in East Africa and even disposed of a special steamer to keep these in touch with the mother house in Hamburg.[10] With the growing competition in the colonial trade, conditions became less profitable, which eventually would be fatal to our poor friend. At the time we knew him, Mr. O'Swald was a very good-looking, smart young man of aristocratic demeanor. Business acumen was not his strong point, however, and I suspect he very much resented not having been born a lord or a count. He loved to keep an open house and to have many guests at dinner, and the more sumptuous his dinner parties, the happier he was. Following the then-prevailing views, he thought that the cultivation of tobacco was the way to increased prosperity, and he took to it on a large scale, with great energy, and at considerable expense. This unfortunately soon turned out to have been a mistake, for the speculation was a failure. Since his excitable and proud temper did not permit him to get over the heavy losses he had caused the firm, he voluntarily expiated them with his life.

While we assiduously devoted the weekdays to making the necessary travel arrangements, we enjoyed our Sundays by idling them away in the company of the admiral, his aide-de-camp, and Mr. O'Swald in the latter's fine country seat near the seashore. There we feasted and reveled and spent the hours puffing away in pleasant talk in the cooling air of the sea breeze, stretched out on the veranda in comfortable easy chairs.

Among the beautiful guns that the count had brought from London were two 8-caliber elephant rifles, which fired ten drachmas of powder. These were short, formidable-looking double-barreled weapons weighing eighteen pounds; as the count observed, firing them was not very pleasant. Except for the count, none of us had ever handled such a rifle, and since I was of very slim build the others liked to amuse themselves with the thought of what would happen if I were to shoot with one of these blunderbusses. Being curious myself to know the effect, I agreed one Sunday to have a try; an empty beer bottle was to serve as target. The merry company made fun of me by taking touching leave of me, and the bottle was then placed in the sand at 50 yards' distance, the farthest range at which this kind of rifle shoots accurately. They then retired to a safe place behind the house, while I betook myself to the stand. The sun was burning with scorching heat, the barrels were glowing hot, and it was not easy to keep the heavy rifle leveled at the mark. I pulled it up, however, took quick aim, and fired. What I thereafter felt was by no means pleasant. My helmet flew away, and I received a blow right in my face that almost moved me to tears. But to my comfort I heard the merry jesters sing out repeatedly "by Jove," and I saw that the bottle had disappeared. When fired, these short rifles bolt up and therefore must be held fast with the left hand, a lesson my painful nose taught me. Being now aware of their rudeness, I wiped away the second and the third bottles without any more ado, and there was no end of "by Jove" calls. Mr. O'Swald, who previously had made the most fun of me, was now so gallant as to trumpet my shooting skill for days all over Zanzibar.

Count Teleki, being forty-one years old when he started on his expedition, was twelve years older than I. We were both the proper age for enduring physical exertion—not yet too old, but not too young. He had grown up in Transylvania and came from a healthy and tough race. Since his early days the count had been a passionate hunter and was very experienced in bush life. He was of medium size, vigorous, and a splendid hiker, and he was also at home in the world of high mountains, having hunted many a chamois. My companion, disposed of very good nerves, had a great knowledge of all shooting matters and was a capital marksman. On his arrival at Zanzibar he was fat and plump and probably did not reveal what a thorough man he was. Six months later, his skin was tanned; hunger, thirst, and fatigue had done away with the superfluous fat; and only sinews and bones were left. In short, he had become quite a different man. I, on the other hand, was of a slender build but was healthy and tough. We were both passionate smokers and very indifferent drinkers, though by no means teetotalers.

Count Teleki had gone through some schooling at various German universities. Much of what he had learned was of course forgotten, but a stock of elementary knowledge and a great interest in science remained. The natural sciences, history, and astronomy were the subjects he particularly favored. The count had a beautiful singing voice, and on quiet evenings in the wilderness he often made himself heard, always beginning with some French songs. These soon gave way, however, to melancholic Hungarian tunes. His most winning characteristics were simplicity, kindheartedness, and carefulness. To get to know the inside of a man takes time. In that respect one was not disillusioned by Count Teleki, and the longer one knew him, the more one appreciated him. When we met in Zanzibar we knew virtually nothing of each other, but we got well acquainted later on under conditions that either bring people very close or separate them forever. The years we spent in the interior of Africa, during which we were entirely dependent on each other, were the foundation of a friendship that united us for the rest of our lives.

The English sporting party, consisting of two Harvey brothers, Sir John Willoughby, and a Mr. Hunter, arrived with the same boat that had brought the count. They left Zanzibar within a few days and set out for the Kilimanjaro district, where we would meet them again. The party was able to get away so soon because their caravan leader Martin had made the necessary preparations in advance. In contrast, we had to do the work ourselves, which took weeks, in a temperature that made us sweat not a little. The contents of the many cases that we had brought had to be classified, checked out, and converted into heavy loads weighing seventy pounds each. To these were added the large quantity of trading goods that were procured on the spot by Jumbe Kimemeta. They consisted of such items as beads and wire of iron, copper, and brass about 3/16 of an inch thick. Much valued in Africa then was a good quality cloth of white drill that went under the name *merikani* because it was made in Massachusetts. An inferior kind, named *gamti*, was imported from Bombay in large quantities. We had, furthermore, to carry with us a dark blue kind of cheap calico called *kaniki* and a better quality of bright red material named *bendera assilia*. Most of the beads used in the interior of Africa were then imported from Bohemia, with only a few kinds coming from Venice. The bartering value of these trading goods varied, and as there were no wholesale dealers in the interior, one was compelled to buy up the rations for the men little by little and therefore to carry small change in adequate quantities. The total of our loads, which had to be carried across mountains and through waterless steppes for hundreds of miles on the backs of men and a number of donkeys, amounted to eighteen tons and was divided into 495 loads.[11] To each load of seventy pounds that the caravan people were obliged to carry must be added a heavy rifle, a powder horn, a water bottle, personal property, and, for every fifth man, a copper cooking kettle. The total weight the men had to carry amounted at times to one hundred pounds and more. I cannot imagine a harder and more pitiable lot than that which caravan men had to endure on travels of discovery in Africa. Without a tent, with hardly a rag on their backs, with no sandals to protect their feet from thorns, and more often than not greatly underfed and exposed to all inclemencies of the climate and weather, they had to put up with the bare ground as their sleeping place at night after a march of from six to twelve hours and more. This life they bore for starvation wages, amounting to five Maria Theresa dollars a month. Science is hardly aware of how much is owed to these so-called Zanzibari men— for the most part slaves—and surely does not think that the discoveries in which it rejoices were paid for with the lives of thousands of these poor devils, who have never obtained their due reward.

One day Zanzibar was surprised by the arrival of Professor Oskar Lenz, an Austrian explorer famous because of his successful trip from Morocco to

Timbuktu and Senegambia.[12] This time his aim had been to bring help to Emin Pasha, who had retreated to Wadelai for fear of the Mahdists.[13] To accomplish that goal, however, Lenz did not possess the necessary means; he did not even get near to Wadelai, and he merely crossed Africa from west to east without having accomplished anything. Soon after, on December 4, a Dr. Wilhelm Junker arrived in Zanzibar after having spent seven years in the very heart of the dark continent. This Russian of German descent had thoroughly explored the provinces inhabited by the Niam-Niam and Mangbetu tribes. Like Emin Pasha, he had been forced to retreat to Wadelai in consequence of the Mahdist uprising, there to await further developments.[14] After having lived there for several years with Emin Pasha and the Italian Gaetano Casati,[15] he had set out to the coast by way of Unyoro and Uganda to apprise the world of the conditions prevailing in the central equatorial provinces. Lenz and Junker were the first Africa explorers I had ever met. From the many books of travel I had read I had formed a certain conception of the type of explorers whose names were written in gold letters in the history of discoveries. I confess that these two specimens did not correspond to my idealized conception. They certainly were sympathetic and learned men, but they did not impress me as being explorers filled with a great spirit of enterprise and daring.

Every Friday morning a parade of the sultan's troops, four hundred to five hundred strong, and of his irregular army took place, a spectacle one always enjoyed watching. The regular soldiers under the command of General Mathews marched from the barracks to the street leading past the customs house to the sultan's palace, where they drew up, while the irregulars, a motley, picturesque crowd of Arabs, half-Arabs, and blacks in everyday costume, were slowly and solemnly tripping along to the rhythm of the drums past the marketplace that lay in front of the sultan's palace. The regular troops were well dressed and armed, and their general, attired for the occasion in a gorgeous and elaborate uniform, was a fantastic sight. But it was much more fun to watch the irregulars. Now and then one of them suddenly rushed forward brandishing his long, straight sword, as if he could not check his eagerness to fight any longer. Sometimes two brawlers jumped ahead, faced one another with wild eyes, and clashed their swords against each other; it was of course all a sham. These irregular troops are of no use whatsoever in battle and are probably maintained only as a symbol or reminiscence of Arab sovereignty.

Amid such military splendor the sultan was accustomed to hold audience whenever prominent figures were in attendance, and one day the count and I were accorded such an honor. Sayid Barghash was certainly not an insignificant sultan. Under his rule the Muscat realm reached its apogee, whereas, after his death, it crumbled bit by bit into insignificance. The sultan received us with great affability, assuring us that he was pleased to further our plans in every possible way and as far as his influence reached. A Dr. Gregory, the doctor of the sultan's harem, acted as interpreter, but I already knew enough Kiswahili to take a part in the conversation. In leaving the sultan I awkwardly forgot my helmet in the audience hall. I became aware of this only when the kind Sayid Barghash himself, who had hastened after me, brought it, in spite of his clumsy left leg, which had been enormously deformed in consequence of elephantiasis. The sultan's kindhearted disposition was also demonstrated by his never allowing a death sentence to be carried out. Another little episode will further demonstrate his humanity. A German, Braun by name, lay ill with an extreme fever, past all hope. An ice bath alone could perhaps save him, but it was nighttime, and no ice could be found anywhere. Finally someone thought of asking the sultan. Sayid Barghash at once sent messengers to his various country houses where his ladies lived, ordering them to give up all the ice they had, and the man was saved.

It was not until the end of January 1887 that our traveling arrangements were finished. We had engaged nine headmen, as many overseers, and two hundred porters. On the advice of Sir Richard Burton, the well-known explorer of Africa and Arabia, Count Teleki had enlisted seven Somalis in Aden, who, with one exception, behaved extraordinarily well. Their leader, Qualla Idris, was a twenty-six-year-old Habr Gerhadji Somali who was entrusted with the duties of manager of the trading goods and who acted as general overseer of the caravan. He was soon the most important of our men and was appreciated by all. Qualla Idris spoke fluent English, Arabic, Hindustani, and Kiswahili. As a youngster he had been in the United States and afterward had been in the service of Mr. Henry Morton Stanley on the Congo for six years. His master had taken him to England several times, which gave him some knowledge of the world and its ways, something our other Somali utterly lacked. We could speak directly with the latter only after they had picked up some Kiswahili, which took a while. Qualla Idris was acquainted with large parts of Africa, knew many native tribes, and was an expert in judging and handling them. He was an exceptionally fine fellow: very intelligent, brave, handsome, and well mannered. His only fault lay in his inability to read and write.

The expedition was to start into the interior from Pangani. There we had to enlist some more men who were accustomed to travels in Masailand. Awaiting us here were twenty-five donkeys which had been purchased by Jumbe Kimemeta. Our men were shipped to Pangani by way of a dhow, while we and some of our followers made the passage on board a steamer that the sultan had graciously placed at our disposal. With regard to details of the expedition I refer the reader to my publication *Discovery of Lakes Rudolf and Stephanie*[16] and will confine myself to a rapid sketch.

The outfitting of the expedition had been made with great care. For the armament of the caravan we disposed of 200 muzzle-loaders, 80 Werndl breech-loading carbines, and 15 Colt repeaters. This power, when compared with that of other expeditions in Africa, was quite unusual and allowed us to proceed with determination and at the same time with moderation wherever we wished. As an exception to the rule I may mention that no women were permitted to join the expedition; made up of only men, the caravan was not encumbered by idle folk. According to our plan, the first goal was the Kilimanjaro district. At that time this highest peak in Africa had not yet been climbed, nor had the surrounding country been adequately surveyed. Our journey along the Pangani River to the foot of Kilimanjaro went off at a slow rate and not without desertions of men and the loss of loads, which was always the case at the beginning of such expeditions. One night the loss of no less than fifty porters compelled us to halt and take special measures. Much more were we aggrieved by the irreparable loss of a tin case that contained all of our maps, astronomical tables, and drawing paper and utensils. We had started with a splendid, thorough outfit in this regard, and though the whole country was closely searched for one entire week, the missing tin could not be found. Thus we were obliged to proceed without the smallest map of Africa at our disposal, and all my cartographic studies had to be carried out with very poor materials.

In Taveta, a small settlement of friendly natives lying hidden in a dense forest at the foot of Kilimanjaro, we made a prolonged halt, during which we explored the mountain and its nearer and farther surroundings. We did not nearly succeed in climbing Kibo, the higher of the two peaks, to which alone our efforts were directed; it was much higher than was thought at the time, so that the temperature was much lower than we were prepared to withstand. Already at a height of 13,840 feet (4220 m) we had to spend one night without disposing of fuel in a temperature of −11° C. A sleepless night passed under such conditions was certainly not the proper preparation for a difficult and fatiguing climb, and I gave up after having reached a height of 16,300 feet (4960 m); my companion did so at 17,475 feet (5310 m). It is surely a surprising circumstance that the Kilimanjaro, which had so long towered over the surrounding plains in majestic solitude and quiet, was visited within a few days by yet another party. The same day we were back again in Taveta, where we had the pleasure of welcoming Dr. Hans Meyer and his companion Baron Eberstein, who had arrived with the intention of conquering Kibo. Although they had the benefit of our experience, their efforts were not crowned with success. Only on his second attempt, which Dr. Meyer undertook two years later in the company of the renowned Alpinist Purtscheller, did he succeed in conquering the Kibo for the first time.[17]

Our further route took us through Masailand to the forest frontier of the dreaded Kikuyuland, which we intended to explore. We had been warned not to do so, and Jumbe Kimemeta showed much faintheartedness on this matter. But we thought that if an expedition that was as formidably outfitted as ours would not risk it, then another was hardly likely to explore the area. We succeeded in traversing the whole country in the course of four weeks, unfortunately not without bloodshed, being on three occasions forced to take up arms. The enterprise turned out to be altogether more difficult than we had anticipated, especially because the burden of responsibility had to rest almost entirely on Count Teleki's shoulders, since I was severely ill with dysentery. For this same reason my companion was subsequently compelled to climb Mount

Kenya alone. He only succeeded in reaching a height of 15,240 feet (4680 m) and then returned out of consideration for the one Somali he had brought with him, who could not stand the extreme cold any longer.

After crossing the Laikipia Plateau, peopled by nomadic Masai, we finally reached Lake Baringo, from where we were to enter entirely unknown regions. The natives living at the lake were unable to give us any definite information concerning the country lying farther north, as none of them had ever been there; they had only heard of the existence of a lake far away. How far? Their answers varied between thirty and one hundred days! Now even Jumbe Kimemeta did not feel on sure ground, and he no longer claimed that the lake of which he had spoken in Zanzibar was within our reach. We could only find out that to get there we would have to carry an enormous amount of food, since the vast tracts of land through which we would have to travel were almost entirely uninhabited. The natives on Lake Baringo were themselves suffering in consequence of a crop failure and could not afford to sell us even one day's ration. Several detachments that we had sent out to far-distant districts lying west, toward the Victoria Nyanza, had returned either empty-handed or with quite insufficient supplies. For many weeks, therefore, the caravan was entirely dependent on our huntsmanship, luckily in a country that was not lacking in game. The provisioning of a large caravan in the interior is in general a serious question and a constant worry. The large quantity of foodstuffs that we needed could only be procured from Kikuyuland, which abounds in them. We therefore sent the main body of the caravan there under command of Qualla Idris, while we set out south of Lake Baringo to a district that swarmed with all kinds of game so that we could lay in a large store of sun-dried meat. Only after such tedious arrangements, which hindered the progress of the expedition for over three months, did we collect sufficient provisions for the caravan to live for thirty-five days, the largest quantity it was able to transport.

On February 10 we were ready to start. In addition to the Somali and our personal attendants, our caravan consisted of seven headmen, fifteen overseers, 197 porters, nineteen donkeys, twenty-one oxen and sows, and some sheep and goats; every man and donkey was laden to the limit. All the sick and feeble had been left behind to guard the loads that we did not take along. With us we had three natives as guides, but they were of use only within a limited range of Lake Baringo. We pursued a north-northwesterly course, and after seventeen marches through uninhabited land—on one day we lost four men for want of water—we fell in with a small settlement of natives on Mount Njiro (Nyiru). From them we obtained exact information as to the whereabouts of the lake for which we were searching, and also a guide who was willing to take us along. After resting a few days we went on traveling over difficult terrain. On March 10 we reached the southern shore of Lake Rudolf (Lake Turkana) and at the same time discovered the first active volcano known in Africa. The water of the lake tasted like lye, but in default of anything better it was just barely potable.

The shores of the lake were desolate and devoid of grass, which compelled us to slaughter our herd of cattle, whereby we suffered a great loss in foodstuffs. We then wandered northward along the lake's dreary and gameless eastern shore, doing so in considerable anxiety now that we knew how far away the Reshiat were, a tribe that lived on its northern end.

Fifty-four days had passed since we had started from Lake Baringo when we finally fell in with the Reshiat. The reader will hardly realize what it means to a caravan two hundred strong to be almost entirely dependent on its own means for so long in a dreary, desertlike country. We were indeed nearly finished by the time we reached the Reshiat, but there we were relieved of our cares, at least for a while. We discovered farther east a second, much smaller lake, which we named "Stephanie" (Lake Chew Bahir) after our crown princess, but thereafter the course that we had to pursue placed us in a serious predicament. The onset of the rainy season made it quite impossible to round the lake and to return along its western shore, since two large rivers that we would have to cross had become quite impassable. We had no choice but to return the same way we had come, the mere thought of which made us shudder. During our stay with the Reshiat our men had recovered and gained somewhat in strength, but many of them had succumbed, as had many of our beasts of burden, so that the loads each man now had to carry weighed over one hundred pounds. The elephants having left the lake shores, we did not see one on our return journey, and we therefore arrived at the south end of the lake with almost no food reserves and were obliged to wind our way westward round the active volcanic region. There we discovered the Turkana, a hitherto unknown tribe of natives who inhabit the poor, desertlike western side of the lake. They were friendly but could not afford to sell us more than about a hundred sheep and one camel, the minimum necessary for the maintenance of the caravan in their country. We finally came to the Turkwel, a dry river bed that takes its course through a dense forest. There was no game whatsoever, and our men had to live on berries, herbs, roots, mushrooms, and eventually on bird nests and the resin scraped off acacia trees. Finally, after twenty-nine days of such an existence, we came to a country inhabited by natives (the Suk) who, to our consternation, were themselves starving, their crops not yet being ripe. Just then heavy rains came pouring down for several days and nights, and this finished the power of endurance of our emaciated men. One day ten were missing, having remained behind because of exhaustion. Our caravan was on the verge of dissolving into pillaging gangs, and to avoid this a decisive step had to be taken. The cattle, which the natives would not—and admittedly could not—sell, had to be taken by force. Necessity knows no law. Of our once proud caravan, only ninety men were fit enough to carry out the unavoidable depredation; the rest were too weak for any great exertion. At the time I was unconscious for three days with high malarial fever. Acts of violence, of course, do not go off without bloodshed, and this grieved us more than I can say, for the natives had been friendly, and we were the first Europeans they had ever met.

After an absence of 169 days, we arrived at Lake Baringo on July 29 and returned to the coast by way of Lake Naivasha, Ukambani, Taveta, and Mombasa. The first sign that we were nearing civilization consisted of footprints that we hit upon one day in the vicinity of Kilimanjaro, which we thought were made by some American because of the hobnailing. And indeed, in Taveta we fell in with a young, very tall American by the name of Dr. Abbott, who was engaged in zoological studies.[18] He very kindly presented us with a whole side of smoked bacon, which Count Teleki and I pounced upon with a wolfish appetite. Seeing this, Dr. Abbott invited us to dinner, which we gladly accepted. Before going away he asked us to bring our own table utensils, not being equipped for three, and to come with our chairs. We said that we would do so. But when he turned around once more and revealed that we would have a roast hornbill for dinner, we heartily thanked him for the treat, saying that we had no special predilection for croaking hornbills and similar delicacies.

We arrived at Mombasa on the afternoon of October 24, 1888. Great changes had taken place as to the sultan's sphere of influence on the continent. Opposite Zanzibar a German East African Colony had been founded, and the exploitation of the northern territories had been ceded to the British East Africa Company. Our first steps were therefore directed to the house of a Mr. J.W. Buchanan, who acted as the company's representative at Mombasa. He received us charmingly, put a plum pudding on the table, and discreetly left us alone with it. We had lived so long on the most simple diet conceivable that for us even a so-called *ugali*, a grayish, tasteless porridge made of coarse durra, was such a delicacy that we quite seriously thought of making it our favorite dish in Europe. And now we found ourselves before a fragrant auburn cake, the mere sight of which made our mouths water. It did not take us long to finish it, and when Mr. Buchanan returned sometime afterward we felt quite ashamed at having been so greedy, though his amused smile told us that he had not expected otherwise.

It was a lucky chance that General Mathews and Mr. George Mackenzie, the chairman of the British East Africa Company,[19] happened to be on the spot. We spent the evening as their guests and found ourselves seated in patched flannel shirts around a beautifully decorated table, looking like ruffians in the midst of festively dressed gentlemen, drinking delicious iced champagne out of fine crystal. We had to answer a hundred and one questions and were congratulated, admired, and honored with heartfelt speeches. Civilization had pounced on us suddenly, without transition. Two days later a steamer took us and our men to Zanzibar, where, at General Mathews' kind invitation, we put up in his country villa. Unburdened from every care, we dreamt away two months there. Our men were paid off and got their hard-earned wages. Not a few of those who had started on the expedition were, alas, unable to answer the roll call, and the small pile of silver due them had to be handed over to their masters, when slaves, or to their relatives. Few of our followers had lost their lives through encounters with natives or wild beasts, but many had succumbed to sickness, hunger, thirst, or fatigue. The Zanzibari are an easy-going lot who often squander within a few days what they have earned through years of hard work. So it could not fail that already a week after our return, some of them came asking us when we would start on another safari.

We had brought with us to Zanzibar the tusks of the forty-two elephants that we had bagged, and we sold them at auction here. It astonished us to see that Hindu merchants were in general the highest bidders, probably because they content themselves with a lesser profit than European ivory traders. After the very active life we had led for so long, complete inertia now got hold of us and made us idle away the days, lying in comfortable easy chairs in the shade of the mango trees that surrounded our house. We were unfit for anything other than a quiet chat and too lazy for the least exertion. It was as if all our former energy had disappeared.

Before starting on our journey I had always firmly refused to partake of iced drinks. After our return, however, I could not withstand the temptation of this poison in the tropics. The many cold drinks impaired my state of health, and in its weakened state my body soon became a victim of malaria, of which I had so long been free. Every move made me shiver a feverish chill, and I passed many a day half-conscious in dreams, until I almost got to like it. I hated to be torn from this torpor by visitors, and I even stubbornly refused the British admiral's kind offer to take a cruise on board one of his ships so that I could have a change of air. In far-distant uncivilized places, where few Europeans live, one often meets with real sympathy, even on the part of utter strangers, especially by people belonging to the Anglo-Saxon race. Having been for centuries the world's pioneers and accustomed to living in far-away places, their sense of humanity may have developed to a higher degree than other nationalities. With the latter, being removed to an out-of-the-way place is as a rule only a casual episode in their life and does not rouse feelings of solidarity. A Britisher, on the other hand, never knows whether fate will bring him back again to the spot, and it is perhaps this uncertainty that links him with stronger ties to the various stopping places in the course of his life and also to the people he meets there. He never knows whether he himself will not one day be in need of sympathy and help. This, at least, is how I explained to myself the readiness to help that I have experienced whenever I came in contact with Anglo-Saxons.

Zanzibar had meanwhile undergone great changes and showed a very different face. The number of Europeans had grown tenfold; one frequently saw English clergymen and female missionaries, and the Europeans did not greet one another indiscriminately when meeting in the street, as had been the case in olden days. The management of the customs was in the charge of German clerks, and German influence had visibly increased. William O'Swald's place had been taken by his cousin, Mr. Albrecht O'Swald, and both the German and British rear admirals had been replaced. The British India Steam Navigation Company was no longer the ruling shipping line on the East African coast; it now had to compete with the French Messageries Maritimes and the very efficient German East Africa Line. The sultan's state coaches no longer rattled through the streets carrying veiled ladies, and one looked up to the windows of the sultan's harem in vain for a fiery look from one of the pretty inmates. The house was empty, and its tenants gone to other parts—to Muscat and Arabia—the new sultan being no admirer of the fair sex.

There were other signs that proved that a sinister spirit was now reigning instead of the amiable and noble Sultan Sayid Barghash.[20] One of his successor's first acts was to drain the crowded prison cells that had been left by Sayid Barghash, who abhorred capital punishment. Nobody knew what crime the poor devils who languished for years in the dungeons had committed. But they were there and they were certainly not innocent, and so away they went to a better world. For several days, just at the time when the market place was filled with men, women, and girls who were cheerfully chattering amidst heaps of sweet-smelling pineapples, mangoes, oranges, and bunches of golden bananas, one could see a gang of four chained wretches being taken to a spot near the old fortress wall. Here they lay their heads on a wooden plug, where they tamely received the deadly stroke that a hard-hearted Baluchi administered with his sharp, crooked sword. This gruesome spectacle lasted only a few minutes, after which four black heads rolled in the sand. Thereafter the market bustle, which had momentarily stopped, went on as before. In time, however, the Europeans began to murmur and the foreign ministers and consuls remonstrated, so that the sultan began to feel uneasy. In consequence, the drama was no longer played out on the open stage and probably took place in the darkness of the dungeons. In any case, it no longer gave public offense.

The villa in which we lived lay at some distance from the town, but visitors came to see us quite frequently. One day Guy Cuthbert Dawney, the inventor of the 577 Express rifle, appeared together with his friend, a Dr. Buckley, with whom he was about to undertake a hunting trip to the Kilimanjaro district. Dawney was certainly an experienced sportsman and an expert in gunnery, but to our mind his original rifle, which he showed us, was not powerful enough to kill a buffalo or an elephant. We warned him, and Count Teleki entreated him rather to take one of our well-tested rifles, which we would be pleased to lend him. Attached as he was to the rifle he himself had constructed, Dawney would not hear of it and declined the offer. Some weeks later Dr. Buckley again entered our house and told us with tears in his eyes that his friend Guy Dawney had been killed by a buffalo.

Among the officials of the German East Africa Company with whom we got acquainted in Zanzibar were Baron Gravenreuth, Captain von Zelewsky, and Lieutenant von Bülow. Captain von Zelewsky introduced himself to us, saying that he preferred to tell us before others had a chance to do so how cowardly he and his companion, Baron von Eberstein, had behaved on the occasion of their first buffalo hunt. They had both thought it wise to climb a tree and to bang away at the animal from a secure height. We did not judge them severely, however, because the rifles they had used were certainly not good enough to kill one of these tough brutes; to have exposed themselves unnecessarily to the fury of a wounded buffalo would have been foolish. At the time of an Arab uprising Zelewsky was stationed at Pangani. The riot broke out quite unexpectedly, and Zelewsky was taken by surprise in the street with no weapon at hand. He hurried home but was intercepted on the way by a band of rioters, who ordered him to surrender at gunpoint. Zelewsky merely crossed his arms, stood erect, and defiantly said, "Shoot!" This bold attitude so impressed his assailants that they lowered their guns and told him to go. This brave man did not escape his fate, however, for one year later he fell in a fight against the Wahehe. Not long thereafter von Bülow's mortal remains were covered by the cool soil on Kilimanjaro, where he found his death fighting Mandara, one of the petty mountain chiefs.

Finally, after many weeks, I slowly got better, the fever attacks becoming less frequent and severe. I could not say why we stayed in Zanzibar instead of moving to a cooler and healthier place, since the count was also suffering from malaria, though less than I. Probably it was because of our growing indolence, for we were quite happy lying on easy chairs in the shade of the trees, with our pipes in our mouths.

Pleasant though it was to spend the days dreaming in the cool shade of coconut palms and mango trees, we finally had to think of making an end of it. At the beginning of January 1889 a French Messageries steamer brought us to Aden, where we put up at the Hôtel de l'Univers. There we had the pleasure of meeting Professor Georg Schweinfurth, the well-known explorer, whose famous book of travel *Im Herzen von Afrika* Count Teleki had held in his hand when he first came on board the *Greif*. Schweinfurth was not a traveler of Mr. Stanley's stamp, but he was nevertheless one of the most important explorers of our time—a thorough expert in matters concerning the dark continent and a scientist who combined in a rare degree a many-sided knowledge with power of observation and literary ability. He had just completed a trip in Arabia and reported to us that the population of Yemen was destined to die out in consequence of their anomalous morals. Professor Schweinfurth and Dr. Junker were great friends; he also spoke highly of Major Hermann von Wissmann's travels and accomplishments and he urged me to read his books.[21] In a passing way we also made the acquaintance of Dr. Karl Peters, who was about to start on his much commented-upon but not duly appreciated expedition to Uganda and who was consequently in a merry farewell mood.[22]

The sea air and the excellent food that was served on board the Messageries boat greatly improved our state of health. When landing at Aden, Count Teleki was almost well again. I looked somewhat pale and was still weak, but our spirit of enterprise was reawakened and we soon began to think of some other job, just to kill one more month of the prevailing European winter. Qualla Idris suggested a trip to Harar, the famous Ethiopian town lying near the Abyssinian frontier. It was all the same to us where we went, so we took up this idea, and although our acquaintances shook their heads in view of my doubtful fitness, our Somali were ordered to make the necessary preparations. The resident of

Aden, Lt. Colonel Stace, and the ever-obliging Italian consul general, Antonio Cecchi,[23] furnished us with letters of introduction. Some other men were engaged in addition to our old Somali guard, and the small local steamer *Binger* took us to Zeila, where we were to start our journey into the interior.

Our caravan was small, consisting of a dozen Somali and some camels that we had hired; we and some of our followers rode on ponies. In accordance with the custom of the country, we engaged as leader of the caravan a so-called *abbân*, one of the more prominent Somali of the place, who knew the road and had some influence over the natives of the country through which we were to pass. This was necessary because of the feuds that prevail between the various Somali tribes, which can cause difficulties for passing caravans.

It took us about twelve days to reach Gildessa, an Abyssinian frontier place three days distant from Harar. The route led through very unattractive lands— steppes, denuded hills, and dry river beds. On rare occasions we met natives watering their herds at water holes dug out in these beds, but we never came across villages or cultivated ground, and we never saw a single head of game. The journey was monotonous and uninteresting. On account of the fierce sun we journeyed mostly at night, or at least during part of the night, always making a longer halt during the hot noon hours. On our fourth march we were overtaken by an express messenger who had been sent by our consul at Aden with a dispatch, the contents of which filled us with utter consternation. It only said that our crown prince, Archduke Rudolf, was dead. This news struck us like a bolt out of the blue. The heir to the throne, its only mainstay, with whom all the people of the Monarchy had associated proud hopes for the future, the beaming young man who was full of life when we last saw him, was no more! Of this we could not doubt, but how it had come about remained a mystery. As many times as we might turn over the ominous telegram, it only said "Dead."

Feelings of true friendship had tied the count to the crown prince for many years. He looked back on many an intimate hour spent in his company and on their many successful hunts together. The crown prince's vivid interest in his expedition to Africa had tightened these bonds of friendship. I knew how happy my companion had felt when chance permitted him to express his veneration for his august friend by joining his name forever with the discovery of the large lake we were seeking. Now came this crushing news, which drove my companion into despair. He did not want to hear of anything, and to all my comforting words he only answered that he wished to return at once to the coast. It was hard work to persuade my utterly broken companion that new impressions and adventures and an active life would soothe his woe, but I finally succeeded in persuading him to go on.

Two days later a traveler coming from the interior passed our camp in the early dawn. It was Alfred Ilg, the Swiss engineer who acted as Emperor Menelik's minister and adviser—a man who rendered Abyssinia inestimable services.[24] He seemed to be in a hurry, for he did not get off his mount and only exchanged a few words with us. In trotting away he warned us that we would have to leave our rifles behind at Gildessa, since no one was allowed to enter Harar with arms. Thereupon he disappeared into the dusk. Count Teleki did not want to hear of this; he would go to Harar with arms, or not at all. This question, therefore, had to be settled before we went any farther. After some thought we remembered that a parcel of letters had been given us at Aden with the request that we forward them to Harar. We looked through to decide which of the addressees to ask to settle the arms question with the ruling authorities; we then wrote a letter to a certain Dr. Cesare Nerazzini, the Italian vice consul in Abyssinia,[25] indicating we would await his answer at Gildessa. While one of our Somali hurried on to Harar with our letter, we continued our journey to Gildessa in easy marches, ill-humored by the new difficulty that had arisen so unexpectedly.

At that time Gildessa was not a village but rather a more or less permanent camping place of natives and caravans, with only a few stone houses in which the Abyssinian officials abided. The population consisted in the main of Somali and Galla (Oromo) and varied much at different times as to their number. At Gildessa the dry steppe comes to an end; farther on the country forms a plateau of some height, shows more vegetation, and is inhabited by Galla (Oromo), who live on farming and agriculture. The *shum*, the Abyssinian resident at Gildessa, received us in a very friendly manner, and within a few days an obliging letter came from Dr. Nerazzini saying that Ras Makonnen, the governor of Harar, was pleased to see us and that we were welcome to enter the town with our arms.

The two following marches took us over the mountainous plateau that farther on slopes down to a wide valley, where we could distinguish Harar in the distance. Expecting to view a grand sight, we were much disappointed. The famous old town presented itself as a disorderly accumulation of small gray stone houses with flat roofs, out of which only a few larger buildings and an insignificant minaret protruded. According to his description, twenty-six years earlier Sir Richard Burton had viewed the then holy city as the first European from exactly the same spot where we were camping. From there he had started his negotiations with the townspeople before he ventured to commit his life to the then purely Mohammedan and very fanatic population of the walled-in town.

One more march brought us to one of the five gateways through which one enters the town, which is encircled by a high wall. I had remained behind for some reason and only later learned that Dr. Nerazzini had very obligingly gone some distance to meet the count and had taken him to the house he had rented for our accommodation. The Abyssinian soldiers in general were an impudent lot who liked to behave in a self-conscious and defiant manner, and at first the guards at the gate were not inclined to make an exception for me by allowing me to pass the gate with my arms. Their attitude may, however, have been influenced by my rather shabby exterior, for I was attired in the same old and unimposing garment I had been wearing for many a month in the interior of Africa. Teleki did not look much better; I can imagine how the always tidy and elegantly dressed Dr. Nerazzini must have been struck when first encountering the count's sunburned and weather-worn figure, which certainly must have reminded him more of a cowboy than anything else. Arrived at our abode, I was told that Nerazzini and the count had gone to see the governor, Ras Makonnen, where they were waiting for me. I found the whole company assembled in the only larger house in the town, in a room of modest dimensions on the first floor, with bare whitewashed walls and no furniture whatsoever. Wrapped in a simple white Abyssinian toga, with which he covered the lower half of his face, Ras Makonnen was sitting squatted down on a shabby carpet. At his feet cowered Dr. Nerazzini, his eyes riveted on the ruler of the town, and opposite them sat the count on a Viennese bentwood chair; a number of Abyssinians were leaning against the wall. The floor of the room was covered with banana peels, and the scene in no way corresponded to what I had anticipated. I could see that my appearance caused a sensation, bringing the conversation to a sudden stop. I looked into very astonished faces, which in an unmistakable way betrayed the thought, "What on earth is this suspicious-looking European doing here?"

At that time I knew little of Abyssinia and the Abyssinians and was very much inclined to treat them like savages, which of course was a mistake. As it was I felt amused by the general embarrassment, and as they went on staring at me and as there was no chair on which I could sit, I smilingly said to Count Teleki that I hoped they did not expect me to squat down on the floor. Thereupon the governor, as if understanding what I had said, nodded to one of his followers, and a second chair was brought in. It did not take long before kinder, more conciliatory feelings began to rise in me, first toward the amiable Dr. Nerazzini, who spoke the Amharic language fluently and acted as our interpreter. Ras Makonnen expressed his friendly feelings and assured us that we could go and do what we liked; he would attend to our safety.

We stayed in Harar about ten days. In its way it was a strange town, but it offered little of interest. The small, very primitive flat-roofed houses were constructed of rough-hewn stone blocks, and were all more or less alike. They stuck together like honeycombs and formed narrow, tortuous, ill-paved, and unclean slums. I have nowhere seen more offal lying about in the streets, which, judging by the loud howls that one frequently got to hear at nighttime, lured jackals and perhaps even a hyena into town. Meat was very cheap, the average price of an ox being between eight and ten Maria Theresa dollars. This silver coinage, which was in general use in the Near and Far East since 1780, shows the image of the Empress Maria Theresa and was then worth about half a dollar. In vast parts of Africa it formed the only and much-preferred currency until the end of the last century. With the increase of international influence in these countries, however, its former sphere of circulation became more and more restricted, other currencies being introduced by force and gradually displacing it.

We soon became acquainted with the few Europeans of the place. They were all Italian, the Greek in the Orient not being considered as such. There was a fever-stricken manager of an Italian firm, I think named Rosa; a Captain Camperio of the Italian merchant marine, who was a very sympathetic man;

and finally the engineer Robecchi-Bricchetti,[26] who had come to Harar several months earlier to undertake, as he said, certain scientific studies. None of these men was blessed with riches. Dr. Nerazzini was the acting Italian vice consul at the place. Years later, in 1896, when the Italians were thoroughly defeated by the Abyssinians in the disastrous Battle of Adowa and lost numerous dead as well as about two thousand prisoners, Nerazzini rendered his country valuable service by cleverly negotiating the exchange of prisoners of war. Camperio looked healthy and always displayed a jolly and happy disposition. Like all sailors, he was a practical man who knew how to reconcile himself to all conditions of life. In later years the Italian government made him station-holder of Bardera, a place in Somaliland on the Juba River, where the well-known explorer von der Decken was murdered by natives in 1865.[27]

Robecchi-Bricchetti was a jolly fellow and an enthusiastic traveler, but being without means he had had to forgo his wanderings. In Harar he was deeply concerned with anthropological studies, in the course of which, to all appearances, he did not shrink from examining pretty Abyssinian women and young Galla (Oromo) maidens. It is true that on one dark night he dug out with his bare fingers somewhere in the surroundings of the town several Harari skulls—a rather risky undertaking—for which he hoped to get a good price in Italy. In his scientific research he said he was much handicapped by mistrustful town authorities, whereas we could do what we liked. Wishing to profit by this chance, during our visit he pursued his studies under our wings—only insofar as they were not of an anthropological nature. One evening Robecchi asked me to dictate to him an account of our discovery of Lake Rudolf which he could sell to newspapers and thereby slightly replenish his meager purse. I willingly complied with his demand, and so it came about that the first detailed news of our discoveries found its way to Europe from Harar.

Harar did not offer any remarkable sights, but its street life was quite interesting, especially on market days, when the natives flocked to town from far and wide with their products. We often saw soldiers simply take what they wanted, without thinking of paying for it. They were a brutal lot; one did well to get out of their way as they strutted about in the streets, shiny breech-loader on the shoulder, a row of cartridges round the waist, and a razor-sharp sword at the side. More often than not they were under the influence of the native beer known as *tej*. Although everyone in Harar knew that we were foreigners of distinction who enjoyed the special favor of the governor, it nevertheless happened several times that soldiers behaved overbearingly toward us, defiantly demanding that we shake hands with them. One afternoon we were sitting in one of the Greek coffee shops, where one could comfortably watch the proceedings at the market without being in the bustle. I was leaning crossed-armed on the rail of the veranda that separated the coffee shop from the marketplace when a probably drunken soldier planted himself in front of me and in a provocative way demanded that I shake hands. At first I did not pay any attention to the man, but he grew more and more excited and insisted on a handshake, until I finally lost patience and threatened him with my heavily mounted camel stick. Seeing this, the man unsheathed his sword in a twinkling and raised it to strike. I do not know how things would have ended if people had not caught the man's arm and pushed him aside. I was afterward seriously warned against letting matters come to blows with soldiers.

After a stay of ten days we had had enough of Harar, being more interested in wilderness than in towns. In setting out on our return journey I felt first-rate, but the count had not yet fully recovered from a fever attack. Our camels started out early in the morning, and the count and I rode off alone one hour later, without any followers, while some of our Somali remained behind in order to pick up after us. After an hour or two we came to a clearing and saw our camels. The count, who was about ten paces ahead of me, gave spur to his horse to overtake them. In that very moment I was quite suddenly overcome with a terrible ill feeling. I had just enough strength to call out with a faint voice that I felt sick, whereupon I sank from my horse to the ground. There I remained, lying in the sand on my stomach, feeling so ill that I was sure my last hour had arrived. I was almost beside myself. After some time I began to vomit, which gave me a little relief. With my face on the ground and utterly unable to move, I may have lain there about an hour, when one of our Somali, a youngster twelve years old, came along. He stared at me from a distance with an anxious, astonished look and then sat down on a boulder with his rifle between his knees. I remember that I was all eyes for his rifle and that my only thought was to get at it to make an end of my misery. But I could neither speak nor move. Then I lost consciousness, for how long I cannot say. Toward evening I felt in an indistinct way, as if dreaming, that I was being raised on a stretcher and carried off.

Not having heard my call, Count Teleki had gone on, wondering why I had remained behind. Only later did he learn in camp what had happened to me and make the necessary arrangements for my transportation. On the following morning I felt very weak but better; the terrible fever attack was overcome. We then proceeded to Gildessa, where we stayed a few days to give me a chance to recover. The next day Signor Robecchi-Bricchetti surprised us by his arrival; he had come to investigate a hot spring he had heard of in the vicinity of Gildessa. He shared our tent but had to sleep on the bare ground, which, however, did not prevent him from being as happy and jolly as ever. On one of the evenings he gave us a very candid picture of his further plans. It was true that his means for traveling were nearly exhausted, but eighty Maria Theresa dollars were due him for some work that he had carried out on the minaret at Harar. If he traveled in the way to which he was accustomed, this would suffice to take him to the coast, perhaps even to Aden. Once there he would blow his trumpet, and he was convinced that a famous explorer such as he would surely be furnished with a free ticket for passage home on board one of the Italian liners. Thus he went on embellishing his visions with southern imagination, concluding with the assurance that should we have the chance to meet him three months hence on the Corso in Rome, we would surely think him a count.

The following journey to the coast, which, though I was feeling miserable, I somehow managed to accomplish on horseback, was uneventful. Shivering with fever in spite of the scorching weather and the fur coat I was wearing, I trotted along, utterly indifferent to what was going on around me. Whenever a short halt was made, I sank to the ground, dozing there until somebody hurried me on again. In spite of all this I gradually recovered a little, and when on the last afternoon we reached the wells at Warabot near Zeila, which, being hewn deep in a rocky cleft, contained deliciously cool water, I even felt tempted to take a long-overdue bath. That certainly was very refreshing, but it was also ruinous. Soon afterward fever set in with rapidly increasing vehemence, and on our arrival at Zeila I hurried to bed. Colonel Stace, who had arrived on a fine government steamer, invited us to dinner, of which only the count could partake. I only vaguely recollect that two days later I was carried on a stretcher in an almost insensible state through the shallow shore water on board the steamer *Binger*. There I soon after lost all consciousness, to recover my senses only in Aden, after lying I do not know how many days in bed at the Hôtel de l'Univers.

At Aden we got acquainted with two Frenchmen from Paris, Dr. Eugène Simon and a Dr. Jousseaume, who were concerned with scientific studies. The latter was an anthropologist, while Dr. Simon was an authority on spiders.[28] He diligently went out hunting for them every day and was delighted when I promised to let him examine the spiders I had collected during our journey in Africa. On one of the last days in April, shortly before our departure from Aden, we saw the Austrian corvette *Fasana* go at anchor on the roads; she had come from the Far East and was on her way home. Her captain was a certain v. W., and among her staff was Lieutenant Archduke Leopold of Tuscany, who in later years withdrew from the imperial house and lived as a simple commoner under the adopted name Leopold Wölfling.[29] As one may imagine, the unexpected meeting with one of our ships filled me with joy, and though still a feeble convalescent, I nevertheless hurried on board. To my disgust, however, I found a very cool reception on the part of the captain, which soon put an end to my joyous mood, and I denied myself the pleasure of seeing any of the officers on board. Although the captain must have been aware that he was dealing with a sick man, he nevertheless wished me to furnish him with a detailed report on our journey to forward to the Admiralty. He certainly did not have the right to give such an order, and I would have been justified in refusing to comply with his wish. But as it was, out of an exaggerated sense of duty I sat at my desk for two long days in tropical heat working on the report, which I sent to the captain without calling on him again.

A French Messageries boat brought us to Suez. On board I suffered a last serious attack of fever while I was enjoying a fine dinner in the company of pretty and charming Parisian ladies. The ship's medical officer fetched me away from them and put me to bed, ascertaining a temperature of 105.8° F. After resting a day at Suez we went on to Cairo, where we stayed several weeks. There the pure desert air and the excellent fare at our hotel soon set us right. We spent many a quiet hour at the foot of the pyramids, which impressed me more than anything I had seen in all my life. But we also enjoyed social diversions, which were never lacking. When society heard of our African adventures, it began to take an interest in us. The Société Khediviale de Géographie interviewed us and conferred honorary membership upon us, and one day we paid our respects to the Khedive. In the hospitable house of our ambassador we made the acquaintance of various notables, among them Sir Evelyn Baring, later Lord Cromer, and Mr. Borelli, a prominent Egyptian financier who was the proud possessor of a very fine collection of Egyptian antiquities.

One day a Mr. Jules Borelli, the younger brother of the afore-mentioned financier, called on us. He had recently returned to Cairo from a successful journey to Abyssinia which had taken him to regions south of Shoa, about which he was to lecture before the Geographical Society.[30] It was fortunate for Mr. Borelli that he met us and showed us the map he had constructed during his journey. This map amused us greatly, since according to it, Mr. Borelli had penetrated south, right across the country in which Lake Rudolf lies, without seeing it. Moreover, the map connected Lake Baringo (1120 m. above sea level) by way of an outflow with the Victoria Nyanza (1190 m. above sea level), in spite of the intervening high mountain ranges. In constructing his map Borelli had taken whatever was told him to be fact. I advised him not to show this map to anybody and promised to set it right by harmonizing it with our discoveries. This was no easy task, and I had to work hard for three days.

When the end of May had come, we stepped on board a Lloyd steamer in Alexandria and therewith brought the last leg of our journey to a close. This thought filled me, at least, with feelings that were far from cheerful. I certainly could not foresee what the future would hold, but I knew that it meant parting from the wilderness I loved so much and from a free, untrammeled life. The skipper's name was Mersich, and he was a younger brother of the unfortunate captain of the *Titania* who had taken me to Aden three years earlier. One day I complained to him about our never being served the famous Lloyd risotto, a dish I very much desired. My wish was realized by the kind captain on the very same day.

When the Istrian coast and the familiar surroundings of Pola finally came into sight, my heart was heavy. Grayish-brown clouds of smoke rising high up to the sky from the practice ground revived old memories. Were they perhaps already firing brown prismatic powder? Then came Trieste. The ship had hardly come alongside the wharf when a band of customs officials came rushing on board, making me suddenly think of the more than twenty thousand cigarettes I had purchased in Cairo. What should I do? Pay the duty? No one in our navy ever thought of being so foolish when there was a chance of avoiding it, and considering the great quantity of cigarettes for which I would have to pay duty, the mere thought seemed ridiculous. I was still undecided as to what I should do when I perceived among the revenue officers a former navy officer who had left the service and joined this department. He was much older than I, and I surely had never spoken with him in all my life, but I now treated him like an old friend whom I was delighted to see again. I then casually asked him whether the count and I were at liberty to go on shore with our bulky luggage. My question seemingly aroused his soul as a revenue official, because he at once asked whether there were any cigarettes in it. It seemed to me so absurd to put such a question to a man who, as he could see, was a smoker and came directly from Egypt that I answered in astonishment, "But of course." The good man luckily understood this as a "no," made a sign to one of his subalterns, and gave the order to let us pass with our things. At the landing a friend of Count Teleki, Baron Giuseppe Sartorio, was waiting for us with his fine landau and took us to town. The count, after having been away so long, was of course eager to get home. I, on the other hand, was again in the bond of service and had to proceed to Pola to report and—what was more important—draw my outstanding salary for three years, a quite considerable sum. From letters that I had received in Zanzibar I already knew that I had in the meantime been promoted to the rank of lieutenant.

At Trieste I had the opportunity to make the acquaintance of the famous explorer Sir Richard Burton, who was serving as British consul general. So far I had only read his book about the journey that he had made in Africa together with John Hanning Speke,[31] but I of course knew that he had been in Mecca and Harar and that he was a great scholar in Oriental matters. It was on his advice that Count Teleki had taken some Somali on his expedition. I was eager to get acquainted with this great man and was very pleased when one day Lady Burton invited me to tea. I first had to pass some time in the pleasant company of the mistress of the house, who, as I was soon aware, was a most passionate admirer of her great husband, speaking all the while of nothing but him in words that were well-nigh idolatrous. She said that Sir Richard used to sleep chiefly in the afternoon but assured me that I would have a chance to meet him. A door finally opened, and a tall, gray-haired man with a worn yellow face entered and sat down silently at the table opposite me. When looking into his marble face and the cold gray eyes that gravely stared at me for a while, I certainly had the impression of being in the presence of an uncommon personage. I do not, however, remember any memorable expressions on his part, probably because Lady Burton went on doing all the talking. Sir Richard Burton withdrew very soon. The impression that I took away with me of this interview was an unpleasant one, in spite of a deifying pamphlet given to me by the hostess when parting, which I later noted she had published herself.

At Pola I stayed only a few days, no longer than necessary. The younger officers received me kindly, some even cordially, but I could not help feeling quite estranged in their midst. Their interests and their way of thinking did not agree with my frame of mind. The superior officers hardly took any notice of me, for what did Africa matter to them? One night, however, I was honored with a grand banquet given by the junior officers, which a few older officers attended. This solemn occasion, of course, did not pass without appropriate speeches, which reconciled me somewhat with Pola. The finest speech was made by a captain with whom I had spent many a night at the gaming table in former years. I therefore was not quite sure whether it was my African exploits or his satisfaction about the gambler's return that had animated him.

I then went to Gorizia to see my old mother and hopelessly sick sister, but I stayed there only a few days. Fever had again set in and made me nervous and whimsical.[32] Unaccustomed as I was to tender female care, I could not stand being continually looked at anxiously and being bothered with questions about how I felt. But what really drove me away so soon was the distressing sight of my poor, doomed sister. As it was I packed my trunk after a few days and left the two good, tender-hearted souls behind, unfortunately not to see them alive again. One year later they were both laid in a cold grave on the same day.

5

In Vienna
(1889–1892)

The big city absorbed me. Nowhere could I better live a retired life and disappear into the crowd. Although I cannot remember, I probably spent the first weeks very quietly, until my return from my travels became known in wider circles. I was spared publicity and was not bothered by requests for interviews. Only the representatives of the *Standard* and *Budapesti Hirlap*, a Hungarian daily, honored me with such a request later on.

One day I had to express my thanks to His Majesty the Emperor for the extraordinary leave that I had been granted. It was the first time that I faced the ruler and heard him utter words of praise, but years spent in the wilds in a constant struggle for life helped take the edge off things. I was therefore able to meet this special event in a perfectly calm frame of mind. On this occasion I could see, not for the first time, how very little our navy was known beyond our maritime borders. Before my turn came I had to wait for some time in the large antechamber to the audience room, and I spent this time walking up and down, as sailors are wont to do. It did not escape my notice that three colonels in richly braided hussar uniforms were discussing me in detail for quite a long while, until one of them boldly approached me with the unexpected query as to who I really was.

From the imperial palace I betook myself to the Admiralty to report on my audience. The commander in chief of the navy, Vice Admiral Sterneck, whom I wished to thank for all the assistance he had give the expedition, was staying in the south because of his health. His representative received me amiably, in his usual urbane manner, and said that an aide-de-camp of His Majesty had just called by order of the emperor to make inquiries concerning my activity in Africa and my person in general. "What answer did Your Excellency give him?" I asked. "Well, I just said that we don't know much about your travels ourselves and that I have not even seen you yet." These few words, uttered in Viennese patois, were all I could elicit from him. Given the many important affairs that take up the time of a ruler of so large a realm, the return of a young officer from his travels cannot, of course, play any role worth considering, and the same is true of a vice admiral encumbered with a multitude of administrative duties. By sending his aide-de-camp, however, His Majesty had shown a certain interest in the matter, a circumstance that had not met with the proper response from the vice admiral. And that could not fail to make an unfavorable impression on the old emperor. At any rate, my merits regarding the results of the expedition received no official mark of recognition whatsoever. I regretted this only because I considered this neglect a lack of respect for research in general, for I never strove for the usual signs of recognition and reward. I was therefore all the more pleasantly surprised to receive a letter from the chair of geography at the University of Vienna that emphasized the significance of the discoveries our expedition had made and was accompanied by words of praise for my own activity. The Vienna Geographical Society also turned its attention toward us and wanted to honor Count Teleki and me with a banquet. We both preferred to be left in peace, however, and declined the invitation, though I did promise to give a lecture if the occasion arose.

There was another reason why Count Teleki did not reap his deserved reward for his enterprise. Following the tragic death of Crown Prince Rudolf, one searched for scapegoats whom one might hold responsible, and the friends of the crown prince were of course seen as the cause of the tragedy. My traveling companion had been one of these, and though utterly innocent and a devoted friend to the prince, abstemious in every way, he had to suffer for his friendship. His name was unpopular in high circles, and this was a reason not to speak of his travels and achievements.[1] Furthermore, certain other persons who liked to pretend that they were the only protectors and promoters of geographical research had not taken the expedition seriously from the outset. Now that they saw they had been mistaken, they buried the enterprise in silence. This was the atmosphere I found when I came to Vienna. It was, however, of greater importance for me that thanks to the broad-minded spirit of Baron Sterneck I met with a most liberal treatment regarding my service. Thus, although I was nominally attached to the Admiralty, I was as a matter of fact perfectly free of formal responsibilities for a number of years.

Naturally I realized that something was expected of me in return, since the results obtained during our travels would be of no use unless they were available to experts in published form. I had at my disposal a great amount of geographic material, astronomical and meteorological observations, vocabularies of African languages, and extensive collections of every kind. I was no doubt expected to write a description of my travels, an idea which, being most uncongenial, I kept putting off. There was no lack of work to be done, but I was at a loss where to begin or how to evaluate the results of our expedition. Only gradually did it become evident that some of our discoveries were of fundamental importance and constituted great surprises for the scientific world. No one had thought it possible that there could exist an unknown lake of such great dimensions in that part of Africa. The full significance of this discovery was only recognized in the course of time by Professor Eduard Suess, the famous author of *The Face of the Earth*.[2] Our discovery of an active volcano far in the interior of a continent supposed to contain only extinct ones caused a still greater sensation. And just as our trip had provided geographers and geologists with the missing links for the recognition of the structure of Africa, only now was it possible in ethnological and other regards to gain a general idea of the connection of various tribes and of the distribution of fauna and flora.

The scientists who paid attention to such matters began to show some interest. This brought me into personal contact and correspondence with some of them, and that opened my eyes to the great importance of the results of our expedition. During the trip I had, for example, drawn an uninterrupted series of mountain profiles.[3] These hundreds of folios, with their thousands of bearings, gave an explicit picture of the areas through which we had traveled. It represented a great deal of labor that had been achieved under difficult circumstances and with much personal sacrifice, and I took great pride in this work. I had these folios lithographed and published for private circulation. This meant a certain expense, and as I sent this publication to the interested parties free of charge, I was rather disappointed that in spite of the general admiration accorded the work, not a few of the recipients, among whom figured well-known geographical societies, did not find it worth their while even to acknowledge its receipt. Perhaps it would have been different if I had published these folios at a high price. Many people do not prize what they get cheaply.[4]

When still in the interior of the African continent I had calculated the simpler astronomical observations and summed up the daily route on a succinct map so as to be able to rectify any mistake on the spot. In this respect I differed greatly from other explorers, who as a rule have their notes and sketches of the route worked out by a professional cartographer into a more or less imaginary map only after their return. The latter is, however, utterly unable to judge the exactitude of the material transmitted to him. He treats good and bad material alike, and this is the reason why maps of distant, uncivilized countries so often do not correspond to reality. I, on the other hand, only had to reduce my maps to a determined uniform scale and enter them into the geographical map of Africa. When working at this, I discovered that all of my observations of the eclipses of Jupiter's moons and also the lunar distances that I had observed in order to determine longitudes were useless. At that time one did not yet know that the occultations of Jupiter's moons are not suitable for this purpose because of their variable orbits. I could boast of having had great practice in observing lunar distances and had therefore given special attention to this means of determining longitude. It was therefore a bitter disappointment to learn that the large pistor prismatic circle that I had used had a very small but varying error that rendered useless the many observations of lunar distances, which require the greatest exactitude. The instrument in question had been carefully carried on the expedition in a padded case, but on one occasion its bearer had been charged by a buffalo and had dropped it, whereby the mishap occurred. The repeated examinations that I undertook in the interior of Africa had never shown an error. How difficult an examination of this kind is may be seen from the fact that neither the geodetic section of the Technical University nor the Vienna Observatory was able to prove the inexactitude of this instrument. Only the observatory at Pola, especially trained for this purpose, discovered it. I have treated this subject, which lies rather apart from general interest, with some detail to show how difficult cartographic survey work is in distant, unexplored lands. Often only disappointment is the reward for much trouble and effort. This is also true in many other respects. The collections accumulated with passionate zeal and at the cost of many sacrifices may spoil or go astray, and the finest photographs may arrive in an unsatisfactory state. Pioneer expeditions are carried out under the most difficult conditions.

In order to finish my work I fortunately was able to use my brother's room at the Technical University. I spent a great deal of my time there looking over maps with rulers, pantographs, and compasses, or working at my desk. In consequence of an invitation from *Petermanns Mitteilungen* in Gotha I had decided to publish the chief results of the expedition in a special supplementary number of that famous geographical monthly.[5] Since I had no literary experience, I had started the writing rather indifferently and was not a little surprised and elated when Professor Alexander Supan, the well-known editor of the *Mitteilungen*, acknowledged the receipt of my manuscript with the following words: "The eager perusal of your work shows that you have written a masterpiece and in its way a unique contribution to our knowledge of the African continent." That an experience of this kind was calculated to make me consider my achievements with some pride is comprehensible, but a certain shyness prevented me from growing conceited.

Amusements played a very small part in the first months of my stay in Vienna. It is true that in Africa I had often thought of the theater and similar pastimes that awaited me on my return. Yet though I soon went to the Burgtheater to witness a classical performance, I was much disappointed. One must be a frequent visitor to theaters in order to overlook certain imperfections. If at the same time one prefers nature to art, crowds are oppressive.

The first summer did not pass without any change, however. In 1889 a universal exhibition took place in Paris, preceded by a great deal of advertising. In August, moreover, an international geographical congress was to take place there, and the organizing committee invited me to give a lecture on the discovery of Lake Rudolf. The Vienna Geographical Society was eager for me to accept this invitation, and since Mr. Jules Borelli—the Abyssinian traveler—had urgently asked me to come and since I did not yet know the French metropolis, I was prevailed upon to accept. I had to compose a French text for my lecture, and in Gotha, where all my maps happened to be at the moment, I quickly had to order a large map, which was promised for the date on which I required it.

What am I to relate of the city of Babylon on the Seine? Borelli met me on my arrival and we drove to my hotel, where he was also staying. The next day was passed in serious interviews with Prince Roland Bonaparte, the president of the congress, and the organizing committee. We thought that herewith we had done our duty as far as science was concerned. Borelli's lecture and mine were to be given only a week later. I must confess that in the meantime we were active not so much in contributing to the brilliance of the congress as in doing our best to get acquainted with the interesting city. My friend turned out to be an indefatigable tourist and a real tyrant. We never returned home before dawn, and at eight o'clock in the morning he would wake me up, explaining, "Il y a l'exposition." Day by day I wished him and all exhibits to the end of the world. At the same time we lived a life of dissipation, dining and supping until the wee hours of the morning, always in first-class restaurants, always ordering the very best. One forenoon, however, I attended to some calls, and on this occasion I met the aged Abyssinian explorer d'Abbadie, the Portuguese traveler Ivens, and also Savorgnan de Brazza, Stanley's famous competitor on the Congo.[6] D'Abbadie bored me to tears with endless talk on the value of the lunar distances for determining longitudes on expeditions. I knew more about this than he did but could not say so to the old man. Savorgnan de Brazza was condescending. "Où avez-vous voyagé?" he asked, and then responded to my answer in a bored voice, "Oui, oui j'ai en entendu parler." I soon had enough of this sort of thing and turned my back on him. On my way I finally reached the Bois de Boulogne and the vicinity of Dr. Eugène Simon, the great arachnologist. By then it was nearly 3:00 P.M. and I was tired and hungry, but I wanted to pay this call and have done with it. Dr. Simon received me with surprising coldness, and this mood endured until at last he asked me whether I had already lunched. "No, and I am terribly hungry." It turned out that he had heard of my arrival in Paris and had invited me by note to lunch at one o'clock. He had waited a long time for me and was so indignant at my late appearance that I was hardly able to convince him that I had not received his invitation. Finally he had the warmed-up lunch served, and after I had duly admired his large collection of spiders we parted good friends. Only late in the evening did I receive his letter.

On my trip to Paris I had brought nearly all the money I had at my disposal. My cash melted away like snow in the March sun, however, so that I repeatedly reproached Borelli for the extravagant life we were leading, especially whenever a plump maître d'hôtel presented our check. This, however, only made my friend madder; he then dived into his trouser pockets with both hands, hauled out two fists full of Abyssinian gold lumps, threw them on the table so that they rolled into all the corners of the room, and screamed, "Ah, tant que nous avons ça, nous ferons la noce." The day came, however, when both our resources began to be exhausted. The approaching end of the congress would have solved the difficulty had Gotha not left me in the lurch, for the large map I had ordered still had not arrived. My lecture was therefore postponed, first for a day, and finally to the last day. A further delay was out of the question, and so I had to content myself with a map that I drew with chalk on a blackboard. Altogether I only attended three of the lectures. A young Frenchman spoke with animated pathos of a small tour in western Africa; Borelli's lecture was good; but the greatest applause was given to the lecture of a Hungarian

Alpine climber who spoke of his ascent of the Demavend.[7] My lecture did not compare very favorably with those of my predecessors, though my subject was far more interesting. It was my first public lecture, I had to give it in a foreign language in which I was not very fluent, and my presentation suffered from the lack of a proper map, so that the audience had some difficulty in following my explanations. When I entered my room on my return to the hotel, I found the notification from the railways authorities that my map had arrived. Such is the irony of fate!

Thus the eleven days that I spent in Paris passed quickly. The hotel bill was paid, and the examination of all my pockets revealed that their contents just sufficed for a third-class ticket from Paris to Vienna. On my return, I set to work with renewed diligence, and my mental balance was soon restored. As far as social life was concerned, I only sought out persons with interests similar to mine, of whom fortunately there were many in Vienna. Above all I must mention Dr. Wilhelm Junker, whom I had already met in Zanzibar. Though a native of St. Petersburg, he had preferred to settle in Vienna, there to write a three-volume work on his travels, which had extended over eleven years.[8] His pleasant little flat in the Maria Theresien-Strasse soon became a meeting place for all who bore Africa in their hearts, knew it already, or longed to go there. Junker was the right man to unite a circle of this kind because of his mature age and winning ways. In the course of time we grew to be great friends, and hardly a free evening passed that we did not spend together. Dr. Oskar Baumann, another celebrated Africa explorer, often figured as a third. He had started in 1885, accompanying Professor Dr. Oskar Lenz in order to relieve Emin Pasha, but had soon recognized the hopelessness of this task and separated from his leader at Stanley Pool. While Lenz contented himself with crossing the African continent on well-known routes,[9] Baumann explored the Spanish island of Fernando Po and published a valuable monograph on this subject. Hitherto Baumann's explorations had been limited to these exploits, but later on he turned toward vaster undertakings, which were brought to an untimely end through a malignant disease that carried off the talented traveler.[10] Whoever had any interest in the dark continent sought to form part of this circle—explorers whom chance brought through Vienna, sportsmen planning a hunting expedition, and geographers and other scientists who sought direct contact. So it was that although we lived in a large, civilized center, we were able to dwell in our thoughts in distant deserts and wilds.

A young officer who is reduced to living on his pay finds it difficult to make both ends meet in the expensive capital. Extravagances were impossible. This was hard to bear in those years; it prevented me from going into society and moving freely. Knowledge of the fine results of our expedition had gradually penetrated into larger circles. Flattering communications from savants and explorers bore witness to this, as did election to honorary membership in several geographical societies. Cairo, Vienna, Florence, Naples, Neuchâtel, Amsterdam, and Berlin in turn sent us their diplomas. Bern and Budapest made this honor dependent on giving a lecture. My means did not permit my undertaking such trips, however, and for this reason I also had to limit my social life. I have already mentioned that of the newspapers, only the correspondent of the *Standard* had shown any interest in our expedition. In his house I spent many pleasant hours, and there I met for the first time with Professor Eduard Suess, with whom I soon developed a warm friendship. Together with him and Professors Toula and Rosiwal I arranged for the publication of the geographical, petrological, and geological results of our expedition in the proceedings of the Imperial Academy of Science, in which work Professor Suess for the first time established his new hypothesis—the so-called Graben-Theorie—regarding the tectonic structure of Africa, which has now been generally accepted.[11]

The fat days of Paris were followed by lean ones in Vienna. I was forced to take my meals in a cheap suburban restaurant, and I did this at a rather late hour so as to be alone. Once—it was toward the end of October—I saw a very smart gentleman enter the room. He first gazed around him in astonishment at the simple surroundings, asked the waiter something, and then approached me. "His Excellency Count Kálnoky, the minister of foreign affairs, wishes to see you at four o'clock." I looked at the unknown messenger in surprise, did not ask why I was being invited, but simply accepted. Time pressed, and I had to hurry in order to exchange my rather shabby plain clothes for a uniform. I was cross at having been found in this cheap restaurant, and I went home very much put out at this disturbance. On the way I concluded, however, that it was not I who wished to see the minister but he who desired to see me. Therefore he had to receive me in whatever I happened to be wearing, and I betook myself to the Foreign Office as I was.

Count Kálnoky did not take any notice of my costume, for he was waiting to speak with me on quite another matter. Three Arabs who had been sent on a mission by Sultan Said Ali of Zanzibar were expected shortly in Vienna.[12] I was asked to take these men under my wing and act as their guide and pleasure cicerone during their four-day visit. It was entirely left to my judgment how to entertain the evidently unwelcome mission. On one day they would, however, have to be presented to the emperor. I took the liberty of remarking that I did not speak Arabic and explained that Kiswahili, because it lacked high-sounding words, was not suitable as a mediating tongue for formal occasions. It would therefore be better to appoint one of the scholars of Arabic at the Oriental Academy as interpreter for the audience. Count Kálnoky promised to arrange this, but on the day before the mission's arrival he told me that the professors had made all sorts of excuses and that none was willing to act as interpreter. I therefore had to do my best with Kiswahili.

One evening three old Arabs wearing sandals and shivering with cold arrived from Berlin. They were quite happy to hear me hail them with "Sabal cheir" (good evening) and "U hali ghani?" (how are you). They were accompanied by an Egyptian courier and a black boy as servant. With this strange company I drove to the Grand Hotel, where princely apartments had been prepared for us. The mission had been made much of in Berlin, where military reviews had been held in their honor. The power of the German Reich had been demonstrated before their eyes and had not failed to impress them profoundly. Unfortunately, they had come to Vienna expecting to meet with the same reception. When on the first evening I asked them what they would most like to see, I received only one reply, "Askari a frasi" (cavalry), and this was repeated on every discussion of the subject of their entertainment. But there could be no question of this. Unlike Germany, Austria-Hungary had no political aims in East Africa, and thus there was no special reason to make a fuss over the mission. This put the Arabs out and made them recalcitrant regarding all my proposals. When, for instance, I managed to persuade them to go to some theater or other place of amusement, it was certain that after a short time they would ask to be taken back to their hotel. Furthermore, they were too old and the autumn season was too advanced for sandal-wearing Arabs, so that they constantly complained of the cold. To make matters worse, on every possible occasion the Egyptian emphasized the grand reception the mission had received in Berlin. It was not a very pleasant situation.

One afternoon I arranged for a lovely party in the big palm house at Schönbrunn, an event that had required extensive preparations. There the guests could eat their fill of all sorts of sweetmeats, and I hoped that in the shade of palm trees and in a nearly tropical temperature they would feel happy. To my great disappointment, however, they soon begged to be taken home even from this treat, alleging that they had to say their prayers. The next evening my patience was finally exhausted. After an agitated discussion I slammed the door and retired, firmly intending to take no further notice of this ridiculous mission. When I stepped out of my room the next morning somewhat later than usual, I found the three old Arabs humbly waiting before my door, where they had been standing for over an hour in order, so they said, to beg me not to bear them any grudge. The lesson had had its effect.

Before the audience with the emperor I gave the members of the mission exact instructions on how they were to behave. I insisted that they should ask no questions and always reply with a "yes" to everything they were asked, even if they did not understand the sense of the query. I would explain everything later on. Fortunately the audience passed without a hitch. The oldest of the Arabs delivered the speech I had written for him, and His Majesty replied, though in words that were rather difficult to translate into primitive Kiswahili. I rendered the meaning as best I could, surreptitiously adding recommendations concerning their answer and their behavior. His Majesty, who of course had no idea what was going on, nodded graciously and finally congratulated me, expressing his astonishment at my fluency in Kiswahili. On the same afternoon the mission requested to be allowed to visit the Egyptian Prince Abbas Hilmi, aged fifteen, who was being educated at the Theresianum Academy. No doubt the sly Egyptian had suggested this move, since he was keen on exploiting this occasion to his own profit by appearing in a favorable light before the future khedive. The

Arabs were evidently in the seventh heaven of delight when the prince's reply in the affirmative arrived, even though one day earlier they had probably known nothing of his existence. Whereas hitherto they had looked forward to everything, including the audience with the emperor, with truly Oriental indifference, now that it was a question of seeing a member of their own faith they seemed totally transformed, and when they found themselves in the presence of the Egyptian prince their deep bows and assurances of devotion knew no end. After I had presented the members of the mission with imperial farewell gifts—snuff boxes richly set with diamonds—and the Egyptian with a decoration, very much *contre coeur*, I was much relieved to see them finally start off for their native wilds.

Soon the day came for my lecture to the Geographical Society, a task I approached with great disinclination. I had prepared photographic slides, which at that time were a novelty in Vienna, and which I was only able to show thanks to the special courtesy of the electrical firm of Siemens & Halske. I felt very uncomfortable when I found myself the center of curiosity of a most choice company in the large, brilliantly lit hall. In Paris I had spoken to an expert audience. In contrast, here I felt that the majority of the people who were present were only keen on seeing the traveler, so that what I had to say was of only secondary importance. After a second lecture, public opinion seemed appeased, and I could now start writing a popular description of our expedition.

In this work I had of course to confer on many points with my traveling companion. Already on our return from Africa, Count Teleki had invited me to visit him at his home in Sáromberke, but it was only possible to accept his invitation and leave Vienna in the summer of 1890. I now became acquainted with a circle I grew to like more and more, until finally Sáromberke—for lack of any other—nearly became my home. Sáromberke lies in Transylvania in the Upper Maros Valley. The many century-old oaks in the neighborhood of his seat were the only grand and impressive sight I found there. The buildings he inhabited were as simple as the host himself and the people I first met there. But the count's study, his large desk covered with numerous folios, and the walls of the room, which were studded with many trophies of the chase and old, precious arms, showed that a striking person lived here. I was still more surprised by the material luxury that awaited me—for example, exquisite dishes from the recipes of the best French chefs, old choice wines from venerable cellars, and whatever else makes up the bill of fare of Lucullus. Simple and modest though Count Teleki had shown himself during the expedition, he now proved that he was a gourmet of no mean order. He imported his coffee directly from Mocha and his cigars from Havana, and the same principle applied to everything in his household. I found him surrounded by a number of precious old books, a luxury he could permit himself because he had inherited a famous library containing priceless treasures from his grandfather, a former governor of Transylvania. His greatest pride, however, was his stud. Sáromberke bred half-bloods of special quality—tough horses with gazellelike eyes and Arab heads. In the morning his first visit was always to the breeding stallion and the foals. We spent many hours in a cozy tête-à-tête, chatting about the past or making plans for the future. Drives across country in fine four-in-hands to visit country neighbors also took up some of our time. All the land in the vicinity belonged to him. We could shoot hare, fowl, and fox wherever we went. Count Teleki was not a keen shot; he was more of a sportsman and a gamekeeper. He also possessed the right to hunt in extensive grounds at a distance from Sáromberke, in the northern part of Transylvania and near Szászsebes in the southern part of the province, where in years to come I was to slay many a bear and stag.

The village of Sáromberke had a purely Hungarian population, which, according to tradition, considered the count as lord and master, so that young and old obsequiously kissed his hands wherever he appeared. Power of this kind is not a cheap affair, however, and no day passed without my friend having to put his hand into his pocket or allow one of his many acres to pass into the possession of one of his peasants who had been clever enough to describe his sorry plight eloquently, thereby melting the count's kind heart. This, by the way, was not difficult to do.

The weeks I spent at Sáromberke passed quietly and uneventfully, and I returned to my work in Vienna refreshed in body and soul. Though I continued to live a retired life, it was no rare occurrence for kindred spirits to find their way to my door—sportsmen who came to tell of their adventures in Africa, or others who were on their way there and came to obtain advice. One day a lieutenant of the hussars called on me, and after presenting himself as Baron Ludwig Fischer, spoke of his intention to undertake an expedition to Africa. His well-groomed and smart appearance seemed to me to be in too great a contrast with his words to permit me to take him seriously, and I dismissed him after exchanging a few general phrases. I had, however, been mistaken. In time I got to know the man better, and his serious mind and deep knowledge of zoology caused me to appreciate him more and more. In the sequel I stood by him and helped him follow the path he had chosen. Dr. Junker also liked him and gave him much advice. Baron Fischer only possessed modest means. It was therefore a lucky coincidence that I received a German offer to explore the Victoria Nyanza from the point of view of navigation, a task for which I felt no inclination. After I had declined the invitation it was entrusted to our mutual friend on the recommendation of Dr. Junker. The nearer the day of his departure approached, however, the more depressed Baron Fischer appeared. We soon guessed that it was not the enthusiasm of the explorer that was driving him to Africa but rather a deep sorrow caused by a faithless wife.

The above-mentioned offer was not the only one I received. Various sportsmen implored me to accompany them to Africa, and I was also negotiating with the British East Africa Company. One day Prince Reuss, the German ambassador, asked me to come and see him. I learned that his government had instructed him to win my services for some exploration work in German East Africa. This offer was couched in such flattering terms and the conditions were so favorable that I immediately declared my readiness to study the proposed contract. We devoted an entire hour to this task, and when the document was ready, the ambassador handed it to me with the kind remark that I had better take it home and bring it back, signed, the next day. I had hardly left the embassy, however, when I resolved to decline the offer. When I informed the prince the next day of my change of mind, he was not in the least annoyed, as I feared might be the case, but said quietly that the matter was after all my affair and concerned me in the first place. My refusal was based on a series of considerations, above all that my predilection for exploration only formed an episode in my life and that my real profession was that of a sailor. When, however, in the spring of 1891 I received a rather laconic letter from England in which Mr. William Astor Chanler, who was unknown to me, asked whether I would be willing to accompany him on a voyage of exploration to Africa which would last several years, I was unable to resist the temptation and replied in the affirmative. What came of this will form the subject of the next chapter.

The repeated offers and inquiries addressed to me had one good effect, for they made me set about finishing my travel description with greater zeal. This work was not at all to my taste, and for a long time it did not progress properly. But now I often sat at my desk until late in the night. This was less of a sacrifice now that I no longer could enjoy the company of Dr. Junker. The three volumes of his book of travels, to which he had devoted all his energies in his last years, had been finished in the middle of 1891. He then planned to spend a few months with his relations in St. Petersburg and return, but I was not destined to see him again. Hardly arrived at home, he gave signs of a malicious disease for which there was no help—a cancer of the brain. A few weeks of terrible torment put an end to his sufferings. My friend left me the watch that had struck the hour for him during his eleven years in Africa, the ragged helmet that had protected him against the sun, and the excellent compass with which he had made his surveys.

At the end of the last chapter I had so much to say about my severe attacks of fever that I ought to mention how matters developed in this respect. Soon after my return to Europe these attacks became rarer and less violent without any medical treatment, and after half a year they ceased altogether. On this occasion I would also like to mention that after three years in the tropics both Count Teleki and I withstood our first European winter apparently better than other Europeans. It was as if we had absorbed a reserve of heat in the tropics and brought it home with us. Of course this is nonsense. The explanation is that in consequence of the years spent with bare arms and chest in the open air we had acquired a thicker, firmer skin that afforded us better protection. The epidermis of the Negroes, who always went stark naked, is far thicker than that of the garbed European. We could often convince ourselves of this in the case of surgical operations. In this connection it may also be interesting to note something that is perhaps not generally known. A dark surface attracts the rays of heat in a higher measure, yet nevertheless the inhabitants of hot countries are apparently unfavorably equipped with a dark skin. There is a good reason for this. The black skin, though it absorbs the heat rays in a higher measure, better protects against the ultraviolet rays that alone cause painful burns when one incautiously exposes himself to the sun. That Negroes are black is therefore not a contradiction of nature, as might at first appear to be the case.

The draft of my book had meanwhile progressed so far that I could think of looking for a publisher. That was not an easy matter, for the moment was unfavorable. In the same year Junker's, Stanley's, and Casati's travel descriptions had appeared, and the book market was saturated with African literature. I therefore met with many refusals, until at last I landed with the publishing house of Hölder, which at least deigned to have a look at the manuscript. It met with a favorable judgment, but for a long time Herr Alfred von Hölder could not make up his mind, only scratching his ears whenever I asked him to come to a decision. The thought that I had gone to all that trouble in vain was somewhat humiliating. I had, however, undertaken this task less out of free will than from a feeling of duty, and personally it was a matter of some indifference to me whether or not the book ever appeared. But I wanted to put an end to all this indecision so as to be rid of this care and devote myself wholeheartedly to other plans. With this in mind I called on the firm one day and insisted on a decisive answer. This at last caused Herr von Hölder to decide to publish the book, whereupon I of course immediately demanded an advance on the proceeds. Therewith my task was not finished, for the printing of my work made many claims upon my time. I had to procure illustrations, get in touch with various xylographers and the firm that prepared the pictures, and finally correct proof.[13] But this was a novelty for me and brought me into touch with various professions and interesting matters.

In the summer of 1891, in the midst of this activity, the naval commander in chief surprised me by inquiring whether I would like to accompany him during a two-month inspection cruise along the Dalmatian coast. This meant an interruption of my work, but on the other hand it was proof of his gracious attitude toward me, so that it was impossible to reply otherwise than in a grateful affirmative. Thus after a long interval I was again at sea as watch officer on board the admiral's yacht *Greif*. I hardly played a brilliant role, for the navy had not stood still during the intervening years. The signal service had been reorganized, and many other innovations had been introduced of which I had not the slightest inkling. But one is nowhere as safe as in the lion's den, on the ship of the commander in chief, where no subordinate dare criticize. Thus the blunders I made at the beginning of the cruise probably passed unnoticed.

Returned to Vienna, I was able to resume the interrupted work and conclude it without further disturbance. At the same time I was also able to dedicate myself to new tasks that awaited me.

6

My Second Expedition to Africa (1892–1894)

It is difficult to state why, after I had refused a number of invitations to travel in Africa, I did not hesitate for a moment to accept the offer of Mr. William Astor Chanler. I had no idea who this gentleman was and only supposed that he was a citizen of the United States. I am almost inclined to think that it was the element of novelty that caused me to say "yes." I was able to draw a pretty correct picture of the nature of the other applicants, but a voyage of exploration in the company of an American appeared to me as an equation with several unknown terms, and this tempted me. Thus the magic attraction of a novel and strange experience was the decisive motive—or perhaps it was only fate that guided my pen as I replied briefly to Mr. Chanler that I would be glad to hear more about his plans. Soon thereafter I called on the navy commander in chief, told him of the invitation I had received, and asked him whether there was any chance of my again obtaining a leave of several years. To my pleasant surprise he made no objections and declared that he would only make a definite decision after having made the personal acquaintance of Mr. Chanler. Several days later Chanler arrived in Vienna and took rooms at the Hotel Metropol. Unfortunately I had caught a terrible cold, so that I could barely crawl out of bed. Nevertheless I rushed to the hotel, curious to meet the man who had chosen me as his traveling companion. Mr. Chanler was having his bath but sent word he would appear presently. I therefore entered the hotel lounge, empty at that early hour, and made up for the disappointment of waiting by ordering a glass of brandy, the drink that in our navy could indiscriminately be ordered at any hour of the day or night. Some time passed until a slight, elegant gentleman appeared, immediately betraying his Anglo-Saxon origins. He looked around him, evidently searching for someone, but passed by without looking at me. I thought that this must be Mr. Chanler, but I only felt sure of having surmised correctly when I realized that the sight of the brandy bottle at so early an hour most certainly had driven him away.

Soon we were sitting together, talking of Africa. To my surprise, I heard that this enterprising young man, who was only twenty-three years old, had already undertaken one journey to the Kilimanjaro district and was not a novice as far as Africa was concerned. As chance had willed it, he had used an Austrian man-of-war for the trip from Mombasa to Zanzibar and had thus made the acquaintance of Captain Count Montecuccoli and several other naval officers.[1] He had been struck by the prevailing discipline, and when he heard in Zanzibar of the fine results of the Teleki expedition to Lake Rudolf he had decided to travel to the still unexplored districts lying east of this lake and to ask me to join him. We soon agreed on the route of our travel, and an hour later we shook hands as future traveling companions. Thus occurred my first meeting with Mr. William Astor Chanler, with whom I would be bound in deep friendship for years to come. On the same morning we called on the naval commander in chief, and the quiet and self-assured manner in which Mr. Chanler stepped into the presence of this, our supreme lord, in whose vicinity we all used to feel awkward, impressed me not a little. The friendly look with which the admiral received his guest and still more the hearty "au revoir" with which he dismissed us told me that I had won my battle.

Mr. Chanler's personal affairs and my own unfinished work forced us to put off the journey for some time. It was only in the fall that I was able to go to London to discuss the necessary preparations for the journey. The procuring of the equipment was to be done partly in England and partly in Austria, at Mr. Chanler's expense. I was now not only more experienced but also more assured in my attitude and demands, and I met with courtesy everywhere I turned. The German ambassador, Prince Reuss, arranged for the exceptional permission of the Colonial Office in Berlin for engaging the necessary caravan people in German East Africa—an important concession, and one only granted in view of the expected important results of our expedition. Since the abolition of slavery, Zanzibar had ceased to be a source from which porters could be drawn in unlimited number. I was able to borrow instruments as much as I liked. The chronometer-maker for the navy volunteered to lend us three excellent chronometers, which were first sent to the observatory in Pola to ascertain their response to various temperatures. From the War Office I obtained 220 new Werndl rifles for the ridiculously low price of two florins each, and the naval ammunition depot provided the necessary ammunition gratis. The War Office even loaned us fifteen new Mannlicher rifles; three hundred were specially tested for us at the Vienna arsenal, where the fifteen best were selected for me. Of these, three showed marvelous shooting records, and the best was of such unparalleled precision that every shot at a distance of 300 yards hit a target the size of an apple. In Vienna the government's photographic institute conducted experiments with various plates and films on our behalf, but in the end I regret to say that I chose a new, English invention that did not come up to expectations. Finally, the Court Museum of Natural History placed at our disposal receptacles for collections and the necessary means of preserving specimens, in the hope, it is true, of receiving some of the objects we would bring back.

During my first expedition I had had unpleasant experiences with determining longitudes by observing the eclipses of the satellites of Jupiter. Because the course of Jupiter's moons is subject to disturbances that cannot be calculated in advance, this method of fixing time can only be employed on voyages of exploration if parallel observations are made by other observatories. I had not known this at the time, and perhaps our teacher of nautical lore at the naval academy had uselessly burdened us with this study, for a simple and yet exact method for determining time is afforded by the frequent eclipses of stars by the moon. I was not versed in this kind of observation, and at the University Observatory Dr. Johann Palisa, the well-known discoverer of many planetoids, declared his readiness to teach me.[2] For lack of time, however, I was only able to attend one practical session.

In May 1892 I had another meeting with Mr. Chanler in London, where we discussed the last details of our equipment, our departure from Europe, and our ultimate meeting in Port Said. Finally the last day approached. I expressed my thanks to the naval commander in chief for his interest in the expedition. I also took my leave of Count Teleki, which turned out to be rather trying. My friend pressed into my hand a costly hunting knife with an old Toledo blade that the late crown prince had given him. He wanted me to take it with me as a personal memento, but when I reached the station and looked for the precious weapon I could not find it. Apparently it had dropped out of the carriage during the drive through the crowded streets, and in spite of Teleki's meticulous searches it never turned up. Count Teleki then sent me his oldest family heirloom, a hunting knife dating back to the year 1545, and I need hardly mention that this time I did not lose his present. The next morning found me alone at the station, from which I traveled first to Trieste. There I had to take over the bulky equipment that had been stored there for weeks and months, a matter requiring two days of feverish activity.

Then came the day for the sailing of my Lloyd steamer—June 13, a Friday—and for a second time Trieste saw me depart on my way into the unknown. Though my gaze was turned backward, my heart was eager to meet the future. The president of the Lloyd himself came to see that I was well cared for. This was an act of courtesy, for the ship was virtually empty, the only passenger on board besides me being an Englishman on his way to India. The ship's whistle had sounded for the last time and the hawsers had already been slacked off when a breathless postman brought a parcel with fresh vaccine, just arrived from Vienna and destined for the vaccination of our caravan. This time my path was smoothed for me in a manner far different from when I had started out on my first expedition.

To my joy, the same captain was in command of the ship who had brought Teleki and me from Alexandria to Trieste three years earlier. Soon after we started, dinner was announced. The outline of the city was still in sight when the dinner bell rang, the first course of which was one of my favorite dishes, a delicious risotto. Captain Mersich smiled as he watched me enjoying my meal, and only then did I remember that once before I had owed this treat to his kindness. More than three years had passed since I had confessed my predilection for this rice dish; how amiable of him to remember. On the forecastle, dogs were barking. As an experiment I had brought two Istrian pointers, splendid animals accustomed to great heat and scarcity of water, which I thought would stand the climate of Africa. A third dog, a beautiful Irish setter bitch, belonged to the Englishman and had probably cost three times as much as my two experimental dogs, and yet every day her owner implored me to exchange one of them against her. I could not do so, however, for we required a rougher breed for our purposes, and to take the delicate Irish lady into the African wilds would have been to sacrifice her uselessly.

We reached Port Said, and Mr. Chanler punctually arrived on board. Another traveling companion, George Galvin, was to follow later. George had already participated in Chanler's Kilimanjaro expedition. On that occasion he had supervised the caravan and the stores and had proved exceedingly useful and competent. He was therefore to share in this expedition in the same capacity and free us of an important but time-consuming and tedious encumbrance. At Aden many things had to be attended to, and the connecting steamer to Zanzibar gave us but scant time to do so. We were therefore in a great hurry, but our Lloyd boat did not move from the spot, since negotiations were being carried on with a Turkish pasha who wanted to use it for himself and his family for a trip to Jiddah. This was most annoying but could not be helped. No wonder that I gave vent to my ill humor in a manner that many a reader may possibly condemn. But as it is in a way characteristic, I shall not make a secret of it.

On our further voyage we caught a glimpse of Jiddah, with its white several-storied houses, from where the faithful Mohammedans start on their pilgrimage to the holy tomb of the Prophet. We visited the grave of our mother Eve and also the cool vaulted bazaar halls, where delicious fruit was sold, but soon left because of the scandal that we, being Christians, were causing everywhere. "Get out, get out!" was the cry that greeted us on all sides, and no one would sell us anything.

The vaccine that we carried gave us a good deal of trouble in the Red Sea and also later on, since it had to be constantly kept at a cool temperature lest it curdle and become useless. This time we wanted at any cost to protect our men against smallpox, which so often plays havoc with caravans in Africa. Captain Mersich did what he could, but the lost days could not be made up. Chanler and I therefore arranged that we would separate in Aden. I was to remain behind while he proceeded to Zanzibar with Tommy, one of the two dogs. He, too, had only just enough time to get on board his boat, and an hour after our arrival he was again at sea.

I knew Aden well. I liked it in spite of its brown scorched rocks, and I had good friends there. Colonel Stace was still at his post, as was the Italian consul general, Antonio Cecchi. If at all possible we wanted to engage the same Somali boys who had proved so serviceable during the Lake Rudolf expedition. I had previously made arrangements to this effect by letter, but these people lived with their tribes somewhere in the interior of Somalia. Colonel Stace had sent out people to search for them, and he actually managed to engage two. Unfortunately, their former leader, Qualla Idris, was in Uganda in the service of the British East Africa Company and was not available.

First of all I had to get camel saddles, water bags, and a few other things, and also two tough Somali ponies. Some of these errands I was able to entrust to my men. The obliging commander of the Indian cavalry detachment promised to obtain the horses while I carried out a special task. In Egypt Mr. Chanler had received information from English officers concerning the usefulness of the Sudanese, and he wished to take a number of these with him, chiefly to serve as watchmen for the camp. Since these men were only to be obtained at Massawa, I started out for that place one day on a steamer of the Florio Rubattino Line, provided with letters of recommendation. Having lost two of its four propeller blades, the boat could only go very slowly, so that the trip took three full days.

Massawa is one of the hottest ports on earth. Even the air seems to be on fire, and the sea seems as if it is boiling. A stony mountain desert, charred by the pitiless sun, surrounds the city, where one is first struck by the two grand government palaces with broad verandas running along each floor. The governor of the colony, General Baratieri, was absent in Asmara, a cooler mountain resort lying on the high plateau, but I was charmingly received by his substitute, General Arimondi, who housed me in a huge airy room on the top floor of one of the two government buildings.[3] General Arimondi was a manly, soldierly figure with charming and agreeable manners that immediately gained my sympathies. Sudanese could only be engaged with the permission of the government, which required them for its native battalions. The Sudanese who hung about Massawa were mostly tramps and vagabonds. General Arimondi had therefore given instructions to one of the troop commanders in the interior to select for me the twelve best men of the district. Thus the matter was, as I believed, well under way. I was already about to accept the invitation of General Baratieri to visit Asmara when a highly indignant Arimondi came to me with a telegram in which the governor had prohibited the engagement of the men already selected. What had happened? The commander of the troops in the interior had misunderstood Arimondi's instructions, and thinking that he was meant to give away the twelve best of his own men, he had complained to the governor. Arimondi was furious at the circumvention of his person by a subaltern, but this did not mend matters. I therefore thanked General Baratieri for his invitation to Asmara and remained in the brazier of Massawa to try my luck there. Much precious time had been wasted. My steamer was not going to remain in the harbor forever, and I had to hurry and, without much deliberation, take the men who offered themselves for the job. Every one of them was strong and bold-looking, but none inspired much confidence. When, at the signing of the contract, the Italian master of police shook his gray head and warned me that one man, named Mussa, was a dangerous knave, I calmly said that just such people were the very best for Africa. I was glad to have accomplished my task as best I could before the departure of the steamer. Later on, however, I had occasion to remember this warning.

I parted from General Arimondi with feelings of sincere gratitude and returned to Aden with the same boat that had brought me, which now boasted four propeller blades. In the following year General Arimondi gained a fine victory near Kassala; he so thoroughly defeated the Mahdists that they lost all further wish to come near the frontiers of Eritrea.[4] This news filled me with great joy. All the more did I grieve, therefore, when I learned of his death on the field of honor in the Battle of Adowa. The unhappy campaign against Abyssinia, through which Italy suffered not only bloody losses but also the decline of her prestige, had not been in accordance with Arimondi's ideas. Baratieri had thrown himself into this mad adventure thanks to a combination of vanity, a total misconception of prevailing conditions, and the desire to accomplish some military feat before his removal from his post. Fascinated by the idea of winning military laurels, he started out sure of victory but was destined to return after a humiliating defeat. Arimondi was killed on this occasion after vainly trying to resist with his detachment.

Many severe judgments were later voiced concerning Baratieri and his troops. A great deal of the guilt was his, for he had been the leader and instigator of the whole affair.[5] Whoever knows the barren stony territory, charred by a pitiless sun, and the steep slopes over which the three columns had to advance in the dark of night, guided by treacherous natives, will not judge the defeat so harshly, however. Once on the heights, the Italians were met by a reposed and superior enemy force, each man knowing every nook and cranny of the ground, and every man a born soldier. Utterly exhausted, torn and bleeding, scattered, suffering from a burning thirst, and nearly incapable of any resistance, the Italians finally scrambled to the top of the ridge. All the force and lust of battle with which they may have been filled at the outset had been exhausted by the weary climb. It was child's play for the Abyssinians to rout them completely. Besides the dead, missing, and crippled, many Italians were taken prisoner. In the course of the negotiations concerning their liberation, Dr. Nerazzini played a prominent role. Emperor Menelik showed himself in a good light at Adowa as a king as well as a man. When he visited the battlefield and saw the many victims and their hopeless misery, with tears in his eyes he gave orders to his generals to stop the hostilities immediately. He had had enough of war.

At Aden I housed my Sudanese in the courtyard of the Hotel Europe, where they remained until George Galvin arrived. The men behaved themselves as long as I stayed at Aden in the same hotel, but they made all the more noise later, so that the authorities breathed more freely when George's arrival delivered them from this horde. As I had expected, the Somalis had satisfactorily seen to the work I had entrusted to them and were only waiting for George's arrival and the departure of the steamer that was to take them, together with the equipment purchased at Aden, directly to Lamu. From there we would start for the interior. The two ponies, nimble yet strong animals, had been shown to me after a solemn dinner given by the friendly captain who had procured them. A gymk-hana of his men followed this show in which he himself, as was proper, proved to be a master in all sports. On this occasion an English corporal offered me a fox terrier by the name of Felix for the price of £8, praising it as a first-class rat catcher. In the course of time we concluded that the little dog would have been better named "Coeur de Lion" or "Sans Peur," for he attacked rhinoceroses and even elephants with an astonishing unconcern. Finally, the question arose as to how the two horses should be brought to Lamu. This was not a simple mat-ter because the southwestern monsoon, with its towering seas, was at its height, and no captain of a steamer wanted to transport the animals. Everyone who was asked declared that it would be impossible to bring them to their destina-tion alive. Only Captain Frohawk, who was no stranger to me and who com-manded a bigger ship, the *Mecca*, could perhaps undertake the risk of accept-ing this cargo.

The *Mecca* was expected to arrive on the same day I had to sail for Zanzibar, and it was therefore doubtful whether I could see Frohawk and have time to make the necessary arrangements with him. This uncertainty lasted until nearly the last minute. My ship, the *Admiral* of the German East Africa Line, had arrived punctually in the forenoon and was to leave just as punctually at 2:00 P.M. At noon, however, not even a drift of smoke from the *Mecca* was visible. At last she arrived; she had barely dropped anchor when I mounted her ladder. I was very glad to see the captain again, who greeted me most heartily. "You here! What can I do for you? I'll do it, depend on it!" I knew that Frohawk would do all in his power. But without padded horse boxes in which to keep the animals suspended by girths, he would not risk it, for without them the ponies would never arrive alive. But where in the name of Heaven should I obtain padded horse boxes in the last half-hour? Already the whistle of the *Admiral* sounded for the first time. "Ask the governor," suggested my friend. "But I don't know the governor." "Never mind, write him a line." Already he had pushed a sheet of paper across the table and handed me a pencil. Frohawk himself undertook to take the note to the governor and to guarantee for the ultimate return of the borrowed horse boxes, and so matters were arranged.

Stormy days on a good ship like the *Admiral* are a pleasure. By the time we arrived on schedule in Zanzibar, the ship was covered with a crust of salt as far as the funnels. Mr. Chanler was there and took me to his hotel, where of course we had a great deal to tell each other. The name of Mr. William Astor Chanler was well known in East Africa. My traveling companion was the bearer of many letters of recommendation with which he gained access to influential circles; he also had a great many friends from the time of his first expedition at Ngambu. The sultan; Sir Gerald Portal, the British resident; Sir Lloyd William Mathews, the premier; Mr. Joseph Jones, the American consul—in a word, everyone of any importance was most supportive of his enterprise. Thus he was able to engage a great number of the necessary caravan people on the spot, though since the abolition of slavery Zanzibar was no longer an inexhaustible reservoir from which explorers could draw their men. As an official prohibition existed on this point, and as the recruitment of men had only been quite exceptionally permitted to Mr. Chanler, this process had to be carried on discreetly. It was also advisable to get away with the engaged men as soon as possible, since the owner of the slave or the man himself might possibly regret the bargain, as frequently happened among these unreliable and mercenary Orientals. Any additional men who were needed to complete the number of two hundred had to be engaged on the mainland near Pangani, the population of which, being accustomed to traveling, furnished excellent material. Mr. Chanler had already rented an Indian dhow with which I and the engaged men were to start for Lamu on the second day.

The shipping of the men went off quite well. A steam cutter tugged the dhow a couple of miles out of sight of the town and left her to her fate toward sunset. The Arabic or Indian dhows, with their prehistoric shape and equipment, are not very pleasant vessels. Though of considerable size, the boat was uncovered, with the exception of the aft raised platform. On this platform a tiny forward-opening cabin was erected, in which I could neither stand upright nor stretch out full length; baskets with provisions and bunches of bananas and coconuts filled the corners. The dhow was old and rotten and could only be kept afloat by continually bailing out the sea water that penetrated through every seam. The rigging consisted of a single mast at the fore, on which one large sail was hoisted. Everything was rough, primitive, and worn-out. The skipper was an Indian who had not the slightest notion of the coast and the prevailing currents. Lamu was about 300 sea miles distant, which was no small matter for a craft like ours, loaded as it was with more than 130 men. Closely crowded together, they stood and cowered in the hold. A mild evening breeze swelled our sail slightly and made us glide slowly northward.

August 5 found us safe in the quiet port of Lamu. To my joy, George Galvin had already arrived from Aden the day before and undertook the care of the men. I also met Messrs. Denhardt and Tiede, the agents of the German East Africa Line, whose acquaintance I had made on an earlier occasion. A Scotsman, McDougal by name, was acting as the representative of the British East Africa Company and spoke Kiswahili fluently, while an older man named Macquairy was the commercial agent, selling bad whisky, which he also liked to drink. These two men had been instructed to assist our expedition in every manner, an order with which they fully complied. I stuck chiefly to Mr. Gustav Denhardt, however, whom I had known for years and who, being a resident at Lamu for more than a decade, knew the area thoroughly. An agreeable young German, Dr. Hässler, a remnant of the former German Witu colony, often came to his house.

Lamu makes a far more Arabic impression than the towns that lie further south on the East African coast. Here people live less out of doors, preferring the cool houses that offer protection from the glare of the sun. The town is built on the island of Manda close to the coast and is surrounded by a rich growth of mangroves, which gives it an erroneous impression of being unhealthy. It goes without saying that the expedition had to form on the mainland and start from there into the interior. Together with Mr. Denhardt I therefore went in search of a camping place. Without Mr. Denhardt's local knowledge it would have been difficult to find a place in the extensive mangrove wilderness that was suitable to our purposes in every respect. In McDougal's steam launch we went straight to Mkonumbi, a primitive native village lying at the end of a narrow creek that leads fifteen miles inland. There we found a suitable location for a camp under a group of shady mango trees. The site was accessible by water and at the same time was located on the route leading via Witu to the Tana River, along which we intended to penetrate into the interior of the continent toward Kenya. The best of our Somalis, Karsha, was sent with some men to clear the spot of undergrowth, and then George and the other men also transferred there, along with the extensive equipment. When Mr. Chanler arrived on the British East Africa Company's coastal steamer *Juba* on August 13, he found this point satisfactorily settled and ordered that the remaining men and the forty-three beasts of burden he had brought join the others. All this meant days of hard work, often lasting until night.

According to our plan, the expedition's route was to run from the Tana northward through barren country in which camels presumably could be used as beasts of burden. We had originally thought of procuring the camels in Aden. However, the animals we found there did not appear suitable and were very expensive, while the difficulty of transporting them had to be considered. We therefore only purchased the saddles in Aden, hoping to buy better animals less expensively in East Africa. Mr. Chanler accordingly made the necessary arrangements with the British East Africa Company, whose steamer *Juba* was to take me to Kismayu, remain there at my disposal, and transport the purchased camels, cows, and sheep to Lamu. During my absence Mr. Chanler took it upon himself to attend to other necessities, first by getting the caravan into shape, a rather disagreeable task involving a good deal of annoyance. He also had to organize a small transportation flotilla of eight canoes that were to carry provisions as far as the Tana was navigable, there being scant chance that the caravan could be provisioned among the natives living along the river.

I sailed on August 15 to Kismayu on board the *Juba* with four of our Somalis. Besides the captain and the engineer, the only other white man on board was an official by the name of Farrar, a young, stern, and evidently very capable young man appointed to Kismayu. About thirty regular soldiers of the Sultan of Zanzibar's army, who were to relieve the station guard at Kismayu, also journeyed with us. The little 120-ton *Juba* rolled terribly in the high monsoon sea, and though I was never seasick, I nevertheless was glad when after a passage of twenty hours we anchored in the open roadstead at some distance from the coast. Hardly anything was to be seen of the town, which lay inland, hidden by bushes about half an hour's walk from the coast. Knowing that my stay would last several days, I quartered myself in the station house of the British East Africa Company, a stone building capable of defense and situated in the middle of the small town. Surrounding the station were ten or twelve smaller stone houses inhabited by the *wali* [a local governor] of the Sultan of Zanzibar, his subordinate irregular troops, and some Indian traders. This was the so-called European town. The natives' town consisted of a row of straggling brown huts which ran along the shore toward the south, at some distance from the town proper. I was warned not to visit it.

The agent of the British East Africa Company was a Mr. Ross Todd, a very pleasant and courteous young Englishman, formerly a shipping clerk and certainly a brave and respectable man. As far as African matters were concerned, however, he was a greenhorn, and he was not up to the post to which the company had appointed him. The loyalty of the Somalis who lived in the vast district surrounding Kismayu was based exclusively on the subsidies with which the company had bribed them. As long as the chieftains and numerous leaders of the different tribes were paid their considerable monthly salaries, calm and order were maintained. In time, however, these liabilities outgrew the company's resources, to the point that it got into financial difficulties and had to economize in every way possible. It therefore cut the Somalis' subsidy in half. This was of course not to their taste, but for the moment they contented themselves by rallying from the interior at Kismayu in great numbers, including 4,000 Somalis who were under the leadership of one Morgan Yusuf, showing a decidedly threatening attitude. This movement was in full swing when I arrived. Todd and I visited Morgan Yusuf on the very day of my arrival and found him in an uncomfortable little stone house, wrapped in dirty blankets and lying on a kitanda—the native kind of bedstead—suffering from a fever. We soon left him after exchanging a few phrases.

The next day my four Somalis started for a far-away place where a large caravan with many camels and cattle was said to be camping, in order to try their luck there. Meanwhile I sat idly in the house like a prisoner, watching the situation worsen by the day. From early morning until late in the afternoon the hall of the house was crammed with Somalis, all armed with shields, spears, and daggers. These rowdies gesticulated, flashed their teeth, rolled their eyes, and hooted furiously at poor Mr. Todd, who stood in their midst pale with fury and exhaustion, racking his brain for new arguments with which to appease their wrath. The roar of the voices penetrated to my room, and whenever the tumult reached a greater height I hurried down in order to see what was up. Every day passed in this manner, and I foresaw that the affair would not end well. Yet though I often warned the young man not to be so careless and not to allow the fellows to enter the house armed, and though I suggested that he at least hold a revolver under their noses, he always declined my advice, saying that matters looked worse than they were. All this, he maintained, did not mean anything. He only realized the plight he was in when he saw that there was no depending on the sultan's troops. Finally the 150 irregular soldiers, who in any case were utterly worthless, openly announced that he must not reckon on their assistance in a conflict with the Somalis. Meanwhile, on the 19th my Somali men arrived with the splendid animals they had purchased—fifteen camels and ten oxen and cows—and the object of my trip was accomplished. Mr. Todd asked me to remain a few days longer and await further developments, but that did not depend on me alone. I therefore went on board the *Juba* and explained the situation to the captain, who declared his readiness to put off his departure until August 22 but who insisted he could wait beyond then. When I returned to Kismayu, ten or twelve most unpleasant-looking fellows barred my way, evidently wishing to pick a quarrel. I passed them without taking any notice of their insults because my Somalis, who were some twenty paces ahead of me, repeatedly called out, "Come along, sir, bad men." For these insults I wanted to get some satisfaction, however, and I therefore asked Mr. Todd to inform Morgan Yusuf of the incident. He objected, but I insisted for his own sake, and the next day we were amused by the message that the culprits had been arrested and that Morgan Yusuf wanted to know whether they should be hanged. This was of course a farce.

On my advice, Mr. Todd had meanwhile addressed himself to the Italians on the Juba River. When I at last had to leave him and Mr. Farrar to their fate, I did so with regret. I promised to notify the company of the situation by wire in the hope that the two would be helped in due time, either by the Italians or from Mombasa. But one night soon after the departure of the *Juba*, the natives tried to storm the station house. Although it was possible to repel the attack, Mr. Todd was severely wounded; the station owed its ultimate relief only to the Italians, who hurried to give assistance the moment they received an appeal.

To get the camels on board ship was a surprisingly simple and speedy proceeding. Four of them were driven through the shallow shore water to a little dhow that then took them in tow; thus they were brought swimming to the *Juba*, the dhow tacking many times against the stiff southwest wind. There Somali boys slung a rope end under the bellies of the animals, knotting it on their backs; the steam windlass then hoisted the drenched desert animals and lowered them into the hold, where they had to lie closely pressed together with outstretched necks until they were delivered from their pains at Lamu.

Meanwhile our camp at Mkonumbi had undergone a marvelous transformation, as was also the case with the men. Mr. Chanler and George had worked wonders. In the midst of a genuine wilderness they had created quite a little village of tents, storehouses, and huts on a cleared spot surrounded by a thorn hedge. Near the entrance stood a martial-looking Sudanese in a bright red fez, clad in white baggy trousers and a long blue butcher's jumper, with a cartridge belt and a brightly polished Mannlicher rifle on his shoulder. The rest of the men also showed some military discipline.

But it is now time to acquaint the reader with my two traveling companions. Mr. William Astor Chanler was the descendant of one of the most esteemed families of the northern states.[6] His father was from Charleston [South Carolina], however, so that in him North and South had met with all their characteristics. Having lost his parents at an early age, his mind and all his inclinations had been allowed to develop freely, for luck had smiled on him from birth. As soon as he came of age he made a trip to Africa with George Galvin, an even younger man; they wandered through the steppes and forests of the Kilimanjaro district, where he got to know the wild Masai and was perhaps the only white man who spoke with their Leibon Mbatián, or spiritual chief. He enjoyed the free, untrammeled life, and he returned full of new ideas and the wish to undertake some greater enterprise.

Mr. Chanler was twenty-four when he started on his second expedition, above average height, of slim but strong build, and hardened to fatigues. His clean-shaven face showed a well-formed forehead, not very pronounced eyebrows, and bright eyes. A rather full nose of normal shape, lips usually tightly compressed, good teeth, and a strong chin that betrayed energy complete the picture of this interesting and, on the whole, attractive person. I do not know whether this was only in my imagination, but for me his profile always seemed to have something of the Red Indian; at any rate it was not an ordinary one. A special trait of my traveling companion was his vivid imagination. I never tired of listening to his picturesque descriptions of his home or his adventures. How much this young man had already seen and lived through, and how many important people he had met! It was this fact in particular that had impressed me, for in spite of his youth, and though he by no means disdained the society of the gentle sex, he preferred the company of a really prominent man to that of the most beautiful woman. He was acquainted with a surprising number of famous people and could speak about them in a fascinating manner; many doors are open to a wealthy, clever, and agreeable American. Intercourse of this kind adds to a man's knowledge in a way that cannot be attained from books. His vivid imagination was especially manifest when he made plans. He had a wonderful way of starting to describe an extensive project suggested by a mere nothing, of drawing the most fantastic pictures, and of painting all the details of his castle in the air down to the last nook and cranny. No doubt Mr. Chanler had his faults and weaknesses, the worst being his great impulsiveness, but one willingly forgave them and could not be cross with him, knowing that he was a faithful and reliable friend to those to whom he had once dedicated his affection.

George Galvin came of a less illustrious family, but he also hailed from Rokeby on the Hudson, where the Chanlers had their family seat.[7] They had known each other since their youth and were close companions. George was of less than medium height but was strong, very calm, cold-blooded, intelligent, and eager to expand his knowledge. He was interested in everything, and I often had to answer scientific questions on subjects that lay quite outside his usual ken. His practical sense and calm reflection permitted him to solve every problem that faced him in a satisfactory manner, and he was thus a very useful member of the expedition. In the course of our travels he often had to be left to his own devices under difficult circumstances, and he always came up to expectations. He had the ability to master the men merely by his calm, without having to show any hardness. George was also fond of hunting, at which he was very successful. He was the only one of us who chanced to bag a lion's skin in the course of our expedition.

By engaging more natives at Pangani and Lamu, the number of our men had risen to 185. Mr. Chanler had divided these into three companies and had drilled them and made them practice target shooting. Other preparations also required weeks of diligent work. The arrival of the two ponies caused a pleasant change in the monotony. Though rather the worse for wear, they jumped gaily out of the dhow that had brought them from Lamu, rolled over in the sand a couple of times, and were as cheery as crickets. In spite of all the care we had taken, for the most part the vaccine was spoiled when we wanted to use it, for only one of the men reacted. Our camp, situated in the immediate neighborhood of mangroves, no doubt looked unhealthy, but it was not so in reality. None of us contracted fever, though we stayed there for many weeks.

On September 18, 1892, we were ready for the start and broke up our camp. Aside from us three white men, the expedition, which was in excellent trim and wonderfully equipped in every way, consisted of 185 caravan people, twelve Sudanese, seven Somalis, the two ponies, fifteen camels, forty-three donkeys, a dozen oxen, and a small herd of sheep and goats. To this must be added the above-mentioned canoe flotilla, which was to serve as a basis for provisioning the expedition until Hameye (Borati), the point where the Tana ceases to be navigable. We intended to follow the course of the river toward Kenya and then branch off to the north into unexplored and completely unknown regions. There we hoped to find the cradle of the Galla (Oromo), a formerly powerful but today scattered tribe that lives in the extensive territories lying between Abyssinia and the Tana River.

The Tana route proved to be difficult beyond all expectation. There was no beaten path and very little game, and the scarcity of the population offered few chances for obtaining provisions. Another circumstance aggravated our difficulties. The river banks were covered by a belt of impenetrable forest thickets of varied breadth, with no paths leading to the water. It was quite possible to die of thirst in the face of a green wall of foliage, behind which one knew there ran a large river. It happened that for one whole night a hundred of our men armed with hatchets and axes tried to penetrate to the water but returned next morning, weary and disappointed. It was therefore not possible to remain in touch with the canoe flotilla or to draw supplies from it, as had been planned. Such difficult conditions, arising at the very outset of an expedition, were not calculated to raise the morale of a young and untrained caravan. Utterly discouraged, some of our men soon preferred to desert. But the worst was yet to come.

After having reached Hameye, an uninhabited site on the Tana River, our beasts of burden showed great signs of fatigue, and many of the men were worn out. They all needed a rest, and there was no thought of pushing on with all our loads without procuring further means of transport. The expedition forcibly came to a standstill. Mr. Chanler and I therefore made up our minds to undertake a journey with a party of men to get more donkeys, while George and the rest of the caravan remained behind in camp. We had brought with us a certain amount of different seeds, intending to use them to introduce new cereals and fruit trees to the natives of the countries through which we were to pass. George was therefore instructed to lay out fields while we were away, to plant them with rice and other grains, and to sow the seeds of mango, orange, papaya, and other fruit trees, which we certainly would not reap ourselves but which we hoped someone else would someday enjoy.

The country lying before us was unknown. Wherever we turned, we moved to unexplored country—to new mountains, new rivers, and new peoples. We at first discovered the Jombeni (Nyambeni) mountain range and then followed the uninhabited course of the Guaso Nyiro until it ends in the Lorian Swamp, hitherto unknown, from where we were driven back toward the west by a terrible mosquito plague. Our provisions had nearly given out when we arrived in the vicinity of the Meru, a tribe inhabiting the western slopes of the Jombeni Mountains; they received us in an unfriendly manner, refusing to sell us foodstuffs or even to allow us to pass through their territory. After three days had been wasted in useless negotiations, several hundred warriors appeared, fantastically draped like the Masai, howling their war songs and dancing round our little camp. This was their last reply to our patiently repeated wish to come to a peaceful understanding. The last handful of maize had been distributed to our men that morning.

We knew that a few years earlier the Meru had cut down a caravan of ivory traders two hundred strong, yet we could not allow them to treat us in the manner they had. In order to show them that we had no fear of them, although we were only sixty strong, and in the hope of thus inducing them to come to an understanding, the next morning at daybreak we marched off through the narrow frontier forest that separated their lands from the steppe. We reached a wide valley covered with bushes, fields, and numerous huts and were soon greeted on all sides with the war cry "Ui, ui," which left no doubt that we would have to resort to arms. We could see hordes of warriors rushing down the slopes, wearing feathers and white, floating sheets, directing themselves against us. We therefore prepared for battle, massing our people, the beasts of burden, and our loads on a slight eminence. Several times the natives bravely rushed forwards to a distance of about one hundred yards, but there our volleys stopped them, causing heavy losses. It took two hours until the struggle was decided in our favor, but we had to pay for our success with three dead and twelve wounded, and our supplies of ammunition had been seriously depleted. When the warriors saw that they were at a disadvantage when attacking us from the front, they changed their tactics and took to the hills, evidently with the intention of intercepting us at some other point along our route. We made use of this interval to help ourselves to the foodstuffs we found in the surrounding huts, filling our empty sacks and rounding up a number of oxen, cows, and sheep, which we intended to carry off as a booty. During our march through their territory the natives again began to harass us, and they continued to do so until late in the afternoon, threatening us with their spears and showering arrows and missiles upon us. It was astonishing how quickly they discovered they could escape our bullets if they quickly fell flat on the ground as soon as a rifle was leveled at them.

Our route led uphill across difficult terrain, and being in constant danger, we had to be very careful. This especially applied to my young traveling companion; he led the vanguard so as to clear the way, which gave him frequent opportunities to show his cold-bloodedness. I could give many examples of this behavior but will restrict myself to only one. The path led across a deep valley, which gave our enemies a favorable opportunity for a surprise attack. We had to descend and again mount on the other side, advancing toward an enemy lying there in ambush. Chanler went ahead with a handful of men, while I, being better able to oversee the situation from my side, stayed behind to cover his advance. Chanler had nearly reached the opposite height and was just about to walk straight into the arms of a band of hidden natives, whom he obviously could not see. I, of course, at once began to fire shot after shot in that direction, my bullets necessarily whistling past Chanler so closely that he turned round in order to see what was the matter. At that moment he saw by chance a Meru armed with a spear approaching me from behind, under the cover of bushes, and without thinking of himself he began to shout, "Look out, look out!" I did not know at first what he meant, but at the same instant I heard one of our Somalis rush by me, saying, "I'll kill him!" A shot rang in my ear, and a moment later Mohammed Aman stood before me with a grinning smile, brandishing a fine Meru spear. We only got into camp long after dark. No one had swallowed a morsel that day. Now, in spite of the risky situation, our men began to milk the cows and to kill some sheep, and the feast they enjoyed after so much hunger and excitement lasted the whole night. No one thought of the danger we had just experienced and which perhaps still threatened us, and only the groans of the wounded reminded us of the day of battle.

Next morning we crossed the ridge of the mountain range and reached the Embu, the frontier neighbors of the Meru. They first received us kindly, with green branches in their hand, but soon they allowed themselves to be incited against us, and the days we had to pass in their country because of our need to tend to the wounded were agitated ones. When it finally became evident that the whole of the population, numbering around 50,000, was vowing revenge, we decided to make our way by a sudden start, breaking up our camp unexpectedly.

After having been away sixty-seven days without attaining our goal, we returned nearly empty-handed to Hameye, where George surprised us with the crushing news that during our absence the greater part of our beasts of burden—camels, oxen, donkeys, and even sheep—had died. I must mention here that long ago, on our way to the Lorian Swamp, my poor pony had become a victim of the tsetse fly; Chanler's horse died a similar death a few weeks later. The two Istrian dogs had both died of sunstroke during the first long and hot march along the Tana River, but to make up for this loss Felix and the mongrel bitch of the flotilla leader had presented us with three splendid puppies, who honored their father by developing into dogs as bold as he. Felix was joint property and recognized no one as his special master. Chanler claimed one of the puppies, which he called Frolic; I kept a nice little female puppy, which I christened Bibi; George's pet soon fell victim to a hyena.

As far as our means of transport were concerned, we were now in a far worse situation than before. Nothing else remained but to draw nearer to the inhabited Jombeni range to a place named Daitcho, which was frequently visited by ivory traders. With our sorely diminished capacity of transport, we could not think of taking all our loads, so whatever we thought dispensable was left behind. In spite of these reductions it was a slow and weary advance. More men deserted, and almost every day we had to abandon precious loads, parts of our outfit, and trading goods along the road. We finally reached Daitcho, where the expedition came to a standstill a second time. With great effort and with the expenditure of the bulk of our trading goods we succeeded in buying over two hundred donkeys. But the tsetse fly, or whatever plague it was, killed them all, no matter what we did, and it was as if an evil star reigned over our enterprise. However, nothing could subdue the undaunted spirit of my young traveling companion. It was decided that Hamidi, our first headman, would proceed to Zanzibar to replenish our stores, while Mr. Chanler and I would go to some far-away area in the hope of obtaining healthy animals. So it was that for the second time we started toward the north, now carrying mostly food and only a few bales of trading goods. This time we were searching for the mysterious Rendille tribe, which we had heard owned large numbers of camels and cattle. George was left behind at Daitcho with the remainder of the men in a stockaded camp, built from many hundreds of trees that had been felled over several weeks.

Without accurate information, it was difficult to go in search of a nomad people in the wide, barren territories north of the Guaso Nyiro. One morning, however, Chanler's happy instinct managed to light on their traces and then actually to find them after a night march he had undertaken with a few followers. According to his description it must have been a thrilling moment when he suddenly faced some two hundred of these mysterious nomads, of whom we had heard only through rumor and who were not a little surprised by Chanler's sudden appearance. No doubt this was a great success from a scientific point of view, but for us it served no practical purpose. The Rendille had thousands of camels, oxen, and cows and also had many beautiful silver-gray donkeys, but they did not want to trade them. We did not impress them at all with our tough, tanned light skins or with our rifles, the reports of which they had gotten to know in the course of a recent struggle with the Barawa Somali. It was therefore only after some time that they realized that we were a type of men they had never met before. Our small party of course made no impression on them, and they even ridiculed our fine trading goods—our red woolen blankets, Scotch plaids, and beautiful beads. With the exception of the good white *merikani*, nothing found favor in their eyes. Why should they trade with us? It seemed such a simple and easy matter just to rob us, and no doubt this thought was taken into consideration. Finally, thanks to a lot of patience and persuasion, we managed to obtain ten fine donkeys, for which we had, however, to pay exorbitant prices.

Wherever should we now turn in this wide, barren, and sparsely inhabited land? From Teleki's expedition I knew that the Turkana, who lived west of Lake Rudolf, had, in addition to a small number of camels, many good donkeys which they willingly exchanged for tobacco, several loads of which we were carrying. We therefore started on this long and weary journey. The route led past the quartz mountains near Barsaloi, and since I surmised that gold might be found there, I was tempted to go in that direction. We first reached the southern end of the Loroghi mountain range and came close to the point where I had vainly looked for the legendary Lorian Lake four years ago. On that occasion our Somali, Karsha, had been with me, but he did not now immediately recognize the spot. The next day, however, he came to me and drew my attention to it. Here we met a small band of shy Wandorobbos who were nearly starving and whom we furnished with elephant meat, thus winning their hearts. The great amount of game we found there and the Wandorobbos' appeal for help induced us to stop for a few days and shoot. While wandering in the hills I came into a most interesting unknown country whose formation and fauna fascinated me. There was an extraordinary variety of birds, among them pretty *Nektarineidae*, the African hummingbird, with a tail a yard long so that it could hardly fly; I also frequently encountered the genuine rare mountain zebra. At the same time I discovered a wonderful waterfall of a hundred feet in height, which I named Seya Fall after the river starting from it. Once a male lion came out of a reed-grown swamp and passed at about one hundred yards' distance without noticing me; being unarmed, I regret that I could only watch him. One moment later a lion that I had evidently disturbed in his slumbers jumped up quite close on my left, roared angrily, and rushed off.

The whole country made a most virginal impression. In one spot I found a veritable roadway cut deep in the hard, stony soil by elephants, evidently a road these animals had pounded out for thousands of years on their way toward the Kenya districts. While I chose to wander about on the mountain side, Chanler preferred to hunt on the plains. These were densely overgrown with a peculiar kind of bush and were a favorite haunt of the elephants. It was easy to approach them noiselessly on the sandy soil, but one only caught sight of them at the last minute and had to face them without cover, since the bushes offered none. Shooting elephants was therefore associated with great danger, and the Wandorobbo followed Chanler most unwillingly. On one occasion he only owed his escape to Felix, the bold little fox terrier.

The enormous amount of game tempted us to prolong our stay, all the more as the hungry Wandorobbo, usually so unapproachable, came in numbers from all parts and appealed to us not to leave them to their fate. Under their guidance we therefore started on August 23 with thirty of our men, six donkeys, and two milch cows on a hunting expedition that took us up the Loroghi Mountains to a district particularly frequented by elephants. Following the course of the Seya River, we marched uphill and camped in the shade toward noon. In the afternoon we hunted a little. Chanler shot two water bucks and I a rhinoceros. Next morning we started northward to the mountains, and we soon came on elephant trails. The path was strewn with foliage, recently broken branches, fresh dung, and other signs that a herd was not far away; we followed the track quietly, sure that we would soon espy the elephants. My friend Chanler was in advance with a majority of the men. I followed him at a distance of 100 to 200 yards with my boy Juma and three or four rifle bearers, admiring the scenery and from time to time jotting down a few observations in my notebook. Toward noon a sudden crash of branches on my right made me think of taking a rifle in hand, and I therefore turned round to Juma, who handed me the 577 Express. A few minutes later a violent snorting on my left announced that a rhinoceros was rapidly coming toward me, whereupon I quickly turned in that direction, simultaneously cocking the right hammer. At the same instant I saw the animal rushing at me with lowered head at a distance of no more than twelve steps. What then followed only took a few seconds, but they were so momentous that it will take much longer to describe all my thoughts and feelings connected with them.

Because I never lost full consciousness, I still have every detail alive in my memory as if the incident happened only yesterday. Should my description not tally exactly with that given by Mr. Chanler in his book,[8] this is no doubt due to the fact that he was not an eyewitness and could only know of it from what was told him by my people, who, scared to death and trembling for their lives, certainly did not follow the different phases of the event as closely as I did. It is known how much the descriptions of exciting incidents vary on the part of different witnesses. Also, one or the other of my men may, without any reason, have felt guilty and reproached himself for having thought only of his own safety. Nobody could have assisted me, however, and I never thought of accusing anybody.

The moment I turned toward the rhino I espied a tree standing to my right which could serve as cover in case of emergency. I did not know what my men had done for their own safety, nor did I think about it. The sight of the rapidly approaching rhinoceros did not frighten me in the least, for I was accustomed to it. My first thought was that because of the nearby elephants I would not shoot, but simply jump behind the tree. To do this successfully, one must allow the animal to approach so close that it cannot stop its course and must rush past. This I determined to do. Fixing my gaze sharply on the beast, I allowed it to approach to a distance of two yards and then jumped aside. But alas, something prevented me from doing so successfully. Whether it was the branches of the tree or the men who had taken cover behind it I could not tell, but I was aware that things went wrong. All that I could do now was to raise my rifle up high and try to fire at the head of the animal, whose snout nearly touched me. It was too late, however. The rifle was knocked away and I was thrown to the ground by a hit in the stomach, which fortunately was protected by two cartridge pouches. I lay on my back, extended to my full length, and saw the dark body rush over me without my being trampled. In the belief that my adventure had ended luckily, I rejoiced at the thought of having got off so cheaply. But suddenly the hideous, huge head of the rhinoceros was again above me, and I felt myself being handled most roughly. It seemed as if my right leg was being trampled, and in order to avoid this I tried in vain to evade the blows. I counted seven hard hits. On receiving the eighth, a most painful shock, I felt myself thrown a distance, gave a cry, and remained prostrate. The rhinoceros seemed to have expended its wrath, for I heard its snorting in the distance, getting fainter.

After a few moments had passed I looked around, wondering where my men were. They had disappeared. I then tried to ascertain what had happened to me. It felt as if my right leg had been crushed. In order to assure myself, I laboriously rose to a kneeling position, felt my leg, and to my great astonishment found that all my bones were whole. Then I sank forward on the ground, my head resting on my arms, and remained in that position. After a short time I felt Chanler cutting up my knickerbockers, which were doubled up with patches, and then heard his excited exclamation: "By Jove, right into the. . . ." This alarmed me, for then I was lost. Having reflected for a few minutes, I had just resolved to ask my friend for his pistol when he, no doubt guessing what black thoughts I harbored, softened his diagnosis by adding that because of the amount of flesh and the great quantity of blood he could not properly diagnose the injury I had sustained. This I did not quite believe, but it made me abandon my original resolve. A rough stretcher was at once improvised. A young tree was cut down, the turban of one of the men was slung round my body, and I was carried back to the spot from whence we had started in the morning. In the evening vomiting set in, a sign that my stomach had suffered. Next day we returned to the camp on the Seya River. News of my accident had already spread, and from my bed in the tent I could see the crowd of Wandorobbo crouching gravely and silently on the ground. These poor devils had brought some honey which they advised me to eat and to put on my wound. There could be no question of this, as for many days I was incapable of swallowing anything, even a sip of water. My stomach was burning like fire as if it was full of red-hot iron, and the agony was so terrible that for more than a week I spent every minute of the day and the endless night in indescribable pain, so much so that I quite forgot about the large wound, which discharged streams of matter and had to be kept open. It was washed twice daily with permanganate of potassium, the only disinfectant we carried with us.

Mr. Chanler realized that we had to return to Daitcho, but he thought it better to remain where we were for a few days in order to see how things went and to determine whether I could stand being moved. My accident was a heavy blow, and not only for me. However things might turn out later, the course of the expedition was again interrupted and delayed. I found this thought as unbearable as my physical suffering. We had to drop the Turkana plan for the present, for we knew that it would take at least several months before I would again be well enough for action. This meant that during all that time I would be a burden to my traveling companion, who already had undergone so many disappointments. But when I think of the heroic spirit that my young friend evinced in spite of all the troubles and hardships he had endured, how bravely he looked to the future, and the efforts he dedicated to keeping me alive, being ready to make any sacrifice to this end, these days constitute one of the most beautiful memories of my life.

In view of our subsequent plans and for many other reasons, it was advisable to leave most of the loads, consisting chiefly of flour and beans, on the spot under the care of some men so as to be as unhampered as possible on our way to Daitcho, which was some 280 kilometers distant. We started on September 1 by another road so that we would have the Guaso Nyiro River to our rear, since once the rains set in it is difficult to cross over. For a whole week we followed its right bank and then branched off on to the old southerly route. The transport over such rough ground in the glare of a fierce sun was a torment for me, but another circumstance made the next few days hellish for all of us. The rhinoceros mating season was apparently at its height, and the part of the Guaso Nyiro that we were following was a favorite trysting place for all the amorous rhinoceros pairs of the entire district, who of course were highly displeased at seeing us disturb their idyll. In the next few days we had a hundred narrow escapes when the caravan was seriously charged and scattered. Many a time the frightened men put my stretcher roughly down on the ground, and the rifle shots of the vanguard led by Chanler, the shots of the guard that surrounded me, the snorting of the monsters, and the constant alarms of the fleeing men created a pandemonium that kept me at a high pitch of excitement the whole time. Under my very eyes one of our men was thrown high into the air and fell head-first on the hard rock; he was buried twenty-four hours later. To all this must be added my own unbearable pain. What my traveling companion experienced in those days he expressed in his book in the following words: "Reviewing in my mind this march from Sayer [Seya] to Daitcho, I can conjure up nothing but a nightmare of continuous horror and anxiety. The anxiety was occasioned by the sufferings of my friend; the horror was caused by the fact that during this entire march, from Sayer until we reached Daitcho, all the rhinoceroses in East Africa seemed to have clustered along our pathway, and to have religiously devoted all their attentions and energies to charging us as frequently as possible."[9]

On one occasion one of these monsters erupted into our camp in the middle of the night, chased our people in all directions, and furiously trampled one of our camp fires, disappearing again like an evil spirit. Once, in the later course of the march, after nightfall, we reached a drinking place that two lions tried to dispute with us. For over an hour their roaring made the air vibrate; although the men were extremely thirsty, it took a long time before they ventured to go en masse near the water, which they finally did carrying torches, drumming their kettles, and making all the noise they could.

The burning sensation in my stomach decreased by degrees, but as my weakness grew, my capacity to endure pain also diminished, and I sincerely hoped for an end to my suffering. During nine whole days I had taken no nourishment whatsoever, nor had I had a minute's sleep. At the same time my wound was continually discharging streams of matter. In the evening of the ninth day, however, I fell from exhaustion into a deep sleep for the first time, which lasted I do not know how long. When I awoke I felt a little fresher, and a weak glimmer of hope began to dawn. But it was destined to expire soon again unless I could take some nourishment, which on account of my injured stomach had to be done by artificial means. On the twelfth day I tried to eat a biscuit, on the next day I consumed two, and I was next able to take some guinea-fowl broth. Thus I improved, slowly but surely. We were nearing Daitcho, where medicines and special articles of food awaited us in abundance.

On September 17 only two marches separated us from our destination, and one can imagine how the thought of that revived us all. We were passing over a wide, barren plain devoid of any bushes, which sloped slightly upward to the right. Chanler was about 500 yards ahead of my stretcher, which was surrounded by half a dozen marksmen, when suddenly a rhinoceros arose from the right and charged toward us in full flight. My men immediately started firing, which only seemed to lend wings to the animal without causing it to swerve from its direction. I saw the danger approaching, and seeing that some of the bullets hit while others merely dusted on the ground, I realized that all this did not impress the brute in the least. My stretcher had been lowered to the ground and my bearers were firing as fast as they could, but all in vain. I heard them say, "Poor *bwana*, this time he is done for." No doubt fate had decreed it so. One moment later the ground shook and the snorting sounded at my left; there the monster was—an ugly sight, bleeding from its mouth and many wounds, rushing past me as if pursued by a thousand furies, just shaving the foot end of my stretcher as it fled off.

The better care and medical treatment that I enjoyed upon my arrival at Daitcho caused my condition to improve somewhat, but a certain state of depression followed which reacted unfavorably upon my health. A complete recovery without the care of a doctor was not to be expected, and the thought that I was now a hindrance rather than a useful member of the expedition depressed me very much, even though my companion looked forward to the future with undiminished courage. That I had to be taken nearer to the coast at any cost was his one idea, and he meant to carry it out. From a caravan of traders that happened to pass we heard that an English physician had arrived at Kibwezi, a locality in southern Ukambani. I was to be taken there, a distance of about 380 kilometers, under George's careful supervision. A light and comfortable stretcher was manufactured, and on September 27 I bade farewell to Mr. Chanler, who in lucky and unlucky days had always proved himself a true friend whom I had learned to love.

Our route led south to the Tana River by the shortest way possible. There we found our first headman, Hamidi, who had been sent to Zanzibar and was bringing back a number of men and some trading goods. He had been away an unduly long time, and the men he had engaged made a bad impression upon me. The Tana could only be forded in this place and formed a considerable obstacle at all times. A long, narrow small island divides its waters into two very unequal arms. While the left part, which is several hundred yards wide and sprinkled with rocks, can be waded through in normal times even though it carries rapidly flowing waters, the right arm thunders past between vertical walls in a mass of spraying foam. George made use of the following day to re-connoiter the condition of the river, and I was glad of this day of rest. A sudden relapse had knocked me down, and for several hours I felt so desperately ill that I thought my end was near. As one may imagine, I was worn down to a mere skeleton, but in spite of my light weight the crossing of the broad part of the stream was the maximum that my bearers, who had to carry the stretcher on their heads, could accomplish. Trembling and swaying, they managed to set one foot before the other, though they were supported, lifted, and pulled by the strong arms of other men. This passage seemed to last an eternity, and when I was finally put down on the rocks of the island, I felt truly saved.

The deep gorge through which the Tana thundered was twenty-five to thirty yards wide. At one point in the middle of the river bed, between the vertical walls, a huge boulder protruded from the foaming spray, over which a passage about four yards long connected the two shores. This bridge was built in a most curious fashion. Because of the lack of any other material, the primitive con-struction, evolved by some bold and unknown natives, was made up of nu-merous short crooked branches, interwoven with roots and creepers. This formed a compact mass that was about a yard in thickness and quite shapeless. The most experienced engineer must have asked himself how the natives had managed without any accessories to execute this masterpiece, which in its way was really a miracle. The whole had no railing, the upper layer of this bridge was uneven, and it took some pluck and a total lack of dizziness to dare to cross over.

George had no confidence in this structure, and for several hours he worked hard at improving it with branches and creepers, which were fetched from a great distance. While this was going on I lay forsaken on my stretcher, exposed to the burning rays of the noonday sun, without knowing what this delay signified, until George announced our start with the words, "I think we can risk it now." The two strongest men lifted the stretcher, started to walk toward the swaying construction, and without difficulty reached the solid part based on the rocky boulder. They showed less courage in taking the second section, however, which on account of its greater length was hanging down more deeply. Until halfway all went well. Then my porters were seized by giddiness and began to hesitate, tremble, and stagger. Suddenly they stood still. Around us the waters thundered, and underneath was white foam. In front of me I saw George's face turn white, and he and half a dozen men rushed forward with open mouths and frightened eyes. They seized the stretcher and my legs, and the porters dragged me as fast as they could to the opposite shore, full of fear that the frail and overloaded structure would tumble down at any moment, carrying us all into the foaming depth. It was the most terrible moment of my life. Once the danger was past and the general agitation had abated, we continued on our way with pulse still hammering, but we were stopped after little more than a hundred yards because the main pole of my stretcher broke in two, bringing me down to the ground very roughly. This accident might well have happened while crossing the river.

Concerning the next weeks I must tell how my doe-eyed Bibi presented me with a litter of puppies but acted toward them in a most unmotherly manner, as if she were ashamed of her faux pas. The little ones developed into fine specimens, however, and did honor to their parents. Near Kibwezi we encountered a large traders' caravan, which, after two years of wandering in the Lake Rudolf district, was on its way back to the coast, loaded with ivory and provided with numerous beasts of burden. Some of the leaders and men knew me, came to pay their respects, and showed their sympathy. Teleki's expedition had opened up a new and vast ivory district; men who have done such deeds are highly thought of by these caravan people, so that their names are remembered for many years. They presented me with fine white flour and other delicacies they were carrying. At the same time George, who had been instructed by Mr. Chanler to buy a good number of donkeys on his way, made use of this favorable opportunity, paying the people with a draft on Zanzibar scrawled in pencil on a scrap of paper; at that time Europeans still enjoyed unlimited confidence.

As far as I can remember, fifty-four days had passed since my accident when we reached Kibwezi. I had got over the journey well, my digestion was almost all right, and I did not feel pains when I lay on my left side, no doubt because only a part of my stomach had been injured. My wound was still open, but its edges had narrowed.

When we approached the village, the attentive George ran ahead in order to prepare the doctor for my arrival. Dr. William Charters, a young man, awaited me before the entrance of a large building of local style, shook hands with a kind smile, and had me carried into the house, where he insisted that I occupy his own bed. All the while his eyes glowed with pleasure, and he seemed happy to be able to follow the dictates of his kind heart and put himself at the service of suffering humanity. From the bed I could see him in the kitchen preparing a porridge which he himself served me, after having assured himself that it had cooled down sufficiently. The young man acted like an affectionate mother. George could return to Daitcho knowing that I was in good hands. We therefore had to bid one another farewell again, and this time it meant severing the last link that bound me to the expedition. During the last few weeks George had given me so many proofs of devotion and self-sacrifice that we became more closely attached than ever.

Dr. Charters immediately examined my wound and declared that an operation was necessary. At the same time he exclaimed, "You have been within an inch of the grave"—words that he often repeated in the course of my stay. To begin with, for two days he studied some surgical texts and anatomical charts because, as he said, a wrong cut might seriously impair my ability to walk. At the operation I saw for the first time his assistant, an English gardener, who acted as chloroformist. I don't know how it happened, but when my face was covered and I was supposed to count from "one" in a loud voice, I had hardly started doing so when I instantly lost consciousness; the gardener had been too lavish with the liquid. Charters pulled me up and bade me expectorate what I could of the narcotic. The second effort was more successful, for I went to sleep very soon, for how long I do not know. Suddenly I felt myself being shaken and heard someone call my name and assure me that everything was over. "What is over?" "The operation, it is done." It took some time before I fully grasped the meaning of this remark.

For three full weeks Dr. Charters kept me in his house, cared for me, waited on me, and looked after me in the most unselfish manner. He even gave me his last bottle of champagne in order to improve my strength. He himself slept on the bare earthen ground floor but seemed quite happy to be able to sacrifice his own comfort to that of a stranger. He was soon able to give me the glad tidings: "You are now safe, but you have been within an inch of the grave."

This true Samaritan was thirty years of age and came from a Glasgow family of strict believers. He was below middle height and of a rather delicate build. From his pale, clean-shaven face a pair of intelligent dark eyes gazed at one, and his hair, too, was dark. His profile so strikingly resembled that of Napoleon that I could not help remarking on it. He knew it, as others had told him so before me. In his youth he had first studied shipbuilding and machinery, and after the close of his studies he had gone out to the Congo. For five years Charters enjoyed good health but was witness to the death of nineteen of the twenty-two missionaries with whom he had been in touch—noble-spirited, self-sacrificing men who often fell victim to the murderous climate. These sad impressions afflicted him so much that his faith in a supremely good and just God wavered. With a broken heart he turned his back on Africa and returned home to his parents. But with the increasing distance from the scene of his sad experiences and with the cheering influences of the fresh sea breezes on the voyage homeward, new doubts began to arise and trouble his mind. What if, after all, an Almighty God existed—a God whose inexplicable decrees we puny men are unable to fathom? Arrived at home in the bosom of his family, he soon found the deity he had lost, and realizing that although an engineer was of good use in African mission work, a physician and surgeon would do better, at the age of twenty-five he zealously set to work to study medicine. He obtained his medical degree at the end of four years. Soon thereafter he accepted the offer of the well-known philanthropist Sir William Mackinnon, who was an enthusiast concerning Africa, to undertake the foundation of an industrial station in Ukambani. This was not to be a religious mission, however; rather it had the aim of raising the cultural level of the natives. Thus two months before I came to Kibwezi, Dr. Charters had arrived there in the company of an English gardener who was to be his assistant.

After three weeks of the most assiduous care and nursing I thought it time to proceed to the coast. The stretcher was fetched, and Dr. Charters insisted on accompanying me there himself. After eighteen days we reached Mombasa. To my surprise there appeared in our camp at the last stopping place a Mr. Younger, a young Scotsman who represented the firm of Smith, Mackenzie and Co. in Zanzibar. He had heard of our approach and had come to ask me to put up at his house. Touched by so much kind attention, I gracefully accepted his offer, and the next day I found myself facing the ocean in a lovely cool house, where I was well taken care of. There I was warmly greeted by a Mr. Jenner, a descendant of the famous discoverer of vaccination against smallpox, who was a judge in the service of the British East Africa Company. He was a friend of Mr. Younger and lived in the same house. These charming young men showed the greatest courtesy and consideration for my health. I could lie in bed as long as I wanted and only put in an appearance at lunch time, and I enjoyed perfect peace and quiet. After two days Dr. Charters returned to Kibwezi. For weeks I had been his personal guest and had eaten his bread and fortified myself with his wine. But how much greater was my debt to this man for his self-sacrificing charity and pure Samaritan heart! And yet all that I was allowed to do in return was to wring his hand warmly in parting. Neither before nor after have I ever met a man of such pure and noble character. When we parted I promised as long as I lived to write him once a year, but already my first letter was returned to me, unopened, with the remark, "Lost in the interior." Soon after his return to Kibwezi he had gone out on a shooting excursion with a Scottish friend, and neither of them was ever seen again. Their fate is unknown. The cruel bush wilderness does not always disclose its secrets. I had been his first and only serious case, and if such a thing as predestination exists, then Dr. Charters had been destined to be my guardian angel.

At that time a Mr. Arthur Neumann was just equipping a caravan at Mombasa with his modest means in order to visit the Lake Rudolf district. He wanted to undertake the shooting of elephants on a business basis. Neumann was about forty, fair, of slight build, and did not look very enterprising, but one is often mistaken regarding the inner worth of a man. He was said to be a crack shot. I was able to give him information about the districts he intended to visit, and he consulted me on many points. After having spent eighteen months in the interior, he returned with a rich booty of ivory, and he has published an interesting book concerning his experience.[10] After Teleki he was the first European to reach the Reshiat country, situated at the north shore of Lake Rudolf; six years had meanwhile gone by. Ten years after Neumann, a British captain visited the Reshiat people, and in his book he gives a detailed narrative as to how he questioned the natives concerning Teleki and Neumann and states that he received contradictory information from them, some of them declaring that Teleki had been the first to visit them, while others said the same of Neumann. The English captain leaves it open, and it appears undecided who actually was the discoverer of the Reshiat—a not very fair way to speak of facts when he undoubtedly knew better.[11] I was also unpleasantly struck by the judgment of this man on the "giant" tribe of the Turkana, which he never got to know personally. He had met a couple of Suk people, a tribe not even related to the Turkana, but that sufficed for him to criticize our description of the Turkana. Superficial travelers have often made for confusion.

On the afternoon before my departure I entered the dining room for a few minutes and met an American unknown to me—a Mr. Lyons—with whom I hardly spoke one word, my wound just then causing me considerable pains. Before leaving he asked me casually where I was going to stay at Zanzibar, to which I replied that I had not yet given the matter any thought. "Oh, then you will stop at my house. There is plenty of room for you there." East Africa at that time was truly a wondrous place, and I would have felt very happy with Mr. Lyons and his young and beautiful wife if only the state of my health had been better. But fever soon set in as a result of the many social claims made by this extremely hospitable house, and at the end of a week I had to move to the new French hospital so that I could have proper nursing care. This excellent establishment was operated by nuns of the Order of the Holy Ghost and Heart of Jesus. With the exception of the Mother Superior, all the nuns were Creoles from the island of Réunion. One of them was so pretty that the whole town of Zanzibar was crazy about her. Because I was a privileged patient, this lovely young person was appointed my nurse, and I suspect that many of the visits I received were intended more for my pretty ministering angel than for myself.

Among my first callers at Zanzibar was the German consul general, who came in the name of the Austrian naval commander in chief, Admiral Sterneck, to inquire after my health. I saw the premier, General Lloyd William Mathews, only once, because I very soon did not wish to have anything more to do with him. As one will remember, our first headman Hamidi had been sent from Daitcho to Zanzibar while Chanler and I had undertaken the trip to the Rendille with the second headman, Mohammadi, and sixty-six men. During this trip Mohammadi had deserted, taking with him two of our men and two elephant tusks belonging to Mr. Chanler. More than that, he had wantonly destroyed a depot of food articles we had established. Having been told that this man, who had behaved so perfidiously, had been seen in Zanzibar, I requested General Mathews to have the fellow arrested so that he could answer for his deeds. This was done, but four days later the general released the man on the plea that he had only carried off the elephant tusks so that they would not be lost. He had thereupon been forced to sell them at Kau on the Tana River in order to pay for the maintenance of himself and his two men. My protests were in vain. In consequence of his long sojourn at Zanzibar, the general had come to love his natives far too much to hurt one of them. As I was unable to obtain redress, I finally transmitted the whole affair to Mr. Chanler's representative, who had no more luck than I. It is incomprehensible how General Mathews, the first personage after the sultan, could in so obvious an instance take the part of an unmitigated scoundrel.

In the hospital I enjoyed capital nursing; my gratitude to the venerable Mother Superior and to the lovely Sister Marie is unbounded. Even the Catholic bishop honored me with calls and often sent some of the delicious grapes grown in his orchard, which were a great rarity at Zanzibar. An English doctor named Gregory treated me, and every second day he extended the edges of the wound, causing me excruciating pain and making me look forward to his visits with considerable trepidation. Dr. Gregory had gone through the Chilean-Peruvian war and had been wrecked on an island in the Straits of Magellan, where he had lived for months among the natives.

Toward the end of January 1894 I thought I should turn home in spite of the northern winter, and I packed my things. While I was thus occupied, a most disturbing letter came from Mr. Younger. Rumors had spread at Mombasa that all the men of Chanler's caravan had deserted him and that he had remained behind alone, with just a handful of faithful blacks. Such an event had never occurred before in the history of African explorations as far as the Zanzibari were concerned. One may imagine how upset I was on hearing this news, and I hesitated to depart under such circumstances. But a second letter from Mr. Younger happily made the matter appear in a less disastrous light, and as my traveling arrangements were far advanced, I consoled myself with the thought that rumors in East Africa always turn out later to have been greatly exaggerated. In any event, my companion would be able to master such a situation without my assistance, which given my state of health would have been of little use.

The commander of an Italian cruiser had most amiably offered to take me on his fast ship to Aden, but I preferred to travel more comfortably on board the Messageries steamer that was due at the same time. At Aden I found Antonio Cecchi still heading the Italian consulate general, and I spent many pleasant evenings in his hospitable house. I also met for the first time the famous African travelers Major von Wissmann and Captain H. B. C. Swayne, the latter well known for his numerous trips in Somaliland.[12] Wissmann and I stayed at the Hotel Europe, and as one might imagine we spent most of the time together, talking about Africa, which this great traveler knew like no other. Four years previously I had met Dr. Karl Peters, also at Aden, to whom Germany chiefly owed her East African colony. These two men had much in common in terms of energy and enterprising spirit, but Peters was the more eminent man as far as intelligence and scientific training were concerned. His spirit of adventure was also based on wider and more practical plans, but he had more enemies and less luck than Wissmann. Captain Swayne had undertaken his many trips to Somaliland in the service of his government, which meant that he worked under more pleasant conditions. He was also respected by the natives because of his perseverance and his truly Spartan frugality. A few months later Antonio Cecchi was transferred to Zanzibar as consul general, and, I regret to say, was killed on an official trip into the interior of Somaliland. Not recognizing the treacherous character and the wild instincts of the members of this tribe, he trusted them too much, and less than a three-day march from the coast he was murdered along with all his companions.[13]

After I had spent ten days at Aden, the Lloyd's *Habsburg* brought me to Fiume. Count Teleki came to meet me, and his right hand was the first that was stretched out to greet me on the home shore. With the special care that formed one of his characteristics, he arranged for my comfort and took me to his beautiful Budapest home, calling in his doctor, Professor Lumnitzer. Count Teleki had meanwhile been in India, hunted bison, and wandered through the forests of Java and the jungles of Borneo; he had accumulated many interesting experiences and brought back many fine trophies. We had a great deal to tell each other, and I would have found it difficult to part from him had not the appearance of Professor Lumnitzer always filled me with horror. No doubt he was a prominent surgeon, but he was even more cruel than his colleague at Zanzibar. He relentlessly scraped my wound with a sharp instrument, causing pains that were all the more unbearable as I really had already undergone enough treatment of this kind.

I therefore fled from my torturer to Vienna. I had left this city full of the keenest hopes, and now I returned a beaten man; no wonder that my mood was not bright. Unkempt, untrimmed hair covered my head, betraying my long stay in the wilds; therefore my first errand was to go to a barber to get myself fixed up. Polite and talkative, this young man tried to cater to my intellectual wants but soon gave up. Seeing that I vouchsafed no answer, he pressed into my hands an illustrated paper that had appeared that day. One may imagine my astonishment when I spied on the front page an account of my accident with the rhinoceros. It was a strange trick of chance that after nearly six months I should arrive in Vienna just on the day that this periodical chose to inform its readers of my adventure. No doubt the barber would have been very proud had he guessed that he had had the honor of clipping the mane of the hero of this drama.

Some months passed before I could resume my duties. The healing of my wound had lessened by degrees, and my recovery progressed slowly, although the chief doctor of the Admiralty, in whose care I stood, did his utmost. When he noticed my growing impatience, thinking that I had no faith in him, he proposed a consultation with the general staff doctor of the army. This man examined the wound and asked who had undertaken the operation. On my reply he said, "That was a thoughtful physician." Yes, Dr. William Charters was indeed a man whose medical knowledge was assisted by a warm heart which wished to benefit his fellow man.

I continued to be in the good graces of the naval commander in chief, Baron Sterneck. My pay for the time of my absence was even handed over to me in gold currency, but this, like the paper bank notes I had received after my first expedition, had no tendency to stay with me. The book that I had compiled about the expedition of Count Teleki had long ago appeared in print, for which His Majesty the Emperor had awarded me a gold medal. The publisher also arranged for an English and a Hungarian translation of the work. I found some difficulty in accommodating myself to the ways and manners of society; I had suffered too much and too long, and my nerves often revolted, which was only natural. Gay laughter, even coming from the lips of the most beautiful girls, irritated me to such a degree that I used to get up and leave the room. I could therefore only meet good old friends, among whom I numbered the family of my wife, who at that time guessed as little as I did that she would one day become my spouse. The idea of binding myself and of sacrificing my personal liberty only occurred to me late in life, and certainly not before I entered my fortieth year. The same was true with my brothers, probably because in younger years we had not known a truly happy family life. Added to all this was the anxiety I felt for my traveling companion left behind at Daitcho. At last, at the end of March, news came from Mr. Younger; soon thereafter Mr. Chanler himself wrote, fully confirming the rumors that I had heard, but also announcing his happy arrival at Mombasa. As I have said before, Mr. Chanler's expedition had been ill-starred to an exceptional degree, and the long series of unhappy incidents found its tragic end in the complete desertion of all the caravan people, who one fine day, without any previous indication of discontent, simply left him. Hamidi, the first headman, cleverly kept in the background, so that it at first looked as if he was not a party to the act. Only by degrees did it become apparent that he as well as the men had acted under the influence of certain intrigues that originated at Zanzibar, though their motives never appeared quite clear.

That men forfeit their claims to their hard-earned considerable wages by desertion without having been assured that they would be compensated by someone else is hardly to be supposed. Nothing is easier than to induce a gang of men of so low an intellectual and moral level, a band consisting mostly of former slaves, to commit any folly by using some fine catchwords. The fact that political unrest prevailed on the East African coast and the attitude in certain circles that the time had come to shake off the irksome European yoke may have contributed to this event. A few days after the caravan people had departed, shooting and crying the revolutionary cry "Haya puani" (Let's be off to the coast), with only a few faithful Somalis and the Sudanese men remaining in the camp, Mr. Chanler was surprised to learn from the leader of the latter that his men had also run off, taking their rifles with them. It is true that on the eve of their desertion Hamidi had had an interview with these men, but a quite ridiculous reason was given for their action. Mr. Chanler, supposing that the caravan people would think better of it and return, had made arrangements to have the ringleaders put in chains. When the Sudanese saw that, they thought that these measures were also to be applied to them, and they preferred to escape this danger by flight.

Mr. Chanler spoke Kiswahili as well as he did English, knew the language in all its shades and idioms, and could make himself perfectly understood by the natives. One might have thought that he therefore would have been able to fathom the psychological trend of their acts. Knowing that he understood their language, however, they took good care during their *wasumgumsu*, or chatter in their huts in the evenings, not to utter any careless word. The moral distance and the instinctive dislike between different races make any kind of intimacy difficult. He only found out many things a few days later, when one of the Sudanese, called Hussein, returned to the camp of his own free will. In his book *Through Jungle and Desert* Mr. Chanler thrillingly describes the situation in which he then found himself—how it was hard for him to renounce his travel plans, and how he was obliged to destroy the expedition's precious equipment, which had been selected with so much care and circumspection, in order not to let it fall into the hands of the natives.[14] His return to Zanzibar was an absolute necessity, however, in order that the culprits should be properly punished and the reasons for their desertion cleared up. He also had to take into consideration his family's anxiety for his welfare, for thus far they had been entirely dependent on rumor.

He left Daitcho with his few companions on January 10, 1894, and arrived at Mombasa on February 10 after thirty forced marches. To his astonishment, when he reached Zanzibar he was faced by a world of enemies. The deserters had arrived there long before him and therefore had ample time to invent explanations for their conduct and to poison the atmosphere. As one may imagine, it had been an easy matter for them to win the good will of General Mathews. A long and most unsatisfactory struggle began between Mr. Chanler and the almighty general-premier. The former of course demanded the unconditional punishment of the deserters, while the general asked for their wages to be paid in full. These contradictory points of view could not be reconciled. Mr. Chanler, assisted by the American consul, fought a good fight.[15] The English general in time began to bargain, declaring that he would be satisfied with half or even with any part of the sum first claimed. But Mr. Chanler remained firm. The men had caused his expedition to fail, and in the interests of future explorers an act of this kind must not be allowed to pass unpunished. A bout of malaria finally forced Mr. Chanler to abandon the hopeless struggle, and after a final protest and with his heart full of bitterness he turned his back on Zanzibar. On a stormy night that gave but scant promise of the arrival of the Lloyd steamer, I had the joy of meeting my friend in the port of Trieste. We had much to tell each other, and Chanler's narrative was only interrupted when the early dawn peeped through the skylight. We then traveled together to Vienna. It was only natural that after his recent experiences Mr. Chanler was attracted for some time by the beautiful city, until the wish to see his own country again arose in his heart and carried him off to his relations and friends across the ocean.[16]

For me, too, the hour of farewell had struck, for naval service recalled me to Pola.[17]

7

Thoughts about Africa

With my sailing orders, the African period of my life came to a close. My accident, which entailed a long period of convalescence, again centered my thoughts on my profession. A period crowded with experiences leaves an aftermath of memories, however, and I cannot easily drop a subject to which I had devoted over eight years of my life.

During that period, chance led me to meet two complete strangers, to enter into intimate companionship with them, and finally to count them among my best and truest friends. Those who are in a position to gain insight into the relations that usually exist between partners in a difficult enterprise will be surprised to hear that from the very beginning no shadow—not even a passing disagreement—clouded the harmony of our companionship.

Voyages of discovery often bring in their train circumstances which, if they are to be overcome, demand special moral as well as physical qualities. Without them, any lasting understanding in the face of privation, excitement, and danger of all kinds is unthinkable. Even little peculiarities of character or personal habits that are merely tiresome in normal circumstances may have a destructive effect in close company. Mutual consideration is above all necessary. A gentleman expects his comrades to have an honorable mind and an unselfish spirit of self-sacrifice; a brave man expects a stout heart. We were especially fortunate in the response these demands found in the three of us. No man knows beforehand how he will bear himself in unusual situations and whether he will be capable of rising to the occasion. I, for example, could not know before I reached Africa whether I would have the necessary physical endurance to meet the privations and hardships with which I would have to cope. In this regard I might have greatly disappointed my comrades.

A forced march, the necessity of which arose at the very outset of my first expedition, proved my physical fitness. We had started from Kwa Mauia, a village several hours upstream from Pangani, and had already progressed for four days when we discovered toward evening that more than fifty of our porters had deserted us. We could not let this pass. It was of vital importance to establish a precedent that would once and for all rob our people of any inclination to desert. I ordered a return and the capture of the men—or at any rate to arrange for their capture on the coast and in Zanzibar. I then not only made the whole distance as far as Kwa Mauia with seven choice men in one forced march lasting from early morning until late at night, but also searched for fugitives in all the villages that lay on my way. With tightly closed lips and in deep silence we thus proceeded through the barren, burning steppe without stopping, until a sunstroke suddenly knocked me over at around 3:00 P.M. I had no idea what had happened to me, and with chattering teeth and a painful sensation of cold I lay prostrate in the hot sand, conscious but yet incapable of rising or thinking coherently. My companions surrounded me helplessly, covering me with their turbans and other items of clothing. About half an hour passed until the idea struck me in a more lucid moment that a violent reaction might help. I therefore made them give me a goblet of brandy into which one gram of quinine had been dissolved. I swallowed the mixture, whereupon the feeling of cold ceased, and in a few minutes I was well enough to continue the march.

The novice is less frightened by incidents of this kind than the experienced traveler, who knows how serious these matters are. Toward midnight we reached Kwa Mauia. After a short meal we boarded two canoes and had a lovely trip all through the night, skirting the riverside, where bushes made a fairylike picture, covered as they were with myriads of fireflies that resembled glowing dewdrops. Toward dusk of the following day we reached Pangani. There I left five of my men behind as a watch and arranged for the seizure of our deserters. Since words and polite requests were of no avail, I forcibly took possession of a small boat; at dawn I left for the open sea and Zanzibar, accompanied by my two servants.

This was a somewhat foolhardy undertaking. We had neither compass nor chart but only a small triangular sail, and in the true sense of the word we were the playthings of luck and the prevailing southwest monsoon. We sailed close-hauled to the wind all through the day and the following night, anxiously looking for our goal, the distance of which we knew only approximately. My two blacks seemed to be indifferent and kept silence; perhaps they trusted my seamanship more than I did. The hours crawled by slowly and often the helm slipped from my tired hands, until at last the first crack of dawn appeared and our fate was about to be decided. Would the rising sun unveil our goal, or would a waste of water surround us? This was the great question that roused us from our torpor and forced our leaden eyelids open. Above the crested waves appeared the delicate outline of palms; this was the first thing that cheered our hearts. Against this background our astonished eyes perceived wavering white spots, like a mirage, resembling houses; in between were delicate vertical lines, which were of course the masts of ships. Gradually the misty picture formed itself into the firmer outlines of Zanzibar. An hour later we could make out ahead the large house of O'Swald, and soon after, just as the first flashes of sunlight chased away the night, we were ashore on the sand in front of his door with the little boat that had rendered us such good service.

Before I started on my first trip I was exceedingly curious to know how moments of acute danger would affect me. Man's ability to control his nerves is not great, and courage seems to be a complicated matter. Even the different races of mankind vary in this respect; the hairs of a native of southern latitudes will stand on end easily. There are also different kinds of courage—an active and a passive courage regarding men, animals, elements, and circumstances. And an individual does not always have the same degree of courage, since the state of one's health, the consciousness of one's physical strength, and the actual condition of one's nervous system all play a part. Age, too, influences courage. Youth develops more active courage, whereas a man of mature age reflects more, shows greater passive pluck, and will probably boast of more cold blood in moments of peril.

One may conclude from what has been said above that Teleki, Chanler, and I were on much the same level. Given the same disposition, courage expresses itself in one case by greater violence and in another by dominating calm; what we lack ourselves, we respect in our companions. As far as age was concerned, Count Teleki was twelve years my senior, and I was as many years older than Chanler.[1] With Count Teleki I had been the younger and therefore the more heedless and care-defying. It did not take me long to find out what an enterprising, high-spirited American Mr. Chanler was, and I realized that on his expedition I would have to be the mother of wisdom. Later on it was indeed a sight to watch my young traveling companion running risks that were not always commensurate with the object to be achieved. He often needed to be cautioned.

It goes without saying that the three of us were different in other respects. Each had peculiarities with which the other had to reckon. However, these were not so great as to become matters of contention. I had made up my mind from the very beginning not to object to the small discomforts that might result from different dispositions and conceptions. My companions bore the great costs of the expeditions and were therefore entitled to expect me to conform to their ways. I had therefore determined that each should be happy in his own way insofar as this depended on me. I only took up another attitude when we dealt with essential questions concerning the expedition. But even in this respect I was amenable to argument.

I was not an inconvenient traveling companion. In opposition to the precepts prevailing at the time, Count Teleki was of the correct opinion that when traveling in the tropics, one must eat well and consume much meat in order to maintain one's strength. On the other hand, he found that one could do without a real breakfast so as not to delay the start of the caravan in the early morning. No doubt this habit dated back to his time of service as an officer, when a glass of brandy in the morning before going to drill was usually the only warming stimulant he could obtain. With Teleki our breakfast consisted of some weak cold coffee that had been brewed the night before, which the boy handed to us in a most unappetizing enameled goblet while we made a rapid toilet. I regularly poured away this "breakfast" because it utterly failed to tempt me and because I did not want to induce any of the men to taste it. One may imagine what a lusty appetite one develops after a march of six, seven, or ten hours, and in the meantime hunger could only be somewhat appeased by smoking innumerable pipes of tobacco. When the camp had been reached, it usually meant another long wait until provisions arrived and the goats and sheep were killed. Our mood during this period of waiting used to be a most explosive one, so that we avoided one another until steaming plates of canned pea soup made it advisable to put in an appearance.

In contrast, Chanler as an Anglo-Saxon was accustomed to a hearty breakfast, and for that reason he voted in favor of it. He alleged that one never knew how the day might end and whether one would be able to obtain a meal. One should therefore start the day's march strengthened by sustaining food so as to be able to face all emergencies. Our meals consisted chiefly of roasted or stewed meat of oxen, goats, sheep, or the game we had killed. Garnishings were for the greatest part lacking, especially during the first expedition. There was no bread at all, and ship's biscuit was a rare delicacy. A stiff, tasteless mash of durra flour was usually the only way in which our bodies received the necessary carbohydrates. Teleki's expedition carried a small quantity of sugar, Chanler's only saccharine; early on we therefore searched for honey. Wine and spirits were easily dispensed with, for one cannot carry a large amount of these on such expeditions. A monotonous diet of this kind produces a ravenous desire for carbohydrates which, lacking anything better, is appeased by the consumption of fats. We were capable of devouring quantities of fat that would have honored the appetite of an Eskimo. Once, without eating any bread, Teleki and I within two days devoured a cured side of bacon that Dr. Abbott gave us at Taveta.

During Chanler's expedition we were not reduced to as exclusive a meat diet. On that occasion we also encountered less game and were obliged to assure the nourishment of our caravan in another way. Count Teleki and I thrived on the exclusive meat diet. It did not agree as well with our men, however, though in time they grew accustomed to it. The fact that animal albumin is more nourishing than vegetable albumin and agrees better with the digestive system was once illustrated in a remarkable manner during Chanler's expedition. When we started out to discover the Lorian Lake, we took two loads of rice, tea, coffee, and other provisions destined for our personal use; our men and beasts of burden were loaded with beans, durra and manioc flour, and some maize grain. As luck would have it, the two porters bearing the provision destined for us soon deserted, and we were forced to live on the same diet as our men. It came to pass that since we were unable to find any game to hunt for an entire week, we had to content ourselves with beans boiled in water and with roast maize grain. It became evident that a European accustomed to a meat diet needs enormous quantities of vegetables in order to keep up to the mark. Three times a day we used to devour a plate heaped with beans, many times the rations of our men; naturally our digestive organs soon rebelled against these quantities. Only the roast maize grain became more palatable as time passed—the blacker it was roasted, the better. We never could get the grains roasted dark enough, however, and the cook was at last ordered to serve them half-charred. We never gave the matter much thought, but our organism clamored for it. Only later, when we learned what a great part carbon plays in digestive functions, did we understand that instinct had correctly guided us.

Our drink in all those years was the water that luck or chance allowed us to find—often a clouded, slimy liquid that every civilized man would have refused with disgust. An Arabic proverb says that the worst water is that which does not exist, and that is true. We often rejoiced to find a puddle, the dirty contents of which we drank with closed eyes and indrawn breath and which in spite of parching thirst one only managed to swallow by trying to think of something else. During the years I lived in Vienna after the first expedition I never passed the dirty Vienna River without thinking how nice it would have been in Africa to have had such good water at our disposal. Water was drunk as we found it; we had neither the time nor the patience to boil or filter it. Besides, every kind of filter was soon so choked up with dirt that it was in itself a source of nefarious germs. During the march we rarely drank at all; we soon learned merely to rinse our mouth with the tepid stuff and then to spit it out. All the more did we enjoy weak and hot, though rather cloudy, tea in the evenings. We grew as thin as whipping posts on this diet, but we felt perfectly fit. Not even the hottest day caused us to perspire, and even a march of sixteen hours failed to fatigue us. Often we had to start off again at the close of a hot day's march in order to shoot some big game for our hungry men or to ascertain from some height a detail necessary for the construction of our chart.

Our marches were made on foot. This is healthier than riding and more advantageous for scientific reasons. A horseman hesitates before dismounting for the sake of a beetle or a plant, reads the compass at rarer intervals, and jots down fewer remarks in his notebook. He is in every respect more indolent and lazy. I experienced this myself during Chanler's expedition, as long as the tsetse flies spared our ponies. In the bush, with its manifold surprises, a horseman is in greater danger than a pedestrian. It is therefore wiser to make these marches on foot. It is, of course, indispensable that one's legs be able to stand the strain and that one have good, serviceable shoes, preferably strong, thickly soled hobnailed laced boots. These protect the foot from the great heat of the soil and resist the often sharp-edged and glass-hard volcanic gravel. I found the common Upper Austrian mountain boot to be ideal. I have heard that Ernst Marno on his expeditions into the territory of the White and Blue Nile carried sixty pairs of light shoes with him. It is no wonder, then, that he often complained of blisters and sore feet.[2] During Chanler's expedition we had to pass through districts where sharp-edged stones would have ruined Marno's entire stock of shoes within a few days.

For the sake of avoiding trouble we wore our hair cut quite short, since one had to reckon with lice. During Teleki's expedition we had our heads shaved, a very disagreeable process, while on the second expedition our hair was kept short by means of a hair-cutting machine. A helmet of aloe fiber or a broad-brimmed double felt hat protected us against the sun's fierce rays, but none of these shapes is ideal. The stiff helmet hampers one when shooting, and the felt hat keeps the head too warm. Early on Chanler experimented with a turban, but he soon gave it up.

The territories through which we traveled on both expeditions were in general situated at a considerable height, were barren, and were therefore not unhealthy. As long as we remained in the heart of the continent, Teleki and I did not suffer from malaria, perhaps thanks to the good mosquito nets under which we slept. Teleki felt quite well during nearly the whole expedition and in every respect stood the hardships as well as anyone. The same would have been the case with me if I had not had the ill luck to come down with a severe case of dysentery, which nearly brought me to an early grave. I suffered from it for short intervals over four months, precisely during the most trying stage of our expedition through the enemy territory of Kikuyuland, a risky enterprise in itself. At that time I rode on a common gray donkey and often had to dismount in order to ease the painful dictates of nature, even though we were surrounded by warlike hordes of natives. The surging crowd of natives found this spectacle so astonishing that their war whoops regularly died away, and poisoned arrows were lowered in hands vibrating in the lust of battle. They evidently thought that a man who had the unconcern to act as I did must surely be endowed with supernatural faculties. In such moments it would have been a matter of utter indifference to me if loaded canon had been leveled at me. At the same time quite a number of our men also suffered from this terrible disease, and the majority died. As I was the one who doctored them, my confidence soon dwindled. None of the remedies I prescribed proved efficacious, and I soon gave up taking any medicine. Probably I owed my recovery to that fact, for *quod natura non sanat, non sanandum est* [What nature does not heal, is not healed]. On Chanler's expedition we knew that disinfecting irrigations are a sure remedy against dysentery, and thus we got rid of the trouble from the very outset. Chanler's case proved that the more mature man has more power of resistance and is therefore better suited for enterprises of this kind. Though never severely sick, he suffered more often from slight fevers and other temporary indispositions.

The greatest danger of a trip through Africa is connected with hunting, especially if, as was the case during our first expedition, shooting has to be resorted to as a means of replenishing the stores of the caravan. The African bush is rich in surprises. The hunter never knows what game he may have to face in the next moment. He may start out to shoot a brace of guinea fowls and return with an elephant, a leopard, or a rhinoceros as booty. This is the great charm but also the great risk of tropical sport. During my first expedition, the task of furnishing the big caravan with the meat necessary for its consumption rested chiefly with Teleki, who was by far best suited to this duty. Trained for hunting from early boyhood, he had shot many a chamois, stag, bear, and wolf in the mountains near his home and had killed ibex in Spain, and he was therefore an experienced shot when he went to Africa. With regard to the necessary shooting outfit and the accessories for big-game hunting, he was far ahead of Chanler and myself, even concerning knowledge of a theoretical nature. Many things important for life in the bush he had acquired instinctively, and he had learned important tricks and feats from the old wood-cutters in the wild mountain ranges of his home. In all these matters Count Teleki was better trained than most travelers and sportsmen who made Africa their traveling ground before or after him. He had brought a number of wonderfully exact rifles from the well-known firm of Holland & Holland in London, which never left us in the lurch. They killed forty-two elephants, ninety-nine rhinoceroses, eighty-seven buffaloes, and a lot of other game, but I must add at once that every one of these animals was necessary for our subsistence. We had not one cartridge to spare for aimless shooting. Ammunition was the treasure we guarded most jealously. The password was "meat" and not "sport."[3] For this reason we did not go in for lion hunting, though we used to hear their roaring night by night and often caught fleeting glimpses of them. On both expeditions only two lions were shot; Count Teleki killed one, and young George Galvin the other. Big game elephants and buffalo demand the greatest sacrifices from the hunter; we soon ceased to fear rhinoceros, however great a first impression they may make upon a newcomer. A series of lucky shots is inclined to make one careless, however, and therein lies the greatest danger for the African hunter.

Before breaking up our camp on Lake Baringo in order to start toward the unknown north, where we discovered Lake Rudolf, we had to lay in a store of from 4,000 to 5,000 kilograms of dried game for provisioning the caravan, a matter that took weeks of shooting. The chief game sought was buffalo, rhinoceros, zebra, and antelope. Luckily there was game in undreamt-of abundance. Since I was laid up at the time with severe dysentery and our men were strictly forbidden to fire a single shot, it became Teleki's task to furnish this enormous quantity of meat. This involved no mean personal risk, as this shooting had to be done within a rather restricted area. When he returned from his daily task somewhat later than was his wont, I was often tormented not only by my racking physical pain, but also by the worry that I might never see my companion again.

Although my scientific activities prevented me from regularly participating in the shooting expeditions, there were nevertheless numerous opportunities, and I can look back on many a thrilling experience. Chance had it that on my first expedition I encountered a number of rhinoceroses, elephants, and giraffes earlier than Count Teleki, who was so keen on shooting, so that I was able to collect some experiences before he did. Quite at the beginning, not far from the coast, a rhinoceros once raced quite close by me, snorting as it rushed past. It was the first one I had ever seen, and I had not expected to meet such big game so soon. I must confess that I was considerably agitated at this first meeting; my excitement only subsided when the monster had reached a safe distance of a hundred yards or so. But then I revenged myself for the start it had given me by firing a shot after it.

In the course of our expedition to Mount Meru it became necessary for the first time to shoot game for the caravan. Teleki and I always went our separate way when shooting so as to cover more ground; we only shot a few elephants together later on, when we had recognized the dangerous nature of these pachyderms. It thus happened that on that day I crossed the brooklet near which we had camped, while Teleki wanted to try his luck this side of it. Luck favored me in far greater measure, however, for within one hour I had killed three rhinoceros. A fourth had passed by me so closely that I might have touched it, but I preferred to throw myself into the thorny bush as rapidly as possible to escape being trampled upon.

Count Teleki had not yet had the chance to fire on a rhinoceros when, later on, I hunted at the foot of the Kilimanjaro. I soon succeeded in shooting a zebra out of a herd that was moving along. My shot had hardly been fired when a couple of rhinoceros suddenly turned up and raced toward me as if joined in double harness. My companions quite rightly immediately took to their heels. Some sought cover behind the dead zebra or on top of a distant tree, and I, too, looked round for some protection. But there was none, and I had to sustain the adventure as best I could. I cannot deny that it cost me a tremendous effort of willpower to remain calm in the face of these monsters, who were approaching me with the speed of a railway engine, snorting violently and heading exactly in my direction. I had always known that flight in moments of danger was the worst policy and that one is better able to grapple with the situation if one faces it calmly. If it had been a question of one rhinoceros only—but two! I seized my elephant rifle, and in order to be sure not to waver or retreat, I dropped on one knee, convinced that only an absolutely straight shot could save me. To be sure of this, I had to allow the clumsy animals to approach very close to me. I awaited their onrush with my rifle cocked and finally pulled the trigger. Through the smoke I saw how the left animal was struck in the shoulder; it dropped but immediately rose again, and how both of them raced on past me at an arm's length. I felt I had experienced enough and did not fire after them. This situation would have impressed me even later on, when I had gained ample experience with rhinoceros, but at the time I was only a novice with regard to African hunting.

I have already mentioned that lion hunting scarcely tempted us. We caught many fleeting glimpses of these animals and left it to chance to add a lion's skin to our collection. When I had barely recovered from my dysentery and visited the bamboo region of Kenya while still weak, our little camp was surrounded one night by several roaring lions, which crept round us so closely that my men said they saw their outlines quite clearly by the flickering firelight. I myself was so sound asleep that I only heard of the incident the next morning. On the way back I wanted to present my thirty men with zebra meat as a reward for the hardships they had endured, and to that end I stalked a small herd of these animals while my men watched me from a little distance in keen anticipation. I had already raised my rifle and was just about to fire when a whistle made me look round. I saw my companions pointing excitedly toward a spot on my left. There, very close to me, were four lions who had been stalking the same herd of zebra. I regret to say that I only caught sight of my rivals when they were already in full flight beyond a gorge, their tails between their legs.

During a march Chanler once saw a lion enter one of the small patches of low-grown bush that were scattered over the landscape. He wanted to drive him out of this retreat and told our eleven Sudanese to undertake this task. To our surprise, these usually plucky men refused to do so. They swore that they would go after men or after any other wild beasts in any number, but they would have nothing to do with lions. They were *sheitans*—that is, devils. We put them to shame with our Zanzibaris, who without hesitation showed great courage and plunged into the bush with loud cries, searching in all directions. Chanler and I had posted ourselves at the outer end of the thicket at a small distance from each other with our rifles cocked, and we waited for the lion. The drive came to an end and the men were already quite close to us, but no lion issued from the bush on any side. Mysteriously, he seemed to have disappeared, and irritably we shouldered our rifles. We had hardly done so, however, when the lion rose up between Chanler and me in front of our drivers, and snarling savagely, it hid again in the next thicket with a few mighty bounds. We were on the march and in a hurry and therefore proceeded on our way.

During my transportation through Ukambani, after having been wounded by the rhino, we came to a place where two years before an Englishman had, so he said, seen twenty-eight lions. He related how the sight of so many regal animals had been so impressive and overpowering that he did not dare fire on them. When I heard this account I was inclined to think it a traveler's yarn; since I knew that Juma, my boy servant who had accompanied me on all my travels, had been the Englishman's servant, I asked him on the spot, without mentioning any numbers, how many lions they had seen on that day. My solemn-faced Juma reflected and then counted on his fingers: so many males, so many females, and so many cubs. The number tallied. Juma never told a lie.

Buffalo have a tough life and are vengeful, so that hunting them is extremely dangerous. The greatest share of the eight of these animals that were killed during the first expedition were victims of Count Teleki's fine shots. I had been very sick when we were in the main buffalo district, and we carried only one 577 Express rifle, the only weapon then in use that was suited for shooting buffalo. Once, after taking cover behind a white ant hill, I fired five shots at a buffalo bull from a distance of a hundred yards, but from the smaller 500-caliber Express rifle. Each bullet hit exactly the right spot, yet the buffalo did not flinch and eyed me so calmly that I had the feeling I was firing at an armored plate. After the fifth shot it fled. I found it later standing in an impenetrable bush thicket with its head turned away at about twenty-five paces; I therefore purposely grazed his spine with a shot. This felled him, and I then gave him the coup de grâce.

Once, during my visit to the bamboo region of Kenya, when issuing from the thicket onto a small clearing, I happened on an old, solitary buffalo bull lying in the grass. When he caught sight of me he rose slowly, stood there ponderously, and eyed me quietly. I happened to have at hand the 8-caliber ele-phant rifle, so I fired at his shoulder blade and rolled him over like a hare, so that for a moment he lay on his back with his legs in the air. I thought he was dead and was about to approach him when Maktubu, Teleki's constant com-panion on his hunting expeditions, whispered to me, "Taratibu bwana"—"Be careful, sir." The same instant the animal was on his feet again as if it had never been wounded. I emptied my second barrel, and again the animal broke down, only to rise once more and move off slowly, hidden by vegetation. The mo-ment he came in sight again he received another shot from the 577 Express rifle, which rolled him over for the third time. Nevertheless, the tough devil managed to rise and disappeared into the bamboo thicket. After such an aston-ishing experience, the greatest care became imperative. We allowed a full half hour to pass before we dared to take up his trail. It was not difficult to find it, for we had but to follow the color, but the bamboo stalks stood as closely as grass blades, and the thicket was too difficult to penetrate. Our attempt being too dangerous, we soon gave it up.

As far as I can remember, buffalo occasioned the maximum of passive cour-age that was ever required of us. After several hours of hunting one morning I had, at some distance from our camp and not far from a reed-grown swamp, killed a buffalo bull after a hard struggle and had used up all my cartridges. I left my men behind in order that they might cut up the buffalo and bring in the meat, and alone and empty-handed I started to walk back to the camp along the edge of the swamp. Plunged in thoughts about the extraordinary harshness of the buffalo's life and of the touching fidelity with which a buffalo cow had stuck to her mate to the last, I had not yet gotten very far on my way when suddenly the rushes parted a few steps ahead of me, disclosing the heavily armed head of a buffalo bull, which eyed me with some astonishment. My path lay close to the edge of the swamp, a few feet past the buffalo. I don't know why just at that moment I was struck with the thought that I must continue to walk on at the same pace and that I would be lost if I turned back or in any way hesitated. At the time I remembered that on an occasion of this kind one must not look one's opponent in the eyes, for the human gaze irritates wild animals and makes them wilder still. I therefore continued to walk on, feeling more like a lifeless phantom than a human being, staring straight in front of me with feel-ings I cannot describe. When at last I had happily gone by the buffalo, I imag-ined I felt the wicked glare of his eyes piercing my back, and I therefore tried to listen with special care to what he was doing. After about twenty paces I heard a rustle, dared to throw a rapid glance over my shoulder, and discovered that the buffalo had, thank God, disappeared. I had not gone much farther and my heart was still beating audibly when, at about ten or twelve yards in front of me, the border of rushes again parted and an ugly, blackish-brown buffalo issued forth, eyed me suspiciously, walked slowly around me, and then to my relief trotted off. This time I had of course shortened my steps. As I heard later, this second buffalo had trotted on straight toward the animal I had killed and, excited by the scent of blood, had thrown himself on my men, forcing them to take refuge in the trees, where he beleaguered them for half an hour before he finally moved off. Possibly my escape was due to the direction of the wind. The two animals had come out of the swamp without any evil intent, the first perhaps prompted by curiosity; certainly an irritating emanation on my part excited them.

During the few years that lay between my two African expeditions, rinderpest had not only decimated the stock of domestic cattle of East Africa but had also played havoc with the game, especially the buffalo. During Chanler's expedition I caught only one or two fleeting glimpses of buffalo, so fleeting indeed that I cannot even be sure of the identification. On the Guaso Nyiro River Chanler encountered a little herd and was able to shoot, but he did not manage to kill a one of them. Wandorobbo told us that we would find a small herd of buffalo on Lollokwui (Lolokwi) Mountain, which has the form of a plateau. We found thousands of skulls, chiefly of buffalo, but also of different kinds of antelope, bleaching on the steppe.

With the big, heavy calibers that were in use at the time it was possible from close quarters to ward off, if not immediately to kill, attacking big game. A buffalo or a rhinoceros thought twice before attacking again after having been greeted with an 8–caliber bullet *à bout portant* [point-blank]. Only the elephant in that case perhaps would shake his head a little but continue advancing on his victim, trying to seize it and trample it to death. For that reason hunting African elephants is comparatively the most dangerous sport. The hunter is nearly powerless when faced by the attack of an elephant that is rushing toward him. It is true that there is one tiny spot on his head—where the trunk joins the front—where the bullet can penetrate into the brain if the head is bent at a certain angle. But this is only a lucky shot, and most sportsmen contest its possibility. Fortunately I was once successful with such a shot, as otherwise Teleki and I would probably have been done for. We had some bad experiences in shooting elephants on the shoulder blade, and we soon went in for the unerring deadly shot in the temple. In order to fire this shot, however, one has to approach very close, and therein lies a certain danger. Luckily for the hunter, not every elephant, just like not every lion or buffalo, is aggressive, but one can never tell in advance. We had many an exciting adventure with these animals, and we felt more and more convinced that this kind of sport demanded great precaution. Of the forty-two elephants killed during Teleki's expedition, six played us some fine tricks. These apparently clumsy animals can be as rapid as lightning and as nimble as cats.

In the preceding statements I have been speaking of the rifles of the period. Because we used black powder, these lacked by far the penetrating force of modern arms used with smokeless powder. A modern sportsman armed with the up-to-date light Cordite rifle is far better off than we were at that time. During Chanler's expedition we also carried, however, a number of normal 7-mm Mannlicher rifles for non-sporting purposes, for which smokeless powder and solid bullets covered with a nickel mantle were used. We had already been in the interior for a long time when I started out one morning with a few men to climb a distant peak, from which I hoped to gain considerable data for map making. On my way I met a pair of rhinoceros, one standing, the other lying beside it in the grass. As we did not require any meat, I had the idea of taking advantage of this opportunity for experimental shooting. Thus I stopped, and from a distance of thirty yards I fired at the shoulder of the standing animal. The rhinoceros that was hit gave a squeal such as I had never heard before, spun round several times, and then slowly trotted off. Its companion jumped up at the sound of the detonation, remained rooted to the spot for a moment, and then followed its wounded companion, trotting along on its farther side. When they were covering each other exactly I quickly fired a second shot at the shoulder blade of the animal already wounded in order to ascertain the projectile's effect on one animal after having perforated the other. To my surprise, the second rhinoceros now also squealed, spun round in the same way as the first, and then squatted down, evidently seriously wounded. The first animal was soon dead, and I gave the other one the coup de grâce.

On another occasion on Chanler's expedition I had the chance to test the effect of the Mannlicher rifle on elephants. We were at that time north of the Guaso Nyiro, marching through flat, open country with an unlimited view on all sides. I could not let this favorable opportunity pass without making drawings of all the visible peaks and fixing their bearings. The large bearing compass was taken out, and I had plenty of work for the next hour, while the caravan moved on unhampered. Juma, my faithful boy, slept near me in the sand. After one half of the horizon was finished I turned the instrument in the opposite direction, and to my surprise I saw five elephants at a distance of about 400 yards, who hurriedly trotted in single file along a low bush thicket. Full of astonishment, I watched the animals for a few seconds. Then, more out of daredevilry than anything else, I seized the Mannlicher rifle and emptied its five shots as quickly as possible, aiming at the flank of the largest and strongest elephant. The distance may have varied between 500 and 600 yards. Hearing the shots, the animals veered round into the bush to seek cover and soon disappeared. The elephant I had hit showed no effect, and when I had done with my cartographic work, prompted by mere curiosity I walked to the spot where the elephants had been and followed the trail, which was easily recognizable in the sand. I had hardly penetrated the light bush thicket when I saw the dead elephant lying with his trunk and head on a bush. In spite of careful examination I could not ascertain any of the spots at which the bullets had entered or come out. When a few weeks later we reached Wandorobbo natives near the Loroghi Mountains, who were practically starving and suffering great want, I perceived two wandering elephants at which, because of the great distance of 200 to 300 yards, I could only fire with the Mannlicher rifle. To the great delight of the natives, we found these two animals dead, close to the place where they had been shot. Thus this little rifle, which one could fire off holding it with one hand, proved itself a quite formidable and on certain occasions an invaluable arm. In the course of time I killed another elephant and quite a number of rhinoceros with it, the latter as a rule when they attacked and rushed toward me, snorting and at a clumsy gallop. Hit at the right spot in the left shoulder, they collapsed each time as if struck by lightning, the bullet having transpierced their entire length.

A repeater compared to a double-barreled rifle is at a great disadvantage. With the latter one can immediately fire a second shot without reflecting, while the repeater requires a certain amount of time, which is not always available. One day in the Loroghi mountain range I had this experience after having followed the fresh trail of a single elephant, which had led me first downhill and then round again uphill to the place whence I had started, which consisted of a rocky flat, surrounded on three sides by thick bushes. Here the trail was lost. The animal no doubt had scented us and strayed off. I told this to my men, turning to them while I placed my rifle near me on the ground. At the same moment a vicious, shrill trumpeting struck my ear, the foliage parted, and from a distance of about twenty yards an elephant cow furiously rushed at me with outspread ears. There was barely time for a quick shot aimed straight at the forehead, which the animal answered with even shriller trumpeting and increased vehemence. It was impossible to repeat the shot, and a sauve-qui-peut being the only thing to be done, I ran off at a right angle as fast as I could. I soon perceived that the trumpeting did not follow me and turned back. My companions had, thank heavens, disappeared; only the elephant stood at the edge of the clearing at a distance of fifty yards, swaying to and fro so strongly that I expected it to drop at any moment. I thought it was dying and, alas, did not fire, though there would have been ample time. Then it quite suddenly disappeared downhill so quickly that all I could do was to fire a badly aimed shot at its side. Because this elephant had splendid tusks, we followed its trail for two days for fifteen miles, until it reached a broad, rushing stream, where we had to give up further pursuit as hopeless. The native guide of my party got such a fright on this occasion that he ran back for many miles as fast as his legs could carry him until he reached Chanler's camp, to whom he described my death in such detail that my companion could hardly doubt that I had met an untimely end.

The results obtained with the Mannlicher rifle caused Mr. Chanler, when still in Africa, to send a report on the matter to *The Field*, a well-known sporting periodical. One can hardly imagine the consternation this bomb, directed against the English rifle market, caused in interested circles. The firms had adapted their workshops for big calibers, had purchased patents, and had spent large sums on advertising—in fact had raised the art of big-bore rifle-making in England to a fine art. Now all this was to be jeopardized by a rifle that one could get for a few shillings! The danger was too great. The sportsmen of the whole world were asked to express an opinion, and for a while this subject filled the columns of *The Field*. This, however, did not help the English rifle makers. They had to change their methods and convert to small bores and to smokeless powder. No doubt this would have happened in due time without our interference, but as it was, Chanler's expedition had the merit of providing the first incentive.[4]

The natives of the territories through which we traveled impressed us less than the great quantities of game; they in no respect appeared to be on a higher plane of civilization, as was to be expected from nomadic tribes. The low level of their civilization was defined in particular by their very vague conception of the deity. As concerns the ethics of the natives we met, however, I can only say that we never made the slightest observation contrary to morality. Until their marriage the Masai girls live away from the house of their parents with the moran—the warriors—in separate kraals in charming free community. Such is the custom there. But even these moran kraals only showed scenes far more reminiscent of *Paul et Virginie*[5] than certain streets in our large cities. One day in the lands of the Turkana we saw among the girls who visited our camp a young creature who wore two instead of only one of the little petticoats that were the fashion there. It took us a long time to persuade the young beauty to part with the one dispensable article of clothing for a number of fine glass beads. But barely an hour later she returned and insisted on undoing the bargain, being bitterly ashamed of having given us this intimate item of her toilet. In Europe we were often asked whether the fair sex in Africa deserved this name. It is, of course, impossible to draw a parallel between the white and the black races. To us they certainly were not tempting, although I admit that their evenly brown skin, with its soft velvety gloss, is not unattractive, and as the dark coloring in a certain sense has the effect of clothing, the scantily clad savages therefore do not make an obnoxious impression of nudity. Speaking of beauty, one can only refer to young girls; they fade very early, and at a more advanced age they often look hideous. We saw well-proportioned figures with splendidly developed extremities and fine busts, but imagine the whole, smeared with a coat of rancid terra-cotta–colored grease![6]

The impression we Europeans had upon the natives varied. In the coastal districts they often admired our light, sunburned skin. Far in the interior, on the other hand, where no white man had yet penetrated, the natives often turned from us in disgust, a dislike that only disappeared in the course of time, when they realized that we belonged to another race of men and were not niggers [sic] who had been discolored by leprosy. We cannot state that we made any particular impression on the young women of the country. I am inclined to think that the two African expeditions of which I speak were the only ones that consisted exclusively of men and had no women in their train. This astonished some of the natives, and for that reason the Rendille treated us rather disparagingly. None of them could understand why we had no females in our caravan. We did not always meet with a friendly reception on the part of all the peoples we visited, and though we were always animated by a sincere desire to maintain peace, this was not always possible. On the first expedition it was the Kikuyu, and on the second it was the Meru living on the west slope of the Jombeni (Nyambeni) Mountains who forced us to resort to arms. This was not undertaken on our part for any frivolous reasons; one may well believe that we would have preferred to act as apostles of peace in the heart of Africa. In truth, it is no pleasure to fire with repeaters and other modern rifles into a crowd of defense-less natives.

There are many other things I might still relate concerning Africa, the black and white men we met, and the explorers who, before and after us, visited this part of the world. I will not dwell on these matters, however, which, though they preoccupy me greatly, are not everyone's affair, and will therefore close this chapter, which deals with the most important period of my life. I feel all the more prompted to do so because our opinions and hopes regarding the future development of Africa have not, as a consequence of the Great War, been realized.

8

At Sea Again
(1894–1899)

F or more than eight years I had been away from the navy and had led a free life, responsible only to myself and God for my actions. Now I again entered into the routine of the navy as a subaltern officer and had to remember the superior and inferior order of things and regard the most secondary duties as extremely important. It was a bitter pill, but it had to be swallowed. Added to this, my professional ability had hardly increased during my absence, and there was much I had forgotten. Moreover, the navy had not stood still in all these years, and many an innovation of which I had no idea had been introduced in the meanwhile. I therefore looked forward to the future with much uncertainty. Fortunately the naval commander in chief, Vice Admiral Baron Sterneck, made the bitter pill more palatable by appointing me gunnery and watch officer of the corvette *Donau*, which was just being outfitted and was destined to start on a cruise in the Atlantic in the fall of 1894 with the new midshipmen on board. I was thus introduced to conditions that were as new to the others as they were to me, so that it was easier for me to adapt. I would also have a period of time at my disposal to refresh my acquaintance with the requirements of the service. As we were to sail for countries and ports that were unknown to me, my last gold sovereign gone from my purse, I was not displeased to turn my back on Vienna.

Pola seemed strange at first, and I found it difficult to feel at home in the company of my brother officers. I met with little interest in the matters that had completely occupied me for many years, and I was hardly asked about my experiences and adventures. The visitors to the casino and its coffeehouse were far more interested in their games, and there were very few among my comrades who really knew where I had been for so long. I think that the publisher of my travel book did not sell a single copy in Pola.

The corvette *Donau* was not the boat of the same name on which I had made my first cruise as a midshipman. The former, an unfortunate construction, had been hulked long ago. The new *Donau*, painted a snowy white that suited a ship going to the tropics, was just being equipped and laid to a buoy under the command of her executive officer, Lieutenant Lazar Schukic. This officer was a typical

Croat in that he was an excellent sailor, well versed in all technical fields. I had been with him on board the small ironclad *Kaiser Max* as a midshipman many years earlier and had found him a manly, energetic figure and a good comrade. I knew that he would be a friend on whom I could rely in case of need. The commander of the ship was a Captain von Rottauscher, one of the more experienced mariners in our navy, who possessed many good qualities. The rest of the wardroom was made up of pleasant fellows, so that I expected a quiet and agreeable voyage, which indeed proved to be the case.

The hour of departure finally struck. The ship left the harbor under steam, but once in open waters she set her white sails and trusted to a fair wind. In our navy at that time, great stress was put on full-rigged ships using their sails as much as possible, and captains were praised or criticized accordingly. This was done not because sailing provided the crew with better professional training, but because of the cost of coal. This was a fallacy, however, since the continual use and wear of sails and rigging was by no means more economical. While still in sight of Pola, therefore, we strove to show how obediently the *Donau* was following instructions. It seemed to me that we were too rash about it. In my young days I had had to work sails, but that was long ago, and what I had known about it was more of a theoretical than a practical nature. I had never before had to command a sail exercise, and now as watch officer I was supposed to do so independently and to be responsible for the weal and woe of the ship, by day and by night, in every kind of weather. The sea was smooth, however, and the breeze was light, and since I was the oldest watch officer, my turn only came at eight o'clock next morning. I therefore slept calmly the whole night until I was suddenly awakened by a dragging of ropes on deck. To my considerable alarm, I heard the mate tell me that the studding sails would be ready by eight o'clock. What was he saying? I had not the faintest idea of how studding sails were set, and muttering to myself, I jumped up and buried myself in one of the maneuver books. When eight bells sounded, I stepped onto the bridge, and when I received the order to set all studding sails on starboard, I complied with a natural air, as if I had done nothing else all my life.

This really was the only time that I could have made a fool of myself. As a rule a summer cruise does not require much seamanship, and a few months are enough to gain the necessary practical experience. To tell the truth, with the exception of the old hands, the officers in most navies are only theorists in sailing matters. Average seamanship such as is generally required, apart from exceptional cases, can be acquired in a comparatively short time with a little good will and a modest amount of brains. But that, of course, does not suffice if it is a question of handling critical situations or when one has only old and worn equipment to work with. Then special experience and practice are essential.

Our voyage took us through the Straits of Messina to Gibraltar, and we touched Tenerife, Dakar, Sierra Leone, Cape Coast Castle, Lagos, Victoria, and the Cameroons. On the whole our cruise was uneventful. Having lived so many years in East Africa and witnessed the influence of Mohammedanism on the character and living conditions of the native population, I was interested in seeing its counterpart, the development of these people under western influence. A naval officer whose time is filled up by many duties does not have much leisure during the usually short calls in port, and as a rule he can only make superficial observations. My first impression was an unfavorable one. The western niggers [sic] may perhaps be better educated and more civilized, but they certainly are not more sympathetic than their brothers in the east, whose customs and traits of character often struck me as unpleasant. East Africa, with its patriarchal, Arabic conditions of life, is a paradise for the black population compared to the west, this in spite of slavery—which by the way, is not half as bad as is usually thought. What one witnesses here in the way of civilization gives the impression of a poor and superficial imitation of our European customs, with no real depth, no doubt because our ethical conceptions correspond less to the life that the blacks lead under different climatic and material conditions. Of course the niggers [sic] in East Africa are no more true Mohammedans than their brothers in the west are true Christians. Even Mohammedanism does not penetrate to the depths of their primitive souls.

The year 1894 came to a close as we left the islands São Tomé and Principe, and this also ended the African part of our cruise. New Year's Eve found us under sail on a smooth sea with a light breeze, the course heading to Brazil. The last night of the year used to be very gay on board Austrian men-of-war. I knew this and retired to my cabin at eight o'clock, since my watch began at midnight. I wanted to have my full sleep and be quite sober. Midnight came. I took the bridge, the preceding officer delivered me the watch, the bell sounded, and the year turned. With the last stroke of the bell, the traditional pandemonium began. The captain stood aft, and round him crowded the officers, midshipmen, and sailors, wishing him a happy New Year and congratulating one another in the best of humor. All this was deadened by the frightful noise made by the men's clanging and banging of hundreds of pots and pans in order, according to an old tradition, to chase away the old year—as if the new one was so certain to be better. Officers and midshipmen lifted their champagne glasses, toasting the captain and crying "Prosit, Prosit!" again and again. Then came the boatswains, the mates, petty officers, and sailors, who marched up to the captain with their glasses full of Dalmatian red wine, shouting "Hurra!" This lasted a good while and gave the impression of a complete dissolution of the usual discipline and strictly observed etiquette. The sight of this crowd, more or less under the influence of liquor, was to a cool and sober observer not very favorable, and after having let them have their fling for a quarter of an hour I collared the first bugler and ordered him—without regard to the superiors who were present—to sound the tattoo. This had the sobering effect of a dash of cold water. The captain retired, the crowd dissolved, and all was soon quiet.

Bahia was the only South American place we touched. There we had to conduct the semiannual gun practice, which kept me, as gunnery officer, rather busy. I never went on shore and saw nothing of the town. Every morning the ship made up steam and went farther into the great bay from which the place derives its name, there to do the gun practice, which was carried out from the moving ship toward a floating target. In the afternoon we returned to our old anchorage opposite the town.

Soon thereafter we set out on our trip across the ocean to South Africa. Followed by albatrosses and frigate birds, we at last came in sight of Table Mountain and Cape Town. Under the guidance of the port pilot the ship was taken to one of the piers and fastened with foot-thick hawsers. I had private letters of introduction to the governor, General Goodenough, whose wife was an Austrian, Countess Kinsky.[1] I therefore spent most of my time in government circles, which somewhat curtailed my liberty; I had less contact with the remainder of society than my brother officers. I had reason enough to envy them because they met quite a number of young ladies who could make a sailor's heart beat faster. But I was charmingly received by General Goodenough and his wife and daughter. The general was a grave-looking but attentive and amiable officer who had lost his left arm in India. A very scientific man, he drew my attention to the observatory directed by the famous astronomer David Gill, which was situated in the neighborhood of Cape Town;[2] he also arranged my visit there. Over many years Gill was extraordinarily active in the domain of practical astronomy and geodetics. Science owes much to him, among other things the complete photographic survey of the southern sky, a work of monumental size and importance. For several hours this famous and yet unaffected man accompanied me through his extensive observatory and did not tire of explaining every detail. He also showed great interest in my activity in Africa insofar as it touched his domain. For example, he explained to me why I did not get exact longitudes by observations of the eclipses of the moons of Jupiter. He even begged me to let him know whenever I should undertake another expedition into the interior of Africa so that he might arrange to have parallel observations made of all intervening eclipses of Jupiter's moons at his observatory and other great observatories for the control of the observations that I might make.

For many on board, every parting after a longer sojourn is combined with a bitter pang. When we left the hospitable Table Bay, a good deal of sighing and groaning went on in the officers' mess room, which would have been touching had it not been ridiculously serious. The southeast trade wind soon brought us to St. Helena, our next destination. That strong current of air passes over this barren, uninviting island all year round, covering the sky with heavy banks of clouds and making the island a cold and inhospitable spot in spite of the semitropical latitude. I can well imagine with what feelings of disgust the ever-shivering Napoleon must have felt when he set foot on this place of banishment. As long as one remains in protected Jamestown, which is situated in a narrow valley, the climate is bearable. But higher up on the plateau, where Longwood lies exposed to wind and weather, one is filled with sincere pity for the great Corsican—still more when one sees the modest, inadequate little houses in which he spent his exile.

I visited Longwood in the company of the captain. Arriving there, we saw a young lady near one of the houses in which Napoleon had lived and, a little farther away, another young girl. They declared their readiness to show us over the place and took us to the several small rooms of the house, all covered with plain, brown wallpaper. Thanks to the care of the French government, these are kept in the same condition as they were in Napoleon's time. There was no furniture, but in the mortuary chamber there was a copy of Napoleon's death mask. The young girls then took us to Napoleon's original burial place, which lies a little lower down, in a protected site near a spring. The weeping willows shown in old pictures of this place had disappeared long ago, and only a few young grafts of the mother tree still stand. Several cypresses now surround the simple iron railing that encompasses the grave.

From St. Helena we sailed to St. Lucia and then to the sunny island of Martinique. There we admired the beautiful marble monument of the Empress Josephine, surrounded by a group of magnificent palm trees, some of which have since been split by a hurricane. We also threw a glance at the fine-eyed local girls, who are particularly attractive and engaging. The colored population of the island is much better looking than that of the other Antilles, and this is no accident. Long ago the French allegedly transplanted the most handsome female types of their West African colonies to Martinique, a fact one willingly believes.

On leaving Martinique we stopped for only a few hours on the English islands of Nevis and St. Kitts on our way to New York, where I was again to meet my traveling companion, Mr. William Astor Chanler. The ship was scheduled to stay there for three weeks, and the captain, who was kindly disposed toward me, gave me leave and complete liberty for that time. As one may imagine, I looked forward to these days with considerable agitation. The corvette had hardly cast anchor when Mr. Chanler came on board with a beaming smile and shook my hand. He had all sorts of plans for me in a grand American style. He wanted to show me New York at its best; to introduce me to all his relatives, many prominent men, and, of course, some American beauties; and also to give no end of grand dinners in my honor. The mere enumeration of his plans frightened me. He had even leased a fine sailing yacht for when we tired of city life. We soon left the ship, and while we sauntered through the streets arm in arm, my friend developed his plans, which grew bolder and wilder as he spoke, until I finally protested. His plans were unlimited, and how should I manage on the £75 I had managed to save for New York? Thereupon he slyly smiled and told me to throw my treasure into the lap of some pretty girl and not to talk any more about money. Things had to be carried out just as my friend had planned them, and in his honor and in honor of the country of which he was so proud, I had to dance to his tune. All I can tell of these three maddest weeks of my life is that we lived royally, untroubled by care, as is possible only for American millionaires. One splendid dinner followed another, and finally I did not even ask which nabob of Fifth Avenue had been my host. From time to time we had clearer moments in which we met serious men, prominent politicians, famous travelers, sportsmen, and also a great artist, but this was not the rule.

One day we went to Rokeby on the Hudson River, the old family seat of the Chanlers, to visit his three sisters. Of these the eldest, Miss Elizabeth, impressed me most by her fascinating character. Once she took me aside and implored me to persuade her brother William to undertake another African expedition and to accompany him. I took the liberty of pointing out the dangers associated with an expedition of this kind, which were greater for her high-spirited brother than for a man of calmer temperament. The young lady thereupon drew herself up—she seemed actually to grow—and replied with glowing eyes, "I'd rather see him die gloriously in Africa than lead a dissipated life in New York." She was quite Roman. At dinner in the company of the three still unmarried sisters and one of their lady friends, the conversation turned to capital executions. I permitted myself to ask whether female criminals were also hanged in America, the proverbial paradise of women. This remark caused a storm such as I have never witnessed in so fair a company. "Hang? Hang?" was the cry that broke out on every side, while excited girlish faces and furious glances were leveled at me. I did not know at first against which paragraph of the American code of gallantry I had sinned, but I was soon to be told. "Do we women not know what we are doing?" said one of the young ladies. Another exclaimed, "Are we intellectually inferior to men?" And the third murmured something like, "We are just as good. Why should we not be hanged?" So that was it. I excused myself as best I could, begging them to forgive my ignorance of the fact that American ladies were so fond of being hanged.

On another day we traveled to Washington, did a lot of sightseeing, and met a good many people, but all in a hurry. With greater leisure we inspected the admirable Smithsonian Institution. What impressed me most, besides the serious work of research done there, was the great quantity of natural history specimens that came from the before-mentioned Dr. Abbott. Nearly every second or third specimen was marked "presented by Dr. Abbott."[3] For several decades this remarkable man had explored large parts of the globe in a most thorough manner; science is indebted to him for the knowledge of many new kinds of smaller animals. His uninterrupted life in the wilderness, in the exclusive company of natives, finally made him little suited to civilized conditions. He had long ago broken all ties with the former; letters from his friends either did not reach him or were left unanswered.

I once had the opportunity to see the celebrated sculptor [Augustus] Saint-Gaudens at work. He was modeling the bust of my traveling companion, which he finished in an uninterrupted session lasting thirteen hours. Mr. Chanler was allowed to eat a few mouthfuls while the artist went on working feverishly, talking all the while in order to keep my friend in an animated disposition. I noticed that his eyes hardly ever rested on the block of clay that he was forming and that he only rarely took some measurements. When I expressed my astonishment, he said that he worked with his heart, which directed his hands. On another occasion I accepted an invitation by Mr. Theodore Roosevelt, then the much-feared police commissioner of New York, to visit him on Long Island at Oyster Bay. I saw this man in his study, surrounded by innumerable books; I admired his universal knowledge, untiring energy, intellectual perseverance, and joy of work, to which he could devote himself undisturbed, being well-cared-for by his charming wife. Later on I was not astonished when he was elected president of the United States.

Whenever we needed some rest during our many and varied experiences, my friend and I spent a couple of hours at sea on board the sailing yacht. When finally my ship left New York for Newport, I made the cruise with Mr. Chanler. Newport is famous for its marvelous country houses belonging to the upper crust. It is also a naval base and the seat of a college for the higher instruction of naval officers. Here my free life came to an end. I had to live on board and, in addition to performing other duties, inspect the before-mentioned naval school and report on it. I therefore could not visit my friend Chanler and his elder married brother Winthrop in the latter's country house as often as I wished. I spent all my free time in this distinguished circle, over which the smart lady of the house presided with particular charm, until this period came to an end and we sailed home by way of the Azores.

Our cruise ended with our arrival at Pola on October 4, 1895. This voyage had contained some charming days. Fourteen months had passed in untroubled harmony, and it was all the more regrettable that a false note should be struck at the very end. Somewhere, either in Bahia or in Cape Town, the ship had struck ground. Such incidents had come to the knowledge of the Admiralty, having probably been mentioned in private letters home. The captain had passed over them in silence in his reports, however, and this circumstance was used against him. Many people gladly seize upon any suitable opportunity to rid themselves of a senior ahead of them when there is a chance of doing so, and they now made a mountain of a molehill. To this came another matter that was fatal to the captain. At Cape Town he had been invited to a solemn Bismarck celebration and had, by request, allowed the ship's band to perform the musical part of the ceremony. Among the pieces played on this occasion was the Rákóczi March, a tune commemorating the revolutionary days of Hungary, which for that reason was forbidden in military circles. Unaware of this, the captain had attached to his report a copy of the musical program.

The emperor, to whom the reports of ships on mission were regularly submitted and whose eye nothing escaped, was extremely annoyed to find the offensive march on the program and had demanded the captain's immediate recall. It required great persuasion to make His Majesty desist from this wish. The unfortunate man did not enjoy the imperial favor; this circumstance probably contributed to the inconsiderate proceedings that followed. The ship having been immediately ordered to dock, it turned out that several copper sheets were missing and that the false keel was injured to some extent. The captain was thereupon court-martialed. He had the satisfaction of seeing all the officers of the *Donau* make statements in his favor under oath. But this was of no avail; his fate had been decided long ago. But what hurt him and every decent officer in the navy was the offensive, nay, brutal style of the decree, with its note of distrust, that communicated his transfer onto the retired list.

My next assignment was an indifferent one. I was attached to the naval technical board, a sinecure that lasted five months and from which I was released in March 1896 when I was appointed to the ironclad *Tegetthoff* as officer of the deck. The *Tegetthoff* was the flagship of the officer commanding the squadron, Vice Admiral Baron Spaun. The flag captain's name was Sachs, and the executive was Commander Anton Haus.[4] As the presumptive commander in chief of the navy, Vice Admiral Spaun was the permanent commanding officer of the summer squadrons, which were set up every year during the three hottest months for the instruction of captains, officers, and crews. The program usually consisted of all sorts of drills and of signaling, frequent maneuvering, and executing tactical problems. At the end, the annual program of firing practice and torpedo launching was carried out. These three months were, as a rule, a hard time for all on board.

Vice Admiral Spaun had had the chance to see and experience more than any other officer of our navy. For many years he had been the tutor and later the chamberlain-in-waiting of Archduke Carl Stephen, who, as a member of the imperial family serving in the navy, had been promoted more rapidly than ordinary mortals to the rank of rear admiral.[5] Thereafter Spaun had been naval attaché in London for an exceptionally long time. In a word, without having seen much practical service or exhausted himself in the fulfillment of inferior duties, he had attained in the most pleasant way possible not only high rank, but also a great reputation. As the permanent companion of a very clever and intelligent member of the imperial house who was passionately interested in naval matters, he had had many opportunities to see things that were not offered to the ordinary officer. No doubt his long sojourn in England and his intercourse with old admirals and experienced mariners had given him valuable insight into naval matters. Spaun was very popular in all the ranks, and justly so, for he was an agreeable and pleasant companion who felt at home in every circle. He never acted as a killjoy or hurt anybody's feelings, and he was exceedingly courteous both to his superiors and his subordinates. Spaun had great experience in the handling of a fleet, and it filled me with satisfaction to be on board his flagship.

The admiral came on board one afternoon toward five o'clock and assumed command of the squadron in a matter-of-fact fashion, so that the hoisting of the vice admiral's flag, followed by the thunder of the guns, was the only solemn moment. The officers and men then retired. Being officer of the deck in harbor, I stood about idly on the quarter deck and noticed the admiral standing bareheaded and undecided in the doorway of his cabin with a questioning expression on his face. I asked him what his wishes were. "Could I have an electrician?" "Certainly, Your Excellency. What for? Can I see to it?" He led me through the admiral's cabin to the balcony that ran round the stern of the ship and pointed out that no arrangements had been made for lighting. "Do you see? I should like to have a light fixed here." "Of course, there must be a light. Your Excellency must be able to read at night." "Oh no," was his reply. "I only want to drink my beer here in the evening." Though I knew that Spaun was fond of the bottle, I had not expected that his first care would be in that direction.

Concerning this period of sea service I have little to tell. It was by no means as hard as I expected; on the contrary, things went quite smoothly. We first spent two peaceful weeks on the roadstead of Fasana (Fazana), now and then putting to sea, returning again to our anchorage after a few hours' fleet maneuvering. I rather liked this kind of life. I was thus introduced in the most pleasant manner to tactics, duties in squadron, and the signal service, all areas in which my knowledge and experience were deficient. My other duties as officer of the deck on board an ironclad mostly consisted in rowing drill on two afternoons every week.

Anton Haus, the executive officer who was later to become the first "Grand Admiral" of our navy, was in no way fussy or pedantic. He accomplished what he had to do with the greatest of ease; one often marveled at how many hours of the day he managed to spare for private matters. Haus was a peculiar fellow. He was of middle height; only his dark eyes and his wide, well-developed forehead were striking as far as his exterior was concerned. He was not only highly cultivated but was also endowed with an incisive, deep intelligence. He remained a riddle even to those who had known him since youth. All admired him, but I don't think there was anybody in the whole navy to whom he had given his heart completely or to whom he permitted any insight into his soul. Of rather slight build, he was tougher than one would have supposed. He was an elegant athlete and an excellent pianist, but nobody could persuade him to show off in this respect. He was also a remarkable linguist and was well versed in classical literature, philosophy, history, natural science, and of course in all the technical branches of his profession. He laid stress upon exterior neatness, though not to an exaggerated degree; he was conscious of his worth; and no doubt he was also proud of his knowledge and his intelligence, without, however, parading it about. The fundamental trait of his character was a certain gravity, but he had a sense of humor, which usually showed an ironic, biting tinge. It always seemed to me that his was a dual nature, by which he was governed independently of his will. Haus was no doubt a brave man and could be very energetic if necessary, though in this latter respect I remember a few incomprehensible instances of passivity on his part. Various indications that only came to surface much later allow one to suppose that at heart he was a democrat.

Haus came from Carniola (Kranj), I believe from the Slav district, but was German by nationality. He had not gone through the naval academy at Fiume but had entered the navy as a civilian. This class of midshipmen distinguished itself from the one that came from the academy in a manner that is difficult to define. In their manners and knowledge, their way of thinking, and their atti-

tudes toward life they did not show the leveling influence of a uniform education. While all the academy boys more or less belonged to one type, each of
these midshipmen who had entered the navy at a riper age represented a type
by itself, and that for life.

At the time of which I am speaking, Haus was already married to a cousin, a
lady who always kept in the background. On board the *Tegetthoff* he showed
no particular care for excessive neatness regarding the ship, the boat, or the kit
of the men—perhaps, though this is only a surmise, because this would have
meant more trouble for the men. He did not spare them any more than was
proper, however.

As his sincere admirer I was happy to be in his company and to sit at his
right every day at table. Yet Haus was not a talkative man. He preferred to listen to others and to the empty chatter of his companions, no doubt forming a
judgment of them, though it may be that he was often plunged in deeper meditation than we thought. But whatever I may write, I shall not be able to draw an
adequate picture of this man, for he was too secretive and reserved.

As a final point of this sketch of his character I should only like to mention
one incident that occurred early during our service on board the *Tegetthoff*. One
evening in Trieste we were alone in the officers' wardroom. Haus was playing
patience, one of his favorite occupations, for which I had no interest. Behind
him, fixed to the bulkhead, stood an upright piano. I knew that he was a wonderful pianist who never played in the presence of others, and I casually asked
him whether he was fond of music. His reply was, "Do you want to hear something?" Upon my answering in the affirmative, he turned to the piano, struck a
few chords, and was soon lost in melody, wrapped in his own thoughts. I
watched him silently from my place at the table and perceived how his eyes
grew dim and saw tears roll down his cheeks, whereupon he shut the lid of the
piano with a clash, got up, and hurried away.

Next to Haus in rank was the gunnery officer, Lieutenant [Alexander] Baron
Taxis de Bordogna et Valnigra. He also had not studied at the academy and was
quite an original in his way, being very aristocratic in his appearance and in his
manner of talking and moving. He used to address all inferiors in a very familiar way, as was the custom in feudal circles, whether they were officers, middies, or men. Although this was not the custom in our navy, it was certainly
second nature to him and not some role he was playing. Taxis was an astonishingly good hiker, a passionate sportsman, and a good shot. However, he only
hunted in the stony deserts of Istria or occasionally in Dalmatia, and he loved
his dog above all things. But here I exaggerate, for above all things he loved his
family. This elegant aristocrat was happily married to a lady of Pola who was
not of a high social extraction, and he had several children. He loved them dearly
and spent every minute he could with them, so that he only gave the absolutely
necessary time—and often not even that—to the service. For Pola society he
had hardly any time to spare. He did not take his duties on board the *Tegetthoff*
terribly seriously, for whenever possible he left the ship and hurried off to see

his family. When at the beginning we lay for some time on the roadstead of Fasana, he rushed home on foot to Pola in the scorching sun, every day shortly before noon. There he lunched quickly with his family and returned on board, where he was due at 2:00 P.M. This was a hiking feat that impressed even me, the old Africa explorer.

Quite indirectly, his exaggerated family sense soon caused a break between Haus and me. Taxis and I were only allowed to go on shore at the same time when the executive officer remained on board. Taxis did not bother about this, even less so as Haus or I rarely left the ship. Neither did he ask permission, however, for he simply disappeared as soon as the drill was over, day after day. One evening—the moon had just risen—Haus invited me to take a walk with him in the neighborhood of Fasana. I was very pleased at this first friendly approach, and in a happy mood we strolled about for a couple of hours in pleasant talk in the mild evening air, which was scented with juniper and wild laurel. At 4:30 the next afternoon we sat as usual at dinner. Taxis, of course, had gone home. Haus was in an agreeable mood, more talkative than usual, and I was also feeling jolly. On this afternoon I had the firm intention of going to Pola, and when the harbor vessel that took the furlough men of the squadron to the town had come alongside the *Tegetthoff* and sounded her steam whistle, I asked Haus whether he was going ashore. His face grew dark, and his curt reply was, "I don't know." I had to hurry if I wanted to be in time, and I rose from the table and said gaily, "But *I* know that *I* am going ashore." At this I saluted smartly and said with jesting solemnity, "Commander, I have the honor to report myself from board." Thereupon I flew to my cabin, seized sword and cap, and rushed up the companionway, for already the tender's whistle was sounding for the third and last time. But Haus intercepted me on deck and ordered me to report to the captain, which was quite unusual. I still thought he was joking and replied lightly that he was just at dinner with the admiral, and left.

The following morning came. I had attached no importance whatever to what I have just related and had not thought about it half a second. One can imagine my astonishment as I stepped on deck when Haus addressed me in an overbearing tone with the words, "You will have to justify yourself at ten o'clock at the captain's." I could hardly believe my ears, but only bit my tongue. Such a report is always a painful matter. Haus did not make a charge against me. The captain delivered a fine speech, blaming me because of my conduct, to which I listened in silence. I regret to state that from that moment on everything was at an end between Haus and me. During the remaining nine weeks that we were together on board the *Tegetthoff* I never again addressed a word to him, excepting official reports. Dumbly we faced each other during meals, and as much as possible he even avoided giving me an order. Thus matters remained until I left the ship, and for a number of years thereafter.[6]

The squadron spent most of the time it was in commission in the Bocche di Cattaro, at the naval station of Teodo (Tivat). Twice a week I had to oversee

146 ✠ OVER LAND AND SEA

rowing exercises, which I regularly ended with regattas with ever more distant goals. The boats were very unequal, of course, and this had to be made up for by distance handicaps. To keep the zeal of competition alive, the crew of the winning boat received a gift of wine. Through this systematic training I obtained considerable results, for my men rowed far better and with greater endurance than those of the other ships of the squadron. And though none of these followed my example, whenever the boats of the squadron met while rowing in the same direction, they immediately began to race without being told to do so. Thus I had lit a little flame of ambition in the otherwise dull hearts of the men. The dockyard authorities were less than delighted, however, when they saw the number of oars that had gone to pieces in these contests, made as they were not of ash but of cheap beech wood.

After the squadron had been put out of commission, about the middle of August, I was transferred as gunnery officer and watch officer to the frigate *Laudon* of the so-called winter squadron. The sister ships *Radetzky* and *Laudon* were big, unwieldy frigates that had been built under the command of Vice Admiral Pöck—this at a time when other navies had long since discarded vessels of this type. *Laudon* was the flagship of the commanding officer of the squadron, Rear Admiral [Karl] Seemann von Treuenwart. The squadron was composed of the *Laudon*, the sloop of war *Zrinyi*, and the three-masted schooner *Albatros*. As far as I can remember, we first steamed to the Bocche di Cattaro for a preliminary drill. This, from the very outset, was an unhappy idea, for the Bocche counts among the spots in Europe with the greatest rainfall, which of course was not favorable for working sails. Life on board was not pleasant because of the cold and exceptionally rainy autumn weather. The cabins were dark and damp; under these circumstances it was impossible to keep the ship dry and spick-and-span.

The admiral was soon bored by having to lie quietly at anchor in this cheerless hole, unable to exercise his power on a vaster field. He therefore was tempted to take to sea before the men, most of them recruits, were properly trained. If only he had been wise enough upon reaching the open sea to give the ships liberty to act as they pleased for some time and to drill their crews! But hardly had we reached the main than he gave orders to get under sail and begin maneuvers in line. As long as daylight lasted, all went as well—or as badly—as was to be expected. During the first watch, which was my turn, the three ships somehow managed to keep formation, though light rain had set in and the night was dark. Tired and drenched, I retired to my cabin after my watch, crept into my bunk, and was soon fast asleep. Barely two hours later I was awakened by my servant with the anxious cry, "Sir, we are sinking!" Of course this roused me, and barefoot though I was, I hastened to the main deck to hear the rain pouring, the wind whistling through the rigging, and the trampling of many feet, while loud orders of the executive officer rang through the general din. Yet I could not gather what was really the matter.

I put on my boots and rain kit and went back on deck, where it took me some time before I fully realized the situation. With her bowsprit, *Laudon* had gored the much smaller *Albatros*, which lay struggling and tugging across our bow. Our rig was in a deplorable disorder. The yards were braced in all directions, some sails were kept full, others aback, and the executive officer, trying to put some order into this chaos, incessantly shouted commands of which nobody took the slightest heed. The inexperienced crew stood about helplessly in the dark rainy night. What else could one expect of these greenhorns? Once I had sized up the situation I hurried to the forecastle to see how matters stood there. Our bowsprit lay across the deck of the *Albatros* between her main mast and her mizzenmast and had torn stays and backstays, so that her masts were swaying back and forth in an alarming manner. *Laudon* forged astern before the wind, and *Albatros*, entangled with her, could not get free. I found our boatswain and a few men standing about helplessly, with a good deal of useless shouting going on between the two ships. They could not free themselves as long as the cordage that held them was not severed. I therefore had axes brought, but it took an awfully long time before they were found, since they had evidently been hidden away somewhere in the boatswain's storeroom. The admiral came and stood near me for a while without uttering a word, contemplating the mess. I drew his attention to the danger that threatened from the swaying masts of the *Albatros*, but he waved me off and retired again. When the axes came, we went to work cutting the entangled cordage right and left.

In the midst of this work I happened to glance to port, and there a picture met my gaze that was so extraordinary that I thought myself the victim of hallucination. The third ship of the squadron, the *Zrinyi*, was bearing straight down on us, all sails set, and she rammed the *Laudon* somewhere near the fore channels. She then swung round and came majestically along our side, as if she were executing a fine maneuver, clinging to us with yard arm and everything else that takes a hold. Thus the whole squadron lay there, clogged together in an almost indissoluble tangle. As it turned out, *Zrinyi*, ignoring what had happened, misguided by our lantern signals, and thinking that *Laudon* was making headway, had wanted to turn into her wake and take up her place. *Laudon* was drifting about, however, and thus the collision had been inevitable.

I do not want to enter further into the details of this tale of horror. The three ships made steam up and then started to free themselves, which they did with more brute force than art. Somewhat crestfallen, we returned to the Bocche, which we should never have left with such inexperienced crews. The damaged squadron was ordered to Pola for repairs and then back to Teodo. One day the naval commander in chief announced his visit and soon thereafter appeared in our midst, breathing fire like an angry god. The judgment that he held over the poor admiral in the presence of officers and men was so brutal that I prefer to pass over it in silence. A few weeks later the squadron went to Rovigno (Rovinj), where the change of command took place. Rear Admiral Seemann was put on the retired list, and the two other captains were given shore appointments. Rear Admiral Johann von Hinke was appointed commanding officer of the squadron for the remaining period of commission.

These events did not remain without influence on the mood of the officers and the crews. There could be no doubt that the squadron had bungled things, and everyone on board was glad when March 1, 1897, came and the ships were put out of commission. I had always disliked shore service, and thus I was glad to be appointed executive officer on the *Donau*, which was preparing for sea in the navy yard in Pola. These months were pleasant ones, and I would have found the task of outfitting a ship for a subsequent cruise even more agreeable had I not been obliged to work under the critical eye of Captain Count Montecuccoli, the second superintendent of the navy yard, who was by no means my friend. Fortunately, however, I had generally been much favored in my appointments. I could therefore hope to participate in the coming cruise of the corvette as her executive officer and see further countries and ports, knowing that such was the wish of the naval commander in chief, in whose good graces I stood. Most officers preferred to spend their time on board ship on interesting voyages rather than in home waters, which one knew by heart, or in squadron service. It is therefore comprehensible that the admiral's manifest favor that I enjoyed caused feelings of envy among my fellow officers. There was no doubt good reason for this. Nevertheless, I can affirm that during all my years of service I never applied for any of my appointments. Whether good or bad, they were allotted to me without my interference.

I devoted all my efforts to the outfitting of the ship with honest joy. In this undertaking two old and experienced friends, Captains Paul and Constantin von Pott, gave me much good advice and many a practical hint. The ship and my preparations for the campaign left nothing to be desired when the day came late in June on which we could show what we were worth. The name of the captain who was appointed commander of the corvette was Emil [Edler von] Hermann. In our navy there had been two brothers Hermann, who, though of much the same age, were most dissimilar in appearance and character. The amiable younger brother had died young as a lieutenant on a cruise in Ceylon; the elder—my captain—was a grumpy sort of fellow and was known in the navy by the nickname Vinegar.

The *Donau* was to make two short trips with the pupils of the naval academy on board and then to undertake a one-year cruise in the Atlantic with a batch of newly appointed midshipmen. Of the feelings that my captain harbored for me I was soon to have striking proof. He came from Vienna, where for three years he had been head of the first department of the Admiralty. There he had been at the source of all things, and he made up his mind to have as his executive officer not me but another lieutenant, who was a year older in rank and had also been attached to the Admiralty. He had discussed the matter with his friend and had made every effort to have him appointed in my place. The naval commander in chief, Baron von Sterneck, declined any such suggestion, however; without having the slightest notion of these machinations, I unexpectedly found myself facing a bitter enemy when I first saw him after his arrival in Pola. He immediately ordered me to come to his cabin, gazed at me for a few minutes with an angry stare, and then, without any ado, said, "Let me tell you at once that you are laboring under a delusion if you think that you are going to have a pleasant cruise." I cannot remember my reply, but probably all I answered was, "Very well, Sir." But one may believe that a host of unpleasant thoughts came crowding into my brain. Even before this strange interview I intended to fulfill my duties in a spirit of inimitable correctness. Nobody should find reason to call into question my good will, diligence, and discipline. In spite of the astonishing reception accorded me by the captain, I only needed to keep to my good resolutions. But of course my joy and satisfaction had suffered a setback, and what under other circumstances would have filled me with delight now appeared as a stern duty.

Before starting on her cruise, every newly manned ship is granted a period of two weeks for practicing the various alarms and for sail exercise. As far as working sails was concerned, the captain did not feel quite sure of himself, as was the case with many in the era of steam, and he gave me a free hand in this matter. At the end of ten days we left the harbor with the intention of finishing the days of preparation on the high sea. I think it was on the second day that we were at Rovigno, sailing with a light breeze. After the midday rest daily sailing practice had taken place, for which all hands had been ordered on deck. This drill, which lasted two hours, had just been finished and the starboard watch had been sent below deck to change to night kit. I had gone from the bridge to the main deck in order to watch the men change their dress. I was about to roll a cigarette when, to my indescribable horror, I saw the sentry of the aft magazine rush up the companionway from the lower deck with a heart-rending yell, followed by a column of fire at his rear. At first I did not know whether this terrible sight was real or only a delusion. My bewilderment lasted only a second, however, and I quickly realized that something awful had happened. Great danger threatened the ship, and immediate measures were necessary. Smashing with my foot the glass pane of the casing containing the socket key for flooding the magazine, I flew up the companionway onto deck and beat the fire roll. Then I hurried back to the main deck, without even thinking of making a report to the captain. The fire drill had been practiced every day, and though the men were young and inexperienced, they nevertheless rushed to their stations with surprising promptness and extended the hoses in all decks, maintaining splendid discipline and calm. There was no sign of panic. Hardly a minute after the fire alarm had been sounded, nine thick jets of water poured forth into the steward's room, where evidently the hotbed of fire was located. Clouds of black smoke filled the main deck, and breathing soon became so difficult that the gunports had to be opened, in spite of the increased draught. In time one could venture down to the lower deck and get nearer to the center of the fire, which was close to the aft magazine.

I had made my report to the captain on the danger of the situation as soon as this was possible and insisted that the magazine be flooded. The ship had on board a supply of provisions for three months, and the steward's room was crammed with hundreds of cases, many of which were the private property of the ship's steward, a civilian. All this was now prey to flames that were raging underneath the lower deck, all through the afterbody of the ship as far as the engine-room bulkhead. The enormous quantities of water being discharged in there at random did not seem to have much effect on the fire, though one waded ankle-deep in water in the lower deck. When the fire seemed to be quenched in one spot, it flamed up all the more violently elsewhere. The fire lasted over two hours, and for a long time it looked as if all our efforts were in vain. Standing on top of the magazine's hatch, I watched with alarm how the caulking of the deck melted away and dripped into the sweltering furnace below, now plainly visible through the seams of the deck planking.

When finally I saw the flames leaping up in some of the lower-deck cabins, I gave up all hope. To my great astonishment, however, shortly thereafter the fire seemed to abate, and half an hour later, toward 7:00 P.M., it could be considered extinguished. I want immediately to give the explanation for the remarkably sudden extinction of the fire, though I only realized the reason a couple of hours later. I had been struck by the great quantity of water that flooded the lower deck, and also by the fact that it was quite tepid. I had supposed that it came from our hoses, but this was not the case. The magazine, a big iron tank built into the ship, was surrounded by the fire and therefore had very soon been flooded. In order to do this, its sea valve had been opened, and naturally it had not been closed again. Thus tons of water, entering continually and flowing out through the air valve, had caused the inundation of the lower deck. After the caulking of the deck planking had melted away, this mass of water could steadily pour down on the fire, and that had been our salvation.

In the meanwhile the captain had undertaken the other necessary measures. After the fire had been extinguished, sails were furled and we went under steam to Pola, where we arrived toward midnight. The captain had to make the unpleasant report to the admiral of the port on the accident that had befallen his ship. Afterward, a prey to sad thoughts, he promenaded the deck with me for some time, and in spite of all I could say he was disconsolate. I finally asked him whether he or anyone else on board was guilty of the accident, adding that I at any rate was not conscious of any duty left undone; and if this was to all appearances the case, our accident must be accepted as vis major [circumstances beyond our control] and nobody could be taken to account. In spite of the misfortune, it should be a comfort for him and all to realize how well the crew had behaved. Thus I managed to calm him a little, but it was only in the small hours of the morning that he dismissed me. Exhausted by the excitement, I now had to start writing my report.

There could be no thought of rest that night, and in this state of mind I was surprised at daybreak by the visit of a judge advocate. So this was the first greeting, the first expression of sympathy vouchsafed to us on the part of the port admiral, an act that characterized the nature of the man, who always and everywhere searched for a scapegoat! I was unable to suppress my indignation at such a proceeding and showed my feelings plainly to the military judge. This man, who was a warm-hearted fellow, understood my anger, but what else could he do but follow his instructions and start a preliminary examination? Subsequently a court of inquiry was held that thoroughly investigated the case, whereby I, to the disappointment of my dear captain, came off gloriously. The evidence showed that I, being responsible for the good working of the ship, had exaggerated rather than neglected the safety regulations. While these directions permitted the ship's steward to take along any amount of methylated spirit and authorized every officer and midshipman to have a small quantity in his cabin so as to be able to brew tea or coffee at night, in a special order I had abolished all these privileges. The ship's steward was not allowed to carry alcohol or to deal with it. I had further ordered that it be kept under lock and key in the mizzen channels and passed on by the boatswain to mess rooms only, and *not* to individuals. By this same order spirits were only to be used for cooking purposes in the pantries under the control of a lantern trimmer. All persons in question had read and signed that order. The ship's steward had stated under oath in the presence of witnesses that he did not have a drop of methylated spirits. Nevertheless, the wretch had smuggled twelve liters on board, perhaps even more, and had told his two assistants to fill this quantity into small bottles, which they were doing in the dark steward's room by the light of a lantern. In order to see better, they had removed the glass cover of the lantern, and so the unfortunate accident had happened. The chief culprit had not been below, but his two assistants were badly burned, one of them mortally. The ship's steward was sentenced and lost all his fortune. The cruise with the pupils had to be put off for several weeks, though the navy yard people contented themselves with quite superficial repairs of the fire damage, simply scraping and whitewashing the charred beams, bulwarks, and walls. A tedious process was the drying up of the magazine, from which every vestige of salt had to be removed by repeated washings with fresh water. A thorough airing was also necessary, as otherwise the hold would always have remained damp.

With some delay in the program, we then sailed to Fiume and took on board the youngest class of pupils, the staff of the academy, and all their paraphernalia, which included an immense number of packing cases. It is natural that this crowd was not very enjoyable on board a ship that had not been built for that particular purpose. During this cruise I often had to overlook things and to make the best of them. After all, it was more or less only a pleasure trip of young folks who were to be introduced to life at sea.

We first touched some of the Dalmatian ports—among them San Giorgio on the island of Lissa, which was meant to remind the youngsters of the glorious victory that our Admiral Tegetthoff had gained over the Italian fleet in 1866, which was the most brilliant page in Austria's naval history. The program we had to follow was exactly prescribed. After Lissa we were to call at Ancona, on precisely the day that thirty-one years earlier, Italy's Admiral Persano, beaten by Tegetthoff at Lissa, had withdrawn to that port with his fleet. This had been a regrettable oversight on the part of the Admiralty; we could not run into Ancona, coming from Lissa, on that very day without giving the impression that we were following Persano's line of retreat. The captain therefore decided to remain at sea twenty-four hours longer and to go to that port on the next day. But this did not make things better. The population felt offended, and this was manifested by the very frigid courtesy of the authorities, by hysterical press articles, and by the unfriendly reception that our men met wherever they went on shore.

To this was added another circumstance that was not calculated to make our relations any more pleasant. The salute that the *Donau* had fired when entering the port had not been correctly returned, for one shot had been omitted, and of course we had to voice recriminations. After the local authorities had first contested the accuracy of our statements, they started to parley and finally declared their readiness to fire the supplementary shot that had been omitted. This, however, was against international rules. An incorrectly returned salute does not count at all and has to be fired anew. The affair took on greater dimensions, was telegraphed to Rome and to Vienna, and ended with our being given full satisfaction. General Baldissera, the military commander in chief of the district,[7] came on board the *Donau* in full dress in order to express the customary excuses. Thus we had the pleasure of greeting Baldissera, a former Austrian general staff officer, and of conversing with him in fluent German. The examination that the Italian authorities had conducted revealed that one man of the salute battery had pilfered a cartridge in order to make use of the powder for the manufacture of firecrackers, so popular on holidays in Italy.

After the end of this four-week trip the youngsters were landed at Fiume, and in their place the second and third classes were taken on board. This second trip lasted six weeks and had Naples as its farthest goal. These older pupils were doing the service of midshipmen and had to work the mizzenmast, so they were no mere pleasure-trippers. During this whole time I was exceedingly busy and did not find time to set foot on land—nor had I the slightest inclination to do so. I was glad that the captain left me to my own devices, allowing me to devote myself to my duties without his interference. I did not, however, owe this to friendlier feelings on his part but rather to the presence of the academy officers, who kept him company and diverted his attention away from me.

One evening I was standing on the port gangway remembering former visits to this place and surveying the wonderful scenery when I heard someone address me from behind in Trieste dialect, "Sior paronzin, would you allow me to give some sugar to one of my friends who has begged me to do so?" The questioner was the chief steward of the naval academy, an old man who had fed not only me but also the captain when we had been youngsters in Fiume. I turned round for a moment, looked the old man in the eyes a while, and then said, "I don't care what you do with your sugar." He thanked me profusely and went his way. I should perhaps explain that the ship and the administration of the academy ran their accounts separately, and for want of a separate storeroom their provisions had been piled up in cases on starboard in the fore main deck. I did not give the matter any further thought and was sitting in the mess room toward ten o'clock when the officer on watch sent me a report saying that a number of cases had been passed through the gunport on the starboard side of the ship into a civilian boat, which had made off with them in great haste. This had been reported to the watch officer, and as it appeared suspicious, he had given the order to man a boat and to give chase to the civilians. When these saw themselves pursued, they threw their cargo overboard, so that it was impossible to report what had really happened. This was no secret to me, however. On account of a high duty, sugar was dear in Italy, while it was cheap at Fiume. It had struck me as odd that the academy had shipped such large quantities of sugar at Fiume, and now I knew why—and also what the chief steward's seemingly innocent question had signified. A smuggling transaction in sugar had been carried on.

The matter was unpleasant for me because of the captain, for I supposed that he would make a lot of it. I explained everything to the young watch officer and made no secret of the possible consequences. He was sorry to have acted so rashly and suggested passing over the incident in silence, an offer that I declined. Everything had to be put down into the ship's journal exactly as it had happened. I myself reported the details to the captain the next morning and was surprised that he seemed to attach very little significance to the matter. A few days later we were again at sea, under way to Messina. After clearing hammocks it was reported to me that during the night the cook of the academy—but not the chief steward—had been robbed of a hundred lire. Whenever thefts occur on board ship they are always severely followed up, and though it may only be the question of a trifle, a careful investigation is conducted. But it is rarely possible to catch the thief, since as a rule he has ample time to throw the article overboard if he feels he is in danger of discovery. When I cross-examined the cook as to how he had come into the possession of so large a bank note, the whole sugar smuggle came to light. He had smuggled sugar for 100 lire, and the old man from the academy for 900 lire. Thereupon I, of course, also tackled the chief culprit and ordered him to give up the money received. When he brought it and counted out the 900-lire notes onto the table, I saw at first glance that they were forgeries. The *caro amico* had swindled him.

Thus the unpleasant sugar-smuggling affair was revived and was destined to remain alive for some time. While at first the whole matter had not seemed to trouble the captain, he now suddenly made a tremendous ado about it. The incident had to be reported in every detail, not only to the Admiralty but also to the Foreign Office. It was our duty to notify the Italian government that we had traced forged bank notes, and so forth and so on. It was most ridiculous, and I soon guessed that all this was directed against me. I did my best to point out the exaggeration of such proceedings and the consequence of such an action, stating that every child knew that Italy was swamped with forged bank notes, and warning him against undertaking any hasty step. All my arguments shattered against the armor of his pigheadedness. He hated me and hoped to harm me by means of this affair. Later I pointed out to him the inconsequence of his not punishing the principal culprit, the chief steward. This evidently was very much against his liking. But being unable to avoid it, for show he went in for some sort of inquiry which, however, was a mere farce. Summoned up, the old sinner uttered one *Sior paronzin* after the other, and then with tears in his eyes he began to bring forward touching reminiscences of the old days, while swearing holy oaths that this was the first and only smuggling he had done in his whole life. He added that he had been cheated by his false friend and was now a pauper. How could I have expected that the captain, whose sternness was clearly make-believe, would do more than remonstrate with this old food caterer of his boyhood days?

This took some weeks, during which I had the pleasure of figuring in another court of inquiry on account of the smuggling affair. I was at first rather indifferent, until one day the course of the proceedings caused me to prick up my ears. Paragraphs from the *Diritto Marittimo*, a code dating back to the days of Empress Maria Theresa, and old court decrees were cited, all of which applied to the impeachment of the captain of an imperial vessel from which smuggling had been carried out or had been tolerated by her captain. In one word, it looked as if I was going to be sentenced as the only guilty man in the whole affair, while there was no talk at all of the actual smugglers. This was too much, and I pointed out with strong words the views that prevailed in our navy and probably also in other navies in this regard, which caused the gentlemen to stop further legal proceedings. None of us did business based on smuggling, but we did find it unjust to be required to pay duty on our personal requirements, and I frankly confess that I have smuggled many a parcel of tobacco and bottle of port wine, not only for myself, but also for the commander in chief and the head chaplain of the navy. I remember a court dinner of Field Marshal Archduke Albrecht, during which, to the great amusement of the august host, his guests had recounted nothing but witty smuggling tales. Under these circumstances, it was very strange to accuse me because someone who had not been under my authority had chosen to smuggle sugar.

After an uneventful homeward voyage we arrived at Pola, where we were to provision the ship anew before starting on our cruise to the Atlantic. The ward officers of the *Donau* were pleasant companions who regretted the tension that existed between me and the captain. Our next cruise went via Gibraltar, Tenerife, and Dakar—places I knew—to the Antilles. For me it was a painful time because the captain incessantly vented his morbid ill-humor on me, though by reason of my duties I was the most hard-working officer on board. Toward the others he was amiable. Nothing I did found favor in his eyes; he criticized everything. The continual humiliations to which one is helplessly exposed impair one's self-respect, and in a matter of time my nerves were ruined. After a while I decided to leave the ship at Tenerife, but my comrades persuaded me to desist, declaring that this would end my career. Since I knew that this was true, I dragged on under the yoke. We next called at Barbados—where the news reached us that Baron Sterneck, the commander in chief of our navy and my protector, had departed for a better world—and then at St. Lucia and Martinique, where as usual pretty brown minxes came on board under the disguise of laundresses, inviting us to see them on shore. But I had received orders to have the ship repainted, and in spite of my protest that the time was too short for the paint to dry and that rain threatened, the captain insisted on it. He had done so on purpose, for hardly had we finished than it began to pour and everything was spoiled! The captain did not mind a bit, for he had succeeded in clipping my budget and could, whenever he wished to exasperate me, justly exclaim, "I am ashamed of the ship! She looks scandalous!"

In Guadeloupe one of the men deserted from the last boat that we had sent on land just before leaving. Of course, this too was my fault. I ought to have known the crew better and should not have ordered an unreliable man to the boat. In St. Thomas my innermost being was so revolted that for the second time I decided to part from the ship, but again my comrades interceded and made me abandon my plan. After San Juan, Puerto Rico, we went to Santo Domingo in Haiti. In none of these ports had I been on shore. Of Santo Domingo all on board only caught a distant glimpse, for here, as in Ancona, the shore battery had returned our salute with one shot less than was required, whereupon an officer was delegated to the president of the Negro republic with instructions to demand satisfaction. The president, as the officer reported, indifferently listened to our recriminations and only shrugged his shoulders, saying that this matter did not concern him and was the business of the garrison artillery. Its general was at his country place in the interior, however, and was therefore unable to correspond with our wish. We waited for two days, during which nobody was allowed to go on shore. Meanwhile the ship rolled in the swell with the rhythm of eternity, which made the captain guess that he would have to wait for satisfaction longer than his time permitted. He therefore punished the president by ordering the anchor to be weighed, sailing for Port au Prince, the chief port of the second Negro republic on Haiti, and from there to Santiago de Cuba. The officers reported many pleasant things about kind invitations and agreeable gatherings in the various ports, and I was glad when they all went from board and left me alone in my despair.

In leaving Santiago de Cuba, after some trifling incident connected with anchor work, I had had enough. After we passed through the narrow, tortuous entrance to the port I went to my cabin, retired to bed, sent for the doctor, and told him that I would leave the ship at New Orleans, our next destination. He should report me as suffering from malaria. The doctor agreed that nothing else remained for me to do; there was not room on board for both the captain and me, and one of us must retire from the scene. He would report me as seriously sick and urgently recommend my removal. I not only remained in bed in spite of the tropical heat, but in order to look ill I took no nourishment during the following four days. Ten days passed. Though the entrance to the captain's state-room was next to my cabin, which he passed many times during the day, he never thought of paying me a visit or inquiring after my health. I was therefore astonished when, on the eleventh afternoon, the door opened and the captain entered, exclaiming, "What are you doing in bed in this heat?" He took a seat and said, "You must not think that you alone are ill." To my laconic "Is that so?" he explained that the doctors had informed him that his liver was the size of that of an ox; his legs were beginning to swell in an alarming way. He made no further comment on that day, nor did I pay much attention to these remarks, but on the next afternoon he came again and in a fit of deep depression told me that the doctors had declared that his condition was worse, and at their advice he would go on shore at New Orleans and live there for some time in order to get well. His legs were swollen still more since yesterday. One may imagine that this time I listened attentively to these communications, and gradually a slight hope grew in my breast that I might possibly be released from this torturer. On the third day he informed me that he would have to leave the ship and return home. As if feeling the shadows of death, he repeatedly groaned, "If only I see my children again!" It was clear to me that now, while maintaining certain ex-terior formalities, I could recover. And when a few days later we approached the mouth of the Mississippi and an old Swedish pilot came on board, I could consider myself master of the ship.

The Mississippi flows with a considerable current into the sea and colors the blue waves of the Gulf [of Mexico] with a muddy tinge. It was with great trouble that the *Donau* made her way upstream, and only the next day did she reach her anchorage opposite the city. Captain Emil Hermann left the ship and moved to a hotel while arrangements were made for his homeward journey. He went to New York, accompanied by the ship's second doctor, and from there imme-diately started for Genoa on board a North German Lloyd steamer. He died at Genoa shortly after landing. The liver complaint from which he had been suf-fering for many years had fully developed of late and may serve as an explana-tion for his attitude toward me. That was no excuse as far as I was concerned, for I had suffered too much. My entire nature had undergone such a change that even the lucky circumstance that we arrived at New Orleans, the gayest city of America, just in time for Mardi Gras, could not mend matters. In those weeks the whole town is dedicated to merriment to an extent unlike anywhere else. At that season men and women flock to New Orleans from all over in quest of entertainment, and every hotel and house is packed with guests. Our ship, whose arrival was known to the town, had received invitations to entertainments, balls, and all sorts of festivities weeks before, but we had never dreamt that the general fever would take on such dimensions. New Orleans appeared to be stand-ing on its head. Daily the *Donau* was inundated with visitors. We were powerless in face of this crowd; moreover, we did not want to spoil their fun. Under these circumstances regular service was impossible.

Close to us an old French frigate, flying the flag of a rear admiral, and a middle-sized American cruiser lay at anchor. These two had had their day in the sun and were no longer a novelty. The *Donau* was now the chief attraction. Besides, the American ship demanded an entrance fee from visitors, whereas we charged nothing. One day we received a written, formal communication from the mayor of the city announcing that on a certain afternoon at three o'clock Prince Carnival would make his solemn entrance into the city, along with his retinue. The men-of-war lying at anchor in the river were requested to receive him with royal honors. This was too much of a good thing. Royal honors indeed! This would mean that we should have to greet the joyous imp with a royal gun salute and man the yards. I called on the French admiral in order to express my astonishment at this idea and hear his opinion. He replied with a smile that this reception of Prince Carnival was a very old custom and that all men-of-war had always participated in the manner desired. He advised against manning the yards, however, as this was too dangerous due to the river's swift current. I shook my head; what would Vienna say to this? Finally I decided to do in Rome as the Romans do, but to salute the mysterious prince on the occasion of his entrance *reservatio mentalis*, so to speak, not with full twenty-one but with only twenty guns, the unlucky experience of my former Captain Rottauscher with the Rákóczi March being still fresh in my memory.

The great day arrived. Long before the yacht of the tinsel prince came in sight, the howling of hundreds of steam whistles and sirens announced his advent. More and more ships joined in the wild and noisy chorus, until finally, when the prince's yacht had reached the city, the voices of the many steamers anchored in the Mississippi produced such a monstrous orgy of roaring sounds that even the thunder of the guns was hardly heard. My gaiety, which the long period of suffering had shriveled, did not revive even in this joyful atmosphere, and the frivolities of the carnival did not touch me at all. Without envy I allowed my brother officers to drink the pleasures offered them to their dregs. Under these circumstances no mean responsibility rested on my shoulders concerning the ship and her crew.

I was great friends with the French admiral, who perhaps only showed me, the young lieutenant commanding a ship nearly equal to his in tonnage, so much courtesy and fatherly condescension for that reason. When I went on board his ship, which was often the case, it was painfully embarrassing when her executive officer, many years my senior in rank, received me respectfully and showed me to the admiral's stateroom. I was still greater friends—one will be astonished to hear this—with the Archbishop of New Orleans and his two secretaries. Though I myself always managed to live without the formalities of the Church, I insisted that my subordinates should have the opportunity to exercise their religious needs, and I therefore had a Mass said on board on Sundays whenever possible. This had been the point that linked me with the episcopate and which grew to be a bond of true friendship. One of the two secretaries, Father Prim, a cheerful young priest, felt so much at home on board the *Donau* that he spent every free minute with us. He was a native of Alsace and spoke fluent German, but his whole nature betrayed his French origin. I once told him that I could not believe that he had been a priest since his young days; surely he must have had a worldly profession at one time. He then confessed that he had once been a cavalry officer.

I saw very little of the carnival. We had 400 to 500 callers on board daily who filled all the decks, stopping neither before any cabin or even before the stateroom, evidently feeling so happy on board that they could hardly be persuaded to leave the ship at night. I therefore had to stick to my post to see to things. Added to this was the circumstance that the ship's position was not always safe, since the river sometimes ran very high. Uprooted trees and sometimes enormous trunks came drifting past us, constituting no mean danger. Our work was therefore cut out for us, and it was often quite a problem to disentangle and get rid of a whole forest of branches and entire trees that had accumulated on the bows overnight. We also had to contend with stormy weather. Of course I went on shore sometimes, moving only in official circles, and I enjoyed some invitations to dinner.

The carnival came to an end and the day dawned on which we had to start for Havana. The American battleship *Maine* had been blown up shortly before, it was said by a Spanish mine, and lay sunk in the port. Like the rest of the world, our Admiralty sympathized with this regrettable and mysterious catastrophe, and it had cabled me to report in detail on the circumstances of the occurrence. The farewell from New Orleans was a sad moment for many on board. The weather was very stormy when we left the river, and in view of the strong current and the heavy gusts of wind it was no easy matter to turn the ship round. The same old Swede who had piloted us in three weeks earlier was a very experienced sailor, however, and he took us safely as far as the outer lightship, where he bade us a hearty farewell after giving many warnings and much good advice concerning the threatening weather. Dark night fell in, and a roaring wind and sea greeted the ship the moment the old sailor left her. I was not so arrogant as to consider myself an experienced seaman and therefore wisely kept the engine going to avoid the dangers that the darkness might hide, for the night is no man's friend. At daybreak the situation looked less threatening, and we set sail and worked our way toward our goal. In the following days the wind calmed and the currents drove us westward.

It took us ten full days to reach Havana. Thanks to our consul general, we were soon on friendly terms with quite a number of families and lovely girls, which quickly caused the faithless to forget New Orleans altogether. The eye of the northern beauties may be deeper and full of soul, but the glance of the Creole, betraying her southern blood, has a more fascinating effect. In addition to the *Maine*, of which only one of the masts and part of the superstructure loomed out of the water, and the American cruiser that had been our neighbor in New Orleans, we found a number of Spanish men-of-war lying at anchor, all of which would be condemned to a glorious end not long afterward. I visited them all and got to know the heroic figures who, with much courage, were to meet their doom facing a far superior enemy. In the narrow harbor of Santiago these ships were caught as in a trap and were beleaguered from inland and from the sea, so that the Spanish admiral Cervera had no choice but to break through the iron ring that hemmed him in from all sides.[8] It was a heroic though hopeless enterprise that ended with the loss of his entire fleet.

On the occasion of my visit, one of the Spanish captains told me that the officers and men of all these ships had not received any pay for several months. I do not think that we Austrians would have shown the same patience in the face of similar behavior on the part of our government; with them this was no doubt a matter of habit. In spite of the strained relations then reigning between Spain and the United States because of the *Maine*, life on board the Spanish men-of-war went on as if deepest peace prevailed. One never saw them drill the men or keep them busy, and at all hours of the day boatloads of well-dressed women and men went to and from the ships, where no doubt the spirit of carnival still dominated. Entertainments of every kind seemed to be the order of the day on board. In contrast, the American cruiser kept a close watch, as one could see by her surely loaded guns, which were pointed at every boat that came near her.

As already mentioned, I had received orders to furnish a detailed report of the sinking of the *Maine* and unofficially to collect as much information as I could. Diplomatic ways have never been to my taste; I always preferred straight proceedings. I therefore asked the captain of the American cruiser to introduce me to Captain Sigsbee, the former commander of the unfortunate ship. This happened the next day. Sigsbee, a friendly little man, was a typical American man-of-war captain of those days. With few exceptions they reminded one more of savants than of sailors. They were comparatively old for their rank and often wore glasses. I believe that later on President Roosevelt caused some changes in this respect by passing ordinances that raised greater claims on the physique of higher-ranking naval officers; whoever could not meet the stipulated conditions had to retire. In order not to come out plump and plain with the object I had in mind, I first spoke to Captain Sigsbee of indifferent matters, but he soon interrupted me by asking, "Well, what can I do for you?" I then told him frankly what had brought me and begged him to tell me as much as he could. He gave me a detailed description of the catastrophe and of all of his and his officers' impressions and observations, speaking as unreservedly as only a truly straightforward man can. When we parted, he presented me with a photo showing the *Maine* as she looked before and now, bearing a dedication in his own hand. I still possess one of the cleverly drawn little pictures that were sold by the score in America in those days. It shows in simple outlines the proud *Maine* in the port of Havana, while opposite, on the shore, a Spaniard kneels with a burning fuse in his hand; the inscription runs "Who did it?" The reply is given when, with a burning cigarette, one touches the spot on which the Spaniard kneels; with a hissing sound a thin fire line runs across to the *Maine* and blows her up. In any case the Spanish-American war was the consequence of the *Maine* catastrophe.[9]

America had an easy role not only with regard to Spain but also Cuba, as the majority of the population desired separation from the mother country, against which it entertained inimical feelings. Of the attitude of at least part of the social circles of Havana toward the Spanish supremacy no secret was made, so that I once felt obliged to take a stand. As everywhere, the *Donau* received many visitors. One afternoon a particularly large number had come on board, filling all decks. I was standing on the bridge with a number of gentlemen and ladies, all belonging to the best society, when at sunset the colors were hauled down with the usual ceremony. Our ship's band began by intoning Schubert's wonderful melody to Körner's "Gebet vor der Schlacht" ("Prayer before Battle"), and afterward it played the Austrian national anthem and the anthems of the other states represented by men-of-war in the port. This ceremony, however often one may have witnessed it, always impresses with its solemnity. Everyone listened to the strains of the music with bare heads until the Spanish national hymn began. Suddenly the mood of my guests seemed to change. The more impulsive ladies gave vent to their indignation by exclamations, the men ostentatiously put on their hats, and they all behaved in a manner that obliged me to remind them where they were.

The officers and midshipmen were often invited to dances and ran great risks of again falling victim to the tender passion. No wonder! Who could withstand the charm of a Spanish Creole or remain cold under the gaze of her flaming eyes? In spite of the many appeals to put off our departure, the hour of farewell also struck here. This time I not only had to turn a deaf ear to the entreaties of my officers, but I had myself to resist the attacks of charming women and girls, which was far more difficult. When even the most entrancing of the Circes met with a refusal, they would not give in; behind my back they telegraphed to Vienna asking the Admiralty to allow the *Donau* to remain in Havana a few days longer. Even at the last hour before our departure a messenger brought a round-robin signed by a number of girls keen on dancing. I fear I left many enemies behind me in Havana among the gentle sex.

On a dark night we steamed through the narrow channel past Morro Castle. We soon set sails with a spanking breeze abeam, and with increasing rapidity we made our way toward New York. We were in a hurry, for an atmospheric depression was threatening. The force of the wind increased, the top gallant masts and yards were bent, and the ship, overpressed with sails and driven by the Gulf Stream, rushed at 16 knots an hour through the Straits of Florida. We had only come as far as Cape Hatteras, however, when a northerner caught us with fury, coming upon us so suddenly that we hardly had time to shorten sails. We had to lay to, and it took us nine days before we reached the Hudson, finally mooring the *Donau* at exactly the same spot she had occupied three years previously.

My friend Mr. Chanler was not there to meet me. His book on our African expedition, *Through Jungle and Desert*, had meanwhile appeared, and different honors had been allotted to him. Harvard University having made him a master of arts, he had gone there to get his degree. All this I heard from his cousin, Mr. Whitney Warren, who came on board the moment the anchor dropped. Messrs. Warren and Wetmore figure among the most prominent architects in America. The stupendous electric metropolitan railway, which runs four underground lines in New York City, Grand Central Station, and many other splendid buildings are their work.[10]

Together with Mr. Warren, another man came on board, and supposing him to be one of his friends, I received him accordingly. As I came from Havana, it was not astonishing that in the course of the conversation the *Maine* catastrophe was touched upon and my opinion asked. I refused to speak of the matter, however. "Ask me whatever you like, only not about the *Maine*," was my reply, and the second man did not insist any further. Nevertheless, the next morning one could read in all the papers that I had given him a long account of the event and had declared that the sinking of the ship had undoubtedly been due to a Spanish mine. This is American journalism. The man accompanying Mr. Warren had been a reporter absolutely unknown to him who had simply pushed his way on board.

Unlike three years ago, this time there was no question of a free, untrammeled life. I had my duties to fulfill as captain, which meant I had to get in touch with official circles. My responsibility was all the greater because the authority of a brother officer only senior by a few years is not as great as that of a real captain. Moreover, the executive officer representing me was not the man to maintain very strict discipline. America, the so-called land of liberty, has a great attraction for elements who do not feel happy in their own country. Desertions are therefore frequent and form a certain danger for men-of-war, and this is nowhere greater than in New York. There exists a simple though not infallible remedy against this, however. It is customary on men-of-war to give the men shore leave, usually in the afternoon until nine, ten, or eleven o'clock at night. That is not wise. The sailor needs time to sow his wild oats and enjoy the pleasures of the city. If he is only allowed to go on shore in the afternoons, night soon sets in with its many temptations, and he more easily deviates from the straight path of virtue, getting into the company of people who make him drink and miss the boat that is to take him back on board. This makes him familiar with the thought of not returning at all. But matters are quite different when the man is sent on shore early in the morning and given furlough until night. Having grown tired by running about seeing the sights of the city and having spent his cash on lunch, he longs to get back on board in the afternoon. The men return to the landing place in crowds at an early hour, waiting for a chance to get on board. The dangerous night is still far away when the majority of the men have returned. I always observed this system and never had desertions.

My life in New York was not devoid of all pleasures, for my former traveling companion and his elder brother, Mr. Winthrop Chanler, entertained me several times. As long as I was the master of the *Donau*, I also spent a couple of nights carousing until the wee hours of the morning. But my supremacy here was to come to an end. A frigate captain, [Viktor Ritter] von Jenik-Zasadsky, had been sent out as the new captain, and this relegated me to my place as executive officer a fortnight after our arrival. In one way I was glad of this, for to play the part of captain with the meager emoluments of a lieutenant was not possible in the long run. In this big, expensive city I suffered from a constant lack of cash, so much so that one night, long before my command came to an end, I heroically resolved not to set foot on shore again and went ahead and spent every cent I still had. This done, I delivered my empty purse to the muddy waves of the Hudson and burned the bridges between myself and New York.

From that day on I refused even the most friendly and tempting invitations and never set foot in the city. Though I was glad to be released from a rather awkward position, I nevertheless looked forward with mixed feelings to the coming of the new captain, whom I knew only superficially. In spite of his serious and quiet manner, he had certain peculiarities that confirmed the rumor that he had once spent some time in a sanitarium. This was hardly calculated to recommend him or put me at ease. One day he arrived and assumed the command, and soon we left New York for Halifax [Nova Scotia]. From there we were to go to St. John's, Newfoundland. Even for New York, the season had been ill-chosen, and we had suffered a good deal from the cold, so that regardless of all regulations I had given the men hot tea and rum at every relief of the watch. St. John's at this time of the year was still blocked by ice; the program makers in Vienna had overlooked this, so we never went there.

Before leaving New York the captain confessed to me that he had not done any sailing since his days as a midshipman and asked me to run the ship as before. This frankness pleased me, and I resolved not to presume on the advantage this avowal gave me. It was not his fault if during all the years of his service he had not had a chance to keep up his knowledge of sailing.

From Halifax we sailed across the ocean to Glasgow, and during the latter part of the cruise we had to struggle with stormy weather. This industrial city lies about thirty kilometers upstream on the Clyde, a deep but rather narrow river. Close to the town all the sewage of the city flows from numerous factories directly into the river, changing its waters into a dark, thick, disgusting mess that hardly deserves the name of water. I could not understand how one could direct the snow-white *Donau* there. No other ships venture so far up, and they all used to anchor lower down near Greenock, on the mouth of the Clyde. What we looked like after twenty-four hours defies description, and one may well imagine that as the executive officer I was mad with fury. I only went on shore once in order to do some shopping, and I had the impression that Glasgow was populated only by factory hands, at least half of whom looked as if they were more or less under the influence of whiskey. It was Saturday, and I did not see any well-dressed people on the streets. It was interesting to see on what primitive wharves ships were built on the Clyde; the space at their disposal is so restricted that ships cannot be launched in the usual manner. In order to get out of this dirty hole again, the *Donau* had to be carefully turned round with warps, there being very little swinging room.

From Glasgow we went to Kirkwall, a little town situated on one of the Orkney Islands. The chief trade here is fishing, especially herring. The fish are smoked for export, which is done by the female part of the population. Anyone who has never tasted a freshly smoked herring has no idea how delicious it is. We then crossed over to Bergen in Norway and next moved on to Edinburgh, the beautiful capital of Scotland, and Newcastle-on-Tyne. I am not sure, but I think it was at Newcastle that we received a strange visit in the mess room one evening. We were just having supper when the door opened and a girlish-looking young Scotsman in a red tartan kilt entered, greeted us with a mild smile, and began playing the bagpipes. This amused us, and the strangely quiet and amiable young fellow quickly made friends with us. We were glad to see him, and he seemed to feel at home, for he remained several hours, and on leaving he refused to accept any reward. Not only was this repeated every evening as long as we were in Newcastle, but the young man even followed us to our next port and appeared on board with his childlike, innocent smile, as if it were the most natural thing in the world. We could not imagine what tied him so to our ship, nor could we discover who he was and what motivated his actions. The psychology of the British is very different from that of other Europeans, so that it is often incomprehensible. But it is just these surprising and mysterious characteristics that make us like that race.

So far I have said very little about my new captain. Generally he kept quiet and seemed to be watching in the background, without interfering much in the service. He did not even appear on the bridge when we ran in or out of a harbor but remained aft on the poop deck. What bored me most was that by his wish I had to trot up and down the deck by his side day after day. I was not always in the mood to do that, nor did I have the time. One morning he surprised me with the utterly unjustified reproach that I drank, claiming that he could smell it! One may imagine that I gave him the proper answer. Another time he asked me with what I dyed my hair! Then, one afternoon, he sent for me in his cabin. I found him standing near his desk and asked for his orders. Instead of giving me any answer, he passed his hand over his forehead, appeared to reflect ponderously, and finally said, more to himself than to me, "I ought to be in a lunatic asylum." No doubt he was not yet ripe for that, but on the other hand he was certainly not perfectly sane.

After the coal city we went to Gravesend on the Thames, and from there to Cowes for the regatta. This visit was not in our program but had been arranged by our embassy in London as an act of courtesy for our widowed crown princess, Archduchess Stephanie, who happened to be staying on the Isle of Wight with her little daughter, Elisabeth. The archduchess wished to watch the regatta from the *Donau*, and we were therefore allotted a very favorable anchorage, from which one could observe the proceedings very well. The archduchess had always given proof of her special sympathies for our navy, which were warmly reciprocated, the naval officers being her most devoted admirers. The illustrious lady knew this, and when moving in naval circles she was always simple and natural, evidently feeling very much at ease. Long ago I had had the honor of being presented to the crown princess, and I was therefore particularly pleased to see her here and to be able to pay my respects to her and her daughter. Every day during the regatta they both spent many hours on board our ship.

The father of the crown princess, King Leopold II of Belgium, had also come to Cowes on his yacht. We knew that the crown princess had begged her father to grant her an interview, something he did not seem to be particularly keen on doing, because he first made excuses and finally—probably only because of the unfavorable impression such a refusal would have created—said he would meet his daughter on board the *Donau*. The meeting took place on deck one morning under our eyes, and as far as we could see it was rather unpleasant. The king's attitude was freezing. He frustrated every attempt of his daughter to approach him confidentially by conversing with the captain and officers on other matters during the whole interview, which only lasted ten minutes. His behavior made a most unpleasant impression on us, but the children of crowned heads grow up under circumstances different from other mortals. They may be more sensitive in some respects, but they do not know the warmth of family feelings. Perhaps, then, the crown princess was less shocked at the meeting than we were. One day she invited the captain, two other officers, and me to lunch. I cannot tell why, but this honor did not seem to please the captain, and finally in the eleventh hour he declared that he would not accept the invitation, ordering me to convey his excuses to Her Imperial Highness. He thus deprived himself not only of a distinction, but of some very charming hours in a social sphere of special attraction.

In Plymouth, our next port, I was very glad to see Admiral Fremantle, one of the most distinguished English admirals of his day, whom I had met earlier at Zanzibar.[11] One day he appeared at lunch as the captain's guest, together with Lady Fremantle and a fascinating niece, whose dark eyes flashed in a most un-British manner. After we had exchanged reminiscences of Zanzibar, we spoke of our present cruise. When Lady Fremantle heard where we had been and that we had visited several of the West Indian Islands, her tired looks suddenly took on a more animated expression. Something had evidently awakened the old lady's interest. "Oh," she said, turning to me with a sigh, "how I envy you your trip! No doubt you have brought back fine postage stamps. Have you already been asked for them?" In those days I was not interested in stamps, but friends at home had asked me to bring them some for their collections. I therefore possessed what the admiral's wife desired, but I was nevertheless astonished at her question and replied with a casual, "No, I have not yet been bothered with stamps." Then I saw the mischievous, smiling face of my pretty neighbor, who turned to me and said, "But you will be bothered now." But "bothered" was not the proper designation for what happened in the cabin after lunch. This was not "bothering" but robbery and piracy, for all my philatelic treasures passed from the drawer of my desk into the old lady's pocket, accompanied by exclamations of delight.

Lisbon was our destination after Plymouth. On our arrival, a conflict with the shore authorities started that lasted a full week and kept all those mixed up in it in a state of great excitement. The officer on watch and the signal midshipman declared, in contradiction to the local authorities, that our salute had not been fully returned. The captain probably thought that the honor of the Austro-Hungarian Monarchy had been compromised. Neither party gave in, the affair drew wider circles, and even the press got hold of it, playfully calling our ship "the ticklish *Donau*." The fort that had fired the salute lay at a good distance from us, and since a sharp wind had been blowing at the time and had made the report of guns nearly inaudible, it seemed to me that we and not the Portuguese might very well be wrong. For that reason I was not much interested in the matter from the outset and do not even know how it ended. I only remember that after about eight days we rendered the honors due to the Portuguese admiral's flag flying on the *Vasco da Gama*, which had not yet been done. Three times within one year I had witnessed this absurd proceeding concerning the salute: in Ancona, Santo Domingo, and now here. After this experience I firmly resolved that under my command the people on watch should never have to report to me the "number of shots fired," but only "salute returned." Where there was doubt, I myself would see that proper control was exercised.

At Lisbon we received orders to return via Palermo and to arrive at Pola on a certain day. The time at our disposal was short, and to be punctual we had either to be favored by fair breezes or to use steam. A telegram awaiting us in Palermo informed us of the death of Her Majesty Empress Elisabeth in Geneva and instructed us to have a solemn requiem celebrated after our arrival at Palermo.[12] This terribly sudden and unexpected news filled us with grief and horror. Who could have been the miserable wretch who had murdered the empress, a woman inoffensive in every way? We knew no details and kept reading and rereading the words of the telegraph. It was too late in the evening to take any steps. Next morning the consul general was awakened from his slumbers and the archbishop was asked to arrange for a requiem. However, the officer who had been sent on shore returned with the information that the day happened to be a high feast of the Church on which no Mass for the dead could be said. It was of no avail that I myself tried to silence ecclesiastical scruples. Everywhere the reply was "non possumus." Finally the captain went on shore to try his best, while I had the ship's coal supply replenished, which soon gave the white *Donau* the aspect of mourning. One will wonder why we were in such a hurry, as surely it would have been the simplest thing in the world to post-pone the requiem to the next day. No doubt this would have been the proper thing, but we were all under the influence of our orders and the date by which we had to be in Pola, with which we could only just comply.

Shortly after lunch the commander came on board, triumphantly exclaim-ing, "At four in the afternoon the fathers in such-and-such monastery will say a litany for the dead empress, and all officers not on duty and half of the men will have to attend." I pointed to the mountains of coal covering the deck and to the great cleaning that was necessary, but it was to no avail. This time the captain remained firm. In any event, I was glad that the requiem question seemed to be resolved; none of us knew that a litany was not a substitute for a Mass. We left Palermo on the same evening, steaming toward the Straits of Messina. We had hardly passed through them when the captain's sailor heart was so stirred by this sight that to my unbounded astonishment he gave orders to set all sails, even though not the gentlest breath of air rippled the perfect smoothness of the sea. All my arguments that the heavy masses of black smoke that rose from the funnel and moved right astern would suffocate the men on the yards and also spoil our white sail forever and cause us trouble on the part of the navy yard people were of no use. I had to obey orders. But the sails had hardly been let fall and the topsails were not yet hoisted when he realized the senselessness of his order and countermanded it. It often takes a good deal of patience to be a subaltern.

By the time we reached Pola I had exhausted my capacity of forbearance. For sixteen months I had had to struggle, at first against hatred, then against unreasonableness. This had made me tired and indifferent. Every campaign of this kind closes with a thorough two-day inspection of the ship by the port admiral, during which all sorts of exercises have to show the degree of training of officers and men. To this tribulation I still had to resign myself; then my days of woe were over. The admiral had announced his visit for the next day but one. The short interval between the arrival and the inspection usually serves for cleaning up the ship to the highest pitch. Scrubbing and rubbing go on day and night, and brushes, soap, and paint are lavishly used until the last moment. For sixteen months I had been a dutiful executive officer, the first out of bed and the last in bed, day after day, had maintained strict discipline, and had practiced drill of every kind. I therefore thought that I had done enough, and my innermost being revolted against any such final humbug. "This ship has been like this all the time. Judge it. I don't aspire to more than that." I said this to myself, stubbornly and boldly, and for the first time I did not bother about clean-ing and polishing, only giving orders that the usual routine should be strictly followed.

On the morning of the day on which Vice Admiral Hinke was to inspect the ship I left my cabin only half an hour before his arrival. Hinke was a true mar-tinet. The perfect tidiness of the men's outward appearance was his hobby, and with the eyes of a lynx he knew how to spot the slightest incorrectness as to

Chapter V. (1886-89)

first Expedition to Africa.

Count Teleki I had agreed, that we
discuss in Vienna about the middle of
some details concerning the Ex-
meanwhile I had without any
y obtained a leave for an indefinite
, was even granted full pay for
le time of my absence. The Com=
in Chief of our Navy, the Vice in
von Sternech, years ago, had himself
a short extratour in Arctic regions
avored any enterprise which contri/
to make the navy popular.
My discussions did not refer to the route
with the Count

Ludwig von Höhnel as a
young Austro-Hungarian
naval officer. (Rokeby
Collection)

Portion of Ludwig von Höhnel's original
handwritten manuscript for *Over Land
and Sea*. (Rokeby Collection)

Ludwig von Höhnel on the
East African coast, 1887.
(Courtesy of Erdélyi Lajos)

Ludwig von Höhnel (*seated at right*) in the camp of the German
explorer, Dr. Hans Meyer, Taveta, East Africa, 1887. (Courtesy
of Erdélyi Lajos)

Admiral Maximilian Freiherr Daublebsky von Sterneck, Commander-in-Chief of the Austro-Hungarian Navy. In 1886, he gave Ludwig von Höhnel permission to travel to East Africa with Count Samuel Teleki. (Courtesy of the Österreichisches Staatsarchiv/Kriegsarchiv and Erwin F. Sieche)

William Astor Chanler in Cairo on his return in 1889 from his first trip to East Africa. (Rokeby Collection)

Count Samuel Teleki at Lake Baringo, East Africa, 1888. (Courtesy of Erdélyi Lajos)

One of William Astor Chanler's East African camps, 1892. *Seated left to right*: Chanler, Ludwig von Höhnel, and George E. Galvin. Standing behind von Höhnel in a striped shirt is Sururu, Chanler's tent servant. (Rokeby Collection)

Ludwig von Höhnel being carried in a hammock after being gored by a rhinoceros. (Rokeby Collection)

Inauguration of the Sayid Ali bin Said (*center left*) as Sultan of Zanzibar, February, 1890. To his left in a white uniform is General Lloyd William Mathews, the prime minister who later instigated the collapse of William Astor Chanler's expedition. (Rokeby Collection)

William Astor Chanler in 1894 after his second East African expedition. (Rokeby Collection).

The Emperor Francis Joseph, for whom Ludwig von Höhnel was an aide-de-camp from 1899 to 1903. (Courtesy of the Österreichische National Bibliothek)

George E. Galvin in 1901. (Courtesy of George E. Galvin, Jr.)

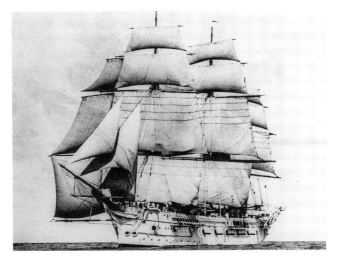

The Austro-Hungarian corvette, *Donau (II)* (2,343.5 tons), under full sail. Ludwig von Höhnel served on this ship as gunnery and watch officer during an 1894-1895 cruise through the Atlantic. (Courtesy of the Österreichisches Staatsarchiv/Kriegsarchiv and Erwin F. Sieche)

The Austro-Hungarian light cruiser, *Panther* (1,530 tons), which Ludwig von Höhnel commanded in 1905-1906. (Rokeby Collection)

The Emperor Menelik II of Ethiopia. (From Prince Henri d'Orléans, *Une visite à l'Empereur Ménélick*, Paris: Librairie Dentu, 1898)

L'Empereur Menélick

The Austro-Hungarian cruiser, *Sankt Georg* (7,300 tons), in the foreground at Hampton Roads, Virginia, 26 April 1907. Ludwig von Höhnel served as flag captain of the *Sankt Georg* during its visit to the United States to celebrate the Jamestown Tri-Centennial Exposition. (Courtesy of the Jahn Collection and Erwin F. Sieche)

Ludwig von Höhnel on the bridge of the *Panther*. (Rokeby Collection)

Ludwig von Höhnel in the uniform of an Austro-Hungarian Rear Admiral. (Rokeby Collection)

The Austro-Hungarian naval station at Pola, Croatia in the 1890s. Ludwig von Höhnel served as commander-in-chief of the naval station from 19 March through 1 August 1909, when he retired from the navy. (Courtesy of the Österreichisches Staatsarchiv/Kriegsarchiv and Erwin F. Sieche)

Ludwig von Höhnel (*standing*) visiting his friend, William Astor Chanler (*in bed*), at a Swiss clinic in 1915, where the latter was convalescing from a leg injury. (Courtesy of William Astor Chanler, Jr.)

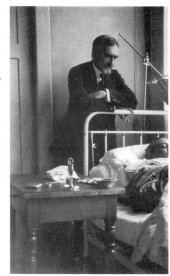

Ludwig von Höhnel (*foreground*) at the wedding of the Princess Maria Antonia de Bragança of Portugal and Sidney Ashley Chanler, Seebenstein Castle, Austria, 13 June 1934. (Courtesy of William Astor Chanler, Jr.)

Ludwig von Höhnel (*center rear with white beard*) at the wedding of the Princess Maria Antonia de Bragança of Portugal and Sidney Ashley Chanler (*in carriage*), Seebenstein Castle, Austria, 13 June 1934. (Rokeby Collection).

Plaque honoring Ludwig von Höhnel erected at the apartment house at Reisnerstrasse 61, Vienna, where he lived from 1909 until his death in 1942. (Ronald E. Coons)

IN DIESEM HAUSE WOHNTE VON 1909
BIS ZU SEINEM TODE DER
AFRIKAFORSCHER
KONTERADMIRAL
LUDWIG von HÖHNEL
1857 – 1942

KULTURAMT DER STADT WIEN
ÖSTERR. GEOGRAPHISCHE GESELLSCHAFT

Bronze bust of Ludwig von Höhnel in the Afrikamuseum, Schloss Marchegg, Austria. (Ronald E. Coons)

von Höhnel monument in Vienna's Central Cemetery. (Ronald E. Coons)

clothing. By his strictness in this regard he had, in the course of several years, really had a beneficial influence on the men as far as neatness was concerned. When I left my cabin at 7:30, the first bugler stood before me. I glanced casually along the deck and at the bugle, and to my astonishment perceived that he was wearing brown laces with his black shoes, which was very much against regulations. I must note that this man had followed me day after day when I had inspected the dress of the men. Thus he himself had escaped my attention. I was astonished that precisely this fellow, who was otherwise obedient and always neat, should be so incorrectly garbed at this critical moment. But I gave vent to my surprise only by pointing to the brown laces, ironically saying they were very beautiful, firmly convinced that he would rush off and change them. The fatal moment approached, and officers and men fell in on deck to receive the admiral. The bugler blared his signal into the morning air in wonderful clarity. Having listened to my report, the admiral approached the front line with quick steps and suddenly stopped before its first man, the bugler, as if stung by a scorpion, exclaiming, "What on earth have we here?" The wretch was still wearing his brown shoelaces! I could not believe my eyes but remained silent. When the admiral next felt under his cloth shirt with an experienced hand and discovered that the man was wearing his strap outside instead of inside, he looked at me furiously and said, "That too!" I thought I was dreaming and said, "Your Excellency will not find another case of this kind." "We shall see," was his ungracious answer. As a matter of fact he did not find any other fault regarding the dress of the men, and he found no reason to criticize anything severely during the two-day inspection. The exercises went off all right, though to work with drenched sails—it had poured the night before—was rather a trial. I was therefore astonished when at the end of the inspection the admiral addressed me as follows: "The ship is clean and well kept, and the men are well drilled and disciplined; I have an eye for that. However, I do not have the impression that the utmost has been reached which might have been obtained." It was a matter of indifference to me what he said. I therefore replied "Yes Sir," faced round, and went my way.

A fortnight later I started on a well-earned three-month leave, which I spent largely in Transylvania at the invitation of Count Teleki. I traveled via Vienna and first went to the Admiralty, there to report my arrival. The late commander in chief, Baron von Sterneck, had been replaced by Vice Admiral Spaun. I was only received by his representative, however, who in a long conversation kindly questioned me about many details of the cruise. I soon had the impression that he was primarily curious about the ship's surgeon, whom he seemed to hold responsible to some extent for the premature death of Captain Hermann, a thought against which I protested most emphatically. It always makes me angry when people hunt for a scapegoat, as if circumstances alone did not in most cases suffice to explain events, and as if fate did not exist.

In the mood I was in at the time there was no better place for me than at my friend Count Teleki's quiet country seat. There I was removed from everything that could remind me of the yoke I had borne so long, and I could breathe freely in a circle of warm-hearted friends, where the months of my leave passed all too quickly. Finally I had to return, not to Pola but to Trieste, there to supervise the progress of the construction of the armored cruiser *Kaiser Karl VI*, a task I gladly fulfilled. I was more or less my own master, and my intercourse was chiefly with ship builders and engineers, from whom I could learn a great deal.

The position of a supervisor of construction was often considered a sinecure. From that point of view the occupation is a dull one, but if one is in the least interested in the matter, the day passes very quickly amidst the animated traffic of a big shipyard. How much there was to be seen! I was able to witness at various stages the gradual evolution of a modern man-of-war, the greatest work of art that technicians have created; I could penetrate into the bowels of these giant bodies and thus gain insights unknown to a naval officer who only sees the finished ship.

The ship whose construction I had to supervise was built at San Rocco near Trieste by the Stabilimento Tecnico Triestino and had already progressed considerably. Next to it were two battleships that were still in the first stages of construction. Moreover, there were furnaces and other plants near the shipyard, and the Lloyd Arsenal was also in the neighborhood. Indeed, there was so much to see that my time was too short. My task consisted in supervising the quality of the material used and the proper execution of the work. The building firms made use of all sorts of devices to distract the attention of the undesired controller. For example, being as a rule the presumptive executive officer, he was begged to inspect his future cabin and requested to express his wishes concerning its arrangements, equipment, paneling, painting, upholstering, and the like so as to concentrate his attention on his cabin and to take it away from other things. They tried the same thing on me and were astonished when I declined their invitation, saying that this was a secondary matter. That made the builders more conscientious in their work, but I must add that the firm in question proved to be thoroughly reliable, meeting all my wishes whenever they could, even though this sometimes involved considerably increased costs.

The shipyard lay at a considerable distance from the city, so that I always remained there over lunch and only started home toward 3:00 P.M. I was tired by that time and usually remained at home, so that the Corso saw very little of me. This pleasant appointment did not last long, however. Already in the middle of April 1899, after hardly two and a half months, I received the unexpected notification during the noon interval that I should present myself immediately at the maritime prefecture at Trieste. I could not imagine what was wanted and why anyone was looking for me at that hour. In spite of all my surmises I could not guess the reason for this call, and in this state of uncertainty I hurried to town. My astonishment may therefore be imagined when the commander of the naval station, Rear Admiral [Franz Ritter] von Perin, holding a telegram in his hand, congratulated me on my appointment as aide-de-camp (*Flügeladjutant*) to His Majesty the Emperor and King. This was no doubt a special honor, and the thought of being brought into the close vicinity of the ruler and highest war lord should have made me proud and happy. To the contrary, the idea of having to live at court and move only in splendid rooms on the slippery floors of the palaces did not tempt me much, since I did not consider myself suited for service of this kind. In time, however, I told myself that since fate had allotted me to this duty, it would also give me the necessary capacity for fulfilling it. I therefore looked to the future more confidently, though I had not the slightest idea of what things would be like. I think one has no inkling of the qualities hidden in oneself, just as one does not know the depths of iniquity to which he might descend.

I was supposed to start my new duties with His Majesty on May 1, at which date my promotion to commander (*Korvettenkapitän*) was due. I did not have many days to prepare for my new existence, so I had to make good use of them. What seemed most important was to practice horseback riding, at which I was by no means an adept, and I immediately put myself in the hands of a riding master, who was an Italian. He was efficient and took a great deal of trouble, so that I made good progress. Thus the fortnight that separated me from the day of my departure for Vienna soon drew to a close, and my confidence gradually increased. My promotion also contributed toward this. A staff officer surely was another kind of man from a subaltern! When I passed the barracks, the sentry called "Gwehr rrraus!" and the soldiers on watch presented arms. On the Corso I was saluted with greater respect, and I gradually began to harbor prouder thoughts, though I did not go to the extreme of imagining that overnight a halo had suddenly adorned me.

9

Aide-de-Camp to Emperor Francis Joseph I (1899–1903)

W hen I arrived in Vienna to take up my duties as aide-de-camp on May 1, 1899, His Majesty happened to be away at Budapest. Thus I did not have to sail full speed into new waters and could devote my time to calls on various people belonging to the imperial household. Without exception I found them polite and pleasant, and in general the tone that prevailed in these circles was very different from the military milieu I knew so well. It was important for me to acquaint myself with the extensive and complicated interior of the old Hofburg so that I was familiar with its numerous exits and entrances, its various apartments, and its many twisted staircases and corridors. I also had to reconnoiter the palace and park of Schönbrunn, on the outskirts of Vienna. Finally, I had to think about my riding, which I immediately resumed in the riding school on a noble Lipizzaner by the name of Kossack who had helped many a beginner over the first difficult stages.

In the course of all these first moves a fellow officer, Lieutenant M. Huber, acted as my faithful mentor. For some years he had been attached to the military chancellery of the emperor and was a favorite with its chief, Field Marshal von Bolfras.[1] A keen observer of men and experienced in court life, Huber was able to give me valuable pointers. This was all the more useful as I otherwise would have received no instruction whatever on my duties. I often wonder whether envy, a plant that flourishes in the atmosphere of courts and rejoices the heart of every true courtier when he sees others make a faux pas, was at the bottom of this omission.

The apartment allotted to me in the Hofburg consisted of two rooms plus a servant's room and was situated on the third floor of the Amalienhof. The rooms had vaulted ceilings and were low, as were the windows, which reached down to the floor. The furniture was worn and threadbare, and the whole did not make a very imperial impression—all the more so as there was no bathroom or any other convenience. On the same corridor the other aides-de-camp and some of the ladies-in-waiting were housed—countesses, as I saw from the inscriptions on their doors.

As aide-de-camp to His Majesty I was not subordinated to the Admiralty and also drew my monthly pay and the imperial allowance of 200 florins from the court exchequer. I was, however, allowed to continue to wear my navy uniform.

One day I had to go to Budapest to report to His Majesty and be received in audience. On this occasion I learned for the first time how agreeably one traveled as an imperial aide-de-camp. Every possible arrangement was made for my convenience without having to ask for it. Porters came unbidden to carry the luggage to the court fourgon, which then took it to the station. There I did not have to trouble myself about any detail; I entered the hall like a grand seigneur and was quickly taken to my compartment by the official on duty. I really had to fight against the idea that overnight I had been transformed into some grand personage. Upon arrival at Budapest, I drove in a gilded coach over the beautiful suspension bridge and up the steep mountain street to the Hofburg, situated in a picturesque position on the heights of Ofen (Buda); my heart beat violently for joy and happiness.

I first had to report to Count Paar, the adjutant general.[2] He received me with a winning smile and a friendly "Hello, so there you are." Whistling softly to himself, he pointed to the sofa and asked me a few indifferent questions. Count Paar was a most distinguished gentleman: kind and even-tempered, quiet but amiable with everyone, and in no way condescending. His most severe displeasure was marked by silence. Unfortunately, my audience with His Majesty has completely escaped my memory. At luncheon I made the acquaintance of the three other aides-de-camp—Lieutenant Colonel Prince Hugo Dietrichstein and Majors Wessely and Pitlik—and the members of the imperial suite. I then returned to Vienna, where I had other calls to make. The most winning impression I received was that of the above-mentioned second adjutant general of His Majesty, Field Marshal von Bolfras. I should also mention Prince Rudolf Liechtenstein, the first grand master of the imperial household, who was a supple, elegant horseman and who radiated a general warmth and simplicity.[3] Day by day my insight into this new world increased and my confidence improved. Nevertheless, I felt very awkward when for the first time I had to ride out of doors through the city, which occurred about ten days later. Flanked by two court riders in brown tail coats, I rode along the Ringstrasse to the large park known as the Prater. As I hated every kind of ostentation, this was always like running the gauntlet, and I never grew accustomed to it.

With considerable nervousness I looked forward to the day when I should have to do duty as aide-de-camp in His Majesty's presence for the first time. There were four of us. Every year one of these left and was replaced by a new arrival. In their selection a certain rule was followed regarding the different branches of the military, for none of these should feel neglected. Nevertheless, cavalry officers were favored, probably because of the orderly duties that had to be made on horseback, and usually there were two of them. His Majesty had only included the navy rather late, in fact not before 1889, and its turn came every ten years. The later Vice Admiral Sachs was the first sailor aide-de-camp to the old emperor; the last in this capacity was Horthy, the present viceroy of Hungary.[4] Service in Vienna was carried on in turn by four, in Budapest by three, and in Schönbrunn and everywhere else by two aides-de-camp. As everyone knows, His Majesty was an early riser. Duty therefore began at the cold, raw hour of 4:00 A.M., no matter what the season, and it often continued until late in the afternoon or even into night. In order to be sure to be ready in due time, one had to get up earlier still, and for that reason there was a special bedroom in the Hofburg reserved for whichever aide-de-camp happened to be on duty in the morning. When the court resided in Vienna, only the aide-de-camp on duty was fed from the imperial kitchen, and not the others. In all other instances—at Schönbrunn and Bad Ischl, and in Hungary, for example—one not only got all his meals served, but in the bargain received a daily remuneration, which alone, as I freely avow, permitted me to keep myself financially above water. Of my companions in the first year, Prince Dietrichstein was of the cavalry, Wessely of the artillery, and Pitlik of the infantry. They were all married men and did not live with their families in the Hofburg; they rarely used the official quarters allotted to them. I should mention that the wives of the imperial aides-de-camp played no official part at court. It was as if they did not exist.

My first day on duty came in the second half of May, when the imperial household had returned to Vienna from Budapest. It was customary that one of the off-duty aides-de-camp should assist the newcomer at the beginning and keep him company. Two rooms, the audience hall and a council chamber opening out of it, separated the aides-de-camp from the emperor's study, in which the venerable ruler sat at his desk from early morning until about 5:00 P.M., hardly allowing himself time for a simple lunch. Here he received the rare calls of members of the imperial family, the occasional reports of ministers, and the daily reports of the two adjutants general. The connection with the room of the aides-de-camp was established by means of an old-fashioned bell, which all too often acted only by a slight swing of the contrivance. We therefore had to keep a sharp lookout and often throw a glance at the rusty bell crank to see whether it was trying to ring, for His Majesty was impatient and was accustomed to being served with lightning rapidity.

Given the emperor's full schedule, every minute was precious. It rarely happened that the aide-de-camp on duty was called before 7:30 in the morning. Until that hour, from four o'clock on, one filled the time by breakfasting, reading the papers, and being extremely bored. When the bell at last rang, it used to give me quite a start, but the interruption of monotony was a relief. It then was a question of rushing through the two adjoining halls to the emperor's door, which I would open without knocking but with an audible, though not violent, shove in order to announce myself to His Majesty, who had his back turned to the door. The emperor would greet me with a "Good morning," to which, however, one did not reply. I would then take from his hands the leather bag containing his finished morning work and receive instructions to notify various ministers or other individuals to appear at a certain hour. This meant listening carefully in order to remember the various names, hours, and minutes, for woe would result if the carefully prepared daily program was upset by forgetfulness or mistakes. The forms printed for this purpose were quickly filled out and sent to the respective addresses by a horseman of the guard. Every day, usually before 9:00 A.M., Count Paar appeared, his report as a rule only taking a short while. Meanwhile the always-welcome head of the military chancellery, Bolfras, turned up in order not to miss the chance of seeing His Majesty. We always looked forward to the appearance and animated chat of this important yet charmingly cordial personage. In the course of time the ministers and court functionaries who had been sent for arrived, in evening dress and black tie if they belonged to the civil service. With all of them we had to be polite and diverting in conversation. For their part, they did not lack in animation; sometimes, if they had a long wait, they disclosed matters that remained hidden from the general public, thus permitting an interesting and amusing glance behind the scenes.

Under these circumstances the hands of the clock moved slowly toward the noon hour on uneventful days. I would have been on my legs since the early morning and for a couple of hours had been polite, amiable, and in a state of tension. It was time to send to the imperial kitchen for lunch, but there was not always time to enjoy it *cum otio et dignitate* [with leisure and dignity]. At the same hour that we received our meal, the lunch tray had been placed on the emperor's desk, only to be pushed aside very soon again; often I had to drop the fork I was lifting to my mouth and obey the ring of the bell. The afternoons were usually quieter; sometimes I only had to receive a portfolio or two from the emperor or take one to him. When this was the case after four o'clock, the greed with which His Majesty used to seize the bag showed how impatiently he had been waiting for it. At five o'clock dinner was served, which His Majesty took alone in a room adjoining his study and which the aide-de-camp took in his "duty bedroom." The dinner was excellent. There were two kinds of wines, and on Sundays and holidays there was half a bottle of Moët et Chandon, the only brand drunk at our court. We were served during this solitary meal by a number of lackeys in rich liveries, assisted by a kitchen official armed with a sword. But I could not say that this solemn and obsequious crowd enhanced my pleasure. After about twenty minutes it was advisable to return to the room where one was on duty, since His Majesty had the habit of appearing personally soon thereafter to dismiss his aide-de-camp graciously with the stereotyped words, "I thank you, I do not require you any more, good night."

This simple daily routine was sometimes pleasantly interrupted, either by official functions, royal visits, or the many other duties of a ruler, of which I will speak in due time. I had no difficulty in adapting myself to the different roles I had to play, and I cannot remember having made any mistakes. At the beginning, however, I did shock my surroundings by the cut of my beard, though not, as far as I know, the emperor. At first my short-cropped sailor's beard was pronounced "impossible at court" by the eldest aide-de-camp. There followed some remarks from higher worthies, though these hints were uttered with a smile and I took no notice of them. When finally the first master of the imperial household addressed me in a pleasant, joking manner as the "man with the incorrect beard," I took the liberty of replying that I would of course modify it on special order from His Majesty, but otherwise I would prefer not to do so. From that moment on I was left in peace. Full beards were not worn at court, and Vandyke beards were so disdained in the army that the slightest attempt at such was criticized by His Majesty at every opportunity in a most ungracious and irritable manner, without regard to the rank of the person in question.

Among the periodic interruptions of daily routine were the general audiences. These receptions, which were exhausting for the old emperor, at first used to take place twice a week, on Monday and Thursday, but later on only once a week. Between ten and twelve o'clock, anywhere from fifty to eighty persons had to be received by the old gentleman, listened to, and then dismissed after a suitable answer had been given. This placed great demands on His Majesty's marvelous memory and experience, lest the whole thing become a mere formality. It was also trying for the aide-de-camp to remember the rank and name of each of the many applicants for audiences and to announce them without making a mistake. Everything had to be done at tremendous speed, moreover, in order to avoid any loss of time. One can realize what it would have meant if ten seconds had been wasted eighty separate times and if the entrance door had had to be opened and shut by the doorkeeper twice instead of only once. At the same moment that the dismissed person issued from the door, one had to glide past like an eel, announce the full rank and name of the next applicant, and then disappear again. The sequence of announcements closely followed rank; with princely persons, there sometimes arose difficult problems of protocol for the aide-de-camp. Incredibly, it was not the ceremonial department, whose task it should have been to establish the sequence of rank, but rather the aides-de-camp who dealt with any problems that arose. We were handed alphabetical lists of names and the corresponding titles, and it was our affair to settle the sequence of reception. There was a good reason for this. With regard to personages of high rank it was not always possible to arrange matters so that the one or the other would not feel neglected. To avoid recriminations, the ceremonial department hit on the simple idea of leaving the responsibility up to us. If at any time a faux pas was committed, one could accuse us of the mistake; out of respect for the emperor, nobody would easily approach him to lodge a formal complaint. At the same time we were absolutely forbidden to ask His Majesty for instructions in especially delicate cases, although sometimes he used to give us some advice shortly before the beginning of audiences, especially when it was a question of noble ladies. One will smile at the importance I allot to this subject, but I am relating my experiences at court, where so much revolved around rank and precedence.

Much sooner than I cared for I was called upon to show myself as a horseman. This was at the beginning of June on the occasion of the inspection of one of the Vienna regiments in the Prater. Being the aide-de-camp on duty, I first accompanied His Majesty to the forester's lodge lying near the entrance to the Prater. Here the horses were waiting, which we immediately mounted, riding off at a brisk trot. We followed the Hauptallee until a road branched off, where we met a large mounted party of generals who were awaiting their war lord. When he arrived, His Majesty slackened speed for a moment and acknowledged the respectful salutes of the assembly. The two adjutants general followed in his wake, and the aide-de-camp eldest in rank made haste to reach the head of the procession, while my other two comrades rode on at my sides. The remainder of the suite followed in an informal crowd. The formation of the procession took place at great speed and with wonderful precision, for everybody except me was acquainted with the spot and place he had to fill and knew that His Majesty was wont to proceed toward the neighboring maneuver field at a rapid trot.

Early in July I was introduced to an important phase of my life as an imperial aide-de-camp when His Majesty, as was his custom, moved to Bad Ischl for the summer season. This was the happiest time of the year for the old emperor, and he looked forward to it with joyful anticipation. There, in delicious aromatic mountain air, released from the daily round of business, he could lead the life of a country gentleman; in these congenial surroundings he devoted himself to the shooting of deer or chamois. He could also experience at least a semblance of family life in a smaller circle. His suite consisted of Count Paar, two aides-de-camp, preacher to the court, Dr. Mayer,[5] and the court physician.

The imperial villa was modest, and together with some outbuildings it was not very spacious. In consequence, the higher court functionaries only appeared singly and for a short visit, usually stopping at Ischl hotels. During the whole of the emperor's stay his daughter, Archduchess Valerie, used to be her father's guest, along with her numerous children and her retinue. His elder daughter, Princess Gisela, her husband Prince Leopold of Bavaria, and their sons Princes George and Conrad also used to stay for some weeks; they lived, however, in another villa in Ischl. Short visits by royalty were comparatively rare. We aides-de-camp had no regular or noteworthy duties to perform, which was quite exceptional. We only had to put in an appearance daily at the family meal, which was served at 3:00 P.M., and we always participated in the shooting parties as guests. For the rest of the time we were free. Together with the court riding master, I used to take long morning rides in the surroundings and thus got to know the area extremely well.

I looked forward to the first "family dinner" with considerable curiosity. Previously I had only come into contact with His Majesty in a military function; now I was about to get to know him from a more human point of view. The pavilion in which we were housed lay removed from the actual imperial villa, but a covered wooden gallery, open at the sides, led there over a distance of several hundred paces, so that even in rainy weather one could reach the villa without getting wet. As the dinner hour approached, Count Paar, Prince

Dietrichstein, and I started for the villa, in the hall of which the guests assembled in order to await the appearance of His Majesty. The Archduchess Valerie soon appeared with her ladies-in-waiting, and also her husband, Archduke Francis Salvator, with his chamberlain. The attitude of the assembly was very stiff and the prevailing mood solemn. Whispered presentations took place which were confirmed by a nod of the head or a limp handshake, according to the person. Coming from the park, His Majesty then entered at a quick pace and was greeted by all with graceful curtsies and deep obeisances. These he answered after a rapid glance over the assembly with a slight bow, less rigid than was his wont because of the ladies present. Possibly a few commonplace remarks on the weather or some such subject were then exchanged between His Majesty and his daughter or her ladies-in-waiting, but one soon passed on into the dining room. There we were served by a dozen lackeys in rich liveries, who watched the table from behind a screen but could only see His Majesty and his immediate neighbors. The dinner passed quietly and, to my relief, very quickly. There was little talk. From time to time His Majesty addressed a question to the archduchess or one of the high functionaries; a concise low-voiced reply was given, and silence reigned once more. To talk among ourselves would surely have been considered a grave lapse of etiquette. The lackeys took little notice of us, who as aides-de-camp were the lowest-ranking guests. We were of course served last, and plates were often removed again without regard to whether we had finished our dish or not, so that many a good morsel was only glanced at and never tasted. But even if no such hurry had prevailed, one could not have called it a pleasant feast. When the dinner was over, we went into the adjoining room to smoke and stood about uncomfortably for a short time, until His Majesty retired with a nod of his head and we were free to leave. In the vicinity of the villa one then saw the emperor sitting in the open air in a wicker armchair, surrounded by his grandchildren, who were playing on the grass.

Such was the first family dinner in the imperial villa, and the two following meals were as like it as two pins. I certainly had not expected to be received in this exalted sphere as one forming part of it, but I had not realized that I would be so completely ignored. Hardly a glance and not a word had I been granted in these three days, and an attitude of this kind was certainly more than I had bargained for. I had not evinced any desire for an appointment as aide-de-camp, not even in my dreams, and if this was what it was like, then I would gladly renounce the honor. My nature, which inclined more toward simplicity and natural manners, revolted against such treatment, and my dissatisfaction grew day by day. I felt that I had to leave these surroundings at least for a few hours and breathe less rarefied air. In this mood, I changed into mufti after the third family dinner so as not to be reminded by anything of my life so brilliant on the outside but so unsatisfactory in truth, and I sallied forth in no definite direction. In my desire to get away from the place where I was feeling so uncomfortable I moved toward the station, took a seat in the train that was just starting, and left. Where should I go? I didn't know and I didn't care. Then the idea struck me that I might visit the Schafberg, one of the mountains of the Salzburg Alps, which is topped by an Alpine hotel and which one reaches by a cog-wheel railway from St. Wolfgang. I spent a misty evening at a height of 1,780 meters above sea level, had a bad supper, and slept miserably. But at least I had been my own master.

The next day, when I reached Ischl in time for the family dinner and again solemnly accompanied Count Paar and Prince Dietrichstein to the villa, I felt freer and looked forward to my duties in a calmer frame of mind. As it happened, matters turned out differently than I had expected. Again we were all assembled in the hall, awaiting the appearance of our liege lord. His Majesty had hardly entered the room when, perceiving me, he approached me with rapid steps and addressed me, evidently full of interest, "So you have been on the Schafberg! How did you like it? Was your bed not damp?" And so forth and so on. His Majesty had deigned to show some interest in my humble person, and now the finely strung worthies, so sensitive to the faintest breath of imperial favor, also had to show a lively interest in my doings. The ice was broken. The way these high personages had acted is no doubt based on a certain principle. One evidently wishes to watch the newcomer for a certain time and form a judgment before first extending one and then two fingers to him, and in time the whole hand. His Majesty was not profuse in his handshakes; he never did so on the impulse of the moment but only in accordance with principles he had established. Aides-de-camp were distinguished by handshakes for the first time on the occasion of the birthday congratulations, which took place during the sojourn at Ischl, later on when meeting again after a separation of several months, and finally when they took their definite leave.

It was the shooting parties that made the sojourn at Ischl so desirable. His Majesty looked forward to them with keen pleasure and could never start early enough, although his enthusiasm for shooting waned year by year, a fact that is hardly astonishing in view of his old age.[6] Yet though we were well-off in Ischl with regard to shooting, it was sometimes too much of a good thing. After the arrival of the Bavarian prince and other occasional guests, the chain of shooting days was uninterrupted. For weeks we never had an undisturbed night, so that we finally felt the consequences of this pleasure in all our limbs. Then His Majesty only participated in some of the shootings, often offering the pretext of work. I wondered, however, that the others, most of whom were old gentlemen, kept up so well, and I strongly suspected that they made up for what they had been robbed of at night by taking a nap at their shooting stands. Humanity is given to exaggeration, and I agree with the Englishman who expressed his conception of existence with words to the effect that life would be tolerable if it were not for its pleasures.

The advancing season occasionally brought court functionaries, ministers, and ambassadors, who created an agreeable change. Among the repeated visits which had grown to be a formal annual tradition and which were always connected with court dinners were those of the aged but beautiful Dowager Queen

Marie of Hanover, the Duke and Duchess Robert of Württemberg, Don Alfonso of Bourbon and his wife, and finally the family of the Duke of Cumberland,[7] all of whose summer residences lay in the neighborhood. The aged emperor, who was particularly chivalrous with regard to ladies, of course returned these visits even if they entailed a long and tiring drive. He never accepted invitations to dinner, however. From time to time members of foreign royal families turned up, but as a rule their visits were not much desired, as they meant an interruption of the old emperor's short summer holiday. I only remember a very few of these visits. We all regarded the stricter formalism and etiquette that accompanied these occasions as an intrusion into our quiet life, for etiquette relaxed somewhat in the course of the summer, and one even looked forward to the dinner hour with a certain pleasure. This pleasure was often diminished, however, by the fact that one's female neighbor at table very rarely came up to expectations. Only once in every season, when the family of the Duke of Cumberland came to visit the old emperor and the three charming young princesses graced the table, could one see that no one was immune to the charm of these three graces—especially the eldest of the sisters, who was just blossoming into womanhood.

In saying that etiquette relaxed somewhat, I mean that one could, with occasional glances at the dominating figure of the emperor, chat with one's neighbor and that one was also honored from time to time by a question and drawn into conversation. The talk always turned on superficial subjects and never dealt with important events or politics. In the course of time it increasingly happened that the company used me as a sort of encyclopedia, as if I knew everything. This often got me into hot water, all the more so as one was supposed to answer in a few concise words and not try the patience of the old gentleman by a long-winded explanation. In a few words it was not easy to answer such questions as how a film is produced or how long butterflies live or to explain the principles of Buddhism. One never spoke of my adventures in Africa, though whenever His Majesty presented me to some foreign royalty he never missed pointing out that I had made travels of exploration and had been wounded by a rhinoceros.

August 18, the emperor's birthday, was celebrated at Ischl with great solemnity. The townspeople were of course very happy to have their ruler in their midst for several months, year in and year out, as this gave a certain prestige to the locality and brought them many advantages, since the glamour of the court naturally attracted many visitors. Following the example of the court, many a faithful subject established himself at Ischl for the summer, and the majority of tourists came not because of the climate or the waters but because of the court. The population showed its gratitude by arranging a splendid illumination of the surrounding heights, which could be seen far off and which on the eve of August 18 made all the mountain peaks in the vicinity glow. The fairylike aspect of Ischl on one of these evenings drew everyone into the open air, and a large crowd of joyous people moved along the banks of the Traun River and through the streets and squares.

The next morning a solemn service in the parish church of Ischl assembled all the notables and all the members of the court and of high society. After the service, the court functionaries betook themselves to His Majesty's study under the leadership of the first master of the imperial household in order to offer their congratulations. The room was so small that it could hardly hold the dozen people. The venerable emperor separately received the congratulations of every member, who was limited to a respectful obeisance and to whom he replied in a manner that showed that he was touched. He shook hands with every person, which was the first occasion on which he so honored an aide-de-camp. Dinner was served in two rooms, because the usual dining hall could not hold all the guests. When the champagne was served, the senior aide-de-camp who presided at the second table, the so-called marshal's table, lifted his glass, and after saying a few words appropriate to the occasion he gave three cheers for the lord and emperor, in which the whole company joined and which echoed throughout the usually so quiet imperial villa.

In the last days of August, the sojourn at Ischl drew to a close. The annual army maneuvers were about to start, and these coming events threw a shadow before them in the shape of travel plans, maneuver programs, and general staff maps. The latter mysteriously arrived one fine day and covered our desks, as if placed there by an invisible hand to remind us that life had a more serious aspect.

During my four years as imperial aide-de-camp I had the pleasure of participating in the Ischl sojourn three times, and I also witnessed the imperial maneuvers on three occasions. In 1900, however, longing once more to breathe sea air, I asked to be allowed to serve on board a ship and was attached for a short time to the staff of Rear Admiral Count Montecuccoli, who commanded the summer squadron.

The maneuvers lasted four to five days and were carried out with large numbers of troops. The leaders as well as the opposing army corps that were subordinated to them had to maneuver under conditions that approached those of actual warfare as closely as possible. Men and materials were not spared, and the strengths and weaknesses of the leading generals were subjected to withering criticism, which for some of them meant the end of their military careers. Each year the site of the maneuvers lay in another province, probably for political reasons as well as because of the varying configuration of the terrain. I had never before had the opportunity to witness a large-scale maneuver on land or to watch the movements of opposing large army corps, and I therefore looked forward with keen interest to the approaching change of scene. I was, however, doomed to disappointment. Modern warfare does not produce those picturesque battle scenes such as we imagine when thinking of olden times. In the course of these maneuvers a situation occasionally arose that was sufficiently interesting from a general point of view and was even thrilling. The leaders endeavored, moreover, to furnish a spectacular final effort, but this was done primarily in order to please the high war lord and was in any event more in keeping with the times of chassepots and needle guns, as even a novice could see.

It was well known that His Majesty had less sympathy for the Kingdom of Bohemia than for other parts of his realm, for reasons that my wholly unpolitical mind did not try to fathom. He had not been there for a long time, and no doubt in 1899 he looked forward to the maneuvers at Reichstadt (Zakupy) with mixed feelings, at least as far as one could judge from his nervous irritability. I may possibly be mistaken, because the mood and attitude of the emperor were always somewhat forced when he acted in his capacity as first war lord. On the other hand, the province and its inhabitants seemed to rejoice over the monarch's rare visit to their province. The imperial special train passed through a veritable *via triumphalis* of flowers and flags to the capital of Prague, where a short stop at the crowded station was filled with deputations making speeches and with parades of veterans.

Reichstadt presented the animated aspect of military headquarters in wartime. Officers of the general staff moving about on foot and on horseback, orderlies rushing back and forth, and units of troops passing through the streets gave an impression of seething activity, while the uniforms of the foreign military attachés gave the finishing touch to this picture. The old chief of the general staff, Beck,[8] felt in his element and appeared rejuvenated, and in spite of the responsibilities of his office a smile always hovered on his lips. Day by day we rode out to the maneuver field, from one prominence topped by army leaders to another, occasionally going into the vicinity of the troops in order to inspect them. We three aides-de-camp followed the war lord in constant readiness wherever he went, but we were rarely entrusted with any orders, for there was no lack of officers younger and better acquainted with the locality than we. I think that during the whole of the three imperial maneuvers I witnessed, only thrice did I do duty as an orderly officer, and I remember the circumstances only because of the events that accompanied them. When one morning His Majesty approached an artillery regiment that was posted along the borders of a wood, the colonel had the misfortune to forget that he was supposed to be in the thick of war and that military honors were reduced to bullets and grenades. He therefore brought the fighting to a stop and ordered the trumpeter to sound the usual signal of reception. His Majesty indignantly turned round in the saddle, caught sight of me behind him, and cried, "Ride there and tell the colonel that he is an ass." I need not say that I fulfilled my task using less drastic words.

Another incident occurred in Galicia. Though we were supposed to reach the maneuver field by special court train punctually at daybreak, we arrived late. The long train with only one engine was heavy and the rails were slippery owing to the cool morning dew, so that at a turn of the line we actually got stuck on a slight gradient. His Majesty's ire was of no avail, and there was nothing to do but take off one heavy car after the other until it was possible to overcome the obstacle with the remainder of the train. By the time we reached our mounts, the ill humor of the supreme war lord, who always prided himself on punctuality, was extreme. For a while we rode silently through the damp forest until a detachment of hussars coming from the right crossed our path. Surmises as to where they had come from and where they were going were now uttered, and His Majesty finally ordered an aide-de-camp to ride after the detachment and question them. The officer in question made off swift as lightning—but to the astonishment of all, to the right and not in the direction in which the hussars had disappeared. One may imagine how this infuriated the old emperor, who already had cause enough for ill humor. "Where on earth is he going?" he questioned irritably, and turning round toward me, he called out my name. Hearing this and having listened to the whole debate, I spurred my horse and started off, but I had barely plunged forward when a flood of imperial displeasure stopped me. "How dare you ride off without knowing what I want! That is how these things happen." Naturally I then executed my orders with something less than enthusiasm. Offended at the reproach, which I deemed undeserved, I withdrew to the rear of the suite for the remainder of the day.

During maneuvers the old monarch spent many hours on horseback. It was remarkable how well he stood this unaccustomed strain, since he only mounted a horse on the occasion of military parades and never rode for the remainder of the year. My opinion is that he had no great interest in horses and did not particularly care for riding. But with his supple figure His Majesty was a splendid sight on horseback, and he was much praised and admired for his horsemanship. In his large suite there were many generals who because of age or their embonpoint did not feel very happy on horseback. During the maneuvers they were often prey to great agitation when the emperor, after a halt at some place, would suddenly and without any warning give rein to his horse and gallop off in one direction or another. How everyone then tried to follow and catch up with him! This caused many a member of the suite to perspire profusely. I made it a rule always to watch the emperor and to try to fathom his peculiarities. In time I flattered myself that I knew him better than many an old courtier. I soon discovered that these sudden gallops were not the result of a whim but were premeditated and that he preferred to do so when his suite was chatting animatedly and had even partly dismounted. I had noticed that before cantering off, the emperor always examined the neighboring ground carefully with his field glasses, evidently to decide on the direction he would take. He then seized the psychologically most favorable moment to give a shock to the old gentlemen accompanying him. I had observed such incidents so often that I always knew what was coming. I enjoyed the joke and was proud when I, the sailor, alone kept close to His Majesty's heels.

I must relate an amusing maneuver story that occurred in Hungary, when one of the opposing armies was commanded by the heir apparent, Archduke Francis Ferdinand. One morning His Majesty found himself on a flat mound watching the movement of the troops. We were within the sphere of the heir apparent's army corps, because he, along with his staff, soon joined us and remained for some time. Thus several hundred horsemen were assembled in one spot. Suddenly, cavalry appeared on the scene, rapidly encircling the hill we occupied and behaving in a strange way. Who were they and what did their attitude signify? For a while we saw only astonished faces. Then it became evident that the opponent had managed a surprise approach and had succeeded in taking prisoner the whole of the enemy's headquarters. Although this action had been carried out in strict accordance with regulations, furious abuse was nevertheless soon heard, and the whole action was declared an unheard-of impertinence—though not by His Majesty. I fear that the commander of the cavalry corps had to pay dearly for the joke he had permitted himself.

The maneuvers always concluded with a discussion presided over by His Majesty and carried on in a huge tent that could hold the large number of generals and officers who participated. The chief of the general staff discussed the events of the maneuvers and dispensed praise and blame in reserved words suitable to the occasion and the presence of His Majesty. Replies and explanations followed, His Majesty taking no active part and only listening. The whole affair was rather boring and made us long for the farewell dinner, which used to be served afterward in the same tent. Although not very sumptuous, the dinner caused the assembled soldiers to unite in an enthusiastic ovation for His Majesty.

The emperor did not have the same keen interest in maritime maneuvers, which did not lie within his ken. It therefore very rarely happened that the navy saw the emperor in its midst. In the autumn of 1902, however, the monarch went to Pola to attend a large maneuver carried out jointly by army and fleet. The maneuver consisted of a supposed warding off of a hostile landing at the southern extremity of the Istrian peninsula. The court was on board the yacht *Miramar*, commanded by Captain Anton Haus, from which His Majesty could easily follow the events and movements at sea and where he would be better housed than would have been possible on shore. Haus was already a person who had attracted general attention, and I may say that I had contributed not a little toward this, in spite of the strained relations that existed between us. As his admirer I had let no occasion pass at which I could point out his remarkable qualities to His Majesty. This was generally known, but Haus did not know it, he at that time having been far away on a cruise around the world. Whenever one of his travel reports came, His Majesty never missed an opportunity to pass it on to me, saying, "Here's another interesting report from your friend Haus." Later on I was delighted when he was appointed head of the chief bureau of the Admiralty in Vienna, and as chance would have it I was on duty and had to introduce him to His Majesty. Since the difference that had occurred between us on board the *Tegetthoff* we had hardly met and certainly had not spoken to each other. But now I greeted him amiably, as if our relations had always been of the most pleasant nature. Haus appeared taken aback for a moment but soon remembered that one had to know how to forget, and he joyously seized my outstretched hand. Subsequently our relations remained the best, and I suppose that he, too, did not judge me indifferently.

It was certainly a sign of high favor that Haus was the commander of the yacht *Miramar* for the duration of the emperor's stay on board. One morning in the course of the maneuvers he executed such a risky movement that the naval commander in chief, Admiral Spaun, and all those on board held their breath, so that even His Majesty noticed it. Luckily all ended well. I bore a grudge against the overly bold commander, however, for having failed to consider His Majesty's presence on board, and I punished him by not mentioning the incident to him with one word. Silence is often more eloquent than words, and Haus no doubt understood me. It amused me in those days to get to know our imperial master as a sailor, to watch the attitude he took up, and to note how careful and reticent he was with his remarks, contenting himself with listening to the remarks of his entourage and often helplessly seeking to form an opinion from the expression on their faces. In short, one saw clearly that he did not truly feel at home at sea.

Speaking of the days of my service as aide-de-camp, I may mention that in those years my interest in geographical matters found expression in the activities of the Vienna Geographical Society. As a member of its board it was my duty to attend the society's meetings insofar as my duties in His Majesty's service allowed. In the course of the winter of 1902–03, I had to give a lecture myself. Although I was always averse to any public appearance of this kind, I could not refuse on this occasion because the society was in a quandary. It had announced a special festive meeting featuring a lecture to be given by the North Pole explorer Julius von Payer,[9] on which occasion he as well as I were to be honored with the Hauser Medal, the only distinction conferred by the society. At the eleventh hour, however, Payer declared that he was unable to appear, and thus there was no way out of the difficulty but for me to take his place. I chose as the subject for my lecture my second African expedition made with Mr. William Astor Chanler, about which very little was known in Vienna. Chanler's description had appeared in America, while I had published nothing in German and had declined all newspaper interviews. My audience, which included a goodly number of members of the imperial family and numerous naval men, was considerably astonished to hear details about this expedition and its various adventures ten years after the fact, and I think that my narrative kept the audience in a state of suspense unusual in these surroundings. My friend Haus assured me at any rate that it had been the most interesting travel lecture he had ever heard.

It is not an easy matter for me to give a comprehensive sketch of my life at court. My period there was unusually quiet and uneventful. Only a few years had elapsed since the tragic death of the empress, and though the consequences of this terrible event in themselves would have sufficed to incline the emperor toward a more retired mode of life, this fact was enhanced by his frequent, if slight, attacks of ill health. After all, it was the court of an old and rather solitary ruler who had no liking for noisy festivities, so that life at court only rarely allowed the ladies to take a more animated part. During my years of service, members of foreign ruling families did not come to Austria as often as formerly or subsequently; I think these visits were not encouraged and were rather considered an encumbrance. Trips abroad to foreign courts did not take place during my time of service. Thus the years passed, apart from the sojourn at Ischl, chiefly at Vienna or Schönbrunn on the one hand and at Budapest or Gödöllö on the other. During the winter months the traditional receptions, court dinners, and festivities had to be endured. Then the court moved to Schönbrunn or Gödöllö as soon as possible, and a constant going back and forth between these two places began, sometimes interrupted for a few days by another sojourn, and resumed again, as circumstances required. His Majesty rather liked the palace of Schönbrunn, though he used to occupy only a few front rooms, situated in the right corner wing of the palace, where no sunbeam ever reached. There was no view at all from the windows, but the air was good, and the emperor led a quiet and pleasant life—enough removed from the hustle of the big city to enjoy not being in the center of the babble and traffic, and yet not so far away as not to know of it.

During one of these sojourns I had the occasion to see His Majesty ill in bed and was more than surprised at the simplicity that sufficed for the wants of the ruler of a great realm. He lay in an iron bedstead under brown camel-hair blankets, and the comforts surrounding him were no greater than those that any lieutenant could dispose of. It is true that a fine prie-dieu stood near his couch and that the walls were covered with brocade. Nothing, however, bore witness to the ministering of a loving hand, and it lacked the cozy atmosphere that women know how to impart to the most barren room. The supreme lord was served by valets and servants, from whom one could not expect any delicate touches. Their master was accustomed to these conditions, however, and did not desire a change or more comforts. But there was also a lack of other arrangements that people with a certain standard of civilization do not as a rule like to dispense with. For example, His Majesty used only a collapsible rubber bath tub, which was laid out to dry on the back stairs after being used.

In Schönbrunn His Majesty could move in good air and enjoy a short walk. This was only the case in the early morning, however, before he went to Vienna for the day's work. The park at that hour was still quite deserted, so that no member of the public crossed his path. Nevertheless, unbeknown to himself the lonely wanderer was closely watched by men of the guards, who never lost sight of him, though they disappeared behind bushes and trees when he approached. Soon after his return, toward 7:30, one started to the Hofburg in Vienna, usually in an open carriage. During such drives, which sometimes took place several times a day, it was forbidden to address the emperor unless an exceptional occasion warranted, lest one disturb his train of thought. As a rule he was plunged in meditation concerning the events of the day or the work to be done. However, he never missed showing the aide-de-camp sitting at his side by some trifling remark that his silence was due to other than personal motives; he always did this at the beginning of the drive. My reply to his first remark about the weather or some indifferent topic was always a laconic "Quite so, Your Majesty." If this first remark was followed by another, my answer remained short, though longer than the first brief reply. Only after being addressed a third time did I feel justified in supposing that His Majesty wanted to be entertained. The conversations that took place on these occasions never exceeded everyday small talk, and as a rule they rarely merited being remembered. It is true that on the occasion of my first drive from Schönbrunn to the Hofburg the talk turned to Africa, but never again after that—except once, and this was at the time when the press, especially in Britain, was full of the Congo atrocities. I had read a good deal about the subject and had also heard some details from eye-witnesses, and when His Majesty expressed his indignation concerning these occurrences, I said that they surely could not be perpetrated without the knowledge of King Leopold. "To be sure he knows of them," was the reply I received. "The King of the Belgians is the worst man on earth, a man who finds pleasure in doing evil." These words surprised me all the more since he usually carefully avoided criticizing any monarch, at least in the presence of others, and he would never have tolerated the slightest disrespectful remark regarding them.

Another time, when we drove into the city on a dull gray autumn morning, the old gentleman began to talk and said that everybody seemed to be thinking of nothing else than getting married. Every day, he explained, he received requests for permission to marry, mostly from officers of the general staff corps and then from naval officers. I had been up since early morning, and not being in a talkative mood I simply sat staring in front of me, replying quietly that I was not astonished that men wanted to fulfill their first duties as citizens. When the old gentleman heard me utter this remark, he may have thought that I was joking, for he suddenly turned round toward me, looked in my face searchingly, and then said seriously, "Thank your Maker that you are not married."

I had often heard it said that the monarch was irresolute and that the last man he had heard was always right. However that may have been, I don't believe it was really true. On questions of traditional matters touching the realm or the dynasty he certainly remained firm and even stubborn, and very rarely did he give in. On questions of government measures and other decisions of a general nature, he may have been more susceptible to influence, and no doubt it often happened that the last man who spoke decided the matter.

I think I am not far wrong when I say that His Majesty was extremely distrustful toward people in general, upon whom he looked down with a certain disdain. Only from the most lofty heights is one able to gaze into the deepest gorges and abysses, and this no doubt also applies to the insight into the depths of human baseness and lowliness. Barras, one of the leaders in the French Revolution, says somewhere in his memoirs that whoever does not despise men at the age of twenty-five is either a knave or a fool.[10] This is of course strong language, but what a sum of unreliability, selfishness, servility, falseness, treason, and lies might not the aged monarch have encountered in the course of his long life! I therefore asked myself which of his subjects he could consider as quite worthy; I reached the conclusion that such a person would have to be a member of the oldest, mediatized nobility, probably of the rank of count, and rich enough not to hold any state or court function.[11] It is evident that everyone who did not correspond to these conditions caused the emperor at least at first to arm himself with a certain armor of distrust, and it was but one short step from this rule to the principle that everyone a priori should be considered as a servile creature until the contrary was proved. I flatter myself that I never gave the monarch any cause for complaint on this score. It was quite evident that I did not thirst for either honors or distinctions, that I did not long for any special favor, and that I did not even cling to my position as imperial aide-de-camp.

Almost every day I risked being dismissed in disgrace because I changed my uniform for a simple civilian suit and disappeared into the crowded streets. This was a rather risky thing to do. A general who was on leave in Vienna happened to have the ill luck to be noticed by His Majesty in plain clothes in the pit of the theater and was immediately relegated to his garrison. Everyone knew that I used to go out in plain clothes. Only the Most Severe did not have an idea of this, but after all, that was the chief thing. Once I very nearly ran into him when he walked from the Hofburg, to which I was about to return, to an exhibition just opposite, but I promptly turned on my heels and fled. On another occasion I avoided meeting an archduchess on whose discretion one could not safely depend. In a small stationer's shop, I was caught in a trap; the door opened and the archduchess and her grand mistress-in-waiting stood before me, looking at me with big, astonished eyes. There was no escape. All I could do was to act as if I were someone else. I succeeded so well that both, as I was afterward informed, doubted my identity.

As imperial aide-de-camp, I was constantly requested to extend protection to comrades, friends, acquaintances, widows, and orphans. In every instance I did my best to assist the petitioners, and in consequence I had to bother many high personages and chiefs of various bureaus. On the occasion of these calls in the interests of my clients it surprised me to see how much even persons who ought to have known better exaggerated the position and influence of an aide-de-camp. Only thus could I explain their extreme readiness to fulfill my wishes. In all those years I only twice met with a refusal—once from Mayor Lueger,[12] from whom I had requested a trifling favor for a poor schoolmistress. When he pronounced his *non possumus*, I laughed in his face and told him that I was pleased to meet a man who knew how to say no. In the second instance it was a question of the transfer of a young count, a lieutenant of lancers, to another garrison. My friend knew that the minister of war, General von Krieghammer,[13] was utterly inaccessible to favoritism but was kindly inclined toward me because I was not his immediate subordinate. Though I knew how unapproachable he was, I thought I might dare to submit my request to him when I happened to meet him one day in a very good humor. He flatly refused my petition; reiterating his assurance of friendship he declared that he was unable to give any suit to the numerous requests with which he was bombarded every day. I could only agree with him, for where favoritism once takes root, it never ends.

When his day's work was done, His Majesty usually drove back from the Hofburg to Schönbrunn at 4:30 P.M. If a gala performance at the court theater, a court dinner, or a *théâtre paré* took place because of the presence of foreign royalty, it was later, sometimes even ten o'clock, before we returned. We had to do duty alternately, which was rather exhausting. Every second day we had to rise very early and be booted and spurred all day long. We also felt the weight of the sword at our sides and therefore rarely felt inclined to do anything in the evenings, while every second day we did well to retire early.

An existence of this kind did not leave much leisure time for wine and the other pleasures of life. Pleasant rides through the vast deer park, where the abundant wild boar caused our horses to shy, or out at a greater distance through the Vienna Woods, used to fill my free mornings. In the afternoon I often used to pay a call on the inspector of the imperial zoo, Alois Kraus,[14] feeding the animals or playing with the lion or tiger cubs, the orangutan, and the parrots. Kraus was prominent as an expert in his field. He had risen to high position from the far more modest one of a marine artillery petty officer, in which capacity, in his younger years, he had participated in the famous voyage of the *Novara* round the world (1857–59) and later on in a trip to China, proving himself to be a very able and efficient collector of animals and preparer of specimens. I used to spend many hours in his company, talking of old times or of the animals he loved so much, or discussing the question how an African rhinoceros, which His Majesty was said to desire, or a hippopotamus might be obtained for the zoo. The bureau of the grand master of the court was not very lavish in matters of this kind, and Kraus liked to avail himself of my assistance, begging me to voice his wishes, and I managed to help him in many ways. This was not very difficult. At the right moment I only had to drop a hint that His Majesty was interested in this or that matter or to indicate that a tank for the hippopotamus was absolutely necessary, and the money question was immediately solved.

So far I have not touched on the personal attitude of the monarch concerning religion and matters of faith. The Habsburgs were at all times faithful adherents of Roman Catholicism and good servants of the Church. The monarch always complied with the customs and claims of the Church to their full extent, though in view of his advancing age some of the functions, such as the Corpus Christi Day procession or the washing of the feet in Holy Week, tired him not a little. The same spirit prevailed among the female and the male members of the imperial house, though as regards the latter this spirit did not go to such depths as to prevent them from enjoying earthly pleasures. Nevertheless, it is certain that they all did homage to the Church and that it received a full measure of what it was entitled to claim. The piety of some members of the imperial house amounted to nothing less than bigotry, but this could in no way be said of the monarch. He was a believer, as is probably every man in so high a position, who only feels God above him and sees all others as subject to himself. One may judge the question of divine right of kings as one likes, but it nevertheless remains a special working of Providence. Naturally the thought arises that the person who incorporates this divine right will believe in a higher and eternal power in a greater measure than others and that sometimes he will feel the desire to communicate his feelings of gratitude, joys, and cares in the form of prayer. That a ruler who devotes himself to his exalted task with holy zeal has more cause to do so than a beggar is self-evident. It was thus that I judged the monarch regarding religious questions. I do not know whether the prie-dieu that stood near his bed was used daily, from time to time, or never. We only had to accompany His Majesty to a short early Mass on Sundays and high holidays. The preacher to the court, Dr. Mayer, only appeared to receive the emperor's confession once a year, at Easter time. This act took place in the emperor's apartment and lasted but a few minutes. What should a man in such a position confess to another, even though a consecrated priest?

On Fridays the imperial family and the ladies-in-waiting were served *maigre* fare; the other guests were not expected to be so rigorous. That a certain tolerance prevailed is illustrated by the fact that there were sometimes imperial aides-de-camp who were non-Catholics. But they too had to accompany His Majesty to Mass, which he heard from a closed oratory, while the aide-de-camp remained in his vicinity, but separated from his imperial master. I used to see the emperor kneel for a while, his face buried in his hands in prayer, and then thoughtfully witness the rest of the service. But he used to be talkative on the way to the chapel, which led through many vast halls and corridors. The washing of the feet, a ceremony that took place every Maundy Thursday, must have been an unpleasant duty for the aged ruler. Picture twelve very old men of the lower class, all over seventy-five or eighty, seated on a row of chairs. The emperor, himself no longer a young man, knelt at their feet in festive array, holding a silver bowl in one hand and a linen cloth in the other. As he glided on his knees from one venerable figure to the next, performing the rite of washing of feet, though merely symbolically, he was assisted by a court functionary with a silver water jug. The old men were then presented with cakes and silk bags containing silver coins that richly attired lackeys brought to them. This ceremony, enacted in the presence of all the finely clad highest state functionaries, no doubt formed an indelible memory for the persons who participated in it.

The winter months formed the chief period for the display of court splendor, for that was when the majority of visits from foreign royal families took place. Only then did His Majesty really reside at the Hofburg; at other times he stayed at Schönbrunn, Ischl, or in Hungary. The New Year's reception inaugurated a series of court festivities that consisted of a number of dinners and gala performances in the court theaters and found their climax in the great Court Ball and the more intimate Ball at Court. In between, the monarch had to hold receptions and perform other functions; he also wished to honor some social functions with his presence, among which the Ball of the City of Vienna figured foremost. In addition, he opened and reviewed exhibitions, received visits, returned calls, and so forth and so on. In the first year I found all this new and interesting, but the program varied only slightly in later years, and insofar as events were enacted in a stereotyped manner, they lost their charm. A gala dinner sometimes was of interest because, in honor of the person being fêted, the meal was served on silver or even gold. The gorgeous display on such special occasions, the profusion of rare flowers, the glimmer of costly silver, the splendid banquet hall, the bright sheen of precious table ornaments, the choice dishes noiselessly served by lackeys clad in rich liveries, the delicate wines fetched from the depths of the famous court cellars, and last but not least the orchestra conducted by Eduard Strauss—all this did not fail to impress even the most blasé courtier.

The Court Ball and the Ball at Court always offered a wonderful sight. The former was an entertainment that included vaster circles of society; invitations were issued to all persons who had the right to be received at court. There one could see assembled all the members of the imperial house, as well as the representatives of foreign states, the highest functionaries, and many officers, all forming a brilliant crowd. In the ballroom were to be admired low-cut rich court dresses, such as etiquette prescribed, costly old family jewels, picturesque national dresses, the manifold colors of Austrian military uniforms, a few simple black evening suits, and the broad ribbons of grand crosses of various orders. The invited worthies flocked into the ballroom in solemn yet festive mood and filled the gorgeous halls with subdued humming until the master of ceremonies knocked on the floor three times with his staff, thus announcing the approach of the court and calling for silence. The double doors flew open and the procession, headed by His Majesty, moved into the hall in couples strictly according to precedence and swept past the assembly, which curtsied and bowed deeply as the procession neared. While the members of the imperial family occupied a raised estrade and watched the gay throng from there, the ruler moved in the midst of the crowd, going from one person to the other, exchanging a few words, never overlooking anyone, and indefatigably carrying out his duties as ruler and host. On a spot that was difficult to clear owing to the throng, a few couples belonging to the highest sets slowly circled to the strains of a Strauss waltz. This lasted until about midnight. Then adjacent rooms were thrown open in which sumptuous buffets were spread and where champagne flowed in torrents, attracting the majority of guests. Toward 1:00 A.M. the court again withdrew as it had come, in solemn procession, and the celebration came to an end.

The Ball at Court distinguished itself from the former function by the smaller number of guests invited, each of whom had to be an excellency, a baron, or a count, so that the affair was not so indiscriminately mixed as the Court Ball. One had no need to trouble about approaching the buffet, because a choice supper served at little tables in adjoining rooms united the guests at midnight. Even as aide-de-camp one had, if not a highness, at least a lady-in-waiting as a neighbor at the dinner table. Even after a festivity of this kind one could see by the brightly lit windows of the imperial study that the ruler was devoting himself to his work at the usual early hour, however tired he might be—this at a time when probably the whole of Vienna still lay wrapped in slumber.

When His Majesty received a call by members of some foreign royal house, he always returned it immediately, after barely half an hour. Upon his arrival, of course, the persons in question were never "at home," since it would have made no sense to meet again after having just spoken a few minutes earlier. The emperor only had himself announced and remained in his carriage, holding in his hand a visiting card bearing his name in German or French. When driving off again he never failed to remark, "That was managed well. They were at home, but true courtesy demands that they deny their presence."

With all its court functions, the winter program must have been a heavy burden for His Majesty. Only his great sense of duty made him assume these obligations, even though he did not bear the yoke joyously. He probably looked forward with greater pleasure to some out-of-the-way visitor, such as the Shah of Persia, though he was rather at a loss to know what to do with him. A visit of this kind entailed no fixed obligations and yet offered a glimpse of other conditions of life and ways of thought. Hospitality was practiced in the full traditional manner, although the shah was not housed in the Hofburg. In 1873 there had been unpleasant experiences with Nasir ud-Din [ruled 1848–1896], or rather with the members of the shah's suite, who had shown that their ideas of civilization were not quite those of more western countries. When His Majesty returned to Schönbrunn after the gala performance at the opera that had been given in the shah's honor, he asked me whether I had heard what had happened to the shah in Ostend. I replied that I knew nothing about it. "Nothing?" he exclaimed, tired as he was and yet amused. "Oh, then I must tell you the story." He then proceeded to tell me the narrative in detail, some of the points of which were so risqué that I cannot possibly confide them to these pages. It was really amusing suddenly to hear the old gentleman talk about subjects that as a rule never passed his lips, the mere mention of which he would not have tolerated on any account. What astonished me still more was the almost feminine, careful manner in which he told the story, and how cleverly he chose his words in order to pass over dangerous ground, showing more delicacy than is usually met with in men. I should be utterly unable to render this tale with the same delicacy with which it was told, even if I wished to do so.

Among the privileges offered to us aides-de-camp were permanent box seats in the two court theaters. We could go there to watch one act or two, just as we liked, or not at all, and this was often the case with me. A totally unmusical person has no business at the opera house; my hearing was too bad for the theater, and ballets soon bored me. We were also often employed to transmit messages, imperial congratulations or condolences, and decorations to high personages. Errands of this kind fell to me more often than to that of the others because I lodged at the Hofburg and was always available, and also because of my knowledge of foreign languages. Once I had to make inquiries about the condition of ex-King Milan of Serbia,[15] who was seriously ill and whom His Majesty favored very much because of the monarch's friendly disposition toward Austria. Ex-King Milan lived in a comfortable but not at all regal apartment. I found the illustrious patient fully dressed, smoking cigarettes, cowering in an armchair, his arms resting on a little table. Apart from the yellow tinge of his complexion, he did not give the impression of being dangerously ill, but perhaps this was due to his general pleasure at hearing of the emperor's interest in his condition. He animatedly expressed his joy and gratitude to His Majesty, and no doubt he would have asked many questions if we had been better able to understand each other. When I met him, the ex-king was so hard of hearing that he was only able to catch a few words of what I said. King Milan died a few days later.

Another time I received orders to remit the Order of the Golden Fleece to Prince Alfred von und zu Liechtenstein, the cousin of the reigning prince of that house.[16] It was toward noon when my gilt court coach drew up before the vast palace, where I was received with the etiquette suitable to the occasion and was taken to one of the apartments. There I was told to wait, a proceeding I at first considered to form part of my worthy reception. But it took a good while before a secretary of the prince appeared, mumbling excuses and asking me to follow him into another room, where I of course believed that the solemn handing over of the order was to take place. Yet nothing happened. Nobody appeared, and the palace remained plunged in silence, as if it were a tomb. When another quarter of an hour had expired, I lost patience and pressed the button of an electric bell. I told the footman who appeared that I would wait five minutes more and would then go my way. This at last had an effect. A door to a third room was thrown open and I was asked to pass into it. In the next moment a half-concealed tapestry door opened and a sight offered itself for which I was really not prepared—the prince, in slippers and night dress, unwashed and unkempt, evidently suddenly risen from bed. This apparition advanced with outstretched hands and assured me that he had not been informed before now of my arrival. "But how can I receive the high distinction which His Majesty deigns to confer on me in this array?" "Of course you can," I replied; "aren't you the Prince Liechtenstein as you are?" I was later rewarded for this service with an invitation to a gala dinner that united the numerous members of this illustrious family.

Aside from the court entertainments that were crowded into the winter months, there were other opportunities for observing the glamour of court splendor. Corpus Christi Day, for example, was celebrated with the greatest pomp. This consisted of a procession in which the emperor, the members of the imperial family, the imperial household, and the knights of the orders walked bare-headed through part of the Inner City. The size of the Habsburg family also meant that there were many engagements, weddings, and christenings to celebrate. The many representative duties that these festivities entailed encumbered the old monarch considerably, though I did not notice his displeasure.

He used to examine the extensive preparations for these occasions with the same conscientiousness with which he did everything else, though one could not help admitting that his aged shoulders bore too heavy a burden in this respect. In the accustomed Viennese surroundings he stood the whirl of gaiety better, but he looked forward with less pleasure to entertainments in the second capital of the realm.

Hungary had adapted the old castle situated on the right bank of the Danube on the hill of Ofen into a wonderful royal residence. From its heights the Hungarians' king was to dwell and enjoy the view over the picturesque capital and the adjoining vast plains. The old monarch had grown up in simpler traditions, however, and preferred a more frugal mode of life. Furthermore, he disliked modern innovations and never really felt at home in this newly created Hungarian castle. Until his death he contented himself with some modest rooms rather than the gorgeous halls and the richly furnished apartments that were added to the original block year by year. In 1867, moreover, Hungary had acquired as a royal residence for her sovereign, the property of the former princes of Grassalkovich, Gödöllö, which after the expiration of this family in 1830 had come into the possession of a certain Baron Sina. Gödöllö was reached by a short railway journey, and as the monarch did not like Budapest, he preferred to reside here in the bracing forest air, only going to the capital on days when he held audiences or for some other solemn occasion, returning to his country seat in the evening. Especially in spring and autumn he used to spend many weeks there in comparative solitude, because the simple little chateau was not suited to receiving guests. For this reason no visits of foreign royalty were ever received at Gödöllö. The emperor's suite, insofar as it consisted of Austrians, also preferred Gödöllö to the capital.

Although we were magnificently housed in the Hungarian Hofburg and though our gaze from the balconies embraced a view of unrivaled beauty, we nevertheless felt as if we were strangers, banished to a high, beautiful watchtower from which we unwillingly descended. We had fewer friends and acquaintances here, and as non-Hungarians we also felt less at home, since the majority of us—I, for instance—lacked any knowledge of the Hungarian language, without which one is lost in Hungary. The process of Magyarization was in full swing at that time. Hungary felt a sovereign disdain for the "stupid Schwaben"[17] and by all the means at their disposal the Hungarians tried to attain the dominant position in the monarchy to which they thought themselves entitled. Of course the upper circles gave the example, as there were only two parties in the country at that time—the oligarchy, from which the politicians were recruited, and the broad inert masses, which had neither opinion nor aspirations. The former party never felt a part of a whole and raised many difficulties that constantly kept the Austrian half of the monarchy in a flutter and paralyzed its activity.

The explanation of the existing contrasts may no doubt be found in the history of the country, the memory of which was still too fresh to be forgotten, and also in the difference of race and the general variation between east and west. One did not notice this so much in intercourse with individuals. The Magyars are not only a chivalrous but also a sentimental and very hospitable people, and it would be a mistake to suppose that we did not meet with sympathy and courtesy on the part of individuals. Even the political leaders and government functionaries with whom we imperial aides-de-camp frequently came into contact never failed in courtesy. Nobody could escape the spell of the royal presence. The cheers that greeted the King of Hungary rang loud and sincere, but the Hungarians' warmth cooled as soon as purely Magyar air again surrounded them. Of course there were exceptional Hungarians who faithfully stood by the imperial house. A rock pillar of this kind, on which the monarch could absolutely rely at all times, was the Honvéd (National Defense) Minister Field Marshal Baron Géza Fejéváry,[18] a plucky statesman who broke many a lance for his emperor-king and who on a number of occasions defended his political opinions against his compatriots with the naked sword. He was devoted to his high master with heart and soul, yet nevertheless was a loyal Hungarian.

The fact that Hungarians are so much more undisciplined and lively than Austrians was manifest in the course of the general audiences, to which for this very reason His Majesty probably always looked forward with a certain nervousness. In the antechamber to the audience hall there was not nearly the same dignified silence that prevailed in Vienna. The assembly chatted in the most familiar manner, and it was difficult for us aides-de-camp to maintain order and control the situation. At a time when I had not yet unraveled the tangle of the many-membered feudal families, it once happened that I committed a lapse. On my calling the first person to be announced for an audience, three magnificently robed Hungarian magnates simultaneously responded to my call, stretched out their hands, and greeted me in the most cordial fashion. I naturally thought the man who had been called up was among them, and accordingly I announced him to His Majesty. Upon leaving the emperor's audience chamber I repeated the name with the intention of ushering in the person in question. It turned out, however, that he had not yet even arrived. Occurrences of this kind were, of course, not calculated to improve the humor of the excessively punctual monarch.

Court festivities in Hungary had some advantage over those of Vienna because of the splendor of the national dress, which made the military uniforms pale in comparison, and also because of a preponderance of aristocratic circles and the comparatively greater number of pretty ladies adorned by jewels. It goes without saying that etiquette was not handled with the same rigor as in Vienna. This was especially true when the Hungarian national dance, the czardas, was played, to the strains of which every true child of the *puszta* rocks in a dream of bliss.

Nevertheless, there was a certain constraint in the air that caused the monarch to dislike the sojourn in the Hungarian capital and his suite not to feel completely at ease. As the years passed, Hungarian chauvinism increased and reared its head ever more boldly. Within a few years the Magyars did more than manage to do away with the ban connected with the memory of Rákóczy, the bitterest enemy of Austria and the Habsburgs, a man who served as a national symbol for a political program that in truth called for national independence. They even succeeded in having a statue erected to this prince, whose memory was in disgrace in Austria, in the town of Klausenburg (Cluj), for the unveiling of which, in the place of His Majesty, an archduke was present. Naturally, from that moment on the revolutionary Rákóczy March was immune from criticism and could be played anywhere, and in the future no commander of an Austrian man-of-war need fear having it performed by his ship's band. In contrast, if one dared to play in Hungary the venerable Austrian national anthem composed by Haydn, dislike of it was freely shown, and in time this hymn disappeared altogether from the Hungarian territory. All these signs and circumstances did not remain hidden from the monarch, and of course they influenced his mood. As soon as possible, therefore, he returned to Gödöllö; we could actually see how he always breathed a sigh of relief when the special court train rolled out of the station at Budapest. This was also shown by the fact that on these occasions, contrary to his usual habit, he used to assemble all the persons accompanying him in the smoking saloon, where one spent a pleasant time chatting and smoking.

The style of life at the country seat of Gödöllö was rather simple, and His Majesty did not want to be disturbed here in any way. Only occasionally, usually at the beginning of the year, Archduchess Gisela or her daughter Augusta came on a short visit, while in the fall Prince Leopold of Bavaria and Grand Duke Ferdinand of Tuscany made their regular appearance during the shooting season. These visits created a slight change in the atmosphere. We had no other resources here, and we spent many a day that was not dedicated to riding or shooting in our four walls, only being called upon to do duty as adjutants when His Majesty went to Budapest. We could not fathom what our imperial master did all day long when there was no shooting. We rarely saw him taking a turn in the park, and as a rule this was only at the dinner hour, which was at three o'clock in the summer and six o'clock in the winter. The dining room was a small one and held hardly more than the usual dozen persons who formed the emperor's suite. Here the meals passed off less stiffly than in other places, especially during the shooting season; the assembly was tired and hungry after a day spent in the fresh air and was less inclined to exaggerated formality. In the fall nearly every free day was dedicated to the chase, which was often too much of a good thing. But great quantities of game had to be shot, and the head forester and manager of the imperial shooting parties therefore insisted on our doing our best. His Majesty did not always join in the shooting, and as the years advanced he increasingly preferred to go alone to special feeding places, which were visited by wild boar, and to wait for them behind a screen of foliage. He was not always successful, but at least the old gentleman could spend a few hours in the fresh air and experience some of the emotions of the hunt without fatiguing himself unduly.

At meals the guests were seated rather tightly round the narrow dining table, and there were fewer servants than at Ischl. The whole standard of life was simpler and more patriarchal, but the cooking was always on the same high level and was everywhere executed by the same staff. The chefs were no doubt eminent cooks, but in my opinion the directors of this department lacked that measure of gastronomic art which would have enabled them to judge kitchen and cellar from the point of view of true gourmets. They were not artists but experienced supervisors, wearing gold collars and boasting high titles. They were too much slaves to old customs and traditions, so that, as mentioned earlier, there was only one brand of champagne drunk at court, and the choicest wines and finest liqueurs were allowed to rest untouched in the depths of the imperial cellars. Traditionalism also explains why only raspberries and strawberries were served at Ischl, day after day, to the exclusion of every other kind of fruit, until one grew tired of them. This was allegedly because His Majesty desired it so. In truth only indolence and habit were at the root of the matter, and also a lack of observation and initiative. The big gala dinners, arranged according to traditional rules, no doubt impressed participants the first time they witnessed them, but a constant guest soon saw that they were no more than well-managed routine work. Being very simple in his tastes, His Majesty did not notice the monotony and was far too disciplined with regard to tradition to think of modifications.

In the course of my four years of service I only once witnessed His Majesty criticize a dish. This happened at Gödöllö. We had spent an entire long autumn day out of doors. His Majesty had remained at home busily working at his desk and was therefore not half as hungry as we when a so-called *Stegschmarrn*, a sweet dish, was served toward the end of the meal, the preparation of which did not make great claims on the art of the chef. His Majesty refused the dish, no doubt because of a lack of appetite. When he saw how eagerly his neighbors to his right and his left nevertheless helped themselves, he grew angry and called the dish a "disgusting mess." No one, however, left off eating, despite the emperor's ungracious side glances and his repeated remark that he could not understand how one could eat anything of the kind. The Prince of Bavaria and the Grand Duke of Tuscany felt rather uncomfortable and tried to defend the "mess" with some diplomatic phrases, but to no avail. The first master of the imperial household being present, he had to listen to a good many ungracious remarks and accept some indignant glances. Nevertheless, nobody was cowed by the ill-humor of the supreme master, and all went on eating as much as they liked. It was truly laughable how seriously the matter was taken up and how thorough were the consequences. The first director of the kitchen department, who was just then far away in the Rhine country collecting the wine tithes, was immediately summoned by wire to come to Gödöllö, and during the next week the first master of the imperial household personally inspected the kitchen every day in order to supervise things. In the future there were always two sweet dishes held in readiness for all emergencies. When after a long time a *Stegschmarrn* was again served, a visible trembling went through the house, and anxious gazes were fixed on the emperor in order to see how he would respond. As on so many other occasions, it was proven how poorly his entourage really knew him, for though he may once in consequence of special circumstances have let himself go and made an unpleasant remark—something that happened very rarely— he always regretted the incident and did not allow it to be repeated soon.

It was interesting to notice how unwillingly he used a table knife; he employed only fork and spoon. The meat had to be so tender that it could easily be broken up with a fork. If perchance this was not the case, he then cut up his meat with the knife into small morsels but laid the knife aside again when he had done so. Especially at gala dinners he would use the brilliantly polished blade as a mirror and often threw a glance at it, stroking his mustache as he did so. During meals he liked to look around the table without adding any remark. Nothing escaped him. For example, when in the fall medlars were served, for which he had a special dislike, he always used to express his astonishment at how one could possibly eat such rotten stuff. It was useless to explain to him that they were just at the right degree of ripeness. But sometimes he watched the assembly out of friendly motives and showed that the cares of a host also occupied him. In my time there used to arrive every spring, in April, a small consignment of delicious white peaches ripened in the Hungarian state hothouses. The quantity was always small and just sufficed to go around the table, and as the old gentleman liked these peaches very much, one would willingly have gone without them. But there was no question of that. Whoever tried to do so was pressed to help himself.

After the meal one passed into the adjoining room to smoke a cigar or cigarette. As soon as this was lighted, His Majesty settled comfortably in an armchair against the wall; his companions sat on chairs in a circle around him. In a corner of the room, whether the weather was hot or cold, large logs of wood burned in a chimneylike stove. His Majesty soon showed signs of fatigue, so that the conversation rarely grew animated. Having only half-finishing his cigar, he usually dropped his head while his eyes closed for a nap of a quarter of an hour. Then one was silent or talked in whispers until the old gentleman awoke. This he did with a short glance around him; then he looked at his cigar, probably to see whether it was still aglow, threw it into the fire, got up with a jerk, said "Good night," and retired. The others then followed suit.

Under the above-described monotonous conditions we were not displeased if from time to time some reason called us to the capital. One of these occasions was a large "carrousel" that the ladies and gentlemen of the Hungarian aristocracy had arranged. This was a wonderful assembly of fine, handsome women and gorgeously costumed horsemen, who sat their noble horses with perfect assurance and thus expressed the characteristic features of this country in a multicolored display, picturesque as no doubt only the Hungarian soil can produce. His Majesty attended the performance with his whole suite, and by his appearance he contributed to the glamour and the purpose of the equestrian feat. Of course the emperor was the subject of loud ovations and was received with royal honors when coming and going.

On this occasion, the playing of the imperial anthem could not be avoided. How much His Majesty was conscious of the Magyars' dislike for this hymn I was destined to learn very shortly. The carrousel was a great success, so much so that it was repeated a few days later. His Majesty had been begged to attend this second performance and had promised to appear. Toward evening, the emperor sent for me on such a trifling matter that I was astonished. On leaving, however, I had hardly closed the door behind me when the exclamation "à propos" recalled me. His Majesty had planned to attend the performance, but now he said that he would not like to appear as monarch. Therefore no solemn reception was to take place, no playing of the anthem, and no pomp and circumstance. I was to see to that. This had of course been the real reason I had been called. Next morning the minister for national defense, Field Marshal Baron Fejéváry, rushed into the room like an angry lion, wanting to know who had had this idea and had ordered its execution. He was most infuriated at the concession made to Hungarian chauvinism and now presented himself to His Majesty in order to express his opinion on this subject. Times had changed very much. A few years earlier a capable general had been pensioned for having neglected to have the imperial hymn played on the occasion of a church festival because he had feared a demonstration.

In the course of several years I met the other members of the imperial house, but not very often, since no very intimate intercourse existed between His Majesty and the members of the dynasty. In their eyes he was the emperor and the regent by divine right, whose majesty had to be emphasized, proclaimed, and respected on all occasions. It was striking to what measure they ostentatiously displayed their veneration at all times. On his part, too, one had the impression that he never forgot his exalted position as the head of the realm and dynasty and took his dynastic rights and duties most seriously. Like very old men in general, whose thinking becomes further and further removed from that of the younger generation, he was not much influenced by family feelings. There was no kind of familiar spirit in his contacts with his relations, not even with his daughters, the Archduchesses Gisela and Valerie.

The members of the imperial family had free access to His Majesty but made little use of this privilege, and when they did so they were always visibly embarrassed. With the exception of the above-mentioned daughters, who could reach their father by a back stair, the members of the imperial house had to have themselves announced by an aide-de-camp, like ordinary mortals. They knew that the emperor did not like to be disturbed at work and therefore came either at an early hour or late in the afternoon, when they knew that he was not otherwise taken up and could not well refuse to see them—for this occasionally happened, though he never caused any disappointment of this kind to an archduchess. Though he might shake his head impatiently when she was announced, he always rose and gallantly advanced to meet her and usher her into his room himself. On the other hand, his brother, Archduke Ludwig Victor, was often refused and had to be told that His Majesty was very sorry but was busy. He showed a certain inclination for the widowed Crown Princess Stephanie, even after her not very popular marriage with the Hungarian Count Elemér Lónyay.[19] Whenever she was in Vienna the emperor honored her with a call, and his granddaughter, Archduchess Elisabeth, was also in his good graces.

Another marriage that His Majesty had only countenanced as the head of the family after a long and tough resistance was that of the heir apparent, Archduke Francis Ferdinand, with the Countess Sophie Chotek, a lady-in-waiting of the Archduchess Isabella, wife of Archduke Friedrich. This morganatic marriage gave rise to a fear of complications in the future, even though the archduke had solemnly renounced for his issue all rights to the throne. In view of his very autocratic nature, a change of mind in this regard was not impossible, all the more so as he could base his claims on one of the articles of the Hungarian text of the Pragmatic Sanction, which admitted even the sons of a morganatic marriage to the succession. The monarch therefore only gave his consent after a severe moral struggle that considerably agitated him and no doubt formed the foundation of the opposition that prevailed between him and the heir apparent. No doubt some dramatic scenes were enacted in the emperor's study in the decisive days. The grave, pale face of the heir apparent and the fact that when entering the emperor's room he first regularly crossed himself, contrary to his usual habit, pointed to this probability. For the monarch and the heir apparent were not on good terms. The rift increased year by year, and they often had violent discussions. On one of these occasions the old gentleman so excited and agitated himself that afterward he was said to have had a severe fainting fit.

Archduke Francis Ferdinand was a great friend of the navy and always appeared in the uniform of an admiral when he visited a naval base. Though a friend of the Emperor William II of Germany, he was politically more inclined to sympathies with Russia; his ideal was an alliance of the three emperors. He made no secret of his dislike for Hungary, and the Hungarians would no doubt have been made to feel this lack of affection if fate had not willed otherwise. Bohemia, on the other hand, enjoyed his patronage, perhaps for the sake of his wife, who was of Czech extraction; because of his dislike of Hungary he tended to favor the Slavs. He considered Italy the archenemy of the Monarchy, but who knows whether later on, like many another crown prince, he might not have realized that theory and practice are different matters. Thanks to his travels he recognized the power and importance of Great Britain, and he showed certain sympathies for Britain until an incident marred these feelings.

The heir apparent's marriage was an unusually happy one, for he adored his wife. Once, when he had to go to England in place of His Majesty, the court there refused to receive his morganatic wife as full-fledged royalty. It must be noted in this connection that ever since the beginning of his union he had sought to advance the rank of his wife, to have her elevated first to the rank of princess and then to that of duchess, and no one knows where his dreams may have ended. In one word, he tried by every means possible to put her on the same plane as himself and to get foreign courts to recognize her. He had managed to obtain this recognition from Emperor William II, so that the British refusal appeared doubly cruel to him.

I once ascertained during the Boer War to what extent this awakened his ire and even influenced his political views. As an old traveler in Africa I was of course interested in this event. His Majesty, too, was keenly interested and like me was a partisan of Britain in the conflict. Queen Victoria knew this and showed her appreciation by the gift of a statuette representing a khaki-clad British soldier, which visibly gratified the monarch. I was therefore not a little surprised when one day the heir apparent openly took the side of the Boers. The occasion he chose was a meeting of the highest military functionaries who had assembled under the presidency of His Majesty to discuss the qualifications of high-ranking generals. The aide-de-camp's room was crammed with ministers and high officers who, with the heir apparent in their midst, were awaiting the beginning of the session. The archduke chose this moment to give a lecture on the South African war, and to my astonishment he expressed his anti-British views without reserve, defending the Boer cause so warmly that I found it difficult to await the end of his peroration calmly. Then I could not help stepping forward and, excusing myself for the liberty I was taking, I emphatically spoke in favor of Britain and disheveled the laurel wreath that the archduke had wound round the brow of the Boers. The flabbergasted faces of the generals clearly showed that I had overstepped the limits of what was permitted, and since the features of the archduke grew paler and graver and his glance more threatening as I proceeded, I expected an ungracious answer. I was therefore very much surprised when he only lightly remarked, "Well, from the point of view of monarchism you are perhaps right." Then, throwing a glance at the clock, he asked whether it was not time to pass in to His Majesty, to which I was glad to answer in the affirmative. When two hours later the meeting was over and the crowd of illustrious sons of Mars filed by me like a powerful fleet, led by the heir apparent, my respectful obeisance was not vouchsafed a glance. A few minutes later, however, the door opened again and the archduke entered, excusing himself courteously for having forgotten to take leave of me. When I was again alone, strange thoughts concerning the importance of an imperial aide-de-camp assailed me, since even an heir apparent to the throne found it wise to be on good terms with him.

At the close of another such meeting of generals I found lying on the table a large notebook bound in red leather which one of the members had evidently forgotten, and in order to ascertain the owner I looked into it. It belonged to the archduke, as I had already surmised by the sumptuous binding, and each page bore the name of one of the generals in our army. As I was in the navy, this did not interest me, and I only happened quite by chance to see that on one of the pages, opposite the name of a very well-known commander of an army corps, was jotted down in pencil only one word: "Ass." This short characterization of an old and deserving general reminded me too much of the jokes perpetrated by schoolchildren against their unsympathetic teacher, and it quenched my desire to peruse the book further.

The archduke was keen on finishing the building of the new wing of the Hofburg. He went in for everything he did with great energy and would not tolerate any obstacle or resistance. If he could not obtain his wish by courteous requests, he was not afraid to take severe measures. Opinions concerning his artistic taste and understanding differed considerably. Some people declared him to be a fine connoisseur and patron of the arts, and some of his creations— for instance, the adaptation of the Belvedere Palace for his residence and the arrangements on his splendid country seat of Konopischt (Konopiště) in Bohemia—to a certain extent made this opinion appear justified. On the other hand, other people who knew what they were talking about said that his discrimination in matters of art was not worth much. They declared that they could prove this by many erroneous opinions he had expressed and mistakes he had made in this domain.[20] They added that a failing of this kind would not be of much importance if the heir apparent had been conscious of his shortcomings and did not insist on carrying out his ideas with so much pigheadedness. His autocracy in artistic matters was similar to that evinced by his friend on the German imperial throne, and it was feared that this would have the same consequences here as there. The difference of character and temperament between the archduke and his imperial uncle was also manifested clearly in this respect. The old emperor's attitude regarding questions of art was most reserved, and he never posed as a connoisseur. In matters that he did not understand he possessed the gift—exceedingly important for crowned heads—of being able to subject his judgment to that of experts.

As a passionate and good shot, the heir apparent, though not a sportsman in the true sense of the word, knew how to make his shooting districts give great returns in an incredibly short time. Bagging innumerable heads of game seemed to be his chief pleasure. I have seen many a good shot at work, but the infallible sureness with which the archduke knocked over a whole pack of chamois flying past him on the occasion of a shooting party in Styria was marvelous. He did not miss one, and I never witnessed anything like it.

The heir apparent had only a small number of adherents who formed his loyal guard, and he was not loved even by them. The general impression he made was that he inspired a sensation of fear. He certainly was not popular, but he did not seem to care about this. Given his peculiar character, he was perhaps glad that the people who were destined in the future to be subject to his sway should see him as a *Jupiter tonans* rather than as a conciliatory father of the people.

His Majesty rather liked receiving famous men, which interrupted the monotony of his daily work. He used to entertain himself with them for a long time and was adept at questioning them, whereby he gleaned a great amount of information. Thanks to his astonishing memory he never forgot what he had once heard, and, apart from technical matters, he was in general surprisingly well-informed. This was no doubt due entirely to such sources or to the explanations he had received viva voce from the best authorities on various occasions in the course of his long life, for I hardly think that after his accession to the throne in his eighteenth year His Majesty had the leisure to study any books. He read the daily news in the *Fremdenblatt* and also the press clippings that various departments submitted to him. Illustrated foreign periodicals were only subscribed to when the Boer War began, and I think I may claim responsibility for that. The emperor's wonderful memory never left him in the lurch and extended even to quite insignificant details and events, a fact proved by innumerable examples. Since the monarch was rarely able to enjoy an hour of leisure, in spite of his wide interest in many matters, and since he also preferred to dedicate such hours to an outdoor life, we may suppose that he had no spare time for idle pursuits.

Whether the emperor confided more fully to other aides-de-camp I do not know; in his intercourse with me he never touched on questions of the day or on secrets. The care that he exercised in this regard is illustrated by the fact that the contents of his wastepaper basket had to be burned before his eyes every evening after he had finished his work. This was in accordance with his strict conception of his duties as monarch, to which he made many a sacrifice in the course of his life. His innate sense of duty and delicacy and his truly high-bred manner of thinking were manifested on many occasions. To cite but one example, the adjutant general, Field Marshal Baron Bolfras, himself a most sensitive and delicate-minded man, once advocated the recall of a foreign functionary but could not obtain the supreme consent to this measure. To his final question of why, in view of the clearly evinced facts, His Majesty declined to act thus, he received the reply, "One can never show enough breeding." That effectively silenced him.

I never saw His Majesty handle money or speak of it and cannot tell whether he despised it, as an Arab proverb wishes it, or considered it an indispensable means of power. Experience no doubt inclined him to the latter view. In his personal habits he was exceedingly simple and frugal, for he had been born at a time that ignored the luxury and the spirit of extravagance of a later generation. Thus he was not ashamed to appear at maneuvers in patched breeches or to wear washable gloves, which he preferred to all others, and he disliked having officers go in for any special elegance. Except on shooting expeditions, I never saw His Majesty out of uniform.

At his advanced age it was no doubt quite unlikely that anyone could have approached His Majesty closely enough to be his friend. He had lived too long enthroned above the clouds and untouched by the soul of the people, and his thoughts and feelings were too different from those of ordinary mortals. In the course of the years he discarded all human passions and soared above good and evil, though if one belonged to his close entourage a slight reduction of the distance maintained was noticeable, as was demonstrated by questions of a personal nature and by various little attentions. If one were a sportsman, for example, he saw to it in the spring that one should have a chance to shoot mountain cocks in the imperial forests, a wonderful sport that was even offered to an aide-de-camp. Not even the most wealthy man could have enjoyed it with more comfort. The emperor knew that every year Count Teleki invited me to Transylvania to shoot stags and bears; he always made me tell him about it and submit the trophies I had bagged. I once received a charming proof of his amiable concern on the occasion of a trip to Ischl that was exceptional because it only included the first grand master of the imperial household and myself. Though we had our own compartments, His Majesty asked us to come to his carriage the moment we boarded the train, and the journey passed in an uncommonly agreeable manner. At lunch he insisted that we share his table, and when he noticed that no rolls had been placed by my plate he asked his valet why this had been omitted. Incredibly, the valet, who had not expected a third guest, had to admit that no other rolls were available. Thereupon, without hesitation, the emperor broke his own roll in two and handed one half to me, saying, "Then we two will share." Such little incidents caused the sincerest gratification, and my devotion to my imperial master was more and more transformed into a feeling of true affection. They even caused my attitude toward earthly grandeur, which had grown extremely sober in the course of a life in close touch with nature and in the frequent struggles with overwhelming forces, to be decisively modified, and I confess that I vowed the most loyal subjection and devoted veneration to his person.

The recognition of the significance of my appointment to the staff of the monarch and the realization that this period of my life had been a particular gift of fate only overwhelmed me, however, on the day of my farewell. Then, on my return to my true profession, as I compared my farewell mood with the mixed feelings with which I had first entered the Hofburg four years earlier, did I fully understand the changes that these four years had wrought in me—not because I had changed from a sailor into a courtier, but because of the pang of the parting from my imperial master, to whom I was now devoted, heart and soul.

10

My First Years as Commander
(1903–1905)

I took my leave of His Majesty according to the usual ceremonial, without any special formality and without any visible sign of favor. To have served the emperor personally and to have lived in his vicinity was a distinction in itself and required no further reward. In one regard, however, the system was ready to make an exception for my sake. The lenient and, let us say, weak naval commander in chief, Admiral Spaun, so disliked rapid personnel changes within the officer corps that during his era promotion had nearly come to a standstill. Thus I had retained the rank of commander (*Korvettenkapitän*) during four whole years, while the imperial aides-de-camp of the army had already been promoted after serving for three years. As compensation, my promotion out of turn had been intended, but since this would have been to the detriment of the first of my class in the naval academy and my best friend, I successfully remonstrated against the proceeding.[1] I also made no use of another tradition, according to which the departing imperial aide-de-camp was allowed the choice of his next post. I was appointed commander of the small torpedo cruiser *Tiger* for the duration of the summer squadron, which nobody could possibly consider the result of favoritism. When I assumed command of the ship, she still bore traces of the navy yard in every way. Since a condition of this kind can hardly be modified within a short and busy squadron period, the appearance of my ship made me the butt of various remarks on the part of the squadron commander and chief of staff, which perhaps was only the expression of the easily comprehensible human envy that my lucky career had aroused on the part of many of my comrades. Ruthless energy soon helped me gain the approval of my superiors, however.

This was my first appointment in the squadron, but I cannot say that it caused me any difficulties, even during the three most busy maneuver days of war practice. Because of the chance absence of my immediate superior, a rear admiral, I was entrusted with the leadership of the entire torpedo squadron. During those seventy-two hours I stood constantly on the bridge and did not sleep a wink. Finally I was so exhausted that when we entered the port I knew so well and where the squadron met, I mistook it for another, until my officers pointed out my error. I had witnessed a similar occurrence years before, when I was a midshipman on the *Kaiser Max*. In Dalmatia two ports that lie in close vicinity bear the similar names of Treporti and Trepozzi, one of which is full of shallow waters and reefs. Into this dangerous port the captain had carelessly steamed one night at full speed, a feat that the admiral had, to the captain's astonishment, praised by signals. It turned out later that he had only been so plucky in the mistaken idea that he was in the other port.[2]

When the summer squadron came to an end I was appointed to command the *Szigetvár* for the autumn months. This small, splendidly kept modern cruiser gave me little trouble during the rather dull time that I spent on her. I should only like to tell one funny story because of the insight it gives into the character of the squadron commander.[3] It happened one morning in the port of Pola, where the proud armada was rallied and the flagship was moored to the buoy next to the *Szigetvár*.

Before telling the story, however, I must recapitulate a little. I had to send off a parcel containing some trifles I had purchased in Pola, and I instructed my servant to take it to the post office. After a short while he returned and reported that the customs officers had taken the parcel away from him. Naturally I was furious. I had my gig manned, and accompanied by my servant I rushed on shore, making for the customs house, where the innocent parcel lay. I seized it and went to the administrator, brandishing it and making such a scene as only an officer could make to a civil servant. I fumed at him and swore—rather rashly—that I would have him dismissed and heaven knows what else, and then returned to the landing stage in a somewhat calmer mood. On my way back, I turned round and noticed to my astonishment that the parcel was in the hands of my servant. In the general confusion, the customs house people had forgotten to relieve him of it. I of course took advantage of this oversight by quickly having my man post the parcel, and I returned on board.

These events had taken up a very short time before 9:00 A.M., just at the hour when the commander of the squadron took his morning stroll on the poop deck of his ship, watching the proceedings in the port with critical eyes. Thus he had of course noticed that my gig had been lowered and that I had been rowed on shore before the hour of schooling and drill, at a time when this was forbidden. He must have grown more and more excited over my absence and had finally eased his mind by instructing his chief of staff to send for me immediately, being sure of catching me red-handed. He had failed to notice, however, that I had returned from shore so quickly, and thus he missed the pleasure of letting me feel his power. When I was about to board my ship again, I saw the flagship hoisting the signal: "The captain of the *Szigetvár* is called on board the flagship," which order I was able to obey at once. The reason why I was called was of course clear to me. To judge by the admiral's expression, when he saw me enter his cabin so unexpectedly he evidently thought he was facing a ghost, for I have rarely seen a more disconcerted and shamefaced superior. At first he found no words at all and tried to master the confusion by offering me a cigarette, dismissing me with a friendly handshake when I had smoked it.

The short moral of my long tale is that this rear admiral was hardly an ideal squadron commander; he himself had certainly never dreamed that his career would take him so high, and higher still. Forty years earlier he and a companion had been simple infantry soldiers in Venice and had stood as sentries in front of some military depot, their rifles slung over their shoulders. The two had had the bad luck of twice failing to pass the qualifying examination to become naval officers and therefore had to quit the navy. According to regulations, they were then required to serve the rest of their legal conscription time—which was then ten years—in the army. This period must have appeared rather lengthy and dull to my future commander's companion, who was the livelier and bolder of the two. One day he started for Trieste, walked all the way to Miramare Castle, and unfolded his tale of woe to Archduke Maximilian, the naval commander in chief, who resided there. Touched by the recital, the archduke ordered that both men should be re-examined regarding their qualifications for naval service; it goes without saying that this time they had no difficulty in passing.

Despite these inauspicious beginnings, both lived to be full admirals. Yet if the beginning and the end of their careers were similar, they were quite different in character and in their likes and dislikes. In the course of time the successful petitioner with Archduke Maximilian grew to be a madcap, the terror of his subalterns and superiors—a commander who found no straits too narrow and no night too dark, and who as admiral took great care that the hair of the captains who were subject to his command should stand on end as often as possible. For his colleague, on the other hand, the motto was "Risk nothing." Whereas steaming through narrow canals at full speed intoxicated the former with delight, the latter found that only the open sea or open roadsteads were the right place for maneuvering men-of-war. Luck was faithful to them both—to the one in spite of all his challenges and bold enterprises, to the other in view of his prudent spirit. Of course the cautious one never had an accident, while the boldness of the other was accompanied by many an injury to his ships. But his adventures had one good result, for his example considerably raised the art of maneuvering in our navy. Feats that formerly had been regarded as more or less impossible were later declared to be quite ordinary. In the course of his two-year command of the squadron, however, the costs of the damages done to the ships amounted to such a sum that the navy yard people began to sigh and to moan, and in spite of its admiration, naval headquarters began to look for a successor who would be less dangerous to the budget. None appeared more suitable for this post than the colleague, and though he was already destined for retirement, he was entrusted with the command of the squadron.[4] So for the second time his former companion in ill-luck in Venice unintentionally helped him and caused him to gain rank and title.

Already on the occasion of my first appointments as commander, I envisaged matters in my own way, not because of any special reflection or pedantry but instinctively; in the course of time I never modified my views in this regard. I do not like to speak of this matter, but no doubt it also forms part of the description of a life. I bore the responsibility connected with the command of a ship at sea lightly. It touched my nerves as little as a command on shore, for one thousand or even ten thousand well-drilled horsepower make maneuvering with a ship a not very difficult matter. No doubt I lacked minute knowledge concerning some details, and I admitted as much to myself. Nevertheless, the wish to complete my knowledge never arose. I told myself that the position of a commander of a ship must be similar to that in former days, when commanders at sea were always military men who used the ships and fleets that formed their war material as a means for the execution of their purpose. To my mind, too much knowledge of details is only apt to confuse a captain and prevent him from daring use of the means at his disposal, to the detriment of his final aim. He who only exacts what is possible will never draw the utmost from men and material. What becomes, moreover, of all the learned principles and of subsequent studies in later years? Does any vestige of all that really remain? This was how I looked at things, and I never dreamed of hiding my ignorance of certain details. If, on the other hand, my subalterns did not know them, then it was a crime in my eyes. I hope not to be misunderstood, for in making these statements I certainly do not speak in favor of ignorance.

Though in private life I was never amiss regarding good fellowship with my comrades, when I was a captain I avoided every kind of intimate intercourse with my subaltern officers. It is true that from time to time I invited them to dine at my table, but I never accepted an invitation to the officers' mess and preferred to bore myself for hours and days rather than arrange a bridge party in my cabin. I was strictest of all with the midshipmen, because it is to their advantage that they ripen to manhood in strict discipline. I was exacting with the sailors, but I looked after them well and was always just. In contrast to the staff, they were complying with the compulsion of a legal call to arms. For them it was often a great sacrifice to serve their country. This had to be considered, and their service could not be made unnecessarily hard. I never particularly respected printed regulations. Who had made them, after all? Some officer who was just as subject to error as I was and who could not foresee every circumstance and condition. What I considered to be right was therefore right for me, whether or not it was printed in books. If this sometimes caused me to be criticized, I did not worry about it.

The exceptional position of a captain causes him to be regarded by everyone on board more or less as an enemy. He therefore does not hear of many things that happen on his ship, for even those whose duty it should be to inform him on all points avoid doing so for various motives. If, however, by chance the captain finds out any abuse, then it is advisable to follow up the matter ruthlessly, even if one should slightly exaggerate, or even if some little injustice occurs. I should like to illustrate this by an example.

On board the *Tiger* it had repeatedly struck me as I watched the men from the bridge at dinnertime that they first carefully removed something from their soup before starting to eat it, without my being able to explain this proceeding. Even with my night glasses I could only see that they were fishing something out with their spoons, but I could not perceive what it was. I therefore once left the bridge, approached the men, and asked them what they were doing. There I heard that their chief meal, consisting of a thick soup, was always full of worms, particularly when vermicelli were used. My poor men were not to have soup with worms, and a stop had to be put to this, for the executive officer and the paymaster received a special lump sum for the proper nourishment of the men. It was noon and the two were just having their lunch, but I ordered them on deck, and in front of the poor worm-fed crew I made a tremendous row, such as they deserved. I immediately had the steward room cleared, had every case opened, and had every one that showed a trace of weevils thrown overboard. How the two men later arranged matters with the commissariat I do not know, but a storm of this kind clears the air and always has a beneficial effect.

On board ship I liked to show everyone that I, their captain, ranked high above them all. Thus I lit a cigarette whenever and wherever I wished, even in front of the open door of the ammunition hold, a transgression that could have cost me a good deal. But at the same time I made ample provision that no one else should dare to take a similar liberty. I was very liberal with officers and men concerning furloughs, because I remembered well from my young years just how unwise restrictions in this direction are.

During the entire following year, 1904, I was on the station list in Pola. This meant that from time to time I had to attend some committee meeting, preside at a court martial, or perform a similar duty. Otherwise I could pretty much do as I liked. This would have been quite pleasant if Pola and its neighborhood had offered more attractions. An amusing diversion did occur that summer, however, during the enlarged squadron maneuvers, which consisted of a three-day warlike practice under the command of the above-mentioned madcap rear admiral. On this occasion he himself was in charge of the battleships, while the cruisers that had to represent the enemy's attack against Pola were under the orders of another rear admiral. The battleships had to frustrate this attack. I was attached to the cruiser squadron as umpire in order to supervise the exact handling of maneuver regulations and the proceedings during the different stages of the fight. The rear admiral commanding the cruisers took his ships to the port of San Giorgio on the island of Lissa, according to instructions, there to await further orders. Even in the depth of peace, Lissa is not an attractive place, but we were playing the war game and were anchored there with our steam up, ready to be roused from our repose at any moment. At first, however, our duty consisted of waiting; since this always allows for a game of bridge, we soon sat down at the card table and played innumerable rubbers. Indeed, we went on playing the next morning and afternoon, nearly forgetting what we were waiting for. The hour fixed for the beginning of the maneuver had long since expired, and the three days passed in the pleasantest manner without bringing either the expected order or the faintest cloud of smoke on the distant horizon to disturb the charming idyll. Though we wondered from time to time how to explain this uncanny state of affairs, which seemed to be utterly unlike the adventurous spirit of the commander of the battleships, we obediently went on living an idle life, which in time we found exceedingly pleasant.

We would perhaps have been less calm if we had guessed that while we were whiling away our time, the commanding admiral was steaming at full speed up and down the coast to the south of Istria, rushing back and forth like a fool looking for us and thirsting for battle. In spite of all surmises and guesses he could not explain our nonappearance, supposing us to be west when he was east, turning his ships about as if hunted by furies, only soon afterward to reproach himself for having done so, imagining that we must be farther east. For wherever he went and in whatever direction he might look, we were nowhere to be seen. These must have been days of misery for his active spirit. Nothing helped to solve the problem—no fits of temper, no strong language, no running back and forth at full speed. And so three days passed without the much-desired fight. The solution to the riddle? The admiral had given his chief of staff the order to notify the cruiser squadron in Lissa by cable of the beginning of the maneuver. As fate would have it, the poor chief of staff, who probably was half-dead in consequence of the constant fuss of his busybody chief, addressed the telegram to Lussin (Lošinj) instead of to Lissa—a similar name. It remained unclaimed until the fatal mistake had been found out, by which time it was too late.

With the fall of the leaves, my sporting spirit again awoke. My friend Count Teleki wrote that the stags in the Transylvanian forests were getting ready for their nuptial rutting time. For the moment the navy did not require my services, and what better could I do than to end the year with a leave? Thus one fine day I was in a train rushing through the plains of Hungary, which had only recently been robbed of their golden harvest, toward Szásebes, a place on the northern slope of the Transylvanian Alps. From there it was still a good distance to the hunting ground up in the mountains—a two-day drive over rough ground, along narrow mountain roads, and through a wild romantic valley along the steep bank of the foaming Sebes River. A whole caravan of ponies carried our equipment and provisions.

After I had passed the greater part of my two-month leave enjoying an ideal sporting existence as Count Teleki's guest, I began to feel a desire for town air. I wanted to devote the remainder of my free days to the city so that thereafter, satisfied with so many varying impressions, I could endure the dull life of Pola with greater equanimity. The worldly aspect of Vienna did not attract me so much, for theaters and similar entertainments had long ago ceased to thrill me. Nevertheless, I had friends there in circles in which I liked to move and to which I felt drawn.

One day Captain Anton Haus, head of the chief bureau of the Admiralty, sent for me. We had long since become good friends again, and he now asked me whether I would care to take charge of the small torpedo cruiser *Panther*, which was to undertake a cruise to Australia and the Far East the following February. This was a ray of light that I had not dreamt of, and one may readily believe that I did not hesitate to accept. Thus again a pleasant chapter of the future was unrolled before me. But better things were still to come.

It so happened that a rather obscure merchant named Arnold Szél, who dealt with all sorts of things but at the present moment was engaged in the paper industry, had suddenly discovered that a country existed in Africa named Abyssinia. At that time the country was more or less unknown in Austria, and as yet no direct commercial relations had been established with it. I did not know this man, nor do I have any idea who or what had aroused his interest in distant Abyssinia. Gifted with a spirit of enterprise, he did not hesitate to risk a couple of thousand Maria Theresa dollars by instructing a friend of his to go to Addis Ababa to study the situation there more closely. This friend returned from a long sojourn in Abyssinia laden with a quantity of data that, embellished with Oriental imagination, fascinated Herr Szél to such a degree that he now harbored the firm conviction that he had made a most favorable discovery for the Austro-Hungarian trade balance. He prepared a sort of memorandum that also contained some information on Abyssinia and its inhabitants, had it hectographed, and took it from one government department to the other.[5] Everywhere he praised his discovery so enthusiastically that like a modern Pied Piper he managed to convince persons in authority that the Monarchy could do nothing better than quickly sign a commercial treaty with Abyssinia, by which he hoped to draw all the treasures of the East to Austria-Hungary. He did so with such success that finally the Foreign Office, which under Count Goluchowski had grown rather indolent and careless,[6] decided to establish relations with Emperor Menelik. The Foreign Office then asked the Admiralty whether one of our men-of-war could be used for the conveyance of the mission to Djibouti. The plan developed gradually, and when at last it had to be decided who was to head the mission, it was probably Captain Haus who suggested entrusting me, the commander of the *Panther*, with the conclusion of a commercial and friendship treaty with Emperor Menelik. The task had evidently not tempted any of the professional diplomats, and Haus knew that I was well versed in African matters.[7] I had been in total ignorance of all the above-mentioned details until Haus surprised me one fine day with the question whether I was ready to undertake the task. One may imagine that I joyously agreed to this chance to visit Africa again, especially a part of that continent that I did not know. Thus it came about that after my leave had expired, I had to remain in Vienna until January 1 of the next year in order to make preparations hastily for a journey into the African wilderness.

In consequence of the rather vague aims of the Foreign Office, there were many changes and modifications in the original plan. For me this meant weeks of feverish activity, which reminded me very much of the times that had preceded my two African expeditions. In contrast to those occasions, however, when I had been my own master, now I was bound to the instructions and decisions of a half-dozen different government departments. An official state mission to the court of a potentate who, though an African, deserves respect differs much from a private undertaking, chiefly because of its political importance and the preparatory diplomatic arrangements. These were of course the affair of the Foreign Office, but they had to be discussed with me. Emperor Menelik at once expressed his great pleasure at the wish of the Austro-Hungarian Monarchy to establish closer relations with him, all the more so as a German mission was to go to Abyssinia at about the same time with a similar aim. The ambitious ruler of Ethiopia was no doubt much flattered that two great European powers were striving to obtain his friendship. It was a lucky coincidence that Austria-Hungary was able to delegate to Menelik's court one of the discoverers of Lake Rudolf, the upper part of which had in the meantime become an important Abyssinian province administered by Ras Wolde Giorgis, the governor of Abyssinia's Kaffa province.

It was my duty to provide all the material necessities of the trip, and in view of the many fingers in the pie this was no easy matter. I had to purchase many things in Vienna against my inclination, knowing that I could have done better elsewhere, such as London or Berlin. And when I heard of the importance that official circles attached to exact and stamped accounts and reports, I begged them to entrust the less important details to Herr Szél, in the erroneous supposition that being the father of the whole idea, he would have a great interest in its execution. But everything, even the writing paper that he furnished from his own stores, was bad.

An envoy to the court of an Oriental ruler must not appear empty-handed. It was therefore important to decide what presents we were to carry. We knew that the Abyssinians were a soldier people par excellence and that they cherished arms and ammunition above all things. Menelik would surely welcome a portable mountain gun that could be taken apart, as well as excellent Mannlicher rifles and repeating pistols. An oil portrait of His Majesty corresponded to the tradition regarding royal gifts, as did the badge of a high order. I saw from the Szél memorandum—which made me feel rather skeptical because of the terrible lack of culture it betrayed—that silks were much in demand in Abyssinia and that good wines were most acceptable. The latter gave me the idea of suggesting a gift of old Tokay wine from the court cellars. To these presents were added other gifts coming from renowned workshops of Viennese craftsmen. Menelik's wife, the Empress Taitu, had also to be considered, as well as some Abyssinian state functionaries. I believed that I had done what was necessary, but I must admit that this was not the case, for we were unable to furnish presents to a number of high personages with whom we came into contact in the course of events. Regarding this part of the preparations I had to deal with the administrator of the imperial revenues and funds, who broadmindedly and liberally granted all my wishes. The War Office also proved most willing to assist our expedition and granted not only the mountain gun and the necessary ammunition, but also five splendid mules for carrying it, some Mannlicher rifles embossed with the imperial coat of arms, and more. Twelve sailors were sent from Pola to the Tyrol to be instructed as gunners for the mountain cannon.

Aside from myself and one officer of the *Panther*, only our vice consul at Port Said, Friedrich Götz, was originally to participate in this mission as commercial reporter, along with the twelve sailors and one bugler. In due time, however, Count Goluchowski gave permission to several other gentlemen to join the trip in no special capacity; they were to enhance the glamour of the mission, but without burdening the state purse. Thus Count Erwein Schönborn, Count Ladislaus Széchényi, Baron Mylius, Mr. Bieber of the Ministry of Commerce, and finally a nephew of Herr Szél, Santho by name, were also allowed to join the mission.[8] The last was not to consider himself as attached to it, however, nor was he to be permitted to do any business during our stay in Addis Ababa. During the trip upcountry I was to treat them all as my guests and see to their comfort and well-being.

Emperor Menelik was a wise and clever ruler who had a keen eye to business and knew how to seize a propitious opportunity. A few years previously an Austrian firm, the Vulkan Werkstätte, had furnished him with a coining plant that did not work properly. Through his premier, the Swiss Alfred Ilg, he therefore expressed the wish that we might put the machinery in order. The firm refused, however, to assume the costs connected with sending a member along. Therefore the only thing to do was to send for one of the engineers of the *Panther* to come to Vienna, have him instructed at the factory, and attach him to the mission. As if I had not yet enough members to cater to, at the last moment Count Goluchowski expressed the wish that we should admit a midshipman of the *Panther*, one Prince Hohenlohe, who had set his heart on joining us. One sees that my task was not an easy one. Nothing makes me more indignant than stinginess in money matters, and in this regard the Foreign Office is not in my good graces. The means provided were small and in the course of the expedition proved to be insufficient. A shipment of French champagne that was already under way from Bordeaux to Port Said I had to countermand by order of the minister for foreign affairs, and I was forced to content myself with cheap Hungarian Törley sparkling wine. For weeks, moreover, futile discussions had taken place between the Foreign Office and the Admiralty concerning the daily allowance that I was to draw, so that I finally—and very superfluously—put an end to the matter by declaring that I renounced any extra remuneration.

The little *Panther* (1,530 tons) did not dispose of any cabins for the reception of guests, and it was therefore arranged that only the vice consul should travel on board from Port Said to Djibouti. The five mules and part of the bulky mission goods were to go by a Lloyd steamer. All these hurried preparations were carried out quietly, because the whole undertaking was kept a secret, an order with which the Foreign Office complies less readily than the Admiralty, which is accustomed to obeying orders and keeping silence. The public knew, however, that the *Panther* was to go for a long voyage, and the Museum of Natural History and other institutions therefore begged to be allowed to transmit their wishes regarding collections of all kinds, even living animals and plants. This desire corresponded to my own inclination, and I declared my readiness to take all the apparatus necessary for catching, collecting, and preserving specimens. All these matters took up my time in an exhausting manner, and the months of November and December passed in a rapid flash of feverish activity. Yet everything has an end, and I was at last able to settle on January 1, 1905, as the day of my departure from Vienna.

As imperial envoy I had to ask for an audience with His Majesty before leaving, and I was notified graciously to appear one afternoon in plain dress. I had not met the monarch since my farewell as aide-de-camp in May 1903, and I looked forward to the meeting joyfully, trying while I waited in the antechamber to picture the course the audience would take. I supposed that the emperor would receive me sitting at his desk and would question me on the details of the mission, but things turned out quite differently. In the last half-year of my appointment as imperial aide-de-camp I had undergone an operation on the sole of my foot, which, badly done, had made me suffer for a long time. Now, when I knocked at the door and entered after being announced by the aide-de-camp on duty, my gracious lord and master strode toward me with quick steps, saying that he was glad to see me again. He then leaned against an upright desk and began to inquire about my operated foot and asked whether it still caused me pain. Assured that I had completely recovered, His Majesty began to talk about Abyssinia, showing a knowledge of the subject that made me marvel. I thus learned some religious and ecclesiastical details of which I was ignorant. Of Menelik he did not speak, and after wishing me a happy journey he graciously dismissed me.

It goes without saying that I also had to take leave of the naval commander in chief, Count Montecuccoli. A clear-sighted, practical man, he immediately began to speak of the *Panther*. "I know the ship is too small; you will have to navigate in stormy waters and have to be extremely careful. You therefore need not adhere strictly to the program you have been given. Before leaving any port, first telegraph and make inquiries concerning the weather. You are at liberty to sail when and where you think fit and need not bother about the program. Only keep us informed in good time where we are to forward the mail. Once more: the ship is too small, but you will surely manage to get her through all right. Good-bye; I wish you a good passage."[9] This sort of rational speech pleased me, and I now looked forward to the interesting cruise with still greater pleasure, for the declarations of the commander in chief made me more or less independent, almost like the owner of a private yacht.

The winter 1904–05 was abnormally stormy and cold, and for many weeks the thermometer showed the lowest temperatures witnessed since 1864. When the express train in which I traveled in the sleeping car en route to Trieste reached the Karst Plateau, an icy cold bora wind received us, which was so violent that we repeatedly had to halt on the line and could only round curves at a slow pace, when the wind had abated a little. The storm beat against the double windows with such fury that one drew back involuntarily, expecting to see the panes smashed to pieces. The wind gave the impression not of air but of some metal fluid that was in violent motion. After a delay of some hours we reached our goal and found the shores of the port of Trieste covered with ice a foot thick, a rare sight in these latitudes. A few hours sufficed for transacting the business I had to attend to there, and I reached Pola after an awful night spent in a train in which the steam heating had been frozen by the severe cold.

The next morning, after a few hours of rest, I had to be on board the *Panther*, ready for a first trial trip. Such claims kept me very busy during the two weeks that preceded our departure. In this short time I had not only to outfit my little ship for a long voyage but also to see that she was made fit in every respect and was seaworthy. She lay deep in the water and had very little freeboard, yet goods for the mission still arrived daily. These rose in great mountains and had to be carried on deck and fastened by means of iron bands. The low ship sides required precautions against the flooding of the deck and to allow its rapid draining. When necessary the forecastle could be raised by one meter by means of a detachable, not very pretty, but effective addition of heavy oak beams; this structure was strong enough to resist even green seas, while broadside ports along the deck permitted the ready outflow of the water.

My desk was covered with piles of materials—letters, notes, instructions, orders from the Foreign Office and the Admiralty, commercial reports, instructions from scientific institutions, and various telegrams—which I could only glance through quickly. After all, I also had to think of my own private matters and to outfit myself completely for a long voyage. Amidst the chaos that reigned in the last weeks I could not possibly know whether the hundreds of objects that I had ordered had really arrived. I had to leave this to luck and restrict myself to keeping my nerves in order and hoping that everything would run smoothly. The major items—His Majesty's autographed letter to Menelik, the three copies of the treaty that I had to conclude, the badges of the decorations, and other gifts—were all there. The remainder was of lesser importance.

In brilliant sunshine—which, however, was unable to mitigate the prevailing bitter cold—and with a rising bora wind, the *Panther* sailed from Pola at 9:00 A.M. on January 15, to the cheers of the other ships in the harbor. All went well as long as we were protected by the Istrian coast, until we reached the Quarnero (Kvarner). We had hardly poked our nose into the gulf when a bitter cold northern began to whiz, throwing salt spray up to the bridge. Higher and higher rose the crystal-clear blue waves, battering against the port side of the ship and making the little *Panther* quiver. I had often heard that it was impossible to cross the Quarnero in a medium-sized ship with a violent bora blowing. But would not the *Panther* have to brave storms of far greater fury in the course of her cruise? Thus I decided to stick to our course and not show a faint heart at the outset. The gale blew harder and harder, and waves came rushing on with ever-increasing violence, shaking the ship, hammering her sides, and washing over the decks as high up as the bridge. There they froze, covering

everything with a thick layer of ice. At the same time the sun was shining gloriously in a blue sky. We did not give in at once. But when one of the booms
was smashed to pieces and the inch-thick glass of one, two, and three bull's
eyes were knocked out on the weather side and water began to threaten the
inside of the ship, we had to surrender and slowly creep nearer to the shore,
under the cover of which we then proceeded southward. How abnormal the
weather was in that year may be judged from the fact that even off Brindisi we
had to sail through a snowblast for several hours.

It was only in those days that I was able to view the ship and my companions more closely. I already knew the executive officer; he was an able man,
though somewhat rough and requiring control. In view of the special circumstances, this choice had not been a lucky one and not quite according to my
taste. I esteemed the torpedo officer, Lieutenant Huber von Scheibenhain, as a
useful assistant and appointed him as my secretary; he was also to accompany
me to Abyssinia. The other four officers I hardly knew, but they made a good
impression. As navigation officer I had selected a rather nervous but very well-
trained ensign, who from the very first day maintained—I do not know why—
a more than reserved attitude toward me, which in the course of time led to
controversies. The six midshipmen who were also on board had excellent records
and were agreeable young people. A mediocre doctor, a good fellow as paymaster, and three engineers completed the staff.

My cabin comprised a little saloon lying in the stern, with an attached sleeping cabin and accessories. The drawing room was ornamented by two revolver
guns which could fire through side portholes; an oblong table that could hold
a maximum of eight guests occupied the middle of the saloon. Two bookcases,
a desk, a couple of sofas, a smoking table, and a small iron fireplace formed the
furniture of the cabin, which made quite a cozy impression.

In the beginning I had neither the time nor the inclination for the usual routine on board ship, for only now was I able to look through the mountain of
papers and letters that had accumulated in the last weeks, to collect my thoughts,
and to concentrate on the necessities that lay before me. Above all I had to make
definite plans concerning my mission to Abyssinia and to draw up instructions
to guide the executive officer during my absence. The unfavorable weather in
the Mediterranean, the touching of Port Said and Suez, and the passage of the
canal disturbed me not a little in my work.

In the first port the vice consul, who was to act as commercial and political
reporter, came on board. As there was no other cabin, he was housed in my
saloon, where a comfortable bed was made up for him at night. This bothered
me less than it did him, since he was a late sleeper and disliked getting up before
eight o'clock. He therefore soon began to look around him and, having discovered the clean, empty, and freshly painted ship's hospital, he asked for permission to occupy it. That made us both happier; thereafter I only saw him at meals.

I joyfully hailed the Red Sea, with its calm and warmth, as an old friend. I
was struck, however, by its appearance in the southern part. Because the cool

monsoon did not set in as it should, the warm north wind continued to blow as far as Perim and beyond. Something was not as it ought to be, and I hastened to reach Djibouti, though the night was dark. Rainy weather set in, hiding from our sight the flat coast that was bordered by coral reefs, and soon we were groping in the darkness, without a guiding lighthouse to help us. Under these circumstances, toward midnight I renounced approaching land until the following morning. Day broke gray and gloomily. Heavy lowering clouds driven by a fresh east wind passed over an agitated, dirty gray sea, and showers of rain hid every outlook. All the more did I think it my duty to try and gain the protecting port, and I directed the ship in the probable course to the Bay of Tadjoura. But the rain fell in ever thicker sheets, and the gray, wet wall encompassed us more and more. The wind and the rough sea increased alarmingly. It was evident that we had come near the range of a cyclonic disturbance, but I nevertheless foolishly clung to the idea that we must reach Djibouti—until eight bells sounded. At this time the scales suddenly fell from my eyes, and in one moment I realized the madness of my intention to approach a flat and dangerous coast, studded with innumerable coral reefs, in such weather. No half-measures, only an entire retreat from the dangers that were in front of us would do, and in the next moment the ship was turned round and headed for Aden. The wind and waves increased, cloudbursts of rain gradually shrouded even the nearest vicinity, and the little *Panther* had more and more difficulty in struggling against the increasing pressure of the waves. By ten o'clock we were making only two knots, but fortunately the wooden breakwater proved to be excellent. Repeatedly Arabic sailing dhows that had lost their masts and had evidently been abandoned drifted past us toward the shore of Somaliland, only to strand there on the reefs. Toward noon, when I was just having a bath, the sudden reversion of the screws with full force caused me to rush on deck just as I was; a merchant vessel lay in front of our bow at half a cable's distance.

It soon became obvious that we could not reach Aden because of the lack of coal and that we must try to gain the nearer port of Perim. But in which direction did it lie? Our position was quite uncertain. Fortunately the heavens had pity on us, for in the west the veil was lifted for a moment, permitting the sun— a gray, indistinct disk—to shine through just long enough to allow the navigation officer to take a sighting with his sextant and chronometer. We now could set course for Perim with some certainty, and flying before the wind and seas at full speed, we were happy, toward sunset, to espy the dark outlines of the island, around which the heavy breakers foamed. It was a question of quickly getting hard starboard into the narrow entrance to the port in the growing dusk. But lo! The ship refused to obey the helm. I immediately recognized the cause. The enormous speed with which we were swept past the island had already caused me to guess that we were running in an extraordinarily strong current brought about by the storm and which was now paralyzing the action of the helm, so that the ship had to be forced to turn round by the screws. A few moments of suspense followed before we were safely in the entrance to the port.

Two hours earlier the British cruiser *Prosperine* had also entered, seeking shelter from the storm; her commander advised me most urgently not to make for Djibouti in anything but perfectly clear weather.

After two and a half days, the storm had spent its fury and the sun again shone from a cloudless sky. Thus on the morning of January 31 the *Prosperine* and the *Panther* could leave the protective port and sail their respective ways. Early in the afternoon we reached Djibouti, where we found a telegram of welcome waiting for us from Minister Alfred Ilg. At first glance this youngest of French colonies showed an astonishing picture of life and movement. But this was only due to the chance presence of a Russian squadron and her immense fleet of transports, which had stopped here for some time. As the officer who had come to pay his respects in the customary manner informed us that the squadron was to sail the same afternoon, I hurried to call on the commander on board the *Oleg*. He frankly admitted that when he had seen the *Panther* approach at full speed with her coat of gray paint and the indistinctly visible red-white-red flag, he had supposed her to be a Japanese vessel and had made ready to receive us accordingly.[10] One may imagine the consequences. However, if it had come to a conflict with the anchored and in every respect unfit squadron, it is doubtful whether the little *Panther* would have suffered much in spite of the great superiority of the Russians. Even my cursory visit on the Russian ships showed me that they were by no means formidable foes, ready for action. Russians are in any case no seamen. The majority of the squadron left Djibouti the next day, leaving behind a few smaller ships.

The other participants of the mission had arrived long before and impatiently awaited the *Panther*'s arrival. They came on board immediately and were glad that we were to start early on February 4. From Perim I had already telegraphed to order the special train that was to take us to Dire Dawa, the terminus of the railway line near Harar. It was still a long way from there to Menelik, and as my ship had to wait for us in this burning region of the coast, I had to shorten this period of suffering as much as possible. During the few days before our start I was exceedingly busy from dawn until late at night, so that it was difficult to fulfill my other obligations, to make use of the invitations that the governor addressed to me, or to reciprocate them.

11

To the Court of Emperor Menelik of Abyssinia (February 4 to April 10, 1905)

The mission's bulky luggage had already been put into the train to Dire Dawa the evening before. When I entered the station shortly before sunrise, I was at first surprised by the courteous manner in which the railway company had provided for our material comfort during the eleven-hour trip through the desert. Mountains of good things, bottles of all sorts of wine, and a quantity of ice were loaded in the cars for our convenience. We traveled as honored guests, and after I reclined luxuriously on the cushions of my seat, my thoughts involuntarily returned to the day sixteen years earlier when I had trodden along this same line in a tiring march that lasted over two weeks. In contrast, we now sat sipping iced drinks, chatting, and smoking—the twelve sailors, the bugler, and my servant in their compartments, and the masters in the saloon carriage. We were all glad that we had come so far and were approaching our goal. Mr. Santho had preceded us some days before, no doubt having been mightily attracted to the field of his future commercial activity.

Our train rolled along through deserts and valleys on bridges boldly constructed over dried-out river beds, while the barren steppes and rocky hills passed before our indifferent glance. Viewed superficially, everything is uninteresting; examined more closely, it may reveal the most wonderful details. Thus the tired hiker rejoices at many things that the man rushing past in a railroad carriage hardly notices. At 9:30 A.M. we crossed the Abyssinian frontier in the midst of a swarm of locusts that whirled through the air like snowflakes. A splendid lunch awaited us at the border station, and the table was laid in the little garden in the midst of the stony desert, thus enhancing our pleasure. In time we felt the heat of the desert, which made us tired and sleepy. We watched the many graceful sand spouts turning and twisting round us and we gazed at shining lakes, fata morgana in the vibrating air. Toward two o'clock the mountains surrounding Harar came into sight, and at five o'clock we reached Dire Dawa. There we were met by Mr. A[dolf] Michel, a charming young Swiss who was the postmaster of Harar, and were welcomed by the Abyssinian authorities. Through a double row of soldiers we walked to the nearby hotel, which

217

was surrounded by a crowd. Only toward evening did we start to unload the goods, provisionally storing them in a heap near the railroad track. Thereafter a good meal helped us forget the hot trip, and we ended the evening pleasantly.

Dire Dawa, a new creation still in development, is of special importance as a storage place for the commercial center of Harar, which lies off the track. From there to Addis Ababa and to Menelik was still a great distance. Today the railroad takes one there comfortably, and Harar is also connected with Dire Dawa by a branch line. In our time, however, one could only reach Addis Ababa by marches. Two routes could be chosen as far as the steeply rising Abyssinian plateau. One led over the hilly district of Chercher and was the more difficult, but it offered better conditions as far as water was concerned—an important matter for a large caravan. The second, the so-called desert route, avoided the mountains but could only be followed with camels because of the prevailing drought. I had often experienced that information given by Europeans on the coast concerning conditions even in the neighboring districts of the "hinterland" had to be taken with caution. Thus it was only here at Dire Dawa, after long consultations, that we were able to settle on the exact plan of our journey. We decided to pass by the Chercher road with the chief caravan, while the heavy gun and its accessories were to travel on camels through the desert.

The necessary mounts and beasts of burden could only be bought and hired at Harar, where we had to go in any event in order to visit the viceroy, Ras Makonnen,[1] who resided there. In the meantime the camp had to be transferred to Kersa, a spot near Harar and favorable as a starting point. When everything had been arranged, we started on our way to Harar early on the morning of February 6, accompanied by the indefatigable Michel and with only a little hand luggage. In the afternoon, near the well of Hakim, we came in sight of the flat, grayish-brown roofs of Harar and its famous coffee gardens. Here the representative of the viceroy received us with the sounding of trumpets, and a large suite escorted us as we continued on our way to Harar. In the midst of a crowd of officers wearing felt hats and bearing shields with silver fittings, surrounded by soldiers and the population, and stared at by curious Galla, we solemnly made our entry through one of the four city gates, while the cannon boomed from the old citadel and trumpets flourished. Then we moved through narrow streets filled with huge crowds to the house of Ras Makonnen—the same simple, one-storied building in which I had visited him sixteen years earlier as a tired and dusty wanderer.

Conducted by various Abyssinian dignitaries, I once more passed over the old wooden stairs into the same unadorned but now much cleaner room that I already knew. Makonnen, wrapped in a white toga, motioned me with a friendly nod of his head to his own seat between the windows, while my companions sat down on chairs in a circle. After having exchanged the usual courteous greetings and having partaken of a glass of *tej*, the drink of the country, we were taken between a double row of soldiers to the viceroy's "palace," which was situated in the vicinity of the horse market and which the *ras* had most amiably destined as our abode. This palace, built in the Indian-Turkish style, had been presented to the viceroy by the railway company, but he could not use it because Emperor Menelik's home was more modest. Makonnen had twice been in Europe and no doubt would have liked to do many things for the development of this country, but he could not live in a more imperial style than the Negus Negesti (King of Kings) himself. Passing through the cool hall on the ground floor of the palace and over a wooden staircase, we reached plain halls and brightly painted rooms covered with a few rugs and containing beds destined for us. From the windows one enjoyed a lovely panoramic view over the low roofs of the city and the surrounding countryside.

Our official audience with the viceroy had been fixed for ten o'clock the next morning. At the appointed hour we again went to the simple house inhabited by Makonnen. The naval people and I were festively adorned in gala uniforms; Count Schönborn and Baron Mylius appeared as smart hussars in top boots, their attila coats picturesquely thrown over the shoulder; and Count Széchényi, who wore Hungarian national dress, was the most magnificent of all. The vice consul and Mr. Bieber wore their official uniforms, and Mr. Santho a frock coat. At a solemn pace we walked through the ranks of the rifle bearers to the same room we had visited the previous day. Here the viceroy received us standing, dressed in a festive garment. After a short greeting I read out a document that indicated the purpose of our mission, and then, according to my instructions, I announced that in recognition of his merits, known all over Europe, I was ordered to present the viceroy not only with the greetings of my imperial master, but also with some gifts. Michel translated this somewhat high-flown speech into Amharic with amazing facility and seemed to make a considerable impression on the intently listening *ras*. In a few words he then thanked us for the gifts and for the honor extended to him by our monarch, saying that he would ask Emperor Menelik to permit him to wear the high order I had presented him.

The return call which the viceroy paid us in the course of the afternoon went off in a similar manner. Like us, he was in full dress, but though his peculiar reserve never left him, the conversation was less formal. As is usually the case in the east, Ras Makonnen had every reason to be reserved and not to give rise to any criticism in high court circles. The fanatic Empress Taitu,[2] an opponent who was always dangerous, did not like him because he had sent back her niece untouched after a year of marriage. In addition, there was the danger that he might aspire to the Abyssinian throne.

During our stay at Harar we were the guests of the *ras* and did not need to bother about anything for ourselves and our men. We could not have expected greater hospitality. In the course of these days we naturally had to exchange calls with other Abyssinian authorities. One day, for instance, Bishop Andrée called on us. He had been in the country for twenty-four years and directed the Catholic mission at Harar, which, as he said, had to suffer a good deal from the enmity of the Amharic clergy. According to him, Russia was slyly pursuing a propaganda campaign for the unification of the Russian and Amharic churches, with the final goal of creating a great Orthodox—i.e., Russian—colonial realm in Ethiopia. He assured us that Abuna Mateos, the head of the Abyssinian Church, who as a rule never left the country, had gone to St. Petersburg on this matter two or three years earlier.[3] Another clergyman, Monsignor [André] Jarosseau, told us many interesting details concerning the Apostolic vicariate in the Abyssinian Galla provinces, which he directed, and spoke of the vast tracts of forests of the old Kaffa realm, of its history, and of its sad end after having been conquered by Ras Wolde Giorgis in 1897.

As interesting as all these meetings were, they nevertheless took up a good deal of our precious time, for our chief duty was to procure a great number of riding mules and beasts of burden, which were only acquired after long and weary negotiations. One evening, however, we accepted the amiable invitation of Michel, the post office director; we admired his splendid lions and other animals, listened to his yarns, and spent some very pleasant hours in his company. This young and efficient Swiss, no doubt according to instructions from his prominent countryman State Councilor Alfred Ilg, put all his experience at the mission's disposal and was indefatigably active in our interest.

On the forenoon of February 10 we were ready to start. We presented our thanks to the viceroy, expressed our wishes for permanent good relations between our respective countries, and parted after having received a gift from the *ras* of three richly harnessed mules. At 2:00 P.M. we trotted out through the gates, accompanied as far as the little Hamaresa River by representatives of the *ras* and his escort. In the uncertain light of the silvery young moon we traversed the wide valley of Kersa and at 8:00 P.M. arrived at our camp, very tired. We found our dining tent fixed and the table laid with plates that gleamed like silver. Mr. Arthur Krupp had lent them, and so we enjoyed our meal until the tattoo of our bugler—for the first time on Abyssinian soil—announced the hour of rest. The sun that awoke me after a night rich in dreams revealed the strange picture of a green tent city in the midst of a gray stony desert, peopled by men of all colors in the most various garbs.

My task was to organize this chaos by kind words, persuasion, or threats. Every beginning is difficult. Everyone is inclined to think only of himself as long as the link of mutual interest is lacking, and this is only forged when joint experiences and a common fate have done their work. Until then everything depends on the will and energy of the leader who bears the responsibility for the weal and woe of all. This is not possible without friction, and no doubt in those days I lost the sympathy of some of my companions. How much there was to be thought of, how many differences there were to settle, and how many decisions I had to make! I had to handle not only natives but also sailors, officers, officials, and aristocrats. I had to consider tastes and outlooks of every kind and deal with men who looked forward to the expedition with distaste, indifference, or in expectation of a large-scale picnic. With two exceptions the men were utterly inexperienced travelers. Count Széchényi had undertaken a short hunting trip in East Africa, while the quiet Mr. Bieber had twice been in Abyssinia and was rather fluent in the language. He was tougher and more capable than I would have thought, judging from his appearance, and was nearly the only one on whom I could lean.

The hired mules gradually arrived from Harar with the *nagades*, the professional caravan people and drivers. The latter shook their heads as they viewed the burdens to be transported and appeared to be dissatisfied. Toward evening the indefatigable Mr. Michel arrived, accompanied by Ato Testa, an Abyssinian official, and six soldiers who had to accompany the mission by order of the viceroy. We were also joined by an Abyssinian telephone man who could connect us with Harar and Addis Ababa at any time during our trip, which proceeded along the telegraph line. Finally, an American physician requested to be allowed to join the caravan. When the bugle sounded the start the next morning, February 13, the general chaos at least superficially dissolved into an imposing column of 220 mounts and beasts of burden, sixty-two native servants and soldiers, and twenty-six Europeans, to which one must add the five large Tyrolean mules that accompanied the mountain gun. Because of their impertinence, the day before I had sacked six Somalis whom the consulate in Aden had engaged for us, even though we thus lost our cook. This duty therefore had to be allotted to a more or less suitable sailor. A first start is always connected with many difficulties, and being the last of the column I was only able to start toward noon, after having searched the deserted camp and picked up a number of objects that had been forgotten in the hurry of departure.

A journey in Abyssinia with a large caravan would not have been possible without the assistance of the authorities of the country, since there was no chance during the march of obtaining the necessary foodstuffs or oats and hay for the beasts of burden. While on Abyssinian territory one traveled as a guest of the emperor and viceroy. The rural population received orders to furnish the passing caravan with all that was necessary, and whenever one reached a camp, natives arrived under the leadership of the chief of the district heavily laden with the so-called *dergo*, the gift of hospitality. It was said that this enforced tribute prescribed to the villages and hamlets is credited to them in lieu of taxes. Mr. Bieber kindly offered to distribute the food brought by the *dergo*, a weary proceeding that repeated itself every day, and it seemed to amuse him to keep a strict account of everything.

Of course, I could only give orders to those of my companions who were my military subordinates. Initially I entrusted Lieutenant Huber with the command of the camp and the supervision of the mission property, but soon I had to entrust the five Tyrolean mules to his special care, since they gave a great deal of trouble. They had been on the road for a long time, and for lack of a smith it had been impossible to have them shod either in Djibouti or Harar; their hoofs had by degrees grown long and become brittle. Thus the shoes and part of the hoofs fell off, and it was to be expected that in view of the bad roads we would only manage to bring the precious animals safely to Addis Ababa with the utmost care. Whenever we started, we had to wrap their hoofs with a piece of fresh ox hide and to take such care of the animals that they soon took up all of Lieuten-ant Huber's time. In his place the midshipman, Prince Hohenlohe, took charge of the sailors and the camp. I appointed Engineer Jina as mess master, and one of the sailors did the cooking. I asked the vice consul to undertake the work of cashier and administrator of the mission.

Being the only man with any African experience, I naturally was destined to be the leader of the expedition, which was no easy matter in view of its hetero-geneous elements. I knew how things happened on these sorts of marches and therefore was always the last to leave the camp. Generally I formed the rear guard of the caravan, to the astonishment of the natives, who asked why I, the leader of the expedition, should take so much trouble. I do not think that we would have reached our goal without heavy losses had I not continually supervised the entire company and driven it before me. The consequence was that the marches were longer and more tiring for me than for anybody else, and I reached the camp many hours later than the others. I found that the tents had been fixed and the pots were boiling over the fires, but the *nagades* were still quarreling with each other over the loads. A lot of screaming went on, and I had to inter-vene to calm them down. It was plain that the whole thing did not yet run smoothly, but that was to be expected.

The sailors took their meals by themselves, while we others dined together in the large dining tent or in the open air. It was not easy to satisfy the various European appetites and to take different tastes into account. Breakfast—we had the choice of tea or cocoa—was not served in common but by my orders had to be fetched from the cook by the servants. Any other proceeding would have delayed the start, as everyone realized, yet this contributed to the ill-humor of the more pampered gentlemen, who no doubt had pictured the expedition as a sort of glorified country excursion. They found fault with many other things, and even the slightest air of military discipline, which was absolutely necessary for so checkered a company, seemed to displease them. The sound of the morn-ing bugle call that roused the sleepers from their slumber offended some deli-cate ears and caused many to use bad language. I could not stop to worry about such things, however.

As has been mentioned, Count Széchényi had been in East Africa on a hunt-ing trip, and on his own accord he offered to undertake the caravan service, an offer I thought I might as well accept on a trial basis. On February 14, after another march, we arrived without any delays at Chalenko, where we camped on a wide meadow surrounded by the most exquisite mountain scenery. When next morning the bugle call sounded, the camp had evidently not completely awakened, for I saw the servants packing their bags and folding up the tents. Yet though I heard Széchényi's voice swearing and scolding, no native hand moved. In the morning mists I calmly awaited the development of events until I received the report that the *nagades* were striking and refusing to go any far-ther. Abyssinians are not Zanzibaris, and one cannot treat them like niggers [sic]. This is probably the reason why Széchényi had failed. I tried to mediate, reminding the men of their contract, but in vain. Therefore I had the five owners of the hired mules bound, and with Mr. Bieber, an interpreter, and two men of our Abyssinian escort I started for the telegraph station of Kulubi to seek the intervention of Ras Makonnen. Széchényi had already tried to do so from the camp by telephone, but without any result. After a hard ride of two and a half hours we reached our goal at a height of 2,600 meters and got into telephonic contact with Mr. Michel, recounting our difficulties. The viceroy was unfortunately in Harar, which was the reason why Michel transmitted the whole matter to Councilor Ilg in Addis Ababa, who replied in a conciliatory spirit. Since Lij Tafari,[4] the 14-year-old son of Ras Makonnen and the future emperor, was residing in Kulubi, we took advantage of the opportunity to pay him a visit. After having been announced a couple of times and waiting in the different outer courts of the vast, primitive residence, we were taken to a well-built round hut, on the threshold of which Bieber and I were received by a much-perfumed, light-colored boy with beautiful large eyes and short-cropped black hair, who was dressed in fine white linen and a black silk cloak edged with gold. This was his little highness. He amiably motioned us to take seats near a table and served us young *tej* and red Chianti wine; he followed this with French champagne and ended up with old, dark *tej*. We had to do honor to this whole succession of wines, and we drank to his and his father's health while telling him many things of Austria, Hungary, and our emperor, which seemed to interest him. The general impression which this youth made on us was excellent.

Meanwhile, a telephonic message had come from Harar, according to which the *shum*, an official with the rank of a colonel, was to follow us to Chalenko with ten soldiers and settle the differences with the *nagades*; we got there in the course of the afternoon. I turned over the *shum* to Count Széchényi and allowed them to telephone to Harar to their hearts' content and to negotiate with the mule drivers, without my taking any personal hand in the matter. I was determined to make an end to the situation by addressing an ultimatum to Addis Ababa if no other means proved effective. Thus the day and the next morning passed. I marveled at the stubbornness of the *nagades* and the lack of energy on the part of the *shum*. Finally, at eleven o'clock the burdens were distributed differently, but I was forced to intervene at the last moment, threatening with chains and tempting with promises before we finally got off.

I have no intention of relating in detail our experiences on the march. As long as we were in the mountain district, where the height varied between 1,600 and 2,200 meters above sea level, the nights were often very cool, and even during the day we did not suffer much from the sun. The road often led through fine forest tracts and wonderful thickets of coniferous trees and high-grown cedars, the delicious wood of which glowed in our camp fires with exquisite scent. From time to time a poor little driblet of a stream was encountered, but in general there was a lack of water, and one could not think of washing every day. Besides, the water was not of the best quality. The trails were surprisingly bad, and their maintenance seemed to have been left entirely to the hoofs of the many heavily laden mules that passed along this route, year in and year out. We saw little of the natives of the district, the Ittu Galla, but only their fields and their straw huts, fenced round by thorny bushes. The district appeared to be sparsely populated, but the *dergo* always put in an appearance in plentiful quantities, and our caravan men had everything they could desire—better, perhaps, than ever before. It always gave me a pang when on the following morning I saw the village people hurry to our campsite after our departure and carefully collect the scattered remnants. Various farmlike houses surrounded by stockades, which we passed on our way, were the seats of the chiefs of the district. Placed as they were on eminences, they bore witness to the careful administration to which the country was subjected.

We traversed the mountainous district that slopes down to the Awash River from Laga Hardine in twelve marches, with only one day of rest at Galanso. Our road often led past burning forests and through smoking grassy plains and whirling swarms of locusts. Some members of the mission made use of the day of rest to undertake a little shooting excursion, which took them to our next camping place by way of Katashinoha. They arrived there at the same time as the main caravan, empty-handed but delighted with all they had seen. They gave glowing descriptions of the splendid vegetation and of strange bird calls, and they spoke of antelope and even alleged to have seen lion tracks.

Katashinoha lies at only 1,050 meters above sea level, and the heat of the sun became more and more apparent as we approached the plain of Awash. On a 35-meter-long iron bridge we crossed the river, which here, at 742 meters above sea level, runs north in a deep bed through the territory of Danakil. In the midst of this wilderness, the bridge is a masterpiece of Ilg's engineering. The flat desertlike country, which extends farther on to the highland of Shoa and which arises abruptly, like a wall, was sprinkled with camels driven by Danakil Somalis. By way of Tedicha Malka we now moved uphill, first reaching Choba, situated in a stony desert, where we quarreled with the local authorities on account of the scarcity of water. The horses were watered out of pails, and our poor burden-bearing mules were ruthlessly chased away by the watches when they only touched the water with their snouts. There was little grass, and when our hungry animals nibbled at the dry cotton plants they were simply seized by the Abyssinians. But then I threatened them with the emperor.

Up to the plateau the landscape was devoid of trees and was almost desertlike; the dried excrement of cattle had to serve as fuel, which did not improve the aroma of the food. For a short distance we rode along a new road that sloped gently upward toward some cotton plantations. Late in the evening a thunderstorm drenched us to the skin. This was accompanied by violent winds which threatened to carry off the tents, and we could only start late the next morning, when the sun had more or less dried everything. On this difficult part of the route we often came upon skeletons of mules and camels bleaching by the roadside. We also had to pay our tribute, leaving behind some burdens that we were no longer able to carry. A day of rest was necessary.

Our road then ran along a deep gorge, mounting nearly vertically over Baltschi, the former frontier-place of Shoa, to Shankora and Chefidinsa. We camped there at a height of 2,390 meters above sea level in the midst of a plain surrounded by low hills near a clear, shallow stream, in the shade of some very old fig trees. From here we had a wonderful view of the distant mountains of Addis Ababa. The air was very cool, and a fresh wind drove great gray clouds before it, making the heat of the sun bearable. On March 8 we reached Akaki and thus were near our destination. The journey to Addis Ababa had proceeded amid the continual telephone inquiries of Emperor Menelik and Councilor Ilg, who were thus informed at every moment of the mission's progress.

On March 8, only one day's march separated us from Addis Ababa. Mrs. Ilg telephoned, however, that the mother of the empress had died. The court was therefore in mourning, and Menelik was inaccessible. We had to be patient a little while longer; the next day we only moved a little farther on to Shola to await developments in closer vicinity to the capital. In the afternoon we were greeted by a Count Eulenburg in the name of the German minister, Herr Rosen,[5] who like us had been sent to Menelik in order to conclude a commercial treaty. At four o'clock Councilor Ilg arrived with greetings from the emperor and a splendidly harnessed mule for me as a gift of welcome. I had seen this talented, efficient Swiss, to whom Abyssinia owes so much, sixteen years earlier on the march to Harar and had spoken with him for a few minutes, and I was glad to make his closer acquaintance. We heard that Ras Wolde Giorgis, the viceroy of the Lake Rudolf province, had been called from Kaffa to the capital because of our arrival; his house was destined for our accommodation, which was a particular honor. Wolde Giorgis would overtake us on the next day and escort us to Addis Ababa.

From Shola one could not see much of the capital, which lay spread out before us at no great distance, and the general impression was very disappointing. In the midst of a barren landscape, on gently rising slopes, one saw the vague outlines of some nondescript buildings—a chaos of huts and little houses, some of them covered with corrugated iron roofs, all half-hidden between low bushes. Here and there a little thicket of eucalyptus trees formed a more prominent feature. The morning of March 11 was nevertheless the dawn of a day that none of us will ever forget.

At 8:00 A.M. State Councilor Alfred Ilg arrived in court dress and hat, wearing all his decorations and a sword at his side. We had also attired ourselves in full dress, and with the Austro-Hungarian flag flying at the head of our caravan we solemnly rode a short distance to a place where thousands of Abyssinian soldiers in full war paint awaited us, drawn up in two lines. Their shields glistening with gold and silver; they were martial figures in white shirts and colored shoulder straps, with panthers' skins on their backs, and with yellow, red, and green headgear fluttering in the wind, or with foreheads ornamented with lions' manes and little silver chains hanging down on their temples. It was a strange and wild sight that I lack the power adequately to describe. In the foreground, surrounded by an imposing retinue of high functionaries of the realm and commanders of the troops, stood an expectant figure: a dark, undersized man with bare feet, wearing a gold crown and a lion's mane on his gray hair. A robe richly interwoven with gold and ending in festoons flowed from his shoulders. Broad, bright strips of fine silk enveloped the body, and at his right side he wore a sword in a gold-ornamented scabbard. This was Ras Wolde Giorgis, the conqueror and lord of Kaffa, Konto, and Kullu, the first paladin and brother-in-law of the emperor. We dismounted and, introduced by Ilg, greeted the *ras*, who amiably shook hands with everyone. He then transmitted the welcome of the emperor and asked how our journey had passed, after which we again mounted and continued the march to the capital, surrounded by all these legendary figures and an immense crowd of warriors. About twenty thousand foot soldiers with glistening rifles formed the vanguard and rear guard; horsemen formed the flanks, armed with spear and shield and with fluttering lion or panther skins on their shoulders. While we slowly trotted along the path, this crowd hurried along in disorderly groups amidst the blare of trumpets.

After a ride of nearly two hours we reached the southern entrance of the imperial residence, which consisted of many buildings and vast courts, and the escort dropped behind. We rode on with Wolde Giorgis and his smart suite into the first large court, where we were saluted with a flourish of trumpets and a march played by a band of about four hundred pitch-black native musicians in dark-brown uniforms. To the right, in front of a barn, were ranged the artillery men of the emperor. In the second courtyard, right and left, were rows of the emperor's bodyguards. We dismounted in front of a building that was simple in its outlines but huge in proportions, with a double-domed roof. This was the reception hall. We brushed the dust of the road off our clothes, and Ilg led us in solemn procession into the vast, high, and pleasantly cool hall. Making the three obeisances prescribed by court ceremonial, we walked along the carpeted middle way to the background, where, on a dais, the figure of Menelik was distinguished from the checkered crowd of strangely robed dignitaries who surrounded him by the glow and shimmer of diamonds in his imperial crown. A dead silence reigned in spite of the many hundred richly clad chamberlains and household soldiers who crowded on both sides. Four torches on high gilt pillars threw a weak light on the throne, reminding one of the distant age of Solomon. The emperor sat with crossed legs in black silk stockings on a raised throne covered with costly rugs; bending forward, he gazed curiously at us strangers. A long flowing robe, richly embroidered in gold and diamonds, hid his figure. Ilg introduced us, and mounting the step we approached the emperor, who shook hands with each one of us. Then the princes and the most prominent court functionaries were introduced. After we had rested a moment on small gilt chairs, I rose to make a speech appropriate to the occasion, which Ilg, in spite of the difficult sentences, fluently translated into Amharic; the emperor nodded his approval. Lieutenant Huber then solemnly handed him the letter of our emperor, a calligraphic masterpiece, in a precious portfolio ornamented with chiseled silver rosettes, which Menelik, rising slightly, received but laid aside without glancing at it.[6]

Menelik thereafter had his greetings presented to the detachment of sailors standing with the Austro-Hungarian flag at some distance in front of the throne, and after a little awkward pause he finally asked whether we were not tired from the journey. Thereupon we rose and left the hall as we had come, to the blare of trumpets, and proceeded to the distant homestead of Ras Wolde Giorgis, who accompanied us. We then offered him and his followers champagne, which after the manifold and tiring experiences was no doubt welcome to everyone, for it was now two o'clock.

The place where we were housed, which must not be judged by European architectural standards, consisted of several buildings in the oriental style, divided by courtyards. The inside, with rough white-washed walls and spare furniture, made a poor impression. A low house near the entrance was suitable for the accommodation of the sailors; the two counts, the vice consul, and we of the *Panther* occupied the one-storied main building. Baron Mylius and Mr. Bieber preferred to lodge in a hotel in the city, and the American doctor and Mr. Santho went their respective ways. Ras Wolde Giorgis lived with his consort and suite not far off in fine large tents.

In the afternoon the German envoy extraordinary, Herr Rosen, called on us and asked us to dinner at the German mission for the next evening. At that time there were permanent legations at Addis Ababa from England, France, Russia, and Italy, where of course we had to call. This required many hours of riding, since they lay scattered all over the city at a great distance from one another. The French legation was situated in the northern precincts and comprised an immense complex of courtyards with eucalyptus avenues and numerous houses. The minister, M. [Léonce] Lagarde—by Menelik's favor the Duke of Entotto—had been here for eight years and had in consequence grown thin; he suffered from stomach trouble and was a grumpy sort of man.

We then rode past a vast enclosure and the fine, well-kept Russian hospital to the Russians at the other end of the city. In the charming flower garden that surrounded this legation a beautiful large monkey of a kind unknown to me showed his teeth as if he had guessed my wish to carry him off. With his well-trimmed red-gray, white, and black hair and an oval face surrounded by regular whiskers he looked ridiculously like an old bearded Muscovite. Mr. Lischin, the minister, was ill in bed but asked me to his room, where he bored me for a considerable time with his memories of the Balkans, which he evidently knew well and liked. He did not change the subject, though I tried to make him do so. Meanwhile the others had a good time with his first secretary, a smart Russian officer of the guards who had been relegated to this post in punishment for some misdeed. He had formerly been the gentleman-in-waiting of some Russian grand duke, knew all the fashionable health resorts of Europe, and spoke German fluently. His vocabulary favored the two words *champagne* and *Quatsch* (bosh); when I asked him seriously of the Russo-

Japanese war, he simply responded, "Dear sir, all that is bosh. Let us rather have another glass of champagne," filling up the glasses. A number of Cossacks of the guard were also attached to the legation. They were huge fine fellows, and with their fair hair and beards and their blue eyes they appeared quite out of place in this exotic landscape.

From here we rode to the British legation, which consisted of a number of round huts, well built and connected by covered galleries, which from the outside did not reveal the exquisite comfort they afforded. We were most charmingly received by the minister, Sir John Lane Harrington,[7] the secretary, George P. Clarke, and the vice consul, W. B. Hurt. As I knew Harrington by fame, so he knew me. We had mutual friends and soon met on common ground. But what was especially valuable for me was the insight into the conditions of the country and the proceedings that were at the present moment agitating the diplomatic world of Addis Ababa. If M. Lagarde had been reserved, Sir John was astonishingly frank.

We could not, of course, compare to the German legation, where we dined that evening. This was a considerable establishment, well prepared and well equipped. Herr Rosen, well-known as a translator of the verses of Omar Khayyám, was an expert Arabist experienced in all questions and matters of the East. He was assisted by a staff of five or six highly educated men, each an expert in his branch; a number of choice, tall soldiers of the royal guards formed his escort. How different our mission was! The Germans, who had come by the same route as we and had already been in Addis Ababa for five weeks, were to start home within a few days via Gondar, Aksum, and Massawa.

In order to fulfill the purpose of my mission, I had asked for an interview with the emperor, which was granted next day. Only Wolde Giorgis and Ilg were present, and everyone, including the emperor, wore everyday clothes. I stated the reason that made it desirable for me to hasten the signing of the treaty; I could not leave my ship unnecessarily long in the hot port of Djibouti, a reason that Menelik understood perfectly well. But the printed text of the treaty that I had brought with me did not correspond to Abyssinian customs and required some modification, for which, of course, I had to obtain telegraphic authorization from our Foreign Office. Unfortunately the reply took a long while to arrive and entailed a great loss of time. Menelik, whom I could contemplate on this occasion in close proximity for nearly an hour, made a pleasant impression in spite of his pock-marked face and his full lips, for he had clever and kind eyes, and I felt I was facing an uncommon figure. During our conversation, which turned on practical subjects and was devoid of ceremony, Ilg translated into Amharic, which he knew better than Abyssinian, while the emperor, with a fly swatter made of white gnu hairs and a beautifully carved ivory handle, drove away the flies that were buzzing round him. When I rose to take my leave he presented it to me, saying that there were many flies in his country. I regret to say that the next day the whisk had already disappeared from my room.

The solemn transmission of the presents that I had brought had been fixed for the following day, March 14. In the morning the mission again proceeded to the imperial compound, where it was received on the half-opened terrace of a stone house, the emperor appearing with a small suite soon after our arrival. After exchanging the usual courtesies I transmitted to Menelik the badge of the Order of St. Stephen. The emperor rose from his sofa, and amid the thunder of cannon I vested him with the ribbon of the order and fixed the star on his side. I then requested that he view the mountain gun, mounted disassembled on the backs of the Tyrolean mules, which were standing at the foot of the terrace in the charge of Lieutenant Huber. The little gun was made ready for use in a flash, making a visible impression on Menelik, and he repeatedly expressed his joyful thanks for the useful gift. Our emperor's large portrait in a gold frame under glass also seemed to please him very much, for he gazed at it long and attentively. Fine silver goblets destined as traveling cups also met with his approval, and he was most interested in the twelve cases of old Tokay when he heard that this was a wine not on the market and of which our emperor drank a little glass every day. Then I presented several bales of white, black, and red silk, expressing my regret at not having known that other colors were also appreciated in the country. Menelik greedily stretched out his hand to touch them and said joyfully, "Never mind, it is silk of excellent quality." Twenty-five Mannlicher rifles, the necessary ammunition, and two fine rugs of Viennese manufacture closed the list of presents.

On my request to be allowed to dedicate a few gifts to Her Majesty, the emperor sent a messenger to her, who soon returned with the reply that she was in deep mourning and begged me to come to her alone. Accompanied by Ilg, I proceeded to the next building, where the Empress Taitu, very simply robed in gray and surrounded by some women whose costume also bore the sign of mourning, received me in a room hung with gray material, in the middle of which she sat on an ordinary chair. She appeared to be small and rather stout, and in contrast to Menelik was of a lighter color. Whether she was pretty or not I cannot tell, for her left hand hid her face with the folds of her cloak as far as her big black eyes. She motioned me to a seat at her side, and I sat while Ilg stood facing her and acted as interpreter. I opened the conversation by expressing my sympathies with the loss that had plunged her into mourning, but could not add another word because the illustrious lady immediately began to speak of our emperor and the many blows of fate he had suffered. She seemed to be so wrapped up in this subject that she could not cease speaking of it in a doleful voice. Meanwhile the gifts I had to give her—perfumes, a mirror, a basin, silver pitchers, etc.—were placed at the feet of the empress, who according to custom did not throw a glance at them. The meeting was not particularly interesting, and I took my leave as soon as etiquette permitted. Then we all rode to Ilg's modest abode to meet his wife and children and to hand over to the worthy man the decoration conferred on him, to which Count Goluchowski had personally added a fine cigarette case.

Aside from the calls at the legations and the return calls that we received, we also had to wait on various Abyssinian notables. First, of course, we visited Ras

Wolde Giorgis, our host, who lived near us in tents made of brown Shoan home-spun. Rugs were spread on the ground before the entrance and inside, and a table was laid for us and another for the sailors, each garnished with vases of flowers and ready for our entertainment. Drinking *tej*, Burgundy, and cham-pagne, we spent two pleasant hours, thanking the *ras* for his attentive hospital-ity and listening to his story of his conquest of Kaffa. Wolde Giorgis had incor-porated the Lake Rudolf district into the Abyssinian realm and knew that this lake had been named after our late crown prince. He told us that the people on the northern shore had fled but were gradually returning and were again culti-vating their fields. The *ras* seemed to be pleased when he heard that Count Schönborn, Baron Mylius, and Herr Bieber were going to travel there and as-sured them that he would receive them as friends. The courtesy of the *ras* fas-cinated us all, and nobody regretted more than I not being able to express our feelings in a more concrete manner. Only one Mannlicher rifle remained, which we were glad to present to him when we saw how interested he was in its mecha-nism. It goes without saying that in the course of time the *ras* received a deco-ration appropriate to his high rank.

One of the most prominent figures in Abyssinia is the head of the Church, who is always a Copt from Egypt. At the time of our mission the head was Abuna Mateos, a little man with a healthy tan complexion, grayish-white full beard, and prudent eyes, who had lived in the country for twenty-three years. He re-vealed an astounding fund of historical knowledge and told us many interesting items about the oldest period of the Ethiopian realm. A less dignified impres-sion was made by the Afenegus Nessibu, chief judge of the country, who, sur-prised by our unannounced visit, did not seem to be quite in his right mind. In a lengthy speech he complained of the lack of affection shown to him, though his judgments and sentences were always just; the lack of friendliness was due only to the fact that he was the chief judge. He repeated this tale twice. Then he began complaining of his gout, which tormented him and which no one was able to cure, not even the doctor of the German mission, though he had prom-ised to do so.

I have a most pleasant memory of an evening I spent with Herr Rosen, Count Eulenburg, and the Englishmen in Ilg's hospitable house. On that occasion Ilg told us of a famine that had raged in 1890, to which one-twentieth of the popu-lation had fallen victim. Menelik had then recognized the importance of a rail-way line for rapid supplies of grain, and only then did he give the permission he had withheld for so long for its construction.

A luncheon party that the British gave us in their round huts made some impression on us. It showed that on every point of the globe these men knew how to establish a home in which they could feel at ease. Rough though these dark huts looked from the outside, their interiors were surprisingly beautiful and comfortable, with fine wallpaper everywhere, good prints on the walls, an astonishingly rich library, and comfortable armchairs. In the dining room every-thing shone, and white-clad Indians served an excellent meal; there was even a pianola. To our regret, Harrington was not well. Ilg, who was of the party, related incidents of bygone days when Addis Ababa had still been a forest and Menelik had had to struggle hard against the Galla (Oromo). After lunch we visited the well-furnished stable of the legation and saw in addition to a number of fine horses a tame zebra. The English, being very keen on improving horse-breeding in the country, had founded an Imperial Club and arranged races.

A short time before our visit, the Bank of Egypt in Cairo had managed to obtain a bank concession, with Emperor Menelik as president. Three-quarters of the capital to be subscribed were taken over by the Egyptian bank, together with Menelik and a couple of *rases*; the remaining quarter was left to the free participation of other powers. The German minister intrigued against this foundation, which evidently favored British influence, and demanded a share for Germany in the administration. His proceedings irritated Menelik and still more the Englishmen, a fact of which they made no secret. Herr Rosen had requested me to join in protesting against this foundation in the name of the Austro-Hungarian Monarchy. The attitude that I had to take in this question seemed to me to be perfectly clear, however, and when Herr Rosen one day asked me whether I would join his action, I replied with a plain "no." Seeing his astonishment at my refusal, I drew his attention to the fact that Emperor Menelik had signed the treaty on March 10 but that I had only arrived at Addis Ababa on the next day and was thus faced with a fait accompli. Furthermore, I had been instructed to sign a treaty of friendship with the emperor, not to start quarreling with him. Finally, I frankly stated that I did not understand the matter and that in any case I did not have the authority to treat of these subjects.

I have often wondered at the number of people who lack the quality of penetrating to the bottom of a matter. Surely in this case it was only a question of giving one or the other financial group the chance to participate in a business undertaking with some amount of capital. How could I know whether Austria-Hungary was ready to participate in the founding of a doubtful bank in distant Abyssinia? Was it worthwhile intriguing to this end, at the risk of burning my fingers? Meanwhile, not only the Germans but also some members of my mission—Baron Mylius and the vice consul—fell in love with the sound of such catch words as "state interest" and "prestige," overlooking the fact that the energetic concessionaires might easily have raised all the capital themselves. They only wished to cede to other powers a quarter of the capital to be subscribed in order to give the foundation an international aspect and to be able to dispose of several state powers in their own interests in case of need. My conception of the whole matter evidently did not please these circles. They did not argue with me on the spot, but by the time I was sailing in the Far East on board the *Panther* they addressed violent accusations to Vienna, stating that I had irresponsibly neglected the interests of the Monarchy. The Foreign Office, to which I had reported my interview with Herr Rosen verbatim, understood as little of the matter as my accusers and therefore did not know what it should believe and how it should judge this unpleasant affair, which later gave me a good deal of annoyance.[8]

We were in continual touch with the German legation as long as it was in Addis Ababa. There was never time, however, for an exchange of opinions on the country, its people, and the commercial possibilities it offered. Shortly before their departure we again lunched with the Germans. At the moment of my taking leave, Herr Rosen asked me for an interview, which I gladly conceded. We were alone. Without preamble he asked me in what sense I would report on Abyssinia and whether I would suggest the appointment of a permanent legation or only a consulate general. The opinion I had long since formed and which I had frequently expressed in my reports to Vienna was that Abyssinia, being a poor country that produced little and had no great purchasing power, was of no importance as a commercial domain. Its export and import figures had been the same for years, and unless I am mistaken, at that time amounted to about fifteen million francs. Because of this wretched bone of contention, hundreds of merchants of all colors and races, French, English, Greek, and Indian, had been fighting for years—men familiar with the customs, traditions, tricks, and measures of the country, with whom it would have been difficult for us to compete. In consequence, establishing permanent and costly representation hardly seemed worthwhile. Added to this was the fact that Menelik as well as his *ras* were themselves traders, importing goods without paying the 10 percent import duty. If they wanted, moreover, they could use their powers to keep back the goods of merchants stored in the custom house as long as they wanted so that commerce would be faced by an arbitrary and absolute regime, in spite of all treaties. I was therefore not at all astonished that the American mission, which had visited Addis Ababa a few years earlier, had returned home after a thorough study of the circumstances and had never been heard of again.

I expressed my opinion perfectly clearly to Herr Rosen, who seemed surprised. I had the impression that I had caused a fine building he and his staff had erected to fall to pieces. "But Abyssinia has products and many requirements!" "May I ask of what these consist, except for rifles, cartridges, cheap enamel goblets and a couple of thousand ox and goat hides?" "But good coffee grows here!" "You will find cheaper coffee in Brazil, and any amount of it. Germany will not grow rich by a coffee trade with Abyssinia." These were the main points of our conversation, after which I took my leave. Because of the brevity of the German mission, however, my comments appear to have influenced considerably the report of the ministers and the plans of Germany with regard to Abyssinia. Germany did not establish an expensive representation in Addis Ababa, nor did she enjoy any commercial profits, but had only losses, as I saw from a publication of a Hamburg and Bremen concern that I had occasion to read a few years later.[9]

Engineer Jina, who had come with us together with a petty officer in order to set the mint going, had started work immediately, but a good deal of other work had to be done which could not be accomplished during our short stay.

Thus Menelik requested that we leave the man, who could also be useful to him in other ways, a couple of weeks longer in Addis Ababa. Of course I had to get permission to do so by telegraph, which in time was given. Jina was a clever engineer, and Menelik, who used to watch him work for hours, soon recognized the treasure he possessed. There were many repairs to be made, above all to the electric reflector that the German mission had presented him that would not work. Menelik also had a large English-made steam roller, of which he was particularly proud, that also would not function. In short, Menelik was happy that Jina was allowed to stay behind, and, to the dismay of the latter, he kept him long beyond the stipulated time period.[10]

Some readers may ask why foreign missions were maintained at Addis Ababa. In view of the not-very-evident need for permanent representations or legations, I myself was not a little astonished to find so many in Abyssinia, which from an economic point of view seemed unaccountable. In this distant frontier realm, however, Britain and France faced each other as political watchdogs, carefully observing one another. Neither of the two states was inclined to allow the other any political preponderance, and each wanted to be able to nip in the bud any slight indication of a protectorate on the part of the other. They observed each other jealously and were informed by paid spies of every word that was exchanged between Menelik and the one or the other.

Italy, with its adjoining colony of Eritrea, certainly took a great interest in events in Abyssinia, and at one time had even intended to lay hands on it. Since the Battle of Adowa, however, this dream had been abandoned. The Italians are not much respected in Abyssinia and still less are they feared, but if their influence and the respect they enjoy are not great, they make up for it in a clever manner by rich presents and bribes—the sum of two million lire a year was mentioned—and thus they were quite popular.

The reasons that have brought the Russians are of a more complex and mysterious nature, but are certainly of greater interest. As will be remembered, Bishop Andrée had already indicated in Harar what aims they pursued in their religious propaganda. Russia's intentions became clearer when it began to make use of the adventurer Leontiev in order to find a firmer footing. In the first place, Leontiev brought 40,000 Berdan rifles into the country as a present from the tsar; thereupon, questioned by Menelik as to his wishes, he begged to be allowed to conquer a province for Abyssinia. Thus was founded the Abyssinian equatorial province. Leontiev was named governor and later was even made a count. The neighboring Congo state soon knew how to make a good friend of Leontiev, who in his turn was supported by Belgium, and together they worked against England. However, the fall of Khartoum put an end to this intrigue and to the role of the Russian adventurer. The Russian colonizing ideas were dropped soon afterward, and only its outward attributes—the hospital and the legation— remained in existence, according to the law of inertia.[11]

Emperor Menelik let us know that he would call on us at nine o'clock on the morning of March 18. We did our best to arrange the house worthily for his reception. We garnished the gateways with green branches, had rugs spread out, and borrowed a fine golden armchair from the emperor's storeroom as a seat for him. Clad in our festive garments, we awaited him near the entrance, together with the sailors' detachment. Mr. Santho also put in an appearance wearing evening dress, but he had to withdraw, not being a member of the mission. That caused him to be my enemy from that day forward, though it was only much later that I began to feel it. The emperor arrived punctually, dressed very simply, wearing the peculiar wide-brimmed gray felt hat that he always displayed; he was followed by a large suite. We received him with all due signs of honor. In our reception room we offered him and his retinue champagne, claret, and biscuits. The conversation at first turned on indifferent subjects such as ships and war, when suddenly an awkward interruption occurred—the old worm-eaten chair on which the emperor was sitting collapsed with a crash. Greatly startled, we all rushed to his rescue, but he did not make much ado about the little mishap and simply took an ordinary chair. I had attached a map of Lake Rudolf to the wall and was glad to be able to impart all the information I could on a country and the inhabitants of a province he did not know and which, to judge from his many questions, interested him greatly. It was evident that although, like Ras Wolde Giorgis, he was unable to read or write, he was at home with a map. As Ilg told me, Menelik knew my book on the discovery of Lake Rudolf, for he himself had had to translate it for him, page by page. After an hour, the emperor left us.

During our stay in Addis Ababa we had of course been the emperor's guests. Besides the daily abundant *dergo*, we had been presented with a number of oxen, sheep, and goats, and once with fine mules for all the members of the mission. One day a chestnut stallion was brought to me, handsomely caparisoned—a fiery animal that seemed to consist of only blood and nerves. A fine shawl of netting thrown over its head and whole body protected it against the pest of flies. It was impossible to mount this splendid animal; it would hardly allow one to touch it, and it took a long time before it deigned to take sugar from my hand. Once, however, it met its master for a few minutes. Mr. George P. Clarke, a perfect horseman, first patiently stood near the pirouetting animal, spoke to it, patted and stroked it until he saw his chance, and then jumped into the saddle quick as lightning. It was like a rodeo show, but he only rode round in a circle once and then dismounted. Horses are valued less in Abyssinia than mules; they cost twenty to forty Maria Theresa dollars, while a mule costs ten to twenty times as much. Of other presents with which the emperor honored me I would mention a richly embroidered Abyssinian gala dress, a gold-embossed shield, a sword, and two fine spears. As chief of the mission I was decorated with the grand cross of the Star of Ethiopia. All the members of my staff received orders according to their rank, and even the sailors were awarded medals. Only Mr. Santho, being merely a commercial traveler, got nothing, to his great distress; he accused me of being responsible for this.

The badges of Abyssinian orders are worn on a red, yellow, and green ribbon and are made of gilt silver. I was entrusted with a grand cross made of pure gold, however, for His Majesty our Emperor. Count Goluchowski and two other gentlemen of our Foreign Office were also not forgotten. In addition, I took back to our emperor four elephant tusks of medium size, an Abyssinian gala dress, a gold-inlaid saddle, a similar shield, and other items. State Councilor Ilg expressed his gratitude to Count Goluchowski by sending a silver-embossed round shield. Ras Wolde Giorgis presented me with a shield, two spears, and a live young colobus monkey, which I particularly prized as a rare specimen.

The manner in which we had been continually distinguished by the emperor and all Abyssinians and the way in which all our wishes had been met caused us to harbor the warmest feelings of gratitude, and no doubt each of us appreciated the happy chance that had allowed him to get to know an interesting country and its distinguished ruler and his court. In combination with the heavy pressures of my official duties, the manifold impressions that had crowded in on us and had held all our senses in a continual tension gradually brought a feeling of fatigue, so that I finally began to look forward to the end of these fine days. No doubt the unaccustomed physical conditions had something to do with this. The tropical sun and the high elevation—2,650 meters above sea level—of Addis Ababa, together with the insufficient amount of oxygen contained in the rarefied air, exhausted one and reduced one's working capacity. I do not think that the average European or white man would be able to stand the strain of a continual sojourn in Abyssinia without his health suffering. The Europeans in Addis Ababa all looked pale and had not the usual healthy tanned color that I and my companions had always shown during our travels in Africa. In consequence of the want of oxygen in the air, the process of oxidation in the human body accompanying nutrition does not take place with the usual perfection, and digestive troubles are very frequent—and for Europeans in the tropics, that means the beginning of the end.

On the forenoon of March 19 a surprising experience awaited us. The emperor had invited us to a so-called *geber*, an imperial banquet in the reception hall. Mr. [Léon] Chefneux, the founder of the railway line and a man who played a prominent role in the country, took us to the hall, which was partitioned off in front of the throne by a curtain.[12] On the left hand of the throne, on a raised platform, a table richly ornamented with silver and flowers had been laid with fine damask and china showing Menelik's coat of arms in gold. The decanters and glasses were engraved with a lion crowned with a miter, while the silver knives and forks showed the monarch's monogram and crown. A succulent dinner of twelve courses, corresponding more or less to European taste, was served by German- and Italian-speaking courtiers, and in spite of the early hour we enjoyed it and did honor to the red wine and champagne. The emperor sat on a throne, his legs crossed, and around him the prominent persons of the realm sat at small tables. According to the custom of the country, the courtiers—probably in order to avert the evil eye—hid the faces of their masters with their togas while they were eating. Thus an hour passed with feasting, staring, and marveling, often encouraged by an engaging smile on the face of our imperial host, who from time to time sent us a friendly message. He finally inquired how we liked the white peaches that he had specially sent from his garden, and four times he even urged us to help ourselves to more. They were delicious, and we gladly availed ourselves of his kind offer. When we had finished dinner, the curtain was pulled apart and the wide hall spread before our eyes, now taken up by a great many small tables. The entrance door was thrown open, and a crowd of strange figures proudly streamed in and sat down in silence at the small tables. Packed closely together, they sat and enjoyed the meal which hundreds of servants carried in. The *tej* flowed in profusion out of a formidable system of pipes, and drinking went on to the sound of curious trumpets—long instruments made of glass. Four times this spectacle was repeated, and on that day about forty thousand people must have enjoyed the emperor's hospitality. The entertainment continued in this manner when we left toward noon; Menelik remained behind with his men until the last of them had satisfied his hunger and thirst. We carried away with us the memory of an experience reminiscent of patriarchal times, when kings had been the rulers and at the same time the feeders of their subjects.

As mentioned above, the British legation was eager to gain influence over the Abyssinians by means of sports. On the following morning we were treated to an entertainment of this kind, a gymkhana given in honor of our mission, which Emperor Menelik also attended. On the race course, a big meadow lying outside the city, a huge Abyssinian tent had been erected for Menelik and his suite. A crowd of many thousand Abyssinians camped nearby in the open air. Mr. George P. Clarke functioned as manager. The games started with a mule ride in which not the first man but the last was the winner. Then followed a horse race in which our midshipman, Prince Hohenlohe, mounted one of Clarke's horses and beat the best horse of Menelik to win the race. There followed a horse race by Abyssinian officers, foot and sack races, and a race in which two men had their legs tied together, which particularly delighted the native youths. Great animation prevailed, and the emperor and all the spectators watched the proceedings with visible interest. One had the impression that the English had succeeded in awakening the spirit of the population for sports.

The mountain gun that we had brought was to be shown in action in connection with this performance. We went to a neighboring hill that sloped down toward a wide grassy plain that was dotted with a few bushes and was bordered on one side by a sheer wall of rock at a distance of 2,000 to 3,000 yards. When I asked what spot was to be fired at, the emperor simply waved toward the plain, though people were moving about there. Since I had no wish to burden my conscience with murder, I pointed to a whitish spot on the distant rock wall and explained that shrapnel was to be fired in that direction, thinking that this would offer the people an interesting spectacle. Beforehand, however, I explained to Ilg, the Englishmen, and everyone else that the projectile would not in fact strike the indicated spot but would burst a little earlier in the air at a certain distance from it. The three shrapnel shots went off regularly but made no impression whatever on the emperor or the others, and I saw disappointed faces wherever I looked. In spite of my explanations, evidently nobody had understood the nature of a shrapnel shot. I therefore sought out another target that would better demonstrate the precision of the gun, choosing a solitary bush on the wide plain, from which the people had meanwhile disappeared. After having carefully estimated the distance at about 2,500 meters, I had three shots fired. As luck would have it, these three shots were precisely on target, and the bush simply disappeared. The general astonishment and delight was enormous. Menelik's eyes shone, and when I asked him whether I should continue shooting, he was most horrified. Most decidedly not; the 125 charges that we had brought were too precious. The little gun was triumphantly carried back to town on the back of the mules and certainly was the best present our emperor could have made to the *Negus* (king).

Late on the afternoon of March 20 we at last received the long-awaited consent of our Foreign Office to draft the treaty in the wording Menelik had requested. Clean copies were promptly made and translated into Hungarian, which luckily could be done by Counts Schönborn and Széchényi; this took the whole evening. Next morning, together with State Councilor Ilg, the treaties were studied and compared; only in the afternoon could they be signed in the presence of the emperor and all the members of our mission. I signed the documents written in Amharic, German, and Hungarian, while Menelik, not knowing how to write, had the state seal impressed by means of an old rusty machine. The object of my mission was fulfilled; I could breathe more freely and think of pitching my tents and starting for home. The mission as such was dissolved. My unofficial companions, who had other traveling plans, remained behind in the country. The two counts were housed with the Englishmen, while Baron Mylius, Herr Bieber, and Engineer Jina moved to one of the inns. March 22 was dedicated to the many unavoidable farewell calls and an audience with Menelik, whereby I was handed a letter destined for our monarch, written in Amharic, and asked to transmit many greetings and blessings to our emperor and realm; we begged to have our respects presented to the empress. Receiving a final handshake and wishes for a happy journey, we went our way with sincere gratitude for the truly imperial hospitality we had enjoyed, conscious that we were parting from a great historical figure.

After a lunch on March 23 that united the members of the mission one last time, those of us who were returning home started for the coast. Councilor Ilg and an escort of two hundred soldiers accompanied us part of the way; those members of the mission who were to remain behind and Mr. Clarke went with us as far as Shola, where the final farewell took place. The moment of parting caused many a sensitive wound to close and rash words to be forgotten; only Herr Santho had excused himself by letter on the pretext of illness. In the evening, two of the sailors who had gone ahead with the caravan in the morning were missing. This was unacceptable. I did not know where the men could have gone or whether they would follow us, but I was so furious that I did not take any steps whatsoever on their account. They turned up later on.

On our journey to Addis Ababa I had followed the caravan in the rear and had borne all the trouble and responsibility. Now I wanted to enjoy greater comfort and entrusted the leadership of the caravan to Lieutenant Huber, thinking that he, being a capable officer, would manage things all right. Five uneventful marches brought us to Katashinoha, where we branched off from the former route, following now the easier desert way leading to Dire Dawa, which could now be taken thanks to the rain that had fallen in the meantime. From Fentale to Katashinoha was a long march, and we therefore started in the dark of night. Knowing the dangers of a night start, I should have taken the precaution to wait until the whole caravan was ready to begin. Instead, I simply warned Huber not to permit the mules to stray in the darkness while the loading proceeded, and then went off to the front. When he reached the camp with the caravan at four o'clock in the afternoon, he surprised me with the unpleasant news that three mules were missing. I did not take the matter tragically at first, but when it turned out that, although two of the loads were of an indifferent nature, the third included a tin box that contained not only the decoration for our emperor but also the key to the code that the Foreign Office had furnished me, I furiously sent the men back to search. Late at night they returned, exhausted, with one of the animals, whose burden consisted only of worthless matter. The incident was telephoned to Councilor Ilg and to Menelik, and both were requested to undertake the necessary measures. At Katashinoha the desert route leaves the telephone line, and thus I could not telephone to Addis Ababa again until we reached Dire Dawa.

I could not think of continuing the march until the important tin box had been found. Next morning I therefore sent all my native men back on search. Three days passed in the suspense of expectation. This at least had the advantage of enabling me to finish my final report for the Foreign Office undisturbed and with all the events still fresh in my memory, though I was tormented by innumerable flies at a temperature of 40° C. Part of this report consisted of the accounts stating the sums spent, which was really the duty of the vice consul, who was the mission's financial administrator. I have hardly mentioned this gentleman hitherto, though he had been attached to the mission as commercial reporter and had lived with me the whole time in the same tent. I could not help noticing that he considered the mission a pleasure trip and never thought of assisting me or of taking any notes that might serve as an aide mémoire for his report. In view of our close proximity I carefully avoided any controversy that might threaten the apparent harmony, but on two occasions I had drawn his attention in a friendly manner to the fact that the rapid succession of impressions would easily fade and that without notes he would find it difficult to comply with the obligation incumbent upon him. He had derided my warnings, however, remarking that he considered his task from a higher point of view and did not require any notes. Yet now, when I demanded material for the financial part of my report, it turned out that except for a few scraps of paper on which some figures were jotted down and which he drew from his pocket, he had no other notes or receipts to produce. I finally requested the efficient and clever Lieutenant Huber to assist the vice consul in his work and to concoct a document that could fairly pass as a financial report. As luck would have it, a sudden storm accompanied by pouring rain upset the tent in which the two men were working and carried off the scraps of paper into the desert. I could therefore state in good conscience that in consequence of a terrible storm our accounts could not be given in an appropriate and detailed manner.

Three days passed, but all our efforts to find the lost mule and its load were of no avail, and in spite of my repeated instigations no comforting news came from Addis Ababa. Our stock of provisions, on which we were dependent on the march through the desert, barely sufficed to take us to Dire Dawa. I could not put off continuing the journey any longer and fixed our start for the next morning, April 2, at 9:00 A.M., with the intention of communicating with Ilg once more before leaving the telephone line. Since the wire ran at a considerable distance from the camp, I went there early in the morning with Ato Testa, the two Abyssinian soldiers, and an interpreter. The telephone man switched on the apparatus in vain; we could establish no connection with Addis Ababa because the intermediate station of Choba, whose authorities we had quarreled with on our journey upcountry as well as downcountry, prevented every conversation—a fact that hardly improved my mood. As we sat there, a small caravan chanced to pass. It turned out that they were taking to Addis Ababa two cases of Tokay wine destined for Menelik and a large pail of fat—items that in fact belonged to us and which we had been obliged to leave behind on our journey to the capital. As we suffered from a shortage of food and particularly of fat, this coincidence was most welcome. The man was told to deliver the fat to us, and he agreed to do so. Meanwhile the telephone man exhausted himself begging and entreating, but it was all in vain. Choba remained adamant. I of course did not understand what was going on, as it was in Amharic, but the leader of the caravan gradually realized that something was amiss, and when I furiously put an end to the telephoning he suddenly refused to deliver our fat. My impatience had reached a climax. I had the man bound and threatened him with devil and hell, which finally made him accede to our wishes. All I could do after that was to send a letter to Ilg by messenger, telling of our departure, begging him to continue the search for the tin box, and finally, if necessary, to send me a substitute for the lost decoration.

In a foul mood I reached the camp toward nine o'clock in order to write the letter and dispatch the messenger. To my annoyance, I found that in spite of my strict orders to have everything ready for the start, the tent the vice consul and I had occupied was still standing, and his bed and belongings had not yet been packed. He himself, I was told, had gone off to shoot. As the vice consul administered the finances, I could not furnish our messenger with money and send him on his way until the consul had deigned to return from his shooting trip. The bugler was sent out in the desert and told to sound the rallying signal continuously, while I, in the mood of an irritated tiger, strode up and down in camp. Very much time did not pass, but it was precious time, and when the huntsman finally came sauntering along, a small drama in the desert was enacted. Out of regard for him and in order to express my justified ire discreetly, I went out to meet him. One word gave rise to another. The continual refrain of his reply was that I was not his commander and could not give him orders. This put an end to my patience, and in the presence of all I threatened to have him put in chains and taken to the coast if he uttered one more word. This finally silenced him, and after dispatching the messenger we marched off. The next day the vice consul requested me to grant him an interview in the presence of Lieutenant Huber. He demanded satisfaction, and if such was withheld he threatened to report to the Foreign Office on the insult offered him and the whole consular corps. My reply was brief. I would not withdraw one word of what I had said, and I told him he was free to make his report. I would do the same. High waves require a certain time to smooth down, but finally they did so, and I behaved in the following days as if nothing had happened. Thus the remainder of the journey did not pass in the way many readers might suppose, but rather in growing harmony.

After seven marches we reached Dire Dawa on April 8. Mr. Michel soon put in an appearance and delighted me with the news that the tin box had been found. Engineer Jina would take it to Vienna. The caravan was dissolved next day, the *nagades* had to be paid, and the property of the mission—beasts of burden, tents, etc.—had to be sold. I entrusted Mr. Michel with this task, and for his trouble I gave him some presents and promised him a decoration. He also got the precious mule Emperor Menelik had given me, along with the ornamented silver European harness that had served me during the trip. Indeed, nobody who had the slightest claim to consideration remained empty-handed, and I was surrounded by happy faces wherever I looked. I presented Mr. Carette with the fine chestnut stallion, a joy that was, however, short-lived. The beautiful horse had arrived in splendid condition, but twenty-four hours later it died in consequence of a sting of a poisonous fly. Mr. Carette was the chief of the police corps, consisting of Somalis, which guarded the railway line. In this capacity his men often presented him with wild animals, which he liked to keep. At that time he possessed a tame half-grown lion that was merely chained to a post on the veranda; sometimes it was even allowed to run free, though under supervision. One could romp with him as with a big dog and put one's hand in his jaw, but the paws of a lion are rather rough and can easily scratch deeply and tear one's clothes. Carette also owned a perfectly tame striped hyena. I was to take her with me to Schönbrunn and succeeded in doing so, and years later I used to play with the animal whenever I went there. With great care and trouble I had succeeded in bringing my little colobus monkey to Dire Dawa in splendid condition and hoped to bring it to Vienna. The animal was quite tame and gave me great pleasure. In my foolish fondness, however, I fed it many sweet things and also almonds procured at Addis Ababa, which it loved more than anything else. On the morning of my arrival at Aden I found my little darling dead in its cage with froth at its mouth, probably in consequence of a bitter almond.

After I had sent a number of farewell telegrams to Emperor Menelik, Ras Makonnen, Ras Wolde Giorgis, Ilg, and other worthies, we took the train on the morning of April 12, and on the same evening reached Djibouti after an absence of sixty-six days. There I found the following paragraph in the final report that the temporary commander of the *Panther* had addressed to the naval commander in chief concerning our arrival: "One could clearly witness the enormous exertions and privations suffered by the commander of the ship and the other members of the expedition from their brown and tanned but emaciated faces. The captain of the ship, *Fregattenkapitän* Ludwig Ritter von Höhnel, assumed the command on the same evening and gave orders to have the ship put under steam and made ready for the start on the following morning."[13]

12

With the H.M.S. *Panther* to India, Australia, and China (1905–1906)

After my return to Djibouti I was back in my proper element. It seemed to me that the officers and crew were pleased that I had returned. Djibouti had offered them little recreation and they had even suffered materially, so that they were now glad to get away. The *Panther* was ready for sea and glittered both inside and out, making a splendid impression. The prolonged stay in harbor had been diligently utilized. The temporary commander had strictly carried out my instructions, but he had ruled with perhaps too much severity.[1]

We left Djibouti at noon the following day and went to Aden, where we provisioned the ship and coaled, all within a few hours. We then proceeded to Colombo with a veritable mountain of coal on deck, the capacity of the ship's bunkers being insufficient for such a long voyage. The surface of the Indian Ocean was as smooth as a mirror and the passage was a delight—from my point of view a great advantage after my months of physical and spiritual toil. I enjoyed these days virtually as a passenger on board an excursion steamer, in an uninterrupted *dolce far niente*. Only one care troubled us; four of the men who had accompanied us in Abyssinia had been ill with a high fever since our departure from Aden, and it looked as if others would follow. The medical man walked about with a grave face and spoke of typhoid fever and of the necessity of returning to Aden. This suggestion I flatly rejected. Instead I had the poop deck transformed into an airy hospital, and as the sick men could nowhere have had it better, we continued our voyage. Later on it turned out that the men had only been suffering from some gastric trouble.

We reached Colombo on April 21, at Easter time. On May 1 we crossed the equator, and two days later we arrived at Batavia (Jakarta). I do not remember ever having seen a darker night than the one that surrounded us in the Sunda Strait. For some hours we had to navigate as if through black ink, without any guiding light to direct us. The sea charts indicated the possibility of a tiny submarine reef lying exactly in the ship's course. It had not been verified after its initial detection, however, and there were doubts as to its very existence. I therefore decided to go on without caring about it. Yet the nearer we came to the doubtful spot, the more my assurance dwindled, and when we came close I thought it wise to pass by at a respectable distance. The captain of the British cruiser *Pegasus*, which arrived the following day, admitted that the astonishing darkness he had met in the Sunda Strait had made him stop and wait for dawn.

On the roads of Tandjong Priok and in the inner harbor of Batavia we found a number of Dutch men-of-war at anchor. Here the pleasant days of idleness came to an end, for at this central seat there were a number of worthies with whom I had to come into contact. It is true that a short sojourn does not allow insight into the conditions of a vast town like Batavia, since one only catches a few glimpses of it in going by rail to Weltevreden, where everyone lives who is not tied to the hot seaport by business. What surprised me in Batavia was the great number of Chinese who have settled down there and their importance in business. I certainly do not despise the Chinese; on the contrary, they made me think very highly of them in their own country. They do, however, show an uncanny ability to get a foothold everywhere, and the world's fate seems to me to be clearly marked out. If one considers the enormous reservoir of unimpaired vitality that China represents, one indeed feels inclined to believe in the "yellow peril."

Unfortunately I could spare only one day for a visit to Buitenzorg (Bogor) and its world-famous botanical garden. This townlet is located in surroundings of wonderful beauty, 265 meters above sea level, at the foot of a volcano, from the forest-clad slopes of which flows down delicious cool mountain air. Buitenzorg is the residence of the governor general of the Dutch Indies, and on account of its healthy climate it is also the retreat of Europeans who are in need of a change of air and relaxation. But it is the botanical garden that has established its wide fame. "S'Lands Plantentuin," as it is called, is a scientific botanical garden of the highest order, the only one that exists in the tropics, to which scientists flock from all parts of the globe. Here they have the opportunity and the facilities to pursue their research under the most favorable conditions possible, assisted by herbaria, an excellent library, and a great number of trained helpers.

Batavia was no longer the most unhealthy place on earth, which it certainly was at the time when the dredging of the harbor was going on. The Europeans here looked much healthier than they did elsewhere in the tropics. One got the impression that the island of Java was a treasure of immense value, but perhaps just for this reason it was a fluttering joy for the mother country, which always had to fear that sooner or later some greedy shark might feel inclined to swallow this delicate morsel.

We left Batavia on the morning of May 9. It was time to get acquainted with another continent—the fourth in the course of our cruise—where a stepmotherly nature offers her children only a scanty existence. As the story goes, in Australia the birds are without song, the trees provide no shade, and the flowers have no fragrance. The soft, zephyrlike breezes and the cozy murmuring sea accompanied us for some distance, but as we moved south these gave way to a freshening northwester and choppy waves. At the same time the smiling blue sky took on a grayish tint. In short, Western Australia received us with an unfriendly mien. The *Panther* shook off the foaming spray and wondered how matters would be later on in the roaring forties if they already looked so bad at the very beginning. We were still more than two hundred miles from the continent when it sent us its first greeting, a winged messenger who settled down on deck, exhausted from his long journey. Elsewhere it would have been a gentle, peaceful dove, but here in the land of sand, sun, and sin it had a pointed beak and sharp claws and was altogether a hawk.

At noontime we passed the Houtman Rocks, a vast and dangerous field of cliffs lying far from the continent in the open sea. I thereafter walked up and down on the poop, wondering at the suddenness with which weather conditions had changed overnight. I then retired to my cabin for a moment to roll a cigarette in quiet, but I had not yet done so when suddenly the ship's strange and confused movements made me hurry back on deck. There to my alarm I found that we were in the midst of irregular and towering waves in a bottle-green sea, evidently in shallow waters. I did not know what this meant, because the ship's day work had been too exactly determined for there to have been an error in navigation, but I experienced long moments of painful tension, until the darker color of the sea and the regular wave lines relieved me of my anxiety. Under these conditions I was glad when on the following morning the abject and desolate Rottnest Island came into sight. Later on we entered the Swan River and came to rest in Fremantle Harbor.

The little *Panther* had hardly arrived when she was welcomed in the name of the governor, the prime minister, the military authorities, and many others. The commissioner of railroads immediately sent free tickets for our use on all lines, and even the crew was at liberty to ride the eighteen kilometers to Perth, the capital of Western Australia, gratis. There was no official representative of our Monarchy here, and even the German honorary consul had left for Europe, but he had instructed one of his clerks to place himself at our disposal. After having been so obligingly received, warmer feelings for the country soon began to fill our hearts. On our way to Perth we soon perceived that the population comprised individuals who enjoyed a moderate income but certainly not great wealth. Probably everyone strives to get away from here as soon as he can comfortably do so. The democratic trait of the country and the fact that the Labour Party was ruling it could easily be recognized in the railway cars by the self-assurance with which workers occupied first-class compartments as a matter of course, feeling very much at home there, reading newspapers and smoking their pipes.

Although Australia is by no means an El Dorado, it nevertheless exerts a great attraction on certain individuals, and desertions by crew members on board men-of-war frequently occur. Sailors, for the most part credulous and inexperienced, are soon misled and easily succumb to the magic of alluring tales or to the thirst for liberty that slumbers in the depth of every man's heart. The men cannot be supervised to such an extent as to make an evasion impossible. They have to get shore leave so that they can have the opportunity to enjoy the sights of the ports they visit. I was always liberal in granting petitions for shore leave. The lost school hours and exercises could easily be made up at a more suitable time, during some long stay in port. On board a small vessel like the *Panther* the crew's training soon attains a high efficiency, and unceasing repetition only leads to disgust. With this announcement I gratified my officers and men on the day we arrived in Australia. At the same time I explained that the seduction to desert would approach them and that I could not hinder them from escaping, but that it was my duty to warn them. They should not think that all that glitters in Australia was gold; they themselves would one day curse the moment at which they were so blind as to sever forever the bonds that joined them to their native country. I had no reason to complain of my liberal attitude.

Weather conditions were not at all pleasant when we put to sea on May 28 to proceed to Albany, our next destination. Near Cape Leeuwin, at the southwest corner of Australia, a nasty cross sea made itself felt in a very disagreeable way, but thereafter we were sheltered by the coast and were better off until we reached the fine port of Albany. This little town makes a snug and dreamy impression and offers a pretty sight, surrounded as it is by dark mountains. We found its wonderful harbor, which is closed on all sides, empty, and nothing on shore pointed to much business life. Albany is all the more condemned to decay because the tarrah and karri trees in the hinterland are exhausted; with the exception of some tanniferous bark of the wattle tree no other articles are produced for export. Albany has some importance nowadays only as an occasional coaling station. One may therefore imagine with what joy the inhabitants of this forlorn place received the news of the arrival of a man-of-war. The mayor and the town clerk, representatives of the Commonwealth army, and other town notables at once came on board to greet us. Albany had little to offer except a small club, but we nevertheless were soon on friendly terms with these simple and good-natured people.

On the second night I had asked the local notables to dine on board the *Panther*. Because of the abominable stormy weather I am sure that a coy person would not have ventured to come on board. My guests were nothing of the kind, however. They arrived in old-fashioned swallowtails and dripping oilcloths, each with a big bunch of beautiful roses in his hand and in such a good and festive mood as if he had come to a wedding breakfast. All were of the typical sailor type, with clear eyes in bearded, wrinkled faces. They were old but still unbent men, in spite of a long and hard life as whalers and gold diggers—and these coarse men had robbed their little gardens to make a stranger happy! But now they could look forward to a hearty welcome; when we sat down at table we all felt cheerful, as if among brothers and friends. My guests spoke of marvelous vicissitudes in life and of olden times, when the feverish greed for gold had mastered all Australians, so that towns were deserted and ships were forsaken by their crews in order that all could rush into the desolate interior in search of the yellow mammon. They also spoke of days of hard toil in the scorching heat of the sun and of disappointed hopes, but also of lucky finds and final success that had enabled them to enjoy the rest of their days in discreet comfort and ease. While they spoke, whizzing gusts of wind and showers of rain were to be heard outside.

I was just hearkening to one of these furies when one of my guests said, "Captain, I am sorry to say it, but you will have a bad time in going to Adelaide; if I were you I would put to sea tonight rather than tomorrow." As I did not at all care to leave the port in this beastly kind of weather, I flatly refused to follow this advice, saying lightly that I liked Albany and did not think of leaving the place so soon. Thereupon another of my guests began to say that unfortunately his friend was right. He explained that they would all be sorry to see my ship leave the harbor, but they were old whalers, had grown up in these waters, and knew them well. I should be glad that the northwester continued to blow as hard as it did and that the barometer was sinking. Only as long as the present weather conditions lasted could my small ship hope to reach Adelaide safely, somewhat sheltered by the coastline, and without having to fear the furious southwester and the huge waves that would certainly follow. All this was said with grave seriousness and of course made me thoughtful. I had not yet made up my mind as to what I should do when the harbor master put an end of it by firmly declaring that he would come on board the following morning and take the ship out of the harbor, asking me to have her ready at daybreak. So to our grief we had to part from our friends in town without even being allowed to say good-bye.

Rough days awaited us at sea. We left Albany on June 3 and arrived at Port Adelaide on June 7 after four days and nights, during which the little *Panther* behaved like a nutshell in boiling water. Eventually the rain ceased to pour down, but conditions as to wind and sea kept on with tiresome sameness until we were close to Kangaroo Island. We went on up a narrow creek to Port Adelaide, where a pilot brought the *Panther* to a well-deserved rest, right in front of the town. Adelaide itself, the capital of South Australia, lies twelve kilometers farther inland.

At the time we were not yet aware that our little ship already enjoyed a certain fame in Australia and that her arrival was an event to which the public looked forward with great interest. The daily papers regularly contained a *Panther* column, and even our names were generally known. The public interest grew with every port that we touched in these waters, and the welcome that government officials and the private world tendered us became correspondingly heartier. We hardly arrived in a port that a flood of callers, official greetings, and invitations showered on us to such an extent that we felt like martyrs. This went on day after day.

The reasons why the *Panther* met with such exceptional courtesy everywhere in Australia are various. In the first place, there was her small size, which in consideration of the rough weather conditions was not thought sufficiently large for a winter cruise in Australian seas. We therefore were pitied by the people, who in general are far more familiar with these matters than is the case elsewhere. Not only men but even women were more or less aware of what it meant to navigate in stormy waters with so small a vessel. In addition, the *Panther* was a smart-looking vessel. Perhaps for this reason one attributed to us an especially high measure of seamanship, a quality that always impresses Anglo-Saxons. It also seemed to me that the official as well as the private world suddenly became aware of the veneration that filled them for the august person of our emperor—the aged "emperor of peace," as they called him—remembering also the traditional good terms that had always prevailed between Great Britain and Austria. On every occasion these feelings were expressed in solemn speeches and toasts, in using our national colors when decorating the dining rooms and tables, and also in playing our national anthem whenever an opportunity presented itself. Though it may appear to be conceited, I cannot leave unmentioned that my travels in Africa and my service as aide-de-camp to the emperor contributed to the exceptional reception my ship received. My great interest in natural history also aroused warm feelings in many people.

The population of Adelaide is of another kind than that of Western Australia. It consists chiefly of permanent settlers who do not consider their adopted country to be merely a passing halting place on the way to wealth. One therefore finds more comfort and sociability here. South Australia has never been a settlement of convicts. On the contrary, it is a foundation of the still existing South Australian Company, a colonial enterprise undertaken in 1835 on an agricultural basis. The beginnings were difficult, and the foundation revived only after the discovery of rich copper mines. Like everywhere else in Australia, the colonists were shaken by the gold fever in 1851, but they soon returned to their abodes and went on living modestly and quietly, without showing much sense of enterprise or higher aspirations. They therefore did not succeed in making the colony thrive. The cause of this circumstance lies chiefly with the attitude of the ruling Labour Party, which for its own sake shrewdly hampers the industrial development of the country. As to democratic institutions, South Australia is the most advanced state in the Commonwealth, being the first that enabled the fair sex to vote.

After a stormy week, it seemed that more settled weather conditions had set in. On June 18 we therefore decided to proceed to our next destination, Melbourne. The many social obligations had tired me to the point that after the ship reached the open sea I at once retired to my couch to give myself some well-earned rest. I could have perfect confidence in my very qualified navigating lieutenant, and since the most reliable of my officers was watch officer on the bridge, I expected to enjoy the rest that I so much needed. But I only turned restlessly in my bed from one side to the other and did not close my weary eyelids. I therefore gave up the attempt to sleep and mounted the bridge. The sea was smooth, but the coastline was half-veiled by fog and could be made out only here and there. The ship's course headed straight to the Backstairs Passage, the channel formed by the continent and Kangaroo Island. The officers reported to me, mentioned the names of the several dark spots visible in the misty gray, and showed me the ship's location on the chart. Leaning with my elbows on the breastwork of the bridge, I listened to them halfheartedly and followed the changes in the coastline with sleepy eyes. Now and then I glanced at the chart, trying to find my bearings. But as time went on I began to entertain doubts concerning the accuracy of my officers' report. I was not able to harmonize their statement with my own observations, and I told them so, but they emphatically assured me that they had correctly identified each and every cape, explaining that because of a contrary current the ship had made less progress than should have been the case. They did not alleviate my doubts, but because I was tired I went on leaning on the railing, gazing about me indifferently. Half an hour later, however, I could stand it no longer. I wished to have certainty, and without offering any explanation I gave the order to stop the ship and to make soundings. It turned out that no contrary current had delayed the ship and that we were much farther south than they had thought—so far, indeed, that a few miles farther on the *Panther* would have grounded in the dirty and shallow waters that spread far out to sea from Kangaroo Island.

Our passage from that point was favorable, and we reached our destination without incident on June 20. Melbourne is the capital of the state of Victoria and lies on the borders of the Yarrayarra River, four miles from its mouth. In 1836 this largest town in Australia was still a miserable village. Nowadays it counts more than a half-million inhabitants, and with its splendid streets and many monumental public buildings it gives the impression of a large, up-to-date European city. Melbourne happened at the time to be the seat of the Commonwealth government; in this it alternates with Sydney. The consequence for me was that in addition to the usual calls, receptions, and invitations came those which had to be made or accepted in regard to the members of the central government.

It goes without saying that the *Panther*'s arrival in distant Port Melbourne did not cause the great sensation it did in lesser places. We lay too far away for the people in the capital to take much notice of our arrival, and in any event the weather was generally very bad. But it would be erroneous to suppose that in Melbourne the *Panther* was denied the same attention it received everywhere else in Australia. To the contrary, the ship was the mark of so many courtesies on the part of the official world that private civilities had to retreat into the background.

It would be monotonous to enumerate the many acts of politeness that were extended to us humble and unimportant representatives of the Austro-Hungarian Monarchy. But it was not only sunshine and happiness that filled my soul in these days, for there was also some cause for ill humor. This came from our own Foreign Office. I had long been deemed unworthy of a single word of appreciation for the services to which I had devoted myself in Abyssinia. I was therefore hurt, for I felt it an injustice and gross ingratitude. But not only did the Foreign Office pass over my work in silence, it did not even seem aware of what I, at least, considered the significant and valuable services I had rendered. And since I did not belong to the diplomatic set, one had gone so far as to molest me continually with semi-official letters in which it was said that many things in my conduct during the Abyssinian mission had incurred the displeasure of Count Goluchowski—for example, the complaint of Messrs. Szél and Santho that I had prejudiced their business interests by not caring that the latter's breast was decorated with the radiant star of Abyssinia, intimating at the same time that if possible I should try to set matters right. In fact, however, I had been good-hearted enough to write a letter to Councilor Ilg about this matter, though admittedly reluctantly, in which I left it to him to decorate the man or not, just as he liked. I am not sure, but I think he did not do it.

Added to this, a letter reached me in Melbourne in which Captain Haus, the head of the chief bureau of the Admiralty, warned me that more mischief-making against me was going on. He had "confidentially" been shown a private report that the vice consul who had been with me in Abyssinia had directed to the head of the consular department in which he lodged a malicious complaint about me, saying that already on our way out on board the *Panther* I had treated him in a shameful manner, making him sleep in the dirty ship's hospital. And that "gentleman" had been my guest for a fortnight, had eaten my bread, and had drunk my wine! He went on to say that while in Abyssinia I had never taken his counsel and that I had decided everything alone, like a lord and master—in short, that I had suffered from megalomania. Having never been allowed to take cognizance of what was going on, he never could use his influence. The Austro-Hungarian Monarchy had therefore been left out in the cold when the "famous" Abyssinian Bank was founded, and her interests had been neglected. He ended his report by stating that Emperor Menelik had been much upset on account of my precipitate departure. The consul wisely did not mention one word of the reprimand to which I had submitted him, the only reasonable complaint he could have made about me. He only alluded in a general way that he was not in need of an official satisfaction on account of the conceit he had had to endure on my part, having himself obtained adequate reparation by way of a discussion that he had on the spot with me as to his grievances!

As Captain Haus wrote, he had told the bearer of this letter that its contents too visibly bore the stamp of hatred and that he regarded it as merely pen and ink. That did not improve my bad humor, however. After having received this news I immediately wrote to request that Count Goluchowski issue an order for the investigation of my conduct in Abyssinia by cross-examining every one of the participants in the mission, and by so doing afford me a chance to refute the inculpations that had been brought against me, of which I did not even have full knowledge. Knowing well enough the ways of these circles and fearing they might simply let the matter drop, I addressed my possibly bothersome note to the Admiralty with the request that it be forwarded to the minister of foreign affairs. But therewith I will make an end of this unpleasant occurrence. I did not succeed in getting any satisfaction whatever, not even an answer, but henceforth I was at least left in peace.[2] When again in Vienna, I happened to meet Count Goluchowski on the very first day. I saw him walk up to me, but I only honored him with a cold stare and simply left him there, without lifting my hat. Subsequently I let matters rest, which certainly was not the right way on my part to proceed, for I should have forced the ministerial Camorra to step up against me with open visor. But one must understand that after the long and very fatiguing cruise, I was too tired and indifferent to do anything of the sort.

After many festivities in our honor, the hearts of several of my officers and midshipmen were sad and their mood was as downcast as the weather was dreary on July 13, the day we left Melbourne to proceed to Hobart. In passing the Bass Strait, ill-famed on account of the unpleasant cross sea that one usually meets there, we were not favored, for a fresh west-southwest wind was blowing and the sea was running high. Later on, however, in the shelter of the steep eastern coast of Tasmania, we enjoyed the stillness that prevailed there all the more. In approaching the famous basaltic formation at Cape Pillar, the high swell that forged its way round Tasmania was again felt and roused our longing to get to the fjordlike Storm Bay and into the well-sheltered harbor of Hobart, lying at the mouth of the Derwent River.

Tasmania was founded in 1803 by a settlement of convicts, and its history was full of gloomy romance until the year 1853, when deportation ceased. Tasmania is about the size of Ireland. Originally a dependency of New South Wales, it was accorded self-government in 1856. At that time its former name, Van Diemen's Land, was changed to Tasmania. Thereafter it developed quietly, and like all Australian states, the island made its way only thanks to the discovery of mineral wealth. The tin layers in the northwestern districts of Tasmania are the largest and richest on earth. The climate is mild and even all year round, with hardly anything like a winter season, and as the heat during the summer months is moderated by fresh breezes blowing day and night, large crowds of visitors flock thither from all parts of Australia. In contrast to the parched continent, Tasmania abounds in water. Sources of fresh, crystal-clear water bubble forth everywhere in the wooded grounds in the interior and turn the island into a country well adapted to agriculture and fruit growing, while the splendid pasture grounds on the tableland in the interior invite stock farming, above all sheep breeding.

Hobart, the little capital of the state, is quite picturesque. It spreads over hilly ground at the mouth of the Derwent River, with beautiful Mount Wellington in the background, the summit of which was covered during our visit with a thin layer of snow. The spacious harbor looked rather empty, and, like the town, it made a quiet, pleasant impression. There was no Austro-Hungarian consul at the place, but the German consul, who had left for Europe, had entrusted his official duties to Mr. A. C. Dehle, a merchant from Bremerhaven, who in spite of his impending departure very kindly placed himself at the *Panther*'s disposal and devoted his fullest attention to her until the very last moment of his stay in Tasmania. After he had left, his brother next in age, Mr. Gustav Dehle, took his place. There were three brothers, and they all had come on board the *Panther* in a body as soon as she had anchored on July 15. It surely was the official debut of these three congenial brothers, and I am almost inclined to think that they had come on board together to fortify themselves in this manner with greater assurance. They first excused themselves for not having any notion as to their obligations regarding a foreign man-of-war, saying that they were eager to do all that lay in their power. I soon relieved them of their anxiety, and it was indeed touching to see how they rejoiced in the discovery that a warship's captain was a human being just like themselves. We soon became good friends, and even today—eighteen years afterward—I still carry on a correspondence with Mr. Gustav Dehle.

A person who soon became inseparably linked to the *Panther* and an almost daily guest was Mr. Alexander Morton, the director of the Hobart Museum and superintendent of the local botanical garden. Mr. Morton was very learned and exceedingly affable, and he had been among the first to welcome us upon our arrival. Before the *Panther*'s departure, the imperial museum in Vienna and the menagerie and botanical garden at Schönbrunn had honored me with a load of orders and wishes of a scientific nature. Mr. Morton met these wishes with surprising obligingness, and he also allowed me to prepare the way for further and lasting relations between our home institutions and his, to which purpose I furnished him with receptacles for various collections and the necessary funds. Through his kind intervention the government promised to effect the capture of a Tasmanian wolf, a very rare marsupial that lives only on this island, and this promise was later fulfilled. I had also been charged [by the anthropological institute] with obtaining the entire skeleton of a native of Tasmania, or at least a skull, for the formidable sum of 1,000 kronen ($200.00). I knew nothing of anthropological matters and therefore had no idea what a ridiculous request this was. Mr. Morton informed me that the aborigines of Tasmania, a race akin to the Australian natives, had died out long ago, and as it had been their practice to burn their dead to ashes, no remnants are found. All endeavors to unearth any by excavation had therefore been futile. Of authentic skulls, only thirteen are known. One is in Edinburgh (the first settlers in Tasmania were Scots), another is in Berlin, and the remaining eleven are in the Hobart Museum. Of these particulars the anthropological institute in Vienna apparently had no knowledge, and it goes without saying that I abandoned all thought of hunting after Tasman skulls.

One forenoon Mr. Morton and the elderly United States consul, Mr. A. G. Webster, appeared on board the *Panther*. The latter, a prominent figure, was the curator of the Hobart Museum. After some preliminary talk my friend Morton said, as if by chance, "Now, Mr. Webster, we are going to taste some of the captain's excellent sauvignon." I was well supplied with wines and was pleased to take the gentle hint; the sauvignon was served and created a very jolly mood. It was early in the afternoon, and Mr. Webster was a gentleman in very advanced years. As my visitors were taking their leave, Mr. Morton turned to his companion and said, "You know, Mr. Webster, the captain is very eager to obtain a Tasman skull for his emperor's museum. Don't you think we should give him one of ours?" In hearing this I was absolutely astonished, for I had never thought of such a thing, and, as one may imagine, I watched the old curator intently. I saw that he was having grave doubts, until he finally murmured twice, though hesitantly, "Yes." No other word was said. No one who is not a passionate naturalist will conceive my happiness upon hearing this or the delight with which I received the precious skull one hour later. I carefully packed it up at once and sent it off without delay in a special mail bag, afraid I might lose my treasure for some formal reason while it was still in my hands.

We left this quiet port on the morning of July 27 and reached Sydney two days later after an exceptionally smooth passage. Port Jackson, as its harbor is named, is said to be the finest on earth, and it is certainly very extensive and picturesque. At first sight the harbor looked surprisingly empty. One saw only the British cruisers, which lay on buoys in Farm Cove, and ships of the Australian station commanded by Admiral Sir Arthur Fanshawe. The merchant vessels were half hidden in Darling Harbor, moored on quays and wharves, while the mail steamers have their own landing places at the Circular Quay in Sydney.

The Austro-Hungarian Monarchy was represented by the consul general, Baron [Otto] Hoenning O'Carroll, with whom I was soon on the best of terms. It was entirely owing to his great influence and general popularity that the *Panther* was received with such distinction. His thorough knowledge of Sydney also made it easy for me to find my way through the bewildering throng of social exigencies in this large city. During her stay the *Panther* was as covered with distinction by the government, military and naval authorities, and private circles as she could desire. In addition to official invitations of all kinds, the various clubs made us honorary members for the duration of our stay in Sydney, and we were given free tickets on all railroad lines. Members of the local Austrian community were pleased to have in harbor a representative of their home country, however insignificant it might be; even those who had long ago changed their citizenship revealed their joy.

Our emperor's seventy-fifth birthday on August 18 fell during our stay in Port Jackson and had to be commemorated with due solemnity. This circumstance required much deliberation and consultation with the consul general, and it finally led to a program corresponding to the solemnity of the occasion. Responding to our invitation, the foremost local authorities, the garrison, and the navy participated in the festival, and even many private individuals decorated their villas with flags. The veneration of our emperor, which was shown everywhere in Australia, found expression on that day in many speeches and in exalted articles in the local press. On the eve of the festival the consul general gave a sumptuous dinner for his friends and the staff of the *Panther*. The following morning dawned amid the roar of hundreds of cannon. At 10:00 A.M. the cardinal himself celebrated a Te Deum in the gorgeous cathedral, at which a wonderful mass by Haydn was intoned. The little *Panther* could only accommodate a limited number of notables, and it could hardly hold the many guests who had accepted our invitation to attend a rout at noontime. After I delivered a speech appropriate to the occasion, the assembled guests gave vent to their feelings in cheers so emphatic that the roar of the guns hardly drowned them out. The day wound up with a large official dinner party given by the consul general that went off amid many toasts, speeches, and remarks.

Probably no other country shows so large a percentage of failures in life, or at least of disillusioned hopes, as Australia. I did not hit on any individuals covered with rags who were reading the *Iliad* and the *Odyssey* in the original while watching a flock of sheep, as others have, but I was told of many a career that had failed. Among the fanatics for the salvation of degenerate souls, upon whom one so often hits in Anglo-Saxon countries, must be ranged Commander W. H. Mason, the superintendent of the *Sobraon*, the recovery and admission ship [*Aufnahmeschiff*] for neglected youths that lay at anchor in the Paramatta River near Cockatoo Island. The government of New South Wales had good reason to be proud of this welfare institution, which had been founded in 1865, and it was pleased to offer visitors a chance to judge for themselves the fine results that were achieved there. Mr. J. H. Carruthers, the premier, had wished to take us there himself, but being unable to do so, one day Mr. O'Connor, the minister for public instruction, appeared in his stead with a fine yacht and took us to the *Sobraon*. We visited the ship quite unannounced, surprising the teachers and their 420 pupils as they were engaged in their usual activities. Commander Mason was absent and had to be fetched from Cockatoo Island. Already the first glances made a thrilling impression. The dazzlingly clean ship, the healthy and happy faces of the boys, and the prevailing order and apparent peace hardly allowed one to think that it was the home of beings who without exception came from the lowest depths of moral depravity. It was quite touching to see the boys look up with love in their eyes to their masters, particularly to Commander Mason, whom they idolized. We remained on board for several hours and were impressed by the astonishing results obtained in educating these boys, who were never punished other than by denying them some privilege. The principles that were followed lay mainly in the endeavor to raise the ambition and moral level of the young souls. Such an education, guided by men of fine character, must develop friendly feelings even in beings whose low and sad origins were often enough written in their faces. Before we left the *Sobraon* the minister delivered a hearty speech to the youngsters, who had gathered in a free and easy crowd on deck. As we parted, the boys spontaneously rushed high and manned the masts and yards of the ship, and their looks followed us a long while, until we were out of sight.

According my orders, the *Panther* was to proceed from Sydney to New Zealand. In consideration of the jealous conditions that prevailed between the several governments, however, our consul general thought it appropriate that the ship should also visit Queensland, the last of the Commonwealth states. Leaving out Brisbane might possibly be construed as a slight, which certainly was not our intention, and would have been all the more out of place since the government of Queensland was the only one that did not oppose the influx of foreign laborers and even favored their immigration. In compliance with these considerations the Admiralty telegraphed orders to call at Brisbane for a stay of ten days.

The succession of farewell entertainments given in honor of the *Panther* ended on the eve of our departure with a dinner party at which the flag captain, Napier by name, was my neighbor at table. Some months before I had received the news that one of my best friends had had an accident with the ship under his command, which at that time meant that his career had come to a close. Then, on that very day, a letter reached me saying that my best friend in the navy, the first in my class, had run aground with his ship and had therefore been put on the retired list. This sad news grieved me greatly, and Napier, seeing me in low spirits, asked why I was so depressed. I told him the reason, adding that I felt sure my turn would come next. My kind neighbor at table did his best to divert my thoughts from the subject, and I finally reconciled myself with the jolly mood that prevailed.

The following morning, August 26, dawned in glorious splendor. A matchless blue sky vaulted over the beautiful landscape, and not the faintest breath of air rippled the surface of the sea. After long weeks of rest the men on board the *Panther* were busy at work, and black clouds of smoke were again rising out of her funnels. At eight bells, after hoisting the colors, she was to leave the hospitable port; close to her, athwart hawse, lay the *Challenger*, a British second-class cruiser. We could see the crews on board all the other ships in the harbor getting ready to extend their farewell greetings to the parting *Panther*. The flagship sounded eight bells, the gangway sentries fired off their shots, and the flags were ceremoniously hoisted high. Then the ships' bands intoned the national anthems. After the last sound had died away, the *Panther* had to turn her keel toward the way out. In order to get clear from the buoy, which was brushing the *Panther*'s head, I wanted first to give the ship some steamway, then swing her round, and in a fine turn take her out of the harbor. Accordingly, the telegraph was set "half speed astern." It came otherwise. The ship made headway and kept on making headway, although the telegraph was again put at "half speed" and a second later "full speed astern," but it was of no use. It only made the *Panther* rush the faster against the *Challenger*'s broadside. Quite at a loss to know what the cause of this mess could be, I was only aware that a collision was unavoidable. Something clearly was wrong, and I thought to myself that the chief engineer had suddenly gone mad. Officers and men rushed down to the engine room and alerted the engineers, and I finally could be sure that the propellers would turn the right way. But all that took time, and only fifty, forty, thirty yards still separated us from the *Challenger*, from where the bugle could be heard calling for the closing of the water-tight doors. It seemed as if the disaster must take its course. For one moment I thought of the apprehensions I had advanced to Captain Napier the night before, and then finally I shouted,

"Let both anchors go," this being the last expedient I could think of. They both dropped simultaneously, missing poor Baron Hoenning O'Carroll, who had come on board in a civilian boat to see us off, by a hair's breadth. The weighty anchors and the exceptionally heavy chain cables with which the *Panther* fortunately was furnished withstood the enormous strain, and the cables were strung like chords. They deadened the ship's speed, stopping her fifteen yards from the *Challenger*, and the danger so imminent a few seconds before was suddenly averted. I saw the men on board the *Challenger* break off the ranks, and one of her officers came on board the *Panther* to congratulate me in the name of his captain on the presence of mind with which I had avoided the disaster.

It goes without saying that the general farewell humor that had prevailed on board the ships in the harbor was at an end. I do not know what Admiral Fanshawe and the other captains may have thought of the incident, and it may be that they were thinking I had cracked. Subsequent court-martial investigations revealed that the connecting wires of the telegraph had been inserted crosswise, transmitting the orders from the bridge down to the engine room in reverse, but correctly returning the answer back to the bridge. The telegraph had been dismounted in Sydney for cleaning purposes, had been adjusted again, and had been twice tested. The return answers being correct, nobody had suspected that anything was wrong. The circumstances were so odd that I could not lay blame on anybody, and I therefore declined to punish anyone on board, although the Admiralty twice ordered me to do so. When weighing the anchors it appeared that they were both foul with the mooring chain of the *Challenger*'s buoy. That had saved us, but to get them clear was not possible without the help of divers.

After a favorable passage we reached Cape Moreton on the afternoon of August 28, and some hours later we anchored at Brisbane, which lies fifty miles farther up the river. After having endured for so long the cold and unpleasant weather that characterizes the Australian winter, it was delightful to be in a region where warmth and sunshine prevailed. While the *Panther* enjoyed a cozy berth in still waters in the Brisbane River, just opposite the town, the seas farther south, from where she had just come, were haunted by strong gales and snowy weather. For one whole week a furious wind raged there with hurricane force, churning the sea to mountain-high waves, paralyzing all traffic and proving fatal to several unfortunate ships. Within the memory of man no storm of like intensity and duration had been experienced in these waters.

The Tasman Sea, stretching between Australia and New Zealand, is in ill repute because of the bad weather conditions that prevail there the whole year round. I once casually asked Admiral Fanshawe at what barometric conditions I should start on my way to New Zealand, a passage the *Panther* could be expected to perform in seven days under favorable conditions. The admiral's response was not very cheering: "I have crossed over seven times and have done so at all seasons and in various barometric conditions. You are bound to have bad weather." What would have become of the little *Panther* if she had proceeded to New Zealand according to the original program, just at the time of a raging snowstorm? According to a telegram from Baron Hoenning O'Carroll, naval circles in Sydney had been of the opinion that she would never reach her destination.

Queensland encompasses the northeastern corner of the Australian continent and spreads over the tropic of Capricorn. The country abounds in water and all kinds of natural treasures and is considered to be the state with the most brilliant prospects for the future. Able to supply the continent with grain as well as sugar and all kinds of delicious tropical fruit, it has the government in which democracy has gained the least ascendancy. We were received with great hospitality, and soon after anchoring we were handicapped in our liberty by a multitude of invitations and social obligations. Our happiest experience was at All Hallows' College, an institution for the education of girls directed by the Sisters of Charity, which we were asked to inspect by the Rev. Mother Pathrik. The exceptional serenity that prevailed soon made us feel at ease in these unaccustomed surroundings, leading us to urge Mother Pathrik to allow the whole lot of pretty young folk to come on board the *Panther* for tea. This wish was granted, and one fine afternoon we had the rare pleasure of seeing nearly a hundred young girls on board, all attired in gay, smart dresses, who had arrived with two of the sisters. The merry young folk ran about everywhere with astonished eyes and delighted, glowing cheeks, filling the *Panther* with gaiety and sweetness and conquering the hearts of all. When at table the schoolgirls discovered small bunches of flowers near their napkins, they were very much touched by this attention and were in the seventh heaven of delight. When they finally had to leave the ship, they could not find words enough to thank us.

Without exception all Australians are great admirers of their country and its riches and are sure of its great future. That showed itself everywhere and was as true with the president of the Upper House, who obligingly invited me to attend one of its sessions, as it was with the captain of the fire brigade, who did not rest until he was assured that some of our officers would be pleased to admire his institution. In most cases, however, it was I, the ship's captain, who was marked out as victim. It was the general lamentation in Australia that the number of inhabitants was insufficient, which certainly is true, and this was the main reason why its economic development advances so very slowly. At the same time the ruling Labour Party impedes immigration by artful laws, and no change for the better can be expected so long as the governments persevere in their present narrow-minded views. In Queensland the Labour Party is in the minority, and fortunately for the welfare of the country the program of the rulers is more liberal than that of the other Commonwealth governments.

We left Brisbane on the morning of September 8 after a stay of ten days. When we passed All Hallows' College, her young inmates hailed us with lusty cheers, waving from the windows with pocket handkerchiefs, towels, and even with sheets, revealing that the recollection of their visit on board the *Panther* still filled their minds. The dreaded Tasman Sea received us graciously and kept on showing its mildest side. In consequence of the foregoing gales, it was of course still agitated by a long swell, but we gladly bore the unavoidable rolling of the ship. Extremes meet also at sea, for the earlier abnormal atmospheric disturbance was followed by a period of calm that lasted until we were near New Zealand. Only there did we again meet with strong gusts of a head wind, blowing directly from Cook Strait—known colloquially as the Devil's Pipe—which made us happy to be near our destination.

We reached the well sheltered and picturesque harbor of Wellington on the morning of September 14 and apparently took the port officials by surprise, because they only became aware of us after the roar of our guns had announced our arrival. Wellington was made the seat of the New Zealand government in 1865, dethroning Auckland because of its peripheral position. The small capital lies almost as in an amphitheater on the slopes of mountains that enclose the harbor and that are so steep that the ground necessary for the erection of the main buildings had to be obtained by filling in the shallow shore waters. On account of the danger of earthquakes, almost all private houses are made of wood. Lying in the windy Cook Strait, Wellington enjoys rather lively air currents all year long, which may account for the surprisingly healthy complexions that characterize the city's females.

The very flattering reception with which the *Panther* so far had been distinguished in all Australian ports here reached the climax of hospitality. We had hardly arrived when the town, government, and military functionaries and the clubs and various unions favored us with invitations. Highly placed persons came on board and made their call before the ship was yet cleared for port. There was no representative of our Monarchy at the place, but Mr. E. Focke, the German honorary consul, at once placed himself at our disposal and very kindly stood by our side during the whole of our stay. It is obvious that in this very democratic country the *Panther*'s crew was not left out in the cold, but was on several occasions favored with entertainments. The Right Hon. R. J. Seddon, premier of New Zealand,[3] the ministers, the mayor of Wellington, and the members of the maritime board all sent word that they would make their call on board the *Panther* on the following morning; there was no possibility for me to make a first call to anyone except the governor. They all, however, appreciated my difficulty in this regard and tried to alleviate the burden of my obligations as much as possible by forming themselves into groups.

Among the many instructions with which I had been so abundantly furnished before starting on the *Panther*'s cruise was a voluminous communication from our Foreign Office concerning the so-called Austrian Question. On my way out I had carefully gone through the whole lot of instructions, but for want of leisure had not looked at them again. Relying on my good memory, I subsequently proceeded with punishable carelessness. As far as I could remember, and I thought I remembered well, these instructions contained the order to settle with the New Zealand government certain complaints with regard to some injustices that Austrian citizens on the North Island suffered while engaged in digging kauri gum, a kind of petrified resin. Because of the ill treatment to which our countrymen had been subjected, rather strained relations had prevailed between Austria-Hungary and the New Zealand government for many years. The interests of about a thousand poor Dalmatian kauri gum diggers were at stake, and based upon my vague recollection of my instructions I very soon and with great emphasis started to settle the Austrian Question, in spite of the friendly relations that I enjoyed with the local authorities. Unfortunately, I did so with such superfluous energy that my doings aroused a great stir in the minds of the general public. The belief that the *Panther* had been sent to New Zealand solely for this purpose soon spread throughout the country and formed the topic of the day. The local papers were full of the Austrian Question, and the matter was taken up and discussed even in Parliament. I finally agreed with the premier that a mixed committee should be appointed to settle the question on the occasion of the *Panther*'s stay in Auckland, where investigations could be made on the spot. Mr. Seddon met with all my demands in a most obliging way, since it was the wish of all to come to friendly terms.

Although my mind is by nature rather serious and quite conscientious, it sometimes happens that a certain carelessness gets hold of me. I remember that on the occasion of a tea party given one afternoon by the wife of the colonial secretary, a very pretty lady asked me with visible emotion whether it was true that the *Panther* had been ordered to New Zealand for the sole purpose of settling the Austrian Question. It amused me so much to see the lady so agitated by this thought that for fun I answered gravely, "Yes, madam." This short reply apparently did not miss the mark, for she thereupon asked me what would happen if no agreement should be secured, to which I, with assumed seriousness, replied, "Then, madam, I should feel very sorry, because in that case I would have to load the *Panther*'s guns with ball and smash your beautiful city of Wellington to pieces." I do not know whether my pretty inquirer took what I had said seriously, but without uttering one more word she suddenly turned away from me and joined the other ladies, as if seeking shelter in their midst from the monster she probably took me to be.

On one of the last mornings of our stay at Wellington I had gone on shore to do some shopping and had ordered my gig to be back at the landing at noon. Having finished with my dealings at an earlier hour, I had to wait for the arrival of my boat. To kill time I was strolling up and down the quay in a drizzling rain when a Mr. Malcolm Ross, whom I knew, happened to pass and asked what I was doing there. Hearing that it would take some time before I could return on board, he asked me whether I had seen the tourist office close by, of which I had never heard. We rounded the corner of the next street and entered a locality that at first sight seemed to be a museum, showing stuffed birds and other curiosities. One may imagine that seeing so many interesting specimens of New Zealand fauna at once awakened my greed. "Hello," I explained in a happy mood, "There are kiwi! Do you think I might get some of them alive?" "We will ask the director of the office," was Mr. Ross's reply, and therewith he took me one story higher and introduced me to Mr. T. E. Donne, the head of the office.

The Tourist and Health Department encompasses many diverse objects. To begin with, it is concerned with advertising New Zealand, its riches, and its scenic beauty. It also aids travelers who wish to visit the interior of the islands, which is not yet developed and is therefore of difficult access, by providing them with guides and means of transport, and by subsidizing out-of-the-way hotels and establishing rest houses. Another goal of this office is to protect the peculiar and not very numerous fauna of New Zealand, which otherwise would certainly soon become extinct. The duties of this office also include the control and execution of certain laws concerning the destruction of injurious animals, such as wild rabbits, and finally the care of the game that has been introduced from other parts of the globe.

Mr. Donne was a very amiable gentleman of about my age, with friendly gray eyes, who, after having been informed by Mr. Ross of my desire, simply asked which of the four existing kiwi species I wished to get. The reader will probably guess what my answer was and that my heart leapt for joy, because I was not prepared to see my wishes met with so obligingly. Still better things were to follow. Mr. Donne began to speak of wekas, keas, and tuis, birds peculiar to New Zealand of which I had never heard, and he asked me whether I would care to have them, too. Seeing my eager and growing delight, he went on telling me wonders of a rare egg-laying reptile, named tuatara, which lives only on some small islands in holes in the ground, generally in company with a petrel of some kind. They look like large lizards, are twenty inches in length, and are of special interest because they show certain particulars that make them very similar to some primordial form of reptiles. When Mr. Donne finally inquired how many specimens I should like to have, in my happiness I could not help answering with an anecdote that I had heard at Adelaide. In that city there once lived a young, very likeable Englishman who had no employment whatever and was thoughtlessly leading a jolly life, which now and then caused him to be short of money. One day he was badly in need of a sum that far exceeded his bank account. He nevertheless went to see the manager of the bank and asked him whether he would not allow him to overdraw his account. "That's very much against our policy," answered the manager, "but as everyone in Adelaide likes you, and as I too sympathize with you, I will make an exception in your case. How much money do you wish to have?" "How much do you have?" was the young man's cool response. Mr. Donne was amused by my little story and said he would give orders for the capture of a collection of animals and promised to forward them, after having accustomed them to captivity, to the menagerie in Schönbrunn, which was indeed done.

With feelings of great satisfaction and sincere gratitude for the kind and obliging way in which we had been entertained, we left hospitable Wellington to proceed to Auckland. We arrived there on the afternoon of September 25 after a rough passage along the picturesque coast and remained until October

16. The presence of the *Panther* caused not a little sensation among the many Dalmatians who lived as kauri gum diggers in the interior of the island. They began to flock to town in great numbers, desirous to see the ship, officers, and crew who had come from afar to see to their welfare. This movement grew to such an extent that it made me feel quite uneasy. It had not been difficult to conjure the phantoms, but would I also be able to fulfill their hopes and wishes? One day I was notified that on a certain day the committee with which I was to investigate the Dalmatians' grievances would arrive. It was agreed that we would visit the main centers of the kauri gum diggers and ascertain whether there were founded reasons for their complaints.

Only now, at this last moment, did I think that it would be well to peep into that bundle of instructions forwarded to me by our Foreign Office, which had peacefully rested for so long in one of my desk drawers. One night I set about studying them, with a result that put me in a state of utter consternation. For though these papers did indeed contain the whole history of the Austrian Question in all its phases, they had been provided only for my information, the question having been settled by friendly agreement and therewith buried several years ago through the intervention of our embassy in London. The actual order contained for me in these files was to investigate whether or not our consul, a trader in kauri gum by the name of Langguth, had perhaps called forth this quarrel for some personal reasons and had thereby compromised for a long time our friendly relations with the New Zealand government.

One can imagine that after all the fuss I had made, this surprising revelation plunged me into deep consternation. For weeks the whole of New Zealand had spoken of nothing else, and the committee of inquiry was to arrive shortly in Auckland. I found no sleep that night, thinking the whole time of how I could appease the storm I had so frivolously roused. I concluded that I had no choice but frankly to avow my mistake and the foolishness and unpardonable way of my proceedings. I relieved my guilty conscience in the early hours of the day by addressing a long letter to the governor in which I mercilessly and without restraint acknowledged the whole truth, requesting him to give notice of its content to the premier, Mr. Seddon, in an appropriate way. I also said that I should like to divert attention away from me by visiting the geyser regions at Rotorua. This done, at sunrise I summoned on board the consul's secretary, initiated him in the matter, and asked him to forward my letter by the speediest possible way to Wellington. He was much surprised at the suspicions the Foreign Office had expressed with regard to Herr Langguth, assuring me that he was an absolutely fair character but stubborn, who for this reason had persistently kept up the fight with the government in the interest of the Dalmatians. I thereupon let the matter rest and filed a satisfactory report regarding the consul, without even thinking of investigating the case further. The next day a charming letter came from the governor in which he thanked me for having addressed myself to him with confidence and frankness. He and the New Zealand government were delighted to hear that there was no longer any such thing as an "Austrian Question," and he assured me that I might put my mind at rest with regard to possible consequences.

The premier was pleased to know that I would like to visit the district of Rotorua and had already made the necessary arrangements and wished me a pleasant time. Somewhat quieted down, I thereafter set out on my way and spent three very interesting days in the volcanic wonderland of Rotorua, 170 miles distant from Auckland. I left it to the *Panther*'s officers and crew to get on with the hundreds of Dalmatians who had come to town from distant inland places. I gave the executive officer the order to entertain them to their hearts' content.

I made the trip to Rotorua by train in the pleasant company of the French consul. I regret that I am unable to give the reader even an approximate idea of what I saw and experienced during these three days. Anyone who has not seen the astonishing number of thermal phenomena one encounters at Rotorua— the endless, almost tiring succession of hot lakes, boiling springs, and mud holes—cannot form an idea of the country. The principal spectacle shown to us was the great Wairoa geyser, which as a rule plays in intervals of eight or ten days but can be roused to activity at any time if a certain amount of soap is thrown into its mouth. This can only be done with the permission of the government, however. In spite of the prevailing heat I was wrapped in a heavy, old, and probably very precious Maori cloak made of feathers and was then photographed with our guide at my side, whereupon, surrounded by a crowd of other visitors who wished to take advantage of the occasion, we proceeded to the Wairoa crater. There a large sack of soap was handed me, the contents of which I had to empty slowly into the mouth of the geyser, which very soon began to show signs that it felt sick. The boiling water in the crater began to foam and gradually rose, until it suddenly rushed up with a crash to a height of 100 or 150 feet, as if shot out of a giant mortar. It was indeed a grand and impressive sight. The geyser went on playing for some while, until the forces that had awakened it from slumber were exhausted; the waters then slowly retired into the cleft. I left Rotorua highly satisfied by what I had seen.

Some days later a sad event cast its shadow upon the succession of pleasant, bright days we spent in Auckland. One morning one of our engine room petty officers, who had already attempted to take his life in Djibouti, was missing, and after a thorough search of the ship he was found hanging dead in the forward funnel casing. This death caused not a little sensation and even led to a lively controversy with the coroner of Auckland, who insisted on making an inquest. I protested against his demand, as he had no right to intervene in a matter that had occurred on board an extraterritorial man-of-war. The coroner only gave in, however, after having received categorical instructions from Wellington. The funeral passed off in an imposing fashion, with the participation of many civilians and all the military and naval forces present at the place. An astonishing number of wreaths covered the gun carriage that conveyed the coffin, and the obsequies were consistent with the exceptional position that was accorded the *Panther* in these waters.

On the day before our departure from Auckland a representative of the New Zealand Press Association came on board and produced a dispatch that had just arrived and asked what it meant. It ran, "London, October 14th: The commander of the warship *Panther* has denied a report that has been published of a mutiny on board his vessel. He has inflicted disciplinary punishment, he says, in a matter of no importance." I could only tell the reporter that I did not know what to make of it but that the news must refer to another *Panther*, since five men-of-war with this name were in other navies. The papers of New Zealand thereupon printed the item, concluding with the sentence: "The above cablegram has no reference to the Austrian warship *Panther* now in Auckland Harbor; Commander Hoehnel, we understand, has not had occasion to send any cablegram to his government denying any report of mutiny. There are *Panthers* in several navies." The matter rested therewith, and I did not give it further thought.

Finally the day came for our parting from the waters of New Zealand and Australia and from cities and people who had received the *Panther* and entertained her officers and crew with rare courtesy. When on the morning of October 16 the *Panther* left the harbor and was already under way, a boat came along rowing at full speed, brandishing a dispatch. I thought it was some local farewell greeting, and being concerned with the navigation, I pocketed it without reading it. We were already far out in the open sea when I came to think of the telegram, which to my astonishment contained an inquiry from friends at home whether I was well. Fortunately we had some carrier pigeons on board that had been given to me in Auckland, and I now furnished them with telegrams addressed to various persons in New Zealand requesting that our consul forward my telegraphic answer to my friends at home. We later learned that all six winged messengers safely reached their destination.

A smooth passage of four and a half days brought us to New Caledonia. I confess that I felt rather uncomfortable upon seeing the surging wall of coral reefs that girds this island on all sides. At first it fills one with anxious suspense to have to take a ship through a narrow passage with walls of foaming water on either side, but the task looks more dangerous than it is, and one soon gets accustomed to navigation in seas sprinkled with coral reefs, which can be perfectly well discerned because of the crystal clarity of these waters. The *Panther* had hardly anchored in the quiet harbor of Nouméa when another wire was handed to me containing another inquiry from home as to my well-being. I was quite at a loss to account for the uneasiness that evidently afflicted my friends, but having already forwarded a reassuring telegram, I left this second demand unanswered for reasons of economy. In consequence of my many representative obligations during the past months, I, the proud commander of a warship, had arrived at Nouméa bankrupt to such a degree that I felt quite ashamed, and I could not think of remaining in port. I therefore decided to put to sea again to conduct the semiannual firing exercises and torpedo-launchings. This would keep us at sea until pay day came on November 1.

We left the anchorage with a pilot on board because of the coral reefs that abounded in these waters. When on the occasion of the first torpedo launching, the *Panther* ran straight toward a sandy beach at a speed of 20 knots an hour, the pilot behaved like a madman. "Stop, captain, for heaven's sake, stop." "Not yet, after 100 more yards." "Stop at once!" When finally the bright fish of steel had left the tube and the ship had been brought to a standstill, I asked the old tar what had made him so nervous, since according to the sea chart this part of the coast was quite safe. "Oh yes, the sea charts! But you can't trust them, not in these waters; there are lots of reefs in them that are not yet surveyed." I took notice of the warning and thereafter was more cautious in my navigation.

We were again in Nouméa on the eve of November 1. Meanwhile a cable had arrived in which Consul Langguth in Auckland notified me that for some reason my dispatch had been returned from Vienna. I was therefore not spared and had to telegraph again. Twelve days had elapsed since my friends' first inquiry, and I could well conjecture the anxiety that must have filled them when their repeated demands as to my health had gone unanswered for so long.

The governor of New Caledonia being absent on leave in France, he was represented by a charming M. Rognon. I had not had very satisfactory experiences with French colonial officials as far as friendly advances were concerned, and I was therefore agreeably surprised to be met with charming obligingness, not only on the part of M. Rognon and his wife, but also in military and private circles. On the governor's beautiful tennis ground M. and Mme. Rognon gave a large garden party once a week, at which one saw assembled what there was of good society in Nouméa. The surprisingly large number of guests plainly evidenced the great hypertrophy relating to civil servants at the place, but it was a pleasant sensation to move in the midst of so many pretty and smart French ladies and girls who, as it seemed, were not averse to a little flirtation. According to the instructions I had received, I had to find a suitable person who was willing to take charge of our consular functions. This would not have given me any trouble if only there had been a necessity for such a post. On the whole island only forty-one Dalmatians were living as miners, and it appeared to me quite nonsensical to think of appointing a consular functionary. I therefore restricted myself to sending home a report to that effect.

I took much more interest in another subject. I knew that the habitat of a certain bird species that by itself forms a family in the scientific classification was confined to the island of New Caledonia. In the world of laymen it goes under the name *kagu*; its scientific denomination is *Rhinochetus jubatus*. The plumage is on the whole unpretentious, of grayish, white, and dun color. The bird is not quite so large as a turkey cock; it has nocturnal habits, and it lives in swamps. I took great pains to get some live specimens of these birds and telegraphed to various places to this end, but only one bird was offered to me for sale. With a second one I was gratified at the last hour by M. Rognon, who had been so kind as to send out a gang of convicts to try to catch one. I was of course most happy at having succeeded in getting these birds, which to my knowledge had not been seen in Europe as live specimens. I kept them on board in a large cage, in which they were not lacking mud or water or plants.

New Caledonia is a French station for the deportation of convicts, but that is gradually being given up because the climate is too healthy. To the sorrow of the French exchequer, the convicts lived too long, and since 1893 no further convicts have been sent out, the object of deportation being not merely the removal of objectionable persons from France, but also to hurry them on as speedily as possible to a better world. New Caledonia does not answer that purpose, for it is a veritable health resort, where even the convicts, in spite of being avowedly undernourished, live to a great age. One frequently meets the so-called *liberés*, who can be easily recognized by their special clothing, carrying out tasks for the government and even acting as servants in the employ of functionaries. But in the penitentiary on the island of Nou there is another class of convicts kept under strict surveillance, and a third category of those who, because of their dangerous disposition, are imprisoned in jail.

Since I wished to see the convicts' station on Nou, the governor very obligingly gave the order for me to be shown round by the director himself. The visit depressed me. A bright sun was shining from a lovely blue sky and did its best to give the establishment a less lugubrious tinge, and although the characteristic marks of a prison were not to be seen in an obtrusive way, one was nevertheless aware of being in a sphere of detention. Added to this was the sight of the many unfortunate inmates, who, though they were allowed to move about freely inside the extensive walls, roused sad feelings that soon drove me away from this site of human misery.

In accordance with its original program, the *Panther* had to proceed from Nouméa through the Torres Strait to China, calling on the way at Amboina and Manila. However, a telegraphic order instructed me to go from Amboina to Makassar, Singapore, and finally Bangkok, where on a certain date I was to be at the disposal of our ambassador to Japan, who was at the same time accredited to Siam (Thailand). The time given me to accomplish what was demanded was short, and we therefore left Nouméa on the morning of November 5 and shaped our course toward the Torres Strait. On the way I had ample time to concern myself with the kagus, which had been brought on board on the eve of the *Panther*'s departure. The question arose of how to feed these birds. In nature they live on snails and worms, which of course were not at my disposal. At first I tried to serve them raw chicken, cut up into small bits. But they did not even look at this food, going hungry for two days. I was already feeling very anxious about them when I thought of trying the entrails of chickens, cut up into pieces about one inch long. This, too, was of no avail. In my despair I hit upon the idea of giving these worm-like pieces of entrails the appearance of living things by moving them about with a rod. I had to do this many times until finally, to my joy, the trick worked. At first one of the birds began to eye these longish, pink-colored things, which indeed looked as if they were alive, and after seriously deliberating what they could be and eventually being convinced that they were something living, he suddenly jumped at one of them and swallowed it. The other bird soon followed the example, and in a day or two I no longer had to use the ingenious trick. The birds took their fill by themselves, without being invited to do so.

It was interesting to watch these birds at sunset, when the day drew to a close. Then they seemed much agitated and jumped up and down excitedly, as if desirous to get away to take up their nocturnal ways. They would have knocked their skulls to pulp if the cover of their cage had not been made of canvas. The most curious transformation occurs with these birds when they are irritated or afraid. Then their long crest feathers, which ordinarily hang down flat on their back, stand up high to their full length in the shape of a beautiful crown. At the same time their plumage ruffles up, the short wings are raised, and the whole bird takes on a form that reminded me of a plump bishop with a huge miter on his head, this all the more so as they moved to and fro with short, solemn steps.

Every day I spent several hours watching my birds and caring for them, until the Torres Strait was reached and reminded me of my more serious obligation as commander. If one casts only a superficial glance at the sea chart of the Torres Strait, which shows almost as many coral reefs as the sky has stars, one thinks it impossible to get through safely, but the task is not nearly as difficult as it looks. The water in all coral seas is so pure and limpid that one can perfectly well discern the submarine reefs and steer through them in safety—especially from an elevated stand if the sun is at one's back. But at night one has to anchor. The sea chart indicates certain main directions, but the ship is steered through this confusion of reefs chiefly by eyesight. On the forenoon of November 12 we reached Thursday Island, where we only called in order to take on a supply of coal. The *Panther* was therefore moored alongside the collier, an old hulk. We had to undertake the coaling with our own men, since the local hands declined to work with people not belonging to the trade union. The small town did not look very attractive, perhaps because of the prevailing dry season. Thursday Island had pearl fishing to thank for its former prosperity, but its importance is rapidly declining, the pearl oyster banks being to some extent exhausted. Many of the Chinese and Japanese shops at the place were closed, and even the hotel bars were deserted. Everything about the town spoke of decline.

Because of its situation at the narrowest part of the strait, the sea around Thursday Island shows currents of surprising speed. In the farther surroundings of the islands one saw many stranded ships lying high and dry on reefs, which gave the impression that navigation in these waters was connected with special risks. In fact, however, the large number of shipwrecks is to be explained by the fact that unscrupulous shipowners take advantage of the easy occasion afforded by the Torres Strait to wreck their old, worn craft without danger to the crew—to the loss, of course, of the insurance company. These proceedings are facilitated through the great distance of the site from the seat of the insurance company, which makes investigation difficult and expensive.

Our route to Amboina took us by Booby (Buru) Island. In times past this small, insignificant island was used as a kind of post office, where skippers who happened to pass by would deposit their letters in a cave; in time these were taken up and forwarded by other ships that came along. Shipwrecked persons could reckon to find provisions there and even some clothes. I had known of the existence of this island since my boyhood, having read of it in writings for the young, so that I now allowed myself to look upon the bare, brown island with more interest and sympathy than otherwise would have been the case. There is, by the way, a similar postal institution on an island lying at the western entrance of the Magellan Strait.

Four days later the *Panther* anchored in the wide bay of Amboina. This small island, which in former times had been the central seat of the Dutch government in the Far East, is now degraded to a mere residency. We had called at the place for the sole purpose of replenishing the ship's coal bunkers and could not think of remaining there longer than two days, though the luxurious tropical vegetation of this island, which is the mother country of the clove tree, tempted me to remain longer. Yet though our stay was short, I took pains to acquire some additional animals for the menagerie I had already accumulated on board. I succeeded in getting a fine specimen of the Amboina red deer and various birds, among others a pair of magnificent New Guinea pigeons, which I owed to a lucky chance. Somebody told me that the headmaster of a school owned two of these birds, whereupon I at once set out in search of his abode. I found the old schoolmaster at home, suffering from gout and couched on a sofa. I was received in a friendly manner, but I was soon disappointed with regard to the birds. He explained that these belonged to his wife and were her pets, and she certainly would not wish to part with them. We were just talking of other matters when a very pretty young woman entered the room, whom the old invalid introduced as his wife. For that she seemed far too young, and I rather bluntly gave expression to my surprise by exclaiming, "Your wife! I should have thought the lady was your daughter." My remark did not quite please the man, but it did not escape me that my words caused a rosy shimmer of happiness to flutter over the young woman's lovely face, and I felt that I had sneaked by a little into her innocent heart. Thereafter I did not think any longer of the object that had taken me there, for the darling, who did not cease blushing, seemed even more desirable than the pigeons. But therewith my adventure in the schoolmaster's house ends. On the following morning, however, the *Panther* was just about to put to sea when an Ambonese hurriedly came on board and delivered the two pigeons, which were accompanied by a note in which the fair donor expressed her pleasure to be able to send me a token of remembrance. Little incidents like this quite often make a greater impression than grand events. On the way of the roaming seaman they are like flowers, which unfortunately more often than not only bloom for a day.

Our next destination was Makassar on Celebes (Sulawesi), which we reached on November 23. The native population of this island is not yet thoroughly subjected to the sway of the Dutch government, and two small warships in the harbor had just returned from an expedition that had unsuccessfully sought to capture the Rajah of Boni. How unsettled conditions still were even in the capital I observed on the occasion of a drive I made with the resident one afternoon. On the outskirts of town we happened to meet a column of soldiers who were evidently prepared for war. On my inquiry, I was informed that they were the usual night guard that had to secure the town from an assault by the natives.

The port of Makassar offered a magnificent sight at sunset, when the land breeze had set in and a large fleet of prams, strange-looking vessels, got under sail, all at the same time. The same thing happened in the early morning, when other hundreds of such craft, profiting from the regular sea breeze, entered the harbor deeply laden with copra, mother of pearl, deer antlers, various kinds of timber, and other wares. At Makassar, like everywhere in the Far East, it is the Chinese who are the main supporters of the small trade.

We did not stay long at Makassar. A passage of four and a half days, which was rather unpleasant because of the prevailing misty weather and a succession of rain squalls, brought us to Singapore after nightfall on November 25. Here we received news that struck all on board with boundless amazement. The *Panther* had not received any letters from home for about two months, and one may imagine that we all looked forward with increased excitement to the arrival of our mail boat and were delighted at the sight of the many mail bags that came on board. Their contents were speedily distributed, and as nobody went away empty-handed, at first only happy faces were to be seen. But only a few minutes later the features of all were changed by what they learned from their letters, all of which spoke in a language that was barely comprehensible. Also on my table lay a pile of letters and newspapers, which I at once set about reading, only to fling them aside scornfully, one by one. All were full of nothing but talk of a mutiny on board the *Panther*, of murdered officers, I among them, and of other such foolish rumors. This, then, was the explanation for the enigmatic dispatch that had been passed on to the press association in Auckland and for the repeated inquiries after my health! How worried my friends at home must have been when their inquiries had been left unanswered. A bitter rancor filled me. Whose were the slanderous tongues that had so grossly defamed my thoroughly disciplined and well-behaved crew, who under trying conditions had attended to their duties without complaint? In spite of the enticements they had encountered in Australia, the land of equality and freedom, not one of my men had deserted ship.

It took quite a while before I calmed down and said to myself that surely the truth had meanwhile come to light. But inward feelings of shame still rose within me when, looking at the other men-of-war in the harbor, the thought occurred to me that they might see in the *Panther* the mutinous ship of which so much commotion was being made. We learned only weeks later that the mischief had been caused by a postal card sent home to Pola by the suicide, in which he complained about being slighted on board, of too much work and small pay, and of general dissatisfaction. This postcard had been followed a day or two later by our telegraphic report of his suicide, and this coincidence had sufficed to inspire the fantasy of some obscure newspaperman, hostile to our navy, to compose a bleeding romance. The Admiralty had never for a moment given any credence to these rumors and had even refused the demand to wire for information. That was all very well and good, but the consequence was that the rumor persisted for some time.[4]

The *Panther* had to be taken to the New Harbor for the purpose of coaling, and I also had to make the many calls that are unavoidable even on the occasion of a short stay. Under these circumstances all I got to see of Singapore were the streets through which the carriage drove me on the way to my calls. The little of my time that was left was taken up by caring for my menagerie, which I could neither keep on board any longer nor forward home on account of the prevailing winter. There being no Austrian consulate at the place, its functions were entrusted to the German consul general. He advised me to address myself to a certain Mr. Loebell, a respected Austrian citizen who lived in a summer house and who, being a lover of nature, liked to keep some live animals round him. This was very fortunate, and Mr. Loebell at once said he would be pleased to take care of my pets and to forward them to Schönbrunn in May by way of an Austrian Lloyd steamer. There is no doubt that he did all he could to keep the animals alive, but as bad luck would have it, the two kagus, to which I attached the greatest importance, fell victim to a poultry plague that was raging at the time—and this only a few days before they were to be shipped.

We proceeded to Bangkok on December 1 and completed the passage under partly rough weather conditions, whereby we got acquainted with a tropical downpour of such density that we sometimes had the impression we were steaming through a compact wall of water. When on December 5 we were at the bar of the Menam, it turned out that we could not cross it because of the *Panther*'s deep draft; we therefore had to anchor on the roads, far away from Bangkok and the flat land. A small coaster that fortunately happened to come along enabled us to notify the local authorities of our arrival and to enter into contact with our consular functionary in Bangkok. A tug that the Siamese navy placed at our disposal later maintained a regular communication between the *Panther* and Peknam, the terminus of the railroad. This, by the way, was the only polite act that we enjoyed on the part of the government. Our ambassador, Herr [Adalbert] Ambró [von Adamócz], had not yet arrived, but on the following morning our acting consular administrator, Mr. F. Lotz, came on board, and it was only thanks to his great amiability that we did not feel quite forlorn in the land of the white elephant.

The next day I had to make my calls, and that obliged me to stay overnight at a hotel in Bangkok. On the occasion when Mr. Lotz and I drove in his fine carriage to the walled inner city, the guards at the gate, a dirty, cigarette-smoking, ragged lot, ordered us to stop, although they could see that I was a foreign officer in full dress. This was not quite suited to cheer me up, and when Mr. Lotz, after a long parley with them, said that we would have to get out of the carriage and tramp on foot in a scorching heat through the immensely extended courtyards, I bluntly declared that I would not walk one step. Thereupon poor Mr. Lotz took to his heels, disappeared behind the wall, and came back after a long while with a written order to the guard to let the carriage pass. This the rag-tag soldiers took very much amiss. They furiously cast wicked glances at me as they slowly and unwillingly opened the wings of the gate. But now I had had enough. I jumped out of the carriage and gave clear vent to my indignation, ordering the impudent chaps to form in ranks and present arms, which they did as promptly as if they had been on the Tempelhofer Heide near Berlin. We did not meet one of the functionaries in his office; all the buildings looked quite deserted.

I spent the following days on board ship in expectation of the ambassador's arrival. On December 10 a German Lloyd steamer approached the roads showing the Austrian colors, and in company with Mr. Ambró I proceeded to Bangkok, where we put up at the Hotel Oriental. The ambassador asked me to accompany him on his calls, and thus I got acquainted with the foreign legations at the place. At the entrance gate to the inner city we experienced the same ill treatment as before, but this time no parleys were of any avail, despite my attempts to stiffen the ambassador's backbone. He submitted to the circumstances, and I had to yield. Thus we finally walked the long distance on foot through the streets and vast courtyards of the city in glowing heat. One will understand that the indifferent and impolite attitude shown us on the part of the Siamese, after the distinguished way in which we had been received everywhere else, put me in an ill humor and caused me to meet all Siamese, not excepting their king and princes, with feelings that were far from friendly.

We stayed in Bangkok until December 23. Part of the days passed away pleasantly with dinners and garden parties arranged in Mr. Ambró's honor by the foreign legations, by our acting honorary consul Lotz, and by a very respectable builder of Austrian descent. Only on December 15 did King Chulalongkorn deign to receive the ambassador and his suite in audience. Two court carriages took us to the royal premises, where we had to wait a long time in a plain antechamber in the company of the minister of foreign affairs, the king's general adjutant, and one of his aides-de-camp. They offered us cigars and a cup of tea, but this done, they went on chatting among themselves without taking further notice of us. We were then taken to the king's palace, to a room next to which His Majesty was to receive us. At first the ambassador's audience went off with doors open and in sight of all. It did not take long, and then my turn came. The king, although attired in a uniform of European fashion, made the insignificant impression of a bon vivant. He gazed at me for a while, seemingly at a loss as to what he should do with me, and then asked in English, "Is this your first time to go on shore?" Somewhat annoyed, I replied that I was the captain of the *Panther* and went on shore whenever it pleased me. That ended my audience.

An invitation to a dinner at court was offered us for one of the following days. It finally came on December 20, and we heard that the departing ambassador of Japan, his replacement, and their ladies were also to attend. On this occasion the generally very unpunctual king was true to habit. He greeted his guests, who were assembled in the hall, whereupon one proceeded through various corridors to the dining room. There were twenty-four guests at table. On the king's right side was seated Mr. Ambró and on his left the Japanese ambassador's wife. I had a princely rear admiral as neighbor, who seemed to be quite intelligent and who had been educated for the profession in England for six years. But I could see from his black teeth that he had not given up betel chewing, about which I took the liberty of giving him a lecture. The dinner was rather indifferent, though the service by the many Siamese flunkies in red dress coats was very attentive and good. The band that played during dinner was hidden from sight; the members were female musicians—from Czernowitz (Chernovtsy), no less—who happened to be in Bangkok. After the dinner, coffee and cigarettes were served in an adjacent room, whereby the king honored his guests by addressing them with a few words. I was favored with a question concerning the state of health of my officers and crew. After a while the king invited us to see the queen. Guided by the minister of foreign affairs, we proceeded to a room on the first floor, where we found her standing in the company of the two Japanese ladies. The queen, who seemed to be about forty and who did not reveal marks of former beauty, had large, dark eyes and a wonderfully shaped hand, which we were graciously allowed to kiss.

In dealing with Siamese of high rank, even with such who had lived a long time in Europe, one was struck by how little they had been touched by western culture. Soon after their return they were again untainted Asiatics. I have already mentioned the betel-nut–chewing prince; as it was with this habit, so things remained as far as ethics and morals were concerned. I do not know whether this is also true of the Siamese fair sex, which in general assimilates with greater facility. A passing acquaintance with the daughter of a Siamese ambassador made on a railroad trip to Paknam seems to speak in favor of the gentle sex. The young lady had just returned home from Europe, where she had spent several years, and she avowed that she was horrified at the want of culture and by the barbarous morals, customs, and notions of her countrymen. For this reason she was going to hide herself away at her father's country seat, far from Bangkok.

What grieved me in Siam was the inferior position that the Austro-Hungarian Monarchy occupied. Germany, Italy, Japan, Belgium, Russia, Holland, England, France, and the United States of America were all permanently represented by ambassadors, whereas we treated this country as a dependency of our legation in Tokyo, thousands of miles distant, to which our ambassador paid a short visit perhaps once every year. A person of German nationality acted as our honorary consular agent. There was certainly nothing to be said against Mr. Lotz, but he was only a merchant and as such was of no importance in comparison with the before-mentioned legations. Siam, moreover, is a rich country and a field of great commercial possibilities. How very different were matters with regard to Germany, 68 percent of whose trade and shipping were carried out by steamers flying the German colors. A similar situation prevailed with regard to the Monarchy's representation in the Dutch Indies and at Singapore. To me it seemed that Austria-Hungary was, so to say, not at all represented in the Far East in a vast field of great commercial importance, so that it did not enjoy the consideration due to a great power. I expressed my opinion about this matter in strong words in a report to the Foreign Office.

On December 21 the king set out on a journey to the interior of his country, and this circumstance determined the moment of Mr. Ambró's return to Japan. There being no conveyance available to get there, I offered to take him to Saigon. We left the roads on December 23 and reached Vung Tau, a place at the mouth of the Saigon River, on December 26; there we took a pilot on board, and at noon we anchored at Saigon, which lies upstream forty-five miles in a straight line from the river estuary. We found quite a number of French warships at anchor, two of which showed the flags of rear admirals. Showing the ambassadorial flag of distinction on the fore, the *Panther* was duly saluted, and our honorary consul came on board at once to pay his respects. The local authorities and the navy vied with one another with regard to civilities, and the *Panther* was received in such a friendly manner that I felt quite confused.

In former times Saigon was the seat of the governor-general of French Indochina. This domain is nowadays ruled from Hanoi; Saigon, being only the seat of a subordinate governor of Cochin China [southern Indochina], no longer enjoys its former importance. The acting governor was a M. Rodier, but it chanced that Mr. P. Beau, the governor-general, was also in Saigon at the time. Mr. Ambró and even I, in spite of our short stay, were made the object of much attention, and one day we were the governor-general's guests on one of his tours of inspection to Tai-Ninh, an insignificant border village close to the frontier of Cambodia. We drove there in two motor cars through flat and not very fertile land over splendid roads that were ideal for motoring. The native Annamites [Annamese who live in southern Indochina] whom we met on the way and at Tai-Ninh impressed us favorably when compared with the Siamese on account of their unassuming character. Not much was to be seen at Tai-Ninh, which is a small place, and we started on the return journey soon after having enjoyed a very welcome lunch with the resident of the district.

Mr. Ambró put up at a hotel after our return to Saigon, but as a favor he asked me to remain with the *Panther* for a few more days. We therefore left the place only on December 28 and proceeded to Hong Kong, where we arrived on the forenoon of January 2 after such a rough passage that we gave no thought to celebrating the New Year. By now the *Panther* was badly in need of certain repairs. Her steam launch, for instance, could no longer be used in its present state. A new set of awnings had come from Pola, but everything else on board that was made of canvas was rotten and had to be replaced. Here we were in a region where the rains and cold made themselves felt in winter, so that the men had to be supplied with new oilcloth, the old ones being worn out. I, too, was in need of rest. I had been in harness for more than a year, had long borne a great responsibility, and had lived under the burden of many social obligations. Supported by the exceptional hospitality with which my ship had everywhere been received, I had cheerfully taken the sacrifice upon myself. Now, however, we were on one of the world's highways, where people meet each other more indifferently, and I could merely observe the usual conventions. Moreover, the much larger cruiser *Kaiser Franz Joseph I* was permanently stationed in China,[5] and since its captain was my senior, the *Panther* moved to a second line. This circumstance touched my independence insofar as I had to inform the superior officer of all the *Panther*'s movements and to accord these to his. Never an enthusiastic subordinate, I made up my mind to avoid meeting with the larger ship as much as possible, and at any rate not to proceed with the *Panther* to the northern Chinese ports before the warm season had set in. But I could not escape receiving letters from the captain in which he gave me some good advice and warnings. Already in Bangkok my attention had been drawn to floating mines, remnants of the Russo-Japanese War which still endangered the Chinese seas. I was too much of a fatalist to be troubled by the phantom of an alleged mine and only smiled at the precautions I was advised to take.

I decided in the future to comply with the incumbent social obligations with more restraint. I could soon expect, moreover, to be relieved of my command, the *Panther* being much too small a ship for my rank. In addition, there were motives of an internal nature that caused me to take a somewhat cooler view about things in general. So far my manifold social obligations had forced me to neglect my duties with regard to the inner proceedings on board my ship, and I had assigned this care in too great a measure to the executive officer, giving him fuller discretionary power than our regulations allowed. Only in the course of the last months had I become aware that this officer did not deserve the confidence I had placed in him. He had treated not only the crew but also the staff in a very frivolous manner and with a severity that was totally out of place.[6] That compelled me to watch him more closely than earlier.

It was a case of court-martial that opened my eyes. According to the rank of the offender, a court-martial was composed either of officers alone, or of officers and men. A professional assessor acted both as accuser and as counsel for the defendant. Independent commanders of ships on mission were endowed with the law to the extent of a supreme commander. A professional judge advocate was only in squadrons; on board a single ship on mission one of the officers specially trained for the purpose was invested with this duty. A sentence passed by a court-martial was incontestable. The supreme commander had no right to interfere and had to sanction the sentence and order its execution. If, for instance, a night sentry was found sleeping, this was a crime that had to be sentenced by court-martial. But it certainly matters very much whether a man is standing sentry on board a large battleship, in a spacious and lofty lower deck, or on board a small vessel like the *Panther*, in tropical heat and close air, within a narrow compass that hardly allowed him to move a yard. It had happened that the sentry at the magazine had been found dozing, and on the strength of the authority that I had transmitted to him the executive officer had ordered the man to be tried by court-martial. This was surely in accord with the law, but such a strict point of view was not generally in use. Ordinarily one was content with punishing the man by disciplinary proceedings, more often than not merely by boxing him on the ear and letting him go. I had never done otherwise. To beat a man was strictly forbidden, but such an offender was glad to get off so cheaply and never complained.

As it was I had to let justice take its course, for I could not stop the proceedings. The man was sentenced to several months' imprisonment. When the two delegates of the court-martial came to me in full dress with the court's sealed sentence, which I had only to endorse with the phrase "Has to be published and enacted" and to sign, I felt so indignant at the monstrosity of the verdict that although I knew it to be against the law, I simply wrote, "Has to be punished with four days close arrest," and without uttering a word I resealed the envelope and returned it to the officers. When they had left me I amused myself by imagining the dumbfounded face the court-martial's president would make upon seeing the extraordinary passage I had added. I was still rubbing my hands in pleasure when the officers, acting as if I had committed an awful sacrilege, returned to my cabin to call my attention to the illegality of my proceedings. I told them bluntly that I knew this just as well as they did but that I was supreme commander; therewith I sent them away. This business was not at an end, however. The Admiralty of course found fault with my proceeding, reprimanded me, and sent a large pile of legal documents for my instruction. These I buried in a desk drawer without even looking at them. To avoid repetition, thereafter I took justice into my own hands.

There was another circumstance to which I had to make an end. The navigating officer, who for reasons absolutely unknown to me had shown his dislike for me from the very first, had to be changed. One day my patience gave way. To his consternation, I made him a simple watch officer and assigned his duties to another man. In a small group, if one of the members fails to show the necessary good will, it disturbs the harmonious life of all. This is all the more the case with the wardroom of a small vessel, when one or the other seeks to tower above the others. That is the beginning of the unavoidable end, which as far as the *Panther* was concerned came six months later under the command of my successor, who finally saw himself compelled to have the evildoer recalled.

According to instructions, the *Panther* had to call at Canton. If we wished to advance up the river to the town itself, it had to be done at full moon because of tidal conditions. We therefore started on January 8 with our vice consul, Mr. [Nikolaus] Post, on board. After having reached the bar of the Canton River, we had to wait for high tide, because only then could we cross it. The port of Canton is very narrow, affording anchorage only for a few ships of greater draught. We were therefore only allowed to take up a passing berth that by chance was unoccupied, and we had to leave on the following morning when its rightful proprietor arrived. For tidal reasons our stay was limited to four days, during which the *Panther* was three times obliged to shift berth. Like no other place on earth, this large, populous, and typically Chinese city reveals the antlike tendency of humankind to crowd together; at the same time it offers a good opportunity to admire the beelike industriousness of the Chinese. For hours I could watch the confusing bustle of life in the narrow slums of the so-called new town and admire the assiduity that fills the old and young alike and the incredible contentment of the sons of heaven with regard to air, sunlight, lodging, and food. They are a race seemingly quite unconscious of having nerves.

We left Canton on the night of January 12/13 and arrived in the course of the forenoon before Macao, where because of the shallows we had to anchor the *Panther* in only three and a half fathoms of water, five miles from land. The sky was overcast, there was some north wind blowing, and the weather was so misty that only now and then could one catch a glimpse of the outlines of Macao. The kind and considerate governor took account of the prevailing weather conditions and at once sent word asking us to abstain from calling on him but to accept his invitation to dinner on the following night. But at daybreak on the next morning I was awakened by some irregular, jerking movements of the *Panther*, caused by movement of the waves, which were breaking athwart the ship's side. Evidently the *Panther* did not swing freely in the direction of the wind. That set me going. To my surprise I found that there were only two and a half fathoms of water instead of the three and a half that we had sounded the day before, so that the ship was aground, though in soft mud. The steady fresh north wind had blown the water away and had diminished the depth. There was no danger, for we could have anchored a mile or two farther out, but as the weather conditions in general were bad, I preferred to leave the place and return to Hong Kong, which I unfortunately had to do without being able to inform the governor of our hurried departure.

There followed five weeks of pleasant rest at Hong Kong, which unfortunately were much impaired by cold and rainy weather. My days passed rather quietly. Now and again I made a call or enjoyed a dinner or gave one on board the *Panther*, but on the whole there was not much going on. Warships, above all those flying the British colors, were continually coming and going, but Hong Kong is too much of a transit place to encourage closer intercourse between them. Even with the commander of the *Alacrity*, a close neighbor of the *Panther*, no relations were maintained. On the occasion of the admiral's one and only call, I felt induced to say that the vessel he commanded appeared to be too small for him. "Too small? The ship that would be big enough for me has not yet been built!" was his prompt, proud answer.

Slowly the time approached when I had to think of proceeding with the *Panther* to Haiphong, and according to instructions also to Kwangchow (Chankiang). I had to go to Tonkin with our consul Post to make economic studies there, but it was a riddle to me why I had to call at that godforsaken place. It was very fortunate that on the occasion of an official dinner the German consul general was my neighbor, because he gave me much valuable information concerning navigation through the Hainan Strait. According to him, this was an extremely dangerous passage that one should venture only with the assistance of the very best pilot available. He advised me to engage not a Chinese pilot but a Dane by the name of Marlees, who was the only trustworthy pilot for these waters. I thereupon immediately secured the man's services.

The *Panther* left Hong Kong on the morning of February 20 and first proceeded to Macao. On her way the *Panther* had to navigate through a fog so thick that I never would have thought of putting to sea without the Dane on board. We proceeded very cautiously, worked our way directed only by compass, log, and sounding, and finally anchored near Macao in four fathoms of water. We had passed close by several large steamers that were cautiously feeling their way to Hong Kong, and the incessant roar of half a dozen steam whistles around us was quite exciting. One must be accustomed to such navigating conditions, and one does get used to them sooner than one thinks, for otherwise no traffic would be possible in certain seas. The ship's position being quite uncertain and the fog getting still thicker, our situation at anchor was not a pleasant one. To avoid being rammed, we lit the *Panther* up with a great number of lanterns and kept a searchlight going all night. This illumination probably seduced the captain of one of the steamers into approaching within hailing distance of the *Panther* to request that we tell him where he was. The weather conditions in the course of the following morning changed so much for the better that we could anchor the *Panther* a little closer to shore and communicate with the town authorities.

Macao is picturesquely situated on a peninsula and connected with the mainland only by a long, narrow, flat strip of land. When seen from the seaside, the town gives the impression of being an important place because of a row of stately buildings that tower above the old fortifications. This appearance soon dwindles down to nothing, however, for if one walks through the still streets he becomes aware of the absence of all commercial activity. Even in the Chinese part of town there reigns a pleasant quiet, until toward nighttime a row of pompous gambling houses, splendidly lit up by electric lights, gives the town the misleading features of sumptuousness. Macao enjoys a fine climate and excellent sanitary conditions, but it suffers too much from the shallowness of its inner harbor ever to rise to greater importance. Nevertheless, Macao is a veritable gold mine for Portugal. With its revenues it not only covers its own expenses but also maintains the totally passive colony of Timor and even manages to pay the motherland a sum varying between $300,000 and $400,000 annually. These revenues in the main consist of the returns of the customs and the rent of the gambling houses.

We left Macao on February 23 and arrived on the following morning at the entrance of the Hainan Strait, with a stiff SSW breeze blowing. These waters are in bad repute because of their many still uncharted shallows, their strong currents, and their quite irregular flood tides. To make matters worse, there are no conspicuous landmarks for guidance. For seven years the Dane Marlees had been the captain of a French steamer on regular service between Hong Kong and Haiphong. After his retirement, the command of the steamer had been entrusted to the officer next to him in rank, who had served under him for several years. The steamer went lost, however, on his very first trip, and we could still see her wreck lying on the north coast of Hainan.

Early on the morning of February 25 we were at the bar of the Red River, on the right side of which lies Haiphong, 10 kilometers upstream. Although pilotage in the river is compulsory, there was no pilot to be seen, and as we were not allowed to waste any time because of tidal conditions, Marlees declared his readiness to take the ship on, which after all was not very difficult, the fairway in the river being well marked. We were already near our destination when a pilot put in an appearance and moored the *Panther* opposite the town, close by the French transport *Manche*. There I at once made my call and was received by her captain very amicably, but as I could plainly see, also with some uneasiness. In his cabin he at first asked me whether I had seen the latest Reuter telegrams. As I had not had a chance to see them for about a week, the captain informed me that the Morocco question had come to such a critical point that matters looked very serious.[7] This unexpected news roused in me an abundance of reflections, for I was sure that in case of a conflict the Austro-Hungarian Monarchy would undoubtedly be involved. And if that happened, the *Panther* would be in a mousetrap from which there was no escape. I thought it very fair on the part of the French captain to have warned me. I thanked him most sincerely, and on his advice I went on shore to obtain the latest news at the naval station. Was the situation indeed so serious as he had pictured it? Then the only thing for me to do was to decamp with the *Panther* at once, without losing much time. I studied the telegrams carefully but was thereafter not any wiser. I then acquiesced in the thought that the Admiralty would not have failed to warn me in time if there was a serious danger of war. But would such a telegram reach me in such a case? Would the French perhaps keep it back? Such thoughts were well suited to aggravate the dilemma in which I found myself and continued to preoccupy me for the next twenty-four hours. But then carelessness and my desire to see something of the interior of Tonkin got the upper hand. I summoned the three oldest of my officers and instructed them on how to behave in case war broke out during my absence. At the first request to surrender, the *Panther* was to be blown up.

After having settled everything to the best of my ability, though not quite reassured and with a slight feeling of guilt, I proceeded by railroad to Hanoi in the company of Lieutenant Huber. We arrived after a four-hour journey across a flat uninteresting plain covered with rice fields. Haiphong and Hanoi are both towns that are plotted on a large scale with a view to the future, with broad avenues and rectangular streets. The very scattered European buildings give both cities the false appearance of importance, all the more so as the indigenous part of the town, which lies in between them, lacks temples and other conspicuous structures of earlier times. I was much disappointed regarding the oriental features of these two towns. A pleasant surprise was the kind manner in which I was received by everyone at Hanoi. Mr. P. Beau, the governor-general, seemed pleased to see me again and treated me like an old acquaintance. The first three days of my stay were profitably employed with studies of an economic nature, in which I was heartily assisted by the officials I encountered. Wishing thereafter to see something of the farther interior of the country, I devoted the following two days to a visit of Langson, a district bordering China.

Langson is a small town of recent vintage, lying 160 kilometers north of Hanoi, close to the Chinese boundary; it takes six hours to get there by rail. Colonel Hocquart, the commanding officer of the military district, received me with charming courtesy and took me to his residence, where a delicious and welcome lunch awaited us. In the course of the afternoon, escorted by several officers and a squad of Annamite soldiers on horseback, I was taken in a carriage to the Chinese frontier gate, a small medieval fortress that protects the road leading to Lungtsin (Pingxiang); we arrived there after a drive of one and a half hours. The guard house is picturesquely situated at the entrance to a narrow valley, hemmed in by precipitous mountains. Old, crenellated fortress walls boldly wind up to the summit of the steep mountains, a work that makes one stare in wonder. At this sight one felt suddenly removed deep into the Chinese middle ages.

The evening was filled with a grand dinner at which the attentive host gave me the opportunity to get acquainted with the other high functionaries of the place and the officers of the garrison. The banquet started with the sound of a popular Austrian military song and ended with fine words of veneration for our emperor, spoken by the host. I confess to never having met a man, either before or later, who combined in such a measure soldierlike straightforwardness with a most refined culture. His mood was somber, however, owing to the loss of his beloved wife. A daughter, about twelve years old, who on that night complied charmingly with her duties as hostess, was the only comfort left to the grief-stricken father. I spent not more than twenty hours in Colonel Hocquart's house and never saw him again, but my visit engendered a friendship that found an end only with his untimely death early in 1914. Hocquart was the first to write, after which we remained in touch. Later on he acted for years as chief of staff in Senegambia, and in its deadly climate he contracted the germ of death. When he finally decided to return to France to recover his health, it was too late. He was already dying when he arrived at Marseilles.

The garrison of Langson consisted in the main of Foreign Legion troops, and it was their band that had played during dinner. Not yet having come in touch with officers of the legion, I was glad to have a chance to learn about this peculiar institution. The officers readily gave me all the information I wanted and allowed me a pretty good insight into its organization. As there were two Austrians among the musicians, I was asked whether I would like to meet them. I do not know what prompted me to say yes, despite the repugnance I felt at the thought, because to my mind these wretches, who had bound themselves to fight even against their own country should the necessity arise, were no longer my countrymen. As it was, they were summoned one after the other into an adjacent room, and I was discreetly left alone with them. The more intelligent of the two hailed from the Tyrol. He behaved with great restraint and would not speak out boldly when I questioned him. The other was a low-grade Bohemian, and with great volubility he told me many intimate details about the men and the service. To my surprise, he spoke of the gross lack of discipline prevailing in the Foreign Legion, claiming that the men were all drunkards and that the pay was insufficient. I was disgusted but let the man talk and left him after giving him twenty francs, which he greedily pocketed.

It would have been a sin to return to Hong Kong without having visited Halong Bay, also named the Bay of a Thousand Islands, which spreads out only a few miles north of the Red River estuary. The bay is prodigiously picturesque; it is of interest because it is the anchorage of the French warships in Indochina, and also because of the presence of enormous coal deposits in the vicinity. We went there on March 4, conducted by a pilot who was well acquainted with the bay's intricacies. After a passage of a few hours we found ourselves removed from the Red River's flat delta region to a fabulous-looking labyrinth of small, rocky islands. On all sides we were surrounded by a confusing number of rocky islets and cliffs, most of them sloping down vertically to the sea; in consequence of the dissolving atmospheric action, they exhibited fantastic forms which it is quite impossible adequately to describe.

Our route took us close by the wreck of the large French cruiser *Sully*, which had struck a reef a few years before and had been entirely lost. We wound through difficult waters that because of their shallowness cannot be navigated by ships with a greater draught, until at sunset we were at Hongay (Hon Gai), a small place lying in one of the extreme corners of the bay. There we anchored for the night. Hongay is an establishment of recent date, sprung into existence as a consequence of coal production and the commerce in that material which goes on there. Coal in an enormous amount crops out at twelve kilometers' distance from the place and is raised by open work; a narrow-gauge line connects the mine with the coast. Being anthracite, however, the coal is not serviceable for ordinary use. It is therefore mixed with soft Japanese brown coal and worked up into briquettes. We profited from the opportunity to fill our bunkers with 150 tons of cheap coal— the so-called *briquettes de guerre*—and then put to sea again on the afternoon of March 5, arriving in Pakhoi the following morning. After a stay of only a few hours, we proceeded on to Hoihao, a small townlet lying on the north shore of Hainan, where we anchored the following morning on the open, extended, shallow roads.

Hoihao looks far more insignificant than it in fact is, for it is the center for the exportation of the products of a large and fertile island. Four freight steamers lay at anchor on the roads in confirmation of that fact. Because of the shallowness of the shore waters, the landing is so difficult that ordinary boats are of no use. One can only get on shore by means of flat-bottomed square punts, which are pushed along for miles with poles by Chinese who are well acquainted with the intricate fairway.

The Chinese government only controls the littoral of the island. Its mountainous interior, inhabited by two tribes of Malay race, is still independent and unexplored. One of the tribes, the Shang Li, are still perfect savages who in the main live on game and beekeeping; an enormous quantity of beeswax is exported from the island annually. The political conditions seem to be similar to those that prevailed on Formosa prior to its occupation by the Japanese. The wilds of the interior of this large island—it is not much smaller than Switzerland—are the haunt of tigers, rhinos, and boa constrictors and are even the home of a species of long-tailed apes. Most of the beetles and butterflies that are found here are limited to the island, and we were told that several Japanese were engaged in collecting them for one of the London Rothschilds. The capital lies farther inland, about a two-hour walk from Hoihao. It is a dreamy Chinese townlet that is reached by a bad road leading right through a large graveyard, the burying place for a thousand years of a population that was once much more dense than it is now. Three of the graves show the names of Jesuits who found an eternal rest on this distant island in 1681. A double wall, partly crumbled and overgrown, surrounds the town, which harbors a *taotai* [magistrate] and a general as representatives of Chinese sovereignty.

The *Panther* could only remain at Hoihao for twenty-four hours. We left the roads on the morning of March 9 and steered through the north passage of the strait toward Kwangchow, a French enclave on the continent lying opposite Hainan. A stiff northeaster made the reefs and shoals in the strait foam up, clearly showing how dangerous these waters were. But the fairway in the creek leading to Kwangchow is well marked with buoys, and in fine weather navigation is an easy matter. We anchored at 4:00 P.M. in the creek, which is about one thousand yards wide, with Fort Bayard on one side and Albiville, the French civilian settlement, on the other.

What on earth had we to do in this godforsaken corner of the world? This was my first thought when looking about at the barren surroundings, which seemed totally deserted. Not a single ship, not even a rowboat, was to be seen. Fort Bayard is not a fortress, for it consists only of a number of barracks and other military buildings, with a new, quite large church in their midst—all of which, with the exception of the latter, were more or less damaged. Albiville, the seat of the civilian government on the other side of the creek, contains several official buildings and looked even more insignificant. Several hours after our arrival a French gendarme came on board the *Panther* and asked whence we came and whither we were bound, establishing thereby the first relation between the ship and the shore. He told us that the year before a typhoon had caused the damages to the structures at Fort Bayard.

Kwangchow is a small enclave that comprises an area of only 700 square kilometers. It had been rented to France in 1898 for a term of ninety-nine years, with the design to develop the place as a naval station. The concession had been wrung from China in retaliation for the murder of missionaries. In question had been either the territory around Kwangchow or the island of Hainan. France, probably hoping to be able in time to push farther inland, right into the gigantic body of China—perhaps as a sanction for the murder of other missionaries—had decided for Kwangchow.[8] There is no doubt that the French soon discovered they had made a mistake, and they no longer seemed to have any interest in the further development of their creation. After having overcome a certain shyness, which quite often fills people who for a long time have lived in seclusion, the few officers and civil servants banished to this out-of-the-way place were delighted by our arrival. At Fort Bayard were garrisoned two officers, a surgeon, and 120 French and 20 Annamite soldiers. The administration at Albiville disposed of a Chinese police force 350 strong, and we were told wonders regarding the valor of these men. Kwangchow had a bad reputation as the haunt of pirates and as a place where in former times the rabble of the bordering province used to hide. To get at them more easily, the Chinese had long ago entirely cleared the country of trees and brush, and this is the reason why it now looks so barren. These circumstances make it necessary for the French to keep a strong police force. We were told that from forty to fifty criminals were caught and sentenced to death annually and that the police forces did their duty unsparingly and with remarkable bravery, knowing well that their adversaries would give them no quarter.

Kwangchow Creek is in bad repute because of the fog that frequently and persistently occurs there. When we were ready to put to sea on the morning of March 10, the ship was wrapped in a fog so thick that one could not see the bow from the poop deck. I should never have thought of leaving the anchorage under the prevailing weather conditions and of running the risk of taking the ship a long distance through a narrow and tortuous creek, but the experienced Captain Marlees explained that we must try and get away, since the fog might keep on for an entire week. By feeling our way from buoy to buoy at a slow, steady speed and with watch in hand, it was likely that we would find our way out; should we miss one of the buoys, we could then anchor wherever we happened to be and wait for a better opportunity. I had not thought that such proceedings were possible, having never done the like, but I had full confidence in Marlees and did not hesitate to agree to his proposal. It was a real treat to watch the clever pilot, used to fog and risky navigation, take the ship out with perfect calm. Several times we could not make out one or the other of the fairway buoys for a while and anxiously strained our eyes until we caught a faint glimpse of a darker spot in the gray mist— the mark that allowed us to get on for a further couple of hundred yards. In this manner we safely reached the open sea and returned to Hong Kong in a fog that could almost be felt and was as wet as rain. I was mighty glad when the *Panther* was again made fast at her old buoy near the *Alacrity*.

In consequence of an order received from the senior captain, the *Panther* had to be off the mouth of the Wusung (Woosung) River on March 25 to execute some gun practice together with the *Kaiser Franz Joseph*. We therefore left Hong Kong the day after our return from Kwangchow, calling first at Swatow (Shantou) and then at Pagoda Anchorage, where we arrived on March 17. Despite its insignificant outward appearance, the place has some importance as the port of the provincial capital, Foochow (Fuzhou), which lies nine miles upstream. The banks of the Min River are high until Pagoda Anchorage; farther inland they are flat. The place boasts a small, neglected navy yard belonging to the government, a dry dock for ships up to 1,000 tons, and several slips for drawing up small craft. Opposite the townlet, on the right side of the river, spreads the stately establishment of the Chinese administration of coastal customs, and farther down river are seen the storehouses of the Royal Dutch Petroleum Company. At Pagoda Anchorage only two personages had to be considered, and I got to know them both soon and all the better, as they were sworn enemies. One of them was the custom house administrator, a tall, white-haired Englishman with a lordly deportment who lived a solitary life in the spacious rooms of a large building. He at once had come on board the *Panther*, there to seek relief with the unknown newcomer for his oppressed heart. The man had been happily married to a Chinese woman but had unfortunately lost his beloved wife some weeks or months before and was unable to get over his grief. Two children had sprung from this union. The son had been bitten in young years by a mad dog and had died; his daughter lived in Hong Kong. The recollection of his son's untimely end had filled the man with an indelible hatred of canines, and that lay at the bottom of the feud that prevailed between him and the British vice-consul. The latter had a little dog that he took to the custom house whenever he had business there, without regard for the administrator's objections. The mere sight of the little dog filled the old man with rage, and on the occasion of his first call on board the *Panther* he gave free vent to his hostile feelings in speaking of the vice-consul's malignant behavior. The British vice-consul, a physician by profession, was also on in years. He had lived for several years on the island of Formosa and was now leading a quiet family life here with his wife, a very sympathetic old lady. They both welcomed me with sincere heartiness, and the more I saw of them, the better I came to like them.

I had called at Pagoda Anchorage at the wish of Herr Post, our consul in Hong Kong, for a rather peculiar reason. A Viennese girl of not quite low descent had been living at this place for twenty months in concubinage with a Chinese. The girl had met the man in Vienna, where he had been in the retinue of his uncle, the Chinese ambassador. There she fell in love with him, and at his invitation she had gone to China after his uncle's employ in Vienna had come to an end. Her lover was neither of better birth nor a wealthy man, had no regular income, and was an inveterate opium smoker. The fate of a European woman in China is deplorable in any case. Despised by the man's female relatives, she is treated like a slave and forced to do all the meanest household chores. Herr Post and the former captain of the cruiser stationed in China had repeatedly sought to free this unfortunate girl from the clutches of her lover. They had tried to induce her to return home, and having met with a flat refusal, they had assisted her with money and had even used their influence to get the man appointed somewhere. But it was all to no avail. The money was turned into opium, and the man was soon dismissed from his job because of his vice.

Out of this union two children had been born, both of whom were still in tender babyhood. The task that had been set to me was to induce the French Roman Catholic bishop at Foochow to christen the Chinese and to sanction his union with the girl by a regular marriage tie. One day I told the vice-consul of my errand, and he at once assured me that all my endeavors to make the bishop give way would certainly be in vain. He and the British consul general at Foochow had done their best, but the zealous bishop would not hear of any compromise with an unbelieving Chinese for the sake of worldly reasons. However, I might go to Foochow and talk the matter over with the consul general. This I did, and when I found that this functionary was of the same opinion, I decided not to trouble the church dignitary with my request.

On the occasion of a lunch with the vice-consul I learned that the Viennese girl was living at Pagoda Anchorage, close to the consulate, and that I could see her if I wished. He summoned her after lunch and discreetly left me alone with her in the next room. I found myself in the company of a very pretty girl, twenty-two or twenty-three years old, whose blue eyes spoke of the many tears they had shed. The girl naturally was much embarrassed. Her outward appearance was plain and she looked worn out, though she probably had done her best to look as advantageous as possible for the occasion. She certainly had donned her best jacket and hat, but they were threadbare, and it was long ago that her gloves had been new. Although I sincerely pitied the unfortunate creature, feelings of anger nevertheless arose within me at the thought that such a nice and comely girl should have so far forgotten herself as to put up with such a degrading life. I consequently covered her with reproaches, which must have sounded brutal, because a flood of tears was her only answer. I told her this was the last chance that would be given her to break with the past. Herr Post at Hong Kong would help her, but only on the condition that she have nothing more to do with her seducer. Tears again flowed from her reddened eyes, but this did not soften my temper. It was probably due to a psychologically favorable moment that she finally gave in and consented to commit herself to the care of Herr Post, though she would not agree to return home to Vienna. I therefore asked the vice-consul to come in. He informed the girl that she was now in the custody of the British consulate and had to obey orders. A consular policeman was instructed to take her home in order to fetch her few belongings and the children, but she was not to see or speak with her lover. One hour later she was on board a steamer on her way to Hong Kong. There she was placed with a well-meaning family, while her two children were given to the charge of an Italian convent.

The *Panther*'s upper deck was badly in need of caulking and her paint had to be renewed. The quiet anchorage was all the more suitable for the accomplishment of these repairs since the necessary workmen were available, and the days until our departure on March 25 could not be employed any better. The ship was resounding from busy caulkers' mallets and smelled of tar and fresh paint, when to my mortification a dispatch came from the senior captain ordering the *Panther* to be off the Wusung River on the morning of March 22 instead of March 26, as had earlier been arranged. I telegraphed at once that we were engaged in work that could not be left unfinished, but the answer came that I had to obey. Discipline and subordination are certainly necessary and fair, but there must be reasonableness in their demand and administration. Only the other day I read that Admiral Sir John Fisher said that too great a sense of subordination in a man was a vice. I should not like to go that far, but I certainly think it is a sign of irresolution. As it was, we had to put to sea with the next tide with a deck not nearly finished and the paint not yet dry.

We arrived at two o'clock in the night at the determined rallying point and met the *Kaiser Franz Joseph* at anchor there. Because of the prevailing beastly weather we were apparently not expected to appear on time, for it took a long while before our signal was answered. The sea was so rough that communication between the ships by boat was out of the question. The gun practice was nevertheless taken up on the following morning, but after some unsatisfactory trials it was abandoned. Thereafter the *Kaiser Franz Joseph* proceeded to Tsingtao and the *Panther* to Shanghai, where we met a number of foreign warships in the Wusung River.

Shanghai is a large center of traffic with a continual coming and going of ships, a circumstance not conducive to a closer relationship. I was therefore very pleased when I unexpectedly found Dr. Nerazzini, with whom I had become acquainted seventeen years earlier at Harar, acting as Italian consul general. I learned to appreciate him better this time as a charming companion, with whom I spent many pleasant hours. One night Herr [Arthur] von Rosthorn, our ambassador in Peking, surprised me with his call. He was on his way to Teheran and was sailing from Shanghai the following morning. Having worked his way up to his present position in the employ in the Chinese customs service, Rosthorn had a thorough knowledge of China, her ways, and her language. He was a very experienced person, and I had a long and interesting chat with him about political conditions in China.

My days in Shanghai passed very quietly. One day for a change I betook myself to Nanking, the former capital of the Chinese realm, on one of the Yangtze River steamers. Since there were no hotels, I was compelled to seek hospitality with the German consul, who at first did not seem overjoyed at the idea but soon reconciled himself to playing the role of an obliging host. Nanking on every quarter reveals signs of decline from its former greatness, for all the old temples and other works of art are neglected and in poor condition. I was greatly impressed by the sight of the vast palace where for centuries the public examinations had been held. On a very extended square many a thousand little barren cells were clustered like honeycombs, one close to the other. For centuries gray-haired, middle-aged, and young candidates had all flocked here annually in the hope of passing an examination, the satisfactory completion of which entitled them to some governmental employ. The candidates had to write the examination paper in absolute seclusion in the course of several days. They were watched like prisoners and controlled from a high tower that overlooked the place. Nowhere else in China did I become so vividly conscious of the gigantic dimensions of the celestial empire and its deep-rooted traditions. At the same time I was troubled by the thought of the immeasurable amount of sorrow, suffering, fear, and final disappointment of which this place had been the tragic scene.

At Nanking a telegram informed me of my impending relief from the command of the *Panther* and also that the third class of the Order of the Iron Crown had been conferred upon me in recognition of my services. My services rendered to the Monarchy as envoy extraordinary to Emperor Menelik, so it seemed, had not been acknowledged. It is natural that Shanghai and the *Panther* thereafter did not stand any longer in the foreground, and the flow of my thoughts took another direction. I had had enough of both of them. The inconveniences connected with so small a ship as the *Panther* were too many not to feel them more and more as time went on. To think, for example, that my stateroom was lit by a single oil lamp! Already in Australia the symptoms of my growing farsightedness had shown themselves and had compelled me to use an eyeglass. My successor in command, a much younger man, wondered at that. "What, you wear an eyeglass?" But when on the same night during our dinner a written message was sent to him by the watch officer, he suddenly became aware that he could hardly read it. With a smile I thereupon offered him my glasses, and lo, the reading went off all right.

Other circumstances too had meanwhile roused in me a longing to be released from the *Panther*. The executive officer had repeatedly given rise to reprimand, and the navigating lieutenant, feeling humbled by his removal from his former post, had become increasingly difficult. The harmonious conditions that had prevailed for so long under brilliant and stirring circumstances had gradually come to naught during the past monotonous months, and life on board was no longer a succession of fine and happy days. Only the midshipmen showed joyful faces, having all been lately promoted to ensign. According to instructions, I was to sail home by way of Suez, the regular route for the reimbursement of expenses. I decided, however, to return home by way of Japan and Canada in order to see some countries that were new to me, if only in haste. But gun practice in common with the *Kaiser Franz Joseph* still had to be carried out. For this reason the *Panther* left Shanghai on the morning of April 18 and met the leading ship in the afternoon at the rallying point near Saddle Island. The target practice occupied two days. The *Panther* was then inspected by the senior captain according to regulations and given over to *Korvettenkapitän* E. Körber, my successor in command. Thus my *Panther* period found an end.

13

My Last Years in Active Service (1906–1909)

I made the voyage to Japan as a passenger on board the *Panther*. The ship left her anchorage near Saddle Island on the morning of April 21, proceeded through the Shimonoseki Strait and the wonderful Japanese inland sea, and reached the splendid harbor of Yokohama on April 28. The steamer with which I had to start on my homeward journey was due in a fortnight, which gave me little time to see the land of the rising sun. Some members of our legation in Tokyo had come to Yokohama to welcome the *Panther*, and in their company I betook myself on the same night to the capital. There I was most kindly received by Mr. Ambró, and I lodged at the legation as his guest.

The cherry-blossom season being just at its peak, I saw the country in its loveliest garb. It pleased me beyond expectation. At the time the population stood under the spell of a grand military review that came to pass on the morning of April 30 in the presence of the mikado as a sort of finale to the Russo-Japanese war and a glorification of the exploits of the valorous Japanese army. Over 30,000 soldiers, the representatives of 119 regiments, were marched out on that day in three battle lines on a vast parade ground under the command of Marshal Oyama.[1] The whole population behaved as if inebriated, and the country, trimmed as it was with countless gaily colored flags and an abundance of flower garlands, put on a fine show. A huge, feverishly excited crowd had flocked to Tokyo from near and far, filling the streets night and day. At the beginning of the parade, at the approach of the mikado's state coach, shouts of *banzai* roared out boisterously from an immense multitude of men, women, and children. In his retinue, in other coaches, came the crown prince and the younger members of the dynasty, followed by a number of foreign princes. High Japanese functionaries on horseback closed the train, in which Colonel Hume, the British military attaché, attracted some attention as the only European. After the mikado's drive past the long lines of troops, the separate regiments defiled with their colors, many of which were riddled with bullet holes and even reduced to rags. The mikado thereafter summoned Marshal Oyama to his side and deigned to express through him his imperial thanks to the troops for their glorious exploits in the Russo-Japanese War. The impressive review came to an end as it had begun, with endless shouts of *banzai*.

285

The war booty, consisting of hundreds of thousands of rifles and an enormous number of guns of all calibers and types, was displayed on a large square near the imperial palace. It was an overwhelming sight in which all Japan, old and young, rejoiced with unconcealed satisfaction. The Japanese press praised the government for having paid the troops a well-deserved tribute by way of this homage, but at the same time it expressed the wish to let the matter rest there and to think now of the more peaceful necessities of the day.

Time passed pleasantly but all too quickly, and the impressions that I took away with me were of a very friendly if all too superficial nature. On May 11 I parted from Mr. Ambró and thanked him for his very kind hospitality. Count [Hieronymus] Colloredo-Mannsfeld, our naval attaché, accompanied me to Yokohama, and after a jolly night spent with him, the hour of my departure from Japan struck. For the passage to Vancouver I unfortunately could not avail myself of one of the fine Canadian liners and had to content myself with a meaner intermediary steamer. When my ship wound its way out of the harbor on the afternoon of May 12, a nasty, uniformly gray sky cast a gloom over a landscape that was so beautiful in sunshine. Quite unexpectedly, however, the heavy cloud banks dissolved for some moments and allowed us to admire once more the snow-covered glittering summit of Mount Fujiyama, which, emerging from a threateningly dark background, formed a wonderful and memorable sight. The saying goes that one returns to Japan if the holy mountain deigns to unveil his face at the moment of one's departure, yet I doubt that this is true in all cases.

It took the steamer fourteen days to get to America, her orthodromic route leading far to the north in sight of the snow-covered Aleutian Islands. The ship was full up. My cabin mate was an elderly New Zealander who had set out with a keen desire to see the Old World for the first time in his life. A young Englishman who was an expert in tea matters and had visited the most important centers of tea production in India related interesting details of what he had seen, seasoning his tales now and then with a cup of exquisite flavor, which he himself used to prepare for us. Another traveling companion was a likeable elderly but good-looking Frenchman, a M. Rosier, who in the evenings liked to favor the company with his beautiful singing. In general I do not like men who sing, but M. Rosier did it without displaying any vanity or affectation and without caring a bit for the languishing looks that the fair sex lavished on him. As he revealed to me one day, he was the happy father of nine children, and that, he thought, amply fulfilled his duty to his native country. A lovely lady passenger attracted the attention of all on board but showed great reserve, for she declined to speak with anybody. She was the young wife of a British naval officer who had been stationed in China and was on his way to England with his ship. He had probably given her strict instructions on how she ought to behave, because she lived for herself, wrapped in absolute silence.

The steamer reached Vancouver only just in time. It was even doubtful that we would be able to catch the train to Montreal and therewith the connecting steamer to Europe. I was in a hurry to get on because I erroneously thought I had to arrive in Vienna at a date no later than I would have arrived had I followed the route prescribed by regulations. The day before our arrival at Vancouver the captain had asked if I was going on to Europe without stopping anywhere, and when I answered in the affirmative, he requested that I take charge of the pretty English lady, who had been entrusted to his care. Shortly before our arrival in port, however, when I asked to be introduced to his protégé, he said that she had declined to be committed to my care. This was probably quite fortunate, for even by myself it was not easy in so short a time to get through customs, arrange for the conveyance of my luggage to the railway station, and take the astonishing number of tickets needed for a journey directly across Canada. When I had done all this I was quite glad to be able to sit down in the train, which left the station but a minute later. If I remember correctly, the train consisted of two Pullman cars, which were only half full, and one dining car. In the same car with me were M. Rosier and several other passengers of the steamer, among them the unapproachable beauty, of whom nobody took notice. She did not wish it otherwise.

The Canadian route in its western part is certainly one of the most interesting and remarkable on earth as far as scenery and the difficulties that had to be overcome in building it are concerned. As it works its way through spiral tunnels up to a glacier region, the track leads straight across a high and steep mountain range on bold bridges built at frightening heights over deep gorges. On some sections of the line six heavy engines are needed to keep the short train moving along. After conquering the Rocky Mountains, the track proceeds through a level and less interesting countryside where the traveler could watch the emergence of human settlements in various stages of development, beginning with the primitive camp of pioneer settlers who have just arrived at the stop, up to established villages and towns in different sizes and states of perfection. One travels through Canada in a Pullman far more comfortably than in Europe in a sleeping car. Each car is cared for by a conductor—ours was a nigger [sic]—who busied himself all day long keeping it scrupulously clean. A sufficient number of washstands with plenty of hot and ice-cold water at one's disposal allowed one to leave the train after a journey of four and a half days as fresh and clean as if one had just stepped into it.

On the second day, on my way from the dining car to my compartment, I was unexpectedly accosted by the pretty English traveling companion. She inquired whether I was also going on directly to England and asked what she should do, for she had just been told that her luggage had been left behind at Vancouver. I could only advise her to ask the conductor to wire to Vancouver to have her luggage forwarded with the next train. That, however, did not remove her embarrassment, since her journey to England had to be accomplished without interruption if she was not to forfeit her passage, which she had paid for in advance. The lady now had in her possession only a little handbag and was desperate, as one might imagine.

The express train arrived at Montreal, the terminus, with considerable delay. The connecting steamer to Liverpool had already left the port, but we were told we would catch up with her at Quebec if we took the next express train. Our fellow travelers had soon disappeared, leaving the young lady and me alone on the deserted platform. To get to Quebec we had to change at the next station. We had already waited there for some time when the train finally came rolling along and my involuntary protégé could step into one of the compartments. I was just about to follow her when by mere chance I detected the lady's handbag lying peacefully on the other side of the track. I had just enough time to fly there and fling it into the luggage van. I then sat down silently at the lady's side and behaved as if nothing was wrong. After a while, however, I could not help mischievously asking her what had become of her hand luggage. As one may imagine, that worked like a bombshell. Now she had lost her last things and was reduced to what she wore—and England was so far away! I was not so cruel as to leave her in despair for long, but in spite of her pretty blue eyes I could not abstain from giving her a stern lecture.

We arrived in Quebec at about 5:00 P.M. and were met at the station by the agent of the Canadian Pacific, who hurried us in a tug to the steamer, which was about to sail. As only one berth was available, which of course was given to my fair companion, I had to betake myself to another steamer, which left the port one hour later. We sailed down the St. Lawrence River in a thick fog, and under rather misty weather conditions we made the passage to Ireland, where for several hours we were prevented from even approaching the coast and calling at Londonderry. An iceberg sighted one forenoon was the only excitement in the course of the smooth passage, which was unpleasant because of the bad fare. From Liverpool I proceeded by way of Harwich and Vlissingen to Vienna, where I arrived on the twenty-ninth day after my departure from Yokohama. I had seen very little of the countries through which I had hurried, but I had caught a glimpse of conditions new to me and therefore did not regret having taken this route. Only later on was I much annoyed at having journeyed in such haste, without stopping at any one of the places through which I had passed, for when I reported at the Admiralty I learned that nobody would have minded if I had stayed away a week or two longer.

Admiral Count Montecuccoli, the commander in chief of the navy, received me kindly with words of approbation regarding the *Panther*'s satisfactory cruise. I was also favored with flattering communications on the part of the Court Chancellery and the various institutions with whose wishes I had complied with such zeal and success. With regard to my subsequent appointment, I was attached to the naval station at Trieste as a mere idler, free from any special duties. This was good news, because with the present commander of the station one could feel like a free man and could even absent oneself for several days without asking for leave. But first I had the pleasure of enjoying a well-earned furlough, which I spent quietly on the shore of the Königssee in Bavaria. At the beginning of September I had to embark as arbitrator on board the store ship

Pelikan in order to participate in maneuvers that the navy carried out in Dalmatian waters in conjunction with the army.

Three uneventful and generally unsatisfactory months followed, a period on which I do not like to think back. I had only rarely to preside at a committee meeting or a court-martial or perhaps to represent the navy at some funeral; other services were not required of me. The few brother officers who were at Trieste generally went their own way. One sometimes met with one or the other of them in the evening in an obscure trattoria, but as a rule we separated soon after supper. The navy had never felt comfortable at Trieste and had not maintained close social contacts with circles in town. It is true that the beautiful Miramare Castle harbored at the time the Archduchess Maria Josefa, the mother of the subsequent—and late—Emperor Karl. That, however, afforded me only an occasional invitation to dinner, a rare bright point in the darkness of my everyday existence. The prevailing awful winter, consisting of a succession of rainy sirocco days followed by an icy cold bora wind, did not at all agree with me and made it ever more difficult to pass the time in idleness. In time these monotonous and unsatisfactory conditions began to affect my mood adversely. Contributing not a little toward this situation was the disappointment that my promotion to the rank of a post captain [*Linienschiffskapitän*], on which I had reckoned with certainty, had not come through as expected on January 1, 1907, since the Hungarian Delegation had voted against any increase in the naval budget. Thus I remained fully eight years in a rank that luckier brother officers had leapt over in three to five years.[2] That was quite enough to put me in a foul humor.

In February 1907 I was delivered from my unsatisfactory existence at Trieste by being appointed flag captain of the *Sankt Georg*, which, together with the smaller cruiser *Aspern*, was to proceed under the command of Commodore Hermann Pleskott to the United States of America to participate in certain festivities there. The 7,300–ton armored cruiser *Sankt Georg* was a fine ship that developed at full force a speed of twenty-two knots an hour. Her executive officer was a very able and reliable corvette captain, to whom I confidently could leave the care for the inner service. Being in a subordinate position, I had no responsibilities to bear, though I did have to cede my stateroom to the commodore and to content myself with a somewhat enlarged officer's cabin. A flag captain messes with the admiral, is freed from the care for kitchen and cellar, and his position is altogether a very easy one. For this, however, he has to pay with the price of his independence, which did not quite conform to my inclination. But I knew that Pleskott was a sensible man with whom I was sure to be on good terms. The commander of the other cruiser was Frigate Captain Rudolf Pajér [Edler von Mayersberg], who was an intimate friend.

The reason for the dispatch of the ships to Hampton Roads was the opening of the Jamestown Tercentennial Exposition in celebration of the jubilee of the first permanent settlement in North America.[3] This was a purely private enterprise promoted by a Mr. Harry St. George Tucker, but the very industrious managing committee had succeeded in rousing a widespread interest in the matter and in gaining official favor. Thus the invitations requesting the various navies to participate in the festivals by dispatching warships had been formally issued by the United States government. From the order of the day we learned that quite a number of boat races and other competitions were planned during this international meeting of warships; unfortunately, however, we had left home waters without any racing equipment.

The commodore's pennant went high on the *Sankt Georg*'s mast top on March 17, and a week later both ships left the home waters to proceed first to Gibraltar. On our way there, two cases of scarlet fever—one on board each of the two ships—compelled us to call at Cagliari in order to commit the sick to the care of a hospital. We left that port at once and arrived at Gibraltar on the morning of March 31. There we met, besides other men-of-war, Vice Admiral Sir Assheton Curzon's flagship *Caesar*.[4] On the occasion of a call by the commodore and myself on board the flagship I was struck by the vice admiral's meeting me with greater formality than was my due. He welcomed me with ostentatious cordiality, for which I was at a loss to account. At the entrance to his stateroom he stopped, looked at me with a smile, and to my surprise asked whether I did not recognize him. I tried hard but in vain to remember when and where I might have met Sir Assheton and therefore begged him to help me. "Have you not made great travels in Africa?" "Yes, but. . . ." "Well, I was commanding the *Boadicea* in Zanzibar at the time you were so low down with fever, and with me you had, at the admiral's invitation, to go on a cruise for your recovery." Eighteen years had passed since then!

On April 3 we left Gibraltar for Madeira. There can hardly be any reader who has not heard of the island. Every cookbook mentions its wine as a necessary ingredient in various sauces, and numerous women have dressed in graceful Madeira embroideries. It is also generally known that people suffering from lung disease go there in the hope of finding a cure. But knowledge about this island generally ends there. Madeira is not suited to agriculture because of its mountainous formation, and the first settlers therefore took to winegrowing. Viticulture was the main source of income of the islanders for several centuries, until the grape disease appeared in 1873 and utterly destroyed the vines. The population thereafter went in for the culture of a certain type of cactus, and the rearing of cochineal living on them produced carmine. Since this trade turned out to produce an insufficient source of income, the people also occupied themselves with the manufacture of the well-known beautiful embroideries. The invention of artificial and cheap carmine put an early end to the cochineal industry, however, whereupon resistant American vines were introduced so that winegrowing could be resumed, though not to its former extent. There is again delicious, golden-yellow Madeira to be found on the island, and not only in the cellar of nabobs, as was the case for quite a number of years.

The two days that we stayed at Funchal passed all too quickly in friendly intercourse with the amiable family of our honorary consul, Ritter von Bianchi.

A man of very advanced age, he had for several years enjoyed close relations with Emperor Maximilian of Mexico and had also been connected with our Empress Elisabeth, who for some time had lived on the island for her recreation. We also spent many pleasant hours thanks to a Mr. Faber, a wealthy and respected person living uphill in a fine country house. His wife was the daughter of an Austrian general, and their daughter was a pretty and spirited girl who contributed not a little to our feeling of well-being.

On April 7 we took leave of this Arcadia and set out on our way to the Bermudas. The Atlantic chose to show its rougher side and did not fail to make an impression on the weaker elements on board the *Sankt Georg*. Since I was accustomed to much worse from life on board the *Panther*, for me it was as if I were in a palace and on solid rock. We sighted the Bermudas on the morning of April 18 and anchored in the midst of two British squadrons. The calls on board these many ships would have taken up much of our time if the practical Englishmen had not simplified the procedure by agreeing that we should meet the two admirals on board the cruiser *Good Hope*, where cards were also exchanged between us and the commanders of the British ships.

Whenever the commodore made his first call somewhere, we, his subordinates, had to accompany him. On the occasion of our call to the governor of Bermuda, his aide-de-camp told me to my surprise that His Excellency would only see the commodore. This, of course, I would not accept. I explained to the man that we were captains and not aides-de-camp and that I had to insist on being received by the governor. That finally enabled us to get acquainted with General Sir Robert M. Stewart, but it did not soften my mood, and I consequently declined his invitation to dinner. Fortunately the reception we received from all the naval circles was far different.

We arrived in Chesapeake Bay on schedule early on the morning of April 25. We first took a pilot on board and soon thereafter an American naval officer, whose business it was to show us where we had to anchor. When we were in sight of the signal station on Cape Henry, a wireless telegram informed us that the commodore had been promoted to the rank of a rear admiral and I to that of a post captain. This tiding came too late, however, to rouse within me any feelings of joy.[5]

By the name Hampton Roads one comprises the historically famous waters of the James River estuary in Virginia, where, as everyone knows, in 1862 a duel had been fought between the *Monitor* and the *Merrimack*. The flat and unattractive surroundings, with their low river banks, would have made a very disappointing impression on us had the roads not been enlivened by a surprising number of fine warships. There we saw anchored in four long lines the entire Atlantic fleet of the United States under the command of Rear Admiral R. D. Evans.[6] Of foreign men-of-war only two German cruisers and one Argentine ship had already put in an appearance; four British cruisers arrived an hour or two after us.

In view of the prevailing conditions, which were exceedingly confusing to a newcomer, it was most pleasing to be cared for in the way the American navy thoughtfully had arranged. The arriving foreign warships were not merely taken to their anchorage, but to each of them the neighboring American ship was assigned as her mother ship, so to speak, to which she could direct all her inquiries and wishes. The American battleship *Kentucky* (Captain E. B. Barry) in this way was attached to the *Sankt Georg* and the *Kearsarge* (Captain H. Winslow) to the *Aspern*. Moreover, to each of the foreign commanders an American naval officer was permanently attached for the duration of his stay. In the case of the *Sankt Georg* this was Lieutenant Commander W. W. Phelps, a very smart-looking officer who was certainly a credit to the American navy.[7] In time we came to appreciate him as a well-versed sailor with whom we all were soon on good terms. The undisputed favorite of all, Phelps passed the nights on board his ship *Kentucky* and spent the daytime in our midst as a guest of the admiral. Altogether our relations with the American navy were exceedingly cordial and form my happiest memory of the time we spent in Hampton Roads.

Unfortunately, if the spectator turned his attention away from the ships to the surrounding countryside there was little to greet the eye. In the distance on the north shore of the river, near Old Point Comfort, was the antiquated Fort Monroe, and hard by was the silhouette of the very large Hotel Chamberlin; farther inland there was Hampton, a small place with some houses. Out of an unsightly landscape on the opposite side of the James River rose the structures of the Jamestown Exposition, which, as one could plainly see, were not yet finished. Under the circumstances it was only natural that interest was generally concentrated upon the ships and the events on the roads rather than on the exposition itself.

On the morning of April 26, the day after our arrival, the yacht *Mayflower* arrived from Washington with Mr. Theodore Roosevelt, the President of the United States, on board. Having dressed with up-and-down flags, the international armada looked magnificent; it welcomed the *Mayflower* with a royal salute, fired simultaneously by all the many units as soon as she came in sight— a grand and impressive demonstration. The yacht at first ran along the lines of the ships and was greeted with shouts of "hurrah" and a renewed royal salute, this time fired by each ship the moment the *Mayflower* passed. As soon as the yacht had anchored in the center of all the ships, the roads were enlivened with swift steam launches and tidy gigs conveying the American and foreign admirals and captains on board to pay their respects to the head of state. I had not seen Mr. Roosevelt since 1898, and it was a joy to meet him in such solemn circumstances now that he had been elected by the millions of a great nation. He seemed genuinely pleased to see me again, for he welcomed me with a happy smile and invited me to a dinner in Washington. Mrs. Roosevelt also very kindly remembered me.

The President and his guests then proceeded to the exhibition ground. No such enterprise was ever finished by opening day, and the Jamestown Exhibition was still far from being ready. The passage through the artificial boat harbor to the landing and our painful walk along the metalled road to the parade ground, where the opening was to take place, clearly showed this. Mr. Tucker, the chairman of the managing committee, welcomed the President with some appropriate words, whereupon the latter bounced up on a round table with youthful vigor and delivered a long speech in a loud and distinct voice. He spoke for a whole hour to a large crowd of people who, in spite of the police, repeatedly tried to get nearer to him, cheering him and occasionally giving vent to their satisfaction with thundering applause, shouting, and whistling.

It had meanwhile struck 1:00 P.M., and according to the order of the day the time had come when the guests could expect a luncheon. A fierce sun had been shining the whole time, parching the throats of all and making the stomach rebellious; a snack would certainly have been very welcome. The whole company briskly trotted along the rugged road to the exhibition headquarters and waited there in painful closeness for the promised meal. An hour passed away, however, without bringing the weary crowd what it was longing for, and the festive mood cooled down visibly, especially since we could guess by the fragrant puffs that reached our noses now and then that some sort of meal was going on for a few lucky diners. In the crowd of disappointed fellow guests I quite unexpectedly had the pleasure of encountering several people whom I knew, among others our ambassador, Baron Hengelmüller.[8] He invited the admiral and me to a dinner in Washington, which was very kind and tempting, but for the moment there was nothing we could do except tighten our belts. As if we had not had enough of this, we were politely asked to return to the parade ground to watch the American infantry, cavalry, and artillery troops march past. They were splendidly equipped and indeed looked first-rate, and by their free and easy carriage they made an excellent impression. It had initially been planned that divisions of all American and foreign ships would participate, but on the previous day the cautious Admiral Evans had inspected the landing conditions and had run aground in the boat harbor with his steam launch. Thereupon he flatly declined the navy's participation in this show. Late in the afternoon, this very fatiguing day came to a close with a large reception hosted by President Roosevelt.

The following days passed more pleasantly, however, after friendly relations had been established among the ships and with the official and private world that had flocked to Hampton in great number and filled the Hotel Chamberlin. The inauguration of the exhibition would not have been a lustrous event without the impressive display of maritime forces. As it was, no day passed without a reception, an afternoon party, a dinner, or even a ball being given on board one of the battleships or on shore. The number of ships continued to increase day after day, to the point that the assembly of so many fine warships put the unfinished exhibition in the shade.

Every day we were either invited somewhere as guests or had to act as hosts. Our admiral liked to entertain, and to be asked on board the *Sankt Georg* seemed to be an honor much sought after, no doubt because of our excellent ship's band, which knew how to execute even classical music artistically. Indeed, it was talked of in such flattering terms wherever we went that it finally bored me. The roads in between were enlivened by various sailing and rowing boat races, which kept the ships' crews and the betting world in suspense. The *Sankt Georg* held her own in these races, coming off rather nicely, which was the more remarkable as she had to compete against overwhelming odds with normal means and without adequate preparation. We carried off the only cup there was, and on two sailing and three rowing occasions we came in first and second, respectively. The boat that took the cup triumphed in boisterous, almost stormy weather, upon which the British admiral put special stress, saying that it proved the superiority of the seafaring skill of the leader of the boat and his crew. There is no doubt that on this occasion the Atlantic fleet and the British division had sent their best means and men to the field. I cannot vouchsafe for the truth of the claim that the Italian racing boat was a craft of special design, but I can state that this boat went flying along like a feather, far ahead of the others. And when after an easy victory her crew had fallen in on the *Connecticut*'s poop deck dressed only in sleeveless singlets in order to receive the prize, the whole assembly showed signs of horrified astonishment at the sight of these Herculean men, every one of whom was an athlete who would have been an attraction even in Barnum's circus.

Our intimate relations with the American navy allowed us a good insight into conditions as they affected the officers. I can only say that our initial favorable impression of them deepened the better we came to know them. With regard to professional ability and universal culture they attained a very high standard. The American naval men appeared to me to differ advantageously from the average American type by their happily combining English straightforwardness with French courtesy. We were very surprised by the officers' comparatively advanced age. With regard to the highest grade we gained the impression that at the time of their promotion most of the rear admirals had indeed or nearly reached the age limit, which according to regulations obliged them to retire from active service. In consequence, a great many able men never had a chance to develop and show their qualification as leaders.

In comparison with all other navies, it is anomalous that in spite of the great size and importance of the United States Navy, the highest rank is limited to that of rear admiral. On the occasion in question it happened that the United States Atlantic Fleet, numbering over forty units, had only a rear admiral as commander in chief. In contrast, the Japanese division, which consisted of only two ships, was commanded by a vice admiral, who, being superior in rank, enjoyed precedence on certain official occasions. Rear Admiral Robley D. Evans was nevertheless the most conspicuous personage in the crowd. As to his appearance, one was struck by his limping a little in consequence of a wound received in the course of the Civil War. Evans seemed a very energetic, qualified, and accomplished leader; he enjoyed the perfect confidence of all his subordinates and was at the same time loved by them. Although still spirited and active, he often suffered from his old wound, and in the course of our stay he was several times compelled temporarily to surrender his functions as commander in chief to his representative, Rear Admiral C. H. Davis.[9] Of the other officers whom we met I should like to single out Captain J. E. Pillsbury, the chief of staff, because of his exceptional professional ability and general learning. It was the regret of all that Pillsbury, having reached the mandatory age limit, was to retire from active service in a few months. Pillsbury had made himself known in scientific circles by his comprehensive studies on the Gulf Stream.[10] We looked forward with great interest and pleasure to meeting General Frederick Dent Grant, the son of Ulysses S. Grant. The general and his charming consort received us with winning cordiality, no doubt remembering their four years in Vienna, where he had served as ambassador.

The American and foreign admirals and captains were invited to Washington for two days as guests of the government, and they betook themselves there, some with their ladies, on the regular Norfolk-Washington boat on the eve of April 29. Both the departure of the steamer and the passage were unfortunately much delayed by fog, and instead of being in Washington early on the following morning, we arrived very late in the afternoon. I had to hurry head over heels to the Willard Hotel and hastily change into full dress uniform in order not to be too late for dinner at the White House. In this dinner, not counting the foremost local authorities, only admirals were to participate, but the President had very kindly made an exception for me. And so it came about that I found myself seated in the White House at a richly and tastefully decorated table, in the midst of many great figures, where I, as the youngest and lowest in rank, could quietly give myself up to the thoughts that crowded into my mind. The dinner was followed by a reception given by President and Mrs. Roosevelt. It was quite interesting to watch the diplomats, their ladies, and a great number of distinguished persons walk past Mrs. Roosevelt and shake hands with her; the President stood back and did not intervene on this occasion. He called me to his side and amused me by telling me who the people were, frequently adding some humorous remark, thereby spicing up the solemn but monotonous proceedings.

The next day my friend Pajér, Captain Barry, and I strolled about in the streets and admired the imposing Capitol and the stupendous Library of Congress. At noon we foreigners were entertained by the secretary of the navy with a luncheon given in the large dining room of the Willard, which was beautifully decorated for the occasion. The luncheon was very pleasantly arranged, the menu was exquisite, and the wines had been selected with taste. We had hardly taken our seats when the representative of the Navy Department presiding at table began to congratulate me because of our excellent ship's band. I had heard that so often that it quite spoiled my humor, and I could not refrain from asking him how he, as a captain of a ship, would feel if the only things that were ever honorably mentioned were his damned buglers and pipers. I said that with a rather annoyed mien, but everyone, including the speaker, agreed that I was right. Thereafter the meal passed off cheerfully and was by far the best and most enjoyable luncheon offered in the course of my stay in the United States. The evening was devoted to a reception given by the British ambassador, J. Bryce.[11] After lunching on the following day in a small circle with Baron and Baroness Hengelmüller and making a tour in a motor car to the surroundings of Washington, I returned to Hampton Roads. Thereafter it was the foreign officers' and chief warrant officers' turn to go to the capital and to be entertained as guests of the government. A few days later the admiral and I again had to proceed there to attend an official dinner given by our ambassador. This time we arrived without delay in the early morning. I therefore had the whole day at my disposal, and since there was not the smallest hole free at the Willard, in spite of its ten stories and thousand rooms, I visited the Smithsonian, eager to see the stuffed antelope, *Cervicapra chanlerii*, which my traveling companion had discovered in Africa. On the occasion of the ambassador's dinner I had the chance to get acquainted with Prince Leopold of Coburg, Secretary of State Elihu Root, Secretary of the Navy Victor Metcalf, the national hero Admiral George Dewey, the postmaster-general, and a number of beautiful ladies.

This time I returned to Hampton by land, wishing to get at least a passing glimpse of Richmond. When I arrived at Hampton after a very hot journey, a surprise was awaiting me. My friend William Astor Chanler had earlier telegraphed from Paris that he was looking forward to seeing me in America, and a telegram from George Galvin had also welcomed me on my arrival in Hampton Roads. But now, to my astonishment, I saw Chanler standing on the platform. With him was a somewhat taller young man of stronger build, unknown to me, who introduced himself as Bob, the youngest of the Chanler brothers.[12] They had not minded the long and hot journey from New York to Hampton, although they were only allowed to stay a few hours, being obliged to return home the same day. My friend of quick resolve had left his things as they were in Paris and hurried to America, and Robert W. Chanler, who was a great admirer of his elder brother, had willingly followed him on his way to Hampton. Since I had last seen him, Mr. Chanler had become a married man, but that had not changed him. His mind was just as unconcerned and sprightly as before— full of enterprise and exploit, as if there were neither wife nor kin for him in this world. I was promised that I would soon have the occasion to meet Mrs. Chanler.

Once more only did the exposition's managers lay the navies under an obligation, requesting them to participate in the celebration of the foundation day of Jamestown on May 13. The American commander in chief at first had declined to accept but had to submit because of orders from Washington. The armada had to dress ships, to make their guns thunder in the interest of a private enterprise, and even to let their landing companies parade to the delight of the visitors to the exhibition. On that day Admiral Evans allowed himself to be represented by Rear Admiral Davis, and it is possible that the cause of his indisposition was the arrival of the Japanese General Kuroki, to whom precedence was due because of his higher rank; he also occupied the place of honor on the parade ground. At the close of the parade Mr. Tucker, the president of the exhibition, intended to deliver a speech and requested the assembly to remain in their seats. The Japanese Kuroki and General Grant did not pay any attention to this, however, and went their way, which induced the other spectators to leave the place as well.

The next morning the *Sankt Georg* and the *Aspern* visited the famous American naval college at Annapolis. Although the director was ill, we were nevertheless given a succession of wonderful parties in the academy's splendid facilities. We met the governor of Maryland and of course got acquainted with the large staff of teachers and their families. When inspecting the academy and its facilities we all were simply lost in amazement to a degree that can only be understood by someone who knows both Annapolis and the Austro-Hungarian academy in Fiume. Only now did I become fully aware of how scandalous the arrangements in Fiume had been at my time, and a deep sadness filled me at the thought of the conditions in which we had been prepared for our profession. In Fiume we had had no textbooks, and on the walls there had been no engineering plans or pictorial presentations for our instruction. Moreover, there had not been a single model or section of mechanical apparatus, not even a rowboat, not to speak of other essentials appropriate to a naval college. I will not dwell on the neat, separate apartments and the many fine bathrooms we were shown and the splendid food the pupils ate, for one can just as well raise proficiency with less sumptuous means. The sinfulness in the conditions at Fiume lay mainly in the absolute lack of teaching tools. Here in a large hall we saw with envy all of the machinery in use in the United States Navy, if not *in natura*, then in natural-sized models, which could all be set into motion by compressed air or electricity. An amphitheater-style lecture room with 200 seats was used for lectures on natural science and for demonstrations. A vast, well-lit hall offered three hundred pupils the opportunity to practice drawing technical designs and plans, while several chemistry and physics laboratories enabled the pupils to perfect their knowledge of these subjects. After that it came as no surprise that for practical purposes this remarkable institution disposed of twenty-five steam launches, twenty sailing boats, many rowing and racing boats, three submarines, two torpedo boats, a sailing corvette, and a monitor. In contrast, at my time in Fiume there had been absolutely nothing in the strictest sense of the word. I quite believe what Rear Admiral Evans said to me on one occasion, that to American naval officers there are no secrets below—he meant the engine room. I rather wondered that the youngsters trained at Annapolis were not mustered out as full admirals.

On May 17 we proceeded to New York and anchored first in the Hudson River, opposite 76th Street. Subsequently, however, we were twice obliged to change the anchorage, being everywhere in the way of traffic. It was the third time that I had come to New York, and I had the chance to admire the magnificent panorama of her harbor. It was fortunate that as the captain of the leading ship I was familiar with harbor conditions, since all others on board, being novices and under the spell of the many impressions that assailed them from all sides, were lost in amazement. Amid the continual fire of an uninterrupted succession of salutes, it was no easy task even for me to take the *Sankt Georg* by the many steamers that were running out and through the lines of crossing ferry boats. After having at first exchanged a national salute with Governors Island, we met the American cruisers *Denver*, *Cleveland*, and *St. Louis*, and soon afterward the battleship *Rhode Island*, the French cruiser *Kléber* with a rear admiral's flag of command on her masttop, and the Italian ship *Varese*. Farther upstream were the Japanese division, Rear Admiral Evans' flagship, and one division of the Atlantic fleet under the command of Rear Admiral Emory. To navigate with such a number of salutes was not a pleasant job.

We stayed at New York until June 5. Our time was almost totally occupied with wearisome representative obligations that were especially burdensome because of the great distances involved. I could not avoid participating in these more-or-less official entertainments, though I would have preferred to spend the days in the company of my friends, particularly with my traveling companion Willie Chanler and his lady, who had meanwhile arrived from Paris. They had built their nest far from New York on Long Island, and it required quite a journey to get there. It was a great and pleasant surprise to meet Baron Hoenning O'Carroll, who had been transferred as consul general from Sydney to New York; but like us, he, too, was sighing under the weight of his position and the many social obligations he had to fulfill.

Most of the new friends we had made in Hampton had come to New York, and the days passed much as before. Two Sundays only—and that in consequence of the prevailing bad weather—could I free myself and spend time with the Chanlers on Long Island, where I had the pleasure of seeing my friend play the part of a tamed paterfamilias and to get acquainted with the Circe who had succeeded in putting him in fetters. I greatly enjoyed the peaceful hours in their midst, near a warm, crackling fire.[13] Of Chanler's brothers I only looked up Robert, the youngest, in his studio, where to my surprise I found him occupied with a strange kind of decorative painting, in a manner quite new to me. What I saw was of striking beauty; it looked very different from what I had ever seen before, and reminded me in some way of antique art; it was altogether a revelation. George Galvin also came on board the *Sankt Georg* soon after we arrived, and I was most pleased to see his face again and to learn that he had successfully worked his way up to a prosperous position.

We left New York on June 5 in order to return to Hampton Roads. Like us, a part of the foreign warships had left the roads temporarily, while others had left for good. The American Atlantic fleet, the Brazilian squadron, and the *Varese* ran in shortly after us. The Annapolis cadets arrived with a special division, and Secretary of the Navy Metcalf came with the yacht *Dolphin*. On June 10 the *Mayflower*, with President Roosevelt on board, reappeared for festivities arranged by the exhibition committee for the celebration of Georgia Day; again the roads showed a multitude of ships dressed in many colors, and the air resounded with the roar of their guns. The parade ground was crowded with American troops, students from Annapolis and West Point, and on this occasion also the leading companies of the foreign powers. It was a grand and picturesque sight, and the marching past of the international military display evoked thunderous applause from the many thousand spectators who attended the show. The President delivered a speech in which he referred to the promotions in the United States Navy, thereby speaking in favor of merit: the efficient to the front, without regard to their less apt seniors! Thereafter in the Georgia House came to pass the solemn presentation of a costly silver dinner service, a gift of the state of Georgia, to the battleship of the same name, in accordance with a nice custom which, alas, was not in use in our Monarchy.

The exhibition was still far from being finished, but some progress was being made. The purpose of this exhibition was to afford visitors the possibility of forming a broad conception of conditions in the United States. There were therefore shown, besides the usual agricultural and industrial products of the country, certain objects and demonstrative exhibitions that permitted an insight into the conditions of the army and navy. Undoubtedly official political aims were also connected with the private part of the enterprise. For example, it enjoyed the maximum of moral and material protection on the part of the government and President Roosevelt, being a means to make the navy popular in the inland states. For this reason the President never failed in his speeches to touch on certain naval questions and to stress the urgency of an increase in American sea power. The American officers suffered visibly from the consciousness that not only they but also the foreign navies were called to serve the interests of a private enterprise and political aims. They therefore did all they could to efface by redoubled attentiveness the bad impression that such proceedings might leave with the foreigners.

Gradually the day of our departure approached, unfortunately not without filling the minds of all with deep grief because of a disastrous accident that cast its gloom over the roads. After one of the festivals the *Minnesota*'s steam launch, with six middies and five men on board, had left the exhibition at midnight and was lost in the darkness of the night, probably foundered by one of the passing vessels. As rainy and boisterous weather prevailed, the steam launch surely was fitted out with the rain awning in use in the American navy. This construction protects the occupants from getting wet, but they are in there as in a mousetrap; an escape in case of an accident is quite impossible. Moreover, the construction does not allow one to look out on the side. I always disliked using these monsters in bad weather, and I could not understand how it was possible that an adaptation so dangerous and unsailorly could ever have been introduced into the United States Navy.

Under these circumstances, the farewell parties with which we thanked our friends in the American navy for the cordial reception they had accorded us passed off in a less than cheerful mood. Baron Hoenning O'Carroll, after having spent the last days with us, had taken leave and returned to New York. But from others, too, we parted with feelings of regret and the sincere wish to meet them again. Commander Phelps had become as dear to us all as if he were a brother officer, and with Captain Barry we were also linked with feelings of considerable affection. On the morning of June 15, the guns of the *Kentucky* transmitted his farewell greeting as we left the roads.

Favored by smooth seas, light zephyrs, and mild air, we crossed the ocean with our minds now directed forward. The days of delight passed and gave way to the exigencies of service, for we could not join our home squadron without being in shape. On the morning of June 25 we came in sight of the Azores and moored the ships in the narrow harbor of Ponta Delgada, inside the breakwater, which we found partially destroyed by a storm. The place made a lovely impression because of its very friendly inhabitants and its stupendous floral splendor. This consisted chiefly of wild-growing Hortensias, which formed thickets of shrubs wherever one went, and of living hedges along the roads, all blooming in various delicate tinges.

After a three-day stay at Algiers we made for home. In accordance with instructions, on our way through the Adriatic we had to guard against falling into the hands of our home squadron, which had been ordered to intercept us. In this, however, it was not successful, and the *Sankt Georg* reached Pola unhampered on the afternoon of July 10, after having detached the *Aspern* to Dalmatian waters. At Pola we were only allowed to remain a couple of days before proceeding to Teodo, there to meet the squadron.

The following two months were devoted to maneuvers in which the *Sankt Georg* participated as the leader of a division of cruisers. The ships thereafter rallied at Pola in order to accomplish changes with regard to the staff. Rear Admiral Pleskott returned to Fiume to his former post as director of the naval college. In thinking back to the day on which he took command of the *Sankt Georg*, I could not say that the hoisting of his flag had roused within me feelings of enthusiasm—not only because at the time I was already used to forming resolutions and carrying them out without asking anybody, but also because I considered myself sufficiently old to be entitled to some independence. The thought that on board my ship I should have to submit to orders and even the wishes of somebody else had hardly been exhilarating. As it luckily turned out, however, the admiral's amiable nature, quite exempt from pride, and his judicious appreciation of the situation never made me feel the curtailment of my independence, and harmonious relations prevailed during his entire stay on board.

The *Sankt Georg* remained in squadron. With regard to personnel, great changes had occurred on board all the ships, and that meant that they had to start anew with training. With regret I saw my excellent executive officer depart, and in his stead another man appeared on board who was not nearly as reliable and efficient. I was, however, fortunate that on several occasions my ship was called to serve the technical committee of the navy for a week or two to perform experiments and trials, this being more interesting and instructive than the everyday routine in squadron. Another pleasant intermezzo was the delegation of the *Sankt Georg* to Piraeus to the Greek court in order to participate in the festivities surrounding the marriage of Prince George with Princess Marie Bonaparte, the daughter of Prince Roland Bonaparte.[14] The *Sankt Georg* was a remarkably fine ship and was well qualified for representative purposes, especially as the sameness of her name with that of the wedding hero could be considered a special attention, and was indeed interpreted as such by the king.[15]

The *Sankt Georg* left Pola on the eve of December 5 and arrived at Piraeus early in the morning on December 9. There we met at anchor only an Italian and two Russian gunboats, but a number of Greek warships and a German and a French gunboat arrived in the course of the afternoon, so that the small harbor was crammed. Because of her heavy draught, the British battleship *Glory* had moored in splendid isolation on the roads of Phaleron. It therefore came about that the *Sankt Georg* by far outshone the ships in port in stateliness and beauty and functioned as their leader on the occasion of simultaneous transactions. The distinguished bride had arrived from Brindisi the day before and was still abiding in the Bay of Salamis on board the king's yacht *Amphitrite*, from which she was fetched by the king in the course of the afternoon and escorted to Athens. The warships had dressed with up-and-down flags, and the streets of the town were adorned with garlands of flowers and triumphal arches, making a fine show. A magnificent blue sky contributed not a little to the splendor of the harbor when the little yacht *Dagmar*, with the king and the bride on board, worked her way through the throng of festively trimmed boats amid the people's ceaseless shouts of joy, the cheers of the ships' crews, and the thunder of the guns.

Frequently ambassadors are not in residence when something important is going on. Our old emperor had once observed as much to me, but instead of "frequently" he had said "never." I therefore was not surprised to discover that our ambassador was absent on leave. This was perhaps fortunate, however, because I do not think he would have advised me any better than the chargé d'affaires, Rudolf Mittag zu Lenkheym, who apparently was most anxious to see the *Sankt Georg* play a prominent part on this occasion.[16] The first feast consisted of a *soirée dansante*, in which only the members of the royal household, the heads of the official world, and the foreign captains participated because of space limitations. On that occasion I had the honor of being introduced to both their majesties, to all the princes and princesses, and also to the bride; I must avow that I was quite fascinated by the charm of Crown Princess Sophia and by the beauty of the dark-haired Russian princess Helena and the blond Princess Alice, a daughter of Prince Battenberg.

The matrimonial ceremonies passed off on the next forenoon but one in the cathedral at Athens according to the Orthodox rite, with great splendor and all the tiresome ritual prescribed by the Greek Church. With the single exception of the bride, the court, including the queen, wore national costume. The evening was devoted to a grand wedding dinner of two hundred covers in the royal palace, followed by a rout of exhausting length. Prince Bonaparte, whom I had met in Paris in 1889 on the occasion of the geographical congress, remembered me, and he entertained me with details of his travels and geographical research. While talking with him it did not escape me that the crown princess and Princess Helena allowed their glances to dwell upon me for quite a while, something apparently having aroused their curiosity. When Prince Bonaparte had left me they discreetly nodded, indicating I should draw nearer to them. It turned out that it was not my humble person that had attracted their interest but an Abyssinian decoration I wore that they had not seen before, and this gave me the chance to make myself useful by amusing the august ladies with stories about Menelik and his realm.

The captains of the foreign warships were ordered to an audience with the king on the afternoon of December 13. When we were assembled in the anteroom to the king's studio, the question arose in what order we should be introduced. To my surprise, the Greek lord chamberlain thought to solve this question by proposing that the seniority of the various ambassadors at the place should be decisive. It goes without saying that I objected against such a funny insinuation, because our seniority alone should determine the sequence. Accordingly, the British Captain R. S. Philipps Hornby went in first, and I followed. The king on this occasion expressed the wish to visit the *Sankt Georg*, remarking that he could only do so in a couple of days, and he asked whether I was allowed to adjourn my departure for so long. It is true that I had been ordered to return to Pola as soon as the festivities were over, but I thought I should accede to the all-highest wish and therefore answered in the affirmative.

Crown Prince Constantine and Crown Princess Sophia had agreed to accept my invitation to a luncheon and appeared on board the *Sankt Georg* the following day with a small retinue. Since in the course of the same afternoon the departure of the newly married couple was to occur, my distinguished guests asked to be brought on board the yacht *Amphitrite* to take leave of them. They returned after a short while, inspected the *Sankt Georg*, had tea, and then left, graciously thanking us for the treat. Since His Majesty the King had deigned to accept an invitation to luncheon on board the British battleship *Glory*, I thought I could not do less than request the same honor, which I did by way of our chargé d'affaires. The king graciously granted my request and came on board, accompanied by all the princes and princesses of the royal household, and since I had also invited some members of our embassy and the consul general, it was a party as large as it was distinguished. In the course of the meal the king rose and expressed his satisfaction at being on board so fine a ship as the *Sankt Georg*; he then drank to the health of our emperor. I thanked His Majesty for the honor of his visit to the *Sankt Georg* and ended with my best wishes for the welfare of both their majesties and the princes and princesses of the royal house of Greece, at which point our band of course intoned the country's national anthem. Although I was not inexperienced in the ways of crowned circles, on that occasion I nevertheless felt a little nervous, it being the first time I had had to act as host for such. The luncheon passed off all right, however, and even in a quite animated mood, thanks to the king's affability and the queen's charming personality.

The *Sankt Georg* left Piraeus on the same evening and after a fortnight's absence anchored again at Pola, where she spent the Christmas week in squadron. With the beginning of the year 1908 I enjoyed a somewhat greater liberty, the *Sankt Georg* having been placed in command of a torpedo flotilla consisting of the transport *Pelikan*, several destroyers, and a dozen torpedo boats. It was my business to school the lot and train them to be efficient instruments of war by giving the officers an opportunity to become thoroughly acquainted with the whole of our coastline, the anchorages, channels, lurking places, signal stations, and other adaptations, in frequent cruises by day and by night. This was interesting and was also instructive for me. In consequence of my unusual career, I was not at all experienced in torpedo matters, but fortunately the *Sankt Georg*'s torpedo officer was a very able man who was happy to be allowed to work in concert with a sensible master. This campaign extended over a period of four months, which passed without any serious accidents or remarks from higher quarters. So long as the squadron was in home waters the *Sankt Georg* was called upon now and then to participate in some combined tactical maneuvers. I only enjoyed complete independence after the squadron had set out on a two-month cruise in the Mediterranean.

Service in our navy was much handicapped by the frequency of changes that occurred regarding the officers and men on board ship. The *Sankt Georg*'s executive officer had already been changed, and that was again the case soon after her return from Piraeus. I certainly did not cry for the man who parted from us, but with his successor things went from bad to worse. I should never have thought that in our navy there was a corvette captain so utterly ignorant of the duties on board and of regulations in general. The new executive officer was almost a danger to the ship, which obliged me to keep him under strict control.

For many reasons I had gradually lost my enthusiasm for the navy and did not wish to continue any longer in the service. Although I was far from being arrogant or filled with pride, in getting older I had become more and more sensitive to unjust or arbitrary acts on the part of superiors. The worst was, and this was a mistake, that I never stood up boldly in such cases but always endured wrongs with a wearied and angered mood, perhaps because I knew that otherwise I would not be able to govern my passion and would surely go far beyond the permitted limits. Constant tension with the port admiral contributed greatly to my weariness of service. I am speaking of that unruly admiral [Julius von Ripper] who had started his naval career as a sentry in Venice and who now interfered on every possible—and impossible—occasion in the affairs of anyone who came near his sphere of command, even the commander of the squadron. In the face of superiors he was without backbone; with inferiors, on the other hand, he was a low-class tyrant, and I came to hate the very sight of him. It was mortifying to witness what even officers of high rank took from him. It would not have helped to rebel against him, however, for he was backed by Archduke Francis Ferdinand and the commander of the navy, Admiral Montecuccoli, who was himself an autocrat.

I have never been ambitious or filled with the desire to rise to high position. When I was aide-de-camp to the emperor I even pitied the old court functionaries and generals who were all "Excellencies" but who to my mind led a dog's life. They were always anxious not to do anything that would cause them to tumble down from the high rungs of the ladder they had climbed. It was then that I said to myself never to be so foolish as to wish to attain high rank. For the higher one's position, the greater are the dangers that lie in wait for him. I always was, and still am, fully convinced that it requires a greater amount of humiliation, self-denial, shrewdness, and even meanness of character to attain and maintain a position higher than any upright man would wish to endure.

These remarks will help explain the rapid course by which my career came to a close. The squadron returned from its cruise on April 30. On June 4, after having been in charge of the *Sankt Georg* for sixteen months, I was relieved. As there never were many shore appointments for a senior captain, I was left unemployed until November 23, when I was appointed as the representative of Rear Admiral Lazar Schukic, the commander of the navy yard. And when he took over the command of a division of ships on March 19, 1909, I was made his successor.

The management of a great navy yard is connected with much responsibility and work, which I tried to fulfill to the best of my knowledge and ability and which I certainly carried out with an enormous amount of good will. It pleased me to show the thousands of workmen under my command that I was on my legs from early morning until often quite late at night, just like them; not even on Sundays did I allow myself a rest. The directors of the various departments were allowed to come and consult with me as often as they liked, at any hour of the day, and not simply at a certain time, as always had been the case in the past. I was—to cut it short—heart and soul in my work, devoting all my time and services entirely to the benefit of the state. Conscious of my utterly self-denying activity, I felt all the more, and in an ever-increasing measure, indignant at the port admiral's constant and unnecessary meddling in my functions,[17] so much so that in a moment of bad humor I decided to make an end of it all. I wrote a letter to the commander of the navy in which I requested to be allowed to retire from active service.[18] This granted, I left Pola after committing my functions to a successor. On August 1, 1909, I could consider myself a free man. His Majesty on this occasion conferred on me the Leopold Order.[19] When in an audience I submitted my thanks for this rather high distinction for one of my military rank, it did not escape me that the Supreme War Lord had been displeased by my decision. Three years later I was accorded the title of Rear Admiral.[20]

Epilogue

Although Ludwig Ritter von Höhnel lived until March 23, 1942, his memoirs end abruptly with his retirement from the navy in 1909. To the intervening thirty-three years Ildikó Simanyi devotes but a brief paragraph in her 1988 University of Vienna master's thesis:

> During his retirement, Höhnel remained active as a scholar. He published his autobiography and a number of articles in various scientific journals, was a member of the Geographical Society in Vienna, and attended virtually all of its public events and lectures until his death.[1]

Except for some valuable information on Höhnel's scholarly reputation, a few details on Höhnel's last will and testament, and material on the distribution to Austrian museums of artifacts he had collected on his expeditions to Africa, this is all she is able to say about the years between 1909 and 1942.[2]

It would be unfair to fault Ms. Simanyi for not having written more. In the absence of Höhnel's private papers, which appear to have been lost sometime after his death, distressingly little information is available on a period that accounts for more than one-third of his life. The major source on these years that was available to Ms. Simanyi were the obituaries that appeared following Höhnel's death, and these are disappointingly sparse in their content. They do little more than state that Höhnel continued to be active as a scholar in retirement and note that increasing deafness caused him to withdraw ever more from the public scene.[3]

Personal recollections add little information. In his foreword to the present volume, Sir Vivian Fuchs observes that Höhnel "had a wide circle of friends among former Austro-Hungarian naval officers" with whom he "greatly enjoyed reminiscing . . . about his years at sea," and he recalls that "one of his hobbies was to follow the movements and exercises of the Royal Navy, for which he had an unbounded admiration."[4] A further personal source is William Astor Chanler, Jr., who explains on the basis of his visits to Vienna in the inter-war period that despite his advancing deafness, Höhnel could engage in lively conversation in at least small social circles, so that he was able to play bridge frequently and avidly with his former naval cronies.[5] And finally, a passage in Admiral Alfred von Koudelka's memoirs suggests that Höhnel's admiration for the Royal Navy was not without limits. Even as he lay dying of pneumonia in March 1942, he tele-graphed the German navy to wish it victory in World War II.[6]

If these were the only sources available on Höhnel's life in retirement, there would be no need to add an epilogue to his memoirs. A footnote reproducing Ms. Simanyi's brief paragraph would be all that the editors could offer to satisfy curiosity about how Höhnel spent his more than three decades in retirement. Fortunately, however, the editors have at their disposal one source of informa-tion on these years that hitherto has gone untapped. At Rokeby in Barrytown-on-Hudson in New York, the Chanler family archive contains a significant por-tion of Höhnel's extensive correspondence with William Astor Chanler. The bond between the two men was extraordinarily close, and they wrote one an-other frequently, often monthly. Although their letters written before 1920 have not survived, many of those exchanged between the fall of that year and the early 1930s have, and they provide insight into three aspects of Höhnel's life following his retirement from the navy: (1) his deteriorating financial situation, (2) his intellectual activity, and (3) his response to the post-war political situ-ation in Austria.

Despite the lack of source material for the years before 1920, there is reason to believe that Höhnel began his retirement in reasonably comfortable circumstances. Upon their marriage, he and his wife established residence at Reisnerstrasse 61, at the corner of the Rennweg and across from the gardens of the Palais Metternich.[7] Höhnel's residence in Vienna's fashionable diplomatic quarter surely indicates that his pension, combined with whatever funds his wife brought to their marriage, enabled him to live in a style that was appropriate to his sta-tus as a retired naval officer who bore the honorary rank of rear admiral.

To the Höhnels' dismay, the outbreak of World War I in 1914 forced them to begin to experience some of the deprivations that afflicted the vast majority of Vienna's more than two million inhabitants. Höhnel referred to his changed circumstances when he reflected on the war years in a letter he sent Chanler in March 1927:

> In 1914, on August 1st, when the *MarineKommando* [i.e., the Admiralty] told me, that England in all probability will join in the war, I hurried home, and started buying non perishable foodstuffs for all the money I could get, foreseeing, that a war with England as adversary would last years. I bought for 900 Kronen flower, rice, beans, macaroni, sugar, tea, tinned meat, sardines, condensed milk etc. Our friends laughed at me. These things we held back, paid them out slowly, but at the end of 1917 the last tin of sardines had to be served out.[8]

The passage is of interest not only for the few details it provides, but also because it indicates that in early retirement Höhnel retained close ties to the Admiralty. It is of further significance because it reveals that unlike many contemporary military men who ought to have known better, Höhnel recognized that the war would not be short.

Höhnel and his wife responded to the collapse of the Habsburg Monarchy in 1918 and the subsequent unsettled conditions that existed in Vienna by fleeing the capital in 1919 and seeking refuge near Sáromberke, the Transylvanian estate of Count Teleki, who had died in 1916. A letter to Chanler written on September 2, 1920, suggests that their experience in Romania was not happy:

> I should like to give you an idea of the train of thoughts, which harass me continually, day and night, since long. We get here only scarce news, rare letters, [and] few local papers, which contain little. But the little we hear does not sound very allaying. A letter, which I received yesterday from a friend, who until recently belonged to the Foreign Office in Vienna, gives an awful and alarming conception of the situation there. He says, that the middle class looks with horror for the next winter. Now, we are here and may stay—should the Roum. Authorities not be against it—until next summer. But even here the living has become with every month more and more expensive, it has trebled since we are here. . . . It is 4 years that on account of the excessive prices I have not been able to buy for myself a suit or books or anything; that cannot go on in this way for many years. So everything combines to drive me to one solution or the other. I must try and find some employment and earn money.

Five years later he looked back upon his sojourn in Romania with bitterness and distaste: "I can hardly tell you how badly, even brutally we have been treated by almost all during our 16 months stay in Transylvania, how they looked down on us as paupers and treated us consequently; we still foam with rage whenever we come to think of it."[9]

Höhnel and his wife returned to Vienna at the end of 1920 after learning that the municipal government was threatening to confiscate their unoccupied apartment. "Unless we . . . return to Vienna at once," he wrote on December 7, "our furniture etc. will be thrown out on 31st Dec. Just think! My wife is desperate, we may lose all we have." Sooner or later Höhnel would in any event have left Transylvania, for while in Romania he was already at work trying to secure employment in central or eastern Europe with an American mission or some international organization. The news from Vienna left him no choice but to return to Austria. Once there, he quickly found a position with the American Red Cross, no doubt thanks to the efforts of friends such as Chanler. As he explained in a letter dated January 16, 1921, his salary, coupled with his pension, for the moment at least "takes all worries for the future of[f] our minds."[10]

Höhnel's joy at finding employment was mitigated, however, by fears that he might not succeed in regaining the economic status he had enjoyed before the war. The sequel would show that those fears were realistic. Indeed, during the next decade Höhnel's lamentations on his financial situation occupy such a prominent place in his correspondence that readers who have not themselves had to confront the dislocation associated first with war and then with the collapse of the existing political order may lose patience with him. They would do well, however, to appreciate the depth of the economic problems Austrians faced throughout the years of the First Republic. Wartime inflation had been bad enough. Post-war inflation brought economic chaos to the country and ruin to many in the middle class, and it was only possible to restore a measure of sanity by imposing strict fiscal controls following the creation of a new unit of currency, the *Schilling*, in 1924. When Höhnel complained, he did so with good cause.[11]

This having been said, it is also true Höhnel and his wife found it extremely difficult to adjust to new economic realities. As time went on, even the sympathetic and well-informed Chanler recognized that the Höhnels were so determined to continue to lead a lifestyle appropriate to their accustomed station in life that they found it difficult even to consider effecting certain economies that the American regarded as reasonable. Chanler was blunt. Writing on September 18, 1930, at a time when Höhnel was truly in hard straits, he observed:

> Despite the fact that you have a very small income, you have at least the satisfaction of knowing that it is a fixed one; and that you get it every month. It is you the man in the house, despite the weeping of the woman in the house, who must live each month within this income: and even set aside a little sum, be it only one dollar. In matters, of this sort, no matter how deep the pity and the affection the man may have for his wife, it is the male who must take matters in his own hands and face facts. . . . You say it would break your wife's heart to part from all her belongings which she has loved from childhood. She does not have to part with them all; but probably most of them will have to go. She can always of course keep those which are dearest to her heart.

Two years later, on June 7, Chanler returned to this theme: "You are not the only one to have trouble with your better half owing to the necessity for the strictest economy, for ladies find it difficult to understand unpleasant realities."

These comments need to be kept in mind when reading Höhnel's accounts of his financial plight in his correspondence of the 1920s. Once members of an elite social group within the Habsburg Monarchy, Höhnel and his wife now had to dispense with some of the amenities that they may earlier have taken for granted. That was even the case while Höhnel was working for the Red Cross:

> We have lived, since our arrival in Vienna, miserably. Without servants [we] had to do all the homework alone, get up early, make the breakfast; our noonmeal, which we got from the next inn, was bad, consisted every day of the same dishes: Soup, a small piece of boiled beef, with plain boiled

potatoes; some cakes and dried figs as dessert. We stuck to this simple diet, because all things are cooked here with bad, stinky margarine, and we refused to eat them. With this I mean to say, that we, and particularly I, with my hard work, have been underfed.[12]

Still, when confronted in April 1922 with the impending loss of his position with the Red Cross, Höhnel faced the future with equanimity:

The A.R.C. stops its work (in all Europe) at the end of June. The loss to me will be the greater, as I am now accustomed to the work and on very good terms with everybody. I like them personally and they appreciated [sic] my services. It will be very difficult to find other suitable work for me here. In consequence of the low economic situation all banks, industries etc. reduce their personel. I was thinking to get a, of course very subordinate place with the American Embassy, but Winti [Winthrop Chanler, William Astor Chanler's brother] wrote, it can't be, it being forbidden to have other than Americans in the personel. So I have made up my mind to finish my memoirs. I think to be able to meet the exigencies by selling my stamps, which fetch good prices. I have already sent some to London for which I hope to get 50£; and I have a lot more stamps. So I am not worried by the future, although life here in Austria is getting more and more expensive. — Both my wife and I are now quite well and even yesterday somebody said— as to me—that I am quite a phaenomenon. I certainly do not feel old and do by far not show my age—65 years![13]

When unemployment came, it even had an advantage, since Höhnel was now able to devote his time to completing his memoirs.

For three years Höhnel survived reasonably well on his pension, his wife's savings, and an occasional check from Chanler, this despite galloping inflation that only ended with the stabilization measures undertaken by the government in 1924. By the summer of 1925, however, the couple feared that its financial resources were nearing exhaustion:

There is now no doubt, that within 5 or 6 months our private means will be at end and . . . our income [will be] reduced to my pension, which allows us only to live on for 8 days in the month. I hate to speak of this, but since the hopes which I had attached to the publication of my Memories in America, have come to naught, there is no day on which I do not rake my brains, in order to find a way out.[14]

Höhnel went on to outline an elaborate scheme whereby he would will to some rich American the couple's entire property, "consisting in jewels, silverware, furniture, carpets, china and glassware etc.," with an estimated value of $15,000, in return for an assured income of $100 per month. "Two or three more years is all there is in store for me, I am quite sure," he explained. "My wife has so many times assured me, that she does not think of outliving me, that I quite believe it." In Höhnel's opinion it would "be nonsense to starve and to leave all our property intact to laughing heirs."

Chanler's response, which Höhnel may well have anticipated, came early in October:

> Now, my dear friend, I am afraid you have got to face the future as calmly and as intelligently as you can. I shall do my best to send you 1,000 francs a month, beginning on the 1st of November. It is also possible, though not probable, that Wintie and Pickman may send you *something* from time to time. I am afraid you will have to do what many of my French and English friends are forced to do on account of the high cost of living resultant from that beautiful Judeo-Prussian movement which began in 1914—viz., cut down expenses in every possible way. For instance, many of my friends here even with children, who had apartments of seven rooms, have sold most of their belongings and now live in lodgings of from three to four rooms. Of course, this is all very sad; but one has to look the world straight in the face at times.[15]

As well he might, Höhnel promptly wrote on October 7 to express his profound appreciation for Chanler's generosity:

> Your good letter was a real deliverance to me . . . it gave me back my faith in humanity. . . . I thank you heartily for this your renewed proof of friendship and magnanimity. With what you so generously will do for us, you indeed save us. By further cutting down as far as possible all our expenses and adding the proceeds from occasional sales of jewelry we will be in position to get along, at least for a time of two years, and that I think is all we need. The imminent danger is averted, time is gained and that was essential. In the course of time the pensions must and certainly will be increased and the general economic conditions will get better. Just now they are very low; we are in the midst of an economical crisis.

As of November 1925, Höhnel became for all intents and purposes Chanler's client.

At first Chanler himself sent the funds he had promised. Then, in October 1931, the Paris office of Bankers Trust Company assumed the responsibility of paying Höhnel the equivalent of 1,000 francs in Austrian schillings on the 25th of every month.[16] On occasion, moreover, Chanler sent an additional check in response to an extraordinary plea for help, as he did on February 12, 1929: "I am making arrangements so that you can have before the end of March 10,000 francs—or roughly $4000. This should pay off what you . . . owe your proprietor [i.e., landlord] and also get the jewels out of pawn." Later in the same year Höhnel wrote an especially poignant letter in which he complained,

> We are both very thin; the weight of my wife is 114½ pds. . . . I am flesh and bones only. I know that one should masticate every mouthful 35 times before swallowing it. To be able to do this, one must have good teeth. And this is the weak point with me. Since 18 months I help myself along with only one tooth in the upper jaw.[17]

As was by now to be expected, Chanler came through on September 6 with funds so that Höhnel could purchase the dentures he needed.

Following Chanler's death in 1934, his lawyers continued to send 1,000 francs monthly as stipulated in his will,[18] and when there was an interruption in the transfer of funds following the German annexation of Austria, it was to his widow, Beatrice, to whom Höhnel expressed his concern in January 1939:

> I know it is brutal of me to importune you at the beginning of the New Year with lamentations. However, I am sure you would pardon me if you were aware of the depression in which I have been living during the past week. December is the most expensive month in the year, and therefore I have been looking forward with growing uneasiness to the arrival of the magnanimous contribution to our support with which you and Willie favour me.[19]

With considerable relief, on April 15 Höhnel wrote to announce that the matter had been resolved:

> I do not find words to thank you for having thought of us. As you may imagine your so very kind letter was a great comfort to me. Since many a month I have lived in a state of continuous anxiety, and as our salvation rests entirely on you, the thought of finding us one day cast off from New York, caused me many a sleepless nights [sic]. The events nowadays develop with a suddenness so unexpected that one never knows what they will be the next day. I therefore about a month ago ventured to ask the Messrs Morris and McVeigh [the executors of William Astor Chanler's estate] if in case of war they could arrange that the remittences are sent by the intermediary of a Bank in Switzerland. In absence of Mr. Morris, the Mr. McVeigh very kindly by return of post freed me of all anxiety, saying that a way will surely be found out.
>
> And just now to my great comfort came your so very kind letter which delivers me from another weight that kept oppressed my heart and allows me now to breathe freely again.

II

Höhnel did more in retirement than worry about money. He also worked. As already mentioned, for a year and a half he was employed in Vienna by the American Red Cross. "My work . . . suits me well," he wrote Chanler in an undated letter sometime in June 1921. "My salary has been increased twice . . . and another title has been conferred to me; I figure in the books as 'assistant to Director' now! But I think, or rather guess, that this will—maybe soon—come to an end." It did so one year later, when the Red Cross wound up its operations in Austria in the summer of 1922.

It was at this point that Höhnel resumed work on the memoirs he had begun to write many months earlier while in Transylvania. Chanler was pleased:

> I am glad that your memoirs have become a hobby. Please look back into our correspondence, if by chance you have kept it, and you will find that it was I who told you to write your memoirs. . . . Now, let me tell you why I asked you to write your life. It was primarily to keep you busy, occupied and therefore alive. Despite your wide travelling—your absolute ignorance of this dreadful world forced me (unlike myself for a moment) to suggest to you how to write this book so that it might be published; because, after all, an unpublished book, no matter how well written, does not exist.[20]

By the end of May 1923 Höhnel was able to report that he had completed the chapter on his service as aide-de-camp to Emperor Francis Joseph and that there remained but two chapters still to write.

From the outset, Höhnel had intended to publish both a German and an English account of his career in the Imperial and Royal Navy.[21] He expressed astonishment, however, when Chanler suggested that he write the English manuscript himself:

> Your wish to have it done in English gave me a shock! I myself do not know near enough English to do the translation. I'll try to find somebody who is willing and clever enough for such work. I have asked . . . Admiral Troubridge whether he does not know anybody, and in a letter, which he wrote me today, he says that his nephew may possibly do it, he being a good German scholar and having a gift for literary expression. The question is whether he has the time, being occupied in business here. In one of your last letters, you said, that the real reason why you made me write my memoirs was, to keep me busy and alive. So I hope that your next letter will not ask me, to have it done in Chinese—to keep me busy.[22]

When Troubridge's nephew proved unreliable, Höhnel accepted an offer from Chanler to provide funds for a typist and for someone who would help him with the English manuscript.[23]

Much of Höhnel's correspondence with Chanler during the next two years concerns his attempt to find a publisher, first for the German original, and then for an English manuscript he hoped would find a market in the United States. After consulting a number of central-European houses, Höhnel was finally able to write on October 18, 1925:

> I am glad to be able to give you a piece of good news: I have succeeded in finding a publisher for my Memories: Reimar Hobbing in Berlin, a good firm. But I have to reduce the content (which now is about 500 pages in print) to 400 pages. The book will appear in the course of next spring. They offer me a royalty of 10% of the bookprice. It is for the second time that I am reducing the M.S. which originally amounted to 600 pages in print. I think this is a pity; a lot of minor details will have to be left out and it is just the little and intimate details which make any story and the more so a life's story, interesting.

When the book appeared,[24] Höhnel was pleased, reporting with some pride that he had received "from a captain in our Navy—to me almost unknown, a letter, in which he speaks in exalted terms of the book. Several of the reviews emphasize the conspicuous truthfulness, and the good, clear style, which some even say, was perfect."[25]

Höhnel never succeeded in placing the English version of his memoirs with a publisher. Similarly, an account he wrote in German in 1929 of Chanler's expedition to East Africa in 1892–94 also failed to arouse interest. On June 1 he informed Chanler that he had "offered the first 16 pages, as specimen, to Ullstein in Berlin, asking them, if they would publish such a book; the answer was negative. I then applied to the firm Brockhaus in Leipzig, but they too declined." By July 4 he had completed 233 pages of the new manuscript but admitted that there "is very little chance to see the work published. I write it because I think it should exist, and also to keep me from thinking. So long as I am sitting at my writing table I forget all around me." When in the following May he announced that he had finished the manuscript, he confessed that he had no prospect of finding a publisher:

> Mentally I am as active as ever. With reading and writing I am fully occupied all day long. . . . I have given up every hope to see my German story of your Expedition printed. I have addressed myself to twelve Editors and they all said "No" without wishing to see the manuscript. I finally asked for advice [from] the publisher of my Memories; he answered that to his mind it is unlikely to find in Germany a publisher for so old a book of travel in view of the economic depression prevailing on the book market.[26]

The book never was published, and there is no indication that the manuscript of what would have been a valuable addition to the historical literature on the exploration of East Africa has survived.

Höhnel had greater success with a number of other writing projects, the most notable of which was his historical survey of the exploration of the Lake Rudolf area. Though the manuscript was not published until 1938, and then in English,[27] he already mentioned a completed manuscript, presumably in German, in a letter to Chanler of February 14, 1928. Other projects included articles on Africa for various Viennese newspapers. He also earned money translating for an American scientist then residing in the Austrian capital:

> During the past week I have been very busy translating an astro-physic treatise from English into German, for a friend of mine, an American Dr. Darwin Lyon, a man of the highest scientific training. It simply fascinated me to talk and to work with him, and I thereby learned a lot of astonishing things about the conditions prevailing in the Universe, a science, with regard to which Dr. Lyon is conversant with the very latest researches.[28]

Höhnel translated a number of articles for Lyon, informing Chanler in February 1928:

> I am now hard at work, the more so as Dr. Lyon still needs me and takes up almost all my time. But, as you said, work keeps one alive. I felt never better, although I rarely leave the house, or make commotion. You certainly have no idea of the high scientific character of the work Lyon is publishing. It sometimes takes me half an hour to merely grasp the meaning of ten lines and to translate them from English into German. But it is fascinating to get acquainted with the very latest theories about the origin, formation etc. of the Universe, the structure of the atoms, the nature of Electricity, of radioactivity, Xrays etc. etc.[29]

Yet as time passed, increasing age and deafness took their toll, and on June 1, 1929, Höhnel confided to Chanler: "My world is getting more and more limited to the number of my friends and the four walls in which I live." A decade later his outlook was no brighter. "I am not at all desirous to see and hear what's going on," he wrote Beatrice Chanler; "[I] live entirely within our four walls and never go out."[30]

III

In the introduction, the editors note that Höhnel's memoirs have virtually nothing to say about the turbulent political events of the last decades of the Habsburg Monarchy. It is therefore entirely true to form that his extensive correspondence with Chanler provides little direct information on his response to the collapse of the Habsburg Monarchy or to the creation and the subsequent tribulations of the Austrian First Republic. Unfortunately, much of what he does have to say about politics he writes primarily in response to Chanler's repeated importuning on the subject of anti-Semitism, and it is never certain to what degree if any he shared his friend's right-wing ideology. Whenever Chanler sought to draw him out, Höhnel was cautious. Such was the case when he was asked early in 1923 to comment on the future of the Fascist movement in Austria:

> Fascisti in Austria! Dear me, you do not know the Austrians. They are not good for systematic, serious work; impulses puff away with them without leaving much impression and there is besides no national spirit in them. Austria [is] too far gone. You cannot expect to find in a country so utterly prostrated other ideals, than material. . . . I myself have no interest whatever for Austria. Since the downbreak [i.e., the collapse of the Habsburg Monarchy] I feel like an uprooted individual, who does not belong to any community. Austria won't and can't recover.[31]

Later, in an undated letter that appears to have been written in June of the same year, Höhnel went so far as to suggest frustration with Chanler's harping on the anti-Semitic theme:

> You . . . seem to be vexed on account of my inactivity as to Antisemitism. I have told you repeatedly, that since our downbreak I have become another man, an individual who has no interest for this world. Our former family motto I have changed into: Après moi le déluge. Besides[,] 90% of the amount of hatred, which is in me and I can raise, is directed against the French. I think them to be the greatest criminals, that have ever lived, the ruin of Europe, since Centuries and without question, the gravediggers of western Civilization. Bismarck was far from the mark, when he characterised them as Red Indians in patent leather shoes; in my eyes they are horrors. So you see that only 10% of hatred are left within me, as a reserve against the Jews and [the] Socialists.[32]

Elsewhere Höhnel gives the impression that try as he might to satisfy Chanler's desire that he openly embrace anti-Semitism, he was primarily concerned about the danger posed by the Social Democrats.[33] He explained his view of the political situation in a letter written on May 3, 1927:

> In 1923 the percentage of Bourgeois versus Socialists was 60:40; now it is 58:42. They have won some mandates. The Bourgeois have still a slight majority, but they are split up into five parties, whilst the Socialists form a solid block and will, as before, play the first violine in the Government, condemn it to inactivity, pass only laws, which are in their favor. The political situation is worse than it was, and the rabble shows it already. No change for the better can be hoped for, so long as the 10 or 12 socialist leaders, namely Adler, Seitz, Bauer, Danneberg, Deutsch etc.[,] all very clever men, but more or less Communists, are not put out of the way; but

[since] there is no probability that this will ever happen, Austria is therefore irresistibly drifting toward a Dictatorship of the Proletariat.[34]

This interest in Austrian internal politics was but passing, however, for subsequent letters make no mention whatsoever of such important events as the July 1927 riots in Vienna or the collapse of the Austrian Creditanstalt in 1931. There is also no reference to the growing importance of the authoritarian Right in the late 1920s and early 1930s, which is surprising in light of Höhnel's knowledge that Chanler was fascinated with the subject. Höhnel apparently meant it when he referred to the four walls that encapsulated his world.

By the time of the Anschluss with Germany, Chanler was dead, so that Höhnel never had an opportunity to comment upon the most significant event in the history of Austria during the inter-war period. His only reference in the Rokeby Papers to his experience under Nazism is indirect and appears in the letter he sent Beatrice Chanler on April 15, 1939, to thank her for her solicitation in the matter of his monthly remittance. It reveals very little:

> Laska grieved over the changes that have taken place and took them at heart in an alarming way, so much that she now is really skin and bones. What we had to go through in [the] course of the past twenty years was too much for her. I had hoped that the peace of God may be again between all men, but I very much fear that a second world war is unavoidable.

Meager though his gifts of political prophesy may have been, on this score, at least, Höhnel was right.

IV

Höhnel did not survive the war he foresaw, which began but a few months after he wrote Beatrice Chanler in April 1939. The last letter from Reisnerstrasse 61 that is found in the Rokeby Papers is a brief note from Laska von Höhnel to Beatrice Chanler and was written on January 5, 1946, following the reopening of regular postal communications between Austria and the United States: "I had a very sad and sorrowful life;—my beloved husband died in March 1942.—It was not possible in that time, to send you the news. The Hitler-regime was terrible and the actual time with hunger and misery is still depressing. God bless you and your family."[35]

Ludwig Ritter von Höhnel died at 12 o'clock noon on Monday, March 23, 1942, and following cremation was buried on March 31. Valeska von Höhnel lived until Saturday, June 14, 1947, when she died in her seventy-seventh year after a long illness. Upon the restoration of the war-damaged grave of honor that the city of Vienna had erected for her husband, she, too, was buried in Vienna's Central Cemetery.[36]

NOTES

Introduction

1. Höhnel bore his title, "Ritter von," by virtue of his father's having been knighted shortly before he died in 1868.

2. Herbert Tichy, *See an der Sonne: Auf den Spuren der frühen Menschen* (Vienna: Verlag ORAC, 1980), 104–05. For a recent and thorough discussion of the geology of the Rift Valley see Walter W. Bishop, ed., *Geological Background to Fossil Man: Recent Research in the Gregory Rift Valley, East Africa* (Toronto, Buffalo, and London: University of Toronto Press, 1978). It should be noted that the German name for the area, *Graben*, was first used by Höhnel and was then placed into currency in the German-speaking world by the distinguished Austrian geologist Eduard Suess; see Ildikó Simanyi, "Ludwig Ritter von Höhnel (1857–1942): Leben und Wirken" (unpublished master's thesis, University of Vienna, 1988), 119, and Eugen Oberhummer, "Ludwig Ritter von Höhnel," in *Petermanns Mitteilungen*, 88 (1942), 183.

3. As Sir Vivian Fuchs wrote in 1938, "Rear-Admiral Ritter Ludwig von Höhnel is the only living explorer who has made a major geographical discovery in the African Continent," in "Foreword to Admiral von Höhnel's Manuscript," which introduces Höhnel's article "The Lake Rudolf Region," *Journal of the Royal African Society*, 37 (1938), 16, 21–45, 206–26.

4. For an evaluation of the cartographic importance of these expeditions see Ingrid Kretschmer, "Österreichs Beitrag zur kartographischen Erschließung Ostafrikas bis zum Ersten Weltkrieg," in the exhibition catalogue *Abenteuer Ostafrika: Der Anteil Österreich-Ungarns an der Erforschung Ostafrikas* (Eisenstadt: Amt der Burgenländischen Landesregierung, 1988), 143–46.

5. William Astor Chanler, *Through Jungle and Desert: Travels in Eastern Africa*, (New York: Macmillan & Co., 1896). There is a brief account of Chanler's life (1867–1934) in *National Cyclopædia of American Biography*, 25 (1936), 279.

6. *Denn Österreich lag einst am Meer. Das Leben des Admirals Alfred von Koudelka*, ed. Lothar Baumgartner (Graz: H. Weishaupt Verlag, 1987), 90.

7. See Chanler to Höhnel, Paris, March 22 and October 2, 1923, and Höhnel to Chanler, Vienna, December 8, 1923; William Astor Chanler Correspondence, Rokeby Papers, Barrytown, New York (hereafter cited as Rokeby Papers).

8. For a brief profile of Pickman see Lincoln Kirstein, *Mosaic: Memoirs* (New York: Farrar, Straus & Giroux, 1994), 109–10.

9. Ludwig Ritter von Höhnel, *Mein Leben zur See, auf Forschungsreisen und bei Hofe: Erinnerungen eines österreichischen Seeoffiziers (1857–1909)* (Berlin: Verlag von Reimar Hobbing, 1926).

10. On March 12, 1927, for example, Lyman B. Sturgis, book editor at The Century Co. in New York, wrote to Chanler's intermediary, Dr. Herbert Adams Gibbons of Princeton (Chanler resided in Paris in the 1920s and visited the United States but rarely): "We much appreciate your having brought to our attention a copy of *Mein Leben zur See* by Ludwig Ritter von Hohnel [sic], which is offered to us for translation. It is our belief . . . that no biography of the type could be published to advantage in this country, since the author is not well enough known and is not a world figure in the ordinary sense. We decline with thanks, therefore, the opportunity you offer us." Rokeby Papers.

11. Maddie DeMott, "William Chanler," in *Africana*, 3/1 (March 1967), 15–19.

12. Pascal James Imperato, *Arthur Donaldson Smith and the Exploration of Lake Rudolf* (Lake Success, N.Y.: Medical Society of the State of New York, 1987).

13. See, e.g., Ronald E. Coons, *Steamships, Statesmen, and Bureaucrats: Austrian Policy towards the Steam Navigation Company of the Austrian Lloyd 1836–1848* (Wiesbaden: Franz Steiner Verlag, 1975); Ronald E. Coons, "Kübeck and the Pre-Revolutionary Origins of Austrian Neoabsolutism," in *Gesellschaft, Politik und Verwaltung in der Habsburgermonarchie 1830–1918*, ed. Ferenc Glatz and Ralph Melville (Stuttgart: Franz Steiner Verlag Wiesbaden, 1987), 55–86; and Ronald E. Coons, "Steamships and Quarantines at Trieste, 1837–1848," in *Journal of the History of Medicine and Allied Sciences*, 44 (1989), 28–55.

14. Höhnel, *Mein Leben zur See, auf Forschungsreisen und bei Hofe*, 324–26.

15. Personal communication from Géza Teleki to Pascal James Imperato, Washington, D.C., August 13, 1996.

16. Ludwig Ritter von Höhnel, *Zum Rudolf-See und Stephanie-See: Die Forschungsreise des Grafen Samuel Teleki in Ost-Aequatorial-Afrika, 1887–1888* (Vienna: A. Hölder, 1892), translated as *Discovery of Lakes Rudolf and Stefanie: A Narrative of Count Samuel Teleki's Exploring & Hunting Expedition in Eastern Equatorial Africa in 1887 & 1888*, 2 vols. (London: Longmans, Green & Co., 1894).

17. See William Astor Chanler, "Hunting in East Africa," in *Hunting in Many Lands: The Book of the Boone and Crockett Club*, ed. Theodore Roosevelt and George Bird Grinnell (New York: Forest and Stream Publishing Company, 1895), 13–54; George E. Galvin, Jr., *Chanler Expedition, Kenya (formerly British East Africa), 1888–1890: Diary of George E. Galvin* (Albuquerque, N.M.: George E. Galvin, Jr., 1996).

18. See Pascal James Imperato, *Quest for the Jade Sea: Colonial Competition around an East African Lake* (Boulder, Colo.: Westview Press, 1998), 89–100.

19. The expedition is described by Chanler in *Through Jungle and Desert*.

20. Bairu Tafla, *Ethiopia and Austria: A History of Their Relations*, Äthiopische Forschungen, vol. 35 (Wiesbaden: Harrassowitz Verlag, 1994), 94–107.

21. See, e.g., Anthony Eugene Sokol, *The Imperial and Royal Austro-Hungarian Navy*, Sea Power Monograph no. 3 (Annapolis: U.S. Naval Institute, 1968); Lawrence Sondhaus, *The Habsburg Empire and the Sea: Austrian Naval Policy, 1797–1866* (West Lafayette, Ind.: Purdue University Press, 1989); Lawrence Sondhaus, *The Naval Policy of Austria-Hungary, 1867–1918: Navalism, Industrial Development, and the Politics of Dualism* (West Lafayette, Ind.: Purdue University Press, 1994); and Milan N. Vego, *Austro-Hungarian Naval Policy, 1904–14* (Portland, Oreg.: Frank Cass, 1996). Also valuable are the chapters dealing with the Austro-Hungarian navy in two books by Paul G. Halpern: *The Mediterranean Naval Situation, 1908–1914*, Harvard Historical Studies vol. 86 (Cambridge: Harvard University Press, 1971), and *The Naval War in the Mediterranean, 1914–1918* (London: Allen & Unwin, 1987).

22. John Biggins, *A Sailor of Austria* (New York: St. Martin's Press, 1994).

23. Ingrid Kretschmer, "Die kartographischen Ergebnisse der Teleki-Höhnel Entdeckungsreise 1887–88," in *Mitteilungen der Österreichischen Geographischen Gesellschaft*, 130 (1988), 55.

24. Heinrich Bayer von Bayersburg, *Österreichs Admirale und bedeutende Persönlichkeiten der k.u.k. Kriegsmarine 1867–1918* (Vienna: Bergland Verlag, 1962), 79.

25. See Ludwig Ritter von Höhnel, Marine, Qualificationsliste, Nr. 2118, fol. 36v–37r and 66v, Kriegsarchiv, Vienna. Throughout Höhnel's personnel folder the words "zealous," "talented," and "energetic" appear with monotonous regularity.

26. See Rilke's *Briefe an Baronesse von Oe.*, ed. Richard von Mises (New York: Verlag der Johannespresse, 1945), and Wolfgang Leppmann, *Rilke: Sein Leben, seine Welt, sein Werk* (Bern and Munich: Scherz Verlag, 1981), 72–73.

27. See Sondhaus, *The Naval Policy of Austria-Hungary*, 175–78.

28. Friedrich Werner van Oestéren (b. 1874), *Christus nicht Jesus: Ein Jesuitenroman*, 2 vols. (Berlin: Egon Fleischel & Co., 1906).

29. Höhnel to Emperor Francis Joseph, Vienna, February 26, 1907, and Höhnel to Reichskriegsministerium, Marinesektion, March 12, 1907, M.S./1.GG.1907, 25a/1, Kriegsarchiv, Vienna; *Denn Österreich lag einst am Meer*, 90.

30. "Vortrag des Marinekommandanten und Chef des Reichskriegsministeriums Abteilung 1, ddo 2. Juli 1909, No. 2435," M.K.S.M. 2102 ex 1909, Kriegsarchiv, Vienna; *Fremden Blatt*, Vienna, Sunday, July 18, 1909, p. 4; Military Chancellery of Archduke Francis Ferdinand to Fregattenkapitän Alfred von Koudelka, Vienna, July 20, 1909, M.K.F.F. Res. Nr. E/21 ex 1909, Kriegsarchiv, Vienna; Reichskriegsministerium to Military Chancellery of Archduke Francis Ferdinand, Vienna, July 23, 1909, *ibid*. Emperor Francis Joseph sanctioned Höhnel's retirement on July 4, 1909, to become effective on August 1. See also Simanyi, "Ludwig Ritter von Höhnel (1857–1942)," 8–11, and Erwin F. Sieche, "Austria-Hungary's Last Naval Visit to the USA," in *Warship International*, 2 (1990), 160.

31. Höhnel observes in chapter 9 that his was a "wholly unpolitical mind," while on June 20, 1921, he wrote Chanler: "I remember that you have asked me to write you about the political situation; but I confess to have forgotten it entirely. I am such an impolitic person and so utterly ignorant in these matters, that I never took an interest in them." Rokeby Papers.

32. Eugen Ketterl, *The Emperor Francis Joseph I: An Intimate Study by his Valet de Chambre* (London: Skeffington & Son, Ltd., 1929), 99.

33. Steven Beller, *Francis Joseph* (London and New York: Longman, 1996), 227.

34. *Denn Österreich lag einst am Meer*, Baumgartner, ed, 90.

35. For example, documents at the *Haus-, Hof- und Staatsarchiv* in Vienna concerning his mission to Ethiopia confirm his account in chapter 11 of how his military style of leadership offended his civilian companions and how they in turn irritated him by trying to pressure him to involve the Monarchy in a banking scheme that he justifiably treated with great skepticism. Furthermore, unpublished diary entries corroborate his version of events on two occasions—his description in chapter 8 of his falling out with his superior Anton von Haus, and his mention in chapter 12 of problems that his executive officer caused by his harsh treatment of the crew on board the torpedo cruiser *Panther*.

36. Ludwig Ritter von Höhnel, *Discovery of Lakes Rudolf and Stefanie*, vol. 2, 321–27.

37. Simanyi, "Ludwig Ritter von Höhnel," 103. Willi Senft and Bert Katschner are especially harsh on Höhnel on this issue in their *Bergwandern in Ostafrika: Riesenevulkane und*

Tierparadiese (Graz and Stuttgart: Leopold Stocker Verlag, 1978), 165, where in the editors' judgment, they unfairly blame a child of the nineteenth century for having failed to share twentieth-century sensibilities.

38. Chanler to Höhnel, Paris, November 4, 1923, Rokeby Papers. The book he refers to is *Through Jungle and Desert*, 2.

39. See Lately Thomas (pseud. Robert V. P. Steele), *A Pride of Lions: The Astor Orphans; The Chanler Chronicle* (New York: William Morrow & Company, Inc., 1971), 96.

40. Chanler to Höhnel, Paris, November 4, 1923, Rokeby Papers. As Höhnel wrote Chanler on December 8, 1923: "You must not be afraid, my dear Chanler, not a word will be published, that does not suit you. I never thought of hurting your feelings or of compromising your interests. You will agree with the book or it shall not be published at all. Besides I am well aware that your interests go hand in hand with mine; your great family and your many friends in America would probably stone me, if I would dare to picture you otherwise than you deserve." Rokeby Papers.

41. See Gerald Schlag, "Koloniale Pläne Österreich-Ungarns in Ostafrika im 19. Jahrhundert," in *Abenteuer Ostafrika: Der Anteil Österreich-Ungarns an der Erforschung Ostafrikas* (Eisenstadt: Amt der Burgenländischen Landesregierung, 1988), 171–86.

42. See the article "Ein österreichischer Kolonialpionier" in *Mitteilungen der Deutschen Kolonialgesellschaft*, February 15, 1930, which contains an interview with Höhnel. A copy of the interview is included in the Chanler papers at Rokeby.

43. Like many wealthy Americans of his time, Chanler used prejudice to protect class interests. Thus, many of his prejudices were directed against groups that he perceived as most threatening to those interests. For a fuller discussion of prejudicial attitudes mustered to protect class interests see Ashley Montagu, *Man's Most Dangerous Myth: The Fallacy of Race*, 5th edition (New York: Oxford University Press, 1974), 14–15.

44. On March 30, 1942, shortly after Höhnel's death, his widow signed a declaration formally stating that according to National Socialist legislation she was not of Jewish origin. It is possible that on this occasion Valeska von Höhnel knowingly gave false information. It is equally possible, however, that like many central Europeans of her generation she was unaware of her Jewish ancestry. Whatever the case, on May 7, 1943, the *Gauamt für Sippenforschung* in Vienna informed the *Finanzamt* in the city's Third District that it had become aware that under existing law Höhnel's widow had to be considered a Jew. In consequence, her pension was to be stopped until she appeared before the authorities. Fearing the worst, Valeska von Höhnel took advantage of her late husband's status and turned to high party officials for help. As a letter she sent on June 7, 1943, to the *Versorgungsamt* in the Third District reveals, her appeal was successful, for she was able to inform authorities that the Deputy Gauleiter for Vienna, Karl Scharizer (1901–1956) had declared, "Nothing shall happen to the widow of Rear Admiral Höhnel. It is the will of the *Reichsleiter* that the matter be dropped." Shortly thereafter Frau Höhnel was granted a reduced pension, and she apparently survived the remaining years of the war without further difficulties stemming from her racial background. Materials on the matter can be found in Kriegsarchiv, Vienna, Versorgungsakt für Höhnel, Ludwig, Konter-Admiral a.D.

45. See Chanler to Höhnel, Paris, October 3, 1925, and Bankers Trust Company, Paris, to William Astor Chanler, October 21, 1931; Rokeby Papers. Bankers Trust continued to send payments to Höhnel following Chanler's death.

46. Höhnel, *Mein Leben zur See, auf Forschungsreisen und bei Hofe*, 145.

47. Tichy, *See an der Sonne*, 103, 104. On the attitudes of European explorers toward native peoples see Tim Youngs, *Travellers in Africa: British Travelogues, 1850–1900* (Manchester

and New York: Manchester University Press, 1994), and for those fluent in post-modern discourse, Mary Louise Pratt, *Imperial Eyes: Travel Writing and Transculturation* (London and New York: Routledge, 1992). Highly readable and also valuable is Frank McLynn, *Hearts of Darkness: The European Exploration of Africa* (New York: Carroll & Graf, 1993), 303–59.

48. Höhnel to Chanler, December 8, 1923, Rokeby Papers.

49. Chanler to Höhnel, November 4, 1923, Rokeby Papers.

1. Family, Youth and Choice of Profession (1857–1876)

1. Gottfried Höhnel was born in Vienna on May 1, 1810. Upon completing his legal studies at the University of Vienna, he took his first civil service position in 1833 with the criminal division of the Viennese municipal government, but in 1834 he transferred to the financial administration of the province of Lower Austria. Subsequently he served as a financial officer in the Illyrian Littoral, in northwestern and central Hungary, in the Military Frontier, and in Venice. In October 1861 the emperor awarded him the Order of the Iron Crown, Third Class; late in the same year he was appointed to head the Finanzlandesdirektion of the Austrian Littoral; in October 1862 he received the title of Hofrat; and on December 14, 1863, he was named Finanzdirektor of the province. In May 1867 Gottfried Höhnel exercised his right as a member of the Order of the Iron Crown to request elevation to the nobility. The draft of the Ritterstandsdiplom is dated September 20, 1867; the official document was delivered to the widow of Gottfried Ritter von Höhnel on March 23, 1868, her husband having died earlier in the year. See Vienna, Allgemeines Verwaltungsarchiv, Hofadelsakt Gottfried Höhnel 1867.

2. Karl Rudolf Brommy, *Die Marine* (Berlin: A. Duncker, 1848).

3. On Heinrich von Littrow (1820–1895), the brother of the astronomer Karl Ludwig von Littrow (1811–1877), see Heinrich Bayer von Bayersburg, *Österreichs Admirale und bedeutende Persönlichkeiten der k.u.k. Kriegsmarine 1867–1918* (Vienna: Bergland Verlag, 1962), 113–14.

4. On the career of Ferdinand Ritter von Attlmayr (1828–1906) see Heinrich Bayer von Bayersburg, *Österreichs Admirale 1719–1866* (Vienna: Bergland Verlag, 1960), 11–12.

5. Höhnel's grade reports that are preserved among his service records reveal that whereas his performance in school in Vienna was indeed, as he indicates, mediocre—in general his grades fell in the middle range of the spectrum *ausgezeichnet, vorzüglich, lobenswert, befriedigend, genügend, ungenügend,* and *ganz ungenügend* (distinguished, excellent, praiseworthy, satisfactory, sufficient, insufficient, and totally insufficient), at the academy they generally fell in the *vorzüglich- lobenswert* range. During his career at the academy Höhnel ranked between fourth and eighth in a class that began in 1873 with thirty-six students; he graduated seventh in a finishing class of twenty-nine. See Ludwig Ritter von Höhnel, Marine, Qualificationsliste, Nr. 2118, fol. 9r–15r, Kriegsarchiv, Vienna.

2. Three Years as a Midshipman (1876–1879)

1. There is a brief discussion of the career of Baron Anton Bourguignon von Baumberg (1808–1879) in Heinrich Bayer von Bayersburg, *Österreichs Admirale 1719–1866* (Vienna: Bergland Verlag, 1960), 32–36.

2. Between 1854 and 1864 Emperor Francis Joseph's younger brother, Archduke Ferdinand Maximilian (1832–1867), better known to history as the unfortunate Emperor Maximilian of Mexico, served as Austrian naval commander. For details about his administration see Lawrence Sondhaus, *The Habsburg Empire and the Sea: Austrian Naval Policy, 1797–1866* (West Lafayette, Ind.: Purdue University Press, 1989), 181–236.

3. Höhnel consistently uses the term *Admiralty* for what was in fact the naval or maritime section of the Austro-Hungarian War Ministry. On the administration of the navy during Höhnel's period of service see Walter Wagner, *Die obersten Behörden der k. und k. Kriegsmarine 1856–1918*, in *Mitteilungen des Österreichischen Staatsarchivs*, Ergänzungsband VI (Vienna: Österreichisches Staatsarchiv, 1961), 49–88.

4. Baron Friedrich von Pöck (1825–1884) served as Marineoberkommandant and Chef der Marinesektion from April 1871 to November 1883. See Lawrence Sondhaus, *The Naval Policy of Austria-Hungary, 1867–1918: Navalism, Industrial Development, and the Politics of Dualism* (West Lafayette, Ind.: Purdue University Press, 1994), 35–80 for an account of Pöck's administration of the navy, which, as Sondhaus observes, was characterized by "a dramatic decline in morale" (p. 35). There is a brief biography in Heinrich Bayer von Bayersburg, *Österreichs Admirale und bedeutende Persönlichkeiten der k.u.k. Kriegsmarine 1867–1918* (Vienna: Bergland Verlag, 1962), 139–40.

5. One of the enclaves to which Höhnel refers is the port of Neum, as is clear from a reference later in the chapter; the other would appear to be Dulcigno (Ulcinj), to the south of the Bay of Kotor.

6. The reference is to William Ritter von Lund. On Scandinavians in Austrian service during the navy's revival following the revolutionary events of 1848–49 see Sondhaus, *The Habsburg Empire and the Sea*, 162, 165.

7. From Vienna, Erwin F. Sieche kindly reports that the captain of the *Kaiser Max* was Linienschiffskapitän Adolf Nöltin, while the executive officer was Korvettenkapitän Friedrich Stecher.

8. On the evacuation of the Turkish troops, see *Die Occupation Bosniens und der Hercegovina durch k.k. Truppen im Jahre 1878* (Vienna: Verlag des k.k. Generalstabes, 1879), 367–79.

9. Maximilian Freiherr Daublebsky von Sterneck zu Ehrenstein (1829–1897) served as Marineoberkommandant and Chef der Marinesektion from November 1883 until December 1897; on his administration see Sondhaus, *The Naval Policy of Austria-Hungary*, 80–91 and 123–41.

10. Bayer von Bayersburg, *Österreichs Admirale 1867–1918*, 122–24, offers a more sympathetic summary of the career of Baron Moriz Manfroni von Monfort (1832–1889), who retired in 1888 with the rank of vice admiral.

11. Subsequently, Archduke Albrecht (1817–1895) held the post of inspector general of the army from March 1869 until his death; see Gunther E. Rothenberg, *The Army of Francis Joseph* (West Lafayette, Ind.: Purdue University Press, 1976), 79.

12. The German zoologist Alfred Edmund Brehm (1829–1884), noted for *Brehms Thierleben: Allgemeine Kunde des Thierreichs*, 2d. ed.; 10 vols. (Leipzig: Verlag des Bibliographischen Instituts, 1876–79), shared a strong interest with Archduke Rudolf in ornithology; see the article by Fritz Böck, "Kronprinz Rudolf als Ornithologe," in the exhibition catalogue *Rudolf: Ein Leben im Schatten von Mayerling* (Vienna: Museum der Stadt Wien, 1990), 33–35. Because of his Masonic affiliation, Brehm's close relationship with the crown prince aroused strong opposition at court; see Brigitte Hamann, *Rudolf: Kronprinz und Rebell* (Vienna and Munich: Amalthea, 1978), 112–20 and 124–29.

13. According to Hamann, *Rudolf*, p. 125, the *Miramar's* officers were so accustomed to

the hunting fever that afflicted other archdukes that they failed to realize that Rudolf and Brehm were far less interested in the hunt than they were in ornithology. Having discovered a new species of lark, which they named *Galerida miramare*, they in fact considered the voyage a success.

3. Life as a Subaltern Naval Officer (1879–1886)

1. The Austrian mining expert and benefactor Paul Kupelwieser (1843–1919) purchased the island in 1893 and subsequently developed it as a winter sea resort; see *Österreichisches biographisches Lexikon*, 4 (1969), 360.

2. Jerolim Freiherr von Benko provides a photograph of the church and a brief discussion of its construction in his explanatory notes to Sterneck's correspondence, which the admiral's widow published shortly after his death. See *Admiral Max Freiherr von Sterneck: Erinnerungen aus den Jahren 1847–1897* (Vienna: A. Hartleben's Verlag, 1901), 292–93.

3. Karl Weyprecht (1839–1881) was the leader of the Austro-Hungarian North Pole Expedition in 1872–74; see Heinrich Bayer von Bayersburg, *Österreichs Admirale und bedeutende Persönlichkeiten der k.u.k. Kriegsmarine 1867–1918* (Vienna: Bergland Verlag, 1962), 180–82.

4. Writing four decades ago in his *The Road to Mayerling: The Life and Death of Crown Prince Rudolph of Austria* (London: Macmillan, 1959), 157, Richard Barkeley dismissed the rumor that Crown Prince Rudolf visited the island for the purpose of recovering from venereal disease. In 1978, on the other hand, Brigitte Hamann wrote that the crown prince in fact visited Lacroma to recover from gonorrhea and that while on the island the crown princess discovered that she, too, was infected with the disease; see Brigitte Hamann, *Rudolf: Kronprinz und Rebell* (Vienna and Munich: Amalthea, 1978), 389. Hamann's statement is supported by Susanne Walther, "Daten zur Biographie des Kronprinzen," in the catalogue *Rudolf: Ein Leben im Schatten von Mayerling* (Vienna: Museum der Stadt Wien, 1990), 395.

5. Prince Philip of Coburg married Princess Louise of Belgium, the eldest daughter of King Leopold and the sister of Archduchess Stephanie, in 1875. Her subsequent liaison with a Hungarian count, her confinement and escape from a mental institution, and her estrangement from her father are discussed in Theo Aronson, *Defiant Dynasty: The Coburgs of Belgium* (Indianapolis, Ind: Bobbs-Merrill, 1968).

6. The African adventures of Count Samuel Teleki von Szék (1845–1916) are discussed in Hungarian in Erdélyi Lajos, *Teleki Samu afrikában; az afrika-kutató eredeti fényképfelvételeivel* (Bucharest: Kriterion Könyvkiadó, 1977). See also Pascal James Imperato, *Quest for the Jade Sea. Colonial Competition around an East African Lake* (Boulder, Colo.: Westview Press/Harper Collins, 1998), 49–78, 270–77.

7. Georg August Schweinfurth (1836–1925), *Im Herzen von Afrika: Reisen und Entdeckungen im centralen Äquatorial-Afrika während der Jahre 1868 bis 1871* (Leipzig: F. A. Brockhaus, 1874), translated as *The Heart of Africa: Three Years' Travels and Adventures in the Unexplored Regions of Central Africa from 1868 to 1871*, 2 vols. (New York: Harper and Brothers, 1874).

4. My First Expedition to Africa (1886–1889)

1. On the botanist Franz Ritter von Höhnel (1852–1920) see *Österreichisches biographisches Lexikon*, 2 (1959), 357–58.

2. For a brief discussion of the maps of eastern Africa available to Teleki and Höhnel see Ingrid Kretschmer, "Die kartographischen Ergebnisse der Teleki-Höhnel Entdeckungsreise 1887–88," in *Mitteilungen der Österreichischen Geographischen Gesellschaft*, 130 (Jahresband 1988), 49–50. Jeffrey C. Stone discusses the general topic of mapping the African continent in *A Short History of the Cartography of Africa*, African Studies, vol. 39; (Lewiston, N.Y.: Edwin Mellen Press, 1995). Ernst Georg Ravenstein (1839–1913) was a German cartographer from Frankfurt who began working for the British War Office Topographical Department in 1855. He later became the cartographer for the Royal Geographical Society and actively participated in the debates about East African geography and the source of the Nile. He drew the maps of a number of eminent nineteenth century travelers to East Africa.

3. Leonidas Freiherr von Popp (1831–1908) served as chief of the emperor's military chancellery from 1881 until his retirement in 1892; see *Österreichisches biographisches Lexikon*, 8 (1983), 202–03.

4. On the scurrilous imperialistic activities of Clemens (1852–1929) and Gustav (1856–1917) Denhardt in the phantom sultanate of Witu in the 1880s, see Fritz Ferdinand Müller, *Deutschland—Zanzibar—Ostafrika: Geschichte einer deutschen Kolonialeroberung 1884–1890* (Berlin: Rütten & Loening, 1959), 287–328; for a brief general discussion of German involvement in Witu see Hans-Ulrich Wehler, *Bismarck und der Imperialismus* (Cologne and Berlin: Kiepenheuer & Witsch, 1969), 367–70. Despite its title, Hermann Schreiber's *Denhardts Griff nach Afrika: Die Geschichte einer deutschen Kolonialerwerbung* (Berlin: Scherl, 1938) is not a work of serious historical scholarship but is rather an undistinguished novel that reflects the German political climate at the time it was written.

5. Höhnel consistently refers in this manner to Sayyid Barghash bin Said, who succeeded to the throne of Zanzibar in 1870 and ruled until his death in 1888; Ahmed Hamoud al-Maamiry discusses the reign in *Omani Sultans in Zanzibar, 1832–1964* (New Delhi: Lancers Books, 1988), 18–22.

6. Joseph Thomson (1858–1895), *Through Masai Land: A Journey of Exploration among the Snowclad Volcanic Mountains and Strange Tribes of Eastern Equatorial Africa, Being the Narrative of the Royal Geographical Society's Expedition to Mount Kenia and Lake Victoria Nyanza, 1883–1884*, 3d ed. (London: Sampson Low, Marston, Searle, and Rivington, 1885), 10–11; see also Sir Frederick Jackson, *Early Days in East Africa*, 1930; reprint (London: Dawsons of Pall Mall, 1969), 66–72.

7. At the time of Höhnel's visit Lloyd William Mathews (1850–1901) was serving as general of the Sultan of Zanzibar's army; in 1891 he became the sultan's prime minister. His career is surveyed in Robert Nunez Lyne, *An Apostle of Empire: Being the Life of Sir Lloyd William Mathews, K.C.M.G.* (London: George Allen & Unwin, 1936).

8. James R. Hooker discusses Cameron, the least famous of this distinguished trio of African explorers, in his contribution "Verney Lovett Cameron: A Sailor in Central Africa," in *Africa and Its Explorers: Motives, Methods, and Impact* ed. Robert I. Rotberg (Cambridge: Harvard University Press, 1970), 255–94; the volume also contains valuable chapters by Norman Robert Bennett on David Livingstone (39–62) and Eric Halladay on Henry Morton Stanley (223–54).

9. On Jumbe Kimemeta see Jackson, *Early Days in East Africa*, 193–96, and Thomson, *Through Masai Land*, 126, where he is described as "a little man, deeply marked with smallpox and blind in one eye. The other eye, however, was lively, and he soon proved to be far above the average in gentlemanly character and intelligence."

10. On the early activity of the O'Swald firm in Africa see Ernst Hieke, *Zur Geschichte*

des deutschen Handels mit Ostafrika: Das hamburgische Handelshaus Wm. O'Swald & Co. Teil I: 1831–1870 (Hamburg: H. Christian, 1939), which contains a history of the family Oswald-O'Swald by Percy Ernst Schramm (7–54).

11. Höhnel's manuscript provides a comprehensive list of the items that is drawn from his published account of the expedition; see Ludwig Ritter von Höhnel, *Discovery of Lakes Rudolf and Stefanie: A Narrative of Count Samuel Teleki's Exploring & Hunting Expedition in Eastern Equatorial Africa in 1887 & 1888*, trans. Nancy Bell, 2 vols. (London: Longmans, Green & Co., 1894), vol. 1, 12–14.

12. See Oskar Lenz (1848–1925), *Timbuktu, Reise durch Marokko, die Sahara und den Sudan ausgeführt im Auftrage der Afrikanischen Gesellschaft in Deutschland in den Jahren 1879 und 1880* (Leipzig: F. A. Brockhaus, 1884).

13. The Mahdists were members of an Islamic order who, led by the al-Mahdi (Muhammed 'Ahmed ibn 'Abdallah al-Mahdi) conquered most of the Sudan by 1885. On the movement see Peter Malcolm Holt, *The Mahdist State in the Sudan* (Oxford: Clarendon Press, 1958).

14. See Wilhelm Junker (1840–1892), *Dr. Wil. Junkers Reisen in Afrika, 1875–1886*, 3 vols. (Vienna: E. Hölzel, 1889–91), translated as *Travels in Africa during the Years 1875–1886*, 3 vols. (London: Chapman and Hall, 1890–1892).

15. Gaetano Casati (1838–1902) was an Italian traveler who spent ten years in the southern Sudan. For a time he worked for Emin Pasha, the Prussian physician (Eduard Karl Oskar Theodor Schnitzer, 1840–1892), who was appointed governor of Equatoria by General Charles Gordon in 1878; see Gaetano Casati, *Ten Years in Equatoria and the Return with Emin Pasha*, 2 vols. (London: Frederick Warne and Co., 1891). Roger Jones provides a modern account of Emin Pasha and his life and work in Africa in *The Rescue of Emin Pasha: The Story of Henry M. Stanley and the Emin Pasha Relief Expedition, 1887–1889* (New York: St. Martin's Press, 1973); also see Iain R. Smith, *The Emin Pasha Relief Expedition 1886–1890* (Oxford: Clarendon Press, 1972).

16. See above, note 11.

17. On Ludwig Purtscheller (1849–1900) see *Österreichisches biographisches Lexikon*, 8 (1983), 340–41; on the ascent of Kilimanjaro see Hans Heinrich Joseph Meyer, *Across East African Glaciers: An Account of the First Ascent of Kilimanjaro* (London: George Philip & Son, 1891).

18. The career of William Louis Abbott, M.D. (1860–1936) is summarized in *The National Cyclopædia of American Biography*, 27 (1939), 312–13.

19. George Mackenzie arrived in Zanzibar in October 1888 to organize the Mombasa headquarters of the Imperial British East Africa Company (IBEA), to which the British government assigned responsibility for administering its last African sphere of influence; see John S. Galbraith, *Mackinnon and East Africa 1878–1895: A Study in the 'New Imperialism'* (Cambridge: Cambridge University Press, 1972), 150–52.

20. Sayyid Barghash, who suffered from tuberculosis and elephantiasis, died on March 26, 1888. He was succeeded by Sultan Sayyid Khalifa bin Said, who ruled until 1890. See al-Maamiry, *Omani Sultans in Zanzibar*, 23–30.

21. Hermann von Wissmann (1853–1905) is noted for his *Im Innern Afrikas* (Leipzig: Brockhaus, 1888); *Meine zweite Durchquerung Äquatorial-Afrikas vom Kongo zum Zambesi während der Jahre 1886 und 1887* (Berlin: Globus Verlag, 1890), an English translation of which appeared in London in 1891; and *Unter deutsche Flagge quer durch Afrika: Von 1880 bis 1883 ausgeführt vom Paul Pogge und Hermann Wissmann* (Berlin: Walter & Apolant, 1889).

22. The German explorer and imperialist Karl Peters (1856–1918) wrote *New Light on*

Dark Africa: Being the Narrative of the German Emin Pasha Expedition (London: Ward, Lock and Co., 1891).

23. Cecchi had previously traveled in Abyssinia; see his *Da Zeila alle frontiere del Caffa*, 3 vols. (Rome: E. Loescher & Co., 1886). He is discussed briefly in *Enciclopedia italiana di scienze, lettere e arti*, 9 (1931), 593.

24. Alfred Ilg (1854–1916) came to Ethiopia from Zurich in 1879 and for twenty-seven years served Emperor Menelik in a variety of capacities, including counselor for foreign affairs; see Konrad Keller, *Alfred Ilg: Sein Leben und sein Wirken als schweizerischer Kulturbote in Abessinien* (Leipzig: Huber, 1918).

25. For a brief discussion of the career of Nerazzini (1849–1912) see *Enciclopedia italiana di scienze, lettere ed arti*, Appendice 1 (1938), 897.

26. On the career of Luigi Robecchi-Bricchetti (1855–1926) see *Enciclopedia italiana di scienze, lettere ed arti*, 29 (1936), 505.

27. There is a brief discussion of Baron Carl Claus von der Decken (1833–1865), who conducted explorations to Kilimanjaro, along the East African coast, on the Comoro Islands and the Seychelles, and up the Juba River, where he was killed at Bardera, in Müller, *Deutschland—Zanzibar—Ostafrika*, 293n; for more extensive material see *Baron Carl Claus von der Decken's Reisen in Ost-Afrika in den Jahren 1859–1865*, 4 vols. in 6 (Leipzig, Heidelberg: C. F. Winter, 1869–1879).

28. Höhnel refers to Eugène Simon (1848–1924), the author of numerous papers and monographs—see his *Histoire naturelle des araignées*, 2d ed. (Paris: Roret, 1892–1901)— and to the naturalist Félix-Pierre Jousseaume (1835–1921).

29. See Leopold Wölfling (1868–1935), *My Life Story: From Archduke to Grocer* (New York: Dutton & Co., 1931).

30. See Jules Borelli (1853–1941), *Éthiopie méridionale. Journal de mon voyage aux pays Amhara, Oromo et Sidama, septembre 1885 à novembre 1888* (Paris: Ancienne Maison Quantin, 1890).

31. See Sir Richard Francis Burton (1821–1890), *The Lake Regions of Central Africa: A Picture of Exploration*, 2 vols. (London: Longman, Green, Longman, and Roberts, 1860).

32. The relapsing nature of malarial infections accounted for Höhnel's recurring fevers. He had also resisted taking the required doses of quinine, then the only effective prophylactic agent available.

5. In Vienna (1889–1892)

1. Following Rudolf's death, unfounded rumors circulated in court circles that the heir to the throne had been involved with Teleki and other nobles from the Monarchy's eastern half in a conspiracy to have himself crowned King of Hungary; see Brigitte Hamann, *Rudolf: Kronprinz und Rebell* (Vienna and Munich: Amalthea, 1978), 263–85.

2. Eduard Suess (1831–1914), *Das Antlitz der Erde*, 3 vols. in 5 (Prague: F. Tempsky, 1883–1909); translated as *The Face of the Earth*, 5 vols. (Oxford: Clarendon Press, 1902–1924). The famous geologist and paleontologist was professor at the University of Vienna from 1857 until 1901.

3. These sketches are preserved in the *Kartensammlung* of the Austrian National Library; see Ingrid Kretschmer, "Die kartographischen Ergebnisse der Teleki-Höhnel Entdeckungsreise 1887–88," in *Mitteilungen der Österreichischen Geographischen Gesellschaft*, 130 (Jahresband 1988), 54.

4. In her discussion of Höhnel's cartographic activity, Kretschmer observes, "Today we must be filled with astonishment and respect upon viewing the expedition's cartographic publications." "Die kartographischen Ergebnisse der Teleki-Höhnel Entdeckungsreise 1887–88," 55.

5. See Ludwig Ritter von Höhnel, "Ostäquatorial-Afrika zwischen Pangani und dem neuentdeckten Rudolf-See: Ergebnisse der Graf S. Telekischen Expedition 1887–88," in *Petermanns Mitteilungen*, Ergänzungsband 21 (1890), Ergänzungsheft 99.

6. Antoine d'Abbadie (1810–1897) conducted expeditions to Ethiopia in 1836–39 and 1842–48; Roberto Ivens (1850–1898) explored in Angola in 1876–77; and Count Pierre Savorgnan de Brazza (1852–1905) explored the regions of the Ogowe, the lower Congo, and the area north of the Congo between 1875 and 1878.

7. The highest mountain—over 18,600 feet—in the Elburz Mountains, to the northeast of Teheran.

8. Wilhelm Junker, *Dr. Wilh. Junkers Reisen in Afrika, 1875–1886: Nach seinen Tagebüchern*, 3 vols. (Vienna: E. Holzel, 1889–91).

9. See Oskar Lenz, *Wanderungen in Afrika: Studien und Erlebnisse* (Vienna: Verlag der Literarischen Gesellschaft, 1895).

10. See Oskar Baumann, *Durch Massailand zur Nilquelle: Reisen und Forschungen der Massai-Expedition des deutschen Antisklaverei-Komite in den Jahren 1891–1893* (Berlin: D. Reimer, 1894). There is a brief discussion of Baumann (1864–1899) in the exhibition catalogue *Abenteuer Ostafrika: Der Anteil Österreich-Ungarns an der Erforschung Ostafrikas* (Eisenstadt: Amt der Burgenländischen Landesregierung, 1988), 247–48.

11. L. R. von Höhnel, August Rosiwal, Franz Toula, and Eduard Suess, "Beiträge zur geologischen Kenntnis des östlichen Afrika," in *Denkschriften der kaiserlichen Akademie der Wissenschaften, mathematisch-naturwissenschaften Classe*, 58 (1891), 447–584; Höhnel's contribution, "Orographisch-hydrographische Skizzen der Graf Samuel Teleki'schen Expedition 1887," appears on pp. 447–64. Franz Toula was professor of mineralogy and geology at the Technische Hochschule in Vienna, and August Rosiwal was his assistant.

12. On Sultan Sayyid Ali bin Said, who ruled from 1890 to 1893, see Ahmed Hamoud al-Maamiry, *Omani Sultans in Zanzibar (1832–1964)* (New Delhi: Lancers Books, 1988), 31–40.

13. For the German edition of the book, which subsequently appeared in English translation, see Ludwig Ritter von Höhnel, *Zum Rudolf-See und Stephanie-See: Die Forschungsreise des Grafen Samuel Teleki in Ost-Aequatorial-Afrika, 1887–1888* (Vienna: A. Hölder, 1892). Count Teleki kept handwritten diaries in Hungarian of the trip and a subsequent one to Mount Kilimanjaro in 1895. These original diaries are in the Special Collections of Michigan State University Library, East Lansing, Michigan. An unpublished English language translation of these diaries was completed in 1961 and is in the personal library of Geza Teleki in Washington, D.C. See "A Personal Diary of Explorations in East Africa, October 1886–October 1888, by Count Samuel Teleki, with Descriptions of His Pioneer Climbs on Mount Kilimanjaro and Kenya in 1887, His Discoveries of Lakes Rudolf and Stefanie in 1888, and His Return Safari to Mount Kilimanjaro in 1895." Text translated from the handwritten Hungarian version into English by Charles and Vera Teleki, Warkworth, Ontario, Canada, 1961. Count Teleki also sent several lengthy letters in Hungarian to Crown Prince Rudolf documenting in detail various aspects of his first East African journey. These are currently in the collections of the Austrian State Archives, Vienna. For recent analyses of Count Teleki's 1886–1888 journey through East Africa within the broader context of late nineteenth century European colonialism see Pascal James Imperato, *Quest for the Jade Sea. Colonial Competition around an East African Lake* (Boulder, Colo: Westview Press/Harper Collins, 1998)

49–78, 270–77, and Pascal James Imperato, *Arthur Donaldson Smith and the Exploration of Lake Rudolf* (Lakes Success: Medical Society of the State of New York, 1987) 17–23.

6. My Second Expedition to Africa (1892–1894)

1. Count Rudolf Montecuccoli degli Erri (1843–1922), promoted to admiral in 1897, served as *Marinekommandant* and *Chef der Marinesektion* between October 1904 and February 1913; on his administration see Lawrence Sondhaus, *The Naval Policy of Austria-Hungary, 1867–1918: Navalism, Industrial Development, and the Politics of Dualism* (West Lafayette, Ind.: Purdue University Press, 1994), 170–224.

2. On the career of Palisa (1848–1925) see *Österreichisches biographisches Lexikon*, 7 (1978), 300–01.

3. General Oreste Baratieri (1841–1901) is discussed in *Dizionario biografico degli Italiani*, 5 (1963), 782–85; on General Giuseppe Edoardo Arimondi (1846–1896) see *Dizionario biografico*, 4 (1962), 159.

4. The Italian victory at Kassala in the Sudan on July 17, 1894, is discussed in Emilio Bellavita, *La battaglia di Adua: I precendenti—la battaglia—le consequenze (1884–1931)*, 2d ed. (Genoa: I Dioscuri, 1988), 152–59.

5. Although Höhnel ascribes blame for the Italian defeat primarily to Baratieri, he would have done better to place responsibility on the prime minister, Francesco Crispi, who embarked upon a misguided policy of seeking a military victory at all costs. For a brief summary of the battle and the controversy surrounding it, see William L. Langer, *The Diplomacy of Imperialism*, 2d ed. (New York: Knopf, 1956), 277–80. For an account that places the battle in the perspective of Italian colonial policy, see Raffaele Ciasca, *Storia coloniala dell'Italia contemporanea: Da Asab all'impero*, 2d ed. (Milan: Editore Ulrico Hoepli, 1940), 248–65.

6. Lately Thomas (pseud. Robert V. P. Steele) discusses the Chanler family in *A Pride of Lions: The Astor Orphans; The Chanler Chronicle* (New York: William Morrow & Company, Inc., 1971).

7. George E. Galvin (1872–1951) was born in Red Hook, New York, the son of a gardener, Patrick Galvin, who was from County Cork, Ireland, and Sarah Catherine Corbett, who was from Rhinebeck, New York. In 1905, he married Helen Goldner, and they had seven children. In the early part of the twentieth century, he managed Chanler's horse breeding stables in Leesburg, Virginia. Chanler later set him up as a travel agent at the Vanderbilt Hotel in New York City in which he held an interest. Galvin lived in Jamaica, New York, where he died on February 14, 1951, at the age of seventy-nine.

8. See William Astor Chanler, *Through Jungle and Desert: Travels in Eastern Africa* (New York: Macmillan & Co., 1896), 380–82.

9. *Ibid*, 384–85.

10. See Arthur H. Neumann, *Elephant-Hunting in East Equatorial Africa: Being an Account of Three Years' Ivory-Hunting under Mount Kenia and among the Ndorobo Savages of the Lorogi Mountains, including a Trip to the North of Lake Rudolph* (London: Rowland Ward, 1898); see also Monty Brown, *Hunter Away: The Life and Times of Arthur Henry Neumann, 1850–1907* (London: M. Brown, 1993).

11. Höhnel refers to Captain Chauncey Hugh Stigand, who visited Lake Rudolf in 1909. Stigand clearly stated in his book *To Abyssinia through an Unknown Land: An Account of a Journey through Unexplored Regions of British East Africa by Lake Rudolf to the Kingdom of Menelek* (Philadelphia: J.B. Lippincott, 1910), 221–22, that Teleki and Höhnel were the first white men to

visit the Reshiat people. He was inaccurate, however, in saying that the ivory hunter Arthur Neumann was the second to do so, since the American explorer Arthur Donaldson Smith was actually the second white man to see the Reshiat during his 1894–95 trip to Lake Rudolf. In quoting the Reshiat, Stigand unadvisedly used "first" to mean most recent, and thus confusingly says that Neumann was the first, arriving ten years ago, and that Teleki and Höhnel were the second, having arrived twelve years ago. Höhnel understandably interpreted Stigand's quoting of the Reshiat use of "first" as meaning an event that occurred before the second one. Stigand erred by failing to explain to his readers that Reshiat recounting of history started with the most recent (first) event and worked backward.

12. See, e.g., Hermann von Wissmann (1853–1905), *Im Innern Afrikas* (Leipzig: Brockhaus, 1888), and Harald George Carlos Swayne (1860–1940), *Seventeen Trips through Somaliland: A Record of Exploration and Big Game Shooting, 1885 to 1893* (London: R. Ward, 1895).

13. On Cecchi's career and his death on the night of November 25–26, 1896, see *Dizionario biografico degli Italiani*, 23 (1979), 242–46.

14. See Chanler, *Through Jungle and Desert*, 448–82.

15. For a full account of Chanler's difficulties with General Mathews see James White Allen (United States consul in Zanzibar) to the Secretary of State, Zanzibar, April 2, 1894, in National Archives, Washington, D.C.: Despatch Files, Zanzibar, British Africa, 1836–1906, Record Group 59.

16. For recent discussions of Chanler's expedition see Thomas, *A Pride of Lions*, pp. 152–80; Pascal James Imperato, *Arthur Donaldson Smith and the Exploration of Lake Rudolf* (Lake Success, N.Y.: Medical Society of the State of New York, 1987), 24–31; and Pascal James Imperato, *Quest for the Jade Sea: Colonial Competition around an East African Lake* (Boulder, Colo.: Westview Press/Harper Collins, 1998), 79–102.

17. Höhnel wrote an account of the expedition in German but was unable to find a publisher; see Ludwig Ritter von Höhnel, "Reminiscences: An Interview with William Astor Chanler, Jr., 1935," in William Astor Chanler Papers, New York Historical Society. Höhnel did, however, publish the survey results of the expedition, supplemented with astronomical analyses by Dr. J. Palisa; see Ludwig Ritter von Höhnel, "Zur Karte des nordöstlichen Kenia-Gebiets," in *Petermanns Mitteilungen*, 40 (1894), 193–99.

7. Thoughts about Africa

1. In fact, Chanler was born in 1867 and was therefore ten rather than twelve years Höhnel's junior.

2. The career of the Austrian explorer of the Sudan Ernst Marno (1844–1883) is ably discussed in Michael Zach, *Österreicher im Sudan 1820 bis 1914*, Beiträge zur Afrikanistik, vol. 24 (Vienna: Afro-Pub, 1985), 146–63.

3. Ildikó Simanyi takes issue with this statement and observes in her master's thesis, "The reproach that Count Teleki shot every animal that came before his gun may well be justified." See her "Ludwig Ritter von Höhnel (1857–1942): Leben und Wirken" (unpublished master's thesis, University of Vienna, 1988), 102. In fact, Teleki often shot game for trophies; he was particularly interested in shooting elephants for their tusks, which he later sold.

4. Chanler's article "Rifles and Big Game in East Equatorial Africa," written from Daitcho on July 24, 1893, appears in *The Field, the Farm, the Garden, the Country Gentleman's News-*

paper of November 25, 1893 (vol. 82, #2135), 826. Ironically, whereas Chanler strongly championed the lighter and less expensive Winchester or, more especially, the Austrian Mannlicher rifle, Count Teleki in a letter that appeared in the issue of February 3, 1894 (#2145), 155, expressed his strong preference for the "paralyzing effect of the '500 and '577 Express" rifles. Professor J. Michael McBride of the Department of Chemistry at Yale University kindly located Chanler's article in his university library's run of this rare journal.

5. Title of a prose idyll set on the island of Mauritius, published in 1788 by Jacques Henri Bernardin de Saint-Pierre (1737–1814).

6. Höhnel's comments about African peoples reflect not only his personal opinions but more importantly European racial attitudes of the time.

8. At Sea Again (1894–1899)

1. Lieutenant General Sir William Howley Goodenough (b. 1833), who married Countess Anna Kinsky in 1874, served as British military commander in South Africa—not "governor," as Höhnel erroneously states—until his sudden death in 1898; see *Who Was Who 1897–1915* (London: A.C. Black, 1920), 207.

2. See, e.g. Sir David Gill (1843–1914), *A History and Description of the Royal Observatory, Cape of Good Hope* (London: H.M. Stationery Office, 1913).

3. In a letter of August 15, 1996, William Cox, Associate Archivist of the Smithsonian Institution, explains that Höhnel's comment on William Louis Abbott's contributions to the Smithsonian's natural history exhibits "is not as far-fetched as it sounds," for Abbott "was one of America's greatest natural history collectors, donating enormous collections to the Smithsonian between 1890 and 1923."

4. Baron Hermann von Spaun (1833–1919) commanded the active squadron from April until August 1896 and had done so on five previous occasions; see Lawrence Sondhaus, *The Naval Policy of Austria-Hungary, 1867–1918: Navalism, Industrial Development, and the Politics of Dualism* (West Lafayette, Ind.: Purdue University Press, 1994), 387–88. Subsequently, from December 1897 until October 1904, Spaun served as *Marinekommandant* and *Chef der Marinesektion* with the rank of admiral; on his administration see *ibid.*, 142–63. On Moritz Sachs von Hellenau (1844–1934), who retired in 1905 after having attained the rank of vice admiral, see Heinrich Bayer von Bayersburg, *Österreichs Admirale und bedeutende Persönlichkeiten der k.u.k. Kriegsmarine 1867–1918* (Vienna: Bergland Verlag, 1962), 156–58. The career and accomplishments of Grand Admiral Anton Haus are discussed in Sondhaus, *The Naval Policy of Austria-Hungary*, Chapters 6 and 7; for a more extensive account see Paul G. Halpern, *Anton Haus: Österreich-Ungarns Grossadmiral* (Graz: Styria Verlag, 1998).

5. On the archduke (1860–1933) see Bayer von Bayersburg, *Österreichs Admirale 1867–1918*, 72–73.

6. Höhnel's account of his relations with Haus differs in minor details but largely agrees with that which appears in Haus's diary. The incident to which the author refers occurred on May 7, 1896. On the following day, after Höhnel had been summoned before the captain, Haus noted, "As usual, at lunch I offered Höhnel some of my olives, but he declined, and I can see that it's over between us." On August 15, moreover, he wrote, "The relationship with Höhnel remained until the last the same as it was on May 8. While on duty we behaved perfectly correctly toward one another; off duty it was as if the other did not exist. In any event, Höhnel's way of thinking is so different from mine that even without the incident we never would have been intimate friends. He had a different opinion from me on

almost every person, every book, and just about everything else." See "Tagebuch Admiral Haus. Übertragungen der Tagebücher aus der Stenographie in die Maschinenschrift," vol. 3, 62 and 91–92, B241:5/III, Kriegsarchiv, Vienna.

7. Piero Pieri surveys the military career of General Antonio Baldissera (1838–1917) in *Dizionario biografico degli Italiani*, 5 (1963), 499–502.

8. The fate of the fleet of Rear Admiral Pascual Cervera y Topete (1839–1909) is discussed briefly in John L. Offner, *An Unwanted War: The Diplomacy of the United States and Spain over Cuba, 1895–1898* (Chapel Hill: University of North Carolina Press, 1992), 203–04.

9. The sinking of the *Maine*, which may well have been the result of an internal explosion rather than an act of sabotage, is discussed in Peggy and Harold Samuels, *Remembering the Maine* (Washington: Smithsonian Institution Press, 1995), which also contains much material on Capt. Charles Dwight Sigsbee. Offner discusses the background to the conflict in *An Unwanted War*, 1–193.

10. On Whitney Warren (1864–1943) see the *National Cyclopædia of American Biography*, 34 (1948), 173–74; Charles Delevan Wetmore (1866–1941), who began his career as a lawyer but whose architectural talents Warren discovered, is discussed in *ibid.*, 42 (1958), 213–14. The two men joined to form the firm of Warren and Wetmore in 1898 and gained distinction for their designs of hotels, railroad stations, and other public buildings.

11. According to his autobiography, *The Navy as I Have Known It: 1849–1899* (London: Cassell and Company, 1904), 451–52, Admiral Sir Edmund Robert Fremantle (1836–1929) commanded at Portsmouth from June 1896 until June 1899.

12. On the assassination of the Empress Elisabeth on September 10, 1898, by the Italian anarchist Luigi Lucheni see Brigitte Hamann, *The Reluctant Empress: Elisabeth of Austria* (New York: Alfred A. Knopf, 1986), 367–70.

9. Aide-de-Camp to Emperor Francis Joseph I (1899–1903)

1. Baron Arthur von Bolfras (1838–1922) served as chief of the emperor's military chancellery from 1889 until Francis Joseph's death in 1916; see *Österreichisches biographisches Lexikon*, 1 (1957), 99.

2. Count Eduard von Paar (1837–1919) had served as adjutant general to the emperor since 1887; see *ibid.*, 7 (1978), 275–76.

3. Prince Rudolf von und zu Liechtenstein (1838–1908) served as *Obersthofmeister* from 1896 until his death; see *ibid.*, 5 (1972), 206.

4. Admiral Nicholas Horthy gives an account of his service as aide-de-camp in his *Memoirs* (New York: Robert Speller & Sons, 1957), 43–60.

5. Laurenz Mayer (1828–1912) held the post of *Hof- und Burgpfarrer* and was the emperor's confessor; see *Österreichisches biographisches Lexikon*, 5 (1972), 437.

6. Francis Joseph was born in 1830.

7. Ernst August, Duke of Cumberland and Crown Prince of Hanover (1845–1923), went into exile in Austria following the Austro-Prussian War of 1866 and lived in Gmunden, not far from Bad Ischl; see *Österreichisches biographisches Lexikon*, 1 (1957), 159.

8. On Baron—later Count—Friedrich Beck-Rzikowsky (1830–1906) see Edmund Glaise von Horstenau, *Franz Josephs Weggefährte: Das Leben des Generalstabschefs, Grafen Beck* (Zurich: Amalthea-Verlag, 1930), and Scott. W. Lackey, *The Rebirth of the Habsburg Army: Friedrich Beck and the Rise of the General Staff*, Contributions in Military Studies, no. 161; Westport, Conn.: Greenwood Press, 1995).

9. Together with Karl Weyprecht (1838–1881), the cartographer, alpinist, and North Pole explorer Julius von Payer (1841–1915) led the 1872–74 Austrian expedition to the North Pole following a preliminary expedition to the Arctic in 1871; see Österreichisches biographisches Lexikon, 7 (1978), 374–75.

10. It has not been possible to locate this needle of a quotation in the haystack of Barras' memoirs, which appeared in four volumes in the 1890s. For the German edition, which Höhnel is most likely to have read, see George Duruy, ed., Memoiren von Paul Barras, Mitglied des Direktoriums, 4 vols. (Stuttgart: Deutsche Verlags-Anstalt, 1895–96).

11. See, however, the comment of the emperor's former valet in Eugen Ketterl, The Emperor Francis Joseph I: An Intimate Study by his Valet de Chambre (London: Skeffington & Son, 1929), 54: "Kind as the Emperor was to his servants and subjects, he could be equally hard and pitiless to persons of a rank more nearly approaching his own, and to members of his own family. The Emperor—who never refused to grant to me, his valet, any wish expressed at the right time and in the right place—was, nevertheless, accustomed to taking strict and intransigent measures against people of high degree. It is, however, a matter of absolute fact that he kept this imperious manner, often so stressed, solely for the audience chamber and for his study. I read in a recently published book the statement that the Emperor considered only members of the baronial and princely houses or of the very oldest noble families as really being in the first rank, and then only when they did not hold State or Court appointments, while he mistrusted everybody else. This is an assertion which I certainly cannot make."

12. Karl Lueger (1844–1910) served as mayor of Vienna from 1897 until his death; for a recent biography see Richard S. Geehr, Karl Lueger: Mayor of Fin de Siècle Vienna (Detroit: Wayne State University Press, 1990).

13. Baron Edmund von Krieghammer (1832–1906) served as Austro-Hungarian Reichskriegsminister from 1893 through 1902; see Österreichisches biographisches Lexikon, 4 (1969), 271.

14. Alois Kraus (1840–1926) directed the menagerie at Schönbrunn from 1879 until his retirement in 1919 and brought the institution to international prominence; see ibid., 4 (1969), 222.

15. Milan I ruled as prince since 1868 and proclaimed himself king in 1882; he abdicated in 1889 in favor of his son, Alexander I.

16. The conservative politician Prince Alfred von und zu Liechtenstein (1842–1907) achieved prominence as the leader of the clerical wing of the right in the Austrian Herrenhaus; see Österreichisches biographisches Lexikon, 5 (1972), 202–03.

17. In his English manuscript Höhnel provides the following explanatory note: "A nickname given to the Austrians, being a people who spoke the same language as the Swabians, who, after the withdrawal of the Turks from Hungary, had emigrated in the eighteenth century to Hungary and settled in many localities, to the economic advantage of the country."

18. Baron Géza Fejéváry de Komlós-Keresztes (1833–1914) served as Hungarian Minister of Defense in a series of cabinets between 1884 and 1903 and as Minister President from June 1905 until April 1906.

19. Lónyay (1863–1946) married Crown Prince Rudolf's widow in 1900.

20. Francis Ferdinand's attitudes toward aesthetic matters—though dedicated to the cause of historic preservation, he was by no means favorable to contemporary art—are discussed in Jeroen Bastiaan van Heerde, Staat und Kunst: Staatliche Kunstförderung 1895–1918 (Vienna, Cologne, Weimar: Böhlau Verlag, 1993), 272–78, and Robert Hoffmann, Erzherzog Franz

Ferdinand und der Fortschritt: Altstadterhaltung und bürgerlicher Modernisierungswille in Salzburg (Vienna: Böhlau Verlag, 1994), 39–60.

10. My First Years as Commander (1903–1905)

1. Höhnel's service record indicates that he was promoted to *Fregattenkapitän*, the equivalent of a junior captain in the United States Navy, on May 1, 1903, at the conclusion of his service as aide-de-camp to the emperor; see, Marine Qualificationsliste Nr. 2118: Ludwig Ritter von Höhnel, Kriegsarchiv, Vienna.

2. Höhnel refers here to the anchorages of Treporti (Tri luke) and Trepozzi—"three ports" and "three springs" respectively—which lie not too far from one another on the island of Curzola (Korčula).

3. According to the table provided by Lawrence Sondhaus, *The Naval Policy of Austria-Hungary, 1867–1918: Navalism, Industrial Development, and the Politics of Dualism* (West Lafayette, Ind.: Purdue University Press, 1994), 388, the commander of the squadron from December 1902 until June 1904 was Leodegar Kneissler von Maixdorf (1844–1925), whose career is surveyed in Heinrich Bayer von Bayersburg, *Österreichs Admirale und bedeutende Persönlichkeiten der k.u.k. Kriegsmarine 1867–1918* (Vienna: Bergland Verlag, 1962), 102–5.

4. Admiral Julius von Ripper (1847–1914) preceded Kneissler as squadron commander and subsequently succeeded him in that post; see Sondhaus, *The Naval Policy of Austria-Hungary, 1867–1918*, 388. Bayer von Bayersburg, *op. cit.*, 150–52, provides a biography of Ripper.

5. For an example of Szél's propaganda advocating ties with Abyssinia see the materials in Handelsministerium, Department 35, Fasz. 1163, "Expedition Arnold Szél nach Ethiopia," Allgemeines Verwaltungsarchiv, Vienna.

6. Count Agenor Goluchowski von Goluchowo (1849–1921) served as minister of foreign affairs from 1895 until 1906; his policies are discussed in F. R. Bridge, *The Habsburg Monarchy among the Great Powers, 1815–1918* (New York: Berg, 1990), 207–68.

7. Emperor Francis Joseph formally approved of sending an expedition under Höhnel's leadership in a decision signed at Gödöllö on December 4, 1904; see Kabinettskanzlei Akten, 3236 ex 1904, Haus-, Hof- und Staatsarchiv, Vienna. By a decision signed at Mürzsteg on January 9, 1905, the monarch specifically empowered Höhnel to conclude a most-favored-nation treaty with Menelik; see Kabinettskanzlei Akten, 87 ex 1905, Haus-Hof- und Staatsarchiv, Vienna.

8. Bairu Tafla, *Ethiopia and Austria: A History of Their Relations*, Äthiopische Forschungen, Band 35 (Wiesbaden: Harrassowitz Verlag, 1994), 95, lists the major participants in the expedition as Legation Secretary Count Erwein Schönborn-Buchheim and Vice Consul Friedrich Götz, both from the Foreign Ministry; Lieutenant Leopold Huber Edler von Scheibenhain and Cadet Alexander Prince zu Hohenlohe-Waldenburg-Schillingsfürst from the naval section of the Ministry of War; Friedrich Julius Bieber of the Ministry of Commerce; Alfons von Mylius; the engineers Franz Jina and Paul A. Santho (in some contemporary correspondence the name is also spelled "Szantó" and "Szanto"); and Count Ladislaus Széchényi von Sarvar und Felsö-Bidek, who represented the Hungarian government.

9. There is a description and a photograph of the *Panther* in *Marine—gestern, heute: Nachrichten aus dem Marinewesen*, 13/4 (1986), 175–77.

10. The *Panther* called at Djibouti during the Russo-Japanese War, which began in February 1904 and was not formally ended until the conclusion of the Treaty of Portsmouth on September 5, 1905.

11. To the Court of Emperor Menelik of Abyssinia
(February 4 to April 10, 1905)

1. The title *ras* in Amharic means "prince." Ras Makonnen was the father of the future Emperor Haile Selassie. Menelik had originally designated his cousin, Ras Makonnen, as his successor, a decision contested by other powerful factions among the nobility. However, Makonnen died of stomach cancer in March, 1906. Menelik then designated his own grandson, Lij Iyasu (his daughter's son), as heir, and set up a regency council. Iyasu, still a teenager, launched initiatives such as accommodating Moslems living in the empire. When Menelik died in December, 1913, Iyasu was not immediately crowned emperor. Although he successfully neutralized rival factions, headed the best equipped and most powerful army in the country, and adhered to Orthodox Christianity, his efforts to secure a place for Moslems in the country and his early inclinations to support Germany and Turkey at the outset of World War I caused a powerful reaction against him in Abyssinia. In 1916, the nobles and church leaders decided to depose Lij Iyasu and install Menelik's daughter, Zawditu, as empress with Lij Tafari, Makonnen's son, as heir apparent. The latter eventually became Regent and succeeded Zawditu on her death in April, 1931 as Haile Selassie I. At the time of Höhnel's visit in 1905, Tafari was only fourteen years of age. For a detailed discussion of the power struggles surrounding succession to the throne after Menelik's death, see Harold Marcus, *The Life and Times of Menelik II. Ethiopia 1844–1913* (Oxford: Clarendon Press, 1975), 214–81.

2. On the empress see Chris Prouty, *Empress Taytu and Menilek II: Ethiopia 1883–1910* (Trenton, N.J.: The Red Sea Press, 1986).

3. On unsuccessful attempts by Russians to use an alleged identity between the Orthodox and the Abyssinian churches as a means of advancing their commercial and political interests in Ethiopia, see Carlo Zaghi, *I Russi in Etiopia*, in Quaderni di critica storica, 2 vols. (Naples: Guida Editore, 1972), vol. 1, 42–49. The visit of Mateos is mentioned briefly in Czeslaw Jesman, *The Russians in Ethiopia: An Essay in Futility* (London: Chatto and Windus, 1958), 45, who observes, "Abuna Mateos, who visited Russia in 1902, could find no common theological ground with the Orthodox Church and he was equally unimpressed by the Russian Church and the Russian Government." Also valuable is Patrick Joseph Rollins, "Russia's Ethiopian Adventure, 1888–1905" (unpublished doctoral dissertation, Syracuse University, 1967), 323–26.

4. In Amharic, *lij* means "child of noble birth."

5. The reference is to Friedrich Rosen (1856–1935), who unfortunately includes no information on his mission to Ethiopia in his *Memories of a German Diplomatist* (New York: E. P. Dutton and Co., 1930).

6. The full text of the letter is published in Ludwig Ritter von Höhnel, *Mein Leben zur See, auf Forschungsreisen und bei Hofe: Erinnerungen eines österreichischen Seeoffiziers (1857–1909)* (Berlin: Verlag von Reimar Hobbing, 1926), 267. For a scholarly discussion and evaluation of Menelik's reign, see Marcus, *The Life and Times of Menelik II: Ethiopia 1844–1913*.

7. Sir John Lane Harrington (1865–1927) arrived in Ethiopia as Britain's first diplomatic representative to the court of Emperor Menelik in 1903 and played an important role in

negotiating borders between Ethiopia and British territories. See Edward Coltrin Keefer, "The Career of Sir John L. Harrington: Empire and Ethiopia, 1884–1918," Ph.D. diss., University Microfilms, Ann Arbor, Michigan, 1974.

8. The official correspondence generated on the bank matter can be found in the Administrative Registratur F 23/29: Finanzwesen Banken 1903–1908, Convolut "Banken, Ethiopien," Haus-, Hof- und Staatsarchiv, Vienna. Additional materials can be found in Administrative Registratur F 37/48, Convolut "Ethiopien 1." The archival record suggests that Höhnel's skepticism regarding the bank project was generally justified and that the private persons who accompanied the mission were not disinclined to use the matter for their own potential personal gain.

9. Even Vice Consul Götz, who was by no means an admirer of Höhnel, warned in a report to Vienna in June 1905 against trying to see "in Abyssinia an African Japan and in its inhabitants suitable objects for [economic and cultural] Europeanization;" Administrative Registratur F 23/29: Finanzwesen Banken 1903–1908, Convolut "Banken, Ethiopien," Haus-, Hof- und Staatsarchiv, Vienna.

10. According to Bairu Tafla, *Ethiopia and Austria: A History of Their Relations*, Äthiopische Forschungen, vol. 35; (Wiesbaden: Harrassowitz Verlag, 1994), 179, Franz Jina remained for more than three months, during which time he repaired "not only the mint, but also a steam-roller, water pipe and electrical dynamo."

11. There is a wealth of material on Nicolai Stepanovitch Leontiev and his machinations in Ethiopia in Zaghi, *I Russi in Etiopia*; see especially vol. 1, 244–74 and vol. 2, 70–110, 135–75, and 216–17. According to Rollins, "Russia's Ethiopian Adventure," 256, Leontiev arrived in Ethiopia late in 1897 with 30,000 rifles—and not 40,000, as Höhnel states—as a gift from Tsar Nicholas II. Leontiev's subsequent activities in the Ethiopian equatorial provinces are discussed in Jesman, *The Russians in Ethiopia*, 110–25, and Marcus, *The Life and Times of Menelik II*, 187–89. See also Pascal James Imperato, *Quest for the Jade Sea. Colonial Competition around an East African Lake* (Boulder, Colo.: Westview Press/Harper Collins, 1998), 177–81, 191–96, 222, 225, 234, and Chris Prouty, *Empress Taytu and Menilek II: Ethiopia 1883–1910*, 121–30, 157–58, 184–86, 192–98, 200–04, 262–64.

12. Léon Chefneux was a retired French army captain who had instructed Menelik's military in the use of rapid fire ordinance. He had also expedited arms shipments to Menelik and served for a time as one of his trusted foreign advisers. Although he had previously represented French interests, he later became an arms merchant whom Leontiev consulted when he was exploring private arms trade with Menelik. See Chris Prouty, *Empress Taytu and Menilek II: Ethiopia 1883–1910*, 16, 84, 88, 94, 106–07, 123, 129.

13. For a discussion and an evaluation of Höhnel's mission to Ethiopia, see Tafla, *Ethiopia and Austria*, 96–117.

12. With the H.M.S. *Panther* to India, Australia, and China (1905–1906)

1. In her study of Höhnel's career, Ildikó Simanyi offers the following explanation for this oblique reference: "During Höhnel's absence there was apparently a series of difficulties with the crew of the *Panther*. Precisely what happened can no longer be determined, since the ship's log book and other materials were lost, in all probability shortly after the end of World War I. According to oral evidence, however, while in port in Djibouti the crew of the

Panther, together with the crew of a German ship, had gotten drunk and apparently had shot at lanterns in the harbor area." Simanyi concludes that Höhnel failed to mention the incident because he did not wish to bring dishonor upon his ship's crew. The temporary commander to whom Höhnel refers was *Linienschiffsleutnant* Miroslav Makuc. On this matter see Ildikó Simanyi, "Ludwig Ritter von Höhnel (1857–1942): Leben und Wirken" (unpublished master's thesis, University of Vienna, 1988), 190–91.

2. Götz's letter of complaint, written from Zanzibar on May 12, 1905, is preserved in Administrative Registratur F 37/48, Convolut "Ethiopien 1," #128, Haus-, Hof- und Staatsarchiv, Vienna. According to a marginal notation, the matter was laid *ad acta* on the order of the foreign minister.

3. There is a brief biography of Richard John Seddon (b. 1845), who served as premier from 1893 until his death in 1906, in *An Encyclopaedia of New Zealand*, 3 (1966), 216–19.

4. It is probable that the rumors to which Höhnel refers stemmed from complaints members of the ship's crew had expressed in letters to their families concerning their treatment in port by the ship's executive officer, *Linienschiffsleutnant* Makuc. Such is the conclusion of Ildikó Simanyi, "Ludwig Ritter von Höhnel," 203, who cites a passage from the diary of the ship's cook, Josef Rozehnal. As the Czech cook notes, only late in the voyage "did the commander [Höhnel] realize what was going on. To be sure, he had known the guilty party for some time and was by no means favorably inclined toward him. But earlier he had had no inkling that the man was so coarse and so lacking in humanity, and he was unaware that he was falsifying his reports in a manner that made them seem plausible. That was understandable, since the commander was very much occupied with his numerous official and social obligations in port, which left him little time for anything else."

5. The *Kaiser Franz Joseph I* was a 4,000–ton cruiser that was considerably larger than the 1,500–ton *Panther*.

6. See note 4 in the present chapter for independent confirmation of Höhnel's analysis of the situation.

7. The diplomatic crisis to which Höhnel refers, which revolved around Germany's opposition to French territorial ambitions in Morocco, was occasioned by a visit of Emperor William II to Tangier on March 31, 1905. Here he delivered a speech in which he expressed his determination to do everything in his power to safeguard German interests in Morocco, stressing his intention to keep the area open to competition by all nations. The emperor's action seriously strained relations among the European powers and led to an international conference at Algeciras which met between January 16 and April 7, 1906. At the time the *Panther* called at Haiphong, the crisis had yet to be resolved, and there were indeed fears that war might break out. Eugene N. Anderson thoroughly treats the matter in *The First Moroccan Crisis, 1904–1906* (Chicago: University of Chicago Press, 1930).

8. There is a brief discussion of the origins and the establishment of the French settlement at Kwanchow in Alfred Bonningue, *La France à Kouang-Tchéou-Wan* (Paris: Éditions Berger-Levraut, 1931), 7–22.

13. My Last Years in Active Service (1906–1909)

1. During the Russo-Japanese War, Iwao Oyama (1842–1916) served as supreme commander in Manchuria.

2. In point of fact, Höhnel had not remained in one rank for "fully eight years." Either

deliberately or out of forgetfulness, he overlooks his promotion in May 1903 from *Korvettenkapitän* to *Fregattenkapitän*. See p. 333, note 1.

3. *An Illustrated History of the Jamestown Exposition* (Hampton Roads, Va.: Hampton Roads Naval Museum, n.d.) provides a brief account of the exposition. Erwin F. Sieche discusses Austria's participation in the festivities in "Austria-Hungary's Last Naval Visit to the USA," in *Warship International*, 27/2 (1990), 142–59.

4. For a brief account of the career of Vice Admiral Assheton Curzon-Howe (1850–1911) see *Dictionary of National Biography*, Supplement 1901–11 (1912), 457–58.

5. Höhnel's promotion took effect on May 1, 1907; see Marine, Qualificationsliste Nr. 2118: Ludwig Ritter von Höhnel, Kriegsarchiv, Vienna.

6. In his autobiography, *A Sailor's Log: Recollections of Forty Years of Naval Life* (New York: D. Appleton & Company, 1901), Robley Dunglison Evans (1846–1912) covers his career through the Spanish-American War.

7. William Woodward Phelps (1869–1938) is discussed in the *National Cyclopædia of American Biography*, 30 (1943), 206–07.

8. Baron Ladislaus Hengelmüller von Hengervár (1845–1917) served as Austro-Hungarian ambassador to the United States from 1894 until his retirement in 1913; see *Österreichisches biographisches Lexikon*, 2 (1959), 272.

9. On Charles Henry Davis (1845–1921) see *Dictionary of American Biography*, 5 (1930), 107–08.

10. John Elliot Pillsbury (1846–1919) is discussed in *Dictionary of American Biography*, 14 (1934), 606–07. Pillsbury's scientific publications include *Report on Deep-Sea Current Work in the Gulf Stream* (Washington, D.C.: Government Printing Office, 1886); for a popular account, see his article "The Grandest and Most Mighty Terrestrial Phenomenon: The Gulf Stream," in *National Geographic Magazine*, 23 (1912), 767–78.

11. The jurist, historian, and politician James Bryce (Viscount Bryce) served as British ambassador to the United States from February 1907 until April 1913; see *Dictionary of National Biography*, Supplement 1922–30 (1937), 127–35.

12. The artist Robert Winthrop Chanler is discussed in Lately Thomas (pseud. Robert V. P. Steele), *A Pride of Lions: The Astor Orphans; The Chanler Chronicle* (New York: William Morrow & Company, Inc., 1971), 129–46, 186–87, and 239–41. Since Höhnel and Chanler had last met, the latter had participated as an army officer in the Battle of Santiago (1898) and had been elected to a term in the U.S. House of Representatives (1899–1901).

13. William Astor Chanler married the popular American actress and operetta star Beatrice Ashley on December 4, 1903, at which time she terminated her career on the stage. Their sons William A. Chanler, Jr., and Sidney Ashley Chanler were born on September 24, 1904, and November 17, 1907, respectively. At the time of Höhnel's visit, the family was living in Great Neck, New York.

14. On the marriage of Marie Bonaparte (1882–1962) to George, Prince of Greece (1869–1957), see Celia Bertin, *Marie Bonaparte: A Life* (New York: Harcourt Brace Jovanovich, 1982), 91–94.

15. King George I of the Hellenes (1845–1913) ruled from 1863 until his assassination in Thessaloniki on March 18, 1913; he was married to the Grand Duchess Olga of Russia (1851–1926).

16. For the chargé's account of the *Sankt Georg*'s visit, see William D. Godsey, Jr., *Unter zwei Kaisern. Lebenserinnerungen des k.u.k. außerordentlichen und bevollmächtigten Ministers Rudolf Freiherrn Mittag von Lenkheym*, to be published as a special number of the *Mitteilungen des Österreichischen Staatsarchivs*.

17. The reference is to Admiral Julius von Ripper, who served as port admiral in Pola from December 1905 through February 1913; see Heinrich Bayer von Bayersburg, *Österreichs Admirale und bedeutende Persönlichkeiten der k.u.k. Kriegsmarine 1867–1918* (Vienna: Bergland Verlag, 1962), 152.

18. On the circumstances surrounding Höhnel's decision to retire from the navy, see the Introduction, xix–xx.

19. See "Vortrag des Marinekommandanten und Chef des Reichskriegsministeriums Abteilung 1, ddo 2. Juli 1909, No. 2435," M.K.S.M. 2102 ex 1909, Kriegsarchiv, Vienna.

20. In fact, the title *Kontreadmiral* was conferred by a decision of the emperor on June 18, 1910, less than one full year after Höhnel's retirement, and not, as Höhnel suggests, in 1912. See "Vortrag des Marinekommandanten und Chef des Reichskriegsministeriums Abteilung 1, ddo 12. Juni 1910, No. 5272," M.K.S.M. 1592 ex 1910, Kriegsarchiv, Vienna.

Epilogue

1. Ildikó Simanyi, "Ludwig Ritter von Höhnel (1857–1942): Leben und Wirken" (unpublished master's thesis, University of Vienna, 1988), 11.

2. Simanyi, *op. cit.*, 220–25, provides a list of the many objects Höhnel or his niece by marriage, Rosa Zündel, donated to the Museum für Völkerkunde in Vienna and the Afrika-Museum at Schloss Marchegg in Lower Austria.

3. See Eugen Oberhummer, "Ludwig Ritter von Höhnel," in *Petermanns Mitteilungen*, 88 (1942), 183–84. Oberhummer amplifies upon his brief remarks in the article "Ludwig Ritter v. Höhnel zum Gedächtnis," in *Mitteilungen der Geographischen Gesellschaft Wien*, 86 (1943), 267–70. See also Josef Breu, "Zum 25. Todestag von Ludwig Ritter von Höhnel," in *Mitteilungen der Österreichischen Geographischen Gesellschaft*, 109 (1967), 434–35.

4. In introducing Höhnel's 1938 two-part article on the exploration of the Lake Rudolf region, Sir Vivian stressed that Höhnel "continues to take a lively interest in all African matters;" see V. E. Fuchs, "Foreword to Admiral von Höhnel's Manuscript," in *Journal of the Royal African Society*, 37 (1938), 18.

5. Interview with Pascal James Imperato, Camden, Maine, August 13, 1997.

6. *Denn Österreich lag einst am Meer. Das Leben des Admirals Alfred von Koudelka*, ed. Lothar Baumgartner (Graz: H. Weishaupt Verlag, 1987), 90.

7. The building was constructed in 1873 according to plans of the architect Ludwig Zettl; see Felix Czeike, *III, Landstraße*, Wiener Bezirkskulturführer, 3 (Vienna and Munich: Jugend und Volk Verlagsgesellschaft, 1984), 51. On the Palais Metternich, which was acquired by the Italian government in 1908 to serve as its embassy, see *ibid.*, 56.

8. Höhnel to Chanler, Vienna, March 9, 1927. Because all quotations from the Höhnel-Chanler correspondence are to be found in the William Astor Chanler Papers at Rokeby, footnotes will be provided only where the author of the quotation or the date of composition is not clear from the context. In contrast to the thirteen preceding chapters, where Höhnel's prose has received the same sort of editorial intervention to which it would have been subjected had he succeeded in finding an American publisher in the 1920s, passages from his correspondence are reproduced as he wrote them. Höhnel's faulty grammar, punctuation, and orthography have, in other words, been retained.

9. Höhnel to Chanler, October 7, 1925. Whereas Höhnel here gives the length of his stay in Transylvania as sixteen months, a short time earlier, in a letter of July 2, he states that he and his wife had spent eighteen months in Romania.

10. In his correspondence Höhnel fails to provide on a regular basis the precise sort of information on his salary and pension that might allow for an accurate assessment of the financial situation in which he and his wife found themselves. In the just quoted letter of January 16, 1921, Höhnel writes: "The pay is . . . not quite adequate . . . 7000 Crowns per month. For me this means, that we are out of the water; it is an addition of 84,000 crowns to my pension, which is now about 26,000 crowns, which takes off all worries for the future of[f] our minds." The only other figures he gives come in a letter of November 30, 1921, where he writes, for example, that his pension had been increased to 12,000 Krone monthly and adds, "To this comes the gradually increased salary, which I get from the A.R.C. (it began with 7000, amounts now to 41,000 cr. p. m.) These sums would certainly not [be] sufficient, to cover the expenses, but meanwhile I have discovered, that my postage stamp Collection is a most productive source of money." Because, however, this was a period of rampant inflation, figures such as these give no indication of real purchasing power.

11. It would be inappropriate to encumber an epilogue to memoirs that deal primarily with the nineteenth century with a treatise on the history of Austria's economic and fiscal tribulations in the twentieth. Those unable to read German will find an exhausting wealth of information in Charles A. Gulick's *Austria: From Habsburg to Hitler*, 2 vols. (Berkeley and Los Angeles: University of California Press, 1948); more succinct, and also more technical, is the study by Eduard März, *Austrian Banking and Financial Policy: Creditanstalt at a Turning Point, 1913–1923* (New York: St. Martin's Press, 1984), especially part 5, "Inflation and Stabilization," 383–557. Brief accounts in German of the inflation and the subsequent stabilization of the Austrian currency, and the social consequences of both, can be found in Hanns Leo Mikoletzky, *Österreichische Zeitgeschichte: Vom Ende der Monarchie bis zur Gegenwart* (Vienna and Munich: Österreichischer Bundesverlag, 1969), 3d ed., 90–93, 99–106, and 183–94; also valuable is Karl Ausch, *Als die Banken fielen: Zur Soziologie der politischen Korruption* (Vienna, Frankfurt, and Zurich: Europa Verlag, 1968), and Karl Bachinger and Herbert Matis, *Der österreichische Schilling: Geschichte einer Währung* (Graz, Vienna, and Cologne: Verlag Styria, 1974), 11–146.

12. Höhnel to Chanler, March 7, 1921.

13. Höhnel to Chanler, April 18, 1922.

14. Höhnel to Chanler, July 2, 1925.

15. Chanler to Höhnel, October 3, 1925.

16. "We have taken due note," Chanler's bankers assured him on October 21, 1931, "that no mention of your name is to appear in the correspondence with the beneficiary, for whom we will use a white envelope." Bankers Trust Company, Paris, to William Astor Chanler, Rokeby Papers.

17. Höhnel to Chanler, July 4, 1929.

18. Personal communication from John Winthrop Aldrich, November 2, 1986.

19. Höhnel to Beatrice Chanler, January 3, 1939.

20. Chanler to Höhnel, March 22, 1923.

21. Höhnel to Chanler, December 7, 1920.

22. Höhnel to Chanler, May 29, 1923. Sir Ernest Charles Thomas Troubridge (1862–1926) was appointed British representative to the International Danube Commission in 1920

and served as its president until March 1924; see *Dictionary of National Biography 1922–30* (London: Oxford University Press, 1937), 858–60.

23. Chanler to Höhnel, October 2, 1923; Höhnel to Chanler, October 8, 1923.

24. Ludwig Ritter von Höhnel, *Mein Leben zur See, auf Forschungsreisen und bei Hofe: Erinnerungen eines österreichischen Seeoffiziers (1857–1909)* (Berlin: Verlag von Reimar Hobbing, 1926).

25. Höhnel to Chanler, October 25, 1926. The editors have not succeeded in tracking down the reviews to which Höhnel refers. It appears, moreover, that no journal in the United States, where comparatively few copies of *Mein Leben zur See* exist, gave attention to the book.

26. Höhnel to Chanler, May 3, 1930.

27. Ludwig Ritter von Höhnel, "The Lake Rudolf Region," in *Journal of the Royal African Society*, 37 (1938), 21–45, 206–26.

28. Höhnel to Chanler, December 30, 1927. On the American rocket expert and physician Darwin Oliver Lyon, who died in his fiftieth year in Valhalla, New York, on April 15, 1937, see the obituary in the *New York Times* for April 16, according to which, "Dr. Lyon received the degree of M.A. from Columbia University in 1908 and a Ph. D. in psychology in 1917. His dissertation on 'Memory and the Learning Process' [Baltimore: Warwick & York, Inc., 1917] had a wide sale," (p. 23).

29. Höhnel to Chanler, February 14, 1928. One of the articles, entitled "Das periodische System in neuer Anordnung," appeared on page 17 of the *Neue Freie Presse* for July 28, 1928, and is included in the Chanler Papers.

30. Höhnel to Beatrice Chanler, April 15, 1939. It was not always so, however. Höhnel's correspondence with Chanler indicates that he and his wife on more than one occasion spent the summer in Bohemia and that in the summer of 1925 he visited Chanler in Paris; see, e.g., his letters of July 2, 1925, written after his return from France and immediately prior to his departure to stay for three weeks with friends in Bohemia, and of September 2, 1929, announcing his return from an August vacation in Czechoslovakia. As photographs document, moreover, on June 13, 1934, Höhnel attended—alone, without his wife—the wedding of Sidney Ashley Chanler to Princess Maria Antonia de Bragança, sister of Dom Duarte, Pretender to the Portuguese throne, at Schloss Seebenstein, outside Vienna. (Sidney Ashley Chanler drew attention to the absence at his wedding of Frau Höhnel in an interview with Pascal James Imperato in Camden, Maine, on July 6, 1994.)

31. Höhnel to Chanler, January 31, 1923.

32. The motto chosen by Höhnel's father upon his elevation to the nobility in 1868 was *Respice finem*—"Consider the end." See Hofadelsakt Gottfried Höhnel 1867, Allgemeines Verwaltungsarchiv, Vienna.

33. Despite its age, the most thorough English-language account of the Austrian political scene under the First Republic is to be found in Gulick, *Austria: From Habsburg to Hitler*, which discusses the electoral situation in chapter 14, "Struggle for Majority, 1923–1927" (vol. 1, 683–713).

34. Here Höhnel refers to either Friedrich Adler or his father Viktor, and to Karl Seitz, Otto Bauer, Robert Danneberg, and Julius Deutsch, all significant Socialist leaders.

35. The Hitler regime was terrible for Valeska von Höhnel for at least two reasons. On the one hand, upon her husband's death she became dependent on a reduced widow's pension. On the other, that pension was further reduced as a result of difficulties she encountered as a result of National Socialist racial policies. For details about the latter pension reduction see note 44 of the Introduction.

36. Copies of the death notices for Höhnel and his wife are preserved in Qualificationsliste, Nr. 2118: Ludwig Ritter von Höhnel, fol. 8v, 7v, Kriegsarchiv, Vienna. The location of Höhnel's grave at Vienna's Central Cemetery is Gruppe 15e, Reihe 3, Grab 32; see Simanyi, "Ludwig Ritter von Höhnel," 12, 15. On June 8, 1972, a commemorative plaque was unveiled on the exterior of the building at Reisnerstrasse 61 where Höhnel had long resided; see ibid., 23. There is a Ludwig von Höhnel-Gasse in Vienna's 10th District; see Friedrich Javorsky, *Lexikon der Wiener Strassennamen* (Vienna and Munich: Verlag für Jugend und Volk, 1964), 157.

BIBLIOGRAPHY

Abenteuer Ostafrika: Der Anteil Österreich-Ungarns an der Erforschung Ostafrikas. Eisenstadt: Amt der Burgenländischen Landesregierung, 1988.

Adlgasser, Franz. *American Individualism Abroad: Herbert Hoover, die American Relief Administration und Österreich, 1919–1923*. Dissertationen der Universität Salzburg, 41. Vienna: VWGÖ, 1993.

al-Maamiry, Ahmed Hamoud. *Omani Sultans in Zanzibar (1832–1964)*. New Delhi: Lancers Books, 1988.

Amin, Mohamed. *Cradle of Mankind*. London: Chatto & Windus, 1981.

Austin, Herbert H. *Among Swamps and Giants in Equatorial Africa: An Account of Surveys and Adventures in the Southern Sudan and British East Africa*. London: C. Arthur Pearson, 1902.

———. "A Journey from Omdurman to Mombasa via Lake Rudolf," *Geographical Journal*, 19 (1902), 669–90.

———. "Journeys to the North of Uganda. 2: Lake Rudolf," *Geographical Journal*, 14 (1899), 148–55.

Bairu Tafla. *Ethiopia and Austria: A History of Their Relations*. Äthiopische Forschungen, Band 35. Wiesbaden: Harrassowitz Verlag, 1994.

Baumann, Oskar. *Durch Massailand zur Nilquelle: Reisen und Forschungen der Massai-Expedition des deutschen Antisklaverei-Komite in den Jahren 1891–1893*. Berlin: D. Reimer, 1894.

Bayer von Bayersburg, Heinrich. *Österreichs Admirale 1719–1866*. Vienna: Bergland Verlag, 1960.

———. *Österreichs Admirale und bedeutende Persönlichkeiten der k.u.k. Kriegsmarine 1867–1918*. Vienna: Bergland Verlag, 1962.

Baxter, P. T. W., Jan Hultin, and Alessandro Triulzi. *Being and Becoming Oromo: Historical and Anthropological Enquiries*. Uppsala: Nordiska Afrikainstitutet, 1996.

Beller, Steven. *Francis Joseph*. London and New York: Longman, 1996.

Bonati, Manlio. *Vittorio Bottego: Un ambizioso eroe in Africa*. Parma: Silva Editore, 1997.

Borelli, Jules. *Ethiopie-Meridionale: Journal de mon voyage aux Pays Amhara, Oromo et Sidama, septembre 1885 à novembre 1888*. Paris: Ancienne Maison Quantin, 1890.

Bridge, F. R. *The Habsburg Monarchy among the Great Powers, 1815–1918*. New York: Berg, 1990.

Brooke, J. W. "A Journey West and North of Lake Rudolf," *Geographical Journal*, 25 (1905), 525–31.

Brown, Monty. *Hunter Away: The Life and Times of Arthur Henry Neumann 1850–1907*. London: MJB Brown, 1993.

———. *Where Giants Trod: The Saga of Kenya's Desert Lake*. London: Quiller Press, Ltd., 1989.

343

Bulatovich, Alexander K. "Dall' Abissinia al Lago Rodolfo per il Cafa. Letta nell'adunanza generale della Imperiale Società Geografica Russa il 13 (25) gennaio 1899 con note de G. Roncagli," *Bolletino della Società Geografica Italiana*, Series 4, 37 (1900), 121–42.

Burton, Richard F. *The Lake Regions of Central Africa: A Picture of Exploration*. New York: Harper and Brothers, 1860.

Butzer, Karl W. *Recent History of an Ethiopian Delta: The Omo River and the Level of Lake Rudolf*. Chicago: University of Chicago Department of Geography, 1971.

Cavendish, H. S. H. "Through Somaliland and around the South of Lake Rudolf," *Geographical Journal*, 11 (1898) 372–96.

Cerulli, Ernesta. *Peoples of South-west Ethiopia and Its Borderland*. London: International African Institute, 1956.

Chanler, William Astor. "Hunting in East Africa," in Theodore Roosevelt and George Bird Grinnell, eds., *Hunting in Many Lands: The Book of the Boone and Crockett Club*. New York: Forest and Stream Publishing Company, 1895.

———. "Rifles and Big Game in East Equatorial Africa," *The Field, the Farm, the Garden: the Country Gentleman's Newspaper*, 82, #2135 (November 25, 1893), 826.

———. *Through Jungle and Desert: Travels in Eastern Africa*. New York: Macmillan and Co., 1896.

Chanler, William Astor, Jr. *And Did Those Feet in Ancient Time. A Seven Hundred Acre Island Reminiscence*. Rockport, Maine: Outerbridge Books, 1984.

Collins, Robert O. *The Southern Sudan, 1883–1898: A Struggle for Control*. New Haven: Yale University Press, 1962.

Davis, Richard Harding. "An American in Africa," *Harper's New Monthly Magazine*, 86/514 (March 1893), 632–35.

DeMott, Maddie. "William Chanler," *Africana*, 3/1 (March 1967), 15–19.

Denn Österreich lag einst am Meer. Das Leben des Admirals Alfred von Koudelka. Lothar Baumgartner, ed. Graz: H. Weishaupt Verlag, 1987.

Dyson, W. S., and V. E. Fuchs, "The Elmolo," *Journal of the Royal Anthropological Institute*, 67 (1937), 327–38.

Erdélyi, Lajos. *Teleki Samu afrikában; az afrika-kutató eredeti fényképfelvételeivel*. Bucharest: Kriterion Könyvkiadó, 1977.

Fuchs, Vivian E. "The Geological History of the Lake Rudolf Basin, Kenya Colony," *Philosophical Transactions of the Royal Society (B)*, 229 (1939), 219–74.

———. "The Lake Rudolf Rift Valley Expedition (1934)," *Geographical Journal*, 86 (1935), 114–42.

Galvin, George E., Jr. *Chanler Expedition, Kenya (formerly British East Africa), 1888–1890: Diary of George E. Galvin*. Albuquerque: George E. Galvin, Jr., 1996.

Gavaghan, Terence. *Of Lions and Dung Beetles: A Man in the Middle of Colonial Administration in Kenya*. Ilfracombe, Devon: Arthur H. Stockwell, 1999.

Graham, Alistair, and Peter Beard. *Eyelids of Morning: The Mangled Destinies of Crocodiles and Men*. Greenwich, Conn.: New York Graphic Society, 1973.

Grant, James Augustus. *A Walk across Africa: or Domestic Scenes from the Nile Journey*. Edinburgh: William Blackwood and Sons, 1864.

Gwynn, Charles W. "The Frontiers of Abyssinia: A Retrospect," *Journal of the Royal African Society*, 36 (1937), 50–161.

———. "A Journey in Southern Abyssinia," *Geographical Journal*, 38 (1911), 133–35.

Hall, Richard. *Lovers on the Nile: The Incredible African Journeys of Sam and Florence Baker.* New York: Random House, 1980.

Hamann, Brigitte. *Rudolf: Kronprinz und Rebell.* Vienna: Amalthea, 1978.

Hamann, Günther. "Ludwig Ritter von Höhnel als Forschungsreisender—Eine Würdigung aus Anlass der hundersten Wiederkehr der Entdeckung des Rudolf-Sees (Lake Turkana) in Ostafrika durch Teleki und Höhnel," *Mitteilungen des Österreichischen Geographischen Gesellschaft,* 130 (Jahresband 1988), 10–38.

Harrison, James J. "A Journey from Zeila to Lake Rudolf," *Geographical Journal,* 18 (1901), 258–75.

Heaton, Tom. *In Teleki's Footsteps: An East African Journey.* London: Macmillan, 1989.

Hemsing, Jan. *Then and Now: Nairobi's Norfolk Hotel.* Nairobi: Sealpoint Publicity and Public Relations, 1982.

Hieke, Ernst. *Zur Geschichte des deutschen Handels mit Ostafrika: Das hamburgische Handelshaus Wm. O'Swald & Co.* Teil I: *1831–1870.* Hamburg: H. Christian, 1939.

Hill, M. F. *Permanent Way: The Story of the Kenya and Uganda Railway.* Nairobi: East African Railways and Harbours, 1961.

Hillaby, John. *Journey to the Jade Sea.* London: Paladin, 1973.

Höhnel, Ludwig Ritter von. "Die Afrika-Reise des Grafen Samuel Teleki. Von seinem Begleiter L. Ritter v. Höhnel, k.k. Linienschiffs-Leutnant," *Mitteilungen der kais. königl. Geographischen Gesellschaft in Wien,* 32 (1889), 533–66.

———. "Die Chanler-Expedition in Ostafrika," *Petermanns Mitteilungen,* 39 (1893), 120–22, 146–48.

———. *Discovery of Lakes Rudolf and Stefanie: A Narrative of Count Samuel Teleki's Exploring and Hunting Expedition in Eastern Equatorial Africa in 1887 and 1888.* Trans. Nancy Bell. 2 vols. London: Longmans, Green & Co., 1894.

———. "Die Expedition des Grafen Teleki in das Gebiet des Kilimanjaro und Kenia: Vorläufiger Bericht," *Mitteilungen der kais. königl. Geographischen Gesellschaft in Wien,* 31 (1888), 441–71.

———. "Forschungsbericht [Höhnel's reports from Mkonumbi near Lamu of September 24, 1892, and from Hameye of November 28, 1892, and March 1893]," *Mitteilungen der kais. königl. Geographischen Gesellschaft in Wien,* 36 (1893), 47–50, 127–30, 341–49.

———. *Mein Leben zur See, auf Forschungsreisen und bei Hofe: Erinnerungen eines österreichischen Seeoffiziers (1857–1909).* Berlin: Verlag von Reimar Hobbing, 1926.

———. "The Lake Rudolf Region," parts 1 and 2, *Journal of the Royal African Society,* 37 (1938), 21–45, 206–26.

———. "Ostäquatorial-Afrika zwischen Pangani und dem neuentdeckten Rudolf-See: Ergebnisse der Graf S. Telekischen Expedition 1887–88," *Petermanns Mitteilungen,* Ergänzungsband 21 (1890), Ergänzungsheft 99.

———. "Über die hydrographische Zugehörigkeit des Rudolfsee-Gebietes," *Petermanns Mitteilungen,* 35 (1889), 233–37.

———. "Über Veränderungen im 'Teleki-Vulkangebiet'," *Petermanns Mitteilungen,* 84 (1938), 84–88.

———. *Zum Rudolf-See und Stephanie-See: Die Forschungsreise des Grafen Samuel Teleki in Ost-Aequatorial-Afrika, 1887–1888.* Vienna: A. Hölder, 1892.

———. "Zur Karte des nordöstlichen Kenia-Gebiets," *Petermanns Mitteilungen,* 40 (1894), 193–99.

Höhnel, L. R. von, August Rosiwal, Franz Toula, and Eduard Suess. "Beiträge zur geologischen Kenntnis des östlichen Afrika," *Denkschriften der kaiserlichen Akademie der Wissenschaften, mathematisch-naturwissenschaften Classe*, 58 (1891), 447–584.

Huxley, Elspeth. *White Man's Country: Lord Delamere and the Making of Kenya*. 2 vols. London: Chatto & Windus, 1935.

Imperato, Pascal James. *Arthur Donaldson Smith and the Exploration of Lake Rudolf*. Lake Success: Medical Society of the State of New York, 1987.

———. "Count Samuel Teleki's 1888 Expedition to Lake Turkana," *Swara: The Magazine of the East African Wild Life Society*, 11/2 (1988), 31–33.

———. "Dr. Arthur Donaldson Smith: Pioneer Desert Traveler," *Swara: The Magazine of the East African Wild Life Society*, 4/5 (1981), 12–15.

———. *Quest for the Jade Sea. Colonial Competition around an East African Lake*. Boulder, Colo.: Westview Press/Harper Collins, 1998.

Imperato, Pascal James, and Géza Teleki. "Count Samuel Teleki's Second Voyage to East Africa," *Swara: The Magazine of the East African Wild Life Society*, 15/2 (1992), 23–25.

Jackson, Frederick. *Early Days in East Africa*. London: Edward Arnold, 1930.

Jesman, Czeslaw. *The Russians in Ethiopia: An Essay in Futility*. London: Chatto & Windus, 1958.

Johnston, Harry. *The Nile Quest: A Record of the Exploration of the Nile and Its Basin*. New York: Frederick A. Stokes, 1903.

Junker, Wilhelm. *Dr. Wil. Junkers Reisen in Afrika, 1875–1886*. 3 vols. Vienna: E. Hölzel, 1889–91.

Keller, Konrad. *Alfred Ilg: Sein Leben und sein Wirken als schweizerischer Kulturbote in Abessinien*. Leipzig: Huber, 1918.

Ketterl, Eugen. *The Emperor Francis Joseph I: An Intimate Study by His Valet de Chambre*. London: Skeffington & Son, 1929.

Krapf, J. Lewis. *Travels, Researches, and Missionary Labours during an Eighteen Years' Residence in Eastern Africa*. London: Trubner and Co., 1860.

Kretschmer, Ingrid. "Die kartographischen Ergebnisse der Teleki-Höhnel Entdeckungsreise 1887–88," *Mitteilungen der Österreichischen Geographischen Gesellschaft*, 130 (Jahresband 1988), 49–50.

———. "Österreichs Beitrag zur kartographischen Erschließung Ostafrikas bis zum Ersten Weltkrieg," in *Abenteuer Ostafrika: Der Anteil Österreich-Ungarns an der Erforschung Ostafrikas*. Eisenstadt: Amt der Burgenländischen Landesregierung, 1988.

Leakey, Richard, and Roger Lewin. *People of the Lake: Mankind and Its Beginnings*. Garden City, N.Y.: Anchor Press, 1978.

Lehr, Rudolf, ed. *Bad Ischl und die Habsburger*. 2d ed. Bad Ischl: Kurverband Bad Ischl, 1992.

Lenz, Oskar. *Timbuktu: Reise durch Marokko, die Sahara und den Sudan ausgeführt im Auftrage der Afrikanischen Gesellschaft in Deutschland in den Jahren 1879 und 1880*. Leipzig: F. A. Brockhaus, 1884.

———. *Wanderungen in Afrika: Studien und Erlebnisse*. Vienna: Verlag der Literarischen Gesellschaft, 1895.

Leontiev, Nicholas. "Exploration des provinces Equitoriales d'Abyssinie," *La Géographie: Bulletin de la Société de Géographie*, 2 (1900), 105–18.

Lyne, Robert Nunez. *An Apostle of Empire: Being the Life of Sir Lloyd William Mathews, K.C.M.G.* London: George Allen & Unwin, Ltd., 1936.

Macdonald, J. R. L. "Journeys to the North of Uganda," *Geographical Journal*, 14 (1899), 129–48.

Maciel, Mervyn. *Bwana Karani*. Braunton, Devon: Merlin Books, 1985.

McLynn, Frank. *Hearts of Darkness: The European Exploration of Africa*. New York: Carroll & Graf Publishers, 1993.

Marcus, Harold G. *The Life and Times of Menelik II: Ethiopia 1844–1913*. Oxford: Clarendon Press, 1975.

Maud, Philip. "Exploration in the Southern Borderland of Abyssinia," *Geographical Journal*, 23 (1904), 552–79.

Meyer, Hans. *Across East African Glaciers: An Account of the First Ascent of Kilimanjaro*. Translated from the German by H. S. Calder. London: George Philip & Son, 1891.

Moorehead, Alan. *The White Nile*. New York: Harper and Row, 1960.

Müller, Fritz Ferdinand. *Deutschland—Zanzibar—Ostafrika: Geschichte einer deutschen Kolonialeroberung 1884–1890*. Berlin: Rütten & Loening, 1959.

Neumann, Arthur H. *Elephant-Hunting in East Equatorial Africa: Being an Account of Three Years' Ivory-Hunting under Mount Kenia and among the Ndorobo Savages of the Lorogi Mountains, including a Trip to the North of Lake Rudolph*. London: Rowland Ward, 1898.

New, Charles. *Life, Wanderings, and Labours in Eastern Africa: With an Account of the First Successful Ascent of the Equatorial Snow Mountain, Kilima Njaro and Remarks upon East African Slavery*. London: Hodder and Stroughton, 1874.

Pern, Stephen. *Another Land, Another Sea. Walking round Lake Rudolph*. London: Victor Gollancz, 1979.

Powell-Cotton, P. H. G. *A Sporting Trip through Abyssinia*. London: Rowland Ward, 1902.

Pratt, Mary Louise. *Imperial Eyes: Travel Writing and Transculturation*. London: Routledge, 1992.

Prouty, Chris. *Empress Taytu and Menilek II: Ethiopia 1883–1910*. Trenton, N.J.: The Red Sea Press, 1986.

Ptak-Wiesauer, Eva. "Die Turkana in Kenia und Höhnels ethnographische Berichte," *Mitteilungen des Österreichischen Geographischen Gesellschaft*, 130 (Jahresband 1988), 68–87.

Rodd, James Rennell. *Social and Diplomatic Memories*. 3 vols. London: Edward Arnold, 1922–1925.

Rollins, Patrick Joseph. "Russia's Ethiopian Adventure, 1888–1905." Unpublished doctoral dissertation, Syracuse University, 1967.

Rotberg, Robert I., ed. *Africa and Its Explorers: Motives, Methods, and Impact*. Cambridge: Harvard University Press, 1970.

———. *Joseph Thomson and the Exploration of Africa*. London: Chatto & Windus, 1971.

Sanderson, G. N. *England, Europe and the Upper Nile. 1882–1899*. Edinburgh: University Press, 1965.

Schlag, Gerald. "Koloniale Pläne Österreich-Ungarns in Ostafrika im 19. Jahrhundert," in *Abenteuer Ostafrika: Der Anteil Österreich-Ungarns an der Erforschung Ostafrikas*. Eisenstadt: Amt der Burgenländischen Landesregierung, 1988.

Schmidt-Brentano, Antonio. *Die österreichischen Admirale*. Band I: *1808–1895*. Osnabrück: Biblio Verlag, 1997.

Schweinfurth, Georg August. *Im Herzen von Afrika: Reisen und Entdeckungen im centralen Äquatorial-Afrika während der Jahre 1868 bis 1871*. Leipzig: F. A. Brockhaus, 1874.

———. *The Heart of Africa: Three Years' Travels and Adventures in the Unexplored Regions of Central Africa from 1868 to 1871*. 2 vols. New York: Harper and Brothers, 1874.

Seltzer, Richard, ed. *Ethiopia through Russian Eyes: An Eyewitness Account of the End of an Era, 1896–98, Consisting of the Two Books by Alexander Bulatovich*. [Internet, WWW]. ADDRESS: http://www.samizdat.com, 1993.

———. *The Name of Hero.* Boston: Houghton Mifflin Company, 1981.

Senft, Willi, and Bert Katschner. *Bergwandern in Ostafrika: Riesevulkane und Tierparadiese.* Graz and Stuttgart: Leopold Stocker Verlag, 1978.

Sieche, Erwin F. "Austria-Hungary's Last Naval Visit to the USA," *Warship International,* 27/ 2 (1990), 142–59.

Simanyi, Ildikó. "Ludwig Ritter von Höhnel (1857–1942): Leben und Wirken." Unpublished master's thesis, University of Vienna, 1988.

Smith, A. Donaldson. "An Expedition between Lake Rudolf and the Nile," *Geographical Journal,* 16 (1900), 600–25.

———. "Expedition through Somaliland to Lake Rudolf," parts I and II, *Geographical Journal,* 8 (1896), 120–37, 221–29.

———. *Through Unknown African Countries: The First Expedition from Somaliland to Lake Lamu.* London and New York: Edward Arnold, 1897.

Sondhaus, Lawrence. *The Habsburg Empire and the Sea: Austrian Naval Policy, 1797–1866.* West Lafayette, Ind.: Purdue University Press, 1989.

———. *The Naval Policy of Austria-Hungary, 1867–1918: Navalism, Industrial Development, and the Politics of Dualism.* West Lafayette, Ind.: Purdue University Press, 1994.

Speke, John Hanning. *Journal of the Discovery of the Source of the Nile.* Edinburgh and London: William Blackwood and Sons, 1863.

———. *What Led to the Discovery of the Source of the Nile.* Edinburgh and London: William Blackwood and Sons, 1864.

Spencer, Paul. *The Samburu: A Study of Gerontocracy in a Nomadic Tribe.* London: Routledge and Keegan Paul, 1965.

Stigand, Chauncey Hugh. *To Abyssinia through an Unknown Land: An Account of a Journey through Unexplored Regions of British East Africa by Lake Rudolf to the Kingdom of Menelek.* Philadelphia: J. B. Lippincott, 1910.

Stiglbauer, Karl. "Zum Gedenken an die Forschungsreise von Graf S. Teleki und L. Ritter von Höhnel vor 100 Jahren (1887–1888)" *Mitteilungen der Österreichischen Geographischen Gesellschaft,* 130 (Jahresband 1988), 5–9.

Suess, Eduard. *Das Antlitz der Erde.* 3 vols. in 5. Prague: F. Tempsky, 1883–1909.

———. *The Face of the Earth.* 5 vols. Oxford: Clarendon Press, 1902–24.

Swayne, Harald George Carlos. *Seventeen Trips through Somaliland: A Record of Exploration and Big Game Shooting, 1885 to 1893.* London: Rowland Ward, 1895.

Tablino, Paul. *The Gabra: Camel Nomads of Northern Kenya.* Nairobi: Paulines Publications Africa, 1999.

Teleki, Count Samuel. "A Personal Diary of Explorations in East Africa, October 1886–October 1888, by Count Samuel Teleki (1845–1916), with Descriptions of His Pioneer Climbs on Mounts Kilimanjaro and Kenya in 1887, His Discoveries of Lakes Rudolf and Stefanie in 1888, and His Return Safari to Mount Kilimanjaro in 1895." Text translated from the handwritten Hungarian version into English by Charles and Vera Teleki, Warkworth, Ontario, Canada, 1961. Geza Teleki Papers, Washington, D.C.

———. "Rifles for Big Game," in *The Field, the Farm, the Garden: The Country Gentleman's Newspaper,* 83, #2145 (February 3, 1894), 155.

Thomas, Lately (pseud. Robert V. P. Steele). *The Astor Orphans: A Pride of Lions.* With a preface by John Winthrop Aldrich. Albany, NY: Washington Park Press Ltd., 1999.

———. *A Pride of Lions: The Astor Orphans; The Chanler Chronicle.* New York: William Morrow, 1971.

———. *Sam Ward: "King of the Lobby."* Boston: Houghton Mifflin, 1965.

Thomson, Joseph. *Through Masai Land: A Journey of Exploration among the Snowclad Volcanic Mountains and Strange Tribes of Eastern Equatorial Africa, Being the Narrative of the Royal Geographical Society's Expedition to Mount Kenia and Lake Victoria Nyanza, 1883–1884.* London: Sampson Low, Marston, Searle, and Rivington, 1885.

Tichy, Herbert. *See an der Sonne: Auf den Spuren der frühen Menschen.* Vienna: Verlag ORAC, 1980.

Trzebinski, Errol. *The Kenya Pioneers.* New York: W. W. Norton, 1986.

Turton, David. "Movement, Warfare, and Ethnicity in the Lower Omo Valley," in *Herders, Warriors, and Traders: Pastoralism in Africa*, ed. John G. Galaty and Pierre Bonte. Boulder, Colo.: Westview Press, 1991.

Vannutelli, L., and C. Citerni. *Seconda spedizione Bottego. L'Omo. Viaggio d'esplorazione nell'Africa Orientale.* Milan: Ulrico Hoepli Editore, 1899.

Wagner, Walter. *Die obersten Behörden der k. und k. Kriegsmarine 1856–1918.* Mitteilungen des Österreichischen Staatsarchivs, Ergänzungsband VI. Vienna: Österreichisches Staatssarchiv, 1961.

Wakefield, E. S. *Thomas Wakefield: Missionary and Geographical Pioneer in East Equatorial Africa.* London: The Religious Tract Society, 1904.

Wehler, Hans-Ulrich. *Bismarck und der Imperialismus.* Cologne and Berlin: Kiepenheuer & Witsch, 1969.

Wellby, Montagu Sinclair. "King Menelek's Dominions and the Country between Lake Gallop (Rudolf) and the Nile Valley," *Geographical Journal*, 21 (1900), 292–306.

———. *'Twixt Sirdar and Menelik: An Account of a Year's Expedition from Zeila to Cairo through Unknown Abyssinia.* London: Harper and Brothers, 1901.

Whitehouse, William F. "Through the Country of the King of Kings," *Scribner's Magazine*, 32 (1902) 286–96.

Whitehouse, William F. "To Lake Rudolf and Beyond," in Theodore Roosevelt and George Bird Grinnell, eds., *Hunting in Many Lands: The Book of the Boone and Crockett Club.* New York: Forest and Stream Publishing Company, 1895.

Wickenburg, Eduard. "Von Dschibuti bis Lamu," *Petermanns Mitteilungen*, 49 (1903), 193–99.

Wissmann, Hermann von. *Im Innern Afrikas: Die Erforschung des Kassai während der Jahre 1883–1884 und 1885 von Hermann Wissmann, Ludwig Wolf, Curt von François, Hans Müller.* Leipzig: Brockhaus, 1888.

———. *Meine zweite Durchquerung Äquatorial-Afrikas vom Kongo zum Zambesi während der Jahre 1886 und 1887.* Berlin: Globus Verlag, 1890.

———. *Unter deutsche Flagge quer durch Afrika: Von 1880 bis 1883 ausgeführt vom Paul Pogge und Hermann Wissmann.* Berlin: Walter & Apolant, 1889.

Youngs, Tim. *Travellers in Africa: British Travelogues, 1850–1900.* Manchester: Manchester University Press, 1994.

Zach, Michael. *Österreicher im Sudan 1820 bis 1914.* Beiträge zur Afrikanistik, Band 24. Vienna: Afro-Pub, 1985.

Zaghi, Carlo. *I Russi in Etiopia.* 2 vols. Naples: Guida Editore, 1972.

INDEX

ABYSSINIA

Lake Stefanie

Lake Rudolf

TURKANA

Mt. Kulal

Lorian Swamp

Lake Baringo

Mt. Kenya

R. Tana

Lake Naivasha

Machakos

R. Athi

Lamu

Mt. Kilimanjaro

Mt. Meru

Taveta

Malindi

MOMBASA

INDIAN

Pemba

Pangani

OCEAN

ZANZIBAR

Bagamoyo

36° 38° 40° 42°

4° 2° 0° 2° 4° 6°

0 100 200

Miles